IRELAND IN THE EUROPEAN EYE

IRELAND IN THE EUROPEAN EYE

Edited by Gisela Holfter
and Bettina Migge

RIA

Ireland in the European Eye

First published 2019

Royal Irish Academy, 19 Dawson Street, Dublin 2
ria.ie

ISBN 978-1-911479-02-4 (PB)
ISBN 978-1-911479-03-1 (pdf)
ISBN 978-1-911479-04-8 (epub)
ISBN 978-1-911479-05-5 (mobi)

British Library Cataloguing in Publication Data. A
CIP catalogue record for this book is available from
the British Library.

Editor: Helena King
Design: Fidelma Slattery
Index: Eileen O'Neill
Printed in Poland by L&C Printing Group

Royal Irish Academy is a member of Publishing
Ireland, the Irish book publishers' association

This publication has received support from

An Roinn Gnóthaí
Eachtracha agus Trádála
Department of
Foreign Affairs and Trade

GOETHE
INSTITUT

Ollscoil na hÉireann
National University of Ireland

Contents

Introduction

Gisela Holfter
and Bettina Migge

Ireland has a very special relationship with
continental Europe. Although her relationship with Great Britain, which of course was
shaped by colonial power imbalances, was
for a long time the most significant connection—Ireland has often been described as the
island behind the island—she has also always
had contacts with the rest of Europe. This
is evidenced by Irish missionary activities,
remnants of which could still be found in
the 1950s when Heinrich Böll described the
island as 'the glowing heart of Europe' from
where Christianity and learning found their
way to the continent.[1] There is also a history
of diplomatic relationships with continental Europe from as soon as Ireland gained

independence. Links were established with France, Germany, Italy and the Netherlands in 1922. In 1929 Ireland opened legations in both Paris and Berlin, Madrid followed in 1935, Rome in 1937; connections with countries in the Eastern bloc, however, took much longer: reciprocal embassies in Ireland and Poland, for example, were only set up in 1976.

But how European is Ireland? In terms of everyday reference, in which 'Europe' often means 'the European continent', it might be argued that even some 40 years after Ireland joined the European Union (EU), or to be more precise, the then European Economic Community (EEC), it has not found its feet in Europe. Such a view would be contradicted, however, by Ireland's varied engagement on the European political stage, where it has significantly contributed to shaping the EU. Its increasing engagement on that stage and with other countries within the EU has also helped Ireland to find its own voice and to normalise its relations with its former colonial oppressor. But Ireland's engagement with continental Europe and as part of a continually growing EU has also not been entirely unproblematic, particularly in the recent past. Referenda on the Nice and Lisbon treaties in 2001 and 2008 (and their respective re-runs in 2002 and 2009) incited passionate discussions about Ireland's place in an ever-changing Europe and EU. Also of significance is Ireland's insistence on its maintaining separate relations with the United Kingdom (UK) and with the USA, where its main diaspora communities are located. Such an approach is not always in line with the policies and outlook of the EU (which gives rise to arguments about whether Ireland's focus should be 'Boston or Berlin')—though of course there are many individual facets to outside linkages for all EU member states. The European project itself, especially the common currency, was called into question during the global financial crisis beginning in 2008, which hit Ireland particularly hard. Ireland was one of the few countries subjected to an EU-led recovery programme (widely seen as an austerity programme), causing significant political and social strain. But Ireland became once more a prodigy in European eyes thanks to its comparatively fast recovery.

With the unexpected result of the British vote on Brexit in 2016, Irish–EU relations are again being tested, especially as the Irish–Northern Ireland border has turned out to be an important testing ground with wider ramifications in shaping post-Brexit EU–UK relations. 'Soft' or 'hard' Brexit scenarios are being analysed for their very different impacts on UK–EU and UK–Irish political and economic relations. But despite occasional calls for Ireland also to hold a referendum on leaving the EU, politicians, commentators and the general public alike are, in the overwhelming majority, united in their willingness to stay with the European project rather than to return to a binary relationship with the UK, whichever way it might be defined.

The political stage is, however, only one of the arenas in which Irish–continental European relations are played out. Traditions in different cultural and academic spheres that extend beyond the confines of the EU present, as this volume will show, a much richer tapestry of mutual influences and appreciation that merit greater attention but are often forgotten in the heated discussions of everyday politics. The perspective of the outsider is particularly interesting as it brings with it a multitude of mirroring images. Given the important changes underway both in Ireland and across all of Europe, it seems an opportune time to analyse these differing reflections, and to shine a light especially on the period since the founding of the Irish Free State in 1922, almost 100 years ago.

Reflections on the relationship between Ireland and Europe are not new, of course. A conference took place in Tübingen some 40 years ago, focusing on Ireland and Europe in the Early Middle Ages. It was followed two years later, in 1981, by a conference in Dublin. Luminaries from politics, diplomacy, academia and indeed the clergy took part or at least sent greetings. The proceedings of that event—in almost 50 contributions running to over 1,000 pages, mostly in German but also in English and French—give exhaustive insights into details of Irish–European links (particularly everything to do with the Irish mission in Great Britain and on the continent) and Irish achievements in theology, art and literature, and the influence of these on religious and political developments on the continent up to the eleventh century.[2] This European perspective has been followed up by Irish scholarship in subsequent decades (of course focusing not only on the Early Middle Ages, though that period has attracted ongoing interest).[3] It is easy to identify particular periods or events that have attracted a plethora of scholarship. Ireland's role and engagement in the First World War, or the state's neutrality during the Second World War (including its involvement and relationship with the continent generally and Germany in particular) are two obvious examples.[4] The subsequent engagement with the EEC and, upon becoming a member, with its institutions, as well as Ireland's relationship with and development as part of the EU, have also had their fair share of academic analysis.[5]

The idea for this book developed in the context of the work of the Royal Irish Academy's committee for the study of Language, Literature, Culture and Communication (2014–18). The focus on European awareness of Ireland emerged organically from one of the committee's central preoccupations—the place of European languages and literatures in Ireland. Since literature is only one of the cultural areas that have contributed to shaping Ireland's relationship with the rest of Europe, however, we felt that the focus of the volume should extend to other closely related domains, such as the arts, architecture, politics and European studies, to bring to the fore a more rounded picture of Ireland's relationship with continental Europe. Beyond considering that relationship, we left it open to contributors whether or not they wanted to deal with the whole island or either of its parts. Most chapters deal primarily or only with Ireland. It is hoped that future research will address this imbalance and also consider the relationship between Northern Ireland and Europe.

The book is divided into four parts. The first part, 'Ireland in Europe: Historical Background and Contextualisation', presents historical overviews and a contextualisation of Ireland's relations with the other European countries. The main developments are divided into three distinct time frames: up to the beginning of the twentieth century; from Irish independence in the 1920s to 1973, when Ireland joined the EEC; and finally from 1973 to post-Brexit times.

Thomas O'Connor starts the historical survey, focusing on the Irish diaspora in Europe. Charting the Irish experience from the Middle Ages to the nineteenth century, he provides the context for the successive waves of Irish immigrants to the continent and the Irish colonial experience. Changes in the socio-economic and religious as well as political landscape meant changing destinations: Spain and Portugal were particularly attractive in the sixteenth and seventeenth century, but were soon

Gisela Holfter and Bettina Migge

rivalled by France. Austria and other continental locations drew in Irish immigrants engaging in commercial, military and academic pursuits.

Continuing to the twentieth century, Mervyn O'Driscoll emphasises the geostrategic and historical factors that came to the fore where Ireland was concerned in the eyes of the continental European countries. Most of all, it was its proximity to and relationship with Britain that played a decisive role when assessing Ireland, for example in the context of Irish attempts to gain membership of the EEC. However, the decision to stay neutral during the Second World War also had ongoing repercussions. Eventually, in January 1973, both Britain and Ireland became members of the EEC, following complicated negotiations among the different European countries and amidst the outbreak of the 'Troubles' in Northern Ireland.

As Brigid Laffan argues, EEC membership was also a return to Europe, recalling the early engagement of Irish missionaries. Engagement saw Ireland blossoming from initially being the poorest and most agricultural member state (not helped by the 1973 oil shock and consequent economic turmoil) to the heyday of the Celtic Tiger. Laffan discusses the tensions brought about by the subsequent traumatic economic crisis that brought the troika to Dublin in 2010. Exiting the bail-out in 2013 and managing an impressive recovery, Ireland and other EU countries have since had to deal with the 2016 decision of the UK to leave the EU, a situation that is likely to have enormous repercussions for Ireland.

The second part of the book discusses 'Representations of Ireland in European Literature and Irish Literature in Europe', and provides a historical contextualisation of selected excerpts from works by Dutch, French, German, Polish and Spanish authors. The impact of Irish literatures—both Irish/Gaelic literature and Irish literature written in English—in different European countries is explored in comparative perspectives, including the reception of Irish literature in Germany, Italy and in the Scandinavian countries.

Anne Gallagher's contribution begins with a particularly influential non-literary portrayal of Ireland—the film *Un taxi mauve* (1977). The film was, however, based on a book by French writer Michel Déon, who lived in Ireland from the 1970s until his death in 2016. Both book and film seem to condense recurrent French images of Ireland as 'an untamed land, bathed in mystery and mythology, where rationalism has no place and the life of the imagination reigns supreme'. Only a handful of writers diverge from this perception, taking the Troubles in Northern Ireland or Irish writers such as Joyce as starting points for their literary production.

David Clark's assessment of Ireland in the Spanish literatures points towards an almost unanimously positive perception and portrayal of Ireland. In fact, Ireland served as a role model to some extent not only for the opposing sides of the Spanish civil war but also, since the rise of regionalism in the late nineteenth century, for the regions of Catalonia, the Basque Country and Galicia. The topic of a small nation achieving independence from an oppressive power recurs frequently in the reception of Irish literature in these areas (and their languages), as does Ireland's perceived role as bulwark of Catholic views and practices. Clark detects a 'long-lasting infatuation' with Ireland, 'although varying in scope, perspective, intention, genre and quality', that has resulted in a further increase in literary output focusing on Ireland in the last decade.

Joanna Kosmalska's contribution allows an insight into the Polish perspective on Irish literature, which is characterised by an enthusiastic engagement, not least due to the great number of Polish immigrants who have come to Ireland since the turn of the millennium. Previously there was already a considerable awareness in Poland of Irish literature, but the general view was that of a 'distant, mysterious, evergreen land inhabited by heroic warriors and talented writers who spoke English'. A shared religious background and social-historical affinities have also shaped a generally favourable view, contested only rarely by negative experiences that occurred during the recent economic downturn in Ireland.

In contrast to a greatly increased awareness in Poland and the many historical and especially contemporary links, the perception of Ireland in the Netherlands is more distant, albeit interested, as Marieke Krajenbrink summarises in her chapter. Relations between the Netherlands and Ireland are far less studied than relationships with many other European countries. Nevertheless, history, landscape, music and especially the perceived connectedness with the supernatural have captured the Dutch imagination and led to a varied portrayal of Ireland, which at times takes on a rather ambivalent fascination. Aspects that come to the fore more strongly here than in portrayals of Ireland in other countries include a critical examination of patriarchal traditions and gender issues.

A genuinely comparative view is presented in three further chapters looking at literary perspectives. Fiorenzo Fantaccini and Anna Fattori present both the Italian and German literary interaction, and often fascination, with Ireland. In comparing both perspectives, similarities but also intriguing differences come to light. Taking the long view from the Middle Ages, Fantaccini and Fattori also consider incidences of reciprocal influences, such as Celtic Studies in Germany and the importance of German scholars in the development of that academic discipline. While Irish authors such as Sterne, Swift and Goldsmith lent a decisive impulse to German literature, their influence on Italian writing was more circumspect and, in contrast to the German reception, more encompassing of a shared religious outlook. Catholicism also played a role in Irish interest in Italy as a travel destination, whereas travel literature from the early nineteenth century onwards played a decisive role in the German interaction with Ireland, culminating in Heinrich Böll's *Irisches Tagebuch* (*Irish journal*), which went far beyond German writing and language in its impact. On the Irish side, the 'three giants' Wilde, Shaw and Yeats dominate the literary perception of Ireland in the beginning of the twentieth century in both Italy and Germany, while more recently Beckett and particularly Joyce have subsequently exerted an unparalleled influence.

Similarly, Joyce proves a starting point for the overview of Nordic encounters with Irish literature, in which Anne Karhio argues that the 'international standing of authors such as Yeats, Joyce and Beckett gives their texts a canonical status as *world* literature rather than situating these figures as *Irish* authors'. While she maintains that 'the cluster of countries, languages and various (and often conflicting) historical narratives that constitutes the Nordic region may appear deceptively coherent', she also recognises that Irish representations of Finnish, Swedish, Norwegian, Danish or Icelandic cultures may not always do justice to the diversity between and within them. Karhio focuses on describing the common characteristics of Nordic receptions of Irish literary genres, particularly prose and poetry, while also raising readers' awareness of the considerable differences between them. She points to political issues such as similar experiences of cultural revival in the face of powerful and oppressive neighbours, especially with regard to Finland and Norway, and similarities in historical and socio-geographic conditions such as the dominance of rural living and a defining proximity to the sea. Unlike others, she also emphasises the success of more contemporary and often female Irish writers in the Nordic countries.

An area even larger than the diverse Nordic countries is covered by Joachim Fischer and Éamon Ó Ciosáin in their exploration of the situation of literature written in Irish in European translation. Looking as they do at more than fifteen national literary cultures, they stress the exploratory nature of their overview. Moreover, they place a special emphasis on the reception and translation of Irish-language texts in the French- and German-speaking countries. They also note, however, that smaller language communities, such as Romanian and Czech, form a surprisingly substantial part of their corpus. The wealth of Irish-language material in translation indicates an ongoing interest in literature in Irish but also highlights the difficulties in accessing different genres for authors from the different countries; Fischer and Ó Ciosáin avoid predictions about whether a renaissance of Irish language literature on the continent can be hoped for. They also raise the issue of the variable understanding of what constitutes the focus of Irish Studies on the continent and advocate in favour of a more inclusive approach.

The third part of the book, 'Irish Art, Architecture, Film and Music in European Discourses', analyses Ireland's representation in the European context from a broader cultural perspective. It examines how awareness and reception of Ireland and Irish contributions to these art forms have changed, and how this has contributed to shaping perceptions of Irish culture across Europe.

Finola O'Kane's chapter explores how Ireland has been represented in the tourist literature. She shows that there has been a rarely contested tendency to erase the existence of urban and middle- or upper-class dwellings and to foreground small, decaying, vernacular buildings, typically subsumed into the landscape, suggesting that Ireland is a country devoid of cities and positive architectural traditions.

Caoimhín Mac Giolla Léith's contribution considers perceptions of Irish modern art in continental Europe through an examination of the makeup of art exhibitions selected by continental and Irish curators for consumption by continental and international audiences more generally. He stresses the heterogeneity of the modern art community in Ireland, argues that a simple local/global dialectic informed by discourses relating to national identity is no longer relevant to the assessment of art within the European context, and calls for the engagement of international audiences.

Lynda Mulvin's contribution demonstrates that a close relationship existed between Ireland and continental Europe during the Middle Ages, when Irish scholars and monks migrated throughout the region. Their migrations led to the diffusion of Celtic literacy and learning, and to artistic contributions that have had a profound impact at a European level; many continental libraries have holdings of Hiberno-Latin manuscripts from the seventh to twelfth century, and there are traces of early Christian ecclesiastical sites and Irish medieval ecclesiastical artefacts across the continent, pointing to a lasting cultural and social exchange.

Fergal Lenehan's chapter compares some Irish elements of British cinema with Irish elements of German and French cinema in Irish-themed genre movies dealing with the Second World War, Anglo-Irish conflict, and film noir. He argues that images of green pastoralism and political violence have dominated cinematic portrayals of Ireland originating from Britain and the US; they have tended to vary between 'idyllic or nostalgic "soft primitivism"' (USA) and 'a romantic but harsh and often violent "hard primitivism"' (UK). Corresponding continental European films with little Irish engagement are culturally more detached. In recent years a more variegated image of Ireland has emerged that is less polarised and not only focuses on traditional issues such as Catholicism and political violence but merges traditional and modern themes. Historical films, he asserts, also increasingly shine a light on 'British agency and responsibility rather than inherent Irish culpability'.

In his chapter, Harry White maintains that because Irish music is highly valued among continental Europeans as authentic and 'as a recreational alternative to and distraction from the high seriousness of other art forms', other musical genres and particularly European (classical) art music have not received much attention in Ireland. In an attempt to understand the reasons for this state of affairs, he examines the history of European musical ideas, focusing on how they have shaped continental understandings, reception and perception of Irish music.

The final section of the volume, which considers 'European Studies, Tourism and Journalism', zooms in on the marketing of Ireland to different parts of Europe, explores developments in European Studies and, turning the tables, analyses European discourses in Irish media.

Edward Moxon-Brown's chapter examines the role of Ireland in European Studies, a multi-disciplinary academic field of study that investigates the patterns and processes of European integration and the new realities that it brings about. This field of study emerged after Ireland's accession to the EEC and focused on developing an understanding of Ireland's new reality within that community. Looking at the existing undergraduate and postgraduate offerings, as well as professional associations in the field, Moxon-Brown's comprehensive overview outlines the developments of the last decades as well as existing challenges. He concludes that Ireland offers 'a natural home for European Studies', arguing that both public opinion and political leadership have been strongly in favour of EU membership. He further notes that Ireland tends to be portrayed in a flattering light within the discipline—not least due to its perceived exemplary role in terms of integration and its ability to 'punch above its weight' in Europe. In Ireland's case, this is also due to its neutral status and comparatively small size as well as its lack of a colonising legacy and, not least, its skill in taking advantage of EU redistributive development programmes.

Linda King's contribution explores the commodification of Irish identity initially for European and North American travelling audiences and increasingly also for Irish and a growing range of international audiences in the context of unprecedented economic and aviational change. Viewing these changes through the lens of the Aer Lingus travel magazine *cara*, she proposes that there has been an important shift in Ireland's self-representation. While conventional images of Irishness through architecture, scenery and ethnicity designed to attract inward tourism dominated in the 1990s, this has, with the rise in importance of Irish travelling audiences, given way to a globalised and glossy image of Irish people, lifestyle and culture. *cara*'s current approach to marketing Irish culture by focusing on celebrities highlights a 'newly found confidence' and appeals to a wide range of audiences.

Gisela Holfter and Bettina Migge

Paul Gillespie's contribution explores the editorial structures of and European coverage in the Irish press, focusing on *The Irish Times*. He suggests, on the basis of case studies, that despite important financial and structural constraints, Irish reporting on continental events was much more extensive and balanced in the early years of the state's existence, up until the end of the twentieth century when Irish journalism, middle-class audiences and the political establishment were keen on developing a voice that was independent of British perceptions of the world. Ireland's rise in prosperity during the first few years of the new millennium led to the rise of a new Anglo-centricity in Irish media, despite significantly improved first-hand access to continental events due to a greater network of well-trained correspondents who were well-versed in European cultures. Gillespie argues that the new challenges that have arisen with the advent of Brexit can only be handled successfully if a well-functioning and critical media is in place that defies reducing complex economic, political and social issues to a simplistic 'Boston/London or Berlin' debate.

All of the contributions persuasively make a case for the multi-faceted, long-lasting nature of Irish–European engagement, and they all highlight the richness of reciprocal influences. There is much to discover still—but this volume will, we hope, contribute to kicking off a new round of lively discussions about the relationship between Ireland and its fellow EU and wider continental European partners in the twenty-first century.

Notes

[1] Heinrich Böll, *Irish Journal*, transl. by L. Vennewitz (Melville House; Brooklyn, NY, 2011), 8.

[2] See, Heinz Löwe (ed.), *Die Iren und Europa im früheren Mittelalter* (2 vols; Klett-Cotta; Stuttgart, 1982).

[3] See, for example, Dermot Keogh, *Ireland and Europe: 1919–1989. A diplomatic and political history* (Hibernian University Press; Cork and Dublin, 1990); Thomas O'Connor (ed.), *The Irish in Europe 1580–1815* (Four Courts Press; Dublin, 2001); Colin Graham, Leon Litvack (eds), *Ireland and Europe in the nineteenth century* (Four Courts; Dublin, 2006); Cathal McCall and Thomas M. Wilson (eds), *Europeanisation and Hibernicisation: Ireland and Europe*, European Studies 28 (Rodopi; Amsterdam and New York, 2010); Brian Heffernan, Marta Ramón, Pierre Ranger and Zsuzsanna Zarka (eds), *Life on the fringe? Ireland and Europe, 1800–1922* (Irish Academic Press; Dublin, 2012); Aid-

en O'Malley and Eve Patten (eds), *Ireland west to east: Irish cultural connections with Central and Eastern Europe* (Peter Lang; Oxford, 2013); Raphaël Ingelbien, *Irish cultures of travel: writing on the continent, 1829–1914* (Palgrave Macmillan; London, 2016). In relation to scholarship on the Middle Ages specifically, see Próinséas Ní Chatháin and Michael Richter, *Ireland and Europe in the Early Middle Ages: texts and transmission* (Four Courts Press; Dublin, 2002); Roy Flechner and Sven Meede (eds), *The Irish in Early Medieval Europe: identity, culture and religion* (Palgrave; London, 2016).

[4] In regard to Irish involvement in the First World War, see, for instance, Terence Denman, *Ireland's unknown soldiers* (Irish Academic Press; Dublin, 1992); Keith Jeffery, *Ireland and the Great War* (Cambridge University Press; Cambridge, 2000); John Horne (ed.), *Our War—Ireland and the Great War* (Royal Irish Academy; Dublin, 2008); Kevin Myers, *Ireland's Great War* (Lilliput Press; Dublin, 2014); Gavin Hughes, *Fighting Irish—the Irish regiments in the First World War* (Merrion Press; Dublin, 2015) and, with a wider focus, Jérôme aan de Wiel, *The Irish factor, 1899–1919—Ireland's strategic and diplomatic importance for foreign powers* (Irish Academic Press; Dublin, 2008). For analysis on Ireland and the Second World War, see Horst Dickel, *Die deutsche Außenpolitik und die irische Frage von 1932 bis 1944*, Frankfurter historische Abhandlungen (Franz Steiner Verlag; Wiesbaden, 1983); Mark M. Hull, *Irish secrets: German espionage in Ireland, 1939–45* (Irish Academic Press; Dublin, 2003); Dermot Keogh and Mervyn O'Driscoll (eds) *Ireland in World War Two: diplomacy and survival* (Mercier Press; Dublin, 2004); Mervyn O'Driscoll, *Ireland, Germany and the Nazis: politics and diplomacy, 1919–1939* (Four Courts Press; Dublin, 2004); Gerald Morgan and Gavin Hughes (eds), *Southern Ireland and the liberation of France: new perspectives* (Peter Lang; Bern, 2011); Dorothea Depner and Guy Woodward (eds), *Irish culture and wartime Europe, 1938–1948* (Four Courts Press; Dublin, 2015).

[5] To name but a few, see, Michael Kennedy and Eunan O'Halpin, *Ireland and the Council of Europe: from isolation towards integration* (Council of Europe; Strasbourg, 2000); Michael Holmes (ed.), *Ireland and the European Union: Nice, enlargement and the future of Europe* (Manchester University Press; Manchester, 2005); Brigid Laffan and Jane O'Mahony, *Ireland and the European Union* (Palgrave Macmillan; Basingstoke, 2008); Mervyn O'Driscoll, Jérôme aan de Wiel and Dermot Keogh (eds), *Through European eyes: Western Europe, the EEC and Ireland 1945–1973* (Cork University Press; Cork, 2013).

Gisela Holfter and Bettina Migge

PART I

Ireland in Europe:
Historical Background
and Contextualisation

Prequels: the Irish European diaspora

Thomas O'Connor

Global contexts

The Irish have always been part of the European story.[1] Having received successive waves of European migration in pre-historic times, the island returned the compliment.[2] During the early medieval period, the Irish church, for instance, mounted numerous evangelising missions to the continent. Peripatetic Irish missionaries established monasteries such as Bobbio, in northern Italy, founded cities like St Gallen in Switzerland, and provided ecclesiastical leaders of the highest calibre: Kilian in Würzburg, Finbarr in Lucca and Vergil in Salzburg. Irish scholars like Eriugena and Sedulius Scottus contributed to the learned culture of the Carolingian court. Later on, Muiris Ó Fithcheallaigh professed philosophy in Padua. All the while, Irish traders exchanged goods with a range of early modern European ports, especially in Spain, Portugal and the Netherlands.[3] From the middle of the sixteenth century, however, Irish migrants begin to appear in greater numbers in Europe, inaugurating a complex of migrant patterns, which would persist into the modern period.[4]

To an important extent, this stepping up of the migrant flow, and its diversification, were due to a congeries of global factors that dislodged Europeans all over the continent.[5] The explorations and subsequent exploitation of the New World, coupled with the influx of precious metals, altered the old continent's economic and mercantile habits.[6] The expanding reach of capital and the extension of credit permitted unprecedented commercial expansion, promising wealth to some and economic hardship to others. At the same time, religious, scientific and literary developments shattered traditional intellectual certainties, plunging much of the continent into creedal conflicts and ideological disputes. In the meantime, throughout Europe and its offshore islands, monarchies and administrations were centralising their authority and extending the scope of their activities. They levied taxes with increasing efficiency; they overawed opponents and reined in the traditional privileged orders such as the clergy and nobility. In the Americas, Africa and elsewhere they facilitated the mass exploitation that saw the decimation of indigenous populations. Everywhere, the extension of state authority was accompanied by military conquest, displacement of people and the establishment of state bureaucracies and churches. As monarchs demanded religious as well as dynastic loyalty from their subjects, the influence of older, transnational authorities like the papacy and the empire were questioned.

Diasporic origins

Because of its geographical location on the European periphery and its political and economic links with Britain, Ireland's experience of these changes was affected by political and religious change in neighbouring

England and Scotland.[7] So too were European perceptions of the Irish. In all this, the geo-political context was crucial. The gradual imposition of English authority on the island of Ireland, which commenced in earnest under Henry VIII (1491–1547), included military conquest. This was largely completed by 1603. Conquest was accompanied by the plantation of English and Scots colonists, making Ireland a staging post in the later colonisation and exploitation of British America. The colonisation strategy, soon to be applied across the world, was pioneered in Ireland in the 1550s, greatly extended in the early seventeenth century and continued in the 1650s and, later again, in the 1690s. Conquest and plantation caused the displacement of defeated soldiery in the short-term and, in the longer-term, the dislodgement of dispossessed landowners and their dependents. The English conquest of Ireland had an ideological dimension too, in the form of the Anglicanism that was gradually imposed as the state religion. It largely failed to gain traction with the older Gaelic and Norman-English populations in Ireland; the latter opted for Catholicism, the religion of England's principal European foes, France and Spain. Accordingly, Ireland entered the seventeenth century as a jurisdiction where the majority of the population did not share the religion of its rulers. Irish Catholics were subject, consequently, to civil and economic disadvantage, not unlike that endured by French Huguenots, Dutch Catholics and Ulster Presbyterians. For most of the population, there was no option but to endure the resultant marginalisation. There were others, however, who could and did opt for migration overseas. They included demobilised Irish military, dispossessed landowners, ejected clergy and peripatetic students. Because their economic and social status at home were undermined, they sought both redress and alternative career opportunities abroad.[8] In this sense, the emergence of the early modern British state was the crucible for Ireland's Europe-bound migration.

The trading diaspora

For most sixteenth- and early-seventeenth-century Irish migrants, Spain and Portugal were destinations of choice.[9] This was due both to Spain's status as the global super power and its championing of Catholicism against Protestant and Ottoman foes. From the Spanish Netherlands to the New World, Spain and its overseas possessions provided the sort of opportunities that Irish traders, in particular, found irresistible. Traders were among the first of the early modern Irish to establish themselves there, setting up small Irish trading communities in the Basque ports, in Galicia and, further south, in Portugal, especially Lisbon. The resulting commercial networks linked Irish ports, especially those in Munster, with European anchorages, and soon came to act as bridges for successive generations of Irish migrants.

Lisbon is one of the earliest examples of a protean Irish merchant community abroad. By 1573 there was a small but varied Irish community there, nearly all connected with trade and numbering perhaps a few dozen. The group included several merchants and sailors, with a sprinkling of tradesmen, vagrants, sundry hangers-on and an innkeeper called Catherine Burke, who appears to have played an important role in the life of the local Irish community.[10] She was married to a Portuguese merchant, Antonio Ribeiro, who made frequent trading trips to Galway.[11] Two Irish tailors were also long-term residents of the city, one of whom had settled permanently there with his wife and family. A few years later, in 1577, one of the Irish merchants in Lisbon lodged the eleven-year-old Maurice, son of James FitzMaurice FitzGerald, who was attending the local Jesuit school.[12] Later, in the mid-1580s John Daniel and his wife were running a tavern for foreigners in the city centre, where they lodged fugitive merchants like Patrick Enright who were out of favour with the Dublin administration.[13] Enright, a political refugee from the failed Baltinglass rebellion of 1580, was associated with the Luttrell brothers, Nicholas and William, who got by as street hawkers in Lisbon. They, in turn, were associated with Francis Cusack, a servant of the Portuguese native Alvaro de Sousa. Towards the end of the 1580s, a Waterford merchant, Michael Purcell, was staying in the city.[14] In 1591, Thomas Burke of Limerick, a wine trader, was living in the *calle Grande*, with his wife, Jeanette Arthur.[15] An Irish surgeon called Maurice Daniels was also resident there at this time. In time, an Irish college (1590) and two Dominican convents followed (1632 and 1639), giving the small colony a degree of institutional permanence. Other Irish overseas communities followed a similar development pattern.[16]

Thomas O'Connor

Military migrants

Over time, larger migrant groups gathered around these small mercantile communities. Initially, the most numerous of these tended to be military men, a reflection of the troubled political situation in sixteenth and seventeenth century Ireland. Already in the 1580s, about 1,000 Irish soldiers were in Spanish service in the Netherlands.[17] They were sometimes accompanied by their wives, families and camp followers.[18] Due to danger to life and adverse conditions, military service was rarely the preferred migrant option, but it was on occasion the only one available. In the 1600s, for instance, Spanish service proved a lifeline for demobilised Gaelic soldiery after their defeat at Kinsale. Families like the O'Neills, O'Donnells, O'Sullivans, MacCarthys and O'Driscolls, all on the losing side in the Tudor and Stuart wars in Ireland, had to make their futures overseas, bringing their retinues with them.

This influx of Irish was not always welcome, and the Spanish authorities were inclined to send the Irish—especially the so-called *gente inútil*—packing.[19] Spain did, however, have a use for disbanded Irish soldiery and quickly set up an Irish *tercio* in the Spanish Netherlands to accommodate them. In this self-interested way, the Spanish military establishment adapted the unwelcome migrant inflow to its own geo-political needs in the Low Countries.[20] Over the following decades, up to 20,000 Irish were active in this theatre of war, marking the beginning of an enduring Irish military presence in the Spanish royal infantry and navy. Later in the seventeenth century, due mainly to man-power shortages in Spain, the Spanish monarchy not only accepted migrant soldiery but also recruited men directly in Ireland. During the strife-torn 1640s, it is estimated that over 20,000 Irish soldiers entered Spanish service. Smaller numbers enlisted in Scandinavian and central European armies.[21]

In Spain, the Irish were not always entirely reliable recruits. By the middle of the century, many were deserting to join the armies of Spain's arch-rival, France.[22] Their military reputation in Spain would not be restored until the following century, which saw a fresh influx of Irish soldiers and the formation, under the Spanish banner, of the Irish regiments of *Ultonia*, *Irlanda* and *Hibernia*. Despite the marked xenophobia of the Spanish establishment, migrants of this generation went on to serve Spain at the highest level. Richard Wall (1694–1777) served as Spanish prime minister from 1754 to 1763, Alexandro O'Reilly (1722–94) as captain general and governor of Spanish Louisiana and Hugh O'Connor (1732–79) as governor of Spanish Texas. Irish contributions to Spanish life were neither completely martial nor totally male. Two Irishwomen, for instance, played a significant literary role in the Spanish enlightenment: the poet, María Gertrudis Hore [Hoare] (1742–1801)[23] and the translator and author Inés Joyes y Blake [Joyce-Blake], (1731–1808), whose *Apología de las mujeres* appeared in 1798.[24]

Spain remained a favoured destination for Irish migrants throughout the early modern period, but as its geo-political star waned, Irish migrants, ever sensitive to fresh opportunities, took note. The Irish migrant gaze turned to France, the emerging European land power of the mid seventeenth century. Under Louis XIV, the Bourbons built up a large military establishment, supplied from domestic and foreign sources. As many as 30,000 Irish soldiers entered French service in the first half of the seventeenth century, many fighting in the later stages of the Thirty Years War. Like the Spanish, the French actively recruited soldiers in Ireland in wartime, through a system of military entrepreneurs that included the Barrys of Cork and the Sinnotts in Wexford. As in Spain, the Irish military influx was deployed to French geo-political advantage. Organised into designated Irish army units, the famous *régiments irlandais*, the Irish constituted a durable presence in the French military establishment.

The largest Irish military influx into France occurred in two waves at the end of the seventeenth century, during and immediately following the Williamite wars. In 1690, about 5,000 Irish soldiers sailed to Brest, under Justin MacCarthy.[25] The second wave of France-bound Irish military migration occurred after the defeat of the Jacobite forces at the Boyne. About 12,000 men with a significant number of dependents sailed for France, bringing the total Irish strength in the French army to about 18,000.[26] Peace brought demobilisation and, in its wake, poverty for many Irish military families abroad, obliging some to turn to crime. This earned the Irish a jaundiced reputation in certain French quarters.

Notwithstanding this, Irish service under the French Bourbon banner was distinguished, notably at Cremona (1702), Ramillies (1706) and Fontenoy (1745). As the century wore on, the rank and file of the

Irish regiments grew progressively less Irish. This was because potential Irish recruits now had alternative employment opportunities, often at home. For Irish officers, however, the foreign commissions remained attractive, thanks to the status they conferred and, also, to the strong sense of regimental ownership among certain military families in Ireland. In spite of native French opposition, the Irish clung to their military privileges, which, overall, provided as many as 500 European commissions for Irish officers at any one time. In this indirect way, military service overseas alleviated at least some of the professional frustrations engendered by the anti-Catholic penal laws in Ireland.

Students on the move

Soldiers and merchants, however, were not the only migrant exports from early modern Ireland to the European continent. Irish students began to appear more regularly in European colleges and universities after the middle of the sixteenth century. This was in part due to the lack of a local university until the 1590s.[27] Even when a domestic university was finally established in 1592, its restrictive recruitment, coupled with the fraught political and religious conditions of the time, led many Catholic heads of families to send their male offspring to European universities, shunning not only Dublin University but also the English and Scottish institutions previously frequented. From the 1550s, Irish students began to appear in the registers of European universities, particularly those of Louvain, Douai, Paris, Alcalá, Toulouse, Lisbon, Salamanca and Rome.[28] By the end of the century, they had become sufficiently numerous to warrant the setting up of dedicated Irish hostels, some of which evolved into fully-fledged colleges and seminaries, nearly always in large university towns. These competed well enough with the newly founded Dublin University to supply an alternative Catholic clergy to the Anglicans trained in Ireland. The first of the overseas colleges was in Lisbon, but others quickly followed in Salamanca, Santiago, Louvain, Paris, Prague, Rome and elsewhere.[29] Initially, these institutions were small, housing only a handful of students and staff. Furthermore, they were riven by the inherited inter-provincial and ethnic rivalries that Irish migrants carried abroad. College finances were particularly precarious, with institutions surviving on a combination of donations from family in Ireland and help from friends abroad. The latter included overseas Irish military and merchants. Support, generally quite niggardly, was also forthcoming from European monarchs. For them, the colleges and the clergy they produced represented a means of exercising soft power in Ireland. This was especially important for the French and the Spanish, so often in conflict with Ireland's English rulers. Foreign nobility and ecclesiastics supported the colleges too, combining *Realpolitik* with piety and good works.

These colleges were complex institutions, playing multiple and changing roles over time. On one level, they were intended to provide trained clergy for Irish dioceses. As this was an expensive activity, especially in the early years, only a small minority of Irish clergy could avail of a foreign sojourn. For those Irish students who did go abroad and eventually returned home as serving clergy, their time away could be a life-changing experience, conferring domestic status and a directive role, often as bishops and senior clergy, in the illegal Irish Catholic Church. In the sixteenth century, continentally educated students constituted only a leaven among the mass of Irish clergy and were probably never in the majority. By the late eighteenth century, however, some of the wealthier Irish dioceses could afford to provide at least a short formation period overseas for a substantial number of their clergy. These European-trained clergy, like their relations in overseas regiments, were, moreover, a significant internationalising influence on Irish life.

The production of priests was by no means the sole function of the colleges. This is clear when one looks at student numbers and composition. In the Irish college at Douai, for instance, there were reportedly 100 students as early as 1599. They were not all or even mostly clerics. Indeed, according to a government spy at the time, over half of the student body was composed of sons of gentry families from the Dublin area.[30] For them, the college was not just a seminary but also a secondary school, providing access to the local university and preparing their sons for secular careers at home and abroad.

Given these circumstances, it is not surprising that not all or even most of the Irish students sent overseas to college returned home. In the first place, the best students were liable to recruitment into foreign service, either by the religious orders or other agencies, such as the army and the universities.[31] Talented clerics like Luke Wadding (1588–1657) and Flaithrí Ó Maol Chonaire (1569–1629) joined the Franciscans, with both men pursuing influential ecclesiastical and political careers abroad in papal and Spanish service, respectively. Others, like Waterford native Peter Lombard (c.1555–1625), represented Louvain University in Rome. The Limerick-born Thomas Field (1547–1626) joined the Jesuits to serve on the foreign mission in South America.[32] Other students enlisted in local armies, entered other careers or simply disappeared, not infrequently into poverty and oblivion.[33]

In the struggle to survive on the continent, the Irish clerical diaspora developed an intriguing expertise in colonising troubled or defunct continental institutions for their own benefit and the benefit of the nascent colleges. In Rome, Luke Wadding acquired the failed Franciscan college of St Isidore for the Irish Franciscans. In 1677, the Irish secured a permanent Paris foothold when a number of astute petitioners gained the defunct Collège des Lombards and its endowments for their students. Early in the eighteenth century, Irish clergy in the city gradually took over an association of university masters and students (called the German nation) within the Sorbonne.

As guests of foreign powers and dependents of local ecclesiastical factions, the migrant Irish had to be careful when taking sides in the intellectual rows, which were a feature of European universities at the time. This became an even more important feature of Irish student life in the mid-seventeenth and eighteenth century, during the Jansenist disputes in France and the Netherlands.[34]

Above all, the colleges acted as centres of sociability, helping migrants to maintain contact and to define and celebrate their identity, notably by hosting the national feasts. Certain colleges, including Louvain, Rome and Prague in the seventeenth and Paris in the eighteenth century, went further, playing important cultural roles too.[35] These included work on antiquarianism, history, lexicography, general scholarship and publishing. For the Irish language, the Franciscan college in Louvain was particularly important, providing the resources for the composition, printing and distribution of pious work in Gaelic.[36] It was also the focus for a sustained effort to collect and preserve literary and history sources in manuscript form that were in danger of being lost. In this way, colleges such as that at Louvain contributed to the formation of an image of Ireland abroad, stressing its antiquity, its contribution to European culture and letters, its Catholicism and its distinctive language and historical heritage.[37] More prosaically, the colleges provided the documentation migrants needed to access continental careers. In Spain, college officials assisted Irish migrants in taking out *hidalgo*, that is, noble status, gaining admission to the military orders or obtaining Spanish nationality.[38] Across the Pyrenees, in France, college staff provided similar services. They drew up *actes de notoriété* or certificates of identity for visiting Irish and acted with power of attorney for absent compatriots.

Financial servicing was another crucial instance in which crossover occurred between different strands of the diaspora. Paris college staff played sophisticated financial roles on behalf of compatriots, holding monies in trust, drawing up wills and providing investment advice.[39] College clerics managed *rentes* (annuities) drawn on sums invested by Irish compatriots with the Paris *Hôtel de Ville* and on investments in government stocks such as the *aides* (excise taxes) and *gabelle* (salt tax). These specialist activities had a larger context. The removal of James II from the thrones of England, Ireland and Scotland in 1688 sparked the Jacobite exodus from the British Isles and a flight of capital towards the continent.[40] International bankers, including Irishmen Daniel Arthur in Paris and Edward Crean in Madrid, helped manage this transfer.[41]

Changing contexts

The second half of the eighteenth century saw the gradual erosion of the conditions that had traditionally motivated and sustained the Irish diaspora in Europe. On the political level, Irish attachment to the exiled Stuart dynasty weakened, permitting former Jacobite loyalists to negotiate a *modus vivendi* with the ruling Hanoverians in Britain and Ireland. Moreover, social changes at home, fuelled by a combination of rapid population growth, economic prosperity and heightened Catholic expectations, permitted a partially successful campaign to remove civil and professional disabilities against Catholics, beginning in the 1780s. This hesitant, contested and partial re-entry of Irish Catholics into the political nation, over time, removed a crucial migrant motivation.

Thomas O'Connor

Within the Irish diaspora itself, this was a time of great flux. For fighting men, the appeal of the continental armies had been declining since before mid-century. Alternative employment opportunities opened up at home, in the Americas, and also in the East India Company, the British navy and, with the repeal of some of the anti-Catholic penal laws in the 1790s, in the British army.[42] Even the merchants, who traditionally transported the diaspora abroad, found themselves in an expanding commercial environment wherein the American markets competed with traditional commercial networks in Europe and served to turn their gaze westwards towards the New World. The Irish followed the money and, while by no means abandoning their traditional destinations in Spanish and French ports, opened up new operations across the Atlantic.

For the colleges' network, too, these were years of challenge and change. Their cultural role continued, part of which included work in the Irish language, notably Seán Ó Briain's *Focalóir Gaoidhilge–Sax-Bhéarla* (published in Paris in 1768) and Aindrias Ó Doinnshléibhe's *An Teagasc críosduidhe* (which had also been published in Paris, in 1742).[43] The phased suppression of the Society of Jesus in Catholic Europe, beginning in Portugal in 1759, proved a disaster for the many Jesuit-run Irish colleges in Iberia. A little later, government consolidation in Austria led to the suppression of the Irish Franciscan college in Prague. From the late 1780s unrest in France led to the closure of the colleges there. Later, the spread of the revolutionary wars into the Netherlands and the Italian peninsula put paid to Irish institutions there too. The ensuing difficulty of supplying clergy to the growing Catholic population in Ireland obliged the Irish bishops to set up diocesan seminaries at home, sealing the post-revolutionary fate of the continental colleges. By the early nineteenth century, almost the entire priest-producing capacity of the continental colleges had been repatriated. After the revolution in France a number of the continental colleges were re-established but they never regained their *ancien régime* lustre.

There were other larger changes at work too. In the nineteenth century the rise of European nationalisms acted as a brake on the sort of migrant patterns established by the Irish in the early modern period. European armies were more suspicious of foreigners, like the Irish, in their ranks.[44] The Irish, for their part, now had better military opportunities in the British army and navy. Irish commercial connections grew increasingly intertwined with those of Britain and America, superseding older merchant links with the continent and hollowing out Irish communities in cities like Cádiz.[45] At the same time, the Catholic 'missions' of European monarchies such as Spain and France, so much a feature of the old regime, were replaced by narrower national agendas. These had little place for migrant minorities like the Irish who had traditionally presented themselves as, and sometimes, in fact, were, religious refugees. In Ireland itself, resurgent Catholicism replaced its old-time rhetoric of persecution with a self-confident discourse of religious universalism that took Irish missionaries to every corner of the world, usually on the coat tails of British, not French or Spanish, imperialists.[46]

The Irish remained in the European consciousness, of course, but henceforth as a sometimes romantic, sometimes condescended to, and occasionally nagging, political and cultural reality.[47] They were no longer visible, as of old, in the human shape of soldiers, merchants, clerics, students and vagrants. As traditional forms of direct contact between Ireland and the continent weakened, 'Ireland', the 'Irish' and the 'Irish cause' became rhetorical devices in European political and popular culture, in ways often disconnected from the political and cultural realities on the island. In the 1820s and 1830s, for instance, the struggle for Catholic emancipation briefly engaged elements of the European liberal movement.[48] Not even the cataclysm of the Great Famine, however, could compete for European attention in a time of famine, dislocation and political unrest over much of the continent. It was not until the campaign for Irish political and cultural independence took wing in the early twentieth century that Ireland re-entered the European consciousness as a pressingly contemporary phenomenon.[49] In its newer nationalist guise, 'Ireland' could operate as a potentially subversive entity, a blueprint to inspire Galicians, Basques and Catalans, for instance, in their respective cultural and political conflicts.[50] More generally, in works like Luís Seoane's El irlandés astrólogo, the Irish experience in Spain has been quarried in order to explore the harsh realities of dictatorship and exile.[51]

At its core, the early modern Irish diaspora was a movement of people occurring in historical time. An untidy human affair, it unfolded under the classic early modern troika of state building, religious change and economic dislocation. Although largely Catholic in composition, it included migrants of all denominations. Moreover, the exit of Catholic migrants from Ireland made way for incoming Anglican, Presbyterian, Huguenot and Palatinate Protestants, who were, in that indirect way, a crucial part of the total Irish migrant experience. Recent work has deconstructed hoary traditional myths, revealing the tensions between different strands of the migrant movement as migrant sub-groups developed their own survival and integration strategies.[52] Most importantly, new research shows that, for all their special pleading as a distinctive group or nation, the Irish were *European* migrants.[53] In moving across borders, between dynasties and through cultural spheres, they competed with other migrants for opportunity, patronage and resources.[54] They generated their own migrant myths and were, in turn, subject to the usually self-absorbed imaginings of their hosts. As historians embed them firmly in their European context, the early modern Irish are slowly recovering their original diversity, richness and ambiguity. The other chapters in this volume reveal something of the extent to which the patterns of mobility and exchange, established in this formative period, have persisted into the contemporary era.

Notes

[1] Roy Flechner and Sven Meeder (eds), *The Irish in early medieval Europe: identity, culture and religion* (Palgrave: London, 2016).

[2] Michael Bennet, 'Late Medieval Ireland in a wider world', in Brendan Smith (ed.), *The Cambridge history of Ireland: vol. i, 600–1550* (Cambridge University Press; Cambridge, 2018), 329–52.

[3] María Begoña Villar García, 'Ingleses y irlandeses en España', in Antonio Eiras Roel and Domingo L. González Lopez (eds), *La inmigracion en España* (Universidade de Santiago de Compostela; Santiago, 2004), 31–76.

[4] Nicholas Canny (ed.), *Europeans on the move: studies on European migration 1500–1800* (Clarendon Press; Oxford, 1994); Yosef Kaplan (ed.), *Early modern ethnic and religious communities in exile* (Cambridge Scholars Publishing; Newcastle, 2017); Liam Chambers, 'The Irish in Europe in the eighteenth century', in James Kelly (ed.), *The Cambridge history of Ireland: vol. iii, 1730–1880* (Cambridge University Press; Cambridge, 2018), 569–92.

[5] John Silke, 'The Irish abroad, 1534–1691', in Theodore William Moody, Francis X. Martin and Francis John Byrne (eds), *A new history of Ireland, vol. iii: early modern*

Ireland 1534–1691 (Clarendon Press; Oxford, 1976), 587–633; Timothy J. Walsh, *The Irish continental college movement: the colleges at Bordeaux, Toulouse and Lille* (Golden Eagle Books: Cork, 1973).

[6] Daviken Studnicki-Gizbert, *A nation upon the ocean sea: Portugal's Atlantic diaspora and the crisis of the Spanish empire, 1492–1640* (Clarendon Press; Oxford, 2007), 17–39.

[7] See, Seán J. Connolly, *Contested island: Ireland 1460–1630* (Clarendon Press; Oxford, 2007); Seán J. Connolly, *Divided kingdom: Ireland 1630–1800* (Clarendon Press; Oxford, 2008).

[8] See, Óscar Recio Morales (ed.), *Redes de nación y espacios de poder: la comunidad irlandesa en España y la América española, 1600–1825* (Albatross; Valencia, 2012); Thomas O'Connor and Mary Ann Lyons (eds), *The Ulster earls in baroque Europe* (Four Courts Press; Dublin, 2010); Patrick Fitzgerald and Brian Lambkin, *Migration in Irish history 1607–2007* (Palgrave; London, 2008); Nathalie Genet-Rouffiac, *Le Grand Exil: les Jacobites en France, 1688–1715* (Service Historique de la Défense; Paris, 2007); María Begoña Villar García, (ed.), *La emigración irlandesa en el siglo XVIII* (Universidad de Málaga; Málaga, 2000).

[9] Karin Schüller, *Die Beziehungen zwischen Spanien und Irland im 16. und 17. Jahrhundert* (Aschendorff Verlag; Münster, 1999), 75–106.

[10] Irish women played a crucial role in the passage from traditional religion to 'Tridentine' Catholicism. See Ute Lotz-Heumann, 'Between conflict and coexistence: the Catholic community in Ireland as a visible underground church in the late sixteenth and early seventeenth centuries', in Benjamin J. Kaplan, Bob Moore, Henk Van Nierop and Judith Pollman (eds), *Catholic communities in Protestant states: Britain and the Netherlands c. 1570–1720* (Manchester University Press; Manchester, 2009), 168–82: 174–5.

[11] Archivo Nacional Torre do Tombo, Lisbon (ANTT), Tribunal do Santo Oficio (TSO), Inquisição de Lisboa (IL), proc. 10871, f. 8.

[12] Archivio Segreto Vaticano, Rome, Nunziatura di Portogallo, 2, ff 280v–281, Coleitor apostólico to the papal secretary of state, Lisbon, 1 August 1577; cited in M. Gonçalves Da Costa (ed.), *Fontes inéditas Portuguesas para a história de Irlanda* (Oficinas Gráficas de Barbosa & Xavier; Braga, 1981), 177.

[13] ANTT, TSO IL, proc. 2028 (1587), ff 6v–7r.

[14] ANTT, TSO IL, proc. 2852, ff 1–14.

[15] ANTT, TSO IL, proc. 13124, ff 1–13.

[16] For Madrid, see Enrique García Hernan, 'Clérigos irlandeses en el corte de Madrid', in Declan M. Downey and Julio Crespo MacLennan (eds), *Spanish–Irish relations through the ages* (Four Courts Press; Dublin, 2008), 49–71; for Málaga, see Jimmy McCrohan, 'An Irish merchant in late seventeenth century Málaga', in Igor Pérez Tostado and Enrique García Hernan (eds), *Irlanda y el Atlántico Ibérico: movilidad, participación e intercambio cultural* (Albatross; Valencia, 2010), 23–33.

[17] Gráinne Henry, *The Irish military community in Spanish Flanders, 1586–1621* (Four Courts Press; Dublin, 1992), 43.

[18] On women in the Irish diaspora, see, Jerrold Casway, 'Irish women overseas, 1500–1800', in Margaret MacCurtain and Mary O'Dowd (eds), *Women in early modern Ireland* (Edinburgh University Press; Edinburgh, 1991), 112–32.

[19] Ciaran O'Scea, *Surviving Kinsale: Irish emigration and identity formation in early modern Spain, 1601–40* (Manchester University Press; Manchester, 2015), 46–9.

[20] See, Eduardo de Mesa, *The Irish in the Spanish armies in the seventeenth century* (Boydell Press; Woodbridge, Suffolk, 2014), 216.

[21] Chester S.L. Dunning and David R.C. Hudson, 'The transportation of Irish swordsmen to Sweden and Russia and the plantation in Ulster (1609–13)', *Archivium Hibernicum* 57 (2013), 422–53.

[22] Mary Ann Lyons and Thomas O'Connor, *Strangers to citizens: the Irish in Europe 1600–1800* (National Library of Ireland; Dublin, 2008), 14.

[23] Frédérique Morand, *Doña María Gretrudis Hore (1742–1801): vivencia de una poetisa gaditana entre el siglo y la clausura* (Ayuntamiento de Alcalá de Henares; Alcalá, 2004).

[24] Mónica Bolufer Peruga, *La vida y la escritura en el siglo XVIII: Inés Joyes: apología de las mujeres* (Universitat de València; València, 2008).

[25] John Cornelius O'Callaghan, *History of the Irish Brigades in the service of France* (Irish University Press; Shannon, 1969), 141.

[26] O'Callaghan, *History of the Irish Brigades*, 141.

[27] See, Virginia Davis, 'Material relating to Irish clergy in England in the late middle ages', *Archivium Hibernicum* 56 (2002), 7–50; Virginia Davis, 'Irish clergy in late medieval England', *Irish Historical Studies* 32 (2000), 145–60.

[28] See, respectively, Jeroen Nilis, 'Irish students in Leuven', *Archivium Hibernicum* 60 (2006–07), 1–304; John Brady, 'Father Christopher Cusack and the Irish college of Douai 1594–1624', in Sylvester O'Sullivan (ed.), *Measgra Mhichíl Uí Chléirigh* (Assisi Press; Dublin, 1944), 98–107; L.W.B. Brockliss and Patrick Ferté, 'Prosopography of Irish clerics in the universities of Paris and Toulouse, 1573–1792', *Archivium Hibernicum* 58 (2004), 1–166; L.W.B. Brockliss and Patrick Ferté, 'Irish clerics in France in the seventeenth and eighteenth centuries: a statistical survey', *Proceedings of the Royal Irish Academy* 87C (1987), 527–72; Óscar Recio Morales, *Irlanda en Alcalá* (Fundación del Rey; Alcalá, 2004); Patricia O'Connell, *The Irish college at Alcalá de Henares 1649–1785* (Four Courts Press; Dublin, 1997); Hugh Fenning, 'Students at the Irish college at Salamanca, 1592–1638', *Archivium Hibernicum* 62 (2009), 7–36; Monica Henchy, 'The Irish college at Salamanca', *Irish Quarterly Review* 70 (1981), 220–7; and Hugh Fenning, 'Irishmen ordained at Rome, 1572–1697', *Archivium Hibernicum* 59 (2005), 1–36.

[29] On the colleges in Lisbon and Santiago de Compostela specifically, see Patricia O Connell, *The Irish college in Lisbon* (Four Courts Press; Dublin, 2001) and Patricia O Connell, *The Irish college at Santiago de Compostela 1605–1769* (Four Courts Press; Dublin, 2007); on the Paris college, see Priscilla O'Connor, Irish clerics in the University of Paris 1570–1770. Unpublished PhD thesis, National University of Ireland, Maynooth (2006).

[30] *Calendar of State Papers, domestic series, of the reign of Elizabeth, 1598–1601*, edited by M.A. Everett Green (Longmans, Green, and Co.; London, 1869), 496–7.

[31] Thomas O'Connor, 'Irish collegians in Spanish service (1560–1803)', in Liam Chambers and Thomas O'Connor (eds), *Forming Catholic communities: Irish, Scots and English college networks in Europe 1568–1918* (Brill; Leiden, 2018), 15–38.

[32] Guillermo Furlong, *Misiones y sus pueblos de Guaranies, 1610–1813* (Ediciones Teoria; Buenos Aires, 1962); Guillermo Furlong, *Tomas Fields SJ y su 'Carta al preposito general 1601'* (Casa Pardo; Buenos Aires, 1971).

[33] On this point, see, Louis Cullen, 'The Irish diaspora', in Nicholas Canny (ed.), *Europeans on the move: studies on European migration 1500–1800* (Oxford University Press; Oxford, 1994), 113–49.

[34] Thomas O'Connor, *Irish Jansenists 1600–70: religion and politics in Flanders, France, Ireland and Rome* (Four Courts Press; Dublin, 2008), 45–73.

[35] Raymond Gillespie and Ruairí Ó hUiginn (eds), *Irish Europe 1600–50: writing and learning* (Four Courts Press; Dublin, 2013); Proinsias Mac Cana, *Collège des Irlandais Paris and Irish studies* (Dublin Institute for Advanced Studies; Dublin, 2001); Maurice Caillet, 'La bibliothèque du collège des Irlandais et son fonds des livres anciens', *Mélanges de la bibliothèque de la Sorbonne* 2 (1991), 151–63.

[36] On Louvain's scholarly role, see, Nollaig Ó Muraíle (ed.), *Mícheál Ó Cléirigh, his assoicates and St Anthony's College, Louvain* (Four Courts Press; Dublin, 2008), especially part one.

[37] For an overview, see, Tadhg Ó Dúshláine, *An Eoraip agus litríocht na Gaeilge* (Baile Átha Cliath; An Clóchomhar, 1987). For a selection of original texts, see, Brendán Ó Doibhlin, *Manuail de Litríocht na Gaeilge, fasc I–V* (Baile Átha Cliath; Coiscéim, 2003–9).

[38] Samuel Fannin, 'Documents of Irish interest in the Archivo de la Diputación Foral de Bizkaia', *Archivium Hibernicum* 64 (2011), 170–93.

[39] Priscilla O'Connor, 'Irish clerics and Jacobites in early eighteenth-century Paris (1700–30)', in Thomas O'Connor (ed.), *The Irish in Europe 1580–1815* (Four Courts Press; Dublin, 2001), 175–90. On sources, see, Liam Swords, 'Calendar of Irish material in the files of Jean Fromont, notary at Paris, 1701–30, in the Archives Nationales Paris: part I, 1701–15', *Collectanea Hibernica* 34–5 (1992–3), 77–115 and *Collectanea Hibernica*, 36–7 (1994–5), 85–139.

[40] The classic text on the cultural significance of the Jacobites, both at home and in France, is Brendán Ó Buachalla, *Aisling ghéar: na Stíobartaigh agus an t-aos léinn 1601–1788* (Baile Átha Cliath; An Clóchomhar, 1996). For recent scholarship, see, Vincent Morley, 'Irish Jacobitism, 1691–1790', in James Kelly (ed.), *The Cambridge history of Ireland: vol. iii 1730–1880* (Cambridge University Press; Cambridge, 2018), 23–47.

[41] For Arthur, see, Nathalie Genet–Rouffiac, *Le grand exil: les Jacobites en France, 1688–1715* (Service historique de la Défense; Paris, 2007), 373–400.

[42] For a general overview, see, Thomas Bartlett and Keith Jeffery, *A military history of Ireland* (Cambridge University Press; Cambridge, 1996).

[43] For the Irish-language literature produced in Paris in the eighteenth century, see, Mac Cana, *Collège des Irlandais Paris and Irish Studies*, 97–181. For a more vernacular example, see, Ciarán Mac Murchaidh, 'Text and translation of James Gallagher's "A sermon on the Assumption of Our Blessed Lady" (1736)', *Archivium Hibernicum* 62 (2009), 154–82.

[44] For the case of Spain in the later eighteenth and early nineteenth century, see, Óscar Recio Morales, *Ireland and the Spanish empire, 1600–1825* (Four Courts Press; Dublin, 2010), 269–84.

[45] For the example of Cádiz, see, María del Carmen Lario de Oñate, *La colonia mercantile Británica e Irlandesa en Cádiz a finales del siglo XVIII* (Servicio de Publicaciones Universidad de Cádiz; Cádiz, 2000), 206.

[46] For recent scholarship on changing migration patterns in the nineteenth and early twentieth century, see, Mary Daly, 'Migration since 1914', in Thomas Bartlett (ed.), *The Cambridge history of Ireland: vol. iv 1880 to the present* (Cambridge University Press; Cambridge, 2018), 527–52.

[47] For the case of Portugal, see, Pereira da Conceiçao, *Portugal e Irlanda: laços duma civilizaçao Atlântica na bruma dos séculos* (Sociedad da língua Portuguesa; Lisbon, 1970). For France, see, Pierre Joannon and Kevin Whelan (eds), *Paris—capital of Irish culture: France, Ireland and the republic, 1798–1916* (Four Courts Press; Dublin, 2017).

Thomas O'Connor

[48] Geraldine Grogan, 'Daniel O'Connell and European Catholic thought', *Studies: an Irish Quarterly Review* 80 (137) (Spring, 1991), 56–64; Pierre Joannon, 'O'Connell, Montalembert and the birth of Christian democracy in France', in Maurice R. O'Connell (ed.), *Daniel O'Connell: political pioneer* (Dublin Institute of Public Administration; Dublin, 1991), 86–109; Geraldine F. Grogan, *The noblest agitator: Daniel O'Connell and the German Catholic movement, 1830–50* (Veritas; Dublin, 1991); Karl Holl, *Die irische Frage in der Ära Daniel O'Connells und ihre Beurteilung in der politischen Publizistik des deutschen Vormärz* (Johannes-Gutenberg-Universität; Mainz, 1958).

[49] Jérôme aan de Wiel, 'Ireland's war and the Easter Rising in European context', in John Crowley, Donal Ó Drisceoil, Mike Murphy and John Borgonovo (eds), *Atlas of the Irish revolution* (Cork University Press; Cork, 2017), 227–39. For Germany, see, Wolfgang Hünseler, *Das Deutsche Kaiserreich und die Irische Frage 1900–1914* (Peter Lang; Frankfurt am Main, 1978). For the USA, see, Michael Doorley, *Irish–American diaspora nationalism: the friends of Irish freedom, 1916–35* (Four Courts Press; Dublin, 2005).

[50] Recio Morales, *Ireland and the Spanish empire*, 7–47.

[51] Luís Seoane, *El irlandés astrólogo* (Buenos Aires; Losange, 1959).

[52] O'Scea, *Surviving Kinsale*, 123–87.

[53] Bernardo J. García García and Óscar Recio Morales (eds), *Las corporaciones de nación en la monarquía hispánica (1580–1750)* (Fundación Carlos Amberes; Madrid, 2014); David Worthington (ed.), *British and Irish experiences and impressions of Central Europe, c. 1560–1688* (Brill; Leiden, 2012); David Worthington (ed.), *British and Irish emigrants and exiles in Europe, 1603–88* (Brill; Leiden, 2009); Alexia Grosjean and Steve Murdoch, *Scottish communities abroad in the early modern period* (Brill; Leiden, 2005); María Begoña Villar García and Pilar Pezzi Cristóbal (eds), *Los extranjeros en la España moderna* (2 vols, Gráficas Digarza; Málaga, 2003).

[54] More broad-ranging comparisons are also appearing. See, Tadhg Ó hAnnracháin, *Catholic Europe, 1592–1648: centre and peripheries* (Clarendon Press; Oxford, 2015).

Re-envisioning independent Ireland

Mervyn O'Driscoll

Introduction

Clichéd it may be, but from a European continental perspective, Ireland remained *une île derrière une île* ('an island behind an island') after 1922.[1] The independence of the Irish Free State (*Saorstát Éireann*) was heavily circumscribed by geostrategic and historical factors. The Great Powers were inclined to treat the offshore European archipelago as one security unit, since the complete severing of the Gordian knot tying Ireland to Britain appeared unfeasible from their perspectives.

Dominion status within the British empire-commonwealth highlighted the qualified nature of Ireland's liberation and blocked the Free State's automatic receipt of full international recognition and legitimacy. An illustration of the Irish state's uncertain status was that it was not granted unshackled rule over all of its territory; the Anglo-Irish Treaty of 1921 accorded Britain possession of three strategic ports in peace-time and additional military facilities to defend them 'in time of war or strained relations with a Foreign Power'.[2] Moreover, Ireland was per-mitted to provide for its coastal defence only after a period of time and only with British consent. In addition, the size of its defence forces was restricted, in order to diminish any potential threat to Britain.[3] More generally, imperial custom was that dominions aligned with Britain 'in time of war'.

Consequently, the enigmatic new state struggled to carve out its niche against international resistance. Power politics was dominated by European imperial kingdoms, and among these Britain held global primacy. From a European imperial outlook, it was unimportant if do-minionhood chafed Ireland's republicans. Moreover, the self-interest of European states impelled them to work constructively with Britain and there was little advantage to be gained from nurturing Irish republican-ism or associating with Dublin in a way that was offensive to London.

On the other hand, Irish links and memories were closest to the old West European states, while its connections to the newly formed post-war East European states were meagre. Many of the latter were formed from the debris of the empires of Germany, Austria-Hungary, the Ottomans, and Tsarist Russia, so they were unknown quantities. In these circumstances, and for reasons of a sense of historical and geo-graphical connection, official Ireland interacted mainly with Western Europe after 1922. This chapter, therefore, pays particular attention to Irish dealings with Germany, France, Spain, Italy and the Vatican. The ability to form and maintain relations with traditional West European powers was viewed by the Dublin government as an affirmation of Ireland's emancipation and self-perception as an ancient nation.

The chapter explores how opting for neutrality in 1939 had signif-icant repercussions for Ireland's associations with Europe after 1945. It argues that Ireland's relations with West-Central Europe only flour-ished after its application for membership of the European Economic Community (EEC) in 1961. Yet again, the explanation for this resided heavily in the stubborn external perception that Ireland remained within Britain's sphere of influence. Part of the problem was Ireland's fixation on partition, and that constrained its conduct of foreign affairs. The chapter outlines how Ireland acclimatised to European integration when Dublin progressively retreated from industrial protectionism to concentrate on enticing foreign industrial investment to establish an export-based manufacturing sector. Access to the EEC market and European, especially German, capital was now an essential component of its new industrialisation policy. The chapter contends that the Federal Republic of Germany (FRG) played a seminal role in redefining official Ireland's destiny, since it acted as the economic magnet at the core of the EEC. In addition, it formed the political axis of the EEC in partnership with France (the Franco-German axis). Therefore, the FRG was critical to Dublin's European journey.

The roots of diplomatic relations, 1919–22

When the first Dáil met at the Mansion House, Dublin on 21 January 1919 to secede from Westminster, and declare independence, it issued a 'Message to the Free Nations of the World'. That message requested 'every free nation to support the Irish Republic by recognising Ireland's national status and her right to its vindication at the [Paris] Peace Congress'.[4] This was in expectation that US president Woodrow Wilson's principle of self-determination would be implemented, but the separatist Irish case did not receive a hearing. It transpired that the French and American leaders were indifferent to Irish nationalist claims. From their standpoint, self-government was for the peoples of defeated empires only. (Moreover, Irish rebels' association with imperial Germany during the Great War had endangered the wartime anti-German alliance.)[5] This, therefore, impelled the underground Dáil to broaden its para-diplomatic offensive by creating a putative Department of Foreign Affairs and a Publicity Department.

With the failure of the First Dáil's initiative to reverse the US position by 1920, efforts turned to mainland Europe with the despatch of envoys and negotiators to represent the republican cause in the capitals of Europe. With the exception of the international pariah or 'rogue' state that was Soviet Russia, few states in Europe were prepared to recognise the Dáil or the legitimacy of the Irish cause. In effect, the Irish envoys on the continent were reduced to fundraising and counterpropaganda, as seen, for example, in the production and distribution of the *Irish Bulletin* to offset the British narrative. Irish missions in European capitals operated in a 'grey zone', where they were barely tolerated by European governments. They had to maintain low profiles and evade the attentions and indignation of British embassies. In effect, therefore, republican expectations that European states would support Irish independence were dashed. This laid bare the unreliability of using Irish nationalist memories of Spanish, German and French interventions in Ireland against Britain rule over the centuries as a guide to contemporary international behaviour. Irish disappointment continued after the signing of the Anglo-Irish Treaty on 6 December 1921, and the foundation of the Irish Free State one year later.

In contrast to their political masters, large sections of the publics of West European states nevertheless seemed generally favourable towards Irish independence. Recent analyses of material from Belgium, West Germany, France, Italy, Luxembourg and the Netherlands suggest there was diffuse uninformed, but uneven, support for the Irish nationalist struggle in many national and regional newspapers.[6] Even newspapers in Luxembourg, which 'possessed few significant or direct material or sentimental links to Ireland before the Second World War ... displayed an affinity for Irish nationalism's struggle to secure and consolidate independence'.[7] Religion played a role and there was support for Ireland in Catholic Belgium, Italy and Spain, as well as among the Catholic sections of the Dutch and German populations. Interest in Ireland was high among submerged and minority nationalities in Western and Eastern European states, such as the Flemings,[8] Catalans and Basques.[9] This was foreseeable as they aspired to imitate Ireland's liberation.

The first decade, 1922–32

The Irish civil war (1922–3) enfeebled the infant state's international image further. Adding to the credibility issues raised by Ireland's dominion status, the civil war produced a polarised parliamentary system. The lasting and bitter cleavage between those favouring accepting the constraints of the Anglo-Irish Treaty and those rejecting them defied the left versus right division that dominated West and Central European politics. The national question, rather than social and economic questions, was the defining issue in Irish party politics.

Compounding the state's image difficulties, the civil war tore the budding Department of Foreign Affairs apart. The government closed its wartime missions on the continent and redesignated the department as 'External Affairs', in line with dominion practice. Once the Irish civil war had receded, the government turned towards improving its image in North America. It was anxious to enlist the support of the Irish-American lobby.

The decision to join the League of Nations in 1923, however, demonstrated the ambitions of the state and fortified its status. As the minister for External Affairs informed the senate on this landmark occasion, 'the chief point is that Ireland as a free country, as a European country, takes her place with the other countries'.[10] The Irish self-image was that of an old European nation retaking its rightful position; at this time European states made up the majority of the League of Nations' 40-odd members.

Meanwhile, the nascent Department of External Affairs struggled to exist. It was a completely new department, unlike the other departments inherited from British rule. Although residential envoys were swiftly appointed to London, Geneva and Washington in 1923 and 1924, it was not until 1929 and 1930 that diplomats were exchanged with Weimar Germany, France and the Vatican. At this early point in the state's history, it had limited trade and cultural interactions with Western Europe, except for a few academic exchanges and a handful of tourists. The main exception was Rome, an eternal destination for Irish pilgrims. Ireland's diplomatic expansion did not emerge from an insistent European demand. Instead it was principally an Irish initiative and the intention was explained by External Affairs when it asserted in 1928:

> There can be no doubt that the appointment of Ministers to one or more of the great European Powers would very clearly establish the fact, which is not at the moment appreciated, the *Saorstát* must be regarded as a unit

Mervyn O'Driscoll

in international affairs in no way subservient to Great Britain.[11]

The incursion into Europe was the brainchild of the dynamic new minister for External Affairs, Patrick McGilligan. He also held the Industry and Commerce portfolio and appreciated Europe's likely contribution to Irish modernisation.

In 1925 Siemens-Schuckert's winning of a contract to construct the landmark Ardnacrusha hydroelectric facility on the River Shannon highlighted how German know-how could assist in this goal.[12] Its high profile facilitated other German firms to establish their position as suppliers, delivering electrical goods, plant machinery, engineering products and manufactures to semi-state bodies and local authorities. German firms profited from Irish stereotypes about German reliability. In view of Germany's industrial and political significance, it was not surprising that Berlin was a target for Irish diplomacy. The memory of Imperial Germany's efforts to assist Irish insurgents during the Great War, above all in advance of the 1916 Easter Rising, likely also played a part.

Exchanging diplomats with the Vatican presented no obstacles in view of the religiosity of Ireland's overwhelmingly Catholic population. The first secretary of the Department of External Affairs, Joseph Walshe, a former Jesuit seminarian, was anxious to cultivate relations with the Holy See. France was the third European country chosen for Irish attentions. A traditional power, it occupied a key role in the post-First World War settlement and in the League of Nations, and any self-respecting state needed a resident minister in Paris. Of course, there was an Irish affinity with France based on a memory of the 'wild Geese' and of French interventions in Ireland during the French Revolution. During the late nineteenth and early twentieth century, however, France had moved into the orbit of Britain and the US, for protection against the recently unified Germany. French reliance on Britain increased when the US retreated into isolation after 1918. Ironically, Weimar Germany prized associations with Britain too, but its motive was to temper French vengeance and soften the effects of the Versailles settlement. Therefore, the Irish government was dissatisfied by the tardiness of Paris, Berlin and the Vatican in responding to Irish efforts to exchange diplomats in 1929 and 1930.

The first minister appointed to Weimar, Daniel Binchy, discovered that Ireland was a low priority in Germany. He concluded that Berlin treated Ireland as 'a small completely isolated state' and prioritised the cultivation of German–British relations.[13] Whatever sympathy existed among the German and French populations and elsewhere for independent Ireland, it did not translate into official policy. Even the Vatican was reticent.[14] It would seem that opening diplomatic relations with Ireland was a low priority at the time. Simply put, the Irish state's claim to occupy the moral high ground on the basis of nationalist grievance was not a consideration in Great Power politics.

Binchy reported in 1930 that independent Ireland's 'fundamental enemy in every country' was 'the idea that we are a sort of bastard English nation with no distinctive ancestry or civilization of our own'.[15] During December 1938 the newly appointed Irish minister to Italy also observed: 'To attempt to convince continental peoples of the objectivity of our views in a case where England is concerned is a rather difficult task for they have always regarded the Irish question as something that is, in itself, anti-British.' He suggested that Italians barely gave Ireland a thought, except if it served their interests to use the issue of Ireland as a 'convenient weapon with which to belabour John Bull'. Italy's interests lay in friendly relations with London, so the Irish question was ignored.[16] The Vatican, for its part, desired Ireland's acclimation to dominion status in order to protect Catholic interests throughout the commonwealth.[17]

Moreover, the piecemeal constitutional evolution of the British empire into the commonwealth proved rather arcane to outsiders. The Balfour Declaration produced by the 1926 Imperial Conference might have declared dominions equal to Britain, but it was difficult to predict how this would operate. Then when the 1931 Statute of Westminster granted dominions the right to repeal any legislation that Westminster had passed, its full implications remained to be revealed.

Dictatorships and war, 1932–45

De Valera took advantage of the Statute of Westminster to revise the relationship between the Irish Free State and Britain. A leading critic of the 1921 Anglo-Irish Treaty and the political head of the anti-treaty forces during the civil war of 1922–3, he became the president of the Executive Council of the Free State when he led the anti-treaty Fianna Fáil party to victory in the 1932 general election. Henceforth, he engaged in a trial of wills with London to hollow out the Anglo-Irish Treaty and the Irish Free State Constitution of 1922. He filleted both to suit the republican palate by purging the state of the symbols and processes of subordination. Finally, he capped off the process in 1937 with a new constitution, *Bunreacht na hÉireann*, which transformed independent Ireland into a republic in all but name within the empire-commonwealth. Neither the commonwealth nor the British crown were mentioned in the new constitution, though Ireland chose to associate voluntarily with the commonwealth, at least temporarily. London, of course, was not pleased, but it had failed to overcome de Valera's ability to mould and harness the Irish national will. Despite the retrospective criticisms that can be made of *Bunreacht na hÉireann* today on social and gender equality grounds, in the context of Europe in 1937 it was a statement of the Irish attachment to constitutional democracy, the rule of law and the toleration of minorities.

Meanwhile, Irish efforts at trade promotion had mixed results and the major European countries did not offer a means to diminish economic dependence on Britain: 90% of Ireland's merchandise exports was destined for the UK during the 1920s, and it remained at that approximate level until the late 1950s.[18] The opportunities offered by the global economy after the Wall Street crash of 1929 were limited by the collapse of free trade. In the new protectionist and 'beggar-thy-neighbour' trade environment, Ireland's efforts to break out of its traditional pattern of trade with Britain were doomed and Dublin remained wedded to Anglo-Irish commerce and protecting the commonwealth trading preference. Regardless of the Anglo-Irish 'Economic war' pursued by de Valera between 1932 and 1938, Ireland's overseas pattern of trade hardly changed.[19] Although Germany was established as Ireland's second trading partner behind Britain, its market share was minuscule in comparison to Britain's.[20] Overall, Irish trade with the remainder of Europe at this point was trivial.[21]

The National Socialist Party of Germany's (Nazi) takeover from January 1933 did not dramatically change Berlin's perceptions of Ireland. Regarding the 'Economic war' as a temporary disruption,

Berlin refused to exploit the quarrel and estimated that Irish trade dependence on Britain could not be broken. Berlin would not harm Anglo–German relations for a negligible and peripheral market far from its hinterland.[22] More significant was the Nazi world view, which saw the English as racial equals, indeed partners, so Adolf Hitler aspired to a global understanding between a German European empire and a British non-European maritime empire.[23] There was little incentive, therefore, for Hitler to embolden Irish republicanism as he pursued an understanding with London. Initially the Irish Free State was open-minded about the Nazi regime, but evidence quickly amassed to generate widespread Irish antipathy towards Nazism. In particular, the Nazis' resort to extra-parliamentary violence and intimidation was not in line with the democratic dispositions of Éamon de Valera. The Nazi policy of de-Christianisation alienated Irish opinion, while the murderous brutality of its anti-Semitism caused widespread horror during the pogrom of *Kristallnacht* in November 1938. The German minister to Dublin, Eduard Hempel, appointed in 1937, observed how Irish attitudes towards Germany deteriorated swiftly at this time.[24]

In summation, Dublin disapproved of the internal policies of Nazi Germany but refrained from public comment. It can be argued that Irish–Nazi relations were a good gauge of the general state of Irish–European interactions. The political distance between the government of Éamon de Valera and those of the continental countries grew during the 1930s as Irish adherence to parliamentary democracy and constitutionalism set it apart from the authoritarian drift in most continental states. The anti-government and para-fascist Irish Blueshirts' affinity with Mussolini's Blackshirts served as a salutary lesson for the governing Fianna Fáil party in 1932 and 1933.[25] The early mistake of some Nazi papers in naively labelling the Blueshirts as Irish Nazis and depicting de Valera as a Jew led to Irish protests and a certain reserve in Dublin's attitude to Nazi Germany.[26] Ironically, the growing Irish awareness of the ideological gap between Ireland and fascistic governments in Europe served to accentuate the commonalities between Britain and Ireland.

The 1930s, after all, witnessed the general collapse of the new democracies established in Eastern, Central and Southern Europe. The disruption caused by the Great War had created political space for right-wing extremists of all complexions across the continent. The success of the radical right began in Italy in 1922. Benito Mussolini's fascist coup provided a model of how to overthrow shaky parliamentary democracies. The wave of the democratic collapse became crushing during the great depression in the 1930s. 'Strong men' won power drawing on paramilitary movements, nationalism, paralegal methods, populist messages and calls for law and order as economic collapse created enormous social pressures. The League of Nations failed to face down aggressive expansionist powers, such as Italy and Germany, which were unhappy with the treaty agreed at Versailles. Ireland was a qualified supporter of the League so long as it protected core values such as self-determination, democracy and the rule of law. This sometimes conflicted with a substantial section of Irish opinion when it adopted a simplified Irish Catholic lens. For example, de Valera opposed Mussolini's invasion of Abyssinia in 1935 and refused to recognise Franco's coup against the Madrid republican government in 1936 until it won the ensuing civil war. Ireland implemented sanctions against Italy and chose a policy of non-intervention in the Spanish civil war. Reluctantly, de Valera's domestic critics soon saw the value of his policy, but to many Europeans de Valera's Ireland was an enigma. On one hand, it was a vocal critic of Britain for national reasons. On the other hand, it made common cause with Britain on many major European questions and crises. In the late 1930s Italian fascism's proselytising and the activities of the overseas branch of the Nazi party in Ireland vexed the Irish authorities.

Troublingly, the inclinations of the Irish minister to Germany, Charles Bewley, diverged from those of de Valera. He was favourable towards the Nazi regime and excused its brutal rule, viewing Nazi Germany as a safeguard against the Soviet Union and communism. Moreover, Bewley advised that Ireland should move closer to the Rome–Berlin axis of Mussolini and Hitler after 1936 to distinguish Ireland from Britain.

This general policy recommendation conflicted with de Valera's democratic predispositions. In effect, his approach to European politics after 1936 was to support Britain's appeasement of Nazi Germany, the Treaty of Versailles having stripped Germany of self-respect in his estimation. In the expectation that complying with some tolerable irredentist claims might lead to a return to European normality, Ireland recognised Nazi Germany's territorial acquisitions, including the *anschluss* with Austria in 1937. De Valera fell into step with British prime minister Neville Chamberlain's policy of sanctioning Germany's annexation of the Sudetenland (from Czechoslovakia) to prevent a European war in September 1938.[27] At the height of this, the Munich crisis, de Valera proclaimed it was prudent to concede legitimate nationalist demands, but he cautioned that if Hitler presented spurious demands subsequently, then his true character would be displayed and war would be justified.

By this point, Bewley's unapologetic defence of Hitler's increasing bellicosity and expansionism was intolerable and revealed his complete conversion to the Nazi worldview. He repeated Nazi propaganda in his reports to Dublin in early 1939, declaring that the liberal democracies of France and Britain threatened world peace. Along with Bewley's acute Anglophobia and his evident anti-Semitism, this made him a transparent liability. It was clear now that he had been allowed to remain for too long in Berlin, and de Valera issued the papers for the Irish minister's recall in February 1939. They took effect from 1 August.[28] This was timely because in March 1939 Hitler exceeded the remit of the Munich agreement by conquering the rump Czechoslovakia. On finally appreciating that the German dictator was unlikely to be satisfied by appeasement, Britain and France guaranteed Poland's territorial integrity when Hitler turned his attentions to disputed territories there, including the Free City of Danzig, the Polish Corridor and East Prussia.

In these circumstances, de Valera aired his intention to declare neutrality in the event of a European war. He had retreated from foreign-policy idealism in support of League of Nations principles to conclude that, in a world of naked power, moral principle would be foolhardy for a weak and peripheral state. Policymakers in Paris, Berlin, Rome and London were sceptical about Ireland's will and capability to implement neutrality, even after the 'Treaty Ports' that had been retained in British control were returned to Ireland under the terms of the Anglo-Irish Treaty of 1938. It took Hempel until July 1939 to convince his superiors in Berlin that de Valera would defend Irish neutrality against any British efforts to retake the ports in a war and that, on balance, Irish neutrality was expedient for Germany.[29] When war broke out in September 1939 Dublin was nervous about whether the belligerents would respect Dublin's neutrality, but time would show that de Valera was unwavering in his devotion to a neutral policy. He would not abandon that course when confronted with blandishments, intimidation or inducements. Covert compromises with the Allies would be required, as would firmness in the face of vitriolic external criticisms during and after the war.

Post-war drift

Irish neutrality during the Second World War had complex and unintended effects (because the country adhered to a neutrality policy, an official 'state of emergency' obtained in the country for the duration of the war; as a result, the conflict came to be termed the 'Emergency' in Ireland). On one hand, neutrality can be thought of as the culmination of a steady process of loosening Ireland's ties with Britain and the commonwealth. It expressed Ireland's independent foreign policy and political will in an irrefutable fashion. Any lingering confusions or doubts about Ireland's status and its resolve to dissolve links with Britain were dispelled.

Moreover, Ireland's humanitarian aid package to war-torn Europe after 1945 promoted goodwill. This effort was continental in scope and an expression of collective Irish gratitude for having been spared the ravages of war. The government agreed to give £3 million for the post-war relief of liberated Western European countries in May 1945, and the delivery of Irish aid continued until the end of the decade, by which point most countries from the Atlantic to Albania had benefitted. The Irish public was even more generous; its donations easily surpassed those of the state programme.[30] Consequently, Ireland received many European honours commemorating its relief effort from recipient countries over the course of the next decade.

On the other hand, however, many continentals reckoned that Ireland's wartime neutrality signified a betrayal of democracy. Numbered among the proponents of such views were aggrieved members of the resistance and opponents of Nazism and fascism. Their view was that de Valera's Ireland was pro-Axis.[31] Simply put, Ireland was the victim of European polarised thinking, which failed to recognise the survivalist, nationalist and anti-war mentality underpinning Irish neutrality. Negative European attitudes towards neutrality were galvanised by de Valera's offer of condolences to the German minister on the death of

Adolf Hitler in 1945.[32] De Valera's justification that this was a fulfilment of diplomatic protocol on the death of the German head of state
was unacceptable to European opinion in light of Nazi barbarism.[33] His
argument received little sympathy in the court of world opinion. From
an Irish perspective, however, neutrality moulded a national consensus,
counteracting the poisonous effects of civil war politics and consolidating the independent state.

Despite their criticism of the neutrality policy, it remained clear to
Britain and America that Ireland could make a useful contribution to
the international community in the post-war period. The US, at Britain's
suggestion, invited Ireland to apply for membership of the United
Nations (UN) in 1946, but the Soviet Union took advantage of Ireland's
wartime neutrality and smeared it as pro-Axis as part of its battery of
excuses to justify its annual veto of Irish membership over the next nine
years. The reality behind the Soviet Union's public rhetoric was that
Ireland's application was a hostage to Cold War bloc calculations, but
this was largely not apparent to public opinion. In effect, Moscow prevented pro-Western states such as Ireland from gaining entry into the
UN until a package deal was eventually worked out with the US. This
allowed friendly Western states entry to the UN in return for several
Eastern Bloc states also gaining membership in 1955.[34] The decade of
enforced exclusion from the UN between 1946 and 1955, however, radically reduced Ireland's international engagement.

When combined with wartime neutrality's shielding of Ireland from
the worst effects of the Second World War, it had an unintended effect
of fuelling Irish public complacency about the benefits of neutrality.
Perhaps neutralism during the Cold War could protect Ireland from the
worst effects of all future European and world wars? This was not de
Valera's stated intention when he announced neutrality in 1939. Then,
he had declared neutrality for the duration of the Second World War
only, but in 1949 a new, inexperienced minister for External Affairs,
Seán MacBride, miscalculated, and his actions perpetuated Irish neutralism, or at least military non-alignment, in the public mind. In a
solo run, MacBride, who was the leader of a small, radical republican
party in a precarious government coalition, overestimated Ireland's
strategic importance to the emerging Atlantic alliance. He failed in
his unilateral effort to barter Irish membership of the North Atlantic

Treaty Organisation (NATO) in return for US opposition to partition.[35] This left Ireland 'out in the cold' and laid the foundations for the emergence of a military neutrality tradition. But read another way it was clear that successive governments were prepared to enter a bilateral understanding with the US in the early 1950s. This underscored that Ireland's fundamental objection to becoming a member of the Atlantic alliance was not that it would not countenance joining a military alliance; the real issue was partition. NATO's guarantee of the territorial integrity of its member states, including Britain, meant that the alliance would not consider that Britain's jurisdiction over Northern Ireland was an issue that Ireland had a right to be concerned with. MacBride issued 'tentative' feelers to the US for a bi-lateral defence understanding in 1951, as did his successor Frank Aiken. Aiken, in fact, went much further and made 'sustained efforts' to secure US military assistance in 1952. These Irish efforts at a side deal with the US were rebuffed.[36] To comply with Dublin's wishes would subvert the principles of collective security and assistance that were at the core of NATO. Compliance might also be read as a tacit display of US approval for the basis of Ireland's objection to joining NATO—the ongoing partition of the island—and as far as the Americans were concerned, Northern Ireland was an internal British matter.

Meanwhile, Ireland's continuing unwillingness to join a collective security arrangement with the West distinguished Ireland from the majority of Western European states who joined NATO. Former wartime neutral states made up a large proportion of Ireland's European diplomatic links. Of the nine states on mainland Europe that Ireland had diplomatic relations with in 1951 (France, Italy, the Netherlands, Portugal, Spain, Sweden, Switzerland, West Germany and the Vatican), five had been neutral or non-belligerent in the war.

Irish military neutrality during the Cold War was viewed as un-European and perilous by most European Christian democrats, who believed regional solidarity and defence cooperation were essential to defending Western European states facing the Soviet Union. Ireland's devotion to military nonalignment paralleled the neutralist tendencies of West German social democrats and also found favour with Western European communists. The posture mystified the governments of the Benelux countries, France, Italy and West Germany. Christian democrats were baffled that a country with a reputation for unstinting Catholicism, anti-communism and democracy could refuse to rally to defend European civilisation. For them, the grounds for Irish non-membership of NATO appeared inconsequential in the tense atmosphere of a polarised Europe.

The official Irish diplomatic campaign banged the drum of anti-partition regularly and loudly during the late 1940s and 1950s.[37] Ireland was unresponsive to prevailing West European opinion, and from that vantage point Ireland's invocation of its 'sore thumb' policy (berating others for not addressing the 'injustice' of partition of the island of Ireland) in the counsels of Western Europe (for example, the Council of Europe) was no more than a sideshow to the main European drama. This was the view of Chancellor Konrad Adenauer of West Germany.[38] An article in the West German journal *Aussenpolitik* in 1954 concluded that the Irish refusal to join NATO was an ineffective means to end partition, and it decided that Ireland was not a neutral of conviction—it did not deserve to be counted on a par with Switzerland or Sweden.[39]

From the vantage point of European centre-right democrats, Irish irredentism was self-centred, and Ireland's anti-partitionist propaganda was an uncomfortable irritant, especially to members of NATO with which it had a strong affinity. For example, the Irish protested against the training of Dutch naval pilots by the British Royal Navy in Northern Ireland as part of legitimate NATO cooperation. This produced an embarrassing difference of opinion between Dublin and The Hague in 1951.[40] Ironically, the Netherlands was one of those countries that exhibited positive feelings towards Ireland; the Dutch fondly remembered Ireland's generous humanitarianism in 1945. According to the Dutch regional newspaper *Limburgsch Dagblad* in August 1951, 'Ireland was an island not living in the twentieth century' and 'fear and dismay concerning what is happening [in Europe] rarely reach Ireland'.[41]

Irish propaganda that contended the post-war division of Germany was analogous to Ireland's partition raised uneasy issues for Bonn's mandarins, who viewed the two cases as incomparable. Bonn staunchly advised its diplomatic representatives during the 1950s and 1960s to:

> practise restraint with regard to occasional Irish comparisons of the partition of the Irish and German peoples. The

population of Middle-Germany is robbed of all liberty and political and personal rights, against that the population of Northern Ireland had the opportunity in a free election to express their opinions, and they live in conditions which cannot be compared with those in the Soviet occupied zone.[42]

The FRG's existence partly depended on Britain, an influential senior partner with Washington in NATO. Prime Minister Anthony Eden brokered a European compromise in 1954 that enabled West German rearmament and NATO membership. Subsequently, Adenauer diligently protected these hard-won gains to transform West Germany into a Westernised state. Likewise, other Atlanticist European states such as the Benelux countries and Italy gave little weight to Dublin's anti-partitionist stance. Since London regarded Northern Ireland as an internal matter it was in the general interest of Western Europe to avoid entanglement. In a nut-shell, Ireland's 'sore thumb' propaganda may have played positively with minority nationalists, the de-colonising world and the Warsaw Pact, but it failed to win influential friends in post-war democratic Europe.

Despite the fact that there was no assistance for Irish anti-partitionism emanating from Bonn, Ireland was an indefatigable devotee of Bonn's Hallstein Doctrine from 1955 to 1970.[43] Dublin refused to recognise the German Democratic Republic (GDR) or maintain diplomatic relations with any state that recognised the GDR. It went farther than most. In addition to refusing to maintain relations with any Eastern Bloc state (it recognised the FRG as the only legitimate successor to the pre-1945 German state), Ireland would not respond to Moscow's overtures inviting it to establish diplomatic relations. Ireland finally opened an embassy in Moscow in 1974; NATO countries had already done so many years earlier.[44] To non-communist eyes the unstinting anti-communism of Irish society and its unwillingness to countenance relations with the Soviet Union made the Irish aversion to NATO difficult to comprehend.

If Ireland's political pose diverged from that of much of the rest of Western Europe, it drifted apart from continental economic and social currents too. After all, it persisted with industrial protectionism in the face of American-sponsored trade liberalisation. Ireland became a founding member of the Organisation for European Economic Cooperation (OEEC) in 1948 when its decisionmakers recognised there was no alternative. Ireland's economic dependence on Britain had left it with no choice when the latter decided to join. Nonetheless, Irish policymakers generally disliked the OEEC's liberalisation of Europe's industrial trade in the early 1950s. After two decades of industrial tariffs, Irish industrial employment had grown by less than 60,000 by the early 1950s. By the mid-1950s, 50,000 of those in employment, or 4% of the national workforce, were employed in protected industries.[45] Industrialisation in a small, protected economy was inefficient, and protectionism shut Ireland out of the benefits to be derived from access to a liberalising world economy. Worse still, perhaps, Ireland's agricultural economy remained dependent on raw food exports, especially live cattle, to Britain.[46] After the post-war European and global food shortages receded, food prices collapsed. Some European observers noted the contradiction between Ireland's nationalist aversion to Britain and its unbreakable economic dependence on it.[47] Approximately 91 per cent of Irish exports were destined for the UK as late as 1953, notwithstanding efforts at diversification.[48] Moreover, the country remained in an effective currency union with Britain.

There was a consensus among most European observers that Ireland was insular and detached. For instance, the newspaper *Libre Belgique* argued in August 1947: 'Isolated in the Atlantic for an incredibly long time, the island lived and concentrated on itself alone, quite unaware of the development of the Continent.'[49] William P. Fay, the Irish chargé d'affaires in Brussels, reported a few months later that though the Walloons and Flemish of Belgium were friendly and sympathetic towards Ireland, this was 'modified by the feeling that we are a somewhat peculiar and unpredictable people'.[50]

After a decade of underachievement, Ireland was, by the mid-1950s, in a deep economic trough. Its dismal post-war performance was commented on by representatives of European countries resident in Dublin, especially the West Germans and Dutch.[51] Mass emigration, rural de-population and political instability demonstrated that Ireland's economic model had failed miserably in the estimation of those countries that would go on to form the European Economic Community (EEC) in

1957. These countries experienced speedy post-war reconstruction and their economies witnessed nearly three decades of growth from the late 1940s. There is ample evidence in Dutch, Belgian and German national and regional newspapers that Ireland was depicted as inward-looking, as a producer of literary geniuses, and as backward and poor.[52] It was regarded as a country gripped by the Catholic Church.[53] Hoary negative stereotypes (the Irish propensity to bigotry and drunkenness) peppered European newsprint, while the country was viewed as pre-modern by the urban-industrial core of Western Europe.[54] Ireland and its people were perceived as socially and politically conservative. Criticism of Ireland's stance by the six states that established the European Coal and Steel Community (ECSC) in 1952– Belgium, France, Italy, Luxembourg, the Netherlands and West Germany—and then progressed to establish the EEC mounted steadily during the decade.

It was clear to 'the six' that Irish identification with the vulnerable position of Western Europe and the Atlantic alliance in the Cold War was limited. For instance, Irish members of the Council of Europe repeatedly critiqued efforts to co-ordinate that body's foreign policy. Irish parliamentarians were allergic to any suggestions that the Council of Europe might be subsumed under a broader 'Atlantic community'.[55] To the Euro-integrationist 'six', the Irish displayed a limited affinity for European unity. The attitude of Irish governments until at least 1959 is summarised best by its elder statesman, Éamon de Valera, who cast a long shadow over post-war Ireland. In a meeting with a member of the central committee of the European Union of Federalists in 1948, he offered support for federation but he rejected Irish participation, intimating that it would depend on Britain's position. De Valera stated:

> If Britain found it necessary, owing to her commonwealth, to remain outside a European Federation, then it might be better for Ireland in the first place to belong to some other regional grouping, based, perhaps on the British Commonwealth of Nations.[56]

Ireland succeeded in retaining special trade and travel access to Britain and the commonwealth, even after it transformed into a republic in 1949 and officially left that grouping. Overall, the Irish response to European integration in the 1950s was unenthusiastic and reactive. Ireland was an organic part of the British economic sphere. It was manifest that the Irish government and people lacked a detailed knowledge and understanding of developments in Western Europe. The simple economic reality was that Ireland remained largely an extension of the British labour, capital and factor markets. It can also be conjectured that Irish emigration primarily to Britain (as a result of Ireland's economic difficulties) allowed the perpetuation of the status quo by reducing social pressure for domestic change. Successive Irish governments of all political hues remained firm in their view that growth relied on Anglo-Irish trade. Thus, they sustained a detached attitude towards European co-operation until the early 1960s. Any Irish engagement with European integration would require a fundamental alteration in the Euro-sceptical attitudes of the British.

In such circumstances, Irish diplomats resident in Western European capitals were unable to project Ireland effectively during the 1950s. They were repeatedly apt to argue that Ireland's national message could not break through the British 'screen'.[57] The Irish minister to the Netherlands noted in gloomy resignation in 1951 that the Dutch 'identify us with England to a large extent' and 'the ignorance about Ireland on the continent is truly extraordinary'.[58] This was a common refrain among Irish diplomats in Western Europe and it revealed a lack of mutual comprehension.

Convergence

Britain, and consequently Ireland, could not ignore European integration indefinitely. In Ireland the Department of External Affairs repeatedly encountered European scepticism about Ireland's international posture and became the first department to shift towards a 'European' perspective in the late 1940s and 1950s.[59] The EEC's trade distortion effects on wider Western Europe when combined with Britain's comparatively mediocre economic performance finally required a wholesale change in British and Irish attitudes. After its effort to dilute the EEC within a broader OEEC free trade area had failed, Britain's recourse was to become involved in setting up the European Free Trade Association (EFTA) during 1959 as a defensive measure. The division of Europe into 'sixes and sevens', between the EEC and EFTA, had far-reaching implications. No invitation had been extended to Ireland to join the EFTA industrial free trade zone. It would have been impossible for Ireland to contemplate membership (in light of industrial protectionism), so the founding states did not bother to invite it. Ireland, therefore, suddenly realised its extreme economic vulnerability and international isolation. Its repeated requests for special dispensations on account of its developing status fell on deaf ears in interactions with the OEEC, the EEC and EFTA from the mid-1950s and into the 1960s. The FRG government, for example, observed, in response to Irish pleading during the failed discussions to establish an OEEC Free Trade Area in mid-1957, that Ireland 'should have greater confidence' in its 'ability to overcome' 'difficulties', and Ireland had to submit to the principles of non-discrimination and reciprocity in trade.[60] This became the refrain of West Germany, its EEC partners and the US over the next decade.

Thus, European economic developments played an essential role in inspiring a change in the Irish economic vision.[61] In desperation, the Irish government began, from 1955, to experiment in a piecemeal fashion with foreign direct investment incentives. This transition towards foreign investment was also championed by the OEEC, EEC and EFTA, but, in particular, by West Germany and the Netherlands. In July 1959 the speech at a landmark economic conference in Dublin by John Cahan, the deputy secretary-general of the OEEC, made a major impression. (The conference was organised by the Dublin branch of the Irish Council of the European Movement.) Cahan argued that Ireland was complacent and 'badly needed a jolt'.[62] The division of Europe into rival trade blocs certainly delivered that thunderbolt.

A new taoiseach, Seán Lemass, was already moving in the direction of some policy change, as witnessed in the First Programme for Economic Expansion that ran between 1958 and 1963. Lemass was aware of the need to attract investment and cultivate the dynamic markets of Western Europe. The dual realisation that Ireland was in danger of being shut out of European trade and that its privileged access to the British food market was now in danger of erosion by European competitors (such as Denmark), spurred change. Ireland had a negative trade balance with Western Europe generally. Its balance of trade with West Germany, its primary continental trade partner, would remain acutely and stubbornly negative unless it could find exports that German consumers wanted. Irish civil servants recognised it was inevitable that Irish agricultural commodities would be shut out of German and European markets when the EEC's protectionist Common Agricultural Policy (CAP) was finally negotiated during the 1960s.[63]

Cumulatively, domestic and European forces encouraged a reorientation of Ireland, and Lemass was deeply aware of the requirement to build relations with Western European states. He therefore toned down Irish anti-colonialism at the United Nations and promoted greater consultation with Western Europeans leaders on UN matters generally. He advised the Department of External Affairs on 24 September 1959 that it should not stand on anti-colonialist principle, at least not to such an extent that Ireland would condemn European colonial countries that were at least making an effort to engage in decolonisation efforts. The taoiseach was conscious of the need to maintain good relations with these countries, 'with which we have friendly relations, and with which we trade.'[64] Thus he diluted the neutralist and idealistic rhetoric of Minister for External Affairs Frank Aiken, and he declared continually after 1959 that Ireland's ideological affinities lay with the West.[65] Bonn, Paris and The Hague approved and, in contrast to the unilateralism that had characterised Aiken's approach before 1959, Dublin began to consult regularly with them on UN matters. Lemass's bridge-building and charm offensive began to pay positive dividends—NATO and EEC countries supported Ireland's successful candidature for the presidency of the United Nations General Assembly in 1960.[66]

This paralleled the take-off of foreign industrial direct investment in Ireland during late 1959 and 1960. A surge of German interest in investing in Ireland occurred. The German economic miracle was in danger of overheating, but Ireland's Industrial Development Authority had fine-tuned its pitch to foreign investors. German firms required openings to export surplus capital and access inexpensive labour, and Bonn drew their attention to Ireland as a possible investment destination. For a variety of reasons, approximately 24 factories with German shareholders were established in Ireland between 1955 and 1962.[67] In fact, West Germany vied with the US to become Ireland's second-largest trade partner behind Britain. Throughout the 1960s, German firms were among the top investors in Ireland.[68]

By July 1961 British prime minister Harold Macmillan had concluded that it was not in Britain's interest to remain outside the EEC. For his part, Lemass decided that EEC membership was the best option for Ireland—it was preferable to continued reliance on Britain or an application for membership of EFTA. The Irish pitch to join the EEC came as a surprise. The 'six' correctly surmised that the Irish haste to apply on 31 July 1961, days before Britain lodged its application, was to conceal that Ireland's move was dependent on Britain. The Irish application was also complicated by an exploratory Irish *aide mémoire* sent to the community three weeks earlier, which had expressed interest in associating with the 'common market'. This was an admission that Ireland's economy was reliant on Britain's. Moreover, it disclosed that, notwithstanding Ireland's recently improving growth rate and its modernisation policy, the country was not in a position to comply fully with the Treaty of Rome's provisions on membership.[69]

It was hardly surprising, therefore, that the EEC quickly resolved in October 1961 to proceed with Britain and Denmark's entry negotiations, while attaching a low priority to the Irish application. The prevailing feeling in European capitals was that Ireland was probably only eligible for associate membership. To the European captains, the Irish economy remained underdeveloped. Ireland was weakly prepared for membership and its accession would add to the difficulties of negotiating a Common Agricultural Policy. In late October the EEC Commission requested that Ireland provide detailed statistics about the state of its economy and explain how it intended to withstand the rigours of membership. An apprehensive Irish delegation, spearheaded by Seán Lemass, came to Brussels in January 1962 to mollify 'the six' about Ireland's capabilities and willingness to meet the EEC's membership requirements, although the effort was insufficient to satisfy many in the EEC. The foot-dragging continued.[70]

The Netherlands and West Germany were the first members to favour opening full negotiations with Ireland in late 1961, but they encountered firm resistance from France, which, backed by Italy, Belgium and Luxembourg, overrode the Dutch and Germans in the Council of Ministers. The Atlanticist Dutch favoured the inclusion of Britain and Ireland in the EEC to moderate Franco-German power. Ireland had built a solid relationship with Bonn since 1951 and had opened up to German investment. Ultimately, the success of the Irish application rested on Britain, and, above all, on French president Charles de Gaulle's reservations about the latter's 'European' credentials. Adding insult to Irish injury, when Norway belatedly applied for membership on 30 April 1962, it was quickly informed that it had permission to commence formal entry negotiations on 12 November.[71] This starkly highlighted once again the reservations of 'the six' towards the Irish application.

The Irish formed the opinion that continued insistence on remaining outside NATO was an obstacle to entry. As the secretary of the Department of Finance, Ken Whitaker, put it, Ireland was a 'contrary'. He told Minister for Finance James Ryan in January 1962: 'Nobody has yet told us that this [NATO membership] is a condition of membership of the EEC. On the other hand, nobody so loves us to want us in the EEC on our own terms.'[72] During the first half of 1962 the Lemass government let it be known that Ireland agreed with the aims of the North Atlantic Treaty and recognised it was vital to Western security. Lemass elucidated that Ireland was ideologically aligned with the West but that the 'particular circumstances' associated with partition had prevented Irish participation in military alliances. Irish representatives publicised the fact that Ireland fulfilled the political criteria necessary for EEC membership—NATO membership was not a prerequisite— and that Ireland held no reservations about playing a full role in EEC political and foreign policy co-ordination. Ireland, after all, had sought a defence/military agreement with the US in the early 1950s, but it remained opposed to joining NATO unless there was a move to de-legitimise Britain's unwillingness to end the division of the island.

Dutch and West German impatience with French obstructiveness on expanding the membership of the EEC grew in the spring and summer of 1962. Couve de Murville, the French foreign minister, continued a determined rear-guard action, supported by Italy, to delay a positive response to the Irish. By September and October, the West Germans and Dutch were no longer prepared to accept French delaying tactics, while the Commission and Italy recognised that Ireland had waited an inordinately long time for an answer.[73] The applicant had supplied adequate information and clarifications and it was sufficiently qualified to begin entry negotiations. Ireland's good faith was apparent, and to deny it the right to begin full negotiations served no purpose. On that account, Italy abandoned France, and Belgium and Luxembourg followed suit. This left France in an exposed position, so in October 1962 Paris agreed that Ireland should be permitted to commence entry negotiations. Throughout, Paris understood that the fate of the Irish application would be defined by the outcome of the British negotiations, and that presented a structural problem since President de Gaulle held deep reservations about the direction Europe would take if Britain entered the EEC.

Waiting

Before the Irish negotiations could begin, de Gaulle vetoed the British application in January 1963. Economic realities dictated that Ireland had to allow its application to lapse until Britain applied again. However, the Irish appetite was whetted. From now on the EEC became Ireland's defining foreign policy and trade focus.

Access to a European market, especially the large West German one, and generous CAP funding, held promise. Moreover, membership could boost Ireland's attractiveness as a platform for export-oriented industry. Dublin waited for a change in de Gaulle's attitude towards Britain while Lemass accelerated the country's programme of liberalisation and modernisation. This involved unilaterally cutting tariffs, introducing the Second Programme for Economic Expansion (1964–7) and signing the Anglo-Irish Free Trade Agreement (1965). Such actions progressively introduced indigenous industry to international competition. In parallel, Lemass abandoned the ostentatious anti-partitionist policy of preceding governments, and he signalled his willingness to work on practical economic cooperation with Northern Ireland by extending unilateral tariff cuts on imports from there. He became the first taoiseach of the Republic of Ireland to meet with a prime minister of Northern Ireland (and the first head of an Irish government since W.T. Cosgrave and James Craig met in 1925 to discuss the report of the Boundary Commission) when he visited Terence O'Neill in Stormont in January 1965. O'Neill reciprocated with a visit to Dublin later that year. Such efforts at the normalisation of relations between the two parts of the island and gestures in favour of economic cooperation were a reversal in the traditional north-south frigidity. They were demonstrations of Ireland's shift towards European norms and broadly in line with the example set by Franco-German reconciliation in the 1950s. Lemass's Ireland, unlike de Valera's, reflected a European *zeitgeist*.

European capitals such as Bonn and The Hague, never doubted that Ireland was committed to accession to the EEC. Various suggestions were made for Ireland to consider—such as EEC associate status, joining EFTA, or an interim trade arrangement involving a reduction of EEC tariffs in the short-term—until membership negotiations could begin at some unspecified time in the future.[74] Such counsels were rejected, as Dublin recognised that they did not offer Ireland a sustainable economic future. But they were also rebuffed for the good reason that Irish policymakers did not want the Europeans, particularly de Gaulle, to conclude that Ireland would settle for less than full EEC membership. When Prime Minister Harold Wilson submitted the second British application in May 1967, Taoiseach Jack Lynch duly reactivated the Irish one. He had to shelve it just a few months later when Charles de Gaulle issued his second 'Non' to Britain.

Generally, Ireland played a frustrating 'waiting game' after 1963, while the EEC experienced a taxing period. A lack of trust and common vision ensured that the community lost much of its forward impetus. De Gaulle's unilateralism and his unapologetic defence of French interests brought him into conflict with the EEC institutions and his EEC partners, especially West Germany.[75] Adenauer's successor as chancellor, Ludwig Erhard, would not allow de Gaulle to forge ahead with a Gaullist Europe, at least not until Britain (and by association, Ireland) was granted entry to the community. British entry would, however, prevent the fulfilment of de Gaulle's design, so there was nothing to be done except to wait. In this great European drama Ireland was only ever an incidental detail.

On the other hand, Ireland's enforced and uncertain wait to begin membership negotiations gave it time to prepare better for eventual entry into the 'common market'. It allowed the government to industrialise, liberalise and adapt to European expectations. A decisive change in national mood came about, and urban Ireland became dissatisfied when European media portrayed the country as rural, backward and poor.[76] The prevailing Irish self-image changed as new generations embraced modernisation and modernity and Ireland moved towards Western European economic and social norms. Paradoxically, the Gaullist blockage to Irish entry assisted in another way too. De Gaulle's decision in 1966 to withdraw French troops from NATO and to close down NATO bases on French territory deflated EEC Atlanticist criticisms of Ireland's non-membership of NATO.

Ireland now had ample time to build up its European credentials, which contrasted sharply with its hasty and maladroit effort at securing EEC membership in 1961. When de Gaulle abruptly left the European political scene in 1969, clearing the path for British accession, Ireland's case for membership had been fortified. Ireland's accession negotiations finally commenced in June 1970 in parallel with those of Britain, Norway and Denmark, seven-and-a-half years after the EEC Commission had sanctioned them. Fortunately, Ireland's small size did not present a great challenge and its political leadership adjusted the country's negotiating posture to consent to the Treaty of Rome's requirements without substantive qualification. Its demands for some transitional arrangements were not unreasonable in comparison to the Norwegian and British demands. It was virtually certain that once the British prime minister, Ted Heath, had an opportunity to build rapport and compromise with the new French president, Georges Pompidou, then Ireland's application would succeed.

The outbreak of the Northern Ireland 'Troubles' in August and September 1969 presented a different challenge. Initial European reactions were of horror as the civil rights campaign polarised an already deeply divided society and the crisis created an inflammatory situation on the streets of many Northern Ireland cities. The Stormont government was apparently incapable of even-handedness as it fought without success to re-establish control. This led to the deployment of the British army on to the streets to maintain law and order and that, in turn, gradually transformed the inter-communal violence into a politicised terrorist campaign by 1970 and 1971. There was considerable evidence of European public sympathy for the Irish nationalist case in 1969 and 1970. Likewise, there was much informal and private sympathy expressed to the Irish government by representatives of the governments of 'the six', but the Western European capitals held back from getting involved.[77] Regarding Northern Ireland as an internal British matter, they would not mediate in the Anglo-Irish recriminations about the (mis)handling of the unfolding Troubles. They would not be drawn into making representations on Dublin's behalf to London. Instead, friendly embarrassment characterised official Europe's reactions while Ireland and Britain were in the process of gaining entry to the EEC.

Historical evidence suggests, however, that once both applicants had been approved for EEC entry in 1972, 'the six' played a behind-the-scenes informal role with the general aim of alleviating the situation. A landmark event occurred in the city of Derry on 30 January 1972 that shocked the world and suggested that a completely hands-off approach was unwise. During a protest march against internment, 28 civilians were shot by British soldiers and 14 people died. Bloody Sunday, as it became known, led to the Dutch cabinet's discussion of the possibility of extending Dutch assistance if Britain and Ireland 'needed the good services of third countries' or if peacekeepers were required.[78] This initiative came to naught in the face of British diplomacy. According to recent research in the French archives by Christophe Gillissen, the British suspension of the Northern Ireland parliament at Stormont and the reinstitution of direct rule from London in March 1972 (marking the first time since 1921 that Northern Ireland had been ruled from Westminster) was encouraged 'by certain countries of the Common Market, in particular France and Italy'. This allowed for the negotiation of the Sunningdale Agreement (which was concluded as a result of Anglo-Irish cooperation on 9 December 1973) and the formation of a power-sharing executive in Northern Ireland.[79] European governments clearly wished for a settlement of the crisis if Ireland and Britain were to be official members of the EEC. It was in the collective European interest to calm the situation in Northern Ireland.

Ireland and Britain realised that the disorder in Northern Ireland could injure their EEC membership ambitions. Under Jack Lynch the Irish government endeavoured to somehow ease the suffering of the nationalist minority in Northern Ireland and though it reiterated that its favoured solution was a united Ireland, it promoted a peaceful, consensus-based political solution. It clarified that it wished to work in a helpful fashion with Britain to facilitate the restoration of law and order in Northern Ireland, but that this was a separate matter from the EEC negotiations. The ability of Dublin to work in a productive and co-operative fashion with London on their conjoined EEC applications, despite bi-lateral tensions over Northern Ireland, was a positive portent. The moderating impact of prospective membership of the EEC on the Anglo-Irish relationship from the late 1960s was substantial. To gain entry to the EEC required co-operation and co-ordination between the two countries, if only for self-interested purposes.

In sum, EEC attitudes regarding Ireland's suitability as a member after 1961 underscored the limitations experienced by Ireland in its relations with Europe from 1922 to 1973. That structural constraint was geopolitical: it was an artefact of Ireland's location, history and ties in Britain's neighbourhood. It could not be otherwise. It remained to be seen how Ireland would capitalise on EEC membership to loosen this British hegemony, in line with the aspirations of Irish republicanism. From that perspective, Irish governments viewed integration within Europe not as a loss, but as an affirmation, of sovereignty. Closer ties with Europe presented an opportunity to balance the influence of Britain as part of a healthier relationship of equals focused on constructing a common European future and identity together. Membership of the EEC became a pillar of national strategy. The official and political elites fused nationalism, Europeanism, multilateralism and economic interdependence together as part of Ireland's official national identity. Independent Ireland chose to exchange a dependent economic relationship on Britain for interdependence in an integrated Europe and to leave the implications of 'ever closer union' for future generations to deal with.

Notes

[1] This phrase was first used by the French writer François-René, vicomte de Chateaubriand, who apparently coined the phrase in his *Mémoires d'Outre-Tombe* ['Memoirs from Beyond the Grave'], originally published in six volumes (Garnier Frères; Paris, 1840). The phrase has also been attributed to Jean Blanchard.

[2] Eunan O'Halpin, 'The army in independent Ireland', in Thomas Bartlett and Keith Jeffery (eds), *A military history of Ireland* (Cambridge University Press; Cambridge, 1996), 407–30: 411.

[3] O'Halpin, 'The army in independent Ireland', 411.

[4] 'Message to the Free Nations of the World', 21 January 1919, Item No. 2, in *Documents on Irish foreign policy*, vol. i, *1919–1922* (Royal Irish Academy; Dublin, 1998), 2.

[5] Dermot Keogh, *Ireland and Europe, 1919–1989: a diplomatic and political history* (Hibernia University Press; Cork and Dublin, 1990), 8–9.

[6] See Mervyn O'Driscoll, Dermot Keogh and Jérôme aan de Wiel (eds), *Ireland through European eyes: western Europe, the EEC and Ireland, 1945–1973* (Cork University Press; Cork, 2013), *passim*.

[7] Jérôme aan de Wiel, 'Luxembourg', in Mervyn O'Driscoll, Keogh and aan de Wiel (eds), *Ireland through European eyes: western Europe, the EEC and Ireland, 1945–1973* (Cork University Press; Cork, 2013), 291–313: 313.

[8] Jérôme aan de Wiel, 'Belgium', in O'Driscoll, Keogh and aan de Wiel (eds), *Ireland through European eyes*, 245–90: 250–6.

[9] Keogh, *Ireland and Europe, 1919–1989*, 79.

[10] Michael Kennedy, 'The Irish Free State and the League of Nations, 1922–32: the wider implications', *Irish Studies in International Affairs* 3(4) (1992), 9–23: 11–2. See also, Michael Kennedy, *Ireland and the League of Nations, 1919–1946: international relations, diplomacy and politics* (Irish Academic Press; Blackrock, Co. Dublin, 1996).

[11] Dermot Keogh and Andrew McCarthy, *Twentieth-century Ireland: revolution and state building* (Gill and Macmillan; Dublin, 2005; revised edn), 51.

[12] Cyril Barrett, 'The visual arts and society, 1921–84', in J.R. Hill (ed.), *A new history of Ireland* (Oxford University Press; Oxford, 1976), 587–620: 587; See also, Andy Bielenberg, *The Shannon scheme and the electrification of the Irish Free State* (Lilliput Press; Dublin, 2002).

[13] Mervyn O'Driscoll, *Ireland, Germany and the Nazis: politics and diplomacy 1919–39* (Four Courts Press; Dublin, 2017), 68.

[14] See, Dermot Keogh, *Ireland and the Vatican: the politics and diplomacy of church-state relations, 1922–1960* (Cork University Press; Cork, 1995).

[15] Quoted in: Mervyn O'Driscoll, *Ireland, Germany and the Nazis*, 72.

[16] 'Confidential report from Michael MacWhite to Joseph P. Walshe', Rome, 6 December 1938, Item no. 247, *Documents on Irish foreign policy* vol. v, *1937–1939* (Royal Irish Academy; Dublin, 2006), 372.

[17] For example, see, Dermot Keogh, *Ireland and the Vatican*, 80.

[18] Kieran A. Kennedy, Thomas Giblin and Deirdre McHugh, *The economic development of Ireland in the twentieth century* (Routledge; London, 1988), 182.

[19] The 'Economic War' was inappropriately christened; it was fundamentally a political conflict fought using economic tools.

[20] For a detailed account of Irish–German trade, see Mervyn O'Driscoll, *Ireland, Germany and the Nazis*, 55–61, 102–5, 118–23, 162–9, 200–6, 230–3.

[21] Kieran A. Kennedy et al., *The economic development of Ireland*, 183.

[22] For more, see, Mervyn O'Driscoll, 'The Economic War and Irish foreign trade policy: Irish–German commerce 1932–9', *Irish Studies in International Affairs* 10 (1999), 71–89.

[23] O'Driscoll, *Ireland, Germany and the Nazis*, 113, 148 and 177.

[24] Politisches Archiv des Auswärtigen Amtes, Berlin (PA), R122531, Hempel to Auswärtiges Amt (AA), 12 November 1939.

[25] For a development of this line of argument, see, O'Driscoll, *Ireland, Germany and the Nazis*, 115–17.

[26] Horst Dickel, *Die deutsche Aussenpolitik und die Irische Frage von 1932 bis 1944* (Franz Steiner Verlag; Wiesbaden, 1983), 34. On the attitude in Dublin to the Nazi regime,

see, National Archives of Ireland (NAI), Department of Foreign Affairs (DFA), Berlin Letterbooks 1932–3, Hearne to McCauley, 29 July 1933.

[27] Three versions of a handwritten letter from Éamon de Valera to Neville Chamberlain, 15 September 1938, Item no. 218, in *Documents on Irish foreign policy*, vol. v, *1937–1939*, 337.

[28] O'Driscoll, *Ireland, Germany and the Nazis*, 256–9.

[29] Dickel, *Aussenpolitik*, 89–90.

[30] Mervyn O'Driscoll, '"We are trying to do our share": the construction of positive neutrality and Irish post-war relief to Europe', *Irish Studies in International Affairs* 27 (2016), 21–38.

[31] See, Robert Cole, *Propaganda, censorship and Irish neutrality in the second world war* (Edinburgh: Edinburgh University Press, 2006).

[32] Mervyn O'Driscoll, '"We are trying to do our share"'; aan de Wiel, 'Belgium', 258; Christophe Gillissen, 'France', in O'Driscoll, Keogh and aan de Wiel (eds), *Ireland through European eyes*, 75–127: 81–2; and aan de Wiel, 'Luxembourg', 297.

[33] For a full treatment of this, see, Dermot Keogh, 'De Valera, Hitler and the visit of condolence May 1945', *History Ireland* 5(3) (1997), 58–61; and Dermot Keogh, 'Eamon de Valera and Hitler: an analysis of international reaction to the visit to the German minister, May 1945', *Irish Studies in International Affairs* 3(1) (1989), 69–92.

[34] For a detailed discussion of these issues, see, Deirdre McMahon, '"Our mendicant vigil is over": Ireland and the United Nations, 1946–55', in Michael Kennedy and Deirdre McMahon (eds), *Obligations and responsibilities: Ireland and the United Nations, 1955–2005* (Institute of Public Administration; Dublin, 2005), 5–24.

[35] Eunan O'Halpin, *Defending Ireland: the Irish state and its enemies since 1922* (Oxford University Press; Oxford, 1999), 260.

[36] O'Halpin, *Defending Ireland*, 262; Keogh, *Twentieth century Ireland*, 213–14, 231–3; Joseph P. O'Grady, 'Ireland and the defense of the north Atlantic, 1948–51: the American view', *Éire–Ireland* XXV/3 (1990), 58–78.

[37] See Paula L. Wylie, *Ireland and the Cold War: diplomacy and recognition 1949–63* (Irish Academic Press; Dublin, 2006). Wylie explores how Ireland structured its foreign policies heavily around the international principles of self-determination and anti-partition.

[38] For a detailed discussion, see, Mervyn O'Driscoll, 'Hesitant Europeans, self-defeating irredentists and security free-riders? West German assessments of Irish foreign policy during the early Cold War, 1949–59', *Irish Studies in International Affairs* 21 (2010), 89–104.

[39] O'Driscoll, 'Hesitant Europeans, self-defeating irredentists and security free-riders?', 98–9; NAI, DFA, Embassy files, Bonn, 19/3I, 'Politischer Jahresbericht', Report, Belton to Nunan, 15 June 1954.

[40] Jérôme aan de Wiel, 'The Netherlands', in O'Driscoll, Keogh and aan de Wiel (eds), *Ireland through European eyes*, 190–244: 228–9.

[41] aan de Wiel, 'The Netherlands', in O'Driscoll, Keogh and aan de Wiel (eds), *Ireland through European eyes*, 227.

[42] O'Driscoll, 'Hesitant Europeans', 96.

[43] Mervyn O'Driscoll, *Ireland, West Germany and the new Europe, 1949–1973: best friend and ally?* (Manchester University Press; Manchester, 2018), 135.

[44] See, Jérôme aan de Wiel, *East German intelligence and Ireland, 1949–90: espionage, diplomacy and terrorism* (Manchester University Press; Manchester, 2015); Jérôme aan de Wiel, 'The trouble with Frank Ryan: "corpse diplomacy" between Ireland and East Germany, 1966–1980', *Irish Studies in International Affairs*, 25 (2014), 203–20.

45 Mervyn O'Driscoll, 'Multilateralism: from Plato's Cave to European Community, 1945–73', in Ben Tonra, Michael Kennedy, John Doyle and Noel Dorr (eds), *Irish foreign policy* (Gill and Macmillan; Dublin, 2012), 36–53: 44.

46 Kieran A. Kennedy *et al.*, *The economic development of Ireland*, 193.

47 Mervyn O'Driscoll, 'West Germany', in O'Driscoll, Keogh and aan de Wiel (eds), *Ireland through European eyes*, 9–74.; PA, Berlin, Bestand B31, Band 64, Report, Katzenberger to AA, 25 January 1954.

48 Andy Bielenberg and Raymond Ryan, *An economic history of Ireland since independence* (Routledge; Abingdon, 2013), 129.

49 See, aan de Wiel, 'Belgium', 265.

50 aan de Wiel, 'Belgium', 265.

51 O'Driscoll, 'West Germany', 32–3; O'Driscoll, 'Hesitant Europeans', 99, 101–2; aan de Wiel, 'The Netherlands', 211–12, 218; O'Driscoll, *Ireland, West Germany and the new Europe*, 129–31.

52 See, for example, Fergal Lenehan, *Stereotypes, ideology and foreign correspondents: German media representations of Ireland, 1946–2010* (Peter Lang; Oxford, 2016), 55–104; aan de Wiel, 'The Netherlands', 220–1

53 O'Driscoll, 'West Germany', 27 and 51; Gillissen, 'France', 112; aan de Wiel, 'Belgium', 262.

54 O'Driscoll, 'West Germany', 27–8; aan de Wiel, 'The Netherlands', 221 and 262.

55 See, Michael J. Kennedy and Eunan O'Halpin, *Ireland and the Council of Europe: from isolation towards integration* (Council of Europe; Strasbourg, 2000).

56 Keogh, *Ireland and Europe*, 207.

57 Gillissen, 'France', 76.

58 aan de Wiel, 'The Netherlands', 216.

59 Keogh, *Ireland and Europe*, 209–10.

60 NAI, Department of the Taoiseach, S15281J, 'Free trade area–working party no. 23– Consideration of the Irish case', McCarthy report, n.d. (*c.* 28 May 1957).

61 Mervyn O'Driscoll, ''The "unwanted suitor": West Germany's reception, response and role in Ireland's EEC entry request, 1961–3', *Irish Studies in International Affairs*, 22 (2011), 163–86: 167–8.

62 O'Driscoll, *Ireland, West Germany and the new Europe*, 131.

63 O'Driscoll, *Ireland, West Germany and the new Europe*, 85, 86 and 133–4.

64 Joseph Morrison Skelly, *Irish diplomacy at the United Nations, 1945–1965: national interests and the international order* (Irish Academic Press; Dublin, 1997), 220. Additional evidence of Ireland adjusting its fervent anti-colonial rhetoric has been uncovered. See, Christophe Gillisen, 'Ireland, France and the question of Algeria at the United Nations, 1955–62', *Irish Studies in International Affairs* 19 (2008), 151–67.

65 PA, B20-200, Bd. 585, Prill to AA, 27 June 1959.

66 For a full account of Lemass's Europeanisation of Irish foreign policy, see, Maurice FitzGerald, 'The "mainstreaming" of Irish foreign policy', in Brian Girvin and Gary Murphy (eds), *The Lemass era: politics and society in the Ireland of Seán Lemass* (University College Dublin; Dublin, 2005), 82–98.

67 PA, Bestand B31, Band 238, von Plehwe circular regarding Seán Lemass's visit to the FRG, 'Deutsche Investitionen in Ireland', 18 October 1962.

68 Konrad Adenauer Stiftung, Sankt Augustin, Pressedokumentation, file: Staaten, Irland, 1951–1983, Press cutting, *Bulletin*, Nr 197/S.1663, 23 Ocotober 1962.

[69] Dermot Keogh and Aoife Keogh, 'Ireland and European integration: from the Treaty of Rome to membership', in Mark Callanan (ed.), *'Foundations of an ever closer union': an Irish perspective on the fifty years since the Treaty of Rome* (Institute of Public Administration; Dublin, 2009), 6–50: 12.

[70] Dermot Keogh, 'The diplomacy of "dignified calm"—an analysis of Ireland's application for membership of the EEC, 1961-3', *Journal of European Integration History* 3(1) (1997), 81–102: 87–8, 94; Michael J. Geary, *An inconvenient wait: Ireland's quest for membership of the EEC, 1957–73* (Institute of Public Administration; Dublin, 2009), 31–3; Maurice FitzGerald, *Protectionism to liberalisation: Ireland and the EEC, 1957 to 1966* (Ashgate; Aldershot, 2000), 178–85.

[71] Denis J. Maher, *The tortuous path: the course of Ireland's entry into the EEC 1948–73* (Institute of Public Administration; Dublin, 1986), 138.

[72] John Horgan, 'Irish foreign policy, Northern Ireland, neutrality and the commonwealth: the historical roots of a current controversy', *Irish Studies in International Affairs* 10 (1999), 135–47: 137–8.

[73] O'Driscoll, 'Unwanted suitor', 180–2; Jérôme aan de Wiel, 'The Commission, the Council and the Irish application for the EEC, 1961–73', in O'Driscoll, Keogh and aan de Wiel (eds), *Ireland through European eyes*, 314–82: 343–4.

[74] Maher, *Tortuous path*, 234–9.

[75] William I. Hitchcock, *The struggle for Europe: the history of the continent since 1945* (Profile Books; London, 2003), 237.

[76] A notable example of this is explored in Gisela Holfter, 'From bestseller to failure? Heinrich Böll's *Irisches Tagebuch* ("Irish Journal") to *Irland und seinere Kinder* ("Children of Éire")', in Christiane Schönfeld and Hermann Rasche (eds), *Processes of transposition: German literature and film* (Editions Rodopi; Amsterdam, 2007), 207–21.

[77] O'Driscoll, 'West Germany', 66–70; aan de Wiel, 'The Commission, the Council and the Irish application', 373; Aoife Keogh and Dermot Keogh, 'Italy and the Holy See', in O'Driscoll, Keogh and aan de Wiel (eds), *Ireland through European eyes*, 128–89: 186–7; aan de Wiel, 'Belgium', 287; aan de Wiel, 'The Netherlands', 231–2.

[78] aan de Wiel, 'The Netherlands', 233.

[79] Gillissen, 'France', 123.

Transforming Ireland into an EU member state

Brigid Laffan

Declensions sang on air like a hosanna
As, column after stratified column,
Book One of Elementa Latina
Marbled and minatory, rose up in him.
Seamus Heaney, 'Alphabets'.

Introduction

A full-page advertisement taken out by Aer Lingus in *The Irish Times* on 1 January 1973 to mark Ireland's accession to the European Union (EU) claimed that 'Ireland is very much a part of the new Europe'.[1] This assertion of Ireland's belonging marked a return to Europe for this small island on the north-western Atlantic coast. Writing this chapter from the hills outside Florence offers a perspective on the longevity and depth of Ireland's links to the European continent. In AD 826, Donatus, an Irish monk, was elected bishop of Fiesole where his body still rests in the cathedral. The nearby village of Santa Brigida is named after the Irish St Brigid, whose life was recorded by Donatus. Since that first wave of Irish monks and scholars, there has been continuous interaction between Ireland and the continent. The many Irish colleges across Europe were not just religious institutions but sites of diplomacy. The Irish found refuge on continental Europe and played noteworthy roles in the service of many European armies. Support from the dominant European powers, first Spain, then France and later Germany, was sought in the long struggle with England. Joyce, Beckett and others opted for exile from the strictures of the newly independent Irish state. Down through the millennia, Ireland was tied to Europe through Catholicism, captured in Heaney's reference to *Elementa Latina*, the liturgical language until the early 1960s.[2] While 1 January 1973 was a new beginning for this small country, it was also a reconnection with its deep history with continental Europe. Joint accession to the then EEC with the United Kingdom underlined the closeness of Ireland's ties with its near neighbour, but membership offered the tantalising prospect of a transition from dependence to interdependence.

The focus of this chapter is on the transformation of Ireland from a nation state to a member state. The chapter begins by analysing the initial adjustment as a small, peripheral member state learnt to deal with the demands of EU membership and transformed itself into the 'Celtic Tiger'. The fruits of economic success were squandered during the next phase of membership when Ireland's boom turned into a bubble and finally a severe economic crisis that brought the EU–European Central Bank–International Monetary Fund troika into the heart of Irish government in 2010. This was the most difficult period of Ireland's engagement with the union, which ended in 2013 when Ireland exited the bail-out. Having survived the trauma of being a programme country, Ireland's recovery was quickly challenged by the decision of the UK to exit the EU in June 2016 and the election of Donald Trump as president in the US. Two of the three core pillars of Irish external relations are loose of their moorings. Ireland faces a difficult and challenging adjustment to a post-Brexit EU and a changing international system.

Ireland's choice for Europe: phase one

When Ireland joined the EEC in 1973, it was the poorest and most agricultural member state. Its indigenous industries struggled to deal with the competition emanating from the larger market. The 1973 oil shock and consequent economic turmoil exacerbated Ireland's economic adjustment. Higher prices for agricultural goods involved a major injection of capital into rural Ireland, which greatly eased the transition from a rural to an urban society. It benefited the prosperity of the countryside and prevented a serious urban–rural conflict developing. As a project for Ireland's future, the modernisation push from EU membership led to a battle about equal pay for women. Ireland as an EU member state had to bring its legislation in line with European law on equal pay. It did so through the Anti-Discrimination Pay Act of 1974, which was to come into force on 31 December 1974. Lobbying by the Confederation of Irish Industry (CII) and concern about the cost of equal pay in the public sector led the then government to request a partial derogation for Ireland from the directive. The European Commissioner responsible for Social Affairs, Patrick Hillary, a former government minister in Ireland, sent a delegation to Ireland to investigate the case and later found against the government. Women's groups in Ireland found strong external support for legal equality and an Irish government discovered for the first time what it meant to be a member state.[3]

The impact of membership on British–Irish relations was more direct than could have been expected on 1 January 1973. Just two years later, the UK renegotiated the terms of membership and put the question to the UK electorate in a referendum. Prior to accession, this development would have been anticipated as a major shock to the Irish state, but it proved not to be. According to Garrett FitzGerald, who was foreign minister in the Irish government at the time, there was 'unanimity on the part of political and public opinion that if Britain left, Ireland would remain a member'.[4] This was a remarkable development just two years after accession. It profoundly altered the underlying context of British–Irish relations. It had the dual impact of releasing Ireland from the psychological hang-ups of a dependency relationship with the UK and altered perceptions of Ireland among the other member states. Thus, by pooling sovereignty in the EEC, Ireland gained autonomy and the ability to exercise sovereignty. The benefits of the pooling of sovereignty and the exchange of dependence on the UK for interdependence within the union remained a consistent and central element of Ireland's European narrative.

The transformation of British–Irish relations was felt not just in relation to sovereignty but also in addressing the difficult issue of Northern Ireland and the Irish border. The so-called Troubles raged during the first 25 years of Ireland's EU membership. Here again, the EU was seen as an accommodating context and model. John Hume, a long-serving member of both the European Parliament and the House of Commons, developed a powerful and sophisticated narrative of the importance of the EU for peace on the island of Ireland. When receiving the Nobel Peace Prize in 1998, Hume argued that the:

> European Union is the best example in the history of the world of conflict resolution and it is the duty of everyone, particularly those who live in areas of conflict to study how it was done and to apply its principles to their own conflict resolution[5]

Interestingly, many features of the Good Friday Agreement were modelled on EU governance and institutions. The Single Market project removed the physical barriers on the island of Ireland, thereby diluting the visibility and lived experience of the border.

For the first two decades after accession, Ireland struggled to make good the economic promise of membership. The two oil crises of the 1970s and the prolonged recession of the 1980s underlined how hard it was for a relatively poor state to adjust to the internationalisation brought about by membership. A front cover of *The Economist* published in 1988 predicted that Ireland was heading for catastrophe and described it as the 'poorest of the rich'.[6] Just then Ireland was about to put in place the domestic policies supported by a benign external environment that would lead *The Economist*, only nine years later, to describe Ireland as 'Europe's shining light'.[7] This signalled the arrival of the Celtic Tiger, a *cliché* that dogged Ireland's boom years.

The economic promise of membership

From 1993 onwards, Ireland began to catch up with the core European economies. The vicious cycle of the 1970s and 1980s was replaced by a virtuous cycle that reinforced Ireland's economic performance. The origins of the virtuous cycle lie both in domestic developments and EU changes. Domestically Ireland began to bring its budgetary deficits under control and to regain control over the public finances. This was made possible through the actions of central government, underpinned by a new form of social partnership. During the crisis of the 1980s, Ireland suffered from high unemployment (17% in 1987), inflation (12% in 1987) and trade union militancy (310,000 days lost in 1986). Social partnership was designed to overcome this cycle of economic turmoil. From 1987 onwards, there was a succession of seven national agreements that involved centralised pay agreements and gradually widened to include most areas of social policy and education. The agreements delivered a high level of industrial peace, especially in the public sector.[8]

Two major EU developments at the end of the 1980s played an important role in turning Ireland's economic fortunes around. The Single European Act (SEA) was accompanied by the first major multi-annual budgetary framework. Agreement to the SEA was built on an enhancement of the resources devoted to economic and social cohesion, and in 1988 the EU promised to double the resources committed to Europe's poorest regions, including Ireland. The so-called structural funds led to a significant investment in Irish infrastructure and improved the evaluation of the public investment process. Ireland received the highest levels of per capita EU transfers at that time. Ireland also benefited from the implementation of the single market programme, although at the outset there were fears that it would disproportionately benefit richer Europe. In Ireland's case, the single market reduced the barriers to exports and attracted to Ireland a large flow of American foreign direct investment (FDI) wanting a bridge to the European market. A leading Irish economic historian underlined the importance of EU membership to the transformation of the Irish economy in the following terms:

Ireland's accession to the then EEC in 1973, and the construction of the single market in the early 1990s, were the two crucial turning points that allowed our Republic to put decades of underachievement behind it and become the prosperous and self-confident State that it is today.[9]

As a member of the EU, Ireland was transformed from an economic underachiever in the 1950s and 1960s into an overachiever by the 1990s. A country of emigration was transformed into a country of immigration at a speed rarely experienced by other countries. The inward-looking, protectionist, conservative Ireland of the 1950s was evolving into one of the most globalised countries of the world.[10]

Interestingly, towards the end of the 1990s the centrality of the EU in Ireland's official narrative began to wane and become contested. Two government ministers, Mary Harney and Síle de Valera, delivered speeches in the US in July and September 2000 that openly questioned the benefits of European integration to Ireland. Síle de Valera's speech drew attention to the adverse impact of the EU on Irish identity and argued that 'we have found that directives and regulations agreed in Brussels can often seriously impinge on our identity, culture and traditions'. According to de Valera, '[t]he bureaucracy of Brussels does not always respect the complexities and sensitivities of member states'.[11] She called for 'a more vigilant, a more questioning attitude to the European Union'.[12] In an earlier speech in July 2000, Minister Harney, speaking to the American Bar Association suggested that: 'Geographically, we are closer to Berlin than Boston. Spiritually, we are probably a lot closer to Boston than Berlin', and she went on to rail against excessive European regulation.[13] Both interventions represented a soft Euroscepticism and would not have been voiced when Ireland was a large net beneficiary of the EU budget and still poor. These speeches represented a rising confidence, perhaps overconfidence, that came with the stellar economic performance of the 1990s. Moreover, they highlighted an important facet of Ireland's EU membership, namely the manner in which Ireland anchored itself in three spheres—the UK, the US and continental Europe. Membership had not forced Ireland to choose. It could have both Berlin and Boston.

The confidence of the Irish government in the electorate's support for European integration was severely tested in 2001 when a majority (53.9%) voted down the Nice Treaty in a referendum with a low turnout of 34.8%. Most of the Irish electorate decided to stay at home. The shock to the elite was caused in part by the successful passage of the Single European Act (1987), the Maastricht Treaty (1992) and the Amsterdam Treaty (1998) following the membership referendum in 1972. The Nice Treaty was not a particularly significant treaty, largely designed to open the way for the Eastern enlargement of the union. The Irish 'No' left the government and the EU with a dilemma. Without the treaty, the existing member states were not prepared to conclude the enlargement negotiations, and the Irish government was broadly comfortable with the terms of the treaty. The government therefore found itself having to navigate the multi-level politics of the EU. It was responsive to the Irish electorate and the reservations that it had displayed on the Nice Treaty. A National Forum on Europe was established by October 2001 to deepen and broaden the debate on the dynamics of integration and the EU. The forum brought together the political parties with representation in the Irish parliament and key civil society organisations on both sides of the European question. It continued in operation until 2008 and during that time enhanced the debate on Europe in Ireland and educated a wider number of party-political actors about what the EU meant and how it went about its business. The forum also legitimised the idea of bringing in speakers from other EU states so that they could freely debate with Irish actors on the key integration questions. The forum played an important educational role.

In May 2002, a general election returned the Fianna Fáil-Progressive Democrats government to power and, with its renewed mandate, it negotiated the Seville Declarations on Irish neutrality at the June 2002 European Council. These declarations clarified the relationship between the developing EU security policy and Ireland. Neutrality and non-membership of NATO underlined a significant difference between Ireland and some other member states of the union, because neutrality was more a question of state identity for Ireland rather than a security policy as such.[14] Armed with the Seville Declarations, the government, with the support of the main opposition parties, Fine Gael and Labour, went back to the people in October 2002. With an increased turnout, the electorate endorsed the Nice Treaty. The gap between the elite and the electorate was closed, but Nice was a reminder to the main political parties that favourable attitudes towards the EU in Ireland did not necessarily mean agreement on all facets of this distinctive polity and its policies. Ireland, as president of the European Council, held the welcome ceremony for the ten new EU member states at Dublin Castle on 1 May 2004. The Castle, once the seat of British power in Ireland, was now the symbol of a country comfortable with its place in the world. Ireland was, for all of the countries of East-Central Europe, the model to pursue, as it was and remains the only poor country that has caught up with the income levels of the core EU economy.[15] On the surface, Ireland was enjoying the best of times, with a booming economy, full employment and a deepening welfare state. The excess and bravado of a wealthy Ireland disguised the weaknesses lurking beneath the surface, however, as a catch-up boom was transformed into a bubble and then the inevitable bust. In June 2008, the Irish electorate again rejected a European treaty, the Lisbon Treaty, although this vote was reversed in October 2009 while Ireland was experiencing the chill winds of a deep recession.

Becoming a programme country

Successive governments, public institutions and the wider public disregarded the significant economic, political and social risks that were being generated by an over-heated Irish economy. The boom was transformed into a bubble as a result of pro-cyclical budgetary policies driven by electoral cycles and reckless bank lending to the private sector, which, in turn, fuelled a housing boom. Notwithstanding low public borrowing, Ireland's public finances were vulnerable because of windfall taxes from construction and the fact that both companies and private households were over indebted. The good times came to an end in autumn 2008 with the advent of the global financial crisis. The collapse of Lehman Brothers in the US in September heralded the onset of a major economic crisis in Ireland that lasted into the second decade of the twenty-first century. The crisis had both domestic and European origins. The domestic crisis began as the direct result of the global financial crisis, when the vulnerability of the Irish banking system was cruelly exposed. In the aftermath of the Lehman collapse, the president of the European Central Bank (ECB) contacted the Irish finance minister on the weekend of 27–28 September 2008 to express his concerns about the stability of the Irish financial system. On the evening of 29 September a series of emergency meetings took place in Government Buildings in Dublin, which culminated in what later became known as the blanket guarantee of the liabilities of the Irish banks. The decision to provide such a guarantee was predicated on the belief that the banks faced a liquidity squeeze, not an underlying problem of solvency.[16] The bank guarantee was to have immediate and long-term consequences for the Irish exchequer, government and society. The guarantee was a unilateral move by the Irish government and was done without consulting Ireland's EU partners and the ECB. The implications and costs of the bank bail-out were felt over the next years as the government had to inject massive amounts of public monies into the Irish banks, nationalise and then liquidate Anglo-Irish Bank and create a bad bank known as the National Asset Management Agency. The bank crisis exacerbated the general crisis of the Irish economy characterised by rising unemployment and a marked deterioration of the public finances.

As the toxic link between the banks and the Irish state deepened, the financial markets began to take a very harsh view of the Irish sovereign signature. In summer 2010 the rating agencies downgraded Ireland, with promises of further downgrades to come. During the autumn Ireland's position deteriorated and the ECB turned its attention to Ireland, with growing alarm. From mid-October 2010 onwards, the president of the ECB, Jean-Claude Trichet, wrote a series of letters to Finance Minister Brian Lenihan, outlining the growing concern of the ECB board about the situation of Ireland and Europe's exposure to the Irish financial system. In a letter dated 17 February 2015 to Matt Carthy, an Irish member of the European Parliament, Trichet's successor, Mario Draghi, outlined the scale of ECB support to Ireland in the following terms:

> In the case of Ireland, the level of liquidity provided by the Eurosystem in support of the Irish banking system had reached about Euro 140 billon (including ELA) or around 85% of Irish GDP, by November 2010.[17]

This represented about one-quarter of the ECB's total lending at the time—an unprecedented level of exposure to any country, not least in the light of the fact that Ireland's share in the capital of the ECB was about 1%.[18] The stark message from the ECB was that it was over-exposed to the Irish banking system and that it could not sustain this level of liquidity. Without it, the Irish banking system and the capacity of the government to fund public services would have collapsed. Ireland was asked to enter a programme of financial assistance, to follow in the footsteps of Greece, as a country under Troika rule. Ireland was about to move from interdependence within the EU to the status of a programme country. Put simply, this was a move from interdependence to dependence. The Irish public was informed of what was about to happen not by the Irish government but by the governor of the Irish Central Bank, Patrick Honohan, who called the Irish national broad-caster (RTÉ) from Frankfurt. The powerful symbolism of this was not lost on the Irish public, who were confronting the depth of the crisis that was unleashed in Ireland by the excesses of the early 2000s.

The reaction in the country was one of shock, captured by *The Irish Times* editorial on 18 November, which was titled 'Was it for this?'[19] This stark question was essentially asking, was it for this that the men of 1916 had died and that Ireland gained independence? It went on to say:

> A bailout from the German chancellor with a few shil-lings of sympathy from the British chancellor on the side. There is the shame of it all. Having obtained our political independence from Britain to be the masters of our own affairs, we have now surrendered our sovereignty to the European Commission, the European Central Bank, and the International Monetary Fund. Their representatives ride into Merrion Street today.[20]

Even as a poor country, Ireland had always been able to maintain the state and run its public finances. The editorial went on to say that 'The true ignominy of our current situation is not that our sovereignty has been taken away from us, it is that we ourselves have squandered it.'[21] Ireland's reputation was transformed from that of model state into a country on watch and at risk. Ireland entered a further three-year period of fiscal consolidation, which increased taxes and reduced public expenditure at a great cost to Irish society. The period 2008–13 was one of the most fraught in Ireland's relations with the EU. On the one hand, the bail-out enabled the Irish state to adjust to the changing economic circumstances in a more gradual manner than would have occurred if Ireland simply fell out of the global financial markets with no safety net. On the other hand, the easy financial liquidity caused by global financial deregulation and the establishment of the Euro was what had facilitated the extraordinary bloating of the Irish banking system. Moreover, the design of the Eurozone, with its centralised monetary policy and weak economic policy, meant that it did not have the policy instruments to address the severity of the crisis. The Eurozone reacted with emergency policies and muddling-through, which imposed the cost of adjustment on those countries in trouble, including Ireland.

The events surrounding the bank bail-out and the high cost it imposed on Irish taxpayers will remain contested for many years to come. One important, albeit also highly contested, issue was the treatment of the 'bondholders'. In the 2011 general election, opposition to the bail-out and its attendant conditions was found on the left of the political spectrum. The United Left Alliance and Sinn Féin promised to burn the bondholders and repudiate the EU–International Monetary Fund package.[22] During the election campaign, the leader of the Labour party, Eamon Gilmore, had also flirted with doing this, saying that '[i]t would be Frankfurt's way or Labour's way'.[23] Ultimately, Labour went into coalition with Fine Gael and their programme for government broadly agreed to accept the bail-out conditions with some minor changes. Both the new government and its predecessor tried to reduce the cost to the Irish tax-payer of the bank bail-out by imposing some of the costs on the bondholders. This was fiercely resisted by the ECB, which was concerned not just about Ireland, but the wider European banking system. At the time, Ireland was experiencing deep austerity and the decision not to bail-in senior unsecured bondholders was deeply unpopular. The joint committee set up by the Irish parliament to conduct an inquiry into Ireland's banking crisis concluded:

> The ECB position in November 2010 and March 2011 on imposing losses on senior bondholders, contributed to the inappropriate placing of significant banking debts on the Irish citizen.[24]

Ireland exited the bail-out in December 2013 with an economy already growing again and unemployment coming down. This dampened discussion of the contested issues that remained on the table. Ireland's presidency of the European Council in 2013 signalled the return of Ireland's reputation. In this period, it was not uncommon for other European leaders to use Ireland as a poster child of economic renewal and recovery. Ireland's exit from the economic crisis owed much to the adaptability and resilience of its society and people. That resilience was about to be tested, less than three years following the completion of the bail-out programme. This time the shock would be entirely exogenous, in the form of the UK's decision on 23 June 2016 to leave the European Union. Ireland was confronted with the departure of the UK from the EU, a situation more commonly called Brexit.

Brexit

The UK's decision to leave the EU was a major shock to Ireland, as it affected its geo-political and geo-economic anchors in a challenging world. Prior to the UK vote, the then Irish foreign minister, Charlie Flanagan, speaking in Dublin, concluded that it was:

> in our country's fundamental interests that the UK remains a member of the European Union. There is, I think, absolutely no doubt about that. British membership of the Union is hugely important for this country—for our economy, for the strength of the British–Irish relationship, for peace and stability in Northern Ireland and for our long-term strategic positioning within the EU.[25]

In London, the then taoiseach Enda Kenny emphasised that while it was a matter for the UK electorate to make its choice, he wanted Britain to remain a central member of the European Union because from our—Ireland's—point of view this was a really critical issue.[26] Following the referendum, Irish politicians and public officials had no choice but to begin to address the implications of Brexit for Ireland. The immediate response was to emphasise that Ireland would remain an EU member state. The foreign minister stressed in the Dáil after the referendum that 'Ireland will of course remain in the EU and in the Eurozone while we will also do everything to protect our political, economic and people-to-people links to the UK'.[27] In order to ensure that Irish interests were known and understood across the other 26 member states and in the European institutions, the Irish state engaged in an unprecedented political and diplomatic effort across the EU. Between the referendum and the triggering of the UK's withdrawal letter on 29 March 2017, the Irish held 400 meetings, including up to fifteen meetings at head of state or government level, on the Brexit issue. Prime ministers, foreign ministers and European affairs ministers across Europe were getting a crash course on Ireland and the Good Friday Agreement—the agreement signed in 1998 that provided for a set of complex institutions within Northern Ireland, between the UK and Ireland and on the island of Ireland.

The Irish approach to Brexit has been characterised by a high level of consensus across the political spectrum and concentrated planning by the government and administration. The three important areas for Ireland in the Brexit process were identified as:

- the importance and volume of economic exchange between the UK and Ireland;
- Northern Ireland, the peace process and British–Irish relations;
- the common travel area and shared land-border.

Concern about the potential impact of the Brexit process on peace in Northern Ireland was a cause of deep concern. Ireland's intensive diplomatic efforts paid off, because when the European Council published its negotiating guidelines on the proposed Brexit talks in April 2017, Ireland was one of three priority areas identified as core to the first phase of negotiations. The other member states, known as the EU-27, signalled to the UK that progress on Ireland was essential before the EU would move on to discussing the next phase, the future relationship between the UK and the EU-27. Ireland found itself dealing with its largest neighbour for the first time with the backing of the European institutions and the 26 other member states. Of course, all member states have their own interests to promote and protect in the negotiations, but Ireland's partners and the chief EU negotiator Michel Barnier have been steadfast in their support for the Irish position. This altered the balance of power between Ireland and the UK for the first time in their shared history.

The problem Ireland faces is that nothing short of continued UK membership of the EU is in its interest. Ireland's geographical closeness to the UK and the significance of the UK—both as a market and transit zone—greatly complicate Ireland's post-Brexit economic and social environment. Add to this the challenge that Britain's departure from the EU poses to the Good Friday Agreement, which was predicated on joint membership of the EU, and the danger of the re-introduction of a hard border between Ireland and Northern Ireland. The chief economist of the Irish Central Bank addressed the implications of a *hard* Brexit scenario, and concluded that 'after 10 years, GDP would be lower by 3% and the number of people employed would be 40,000 fewer'.[28] Unlike the other member states, Ireland has core interests at stake in the Brexit negotiations. The decision by the UK to leave both the single market and the customs unions has yet to be reconciled with the stated aim of the UK that it is not seeking to re-introduce a hard border in Ireland. Taoiseach Leo Varadkar, speaking in Belfast on 4 August 2017, displayed frustration with those who were advocating the re-introduction of a hard border, namely those who sought a hard Brexit. In hard-hitting comments he argued that:

> [t]here are people who do want a border, a trade border between the United Kingdom and the European Union and therefore a border between Ireland and Britain and a border across this island. These are advocates of a so-called hard Brexit. I believe the onus should be on them to come up with proposals for such a border and to convince us and convince you; citizens, students, academics, farmers, business people that it's in your interest to have these new barriers to commerce and trade.[29]

Although it was not stated, the taoiseach was, in fact, being very critical of the stance of Prime Minister Theresa May and the British government because of the decision to leave the single market and customs union. The EU task force published a commission paper on guiding principles on Ireland, which has been transmitted to the EU-27. The paper had significant input from the Irish government and was welcomed by the government. The paper began by emphasising that:

> The onus to propose solutions which overcome the challenges created on the island of Ireland by the United Kingdom's withdrawal from the European Union and its decision to leave the customs union and the internal market remains on the United Kingdom.[30]

The document then suggested that Ireland will require unique solutions that would not impact on other aspects of the post-Brexit EU relationship. How this plays out in the Brexit negotiations will have profound implications for Ireland over the next fifty years. Although the primary focus is on Brexit and the withdrawal process, an EU-27 will be a different union for Ireland as a member state. Ireland must begin to address the dilemmas of its future in the European Union, minus the UK.

Ireland's European future

The election of Donald Trump as president of the USA in autumn 2016 served to complicate Ireland's geo-political environment. Ireland was a comfortable member of the EU, with strong ties to the US and good relations with its nearest neighbour, the UK. The shifts and shocks of 2016 undermined two of Ireland's three global anchors. Consequently, membership of the EU assumes even greater strategic significance, but the EU-27 is changing because of the loss of the UK and multiple pressures for change. President Michael D. Higgins sought in a March 2017 speech to business leaders to reassure the Irish people that they could meet the challenge:

> The Ireland in which we live is one that is already embracing challenges at global, European and national level. The Irish people are instinctively international. They are

positive about participation in the European Union and have a mind-set that will be to their advantage in facing our new circumstances, including the immediate challenge of Brexit and, beyond, the challenge of renovating the projects of the European Union.[31]

The EU has experienced a turbulent decade of multiple crises: pressure on the Eurozone, the refugee crisis and the crisis of politics characterised by the rise of right-wing populism in many parts of Europe. Disintegration rather than integration seemed to be the dominant trend in the union. Faced with multiple challenges, the EU has proved resilient but divided. The election of Emmanuel Macron as president of France in May 2017 was a boost to the EU, as he ran on a strong pro-European platform and was not afraid to take on the populists, notably his adversary in the election, Marine le Pen of the Front National. President Macron has set himself the task of a renewal of the EU in tandem with Germany. Historically the Franco–German alliance has been the motor of European integration.

The next phase of integration poses a set of challenges to Ireland, including its relations with the other member states and its approach to particular policy areas. The first challenge it faces, as already noted, is to position itself in the EU-27, minus the UK. Ireland has to establish new working relations across the member states. One of the benefits of the Brexit negotiations is that they have forced Irish politicians and diplomats to exert considerable energy on talking to the other member states. In the longer term, Ireland could become part of a group of small North European states stretching from Ireland to Sweden working together within the EU. Ireland is now a net contributor to the EU budget and these partners are potential allies. This does not, however, preclude Ireland from seeking to develop strong relations with other states in the eastern and southern half of the continent. Following the departure of the UK, Berlin and Paris will require constant cultivation by Irish actors.

There are two issues on the EU agenda that will require considerable deliberation in the Irish political and policy system. These are corporate taxation and developing EU policies in the area of security and defence. Low corporation tax has been at the core of Ireland's economic model since the decision was taken to modernise through export-led growth. Attracting FDI to Ireland, particularly investment by US multinationals, was the central function of the highly successful Industrial Development Authority. By the second decade of the twenty-first century Ireland had experienced waves of foreign investment concentrated in a number of high-tech industries, such as pharmaceuticals and information technology. There were many reasons for locating in Ireland, not least because it afforded access to the large and lucrative EU single market, but the corporate tax regime undoubtedly played a major role. Other member states and EU institutions have expressed opposition to the Irish tax regime over many decades but could do little about it, since setting the tax rate is an exclusive Irish competence. When it became apparent, however, that Ireland's nominal corporate tax rate of 12.5% disguised far lower tax contributions for very large and wealthy corporations, Ireland came under renewed pressure to amend the rate. The European Commission took a case against the Apple Corporation that led to a significant fine on the grounds that Ireland's tax rate was state aid in disguise. The Irish state has begun the process of recovering unpaid taxes amounting to €13 billion from Apple. Both Apple and the Irish government are appealing the European Commission's ruling in relation to Apple, but the judgement has forced Ireland to close down loopholes in its tax code that had seen companies, such as Apple, paying very little tax. Even without EU pressure, it behooves Ireland to ensure that it is not a tax haven.

The election of President Trump in the US and the instability on Europe's borders to the south and east have brought the question of European defence and security policy back on the agenda. Ireland has been actively involved in the European Security and Defence Policy, both at a policy-making and an operational level. It is unclear just how this field of EU action will develop in the years to come, but it is highly likely that there will be continuous pressure to ensure that Europe can guarantee its security and secure its borders. The time is ripe for a discussion in Ireland about how it sees its participation in this facet of European integration. Successive governments have been loath to initiate a public debate, fearful of the strong and vocal pro-neutrality lobby. With Russian president Vladimir Putin to the east and instability and state failure to the south, Ireland can no longer assume that its security will be guaranteed by others within Europe. Beyond Brexit there are issues that Ireland must address as it forges its European future without the UK. Not by choice, Ireland is forced to cut the umbilical cord, while retaining good relations with its nearest neighbour.

Conclusions

Ireland's return to Europe, which began in the early 1960s and culminated with EU membership in January 1973, has been a voyage of discovery and change. Irish public opinion is deeply supportive of EU membership and broadly supportive of what the EU represents. Ireland's most important contribution to the EU has been to make a success of membership and to demonstrate that a small and relatively peripheral member state could modernise within the framework of membership. It found that it was adept at playing the interdependence game, not by losing its identity, but by allowing its identity to flourish in a large multinational framework. This was helped by the fact that Irish nationalism found a relatively hospitable home in the European Union. Membership has not been smooth. In the early decades Ireland struggled to learn the rules of internationalisation, and it took over twenty years for Ireland to catch-up economically with the richer countries. From time to time, both the elite and the electorate have questioned Ireland's European engagement and its impact on Ireland. The juxtaposition of Boston and Berlin as Ireland's main sources of influence highlighted tensions among the elite about Ireland's European home. The 'No' votes in two European referenda strongly signalled that the support for European membership within the wider population was not unconditional. While it watches on as the UK exits the EU, Irish society appears far more comfortable in a world of connectivity with multiple cross-cutting fuzzy identities. Some of the UK discourse is a reminder of the age of empire and a reinforcement of the value of being part of a multi-level polity that embraces the nation states but goes beyond them. An institution based on law and treaties is a far more benign environment for small states than one based on the coercive traditions of empire.

Notes

[1] *The Irish Times*, 1 January 1973, 3.

[2] Seamus Heaney, 'Alphabets' (from *The haw lantern*), in *New selected poems 1966–1987* (Faber and Faber; London, 1990), 211–13.

[3] Barbara Hobson, *Recognition struggles and social movements* (Cambridge University Press; Cambridge, 2003), 352.

[4] Garrett FitzGerald, *Irish foreign policy within the context of the EEC*; address given by Minister for Foreign Affairs, Dr Garret FitzGerald TD, to the Royal Irish Academy, 10 November 1975, 2. The text of the address is available online at: http://aei.pitt.edu/8545/ (17 March 2018).

[5] John Hume, Nobel Lecture, Oslo, 10 December 1998. The text of the lecture is available at: https://www.nobelprize.org/nobel_prizes/peace/laureates/1998/hume-lecture.html (17 March 2018).

[6] *The Economist*, title page. 16 January 1988.

[7] *The Economist*, title page. 17 May 1997.

[8] Seán Ó Riain, *The rise and fall of Ireland's Celtic Tiger: liberalism, boom and bust* (Cambridge University Press; Cambridge, 2013), 309. Paul Teage and Jimmy Donaghey, 'Why has Irish Social Partnership survived?', *British Journal of Industrial Relations* 47 (1) (2009), 55–78.

[9] Kevin O'Rourke, 'Brexit a reminder of how EU has benefited republic', *The Irish Times*, 14 August, 2017; the article is available on the newspaper website at: https://www. irishtimes.com/business/economy/brexit-a-reminder-of-how-eu-has-benefited-repub-lic-1.3185625 (17 March 2018).

[10] David Haugh, 'Ireland's economy: still riding the globalisation wave', OECD Observer 305 (January 2016); available on the OECD website at: http://oecdobserver.org/news/fullstory.php/aid/5456/Ireland_92s_economy:_Still_riding_the_globalisation_wave.html (17 March 2018).

[11] Síle de Valera, Minister for the Arts, Culture, Gaeltacht and the Islands, *Address to Boston College, 18 September 2000* (Department of Arts, Culture, Gaeltacht and the Islands; Dublin, 2000).

[12] de Valera, *Address to Boston College.*

[13] Mary Harney, Tánaiste, *Address to a meeting of the American Bar Association, Dublin, 21 July 2000* (Government Information Service Dublin; Dublin, 2000).

[14] Brigid Laffan and Ben Tonra, 'Europe and the international dimension', in John Coakley and Michael Gallagher (eds), *Politics in the Republic of Ireland* (6th edn; Routledge; Abingdon, UK and New York, 2018), 349–69.

[15] Brigid Laffan and Jane O'Mahony, *Ireland and the European Union* (Palgrave; London, 2008), 48–55.

[16] Patrick Honohan, *The Irish banking crisis: regulatory and financial stability policy 2003–2008. A report to the minister for finance by the governor of the Central Bank* (Government Publications; Dublin, 31 May 2010); Klaus Regling and Max Watson, *A preliminary report on the sources of Ireland's banking crisis* (Government Publications; Dublin, 2010, Prn. A10/0700).

[17] Mario Draghi, 'Letter to Matt Carthy MEP', 17 February 2015, L/MD/15/86; available online at: https://www.ecb.europa.eu/pub/pdf/other/150218letter_carthy.en.pdf (17 March 2018).

[18] Draghi, 'Letter to Matt Carthy MEP'.

[19] *The Irish Times*, 'Editorial', 18 November 2010, 17.

[20] *The Irish Times*, 'Editorial', 18 November 2010, 17.

[21] *The Irish Times*, 'Editorial', 18 November 2010, 17.

[22] Derek Hutcheson, 'The February 2011 parliamentary election in Ireland', *Working Papers in British–Irish Studies: University College Dublin* (UCD, Dublin, 2011), 109.

[23] Hutcheson, 'The February 2011 parliamentary election in Ireland', 20.

[24] Government of Ireland, *Report of the joint committee of inquiry into the banking crisis* (Houses of the Oireachtas; Dublin, January 2016); the complete text of the report is available online, at: https://inquiries.oireachtas.ie/banking/ (17 March 2018).

[25] Charlie Flanagan, 'Speech delivered by Irish Foreign Minister, Charles Flanagan T.D., Leinster House, 25 March 2015, at the launch of the book *Britain in Europe: the end game—an Irish perspective*'; the text of the speech is available at: https://www.dfa.ie/news-and-media/press-releases/press-release-archive/2015/march/minister-launches-iiea-book/ (17 March 2018).

[26] Enda Kenny, 'Remarks at a press conference in London with UK prime minister David Cameron, 26 January 2016'; available online at: https://www.gov.uk/government/speeches/pm-press-conference-with-enda-kenny-january-2016 (17 March 2018).

[27] Charlie Flanagan, 'Statement by Irish Foreign Minister, Charles Flanagan T.D. to the Dáil on the UK–EU Referendum Outcome, 27 June 2016'; the text of the statement is available at: https://www.dfa.ie/news-and-media/speeches/speeches-archive/2016/june/uk-exit-from-eu-mfat-dail-statement/ (17 March 2018).

[28] Gabriel Fagan, 'Opening statement by chief economist, Central Bank of Ireland, at the Seanad Committee on Brexit, 4 May 2017'; available at: https://www.centralbank.ie/news/article/opening-statement-by-gabriel-fagan-at-the-seanad-committee-on-brexit (17 March 2018).

[29] Leo Varadkar, 'Taoiseach's address to Queen's University Belfast, 4 August 2017'; available at: https://merrionstreet.ie/en/News-Room/News/Taoiseach_addresses_Queens_University_Belfast.html (17 March 2018).

[30] European Union, *Guiding principles for the dialogue on Ireland/Northern Ireland*, 21 September, 2017; available at: https://ec.europa.eu/commission/publications/guiding-principles-dialogue-ireland-northern-ireland_en (17 March 2018).

[31] Michael D. Higgins, 'Keynote address by the President of Ireland, Michael D. Higgins to the IBEC Conference, 9 March 2017'; available at: http://www.president.ie/en/diary/details/president-addresses-the-ibec-ceo-conference (17 March 2018).

PART II a

Representations of
Ireland in European
Literature and Irish
Literature in Europe

Destination of the imagination: representations of Ireland in modern French literature

Anne Gallagher

Introduction

'To speak correctly of Ireland, it is preferable not to know what one is speaking about'.[1]

The most enduring image of Ireland in the French imaginative consciousness is only indirectly a product of French literature. *Un taxi mauve*, the film directed by Yves Boisset in 1977 and based on the award-winning

1973 novel by Michel Déon—who co-wrote the script with Boisset—escaped the attention of most Irish cinephiles but went on to form the basis of a significant proportion of Irish iconography in France.[2] It was shot in various locations in the west of Ireland (in counties Sligo, Mayo, Cork and Kerry) and features rugged, untamed landscapes inhabited by a happy-go-lucky people with little regard for the materialism of the modern world: they are dreamers or fantasists.[3] According to Déon, they live like 'holidaymakers in their own country'.[4] The presence of an austere religion is juxtaposed with an irrepressible *joie de vivre*. In contrast, the protagonists, none of whom is Irish, display a great deal of existential angst. In truth, Ireland is merely a backdrop to their story, its oneiric qualities adding a sense of mystery and serving to highlight the brutality and ugliness characteristic of their lives. Although Ireland may only have had a secondary role in the film, in France it emerged as the star turn.

Un taxi mauve, both the film and the novel, is interesting to the student of French literature, since, in many ways, it is a distillation of recurrent images of Ireland in French literature over the centuries: an untamed land, bathed in mystery and mythology, where rationalism has no place and the life of the imagination reigns supreme. Only a minority of works in modern times depart from this stereotype, principally those from the pen of the former surrealist Raymond Queneau in the 1940s and 1950s and, more recently, those dealing with the Northern Irish 'Troubles', such as work by Sorj Chalandon, Yannick Guin, Gilles Rosset and the poet Paol Keineg.

Voyage literature

Early French literary texts refer to Saint Patrick's Purgatory and journeys to the other world in the twelfth century.[5] More noteworthy for the purposes of this chapter, the *Navigatio Brendani*, or *Voyage of Saint Brendan*, a text written at the beginning of the eighth century, had a significant influence on French medieval literature. According to Stifter:

> It tells the story of the voyage of an early medieval Irish abbot, St. Brendan of Clonfert (*c.* 484–*c.* 577), and his crew

Anne Gallagher

on the North Atlantic, and of their adventures on sometimes realistic, sometimes allegorical islands until, after
going in circles for seven years, they reach the goal of their
quest, the *Terra Repromissionis Sanctorum*, 'the Promised
Land of the Saints'.[6]

The story is an early Irish voyage tale and has much in common with
the *Immrama*, in which, according to Fleuriot, 'the voyage serves as
a backdrop to fantastical adventures and the climax is the visit to the
terrestrial Paradise'.[7] The *Navigatio Brendani* itself is also heavily influenced by classical mythology. As we shall see, a significant body
of French literature involving Ireland, whether consciously or uncon-
sciously, draws on this voyage literature.

As has already been mentioned, there were, from time to time, some
unflattering departures from this theme. According to Ó Ciosáin, medieval French literature represented the Irish as wild wood-dwellers,
uncivilised, irreligious and unaccustomed to strenuous work.[8] In a reference to communities of destitute Irish immigrants who had settled in
various parts of France, including under Paris bridges, he quotes from,
among others, Motin, a rhymester, whose suit had been refused, and
who, as a result, wishes that the lady in question would marry a knave,
live in a cellar and:

> then, after some time passes
> hating and beating each other,
> Both in eternal strife,
> with clothes flea-ridden and torn
> under the Pont Saint-Honoré
> You'll die like a poor Irishwoman.[9]

In later centuries, the image of the Irish in French literature is, on the
whole, a more positive one, chiefly as a result of the influence of the
Romantic movement and of the Celtic Revival it inspired.

Unsurprisingly, Ireland features most prominently in Franco-Breton
literature. Brittany, a proudly Celtic country where a Celtic language
is still spoken, has, for more than a century, had a particular regard
for Ireland as the only Celtic land to gain its independence. Breton

intellectuals have frequently seen in Ireland an example of what Brittany could or should be.

In France generally, interest in the Celts and the Celtic world was first sparked by the publication in 1760 by James Macpherson of *Fragments of ancient poetry collected in the highlands of Scotland and translated from the Galic or Erse language*, a text known more popularly as *Ossian*.[10] This interest grew in intensity in the context of the Romantic movement. In 1804 the *Académie celtique* was established in Paris, with the aim of conducting research on Celtic and Gaulish language still extant in France. Scholarship very quickly drifted, however, towards what is usually described as *'La Celtomanie'*, in reference to the theories proposed by Théophile Malo Corret de La Tour d'Auvergne, who held that the Breton language was the prototype for all languages.[11]

In 1839 Théodore Hersart de la Villemarqué published *Barzaz Breizh*, a collection of oral literature in the Breton language, purported to have been gathered in the Breton countryside.[12] This publication re-awakened intellectual Breton pride in the native culture and heritage of the region, and, arguably, played a pivotal role in the formation of a Breton nationalist movement; a movement which, in large part, drew its inspiration from Ireland's efforts to secure its independence from Britain.

In 1854 Ernest Renan published *La poésie des races celtiques* ('The poetry of the Celtic races'), later republished as *L'Ame bretonne* ('The Breton soul').[13] This seminal essay established what was to be the narrative foundation for much Breton literature over the following centuries, particularly when referring to other Celtic countries:

> [t]hus has been the Celtic race: she has worn herself out by taking her dreams for reality and chasing her boundless visions. The essential element of the poetic life of the Celt is adventure, that is to say the pursuit of the unknown, endlessly running after the ever-fleeting object of desire. That is what saint Brendan imagined beyond the seas, that is what the knight Owen demanded of his underworld peregrinations. That race desires infinity, she thirsts for it, she pursues it at any cost, beyond the tomb, beyond hell. The weakness of the Breton people, its inclination to intoxication, a weakness, which, by all accounts in the sixth

century, was the cause of its disasters, is due to that in-domitable need for illusion.[14]

The text features a lengthy description of Saint Brendan's voyage, which, according to Renan, is 'without fear of contradiction the most singular product of that combination of Celtic naturalism and Christian spirituality'.[15] It also describes the voyage of Owen to hell through Saint Patrick's Purgatory in County Donegal. As Renan would have it, all Celts have a thirst for the unknown, for an experience of life beyond the grave, for the Promised Land.

More prosaically, the Celts are individualistic, xenophobic, conservative, proud of their origins, gauche, fatalist and sensitive. He believes that they are a race with:

> all the qualities of a solitary man who is both proud and shy, powerful in his feelings and weak in action: at home she is free and at ease; outside gauche and ill at ease. She distrusts the foreigner, because she sees in him a more refined being than she, and who would take advantage of her simple ways. Indifferent to the admiration of others, she asks for only one thing, to be left alone at home.[16]

In 1905, the Breton writer Anatole Le Braz undertook a journey to experience Renan's Ireland for himself. He went in search of:

> that land whence had come our first Breton saints, the impressions which certain pages of Renan had conveyed many times, the cradle of Celticism and the fatherland of the patriarchs of the fifth, sixth, seventh and eighth centuries and I went there in the end to study the race.[17]

His travels, described in a lecture to the Geographical Society of Lille five years later, first took him to Dublin before he set forth for Donegal. He is struck by the contrast between what he describes as the prosperous Protestant counties of Ulster and the poverty of the Catholic counties. The Irish Catholics he meets are Francophile and very welcoming. 'Not since General Humbert, Wolfe Tone's friend, has a Frenchman come around here', declares a Donegal man, who asks him to sing the 'Marseillaise' to prove his nationality.[18] Later, Le Braz notes the presence of statues of Hoche and Napoleon in even the most modest homes. In his view, the Irishman is the original political animal. Intrigued by the number of Irish who do nothing all day, he learns that this is because 'over three hundred years of despoilment, they were forbidden to do anything'.[19] There is now, however, a great sense of optimism in the air, although it is an optimism not shared by everyone. Le Braz notes in particular the politico-religious divide: 'If one consults the Irish, one hears two refrains: the more numerous, the nationalists, the Catholics, are very optimistic, whilst the others, Protestants, are absolutely pessimistic.'[20] Le Braz also seeks to explain the role of the Catholic Church in the lives of the Irish: they were supported by the priests when all others had abandoned them and, as a result, their places of worship became bastions of national hopes and aspirations. The article confirms many of Renan's theories as posited in *La poésie des races celtiques*. The Irish are, on the whole, fantasists (*rêveurs*) and idealists who care little for material comforts.

The year 1919 saw the publication of *Les bardes et poètes nationaux de la Bretagne Armoricaine*, although most of the poems were written in the 1890s. The fact that the anthology was published after the Easter Rising of 1916 is probably not a coincidence. In his introduction to the work, Camille Le Mercier d'Erm calls for Home Rule for Brittany. The poems themselves, arguably of little literary value, constitute a somewhat naïve display of nationalist sentiment, (Roman Catholic) religious fervour and Celtic mythology. The following example from Alain Gourval is representative of the collection:

> And Brittia suddenly starts to the sound of the Bard
> Keltia! Keltia! Éir-in has her *Chouans*![21]
> Fearless, to their Duty go the Fenians![22]
> When the Englishman strays in the Emerald Isle
> Cunning Punishment around the Englishman lurks
> Keltia! Keltia! Sad until death
> Under the French yoke moans the suffering Armor[23]
> Waiting until the dawn lighting the mountain
> Finally awakens Prince Arthur—and Brittany.[24]

Anne Gallagher

The Breton academic Per Denez draws attention to the stark contrast between the law-abiding, even meek, nature of the poets themselves and the violent, blood-thirsty exhortations which pervaded much of their writing.[25]

In 1961, Michel Mohrt published *La prison maritime*, an adventure novel, which includes a number of thinly disguised events from early twentieth-century Breton history. The novel, for which he received the *Grand Prix du roman de l'Académie française*, is set in the 1920s, when the Breton nationalist movement saw in Ireland a model for an independent, Celtic and Catholic state. The young protagonist, Hervé, is a pupil at a secondary school in Brest, where his English teacher, l'Abbé Guern (Le Grand Foc), attempts to promote some of his Breton separatist ideas among his young charges:

> Not enough is said about Ireland and its example. May I remind you: we are in 1921 and the Republic of Éire has only just been born. Is it the case that not everyone is deserving of freedom, and that a Catholic country does not have the right to demand it? Of course, it is a victory of the old Celtic cause, which can never be totally suppressed … an eternal Vendée emerges from century to century, on the shores of the West.[26] Those men, a Pearse, a Connolly, were giants.[27] James Connolly half-dead, was shot in his wheelchair.[28]

His words echo both the tone and content of a significant proportion of Breton nationalist propaganda from the 1930s and 1940s, such as the following example from a 1942 Breton Nationalist Party brochure.

> We are filled with admiration for the heroes who have liberated Ireland. Their blood has fertilised Brittany and they have engendered a spiritual son…
>
> An activist minority, prepared for the supreme sacrifice, was sufficient to rally the Irish people and banish the foreigner. Like them, let us not expect anything from anyone but ourselves.[29]

The principal characters, Hervé, Olivier de Kersanger and his brother Tugdual, set sail for Ireland on a boat named *Roi Arthur*, in search of arms to bolster the cause of the Breton autonomists. The name of the boat is a strong indicator of much of what lies in store, the Arthurian legend being among the best-known Breton legends. The return of Arthur, also referenced in the poem by Gourval above, signifies the return of hope for Bretons and freedom for Brittany. In line with Fleuriot's definition, the novel describes a voyage from one Celtic country to another, from the continent to a faraway island, a voyage from reality to a dream world and from youth to adult life, a voyage of initiation. Having attempted to take the Island of Couëron for Brittany—a reference to the attempt by the Breton autonomists to take the Chausey Islands—the crew heads directly for Ireland. Hervé says, 'there burned in me the faith of a pilgrim who is heading towards a sanctuary'.[30]

The journey to Ireland is a disappointment. The Bretons are struck by the poverty of the new state, for which they blame the British, and by the ravages wreaked on both people and place by the recent civil war. Hervé also speaks of a pride and wistful irony (*ironie rêveuse*) on the faces of the Irish, which will always have been the 'strongest weapon of the Celtic nations against adversity'.[31] The voyagers' disappointment is compounded by the fact that their Breton origins mean nothing to the Irish, who see them as merely French.

A visit to the Hibernian Hotel, a kind of pseudo-English oasis populated by the gentry, who dress like caricatures of the English, gives the reader a glimpse of another aspect of Irish life. The character of Arthur Saint Arthur embodies (non-Celtic) English rationalism and argues that it is the Catholic clergy and not the English who have been a thorn in the side of Ireland, in a probable reference to James Joyce and other writers who famously expressed the desire to live abroad in order to develop as artists: 'The clergy keeps this country in a state of ignorance and superstition. Censure is applied indiscriminately, prohibiting that which is noble and beautiful.'[32]

Saint Arthur also compares the economic situation in Northern Ireland to that of the new state, arguing that the ambition to separate from the United Kingdom was a form of madness:

Anne Gallagher

'You must read a newspaper from this country', said my companion, 'to see where nationalist passion can lead. Ireland is a country of legends but her legends were no longer enough for her; she had to invent new ones... The Easter Rising of 1917 [sic] is considered sublime, whereas it was a folly committed as a result of misunderstandings between the leaders of Sinn Féin. I knew several of them: they were dreamers with no political understanding.'[33]

Hervé responds that a people may choose poverty if it is the price of independence.

In Mohrt's novel, the Breton dream finally perishes on the rocks off the Côtes du Nord (Côtes d'Armor today) and the boat is washed onto a fictional beach named 'Les Sables d'Or', an allusion to a well-known episode in Breton history. In 1939 Breton militants landed arms near Locquirec in a place called Les Sables Blancs. This operation was an effort to repeat the famous failed attempt by Roger Casement to land arms, originating in Germany, in Ireland in 1916. It is interesting to note that the Breton nationalist operation was named *Abadenn Casement* ('Operation Casement').

The fact that Ireland is merely a backdrop for Michel Mohrt's adventure novel is not insignificant. Mohrt has written that history is made by fantasists (*rêveurs*). We encounter these 'fantasists' in several of his novels, such as Olivier du Trieux in *La guerre civile* and Xavier Lenfant in *Les moyens du bord*. The Ireland portrayed in *La prison maritime* is mainly a figment of the Breton imagination, very much in line with the description of the Celts in *La poésie des races celtiques*, and therefore the ideal location in which to situate a quest-type or voyage novel. Only Saint Arthur attempts to break the spell from time to time. Yet the intellectual writer, who frequents the great modern and modernist writers, fails to destroy the myth. Hervé returns home a little less naïve but the other members of his crew continue to believe in the dream (*rêve*). The Grand Foc will finish his days on the Aran Islands, 'the last land of Europe facing the Atlantic'.[34]

The maritime prison is the prison of rationalism, which attempts to contain human dreams and erect barriers around the imagination, which, like the sea, knows no bounds: *Navigare necesse est, vivere non necesse* ('To voyage is necessary, to live is not necessary').[35]

The Breton theme of the Celtic imagination versus Latin rationalism is also to be found in the writings of Xavier Grall in the 1970s. He presents his book entitled *Le cheval couché* as the antithesis of the well-known, much loved, but somewhat *passéiste* ethnographical autobiography *Le cheval d'orgueil*.[36] Grall cites the Breton historian Morvan Lebesque to illustrate what he identifies as the relationship between the Breton people and the sea and the Breton people and the world of the imagination (*le rêve*), a quest which, once again, echoes both Renan and the *Navigatio Brendani*.[37] For Grall too, rationalism is the enemy of the imagination; Latin rationalism has sought to contain or destroy the Celtic imagination. He believes that there are three places conducive to a voyage to the infinity of the imagination: the southern countries, Brittany and Ireland.

In the chapter he devotes to Ireland, Grall recalls a passage from the writings of the female Breton nationalist Fant Rozec, better known as Méavenn; once again, a passage redolent of Renan's musings on the subject.

> Why do catastrophes so become the Celts, as mourning becomes Electra? Because we are proud of them, enough to cry, enough to die: because suddenly, well, too late, we begin to trust ourselves.[38]

Grall goes on to relate his own trips to Ireland. He writes of a beggar he encounters who seems to be the incarnation of 'Beggar, itinerant Ireland, introspective, wretched but elated'.[39] He feels as though he is 'in a Brittany preserved from, alien to, Latin values'.[40] 'The only escape in this darkening limbo: fantasy (*rêve*), quotidian fantasy.'[41] He is constantly struck by the contrasts and contradictions of Ireland, which give him a sense of being in a surreal country. The men of the Aran Islands are not men of the sea but rather farmers without farms. He describes a bleak, dying land, where rotting *currachs* on the beaches resemble dolphins struck by lightning.[42]

Grall's Ireland is a twentieth-century incarnation of Renan's Celtic country: poor and dreary but managing to survive thanks to its imagination, thanks to the Atlantic Ocean—the saviour of the Celtic countries—and the limitless possibilities it offers, both in terms of physical and psychological escape. Ireland is also an exotic country: the country of European blues, which is mysterious, hospitable, melancholic and merry. There, reason and rationalism remain firmly in the background; Ireland represents an imaginative ideal to which Brittany should aspire:

> Bretons, march, with the little harp on your shoulder, that national emblem of free, heroic Ireland, which the Renaissance, the era of preciosity and elitism, had thrown on the scrapheap![43]

Joyce's Dublin?

> 'Then he spoke to me of a Dublin guy,
> named Joyce, a pornographer who had
> to have his books printed in Paris.'[44]

A very different Ireland is portrayed in the works of Raymond Queneau. In 1947 Queneau published *On est toujours trop bon avec les femmes* under the pseudonym Sally Mara, which was followed three years later by *Le journal intime de Sally Mara*. Both novels were subsequently published together under the title *Les oeuvres complètes de Sally Mara*.

The first novel is Queneau's scandalously satirical version of the Easter Rising at the Eden Quay post office in Dublin. The rebels manage to cause everyone to flee the post office, apart from one young postmistress, Gertie Girdle, who is in the toilets when the building is taken. Gertie is Anglo-Irish, anti-Catholic and loyal to the king. She is engaged to be married to Commodore Sidney Cartwright of the British army, who rescues her at the end of the story. The novel is a kind of iconoclastic homage to James Joyce, the name of the protagonist being a direct reference to Gertie McDowell, familiar to readers of *Ulysses* from the scene on the beach with Leopold Bloom; having Gertie as the protagonist is also a strong hint as to the sexually explicit, even crude, nature of much of the content to come. Gertie repeatedly shouts 'God save the King' in protest at the rebellion, to which the rebels reply 'Finnegan's Wake'. The latter are alarmed to learn that Gertie is a religious agnostic, and one of them exclaims, 'you can see that we're in James Joyce country here'.[45]

Religion and nationalism are intertwined in *On est toujours trop bon avec les femmes*. Another rebel comments: 'As for our motherland, I fear nothing for her. She is eternal, our Éire. Just like the Christian era'.[46] Aside from the somewhat facile pun in French (and perhaps also in English), this declaration summarises what Queneau perceives as the naïvety of the impassioned nationalist and the unquestioning believer. Gertie Girdle seduces many of the rebels from the brigade led by John Mac Cormack, and they fear that this could damage their legacy by sullying their personal reputations, since as Mac Cormack reminds them: 'it is necessary for our cause, that she acknowledges our heroism and the purity of our behaviour'.[47]

In *Le journal intime de Sally Mara*, Mara's diary contains references to her attempts to learn the Irish language. Sally Mara is a young Dublin woman born on Easter Monday 1916. She keeps a diary in French, a language she has recently learned. She describes her life in Dublin, living with a sadistic father with vampire tendencies; a mother who is intellectually challenged; a brother who is both an alcoholic and 'sex mad', who sets up home with one of their maids and is sent to prison for the murder of another; and a sister whose ambition is to work in a post office. Her father goes out to buy a box of matches one evening and only returns several months later. In his absence, her mother, a sort of Irish Penelope, whiles away the time by knitting socks. Queneau made no secret of Joyce's influence on his writing. In this homage to Joyce, many of the proper names are transposed directly from Joyce's work. We encounter Stephen Dedalus's green handkerchief in a scene with Mac Cormack, Caffrey and Gertie Girdle; the latter surname possibly an allusion to the griddlecakes made by Gertie in *Ulysses*. Both writers refer to Fr Matthew and the temperance movement. The revival of the Irish language also features in *Ulysses*.

Perhaps the greater homage to Joyce is in terms of the construction of the novels. *On est toujours trop bon avec les femmes* is constructed like a cinema script, and the second novel is in the form of a diary. Queneau's tribute also contains many of the linguistic and stylistic devices employed by Joyce in the construction of *Ulysses*: puns, alliteration, alexandrines, enumeration and accumulation, interior monologue, as well as parodies. To mention but one example: the list of Irish-speaking intellectuals in Sally Mara recalls the sylvan high society in *Ulysses*.[48]

Queneau's interest in Ireland appears to have been purely intellectual, partly derived from his stated interest in the work of Joyce but also from his particular interest in language and linguistics. A constant theme in his writing is the increasing divide between written and spoken French. He mentions as a turning point in his life as a writer, his first reading of *Le langage* published in 1921 by Joseph Vendryes, the great Celtic scholar and author of several works on the grammar of Early Irish.[49] Queneau also translated *Fiche bliain ag fás* from the English in 1935.[50] Given all of the above, it is unsurprising that Queneau was more familiar with the Irish-language question than most of his French counterparts.

Queneau also had a brief association with the French surrealist movement, which he relinquished as a result of differences of opinion with André Breton. Notwithstanding this, it would appear that, in the case of his two Irish novels, some of the principles of surrealism were to the fore. To quote Durozoi on surrealism 'everything is to be done; any means are admissible to ruin the concepts of family, fatherland, religion'.[51] The aim was, in part, to demystify everything ordinarily treated as sacred. Ireland, famous for its nationalism, religious and social conservatism, all of which Joyce vowed to flee in *A portrait of the artist as a young man*, provided the ideal setting for such demystification.[52]

Northern Ireland

Sorj Chalandon is a French journalist who acted as correspondent for the French left-wing newspaper *Libération* for a number of years; the post included an extended period in Northern Ireland. During that time, he befriended Denis Donaldson, later to be revealed as a British informer. Chalandon's novel, *Mon traître* ('My traitor'), first published in French in 2007 and published in English in 2011, was an attempt to come to terms with the hurt and disappointment of the betrayal of a close friend.[53] It is loosely based on the development of the relationship between Chalandon and Donaldson and the subsequent shock when Chalandon learns the truth about his friend. He presents the reader with a very realistic and accurate account of life in Belfast during the 'Troubles', something not hitherto available to French readers. The narrator, Antoine, describes his view of Ireland before meeting a Breton, who spoke to him of James Connolly, telling him that if he had not been to the North, he did not know Ireland:

> My Ireland was *The Quiet Man, The Purple Taxi*, the Emerald Isle, Aran jumpers, whiskey, the Éire of our crosswords. It was like a glossy picture. It was green grass, red-haired Maureens, stone walls, thatched roofs and Georgian doors. It was happy, laughing, smoky, black with porter and white with sheep wandering around winding roads. My Ireland—I had been there three times—was Galway, Clifden, Lisdoonvarna, Aran. An Ireland that was musical, maritime, agricultural, welcoming, spiritual, poor yet proud, tranquil.[54]

On a trip to Dublin, Antoine decides to go and spend a few hours in Belfast. The contrast with the passage above is stark:

> Near the tall Divis Tower, I saw my first British patrol. I saw my first gun. The soldier was young, crouched down in a garden, behind the gate of a house. I remember his face, a gloomy expression somewhere between fear and boredom. He looked at my violin case. I felt something tremendous and ridiculous. I was happy to be there. Proud to know I was where it was all happening. Dublin seemed far away to me. Another country, almost. Two helicopters dirtied the low sky. Armoured vehicles were constantly driving past. I was on the Lower Falls Road.[55]

For Antoine, this visit to Belfast is life-changing. He values the strong sense of a cause, of a just war, and of community and hospitality in the face of adversity. His Belfast is the Belfast of the Irish Republican Army (IRA).[56] It is the Belfast of commemorations, of surprise arrests and equally surprising releases, of the IRA hunger strike, of Long Kesh, and, finally, of the 1994 cessation of hostilities.[57] He is shocked to discover that Tyrone Meehan, who had become his Ireland, was a British army informer. He questions every aspect of their relationship but finally returns to visit Meehan in the cottage in which he is in hiding in Donegal. Shortly afterwards, he learns of Meehan's death. He returns for the funeral, still seeking answers. Finally, he acknowledges that betrayal is a part of life.

The sequel, *Retour à Killybegs* ('Return to Killybegs'), which was published in France in 2011 and in Ireland in 2013, also won the *Grand Prix du roman de l'Académie française*.[58] The novel tells the informer's story from his own perspective. It begins with the sentence 'When my father beat me he'd shout in English, as if he didn't want his language mixed up in that.'[59] There follows a description of an abusive, alcoholic father, who, on the way from the pub, beats the coal merchant's mule, called George, for the king, eventually knocking the animal over. When this happens, he shouts 'Éirinn *go Brách!*' and reminds his son that 'Speaking Irish is a form of resistance' and later that 'they spoke Irish in paradise'.[60]

We learn that Meehan's father, Patraig [*sic*], was an IRA activist, had taken part in the civil war, and had been tortured (in English); when the war was lost and the country partitioned, he had begun to drink heavily, shout a lot and beat his children. Life was to take a turn for the worse with Patraig's death and ensuing attacks by locals. Meehan's mother and her seven children moved to north Belfast. Many inconsistencies strike the Irish reader: the Catholic father's bible; turf-cutting in November; the Killybegs child's ability to recognise a Dublin accent as being from his own country and that of Northern Ireland as being foreign; bread with dinner; tanks in Belfast in 1942; and the fact that Meehan did not expect to be recognised upon his return to Killybegs. Eventually, the family is forced to flee its home once more, following an attack by Protestants. The Meehans move to a Catholic area, where they will be protected by the IRA; Tyrone joins the organisation four days later. The second part of the novel, which is set in the 1940s, evokes instead, in terms of atmosphere, the Belfast of the 1970s and 1980s, the period in which Chalandon lived there: this part of the text features republican parades, IRA attacks, torture.

Fast-forward to events in Derry and Belfast at the end of the 1960s, which saw the nationalist population accuse the IRA of abandoning it:

IRA equals 'I Ran Away'.[61] The final section of the novel catalogues happenings familiar to most followers of events at the time: punishment beatings, rubber bullets, interrogations, the Dublin and Monaghan bombings, prison and internment, and the Irish language as a military weapon. These latter events are interspersed with reflections from Meehan's diary of his period in hiding in his father's cottage in Killybegs, following the revelation that he was a British informer. The Dirty Protest is covered.[62] So too is the role of nationalist women militants, but also what academic musician Desi Wilkinson refers to as 'a different ambiance, one that was characterised by friendship, music and conversations rich in philosophical anecdote and humour...'.[63] The early chapters of the book are a somewhat stereotypical portrayal of a very miserable Irish childhood and lack authenticity. In contrast, the later parts give a very realistic account of life in Belfast in the 1970s and 1980s in particular, something which few other French writers have managed to do.

Michel Déon, who died in 2016 at the age of 98, first began writing about Ireland in 1970 (*Les poneys sauvages*).[64] His best-known novel set in Ireland was the aforementioned *Un taxi mauve*. His final work *Cavalier, passe ton chemin!*, is an affectionate tribute to Ireland.[65] That book describes the Déons' first visit to Ireland, the Irish countryside, local characters he has met along the way, including writers and lovers of literature. He comes to Ireland to finish a novel, counting on '...whichever unknown force it was that had made this Atlantic island a hotbed for writers, poets, artists and wild dreamers' for inspiration.[66] Déon becomes part of the hunting–fishing–shooting set; castles feature quite prominently and he engages with, among others, eccentric members of the Anglo-Irish landowner class, a class—reminiscent of Molly Keane's Ireland—determined to keep up appearances in the face of impending bankruptcy and loss of social status.[67] Déon paints an affectionate portrait of one member of this class he had befriended.

He also paints an affectionate and touching portrait of some of his other neighbours, in particular Pat-Jo [*sic*], who was a kind of handyman in the area. He is intrigued by the absence of class in rural Ireland:

> I admired the very Irish privilege of being at ease everywhere, being uncomfortable in no situation, an exemplary

absence of barriers between people, a social fabric with no class divisions.[68]

Déon refers to the amalgam of religion and superstition manifested by Irish acquaintances and devotes a long passage to the paedophile past of Fr Seán Fortune. He mentions, in passing, Ireland's cruelty to her writers in former times and, in more detail, his friendship with writers Ulick O'Connor and John McGahern. He bemoans the newly prettified Ireland and remembers his former postman Tim, who was given the opportunity to emigrate to San Francisco with his daughter but decided that he preferred his native village of Ballindereen:

> Would he have liked the changes in his country? The painted or white-washed houses, the abundance of geraniums, the tidily kept gardens, the rented cars that whizz through the village bearing tourists to Kinvara or Ballyvaughan, the drying up of the bogland. Would he shed a tear in memory of the poky little shop-*cum*-post office, the road that flooded under the slightest downpour, the freezing church, and the petrol pump that the shopkeeper manoeuvred with a fierce energy one could only dream of?[69]

Déon is ruthless in his analysis of Ireland's modernity, new-found prosperity and consequent (as he sees it) lack of authenticity. He comments that the competition for bad taste in Ireland is stiff, and he takes a dim view of the new houses springing up in the Irish countryside, where native hedges have been replaced by cement poles and barbed wire. Instead of stopping on the road to allow brown cows to cross, cars are now stopping to have their car tax and insurance, or the colour of their diesel, checked: 'Prosperity has come crashing down on Ireland like paedophilia on base [*sic*] clergymen'.[70]

Referring to the superstition in the Yeats family that the apparition of a seabird in a dream was an indication of imminent danger to a loved one, Déon comments:

> The birds are not wrong. The life of Erin is always in peril. If it wasn't for the deep thinkers keeping them alive, its

history, its nightmares, it wondrous dreams and its extraordinary capacity to escape wearying reality and live
on fantasies would be forgotten forever.[71]

This passage is reminiscent of work by so many other French authors,
including those already discussed, who attribute Ireland's survival as a
nation to the pre-eminent role of the imagination.[72] Déon now suggests
that this is in danger.

It is no coincidence that the final chapter of Déon's final book (the
English version) should be a retelling of the *Navigatio Brendani* and that
this most influential of Irish legends should close his final work:

Navigatio Brendani is one of those books that will go on
forever. Poetic, learned, inspired, it lends the imagination
to terrestrial and heavenly wonders. Each reader can make
it his own.[73]

Conclusion

The works discussed above constitute only a representative sample of
the foremost interpretations of Ireland in modern French literature.
Ireland as a theme in French literature, whether central or incidental,
has evolved little over the past two centuries and, for the most part,
continues in the tradition of adventure or voyage literature. To some
extent, this speaks more to the pre-occupations of the writers themselves than to a deep understanding of the country and its culture. In
the case of the literature of Brittany, it would seem reasonable to attribute its writers' interpretation of Ireland to what Wilkinson terms
'a search for wider frames of meaning and identity'; indeed it is his
conviction that a certain sense of Ireland has, in itself, been an integral
part of Breton identity, from the time when the search for a specific
cultural identity became a conscious endeavour.[74] Ireland, since, and
possibly because of, Renan has been assigned the role of a kind of repository for the Celtic imaginative consciousness of the Bretons, a kind
of promised land of the imagination, beyond the seas. Other French
writers have also promulgated this vision of Ireland, including those
who seek in Ireland an England untouched by progress, with castles,

Anne Gallagher

an old-fashioned landed class and endless days of hunting, fishing and shooting.

Notwithstanding this, there are also the iconoclastic portrayals: Queneau, in his tribute to Joyce, knocks on its head this mystical, fantastical, other-worldly image of Ireland and enlists it in order to satirise many of the pillars of respectable society. Chalondon describes yet another Ireland, the troubled Northern Ireland of the 1970s, the 1980s and the 1990s, far removed from the rolling hills and the Celtic mists, and with only occasional lapses into stereotypes. In the end, perhaps Ireland is merely a state of mind. A 1984 *Artus* publication title corroborates this view: *A chacun ses Irlandes*. In that collection of articles, Pierre Joannon sums up this imaginary Ireland:

> She is all at once a province of the soul, a two-way mirror of the past, a standard riddled with grape-shot which is fraying in the wind, a ship bound for elsewhere, a challenge to the modern world, a laboratory where the violence of the future is incubated, a people which cultivates reason and madness with equal passion, a nation which extends beyond its glens and its coasts, a ghost, a cry, a song. She is a thousand more things which the world could not do without for fear of waning and withering, irredeemably.[75]

Notes

[1] Michel Déon, 'Insaisissable Irlande', in Patrick Rafroidi and Pierre Joannon (eds), *Études Irlandaises VII* (Université de Lille III; Lille, 1982), 13–15: 13.

[2] Michel Déon, *Un taxi mauve* (Editions Gallimard; Paris, 1973).

[3] The word *rêve* whose usual translation is 'dream' may also be defined as 'thought which seeks to escape the constraints of reality' (see *Le petit Robert de la langue française*: 2292). It is also variously a synonym for 'imagination', 'vision', 'fantasy' 'desire' and 'chimera'. All of these connotations apply in the discussion above.

[4] Déon, 'Insaisissable Irlande', 14.

[5] Jean-Michel Picard and Yolande de Pontfarcy, *Saint Patrick's Purgatory: a twelfth century tale of a journey to the Other World* (Four Courts Press; Dublin, 1985).

[6] David Stifter, 'Review of the critical edition of *Nauigatio Sancti Brendani* by Giovanni Orlandi e Rossana E. Guglielmetti', *Speculum* 91 (4) (2016), 1148–50.

[7] Léon Fleuriot, 'Le récit de navigation', in Jean Balcou et Yves Le Gallo (eds), *Histoire littéraire et culturelle de la Bretagne*, (3 livres, Éditions Champion-Slatkine; Paris et

Génève, 1987), livre 1, 131–64: 161.

[8] Éamon Ó Ciosáin, 'Voloumous deamboulare: the Wandering Irish in French litera-ture, 1600–1789', in Anthony Coulson (ed.), *Exiles and migrants: crossing thresholds in European culture and society* (Sussex Academic Press; Eastbourne, 1997), 32–42: 33.

[9] Pierre Motin quoted in Pierre de L'Estoile, *Mémoires* (12 vols; A. Lemerre; Paris, 1875–96), vol. xi, 234–6. Quoted in Ó Ciosáin, 'Voloumous deamboulare', 33.

[10] James Macpherson, *Fragments of ancient poetry collected in the highlands of Scotland and translated from the Galic or Erse language* (Hamilton and Balfour; Edinburgh, 1760).

[11] Hervé Abalain, *Histoire de la langue bretonne* (Éditions Gisselot; Plouédern, 2000), 105–6.

[12] Théodore Hersant de la Villemarqué, *Barzaz Breiz: chants populaires de la Bretagne* (Perrin; Paris, 1959).

[13] Ernest Renan, *L'Ame bretonne* (*La poésie des races celtiques*) (Éditions Philippe Camby; Maulévrier, 1982).

[14] Renan, *L'Ame bretonne*, 17.

[15] Renan, *L'Ame bretonne*, 60.

[16] Renan, *L'Ame bretonne*, 12–13.

[17] Anatole Le Braz, 'Impressions d'Irlande', *Bulletin de la Société Géographique de Lille* (Lille, 1914), 3–19. Bibliothèque nationale de France (BnF): 1914/01/25; the text is avai-lable online at: http://catalogue.bnf.fr/ark:/12148/cb327240723 (12 January 2018).

[18] Le Braz, 'Impressions d'Irlande', 2.

[19] Le Braz, 'Impressions d'Irlande', 13.

[20] Le Braz, excerpt from *Démocratie de l'Ouest*, 1905, in Yan-Ber Piriou, *Il était une voix, Anatole Le Braz. Discours et conférence* (Éditions Apogée; Rennes, 1995), 87.

[21] Members of a royalist uprising against the First Republic, mainly in the western provinces of France.

[22] An organisation dedicated to the establishment of an Irish republic in the nineteenth and early twentieth century.

[23] Another name for Brittany.

[24] This poem by Alain Gourval is published in Camille Le Mercier d'Erm (ed.), *Les bardes et poètes nationaux de la Bretagne Armoricaine* (Kelenn; Guipavas, 1977; facsimile reprint of the first edition, Plihon et Hommay; Rennes, 1919), 321.

[25] Per Denez, 'Modern Breton literature', in John Ellis Caerwyn Williams (ed.), *Literature in Celtic countries* (University of Wales Press; Cardiff, 1971), 124–5.

[26] Refers to counter-revolutionary uprisings in the west of France.

[27] Patrick Pearse and James Connolly, two of the leaders of the 1916 Easter Rising, which led to Irish independence.

[28] Michel Mohrt, *La prison maritime* (Gallimard; Paris, 1961), 50–1.

[29] Parti National Breton, *L'exemple de l'Irlande* (Éditions du Parti National Breton; Rennes, 1942), 5. The suggestion to 'not expect anything from anyone but ourselves' is probably an allusion to Sinn Féin, the Irish separatist party founded in 1905; the words *sinn féin* translate broadly as 'ourselves'.)

[30] Mohrt, *La prison maritime*, 183.

[31] Mohrt, *La prison maritime*, 190.

[32] Mohrt, *La prison maritime*, 213.

[33] Mohrt, *La prison maritime*, 210.

[34] Mohrt, *La prison maritime*, 423.

Anne Gallagher

[35] Michel Mohrt, *La guerre civil* (Gallimard; Paris, 1986), 325. (Attributed to Pompey.)

[36] Pierre Jakez Hélias, *Le cheval d'orgueil* (Terre Humaine; Paris, 1975).

[37] Xavier Grall, *Le cheval couché* (Hachette; Paris, 1977), 111.

[38] Grall, *Le cheval couché*, 125.

[39] Grall, *Le cheval couché*, 126.

[40] Grall, *Le cheval couché*, 116.

[41] Grall, *Le cheval couché*, 128.

[42] Grall, *Le cheval couché*, 131.

[43] Grall, *Le cheval couché*, 183.

[44] Raymond Queneau, *Les oeuvres complètes de Sally Mara* (Éditions Gallimard; Paris, 1962), 189.

[45] Queneau, *Les oeuvres complètes de Sally Mara*, 245.

[46] Queneau, *Les oeuvres complètes de Sally Mara*, 218.

[47] Queneau, *Les oeuvres complètes de Sally Mara*, 307.

[48] Queneau, *Les oeuvres complètes de Sally Mara*, 28; James Joyce, *Ulysses* (Penguin; London, 1969), 325.

[49] Joseph Vendryes, *Le langage : introduction linguistique à l'histoire* (Renaissance du Livre; Paris, 1921).

[50] Muirís Ó Súilleabháin, *Fiche bliain ag fás* (Talbot Press; Baile Átha Cliath, 1933). Raymond Queneau (translator), *Vingt ans de jeunesse* (Gallimard; Paris, 1936), translated from English (Ireland).

[51] Gérard Durozoi, *Le surréalisme* (Larousse; Paris, 1971), 83.

[52] James Joyce, *A portrait of the artist as a young man* (Huebsch; New York, 1916).

[53] Sorj Chalandon, *Mon traître* (Éditions Grasset et Fasquelle; Paris, 2007; Fiona McCann and Kitty Lyddon (translators), *My traitor* (Lilliput Press; Dublin, 2011).

[54] Chalandon, *Mon traître*, 28. All quotes are from the translation by McCann and Lyddon.

[55] Chalandon, *Mon traître*, 35.

[56] Paramilitary movement dedicated to Irish republicanism and independence.

[57] Maze Prison used to house paramilitary prisoners during the Northern Ireland Troubles.

[58] Sorj Chalandon, *Retour à Killybegs* (Éditions Grasset et Fasquelle; Paris, 2011); Ursula Meany Scott (translator), *Return to Killybegs* (Lilliput Press; Dublin, 2013).

[59] Chalandon, *Retour à Killybegs*, 13. All quotes are from the translation by Ursula Meany Scott.

[60] *Éirinn go Brách!* translates as 'Ireland Forever!'; Chalandon, *Retour à Killybegs*, 14, 16.

[61] Details on the origin of this slogan may found in 'No photos extant of "I Ran Away" slogan', *History Ireland* 17(3) (May-June 2009). The text of the article is available online at: https://www.historyireland.com/20th-century-contemporary-history/no-photos-extant-of-i-ran-away-slogan/ (21 March 2018).

[62] This refers to the 'no-wash protest' embarked upon by republican paramilitary prisoners in the Maze Prison between 1978 and 1981 as part of their protest at the removal of prisoner-of-war status. Prisoners resorted to pouring their urine out of their cells and smearing the cell walls with their excrement.

[63] Desi Wilkinson. *Call to the dance*, Wendy Hillton Dance and Music Series, no. 18 (Pendragon Press; New York, 2015), x.

[64] Michel Déon, *Les poneys sauvages* (Éditions Gallimard; Paris, 1970).

[65] Michel Déon, *Cavalier, passe ton chemin!* (Éditions Gallimard; Paris, 2005).

[66] Déon, *Cavalier, passe ton chemin!*, 26. All quotes are from the translation by Clíona Ní Ríordáin, *Horseman, pass by!* (Lilliput Press; Dublin, 2016).

[67] Molly Keane (1904–96), also known as M.J. Farrell, was an Irish novelist and playwright who chronicled the declining fortunes of the Anglo-Irish landed gentry.

[68] Déon, *Cavalier, passe ton chemin!*, 66.

[69] Déon, *Cavalier, passe ton chemin!*, 59.

[70] Déon, *Cavalier, passe ton chemin!*, 141.

[71] Déon, *Cavalier, passe ton chemin!*, 144.

[72] See, for example, the work by René Barjavel and Olenka de Veer, and also Anne Pons.

[73] Déon, *Cavalier, passe ton chemin!*, 182.

[74] Wilkinson. *Call to the dance*, x.

[75] Pierre Joannon, 'L'Irlande, mais quelle Irlande?', in *A Chacun ses Irlandes*, Special issue of *Artus* 15 (hiver 1983–4), 15–17: 17.

Ireland in the literatures of Spain

David Clark

Introduction

Ireland has been the subject of almost unan-imously positive accounts in the literatures of Spain. The island's dominant Catholicism has, of course, been of fundamental impor-tance for such affirmative views, and this was heightened by the country's perceived role as bulwark of Catholic views and practices in opposition to the Protestantism of England—Spain's main political enemy during the Counter-Reformation. Surprisingly, perhaps, the essentially optimistic view of Irish culture and society has survived a number of political and ideological changes in Spanish perspectives, leading to the circumstance whereby, during the Spanish civil war of 1936–9, Ireland could be regarded as a role model for both opposing sides: the Francoist right-wing regarded Éire as a staunch defender of Catholic values of family and tradition, while the Republican left, especially its supporters from the 'historical' regions of Spain, praised Ireland's revolutionary escape from the yoke of colonialism.[1] The rise of regionalism in Catalonia, the Basque Country and Galicia in the late nineteenth century, saw ready acknowledgement of support for Irish initiatives and practices, and writers from these three 'historical regions' produced widely, and in a positive sense, on Irish subjects. Although the period of the dicta-torship of Francisco Franco from 1939 to 1975 would prove relatively barren in terms of representation of Ireland in Spanish literature, after Franco's death Ireland became an important topic in Spanish writing, and a number of interesting texts have been produced in which the island is prominent.

Ireland in Galician-language literature

Ireland was seen as an important example of a small nation achieving independence from an oppressive power by literary figures from many parts of Spain, but most especially from the Basque Country, Catalonia and Galicia. Of the three, it was, however, in Galicia, the poorest of these and the one, thanks largely to a lack of support from the native bourgeoisie, with the least political muscle, in which the exaltation of Ireland and the Irish was greatest. There are, of course, numerous significant reasons for this. Galicia, unlike Catalonia, and unlike the coastal power base of the Basque Country, was not an industrialised territory. Galicia, like Ireland, was a mostly rural area, with subsis-tence farming being the most common occupation. Like Ireland, Galicia was a wet, Atlantic country, where the potato and cabbage were the dominant crops and where most families owned chickens, a pig and, in richer households, a cow. Galicia, again like Ireland, was a country dominated by absentee landowners and worked by emaciated peasants. Galicia had its own language, but unlike in Catalonia and the Basque Country—or, in this case, post-Gaelic Revival Ireland—this language was not supported by the middle or ruling classes. Importantly, Galicia, after the work of nineteenth-century intellectuals such as José Verea y

Aguiar, Antolin Faraldo, Benito Vicetto and Manuel Murguía, started to see herself as part of a group of supposedly Celtic countries lying on the fringes of Atlantic Europe. In Galicia too, the language was a highly-charged political issue, with the entirety of Galician peasants speaking their own language, a historical tongue with the same roots as modern Portuguese.

It is not, therefore, surprising, that when the Galician people started to strive after recognition of their own political and cultural identity in the late nineteenth and early twentieth century, it would be to Ireland they would turn for an example, a model and an inspiration. Support for Charles Stewart Parnell and the Land League, the Gaelic League and the Fenians was common in political texts published in the period, while literary works from Ireland were influential on Galician writers, such as the essayist Manuel Murguía and the poet Eduardo Pondal, who would use the *Lebor Gabála Érenn* and the *Ulster* and *Fenian Cycles* as justifications for the differentiation of Atlantic Galicia from the Mediterranean metropolis. The nationalist movements that grew from regionalism in the early twentieth century drew heavily on Ireland's struggle for independence, and the *Nós* ('Ourselves') movement drank from the twin cups of Irish nationalism and Joycean modernism.[2]

Among the Galician writers of the 1920s and 1930s who were part of this movement were figures such as Vicente Risco, Ramón Otero Pedrayo and Plácido Ramón Castro, all of whom promoted the vision of Galicia as a Celtic country and Ireland as a sister nation in the process of acquiring the independence that Galicia too, they believed, should aspire towards. Otero Pedrayo believed that the Atlantic nations, of which Ireland, Galicia, Brittany, Scotland, Wales and Portugal formed a part, had the moral obligation to regenerate European civilisation, freeing it from what he considered to be the degenerate nature of Mediterranean culture. Risco took Otero Pedrayo's ideas further, adapting them to a political context in which the morally superior Atlantic Europe had been given the role of defending the continent from the degenerate Mediterranean yoke under which it had been subjugated. Both Otero Pedrayo and Risco hailed Ireland and her struggle for independence from Britain as a positive step towards the creation of an Atlantic Alliance in which, they believed, Galicia, with her roots in both Latin and Germanic culture, would play a leading role.

The *Nós* group, based around the eponymous journal, was fundamental in spreading the ideas of Atlanticism and the pro-Irish sympathies of its writers. Translations appeared in Galician of Yeats, Synge and other Irish writers and, most importantly perhaps, of sections from *Lebor Gabála Érenn* and, for the first time in any of the languages of the Iberian Peninsula, Otero Pedrayo translated fragments of Joyce's recently published *Ulysses*. Otero Pedrayo's own fictional output was also heavily influenced by Joyce, and both he and Risco, using modernist techniques taken largely from the author of *Ulysses*, reshaped the Galician literary panorama. Although the nationalism of both Otero Pedrayo and Risco was on the Catholic right-wing, the *Nós* group also produced a number of important intellectuals who held nationalist views, positioned on the political-left wing, and who also applauded Ireland as a sister nation. Daniel Castelao and Plácido Ramón Castro both wrote extensively on Ireland, and the latter's visits to the Blasket Islands of County Kerry were chronicled in a number of newspaper articles.

The outbreak of the Spanish civil war after Franco's armed coup in 1936 effectively divided Galician nationalism; Castelao went into exile in Argentina; Castro became one of the most important voices of the BBC World Service during the Second World War; and Risco and Otero Pedrayo worked within or on the margins of the Franco regime. Under Franco, writing in the languages of Catalonia, Galicia and the Basque Country was effectively prohibited, but despite the harsh censorship laws in place during the 'long night of stone' of the dictatorship, a number of authors from all three regions did manage to work.[3]

One influential Galician writer who continued to write during the years of the Franco dictatorship was Álvaro Cunqueiro (1911–81). Cunqueiro was a journalist, poet, dramatist and translator, and he produced some of the most revolutionary narrative in the Galician language; he was strongly influenced by the Irish writer Lord Dunsany, with whom he shared a number of characteristics. César Antonio Molina collected a number of Cunqueiro's shorter prose work in Castilian Spanish in the posthumous *Viajes imaginarios y reales* ('Real and imaginary journeys'), which was published in 1986 and reveals the extent to which Cunqueiro's imaginary world was influenced by Ireland, a country he never visited, and by the works of Dunsany.[4] In 'Flying with thunder' we see how Cuchulain commands lightning to drown in the ocean, while in 'Against the rain', Cunqueiro's Lady Gregory performs magical ceremonies to halt the rain.[5] Not only does Cunqueiro's fiction reflect his own interpretation of historical figures such as Lady Gregory, or mythical figures like Cuchulain, it is also full of his own imagined characters—Irish inventors Fagha Fiona and Lenke O'Donnell, who, claims the author, invented hair curling tongs and the colander respectively. Although Cunqueiro did not adhere to the concept of 'Atlanticism' as espoused by Murguía and developed by Risco and Otero Pedrayo, he did believe that 'countries like Brittany, Ireland and Galicia herself share, undoubtedly, an incomparable intellectual and spiritual richness'.[6]

Since Franco's death in 1975, the Galician language has undergone a significant revival and, among writers using this language now are many who admit an Irish influence and who use Irish subject matter as a means to help redefine their own Galician identity. Suso de Toro admits to being strongly influenced by both James Joyce and the history—both real and mythical—of Ireland, and this can be seen in works such as the 2003-published *Morgún*, a fable of Galicia's Celtic past that borrows deeply from Gaelic legend, and his non-fiction *The people of the mist* from 2000, which, narrated by two crows, provides a stylishly-written and intelligent re-examination of both Irish and Galician myth and history.[7] Another popular contemporary Galician writer Manuel Rivas also fervently declares the Irish influence on his work, at times even using the pseudonym Manuel O'Rivas, while respected authors such as Xosé Luis Méndez Ferrín, Darío Xohán Cabana, Xoan Bernárdez Villar and Nacho Taibo all make use of Irish subject matter in their works. Xurxo Souto's 2014 work *Contos do mar de Irlanda* ('Tales of the sea of Ireland') is a vigorous and entertaining homage to the Galician seamen and fisher-folk who worked from the coasts of Galicia to those of Ireland, while Xosé Cid Cabido's *Blúmsdei* contains, in its title, a phonetic transcription of the word 'Bloomsday', and, as a novel focused on a single day of the life of its protagonist, reveals the extent to which Joyce's influence has lasted in Galicia.[8]

Ireland in fiction from Franco's Spain:
José María Gironella and Ignacio Aldecoa

The years of Franco's dictatorship, beginning with his victory in the civil war in 1939 and lasting until the advent of parliamentary democracy after his death in 1975, saw a powerful system of censorship, equalled only perhaps, at least in the 1950s and 1960s, by that of Ireland, which curtailed the freedom of writers. Although a number of great works of literature were produced in Spain during this period, including works by Cela, Laforet or Torrente Ballester, two novels by writers of the period are of particular interest in the current context given the relationship of the writers in question to Ireland. José María Gironella (1917–2003) was a Catalan author who supported the Franco uprising in 1936 and whose most famous work, *Los cipreses creen en dios* ('The cypresses believe in God'), published in 1953, was the first part of a trilogy narrating the events leading up to, during and in the aftermath of the internecine conflict.[9] Before this, however, in 1946, Gironella had published an interesting novel entitled *Un hombre* ('A man'), which won the highly coveted Nadal Prize.[10] *Un hombre* features Miguel Serra, born in France to a French mother and Catalan father, who, after owning a bookshop and a circus, travels to Ireland to visit his widowed mother who has bought some land in Donegal. The Ireland that Gironella describes is obviously an imagined territory that an Irish reader would have great difficulty in recognising as home; his descriptions of Donegal and of the Galtee Mountains read more like portrayals of stereotypical Alpine scenery than anything remotely Irish. When coming across the numerous cultural blunders present in the novel, the twenty-first century reader can only marvel at how distant—both culturally and geographically—Ireland must have appeared to both the author and readers living in Franco's Spain.

Although the fact that Gironella never visited Ireland has obvious effects on the representation of Ireland and of the Irish in his work, another writer of the Franco years successfully contrived a magnificent study of Basque fishermen working in the waters of the Sole Bank. Ignacio Aldecoa's 1957 work *Gran Sol* ('Sole Bank') is a wonderful example of mid-century Spanish realism, which describes the toils and hardships of the fishermen as they fight against the elements and the rapacity of their employers.[11] Aldecoa's language is concise, practical,

David Clark

but at the same time highly poetic, and the dignity he bestows upon his characters makes *Gran Sol* one of the masterpieces of Spanish literature produced during this troubled period of the country's history. The author's description of the time his characters spend on shore between Bantry and Castletown is evocative and shows a rare cultural sensibility for the period. The Spanish fishermen participate in the social life of the Irish harbour towns, drinking in the pubs and dancing with the local women. Aldecoa's Ireland is, unlike that of Gironella, recognisable and tangible.

Travel writing

Volumes of travel writing on Ireland by Spanish writers have proliferated over recent years, and some of these works notably transcend the limitations of the genre. An early example is Ricardo Baeza's work from 1930, titled *La isla de los santos: itinerario en Irlanda* ('The island of saints: itineraries in Ireland').[12] The Cuban-born Baeza (1890–1956) was a diplomat for the Second Spanish Republic before the Franco coup, after which he was forced into exile. Highly sympathetic to the new Irish Free State government in Dublin, *La isla de los santos* is a work widely deserving of translation into English. Baeza's descriptions of Ireland in the 1920s are important pieces of social and political commentary, but the numerous anecdotes he recounts are amusing and revealing. In one of these, for example, he tells of when he, along with other foreign journalists (three French and two Americans), was called to a press briefing at the offices of the Young Ireland organisation by Arthur Griffith, then president of the executive council of the Free State. The purpose of the meeting was to uncover a British *agent provocateur*, who Griffith dramatically revealed to the foreign press writers present. Hugely impressed, Baeza comments that Griffith, 'apart from being a great patriot and a talented statesman, was an eminent stage manager'.[13]

The Franco period, with its limited travel opportunities for Spanish citizens, was a relatively fruitless period for literary travel writing, but in the post-transition period travel and travel writing flourished in Spain. The Catalan Valentí Puig's *Dublín*, published in 1987, looks back to Baeza's example and signposts the route that other Spanish writers within the genre would follow in the first years of the twenty-first

Blanco would follow the earl into exile following defeat at the Battle of Kinsale in 1601. Revelles expresses his horror at the brutality of the treatment of Spanish mariners and infantry at the hands of the British troops and, although he follows the usual Spanish opinion that this mistreatment by the English stands in contrast to a general hospitality offered by the Irish, the writer also acknowledges the participation of Irish worthies such as the local chieftain Turlough O'Brien and the high sheriff of Clare, Boetius Clancy, in the torture and execution of Spanish prisoners.

Miguel Silvestre is an adventurer and self-styled 'nomad' who writes illustrated travel books detailing his adventures with his motorcycle, from which he is inseparable. In *La fuga del naúfrago*, Silvestre describes his travels in Ireland, where he follows the route taken by the shipwrecked survivors of the Armada. Silvestre marvels at the loquaciousness of the Irish; bemoans the patent unsuitability of their roads for his large motorcycle; and criticises the waves of Spanish student tourists who visit the country for 'thinking that Ireland is more genuine and cordially hearty than the pompous, arrogant and highly-expensive Great Britain'.[19] He makes a number of blunders, including his mention of 'The Raising [*sic*]' of 1916; citing the four Irish Nobel laureates for literature, 'Yeats, Beckett, Haney [*sic*] and Bernad [sic] Shaw'; or his reference to Irish beers such as 'Murphi's [*sic*] or Smithick's [*sic*]'.[20]

Both Silvestre and Revelles are influenced in their works by an incredible publication that came to light in 1884, when Spanish naval captain and historian Cesáreo Fernández Duro discovered a letter written by Francisco de Cuellar, a ship's captain and survivor of the Armada. After the ship he commanded supposedly broke files, leaving the main body of the Armada following storms in the English Channel, Cuellar was sentenced to death by hanging. The sentence was never carried out and, after the fleet was shipwrecked off the Irish coast, Cuellar made a remarkable escape. His adventures on land were written down in a long narrative letter that the captain sent to King Philip II and that was later discovered and edited by Fernández Duro and published as *Naufragios de la Armada Española* ('Shipwrecks of the Spanish Armada').[21]

Cuellar's correspondence with Philip II has provided a rich source of inspiration not only for the travel narratives mentioned above, but also for novelists such as José Luis Gil Soto and Carlos Carnicer. Gil Soto's

La colina de las piedras blancas ('The hill of the white stones') gives a fictional account of the events following the Armada shipwrecks, based almost exactly on the contents of Cuellar's letter.[22] In *La cruz de Borgoña* ('The Burgundy cross') Carnicer's hero, Guillaume, servant to the noble Juan de Forcada, having been shipwrecked with the Armada is given a Burgundy cross by a mysterious woman who speaks his language. The novel narrates his escape across Ireland as he attempts to reach Scotland, then a Catholic country, from where he would be able to return to continental Europe. Guillaume's adventures also give him the opportunity to observe Irish life and customs, and his observations lead to him change his mind about the land he had initially regarded as savage and heartless.[23]

Ireland in the contemporary Spanish novel

Gil Soto and Carnicer are not the only Spanish writers who have found in Irish history a productive seam for exploitation, especially given the popularity of historical fiction in Spain in the early twenty-first century. Ana B. Nieto published *La huella blanca* ('The white footprint') in 2013 and its sequel *Los hijos del caballo* ('The children of the horse') in 2016, both set in fifth-century Ireland and presenting a family saga that takes place between warring tribes and culminates in the childhood and coming-of-age of Saint Patrick.[24] Giulia Xairen's 2015 work *Iúl* opens in twelfth-century Ireland, where Aidan, a young novice in an abbey, is entrusted with the safekeeping of a secret manuscript.[25] The novel hovers between medieval Ireland and contemporary Galicia; Ciara, a young writer, has returned to her ancient family home, the unlikely survivor of a clan of druids exiled from their Irish home. She is caught up in the mystery of the manuscript under the watchful and suspicious eyes of a former lover, the unfortunately-named Dago. In *Lo que dure la eternidad* ('That lasts for eternity') by Nieves Hidalgo, published in 2012, a young Spanish art specialist, Cristina Rios, is employed to assess the works of art in the medieval castle of Killmarnock in Ireland.[26] Cristina is surprised by a ghost named Drago. Drago, it would seem, was the son of Augustus, Earl of Killmar, guardian of a precious relic—the sandal that once belonged to Jesus Christ. When the castle was attacked by Killmar's enemies in 1535 and the earl left for dead, Augustus blamed the absence of his son Drago for the castle's defeat. Augustus cursed his son, resulting in Drago's ghost being forced to wander the rooms and corridors of the castle for eternity or until, with the help of the beautiful and intelligent young Spanish girl, he is able to recover the relic and his family's honour.

La herencia de la rosa blanca ('The inheritance of the white rose') by Raquel Rodrein is a romantic saga of love, betrayal and revenge set in Ireland, the USA and continental Europe.[27] Starting with the emigration of the O'Connor family to New York from their native Ireland at the beginning of the twentieth century, the novel follows Edward O'Connor and his wife Erin as they return to Europe in the 1940s to fight in the White Rose, an anti-fascist resistance movement. Mercedes Guerrero's 2013 novel, *La mujer que llegó del mar* ('The woman who came from the sea'), although set in present-day Ireland, also looks back to the 1940s, when the mysterious woman of the title drifts ashore in Ireland escaping an evil Nazi who is pursuing her from the Netherlands. The woman is taken in by an Irish fisherman, and her full story is revealed gradually to Martin Condor, a writer, by her granddaughter Amanda.[28] *La mujer que llegó del mar* is, perhaps, unique among novels written by Spanish authors and set in Ireland in that it contains no Spanish characters.

Chesús Yuste, a writer, journalist and politician from Zaragoza in Aragon is an ardent hibernophile whose *blog* 'Innisfree1916' provides a popular forum for matters dealing with Ireland and her culture for Spanish speakers. Not surprisingly, therefore, his first novel *La mirada del bosque* ('The gaze of the forest'), published in 2010, has an Irish location.[29] Set in 1992 on the eve of the Maastricht referendum, *La mirada del bosque* is a crime whodunnit whose action takes place in the imaginary village of Balydungael in Donegal. Police officer Sergeant Eoghan Duffy, helped by the local reading group, comprising the local school-teacher, the mayor, a priest, a radio presenter and a doctor, attempts to solve the murder of the local post-mistress, the first killing in the village for 70 years. Interestingly, Yuste has translated his own novel into his native Aragonese language with the title *A gollada d'o bosque*. Also of note is the writer's 2015 collection of short fiction, *Regreso a Innisfree y otros relatos irlandeses* ('Return to Innisfree'), in which all of the stories are linked by their Irish subject matter.[30] J.L. Rod's 2010 novel, *La suerte de los irlandeses* ('The luck of the Irish'), is a hard-boiled crime novel featuring Pat McMillan, a Spanish detective from an Irish background who, working for the CNI, the Spanish intelligence agency, is taken out of his habitual work routine to investigate a mole from the Basque separatist organisation ETA who has infiltrated Spanish intelligence.[31]

While the historical and crime fiction of writers such as Gil Soto, Carnicer, Xairen, Rodrein, Guerrero, Yuste and Rod is destined for a popular market, a number of writers have approached Irish subjects from perspectives closer to those of so-called 'literary fiction', whereby the plot is secondary to stylistic or intellectual intent. Writers such as Jordi Soler, Carlos Moleno, Diego de Cora and, most particularly, Enrique Vila-Mata have all paid tribute to the narrative methods found in the work of Irish writers and attempt to emulate these in some way in their fiction. Jordi Soler, who was born to Catalan parents in exile in Mexico, was cultural attaché to the Mexican embassy in Dublin between 2000 and 2003. Soler's *Díles que son cadaveres* ('Tell them that they are corpses'), published in 2011, uses the knowledge of Ireland the author acquired during his time in the country to create a humorous but perceptive tale in which a Mexican diplomat assembles a team led by Lear McManus—a Gaelic poet and former seller of peat—to attempt to retrieve Saint Patrick's walking stick.[32]

The plot has it that the stick was allegedly found in France by French surrealist poet Antonin Artaud after a peyote-induced epiphany in Mexico. McManus is a larger-than-life figure, whose past in the business of the selling of peat allows him to compare the task of writing poetry with that of working in the fields, and who is described by Soler as a 'poet of the asphalted meadow'.[33] The novel looks critically and wittily at the hypocrisy the author sees in the world of art when related to the world of diplomacy in economic terms. Soler attacks the uselessness of government-centred cultural initiatives, such as the commissioning of a work from a self-serving Mexican sculptor, apparently designed to show the fraternity between Mexico and Ireland, but really no more than a trick to earn money for a friend of the ambassador. The 'unique' sculpture is but one of a series of 'very large and very ugly' works already spread across a number of Mexican cities.[34] The search for the walking stick takes the group into County Antrim and the world of the Northern Irish conflict, where they uncover suspected contacts between the Zapatista Army of National Liberation and the IRA, and discover the identity of a paramilitary psychotic known as the Antrim Butcher. Soler is a member of Vila-Matas's 'Order of Finnegans', for more on which, see below.

Carlos Maleno's 2014 book, *Mar de Irlanda* ('Sea of Ireland'), is a finely-wrought lyrical novel in which the narrator, haunted by the vision of a woman with pale skin and green eyes, contemplates the Mediterranean from his home in Sitges in Catalonia, converting it poetically into the Sea of Ireland. The story is interpolated by an account of the expedition financed by Pope Gregory and led by Sebastiano di San Giuseppe that took an army of Spanish and Italian soldiers to Smerwick Bay in County Kerry in 1580, where over 600 of them died in a siege.[35] *Tu viaje a Irlanda* ('Your journey to Ireland', published in 2014) by Diego de Cora is set in the year 2080, in a world dominated by women and in which men, given their low birth-rate, are scarce and are held in captivity, forced to act as prostitutes. Only in Ireland are men still free, and so from all over continental Europe men are trying to reach Great Britain, from which point it is easier to reach the free territory of Ireland. De Cora's protagonist, a Galician like the author, seeks solace in Ireland, 'an overcast paradise', in this parody of dystopian science fiction.

Enrique Vila-Matas—Dublinesque

Enrique Vila-Matas, born in Barcelona in 1948, is a Catalan author who writes in Spanish, and among whose works are numerous volumes that have been translated into English. His interest in Ireland—and in James Joyce in particular—is manifest in his founding of 'The Order of Finnegans', an *ad hoc* group of writers, which includes Eduardo Lago, Antonio Soler, Jordi Soler, Malcolm Otero, José Antonio Garriga Vella, Marcos Giralt Torrente, Emiliano Monge and Vila-Matas himself. This anarchic group was created with the purpose of celebrating the work of Joyce and meeting in a Dalkey pub on 16 June, Bloomsday, every year. Two volumes of writing have been published by the group. The first of these, *La orden de Finnegans*, appeared in 2010. Antonio Soler's contribution to that volume, 'A day in June', recalls the foundation of the group. One Bloomsday, on Vila-Matas's first visit to Ireland, members of the order take him around Dublin without ever visiting the centre of the city.[36] Jordi Soler's contribution, 'Dreamery creamery songbirds', is a fantastical tale of MacLir and his magic cape. Eduardo Lago presents a surreal discussion of *Finnegans Wake* in a barroom in 'Speak-Easy', while in 'Leopold', Malcolm Otero Barral has his character, the Spaniard Leopoldo Garcés, show surprise at the extent to which Ireland resembles England. Unsurprisingly perhaps, however, the most accomplished piece in the collection is that provided by Vila-Matas himself. In 'Doctor Finnegan and Monsieur Hire: work in progress', the author's famed erudition focuses on the difference between the concepts of narration on the one hand and art on the other. Vila-Matas ponders on the nature of what he terms 'critical fiction'. Along with his fascinating ideas on literary concepts—'I like literature which is not too sure of itself, which presents itself to us as a discourse which is slightly unstable'—Vila-Matas also discusses the role of Ireland as both a literary and a geographic territory.[37] The second volume, playfully titled *Lo desorden* ('Disorder'), and published in 2013, is a collection of texts centred on the subject of childhood that, although less iconoclastic than its predecessor, offers a satisfying collection of prose. Once again, the contribution by Vila-Matas, 'Would you eat a magnolia bud?' stands out.[38]

The Order of Finnegans was created at a time of personal difficulty for Vila-Matas. Recovering from a devastating, near-fatal illness and having finally managed to battle his addiction to alcohol, the writer found himself in a period of flux and creative crisis. Vila-Matas describes a moment of epiphany, in the form of a dream he had in a Barcelona hospital ward:

> ...it was incredibly intense. I dreamed I was in Dublin—a city I'd never been to before—and that I had started drinking again and I was lying on the floor in the doorway of some pub and crying my eyes out. I was crying while I embraced my wife, sorry for the fact that I had started drinking again. The intensity came from the fact that in the dream, in my embrace with my wife, there was a highly concentrated and palpable feeling of rebirth. I was recovering in hospital and it was as if I'd managed to touch real life for the first time ever. But I haven't been able to transmit all of this intensity. More proof, if you like, of what we call the impossibility of writing. A few months later I travelled to

David Clark

Dublin but could not find the exact place where the dream had taken place. But I remembered it with astonishing precision. It wasn't there, or I wasn't able to see it.[39]

From this experience the Order of Finnegans was born, but it would also provide the basis for Vila-Matas's next novel, *Dublinesca* ('Dublinesque'), published in 2010.[40] *Dublinesca* is the story of Samuel Riba, a publisher from Barcelona who, in a moment of personal crisis, decides to travel to Dublin with a group of like-minded friends from his literary circle in order to celebrate an elegy for what he sees as the death of print literature; to hold, as he says, 'a funeral for the age of print, for the golden age of Gutenberg'.[41] Like Vila-Matas, with whom Riba shares many characteristics, the publisher had never been to Ireland, but thanks to a dream he knew the city 'as if he had lived there in another life'.[42] Riba is scholarly and opinionated, and his reflections throughout the novel provide an oddly satisfying mixture of humour, parody and elegy. Like Joyce's Leopold Bloom, Riba is of Jewish extraction, and like Bloom his opinions range from the quirky and quotidian to the erudite and arcane. Having spent a lifetime as a publisher of 'quality' literature, the valedictory Riba voices his frustration at never having discovered the elusive literary genius, the writer whose works would make sense of the publisher's lifelong quest for perfection. For Riba, good literature must contain 'intertextuality; connections with high poetry; the consciousness of a moral landscape in ruins; a slight superiority of style over plot; writing seen as a clock which moves forward'.[43] He sees some of the greatest examples of this in work by Irish writers, and in this regard Riba mentions Brendan Behan, John Banville, Colum McCann, Elizabeth Owen and, most specifically, Beckett and Joyce.

Vila-Matas's character complains about how, in his native Spain, it is fashionable to boast about never having read *Ulysses*. At Glasnevin cemetery he relives the episode of Paddy Dignam's funeral from *Ulysses*, and amid his re-reading and re-telling of the episode he deliberately parodies Joyce's style. Just as Bloom is surprised by the mysterious stranger in the Macintosh at the funeral, so Riba is surprised at the presence of a Beckett lookalike at Glasnevin, recalling the ghosts he believes he has seen in Barcelona. Dublin and Ireland have a healing effect on the publisher's troubled soul. In Ireland, he believes, he is 'freed from the sweet tyranny' of his parents and he has fallen in love with Ireland and what it would seem to represent.[44] The Ireland Riba discovers is, of course, a landscape of the mind as much as it is a physical space, and he comes to believe that this mental landscape of Dublin and the sea of Ireland has 'always been in his cerebral landscape, forming part of his past'.[45] The visit provides him with new hope; he realises that his version of Ireland is now his country, and this frees him from the stolid reality of Spain and the depression this has provoked in him.

While many of the experiences undergone by Samuel Riba in *Dublinesca* echo those of Vila-Matas himself in Ireland, the author expresses his surprise at the way the work developed. As a reader of his own work, Vila-Matas states in an interview that he 'didn't know very well what was happening, and this led me to write the book as if I were reading it, following, as a reader would, what happens to this publisher in his everyday life'.[46] Vila-Matas shares Riba's respect for the Irish literary tradition but, while marvelling at the sheer number of extraordinary writers produced by such a small country, he recalls replying to an Irish listener at a talk he gave once in Dublin. The interlocutor had asked Vila-Matas if he was aware of how superior Irish literature was in comparison with its English equivalent, in response to which the Catalan author reminded him of the existence of Shakespeare.

Mario Vargas Llosa—The dream of the Celt

Mario Vargas Llosa, the 2010 Nobel laureate in literature, was born in Arequipa, Peru, in 1936. He was granted Spanish citizenship in June 1993, thirty-five years after first arriving in Madrid to take up post-graduate study at the city's Complutense University. In his 2010 novel *El sueño del celta*, published in English as *The dream of the Celt*, he uses as his subject matter the life of Roger Casement, the Dublin-born diplomat who had been knighted in 1911 for his services to the British empire but who would be hanged after his participation in the revolutionary events of Easter 1916.[47] Casement, after unsuccessfully trying to raise an Irish contingent to fight against the British from among prisoners-of-war held by the Germans, landed in Ireland from a German ship, purportedly in an attempt to delay the planned rising.

Vargas Llosa's choice of Casement as a subject for his novel is, perhaps, surprising. Despite early Marxist leanings, the Hispano-Peruvian writer is known for his right-wing libertarian political views. In 1990 he stood for the presidency of his native country as a candidate for the centre-right Democratic Front coalition, and his support for the monetarist policies of European politicians such as Margaret Thatcher and José María Aznar has been widely publicised since the 1980s. His vociferous support as spokesman for the Madrid-led demonstration 'for a united Spain' held in Barcelona in October 2017 in the midst of the Catalonian independence process renders him, it could be argued, as an unlikely candidate to deal in fictional terms with a character as complex as Casement. The Irishman was knighted for his work on behalf of the oppressed natives of the Congo Basin and the Peruvian Amazon, but he later became a revolutionary Irish nationalist whose eventual arrest and execution would be overshadowed by the release of his diaries by the British government; the diaries revealed a sexual history deemed unacceptable to both the British establishment and also, in the course of time, to the fledgling Irish state.

The dream of the Celt does, however, follow the trajectory of other works by Vargas Llosa, in that it is a novel that takes its subject matter from historical sources and deals with the conflict between political idealism and the inner life of the individual. The novel moves from Casement's early life in Ireland through his experiences in the Congo and in South America, before relating his conversion to militant Irish nationalism and his eventual arrest. The odd-numbered chapters tell of the three months of his imprisonment until his death and the even ones provide the analeptic information about Casement's life. Although Vargas Llosa successfully manages his use of the temporal aspects of the novel, certain commentators have criticised some of the stylistic choices he made. For Colm Tóibín, for example, although Vargas Llosa's finest works 'display extraordinary sympathy and a complex command of styles', and whereas he 'is deeply alert to the tricks and ironies of history', in *The dream of the Celt* the over-use of free indirect style, while lending intensity to the work, is also responsible for it lacking 'the sweep and forceful rhythmic power of *The war of the end of the world*'.[48] For Fintan O'Toole, the novel is 'flawed but often fascinating', but the critic voices his belief that while Roger Casement might well be, for his apparent contradictions and complexity, the perfect postmodern subject, Vargas Llosa is far from being the perfect postmodern writer.[49] For O'Toole, the Hispano-Peruvian's sentences regrettably 'trudge through the mire of unprocessed research'.[50]

The complexity of Roger Casement, as a character, is beyond question. Born into an Anglo-Irish family, his experiences working in the Congo Basin led him to formulate a reformist discourse that criticised the inhumanity of the three 'C's'—Christianity, civilisation and commerce—which he had been brought up to venerate. Not surprisingly, Vargas Llosa is at his strongest when dealing with the Roger Casement of the Congo and the Amazon and at his weakest when trying to come to terms with the diplomat's movement towards militant nationalism. Vargas Llosa treats Casement's childhood perfunctorily, only hinting at the contradiction between the Anglo-Irish upbringing in the stern household of his paternal grandparents after his mother's death and the Catholicism bestowed upon him by his mother who, before her death, had her son baptised secretly in Rhyl, Wales. This contradiction, it could be argued, might provide fundamental clues as to Casement's initial fervour for the colonial process, as well as to his disillusionment at the violence and savagery of that process. The imaginary umbilical cord that he sees joining the Congo Basin to the Peruvian Amazon is later used to justify his commitment to militant Irish nationalism as the maternal influence overcomes that of his paternal family.

Casement's conversion to the nationalist cause is, however, never convincing in *The dream of the Celt*, possibly because of the almost total absence of Ireland from the novel. Sam Jones, the Madrid correspondent of *The Guardian* complains that 'we never see him in Ireland interacting with the ordinary people there', and regrets the fact that Vargas Llosa fails to show the reader the process of Casement's conversion.[51] We are told that his visit to the Congo helped him to 'find' his home country; 'thanks to the Congo he had discovered Ireland, he wanted to be a true Irishman, to appropriate her history and her culture'.[52] In his conversion, Casement's mentor is Alice Stopford-Green, who introduces the disillusioned diplomat to Irish language, history and mythology, but Vargas Llosa's portrayal of her character is sadly lacking in depth and sheds no light on Casement's transformation. Colm Tóibín regrets that the reader is 'asked to take Caasement's

David Clark

feelings about Ireland—a country he barely knew and only romanticised—as seriously as his views on the Congo and the Amazon.[53]
For Tóibín, in *The dream of the Celt* Casement's 'thoughts on Ireland
lack substance; because they can't be handled comically, or viewed
by anyone other than the humourless Casement himself, as the novel
proceeds they become repetitive and tedious'.[54]

There would seem to be a wide-ranging critical consensus that,
while Vargas Llosa's treatment of Casement's experiences in Africa
and South America is handled with a degree of narrative skill that at
times verges on brilliance, the author fails when dealing with the Irish
component of his subject's life. The issue of Casement's sexuality is also
one on which the author would appear to flounder. Vargas Llosa's handling of Casement's sexuality is disappointing. Fintan O'Toole bemoans
the Nobel laureate's 'inability to integrate his hero's sexuality into his
narrative'.[55] When details of his diaries were leaked at the time of his
trial, Casement's homosexuality was used against him by the British
authorities as a means of generating an even more unfavourable public
opinion towards the diplomat. These diaries, which would later complicate Casement's incorporation into the pantheon of Irish nationalism,
are dismissed by Vargas Llosa in an unnecessary epilogue in which he
tries to make light of the diary entries. He rejects them as exaggeration
and fiction, arguing that Casement 'wrote certain things because he
would have liked to but could not live them'.[56]

Conclusion

Ireland has long served as a fertile subject for writers from Spain.
Although the novel has been the most constantly-used literary form
to reflect the interest of Spanish authors, non-fiction accounts of Irish
matters have also abounded, especially in the field of travel narratives.
Poetry and drama on Irish topics, or influenced by Irish models, have
been of particular importance, and translations of great Irish poets
and dramatists exist in all the official languages of Spain. As we have
seen, novels on Irish topics have flourished, especially over the last ten
years, and although varying in scope, perspective, intention, genre and
quality, collectively they pay tribute to the long-lasting infatuation that

a large part of the Spanish literary establishment—from all sides of the ideological spectrum—has had with Ireland and all things Irish.

The nationalist longings of the early-twentieth century Galician writers who saw in Ireland a shining example of hope and optimism was transferred into a body of literature that would help shape the development of the literary system in that language and would contribute in no small way to the healthy situation in which both the Galician language and her literature are to be found today.[57] During the difficult years of the Franco dictatorship, writers nevertheless continued to demonstrate an interest in Irish subject matter, as the cases of Gironella and Aldecoa—a Catalan and a Basque, respectively—illustrate, and the post-Franco period has seen the publication of a large number of novels dealing with Irish themes, from the popular historical fiction of writers such as Carnicer, Gil Soto, Nieto, Rodrein and Xairen, to the crime novels from Yuste and Rod. Experimental works such as those by De Cora, Maleno and Cid Cabido use both stylistic and thematic elements that owe a debt to Irish literature, while novels by two of the most important authors writing in the Spanish language, Vila-Matas and Vargas Llosa, have revolved around an Irish subject.

Ireland is often viewed in idealistic terms by Spanish authors, and the positive reading of the country's history, culture, geography and politics can sometimes verge on the stereotypical. Despite certain failings, however, many of the writers who have delved into Irish subject matter are capable of successfully communicating their observations, their often profound analysis, and their appreciation of a small country, which, in literary terms, they believe to have been punching above its weight.

Notes

[1] The 'historical regions' are considered to be those that were granted political autonomy during the Second Republic (1931–9). This should not be confused with the term 'historical nationality' in current use, in which the three 'historical regions' of the Basque Country, Catalonia and Galicia are joined by Andalusia, the Balearic Islands, the community of Valencia Aragón and the Canary Islands.

[2] The *Nós* group was based around the journal of the same name, published between 1920 and 1936. Publication moved between the Galician cities of Ourense, Corunna and Santiago de Compostela during this period.

[3] 'Longa noite de pedra', translated as 'Long night of stone' is the title of a poem by Celso Emilio Ferreiro (1912–79). The title is generally regarded as a metaphor for the period of the dictatorship. Celso Emilio Ferreiro, *Longa noite de pedra* (El Bardo; Barcelona, 1967).

[4] Alvaro Cunqueiro, *Viajes imaginarios y reales* (Tusquets; Barcelona, 1986).

[5] The titles of these works in Spanish are respectively 'Volando con el trueno' and 'Contra la lluvia'; see Cunqueiro, *Viajes imaginarios y reales*, 18–42.

[6] English translation; the original reads *[P]ueblos como Bretaña, Irlanda y la propia Galicia, son, intelectualmente hablando, de una riqueza incomparable*; see, Cunqueiro, *Viajes imaginarios y reales*, 114.

[7] Suso de Toro, *Morgún* (Xerais; Vigo, 2003); *O país da brétema* (Aguilar; Madrid, 2010).

[8] Xurxo Souto, *Contos do mar de Irlanda* (Xerais; Vigo, 2012); Xosé Cid Cabido *Blumsdei* (Xerais; Vigo, 2012).

[9] José María Gironella, *Los cipreses creen en dios* (Planeta; Barcelona, 1953).

[10] José María Gironella, *Un hombre* (Destino; Barcelona, 1946).

[11] Ignacio Aldecoa, *Gran Sol* (Noguer; Barcelona, 1957).

[12] Ricardo Baeza, *La isla de los santos: itinerario en Irlanda* (Igitur/Piedras Vivas; Montblanc (Tarragona), 2010; reprint of 1930 edition, Renacimiento; Madrid).

[13] English translation; the original reads *...además de un gran patriota y un consumado estadista, es Mr. Griffith un eminente director de escena*, Ignacio Aldecoa, *Gran Sol*, 49.

[14] Valentí Puig, *Dublín* (Destino; Barcelona, 1987).

[15] Jorge González de Matauco, *En el purgatorio de Irlanda: Crónicas de un penitente* (Niberta; Barcelona, 2009).

[16] Javier Reverte, *Canta Irlanda: un viaje por la isla esmeralda* (Plaza & Janés; Barcelona, 2014).

[17] León Lasa, *Por el oeste de Irlanda* (Almuzara; Córdoba, 2014).

[18] David Revelles, *En los confines de Hibernia: tras la leyenda de la Armada Invencible en Irlanda* (Editorial de la Universitat Oberta de Catalunya; Barcelona, 2015) and Miguel Silvestre, *La fuga del naúfrago* (Barataria; Seville, 2013).

[19] Silvestre, *La fuga del naúfrago*, 52.

[20] Silvestre, *La fuga del naúfrago*, 10, 54 and 73.

[21] Cesáreo Fernández Duro, *Naufragios de la Armada Española: relación histórica formada con presencia de los documentos oficiales que existen en el archivo del Ministerio de Marina* (Renacimiento Isla de Tortuga; Seville, 2009; reprint of 1867 edition, Establecimiento Tipográfico de Estrada, Díaz y López; Madrid).

[22] José Luis Gil Soto, *La colina de las piedras blancas* (Styria; Barcelona, 2008).

[23] Carlos Carnicer, *La cruz de Borgoña* (La esfera de los libros; Madrid, 2008).

[24] Ana B. Nieto, *La huella blanca* (Ediciones B; Barcelona, 2013), and Ana B. Nieto, *Los hijos del caballo* (Ediciones B; Barcelona, 2016).

[25] Giulia Xairen, *Iúl; Llegó el momento de saber la verdad* (Amazon Digital; Seattle WA, 2015).

[26] Nieves Hidalgo, *Lo que dure la eternidad* (Ediciones B; Barcelona, 2008).

[27] Raquel Rodrein, *La herencia de la rosa blanca* (Roca; Barcelona, 2012).

[28] Mercedes Guerrero, *La mujer que llegó del mar* (Random; Madrid, 2013).

[29] Chesús Yuste, *La mirada del bosque* (Paréntesis; Alcalá de Guadaíra, 2010).

[30] Chesús Yuste, *Regreso a Innisfree y otros relatos irlandeses* (Xordica; Zaragoza, 2015).

[31] José Luis Rod, *La suerte de los irlandeses* (Ediciones B; Barcelona, 2014).

[32] Jordi Soler, *Díles que son cadaveres* (Mondadori ; Barcelona, 2011).

[33] Soler, *Díles que son cadaveres*, 51

[34] Soler, *Díles que son cadaveres*, 21.

[35] Carlos Maleno, *Mar de Irlanda* (Sloper; Palma de Mallorca, 2014).

[36] Enrique Vila-Matas, Eduardo Lago, Antonio Soler, Jordi Soler, Malcolm Otero Barral and José Antonio Garriga Vela, *La orden de Finnegans* (Ediciones Alfabia; Barcelona, 2010).

[37] English translation; the original reads *Me gusta la literatura que no está muy segura de sí misma, que se presenta ante nosotros como un discurso poco estable*, see Vila-Matas et al., *La orden de Finnegans*, 28.

[38] Enrique Vila-Matas, José Antonio Garriga Vela, Marcos Giralt Torrente, Eduardo Lago, Emiliano Monge, Malcolm Otero Barral, Antonio Soler, Jordi Soler, *Lo desorden* (Alfaguara; Barcelona, 2013).

[39] Juan Cruz, 'Entrevista Enrique Vila-Matas', *El País*, 13 March 2010; available online at: https://elpais.com/diario/2010/03/13/babelia/1268442746_850215.html (12 April 2017). My translation.

[40] Enrique Vila-Matas, *Dublinesca* (Seix Barral; Barcelona, 2010).

[41] English translation; the original reads [U]*n funeral por la era de la imprenta, por la era dorada de Gutenberg*, see, Vila-Matas, *Dublinesca*, 37.

[42] English translation; the original reads [C]*omo si hubiera vivido allí otra vida*, see, Vila-Matas, *Dublinesca*, 23.

[43] English translation; the original reads [I]*ntertextualidad; conexiones con la alta poesía; conciencia de un paisaje moral en ruinas; ligera superioridad del estilo sobre la trama, la escritura como un reloj que avanza*, see, Vila-Matas, *Dublinesca*, 15.

[44] English translation; the original reads [L]*e ha liberado de la suave tiranía de sus padres*, see, Vila-Matas, *Dublinesca*, 253.

[45] English translation; the original reads *Hoy da por hecho que Dublín y el mar de Irlanda estaban siempre en su paisaje cerebral, formaban parte de su pasado*, see, Vila-Matas, *Dublinesca*, 15, 266.

[46] Cruz, 'Entrevista', my translation.

[47] Mario Vargas Llosa *El sueño del celta* (Alfaguara; Barcelona, 2010).

[48] Colm Tóibín, 'A man of no mind', *London Review of Books* 34 (17) (2012), 15–16: 15.

[49] Fintan O'Toole, 'The multiple hero', *New Republic* 12 October 2010; the article is available online at: https://newrepublic.com/article/105658/mario-vargas-llosa-dream-of-celt-fintan-otoole (15 September 2016).

[50] O'Toole, 'The multiple hero'.

[51] Sam Jones, 'Nobel winner Mario Vargas Llosa finds perfect protagonist in Roger Casement', *The Guardian* 18 October 2017.

[52] English translation; the original reads ... *gracias al Congo, había descubierto a Irlanda, quería ser un irlandés de verdad, apropriarse de su historia y de su cultura*, see, Vargas Llosa, *El sueño del celta*, 120.

[53] Tóibín, 'A man of no mind', 16.

[54] Tóibín, 'A man of no mind', 16.

[55] O'Toole, 'The multiple hero'.

[56] English translation; the original reads *escribió ciertas cosas porque hubiera querido pero no pudo vivirlas*, see, Vargas Llosa, *El sueño del celta*, 449.

[57] Writing in 2007, Antonio de Toro Santos claimed that over 90% of all literature ever written in the Galician language had been written between the years 1975 and 2005; see, A.R. De Toro Santos, *La literatura irlandesa en España* (Netbiblo; Corunna, 2007), 292.

David Clark

Turning the foreign land into a homeland: representations of Ireland and the Irish in Polish literature

Joanna Kosmalska

The mysterious island

In August 2017, any visitor to Łazienki Park—a popular tourist destination and a venue for numerous music, arts and culture events in Warsaw—was presented with the opportunity to learn about Polish–Irish connections by visiting an open-air gallery located in the centre of the park. It showcased the exhibition whose title *From strangers to neighbours: encounters between Poland and Ireland* aptly summed up the long-standing relationship between the two countries.[1] The exhibition was organised by Gerard Keown, the Irish ambassador to Poland, and it tracked the links between Ireland and Poland from 1698—when Bernard O'Connor published his *History of Poland*, the first account of Polish history in English—to the year 2016, when the Irish government, in collaboration with the Polish embassy in Dublin ran the second *Polska–Éire Festival*, a series of cultural, sports, business and academic events held all over Ireland to foster bonds between the two communities.[2]

The earliest literary encounter that the exhibition mentioned dated back to the nineteenth century, when romantic literature accompanied the struggle for independence, both in Ireland and Poland. At that time, Thomas Moore was in frequent contact with two exiled Polish authors in Britain, Zygmunt Krasiński and Julian Ursyn Niemcewicz. Moore's poetry also became a source of inspiration for Polish national bards: for example, Adam Mickiewicz translated his poem 'The meeting of the waters' and Juliusz Słowacki rendered into Polish *Irish melodies*, the songs that Zygmunt Krasiński used as a pre-text for writing *Polskie melodie* ('Polish melodies'). When the Easter Rising broke out in 1916, the Polish press carried news about the cataclysmic events taking place in Dublin and paid particular attention to the activity of one of the rebel leaders, Constance Markievicz, who was married to a Polish play-wright, theatre director and painter, Count Casimir Dunin-Markievicz. The weekly *Świat* called her 'a modern Irish amazon', and other journals implied her nationalism might have been encouraged by her husband.[3] With their struggle against the oppressor, the Irish were like brothers-in-arms to Polish people: heroes fighting for a similar cause. Their rebellions gave hope that freedom could be won and a national identity could be reconstructed.

Since the turn of the twentieth century, Irish plays have regularly appeared on stage in Poland. The wit and unanticipated twists of action worked into tragic stories draw the attention of local audiences. Among the first Irish dramas staged in Polish theatres were the works by Oscar Wilde, J.M. Synge and W.B. Yeats. But it was George Bernard Shaw who enjoyed the greatest popularity: his plays premiered in Warsaw almost at the same time as in London and were performed repeatedly

Joanna Kosmalska

until the outbreak of World War Two. When the war ended, the work of Irish playwrights—this time it was Seán O'Casey, Brendan Behan and Samuel Beckett—returned to Polish theatres in the 1950s and the 1960s. Since Antoni Libera, a critically acclaimed Polish writer, translator and theatre director, translated all of Beckett's dramatic works and directed many of them, the Irish Nobel prize-winning playwright has established a strong presence on the Polish literary scene.[4]

But the real exercise in translation was *Ulysses*, James Joyce's masterpiece of modernism whose rendering into Polish appeared in 1969.[5] It took Maciej Słomczyński over a decade to complete the work. Throughout this time, he compiled a large collection of Joyce's biographies, Irish history books, old maps, postcards, etc. His office housed a greater number of critical books on *Ulysses* than all of Poland's public libraries combined. On finishing his translation, Słomczyński travelled with his typescript to Dublin to re-enact scenes from the novel: he drank, ate and slept in the places mentioned in the novel to make sure he had captured all of the details.[6] In the 1970s and the 1980s, Ernest Bryll, a Polish poet and diplomat, along with his wife Małgorzata Goraj-Bryll, translated early Irish poetry.[7] And the 1990s saw the publication of Séamus Heaney's poems in Polish.[8] The fact that the poet was friends with his fellow Nobel laureate, Czesław Miłosz, and an eminent literary critic and translator, Jerzy Jarniewicz, has created much interest in Heaney's work in Poland.[9]

The Polish translations of Irish drama, prose and poetry shaped the image of the Irishman as an artist—a writer, a visionary, an intellectual—a person at odds with the social conventions and a fighter for ideals. Only Polish people with a particular interest in Irish studies had a broader knowledge of the country's history and culture. For the rest, the Emerald Isle was a distant, mysterious, evergreen land inhabited by heroic warriors and talented writers who spoke English (which became significant when Poland joined the EU and many of her citizens chose to move to Ireland because they had studied English as a foreign language at school).

The story behind the song 'Kocham cię jak Irlandię' ('I love you like Ireland') by the band Kobranocka illuminates how little the general public knew about Ireland. The song, which was one of the greatest hits in the history of rock music in Poland, appeared on the album *Kwiaty na żywopłocie* ('Flowers on the hedge') in 1990 and remained in the charts for twenty-two weeks: almost everyone, regardless of age, knew the lyrics by heart and could hum the melody. It told of the unrequited love of the lyric-writer, Andrzej Michorzewski, who fell in love with a stranger he met on his way to high school every day. He finally plucked up courage to ask the girl out, but she never showed up for the date. When he met her again as a grown-up man, the feelings revived and he wrote the song. Interviewed on why he chose to compare his object of desire to Ireland, he replied that he had never been to the Emerald Isle and knew very little about it. He adopted the place as a symbol because it was as distant and mysterious as the girl for whom he had fallen.[10] Michorzewski never suspected that a decade later the country would become a home to thousands of Polish people.

Tomographic exploration of Ireland

From the undiscovered land, Ireland grew into the territory well-researched by Polish migrants at the turn of the twenty-first century. When migration began, there was a daily bus service from Warsaw to Dublin, but it was soon replaced by over sixty flights departing from eleven cities in Poland.[11] The newcomers evinced great interest in the new land: they roamed the streets, went to pubs and clubs, visited museums and galleries, and travelled the country, uncovering the layers of Irish life. What they saw and experienced they described in semi-autobiographical, frequently first-person narratives, which had a patchwork structure and wove together disparate elements, such as passages depicting places and people, photos, amusing anecdotes, interviews, scraps of conversations, other narratives, poems, songs, media reports, maps and the like. As the writers recorded their observations, they simultaneously cast themselves in four seemingly conflicting roles: one was that of a reporter who was an eyewitness and therefore a reliable source of information; the second was that of a storyteller who presented his or her experiences and observations in a comprehensive and enjoyable way; the third was that of a displaced person attuned to matters of place and therefore able to depict Ireland in a more 'truthful' way; and the last was that of the local, a person who lived in the place he or she described and with which they were well-acquainted.

Joanna Kosmalska

But as much as the writers reconciled these roles to ensure a more contrapuntal analysis in their work, they never underwrote a claim of objectivity. Some even made sure to mention this fact in their books. For example, in his 2012 collection of essays, *What I got from Ireland?*, Przemek Kolasiński writes:

> I present my deeply subjective depiction of the Green Island, but I don't fantasise, make things up, although I tend to equip the presented reality with some colour. ... This book is about Ireland, the Irish and the Poles living here....[12]

Whether the writers acknowledge it or not, they render Ireland through the prism of their own experiences and the result is a partial and skewed representation, in which certain aspects are inevitably prioritised and exaggerated. Tomasz Borkowski tackles this issue in the opening to *Irlandia Jones poszukiwany* ('Ireland Jones wanted'):

> [This book] is an attempt to describe my personal experiences in Ireland which I have shared with thousands of my fellow compatriots and with millions of Irish people. Presumably, there have been as many perplexities and explanations as there were people involved in that process. Here I put out only one account of what happened. One could call it a 'tomography.'[13]

By comparing his writing to 'tomography,' which is a word derived from Ancient Greek meaning 'to write' (γράφω, *graphô*) and a 'slice, section,' (τόμος, *tomos*), Borkowski broaches the question of reflecting the world and arrives at similar conclusions to those made by Graham Greene in *The lawless roads*: it is impossible to describe a place. One can 'present only a simplified plan, taking a house here, a park there as symbols of the whole'.[14] In the same vein, the depiction of the Emerald Isle by Polish migrant writers is composed of an array of colourful mental images illuminating O'Connell Street, the Spire, the River Liffey, St Stephen's Green, *Busáras*, a row of houses in Howth, the harbour in Skerries, the Cliffs of Moher, and the like. By the same token, the narratives of Polish migrants are as much representing a world as they are a form of world making. Their portrayal of Ireland, which is subsequently passed on to readers, is a product of the way they have selected and presented those places. And the technique of the writers is very much alike: they outline the contours of the place they have lived in (or frequently visited) with great precision and then fill them with vivid and detailed recounting. Therefore, most of the books could pass for fictionalised travel companions, narrated by a pedestrian, *flâneur*, voyeur, the urban stroller who aspires to know the place as well as Joyce knew Dublin.

Some writers even follow in the footsteps of Joyce's characters from *Ulysses*. One of them is Małgorzta Goraj-Bryll, the co-author of *Irlandia. Celtycki splot* ('Ireland: the Celtic wreath').[15] The book begins at the point when Goraj-Bryll leaves her house to join the Bloomsday celebrations and searches the recesses of Dublin in Joyce's shoes. The fact that she was the wife of the Polish ambassador to Ireland, Ernest Bryll, permitted her to have contact with celebrities from the front pages of newspapers, such as the president, Mary Robinson, or Bono from U2, as well as with the people she met in the streets every day. Consequently, the book she co-wrote with her husband portrays a whole variety of people, the representatives of different walks of life. What looms throughout the Brylls' personal narrative is their fascination with Irish literature: their intimate knowledge of Ireland is presented in a literary context, something not completely surprising if one takes into account their previously mentioned translations of Irish poetry or the fact that Ernest Bryll was already an established poet in his homeland before he was appointed Poland's ambassador to Ireland.

Equally predictable are references to Irish literature in other migrants' books. This is, after all, what the Emerald Isle was known for in Poland, even before Polish migrants arrived in the country. For example, Daniel Żuchowski's *The new Dubliners* is an obvious reference to Joyce's 1914 collection of short stories. If *Dubliners* sketches the daily lives of the Irish at the turn of the twentieth century, *The new Dubliners* depicts personal and often tragic stories of migrants in the Irish capital a century later. Joyce peers into the homes of his contemporaries while Żuchowski gives an insight into the lives of migrants who share the space and spirit of Dublin with the Irish.[16]

In *egri bikavér*, Łukasz Suskiewicz invokes Beckett's *Waiting for Godot* when the narrator and his friend spend every night drinking whiskey and conversing on various topics. They are deadened by routine and feel that every day is like the previous one. They waste their time in Ireland, but they have no clear plan for the future. Like Vladimir and Estragon, they are 'educated tramps' (both hold MA degrees and work in positions below what their qualifications make them suitable for) who are waiting without hope for deliverance.[17]

Magdalena Orzeł, whose book ends with a reference to *Ulysses*, ascribes the worldwide popularity of Irish literature to the extraordinary capacity of Irish people to promote their national culture. She remarks in *Dublin, moja polska karma* ('Dublin, my Polish karma'):

> The Islanders are really good at advertising. As hard as it is, they have even invented admiration and craze for literature. They have found and maintained their own brand. They seduce all our senses—greenness caresses our eyes, Guinness finds a way to our stomach, and books get hammered into our heads with a fist.[18]

In this manner, by recourse to a few chosen symbols (literature, Guinness, shamrock, greenness, Celtic knot, sheep, red hair, Ryanair, to name but a few) and the repeated use of them, the Irish have created a set of positive stereotypes, which immediately bring to mind their national identity. For newcomers, these symbols—which obviously comprise only the surface of the local culture—function as signposts that guide them through the unexplored country. They mark the otherness of Irish people and the distinctiveness of their culture, and, as indicators of such features, they adorn covers of Polish migrants' books.[19]

Even more often than the attributes of Ireland, the cover designs on works produced by Polish migrants in Ireland depict the island's breath-taking landscapes, which are also a prominent part of the narratives.[20] Again and again, Polish authors return to the notion of nature providing a shelter from the hectic pace of modern life and a space for spiritual renewal. Their characters travel to the Irish seaside every time they feel stressed, over-worked or frustrated. As they immerse themselves into meditation amid the windswept Irish landscapes, they reconnect to the self, rethink their current situation and make plans for the future. This has given rise to long passages in migrants' writings devoted to observational accounts of sea, cliffs, beaches, pastures, parks, plants, animals and, above all, meteorological phenomena. The weather wields such an immense power over the island that it has even shaped Irish cultural and social life. Gosia Brzezińska jocularly implies in *Irlandzki koktajl* ('The Irish cocktail') that the Irish affection for literature might have been brought about by exposure to frequent rainfall and wind: Irish people cocooned themselves inside their houses and read poetry.[21] According to Agnieszka Latocha, Irish myths and legends arose out of a 'damp and tacky world of greenery' whose fairy-like, magical aura formed a perfect setting for supernatural and peculiar creatures.[22] In *egri bikavér*, Łukasz Ślipko contends that the Irish have developed a fondness for a pint because they took refuge from repetitive cycles of pelting rain in an alcoholic haze.[23]

While it is explored in many different contexts, the weather functions also as a reflection of the characters' emotional states. For example, the worry voiced by an Irishman in Ryszard Adam Gruchawka's *Buty emigranta* ('The emigrant's shoes') is an expression of the fear that some members of Irish society harboured about the massive influx of migrants: 'On a rainy day, a farmer, who was as old as the ocean, sadly confided in me that ever since the wave of migration had begun, the weather had gone nasty, too.'[24] In *Przebiegum życiae* ('Conductum lifae'), the ailing Gustaw is assigned the job of cleaning the lawn in front of the factory. Against the bleak backdrop of a grey sky and the pouring rain, he is down on his knees, picking up cigarette butts, coughing, mopping sweat from his face and singing 'I'm singing in the pain' to the tune of *Singin' in the rain*.[25] In this scene, Piotr Czerwiński achieves a tragic intensity by emphasising through use of bad weather conditions the lamentable plight of his character. Finally, Wowa, the main hero of Łukasz Stec's *Psychoanioł w Dublinie* ('The psychoangel in Dublin') reads meaning into the weather changes: he deduces good fortune from the cloudless sky and awaits troubles when it rains.[26] The use of environment in Polish migrant writing seems, for the most part, to be a resounding echo of the Romantic period: nature aids the characters' intellectual and spiritual development, it exerts a tremendous influence on the island

Joanna Kosmalska

and the island's inhabitants, and it is a medium through which the characters' emotions are expressed.

There are at least eleven novels, a short-story volume, two poetry books and five collections of essays, as well as short stories and poems included in anthologies produced by Polish writers, that purport to record life in Ireland from a Polish perspective.[27] Ever since Iwona Słabuszewska-Krauze's *Hotel Irlandia* ('Ireland Hotel'), the first-published account of a Polish economic migrant living on the isle, came out in 2006, work by her compatriots has appeared quite regularly. One of the most recent is Piotr Czerwiński's 2017 *Zespół ojca* ('Father syndrome'). If Słabuszewska-Krauze's account adopts the coloration of a settler in an exotic country, Czerwiński's narrator conveys the impression of being a member of the local society. Crossing from one country to another, the heroine in *Hotel Irlandia* remarks:

> We came by ferry. In an ordinary way, just like dozens of our fellow countrymen who had arrived here every day. Although I thought of myself rather as a traveller, or even a conqueror, who was sailing to another land which was as undiscovered as a land can be.[28]

By way of contrast, Ireland feels like home to the hero in *Zespół ojca*, and this feeling is heightened by his dissolving memory of Poland. Pondering the ten years he has spent in Dublin, he notes: 'More and more often, I feel as if I have lived here forever. As if I came from here, as if I was born here....'[29] The character has developed such an affinity with Ireland that the country's initial exoticism has degraded to the routine. His sense of belonging to the local place and its history grows stronger as Poland is, for him, slowly turning into a dream world, to which it is impossible to return.

The polarity of the narrators' attitude towards Ireland in both *Hotel Irlandia* and *Zespół ojca* is reflective of two points in time: one is the late-1990s when the economic boom was in full swing and the influx of Polish people was still in its initial stages; and the other is the late-2010s when the country was experiencing a return to economic stability and had become home to thousands of Poles. Throughout this time, the writings of Polish migrants captured Ireland's metamorphosis from the 'Celtic Tiger'[30] into the 'Celtic Phoenix'.[31]

The Emerald Isle through Polish eyes

At the beginning of the millennium, Polish news reports and the first personal accounts of migrants portrayed the Emerald Isle as a paradise: a promise of global capitalism and an easy life. This seductive image was transfigured into a symbol, which grew so strong that Donald Tusk, the party leader of Civic Platform, based his successful political campaign on the assertion that he would turn Poland into 'The Second Ireland'.[32] Like many political promises before, this one remained undelivered, but ever since the 2007 parliamentary election, this metonymic expression was regularly used in the public space, often with wry irony. The powerful myth of the Irish promised land was given a further lease of life by Polish migrant authors who—not unlike the rest of their compatriots—came to the Emerald Isle with this utopian vision aroused by news reports and migrants' stories.

Surprisingly, this idealistic image of the country was ratified by the writers' initial observations: Konrad, the main character in Piotr Czerwiński's *Przebiegum życiae* ('Conductum lifae'), collected coins from pavements because Irish people did not bother to pick up the change they had dropped. This aroused his serious suspicion that they might 'shit with money'. His first impression of the new place was nothing but positive: 'It's perfect: they drink, they sing and they have jobs.' For all these qualities, Ireland earned many telling nicknames in Polish migrant books, such as 'the land of milk and honey,' 'the ultra-divine paradise',[33] 'heaven',[34] or 'the crystal palace',[35] to quote but a few. Implicit in these names was the country's excessive affluence, but also a pervading sense of unreality. As if the place was too good to be true.

The nicknames portended the sad recognition that the Irish idyll was an illusion, which was a theme reworked in almost all Polish migrant books, including *Pokój z widokiem na Dunnes Stores* ('The room with a view of Dunnes Stores') in which Łukasz Ślipko drew up a sort of profit and loss account of migration:

> They took shelter under the umbrella of wealth, leaving their decayed villages, potholes in roads and rust-eaten buses behind. They were let into the crystal palace, but even in this palace they are not devoid of worries and they atone for the high standard of living by being 'the Other', 'proles from the outside'.[36]

Joanna Kosmalska

The topic of migrants being divested of their illusions about Ireland was also put forward by Łukasz Suskiewicz in *egri bikavér*. In that book, two Polish truck drivers travel on a bus to Poland and complain to the narrator about their unsuccessful stay in Ireland:

> They called this smart aleck here to tell him it was a para-
> dise. That manna fell from heaven and that we should come
> because people here had nice cars, earned huge money and
> lived in the lap of luxury. They did a snow job on this fool
> and he followed me around and mumbled, and burbled
> and grumbled. And there was 'Ireland' and 'Ireland.' As if
> he knew no other words. Only this one. This moron had
> dreamt up that he would save for a house, that he would
> buy a car... You've really made a pile! Ha ha. You're coming
> back so well-off! Like from America![37]

In teasing out the theme of disillusionment, America provided Łukasz Suskiewicz, as it had provided many other Polish authors, with a met-aphor for Ireland, offering points of comparison that illustrated how the myth of the Irish promised land had come into being. The projec-tion of celebrated American ideals—one of which was securing a better material future through hard work—onto Ireland, led to a belief that all newcomers would live the 'Irish Dream', a magnified version of the American Dream. It was, of course, a fantasy, unscathed by reality, but it had become the basis of the common perception of the Emerald Isle that had prevailed in Poland for a few years before it was dismantled by a surge of new journalistic articles and migrants' books.

The updated, more realistic literary portrayals depict Ireland as a country of 'new money', where memories of emigration are still vivid and where juxtapositions of poverty and wealth, of backwardness and progress, of provincial and cosmopolitan, of rustic and urban, and of conservative and liberal life lurk in the landscape. For example, the writers recount that Irish cities, including the capital, have a rural structure with low-rise buildings, which look almost the same within each district. In *egri bikavér*, the narrator recalls how he meandered through the narrow streets of Dublin, which—apart from the city centre—is laid out in a relatively geometric pattern as if the capital were designed by mathematicians. His confusion is heightened by the fact that the houses, which have no balconies, no curves and almost identical doors and windows, differ only in that they are buildings of two or three storeys. Worse still, there are much the same road signs on every street corner.[38] With their relatively homogenous buildings and narrow streets, along with a low-rise skyline punctured only here and there by tall buildings (many of which were erected during the Celtic Tiger era), Irish cities seem intimate and provincial to authors who are new to the country.

Polish migrant writers also chronicle how Dublin, having entered into the boom period, had attracted large numbers of young people from all over the world because the place offered a happy and comfortable life. The result was the city's transformation into a vibrant, multi-cultural metropolis, which facilitated liberal lifestyles. Emphasising this metamorphosis, Polish authors reprise in their writings that Dublin had become a true home of personal freedom and ethnic diversity. The change manifested itself in, among other things, the appearance of foreign shops, restaurants, pubs and other business establishments all around the capital. As the main characters in *Psychoanioł w Dublinie* ('The psychoangel in Dublin') walk down Abbey Street in the city centre, they see a number of such places:

> As they were walking towards O'Connell Street, they went past ten Polish, eight Indian and eleven Chinese shops. There were only two Irish stores, and Wowa bought a packet of cigarettes in one of them. Just in case he needed it. Having done the shopping, they went for dinner to an Indian restaurant called Govinda's.[39]

In their narratives, Polish writers compare Dublin, in a sometimes hackneyed manner, to the crucible in which various nationalities have melted into a dynamic, cosmopolitan society. The authors turn to the ethnic diversity of the city for inspiration, since it provides a colourful context for their plots. They paint the spaces where the multi-cultural crowds spend their time with such precision that many texts, some of which are even accompanied by illustrations, could constitute a sort of interactive map: by adducing stories associated with the places, the writers endow them with life and meaning. A clear instance of such mapping is the scene in Piotr Czerwiński's *Przebiegum życiae*, in which Gustaw finds shelter from the rain in 'The Church':

> Gustaw managed to pick up twenty cents from the pavement in front of Arnotts and rushed to the portal of the nearby church, clearly a relic, whose refurbishment must have been well-thought-out by some very noble monks since there was even an inscription over the entrance that read 'The Church' and a macho Garfield for security who opened the door for worshippers. Inside, a spiritual atmosphere prevailed: behind the bar, there were fifty different kinds of whiskey and the Irish toast painted in golden Gothic lettering instead of the altar, from which Jesus usually looks down at people. There was also a DJ who operated consoles standing on two holy water basins and the pipe organ in the loft where the waiters had their rallying. Gustaw suspected that it had to be a church of some very funky sect: the provost was resting after the mass by his console and the sectarians were eating dinner. So, he ordered a steak and a glass of wine and read the leaflet lying on the table which advertised other attractions of this temple. It turned out there was a disco in the underground catacombs. A permanent resident of this place was the English guy who jakieś two hundred years earlier had ordered an execution of a bardzo, very important freedom fighter from the bajabongo land. Gustaw suspected that the sectarians from 'The Church' gathered every night in the catacombs and paid people for dancing on this fellow's tomb so that he would never forget what he had done to this nation.[40]

Running to over a page in length and written in Ponglish—the bi-lingual weave of Polish and English—this detailed description of the modern club located in an old church is Czerwiński's trenchant introduction to the interconnected themes of the consumerism and hedonism of Dublin, themes that also recur in the writing of other Polish migrants. Regardless of their nationality, crowds of Dubliners spend their free time browsing around the city's shopping centres with the aim of purchasing useless and redundant goods just for the sake of squandering money. By recycling somewhat cliched comparisons of shopping malls and nightclubs to 'temples',[41] Czerwiński explores the alarming affection of the city dwellers for excessiveness, which has grown into a sort of religion. The pastime of compulsive buying on weekdays is replenished with binge drinking at weekends. In *Zielona wyspa* ('The green isle'), Mariusz Wieteska castigates young Dubliners for succumbing to witless hedonism:

> Saturday and Sunday were the days when people unleashed their primal instincts. Dazed with drink and dope, they showed how you could fall without touching the ground with your hands. They slipped off their masks and stepped on them with their expensive shoes which reflected the class of their owners, who went to work Monday to Friday.[42]

In much the same way as Wieteska, many other writers provide extensive accounts of Dublin's self-indulgent nightlife and suggest parallels with the Greek Dionysia: Daniel Żuchowski and Przemek Kolasiński quip that the central event epitomising such indulgence is held on 17 March, the feast of the Irish Dionysus—St Patrick's Day. Magdalena Orzeł and Mariusz Wieteska describe how, with the break of dawn on Saturday and Sunday, the city is reminiscent of a waste dump, an incisive symbol of young Dubliners' debauchery: the streets are covered with broken bottles, condoms, fast food leftovers, piss and vomit. On Monday, the litter is scavenged, everybody goes to work, and the weekend wildness passes into oblivion.

This youth drinking-culture, which seems to serve mainly as a distraction from their day-to-day lives, has no resemblance to that of the older generation, for whom a local pub is the basis of communal life, the place where people develop relationships with a whole network of locals. Thus, as Agnieszka Latocha chronicles in *Irlandia, moje ścieżki* ('Ireland, my paths'), drinking in pubs is always accompanied by all sorts of social activities, such as singing, dancing, tale-telling, card games, darts, etc. In the previously mentioned *Pokój z widokiem na Dunnes Stores* ('The room with a view of Dunnes Stores'), Łukasz Ślipko observes that Irish people drink in large quantities but innocently: there is no bohemian ring to it, drinking is more like a 'national sport',[43] like Gaelic football or hurling—a distinctive feature of the local culture. Daniel Żuchowski registers in *The new Dubliners* that although migrants find the rules of Gaelic games very complicated and have scant understanding of them, they enjoy going to the matches because of the friendly atmosphere; the atmosphere that is also typical of Irish pubs and that has arisen from the happy-go-lucky demeanour of Irish people.

A portrait of the Irish as ...

Virtually all Polish migrant writers offer the same portrait of the Irish as blithe, convivial, laid-back, hospitable, friendly and tolerant minimalists. They gave a warm welcome to thousands of newcomers, they have generally avoided mixing local economic problems with the subject of ethnic minorities, they set little store by material possessions, they focus on the present moment rather than muse about the future, and they live by the maxim that Magdalena Orzeł cites in *Dublin, moja polska karma* ('Dublin, my Polish karma'): 'Take it easy, we can do it tomorrow.'[44] Łukasz Ślipko mentions with amazement that even the police force, *An Garda Síochána*, evokes sentiments of social trust and liking. Anna Wolf, a Polish playwright and founder of Polish Theatre Ireland, attests to this in an interview:

> I think they [Irish people] are friendly, optimistic, and helpful. I remember when I first went to Kilkenny. Lost in thought, I stood in the street, and suddenly an Irishwoman approached me and offered to help me find a job. She led me to a nearby supermarket, gave me an application form and went on to explain how to fill it in. Nobody would approach me like that in Poland! I also think that the Irish live on a day-to-day basis. They don't worry about tomorrow and they don't make far-reaching plans. In Poland, it's the other way round. We live on our dreams and we plan everything in hope of a better future. That's why here,

in Ireland, people have their apartments made over only every now and then; whereas every time I visit Poland, I hear the noise of drilling, because of someone redoing their flat. It's partly due to our financial situation, but it's also a consequence of our mentality. [45]

The bitter paradox is that the same traits that the Irish are admired for in personal relationships they are chided for in the work context. Their laid-back attitude has given rise to the different perception of time that prevails on the island, with the result that all sorts of delays are frequent and people just pass over them lightly. In *Hotel Irlandia*, Iwona Słabuszewska-Krauze describes how passengers wait for buses that follow some secret, unpredictable timetable, plumbers promise to come in two days but show up two weeks late, a simple renovation or amendment turns into a long mission, etc.[46] Marcin Wojnarowski in *Okrutny idiota* ('The cruel idiot') jocosely concludes that when a job is two days overdue, it is considered to be completed promptly.[47]

As a consequence of their gregariousness, the Irish have great attachment to their social circles, the inevitable result of which is their tendency to endow greater trust in members of their own community and to prioritise them over strangers. Kinga Olszewska, whose work as an interpreter for Galway Community Services has inspired some of her poems, highlights in 'Site for sale' how migrants occasionally experience prejudice in business relations, only because they are members of the out-group:

> 'Site for sale to locals in the area'
> I go in to inquire.
> Are you local? The man behind the desk asks disbelievingly.
> I have been local for the last ten years.
> But you are not really Irish?
> So I recite: Irish passport, Revenue, Hibernian, Bank of Ireland,
> Áine and Saoirse, holiday house in Wicklow,
> I start quoting national heroes
> When the man interrupts
> In fairness, I don't think it's a site for you.[48]

Joanna Kosmalska

Truth to tell, Polish authors seem to be envious rather than critical of the Irish solidarity and mutual support. When asked how his life would change if he were Irish, Piotr Czerwiński said in an interview:

> I would easily get a decent job. I would quickly get promoted. Seriously. No joke here. I don't refer to any particular situation. It's just a general rule and there is no sense denying that. Good for them, at least they respect themselves. I wish Poles had such an attitude in Poland.[49]

Finally, some Polish migrants struggle to reconcile the affable Irish nature with the assertiveness of their Irish superiors in business situations. In *Pokój z widokiem na Dunnes Stores*, the Irish manager beams at the employee whom she is making redundant.[50] In much the same way, the narrator in Słabuszewska-Krauze's *Hotel Irlandia* is called into the office by her boss, who makes friendly small talk and then dismisses her with a smile on his face.[51] The woman looks back with some bitterness to the time when she worked in the company and complains that her supervisor has never shared his ideas, or for that matter reservations, about her work. As if to vindicate Słabuszewska-Krauze's observations, Piotr Czerwiński points in *Przebiegum życiae* to a major difference between Polish people and the rest of the world: while other nations express their thoughts in a less direct manner, Poles openly state what they think and in return they expect patent sincerity from others.[52] Despite their minor frustrations, however, Polish migrants extol the Irish lifestyle since it renders into reality a place where, in Słabuszewska-Krauze's words, the cashiers are in no hurry, officials are humane, and passers-by smile at one another.[53] Ryszard Adam Gruchawka adds that there is an absence of stark divisions in Irish society, and work, regardless of its nature, is held in high esteem.[54]

In the rudimentary portrayal of the Irish, Polish authors mention also jocularity, garrulousness and a predilection for tradition. Marvelling at the capacity of Irish people to be naturally funny, Przemek Kolasiński notes in *What I got from Ireland?* that everything and everyone is a source of wise-crackery in Ireland, but the jokes always walk a fine line between jocosity and mockery, with the result that they are caustic but never humiliating.[55] Tomasz Borkowski devotes a whole chapter of

Irlandia Jones poszukiwany ('Ireland Jones wanted') to 'The famous Irish sense of humour' and uses the space, first, to outline major historical, literary, social and linguistic influences that have led to the refinement of Irish humour and, second, to give a few first-hand examples of Irish wittiness. The jokes are often woven into wider stories, since the Irish are a nation of gifted tale-tellers who spin their colourful stories for hours on end. As Ryszard Adam Gruchawka asserts, the talkativeness of Irish people, along with their fondness for music, is encoded in their green blood.[56]

Although the Irish have a vibrant contemporary culture produced by numerous professional and amateur artists, they have also retained a penchant for their Gaelic tradition of folk music, dances, songs and tales, which are all bound together by the Irish language. The language, which has been in decline, is a subject widely discussed by Polish writers, who shed some light on how the Irish have been robbed of their native tongue by British colonisers and how they have attempted to revive it. Łukasz Ślipko sadly notes that contemporary Ireland is bi-lingual only in theory because, in practice, the Irish language has been side-lined: few people care about it and even fewer are fluent in it.[57] Tomasz Borkowski bears out Ślipko's diagnosis, remarking that a huge majority of Irish society loses touch with Irish as soon as they graduate from school, even though they are offered a free language course, thanks to the Irish street signs, TV shows, radio programmes and books. The result is that: 'when you ask two Irishmen about the meaning of an Irish word, a dispute breaks out because each of them gives you a different definition.' Fortunately, 'they all agree that *Póg mo thóin* means "Kiss my arse".'[58] Many Polish authors confront the issue of the Irish language with a touch of humour, some take a more serious approach to the subject, and there are also a couple of writers who lapse into a sort of nostalgia for the native tongue that the Irish have lost. In Łukasz Stec's *Psychoanioł w Dublinie*, the main character dies and ascends to heaven where people speak Irish, the language that has always sounded heavenly to the hero.[59]

A whole set of texts produced by Polish migrants attests to the fact that despite the dwindling of the Irish language, the Irish have preserved the wealth of the Gaelic tradition and appropriated the English language to express their own distinctive identity. One result of this

Joanna Kosmalska

is that the newcomers find it challenging on arrival to understand the Irish, and they often talk about the need to learn the local language. When the narrator of Łukasz Suskiewicz's *egri bikavér* lands at Dublin airport, he strikes up a conversation with a bus driver only to realise that neither of them can discern what the other is saying:

> I had thought that I had at least communicative English. But when I articulated my thoughts, the guy just winced helplessly. In turn, when he started responding to what I had said I was convinced I heard the gurgle of water. We probably used different course books to learn the language.[60]

The deployment by Irish people of alternative vocabulary, pronunciation, syntax and accents are elements of Hiberno-English that are repeatedly mentioned by Polish migrant writers, who identify the local language as one of the distinctive features of the Irish nation.

Another trademark of the Irish identified by Polish authors is their clothing: despite wind, rain and low temperature, Irish people, who are surprisingly resilient to the cold, always wear short-sleeves. This is how Piotr Czerwiński and Łukasz Suskiewicz set Irishmen apart from foreigners, and Magdalena Orzeł recounts that 'a December evening is full of bare shoulders, backs, thighs, calves, feet, stomachs', especially those of Irish girls who, like nymphs, waltz through the streets in sheer dresses and high-heels.[61] The female attire epitomises the lifestyle of young Irish women: the skimpy evening outfits, which accentuate their sensuality by night, are replaced with tracksuits, which provide them with cosiness, by day. In *Dublin, moja polska karma*, Magdalena Orzeł refers to a radio show, which was meant to address the question of 'What do Polish people think about the Irish?' but turned into a sort of beauty contest for Irish and Polish women, in which male callers chided the former for their licence and lack of personal grooming and lauded the latter for their restraint and good looks.[62]

If some Polish male authors seem to flirt dangerously with these stereotypes, their female counterparts mock them with devastating wit as nostalgic fantasies of men. Polish female writers extol the self-confidence of Irish women, who, in Iwona Słabuszewska-Krauze's words, behave as if they have no complexes. 'I was really impressed by it', she concludes in *Hotel Irlandia.*[63] An equally animated discussion about fashion in Ireland may be found in *Pokój z widokiem na Dunnes Stores* by Łukasz Ślipko or in *Psychoanioł w Dublinie* by Łukasz Stec.[64] Both writers use the androgynous emo style, which is typical of the contemporary youngster, to highlight a generation gap. The emo, with their figure-hugging, studded clothes in black and pink colours and their dark make-up, are juxtaposed with middle-aged and elderly Irishmen in their V-neck sweaters, shirts and tweed jackets. In Łukasz Ślipko's eyes, a significant difference between younger Irish people and their parents or grandparents, which is embodied by their apparel, is that the older generation fought for their identity and slogged away in Britain, while everything is handed on a plate to modern teenagers who, as a result, have developed a sort of sentimentality that he calls 'Electropop Wertherism'.[65]

Ireland—the other Poland?

Apart from cultural and social issues, the attention of Polish migrant writers in Ireland also turns to some bread-and-butter domestic matters, such as the impracticality of two taps or three-pronged plugs; the superannuated plumbing system in which the water freezes if the temperature drops below zero; the tradition of naming houses and using the name of the property instead of the address in some parts of Ireland; or spongy bread, to name but a few. What these things have in common is that they signify a difference between Ireland and Poland. Establishing the points of comparison and difference between the two countries is an instrument with which the migrant writers investigate the island and its inhabitants. A closer reading of their texts reveals how the authors tend naturally to attach 'the other' to the cultural context they are familiar with, framing the new and unknown in terms of the old and known. Obviously, the ensuing result is also a better understanding of themselves and their country of origin. This method, however, runs the unintended risk of assuming a greater similarity or difference between the countries than is actually the case, which has occasionally led to some overgeneralisations, ill-founded assumptions or biased projections.

Some of the recurring analogies between Ireland and Poland that have been explored by Polish writers include history (fighting against the oppressor for national independence and the experience of forced and economic migration); religion (the powerful influence of the Catholic Church in each country); and culture (which emerged from the folk life of a rural society). In *Przebiegum życiae* ('Conductum lifae'), Piotr Czerwiński derisively sums up the historical links between Ireland (which he nicknamed the bajabongo land) and Poland (called Bulanda):

> Generally speaking, Mickeys and Poms had a long sado-masochistic relationship, which clearly wasn't very happy. It was kinda like the affairs of Bulanda with her exotic neighbours who had desperately wanted to screw Bulanda over for the last thousand years and turn her into soap or send her na holidays in Ciberia. But we didn't give up. Everyone who was still alive fled from Bulanda abroad. A lot of people ended up in England or the USA where the main intention of the locals was to screw them over dla a change. Mickeys had exactly the same adventures, so I think, that both nations should be very happy that they have finally found each other in this world.[66]

Ireland became independent from Great Britain in 1922, but Poland regained its independence from the USSR only in 1990 and the Soviet Northern Group of Forces left the country in 1993. Consequently, as Łukasz Ślipko observes, Irish people seem to have, for the most part, reworked their traumas, recovered their self-confidence and started to work towards utilising their full economic and entrepreneurial potential. Meanwhile, Polish people still nurse their own wounds and read their deepest fears into everything that is strange and foreign, with the result that they live in a sort of seclusion and hibernation.[67] The Poles who sensed a frustration with the *status quo* took refuge from the malaise by moving to Ireland and elsewhere in Western Europe at the turn of the twenty-first century. The same might be said of the Irish emigration in the 1980s, when many people in their twenties and thirties saw no future for themselves in their homeland and pursued an emigrant career and a more prosperous life in the UK or the US.

In their writings, Polish authors indicate a set of connections between the experiences of the Irish and Polish migrants: people who left were young, well-educated, eager to integrate into a developed economy and similar in appearance to the local people. The countries in which they settled differed from their homeland in several important ways, but nevertheless the underlying realities were, in fact, strikingly similar. One of the characters in Magdalena Orzeł's *Dublin, moja polska karma*, Wiola, becomes aware of this when she strikes up a conversation with her Pakistani female neighbour:

> 'Ireland is like Poland, like your home, here is your religion,' said Shazia dreamingly. That was indeed the case but Wiola had never thought about it this way. Until now, she was convinced that they had gone so far. But actually she was at home here. Everybody could visit her and she could fly to Poland. Besides, they had the same churches and McDonalds. People also looked the same because everybody followed the European fashion while Shazia never took off her headscarf. How close were they, and how far has Shazia travelled... [68]

Ryszard Adam Gruchawka phrases the same idea slightly differently in *Buty emigranta* ('The emigrant's shoes') by saying that when he arrived in Ireland the place felt so familiar and ordinary to him that he had an impression he had arrived in a Polish city, which he simply had not yet visited.[69] Similarly, when the narrator of *Hotel Irlandia* goes to Wicklow, she feels as if she were in Kashubia.

In *Pokój z widokiem na Dunnes Stores*, Łukasz Ślipko probes what lies behind the casual ease with which Polish people make the Emerald Isle their new home and comes to the conclusion that it is the shared culture of 'folk songs and dances, drinking, garrulity, pissing in the streets and rural cuisine'.[70] There is also the affinity in terms of religion; the Irish parishes are increasingly populated by migrants rather than natives, but the relationship between the state and the Catholic Church nevertheless seems stronger in Ireland than in Poland (where Communism largely dismantled church–state connections). The recognition of this is implicit, for example, in the bafflement of Gustaw, the character in

Piotr Czerwiński's *Przebiegum życiae*, when he learns that the sale of alcohol is prohibited on Good Friday, or in Daniel Żuchowski's and Marcin Wojnarowski's commentaries on the ban on abortion. That the allegiance of the Irish state to religion has been rapidly flagging can, however, be traced in more recent writings. In the brief afterword to *Zespół ojca* ('Father syndrome'), Piotr Czerwiński remarks, for instance, that Irish family law was changed in 2015, opening up the possibility that in cases where parents are not married, guardianship over children from their relationship may now, in certain circumstances, be granted to the father instead of the mother.

When asked in an interview about his experience of living in Ireland, Czerwiński points to yet another change that the country underwent between 2000 and 2015:

> I like the Ireland that we have now. It's poorer, but it's finally Irish, the way I had always imagined it. People are normal again. Now they are the Irish I always wanted to meet and live among. It's good, despite the price Ireland had to pay to wake up from the prosperity craze. But again, for me, that wasn't Ireland back then—that was a bad dream, in a way.[71]

After the Celtic Tiger dream (or nightmare as some writers would argue) was over, the reality to which Irish society awoke was one in which people were poorer, more secular and more ethnically diverse. If the Irish successfully defined their national character in relation to Britain in the past century, they face an even more complex task at present: to negotiate their identity with reference to the ethnic minorities, which have become constituent parts of their society. Iwona Słabuszewska-Krauze is one of many Polish authors who raises this issue. In *Hotel Irlandia* she briefly introduces Heidi's son: the boy, described by his mother as Irish, has become tri-lingual as a result of being brought up in Dublin by his German mother and Italian father. The same group of writers also registers the astonishing capacity the Irish have demonstrated to embrace foreign elements throughout all their history. It is one of the reasons why so many Polish people feel at home in Ireland.

Notes

[1] The section 'The mysterious island' is largely based on the information presented at the outdoor exhibition *From strangers to neighbours: encounters between Poland and Ireland* organised by the embassy of Ireland in Poland (Open-Air Gallery, the Royal Łazienki Museum; Warsaw, 1–30 August 2017).

[2] Bernard Connor, *The history of Poland; in several letters to persons of quality* (Brown; London, 1698), 2 vols. O'Connor removed the "O" prefix from his surname in 1695; therefore two spellings of his name are in use.

[3] Embassy of Ireland in Poland, 'Constance Markiewicz: the rebel Countess', *From strangers to neighbours. encounters between Poland and Ireland* (Open-Air Gallery, the Royal Łazienki Museum; Warsaw, 1–30 August 2017).

[4] On the impact of Irish drama on Polish culture and literature, see the recent book by Barry Keane, *Irish drama in Poland: staging and reception, 1900–2000* (Intellect; Bristol, 2016).

[5] James Joyce, *Ulisses* (Państwowy Instytut Wydawniczy; Warszawa, 1969).

[6] '„Ulisses" Jamesa Joyce'a – niemoralne arcydzieło wznawiane w prestiżowej serii', in *Booklips*, 10 December 2012. Available online at: http://booklips.pl/premiery-i-zapowiedzi/ulisses-jamesa-joycea-niemoralne-arcydzielo-wznawiane-w-presti-zowej-serii/ (29 October 2017).

[7] Ernest Bryll and Małgorzata Goraj-Bryll, *Miodopój (VI–XII.)* (PAX; Warszawa, 1978); Ernest Bryll and Małgorzata Goraj-Bryll, *Irlandzki Tancerz (XII–XIX)* (PAX; Warszawa, 1981).

[8] Seamus Heaney, *44 wiersze* (Wydawnictwo Znak; Kraków, 1995), trans. Stanisław Barańczak; Seamus Heaney, *Ciągnąc dalej. Nowe wiersze 1991–1996* (Wydawnictwo Znak; Kraków, 1996), trans. Stanisław Barańczak; Seamus Heaney, *Kolejowe dzieci* (Centrum Sztuki—Teatr Dramatyczny; Legnica, 1998), trans. Piotr Sommer.

[9] Jerzy Jarniewicz is the author of *Heaney. Wiersze pod dotyk* ('Heaney: Tangible poems'), the first Polish monograph about Heaney's poetry, which was published in 2011 by Znak, one of the leading publishing houses in Poland.

[10] 'Historia piosenki „Kocham cię jak Irlandię". To się wydarzyło naprawdę', WP Teleshow, 20 March 2014. Available online at: https://teleshow.wp.pl/historia-piosen-ki-kocham-cie-jak-irlandie-6033696284095617g (29 October 2017).

[11] Embassy of Ireland in Poland, 'Building bridges: the Polish community in Ireland', *From strangers to neighbours: encounters between Poland and Ireland* (Open-Air Gallery, the Royal Łazienki Museum; Warsaw, 1–30 August 2017).

[12] Przemek Kolasiński, *What I got from Ireland?* (Xilbris; Bloomington, 2012), 1.

[13] Tomasz Borkowski, *Irlandia Jones poszukiwany* (Gajt; Wrocław, 2010), 10. As all citations from Polish books are translated by the author, the original quotes are provided here in the endnotes:
Jest to próba opisania moich osobistych irlandzkich doświadczeń, które dzielę z tysiącami innych rodaków i milionami Irlandczyków. Przypuszczam, że ile było osób w ten proces zaangażowanych, tyle było zdumień i wyjaśnień. Tutaj prezentuję jedną z wersji wyda-rzeń. Można by powiedzieć „tomografię".

[14] Graham Greene, *The lawless roads* (Penguin Books, 1981), 65.

[15] Ernest Bryll and Małgorzata Goraj-Bryll, *Irlandia. Celtycki splot* (Zysk i Sk-a; Poznań, 2010).

[16] Daniel Żuchowski, *The new Dubliners* (Literary Publishing; Dublin, 2014).

17 Łukasz Suskiewicz, *egri bikavér* (Forma; Szczecin, 2009), 36. The book takes its title from a variety of wine and so does not have a direct translation in English.

[18] Magdalena Orzeł, *Dublin, moja polska karma* (Skrzat; Kraków, 2007), 104. *Wyspiarze umieją się reklamować. Potrafią wykreować nawet rzecz tak trudną jak zachwyt literacki i czytelniczy amok. Odnaleźli i utrzymali własną markę. Kuszą każdy zmysł – zielonością przez oczy, guinessem do żołądka i książkami jak pięścią w głowę.*

[19] See, for example, the covers of Piotr Czerwiński's *Przebiegum życiae* (Świat Książki; Warszawa, 2009) and Ernest Bryll and Małgorzata Goraj-Bryll's *Irlandia. Celtycki splot* (Zysk i Sk-a; Poznań, 2010).

[20] See, for example, the covers of Agnieszka Latocha's *Irlandia, moje ścieżki* (Gajt; Wrocław, 2008), Mariusz Wieteska's *Zielona wyspa* (Anagram; Warszawa, 2009) and Marcin Lisak's *Dwie fale. Przewodnik duchowy emigranta* (Homini; Kraków, 2012).

[21] Gosia Brzezińska, *Irlandzki koktajl* (Wydawnictwo Bliskie; Warszawa, 2010), 10.

[22] Latocha, *Irlandia*, 49.

[23] Suskiewicz, *egri bikavér*, 19.

[24] Ryszard Adam Gruchawka, *Buty emigranta* (Exlibris; Warszawa, 2007), 61. *Pewnego deszczowego dnia farmer stary jak ocean wyznał mi ze smutkiem, że odkąd zaczął się napływ imigrantów, pogoda też zrobiła się paskudna.*

[25] Piotr Czerwiński, *Przebiegum*, 235.

[26] Łukasz Stec, *Psychoanioł w Dublinie* (Akurat; Warszawa, 2014).

[27] The publications that this chapter refers to include:

a) eleven novels: *Irlandzki koktajl* by Gosia Brzezińska (2010), *Przebiegum życiae, czyli kartonowa sieć* by Piotr Czerwiński (2009), *Zespół ojca* by Piotr Czerwiński (2017), *Lenie* by Andrzej Goździkowski (2007), *Buty emigranta* by Ryszard Adam Gruchawka (2007), *Irlandia, moje ścieżki* by Agnieszka Latocha (2008), *Hotel Irlandia* by Iwona Słabuszewska-Krauze (2006), *Psychoanioł w Dublinie* by Łukasz Stec (2014), *egri bikavér* by Łukasz Suskiewicz (2009), *Zielona wyspa* by Mariusz Wieteska (2009), and *Okrutny idiota albo prywatny żart* by Marcin Wojnarowski (2008);

b) a short-story volume: *The new Dubliners* by Daniel Żuchowski (2014);

c) three poetry books: *Mullaghmore* (2016), *Pierwsze wspomnienie wielkiego głodu* (2017), both by Małgorzata Południak, and *Nocne czuwanie* by Tomasz Wybranowski (2012);

d) five collections of essays: *Irlandia. Celtycki splot* by Ernest Bryll and Małgorzata Goraj-Bryll (2010), *Dublin, moja polska karma* by Magdalena Orzeł (2007), *Dwie fale. Przewodnik duchowy emigranta* by Marcin Lisak (2012), *Co mi dała Irlandia?/What I got from Ireland?* by Przemek Kolasiński (2012), and *Pokój z widokiem na Dunnes Stores* by Łukasz Ślipko (2011);

e) short stories and poems included in the following anthologies: *Wyfrunęli. Nowa emigracja o sobie* Wiesława T. Czartoryska (ed.) (2011), *Na końcu świata napisane. Autoportret współczesnej polskiej emigracji* Elżbieta Spadzińska-Żak (ed.) (2007), *Transgeniczna Mandarynka* by Barbara Mikulska, Dariusz Wędrychowski, Marek Zychla, Adam Dzik, Anna Grzanek, Agnieszka Osikowicz-Chwaja, Anna Brzeska, Adam K. Burling, Marek Hołub, Marcin Kasica, Ryszard Machowski, Rafał Piotrowicz (2013), *Landing places: immigrant poets in Ireland* Eva Bourke and Borbala Farago (eds) (2010), and *Yet to be told* Ciara Doorley, Daniel Bolger and Clara Phelan (eds) (2012).

It is worth adding that—apart from four volumes in English—these books were published in Polish, in Poland, and, as such, are primarily addressed to Polish readers.

[28] Iwona Słabuszewska-Krauze, *Hotel Irlandia* (Wydawnictwo Naukowe Semper; Warszawa, 2006), 6. *Przypłynęliśmy promem. Zwyczajnie, tak jak dziesiątki innych rodaków przybywających tutaj każdego dnia. Chociaż ja wolałam czuć się jak podróżnik raczej, a może nawet zdobywca dobijający do kolejnego lądu, tak nieznanego jak tylko nieznanym ląd być może.*

[29] Piotr Czerwiński, *Zespół ojca* (Wielka Litera, Warszawa, 2017), 24.

[30] The term 'Celtic Tiger' as a signifier of Ireland's economic health (or even just the nation's health as a whole) seems to have first been employed by Kevin Gardiner, a contributor to a newsletter produced by the company Morgan Stanley in 1994. See, Peadar Kirby, 'Three tiger sightings, but its stripes are in dispute', *Feasta Review* 1 (2002), 17–18, and Denis O'Hearn, 'Globalization, '"New Tigers", and the end of the developmental state? The case of the Celtic Tiger', *Politics and Society* 28 (1) (2000), 67–92.

As Kirby notes; 'The official Tiger narrative is typically structured around the following explanations of Irish success: consistent macro-economic management of the economy, investment in education, social partnership, EU structural funds combined with the fiscal discipline imposed by the Maastricht criteria and, of course, very high levels of inward US investment'. See, Peadar Kirby, *The Celtic Tiger in distress: growth with inequality in Ireland.* (Palgrave; Basingstoke, 2001), 2.

[31] The phrase 'Celtic Phoenix' seems to have been coined by Paul Howard, a satirist who writes a column under the Ross O'Carroll-Kelly pseudonym in *The Irish Times*. See, Donal O'Keeffe, 'Phoenix Miracle or Celtic Phoenix, Paddy never learns any lessons', *The Avondhu* (19 April 2017). Available online at: https://avondhupress.ie/phoenix-miracle-celtic-phoenix-paddy-never-learns-lessons/ (12 February 2018). The term started to be used irony-free by media commentators to describe a revival of the Irish economy after its severe post-2008 crisis. See, 'Celtic Phoenix; the Irish economy', *The Economist* 417/8965 (19 November 2015), 15–16. Available online at: https://www.economist.com/news/finance-and-economics/21678830-ireland-shows-there-economic-life-after-death-celtic-phoenix (12 February 2018).

[32] Sylwia Miszczak, '„Druga Irlandia", czyli wpadka Donalda Tuska', in *Wirtualna Polska*, 19 December 2007. Available online at: https://wiadomosci.wp.pl/druga-irlandia-czyli-wpadka-donalda-tuska-6037410533958785a (4 September 2018).

[33] Czerwiński, *Przebiegum*, 54.

[34] Mariusz Wieteska, *Zielona wyspa* (Anagram; Warszawa, 2009), 11 or Andrzej Goździkowski, *Lenie* (Lampa i Iskra Boża; Warszawa, 2007), 129.

[35] Łukasz Ślipko, *Pokój z widokiem na Dunnes Stores* (Wydawnictwo RB; Opole, 2011), 21.

[36] Ślipko, *Pokój*, 21. *Schronili się pod parasol dobrobytu, zostawiając za sobą zapadłe wsie, dziurawe drogi i zardzewiałe autobusy. Wpuszczono ich do kryształowego pałacu, ale nawet w tym pałacu nie są wolni od trosk, a wysoki standard życia materialnego okupują byciem „innymi", „zewnętrznymi proletariuszami"...*

[37] Suskiewicz, *egri*, 85. *I temu tu, mądremu, dzwonili, że jest raj. Że manna z nieba leci i żeby przyjeżdżać, bo auta dobre, pieniądze duże i w ogóle luksus. I tak mu w tej pustej głowie namieszali, że cały czas za mną łaził i szeptał, i mamrał i truł. I nic – tylko „Irlandia" i „Irlandia". Jakby innych słów nie było. Tylko to jedno. Wymyślił se durnota, że tam na dom zarobi, że auto kupi... Ale żeś zarobił! Ha, ha. Taki już dorobiony wracasz! Jak z Ameryki!*

[38] Suskiewicz, *egri*, 22.

[39] Łukasz Stec, *Psychoanioł*, 44. *Ruszyli w stronę O'Connell Street, mijając po drodze dziesięć polskich, osiem hinduskich i jedenaście chińskich sklepów. Irlandzkie były tylko dwa i*

Joanna Kosmalska

właśnie w jednym z nich Wowa kupił nową paczkę papierosów. Tak na wszelki wypadek. Po zakupach udali się na obiad do hinduskiego baru „Govindas".
[40] Czerwiński, *Przebiegum*, 107. Since Piotr Czerwiński wrote *Przebiegum życiae* in Ponglish, the bi-lingual weave of Polish and English, I have deliberately included some Polish words in the English translation: *Gustaw zdołał tylko podnieść dwadzieścia centów z chodnika przed Arnottsem i popędził do portalu pobliskiego kościoła, najwyraźniej zabytku, który jacyś bardzo zacni mnisi musieli odrestaurować z prawdziwym pomyślunkiem, ponieważ miał nawet napis „The Church" nad wejściem, a także własnego macho Garfielda dla bezpieczeństwa, który otwierał drzwi wiernym. W środku panowała bardzo spirytualistyczna atmosfera; za barem mieli pięćdziesiąt gatunków whisky i toast po irlandzku, wymalowany złotym gotykiem w miejscu ołtarza, skąd zwykle Jezus patrzy na ludzi. Był też didżej, obsługujący adaptery ustawione na dwóch kropielnicach oraz organy na galerii, gdzie był punkt zborny kelnerów. Gustaw uznał, że to musi być kościół jakiejś bardzo odjechanej sekty, miejscowy proboszcz właśnie odpoczywa po mszy przy swoim gramofonie, a sekciarze jedzą dinner. Zamówił więc stek i małe wino, czytając ulotkę ze stołu, która zachwalała pozostałe atrakcje świątyni. Wynikało z niej, że w piwnicy lokalu znajdują się katakumby, a w nich dyskoteka. Jej stałym rezydentem jest facet, który like dwieście lat wcześniej, zarządził egzekucję jakiegoś bardzo ważnego freedom fightera z krainy bajabongo i był Angolem. Gustaw uznał, że najwyraźniej sekciarze z „The Church" zbierają się co noc w katakumbach i płacą za tańczenie na grobie tego klienta, by nigdy nie zapomniał, co zrobił temu narodowi.*
[41] Czerwiński, *Przebiegum*, 138; 107.
[42] Wieteska, *Zielona wyspa*, 46. *Sobota i niedziela były zawsze dniami, w których ludzie powracali do swych pierwotnych instynktów. Odurzeni alkoholem i narkotykami, pokazywali jak można upaść na ziemię nie dotykając jej rękoma. Zrzucali maskę, depcząc ją drogimi butami, obrazującymi klasę ich właścicieli, chodzących od poniedziałku do piątku do pracy.*
[43] Ślipko, *Pokój*, 17.
[44] Orzeł, *Dublin*, 19.
[45] Joanna Kosmalska and Joanna Rostek, 'Irish-Polish cultural interrelations in practice: interviews with Chris Binchy, Piotr Czerwiński, Dermot Bolger, and Anna Wolf', *Studi irlandesi. A Journal of Irish Studies* 5 (2015), 103–30: 123.
[46] Słabuszewska-Krauze, *Hotel*, 35; 90.
[47] Marcin Wojnarowski, *Okrutny idiota albo prywatny żart* (Wydawnictwo EP; Poznań, 2008), 134.
[48] Kinga Olszewska, 'Site for sale', in Eva Bourke and Borbala Farago (eds), *Landing places: immigrant poets in Ireland* (Dedalus Press; Dublin, 2010), 144–7: 144.
[49] Kosmalska and Rostek, 'Irish-Polish cultural interrelations', 110.
[50] Ślipko, *Pokój*, 7-8.
[51] Słabuszewska-Krauze, *Hotel*, 158.
[52] Czerwiński, *Przebiegum*, 202.
[53] Słabuszewska-Krauze, *Hotel*, 35.
[54] Gruchawka, *Buty*, 81.
[55] Kolasiński, *What I got*, 35.
[56] Gruchawka, *Buty*, 47-8.
[57] Ślipko, *Pokój*, 6.
[58] Borkowski, *Irlandia Jones*, 34.

[59] Stec, *Psychoanioł*, 300.

[60] Suskiewicz, *egri*, 9. *Uważałem, że mój angielski jest co najmniej komunikatywny. Ale kiedy werbalizowałem myśl, facet robił bezradny grymas. Z kolei, kiedy odpowiadał, byłem przeświadczony, że słyszę bulgotanie wody. Prawdopodobnie korzystaliśmy z różnych podręczników do nauki języka.*

[61] Orzeł, *Dublin*, 37.

[62] Orzeł, *Dublin*, 110–14.

[63] Słabuszewska-Krauze, *Hotel*, 187. *To mi naprawdę imponowało.*

[64] Stec, *Psychoanioł*, 118; 192.

[65] Ślipko, *Pokój*, 47.

[66] Czerwiński, *Przebiegum*, 77. *Ogólnie rzecz biorąc, Irole i Angole mieli długotrwały związek sadomaso, który najwyraźniej nie był szczęśliwy. Kinda trochę przypominało to romanse Bulandy z jej egzotycznymi sąsiadami, którzy przez ostatni tysiąc lat desperacko pragnęli wydymać Bulandę i zrobić z niej mydło albo wysłać na holiday in Cyberia. Aleśmy się nie dali. Kto żyw uciekał z Bulandy za granicę. Mnóstwo ludzi wylądowało w Anglii albo w USA, gdzie główną intencją wielu miejscowych było ich wydymać, for a change.*

[67] Ślipko, *Pokój*, 43.

[68] Orzeł, *Dublin*, 129. 'Ireland is like Poland, like your home, here is your religion'. *Rozmarzyła się Shazia. Rzeczywiście to prawda, chociaż Wiola o tym nigdy nie pomyślała. Do tej pory wydawało jej się, że pojechali tak daleko. A przecież tak naprawdę tu jest jak w domu. Każdy może ją tu odwiedzić i ona może polecieć do Polski, poza tym mają te same kościoły i McDonaldy. Ludzie też wyglądają tak samo, bo obowiązuje moda europejska, a Shazia przecież nie zdejmuje szalika z głowy. Jak niedaleko oni wyjechali, jak wielką podróż odbyła Shazia...*

[69] Gruchawka, *Buty*, 18.

[70] Ślipko, *Pokój*, 41.

[71] Kosmalska and Rostek, 'Irish-Polish cultural interrelations', 110.

Ierland is anders: Representations of Ireland in Dutch literature

Marieke Krajenbrink

With its remote geographical location on the western periphery of Europe, Ireland holds a special fascination for many on the European continent, and the Netherlands is no exception. Connections between Ireland and the Netherlands have been much less studied than those between Ireland and other European countries, notably Germany.[1] As Jérôme aan de Wiel points out, over the centuries, contacts and exchanges between Ireland and the Netherlands have been relatively limited, due to Great Britain lying in between, but nevertheless they did exist and were in some instances of particular importance.[2] Relations, which go back many centuries but still reverberate in Dutch cultural memory, include the early missionaries, most notably (the Northumbrian) St Willibrord. Known as the apostle to the Frisians, Willibrord studied for over ten years in the Irish monastery of Rathmelsigi in County Carlow before embarking on his mission of bringing Christianity to the Netherlands, where he became the first bishop of Utrecht in 695.[3] Furthermore, links between Great Britain and the Netherlands had, of course, considerable repercussions in Ireland as well. We only need to think of William of Orange, known in the Netherlands as William III, who is viewed very differently in the two countries: stylised into an icon of Protestantism and unionism in Ireland (north and south) but regarded as a champion of religious tolerance in the Netherlands.[4] Accordingly, Dutch visitors to Ireland have often been shocked to discover how William's role and the Dutch national colour orange have had such a divisive history in Ireland.[5]

By and large, for Dutch writers it is the perceived difference between Ireland and the Netherlands that attracts them to write about the country: *Ierland is anders* ('Ireland is different'), as the title of a travel book from 1959 sums it up.[6] This idea of Ireland being 'different' can be found again and again in Dutch travel books about the country and also features strongly in other literary portraits of Ireland.[7] For Belgian authors, on the other hand, their image of Ireland is often affected by a perceived shared historical experience, notably in relation to contested language and religion, and their key role in constructions of cultural and national identity.[8] In Dutch literature across epochs and genres, we find a broad spectrum of texts portraying Ireland and Irish characters. Particularly popular were the adventures related in the Brendan voyage, of which there is a medieval Dutch version from the twelfth century—the curious poem *De Reis van Sint Brandaen*, which continued to live on in a number of popular prose versions and was rediscovered in the nineteenth century.[9] This is clearly a story that speaks to the imagination of a seafaring nation (and it also lives on in the name of the lighthouse on the Dutch island Terschelling, the *Brandaris*).

The focus of this chapter, however, is twentieth-century narrative fiction. Some of the most interesting examples of the genre will be discussed, with the aim being to shed light on how the image of Ireland in Dutch literature has evolved over the years and what particular aspects of Ireland have captured Dutch writers' imagination. For example, Ireland's turbulent history and the ongoing impact of that history today, the impressive landscape of the country, traditions of music and storytelling, the special relationship to the supernatural and the significance of religion, the importance of language and a Celtic heritage are elements that, in different ways, all feature prominently in Dutch literature about Ireland. As already noted, Dutch authors often highlight how Ireland differs from the Netherlands, giving it the attraction of the strange and exotic; their depictions range from the romanticised image of the green island as a magic land of fairy-tales, to gritty portrayals of poverty and oppression, violent sectarian conflict, and abuse.

The 'Prince of Dutch poets' inspired by the Celtic Twilight

A key figure in the reception and dissemination of Irish literature—especially of the ancient mythology of Ireland—in the Netherlands in the first half of the twentieth century and well into the post-World War Two era is the acclaimed poet Adriaan Roland Holst (1888–1976), also named 'the prince of Dutch poets'.[10] As a student in Oxford, he discovered Celtic mythology, which had a profound impact on him:

> It was in my youth, when I studied, or was a student anyway, in England, that some forlorn afternoon I found, in the Library of the Student's Club, a translation of a Celtic saga, The Voyage of Bran, Son of Febal—Reading those pages it seemed to me as if old memories awoke in me, and when I studied Celtic mythology more closely, this confirmed me in my feeling that I finally had found the road home. ... With the discovery of Celtic mythology I also discovered the literature of the so-called Irish Renaissance. Both discoveries were of decisive importance to me, because this literature too vibrated and sparkled with a mythical and elementary life, a life in which the heart always is in touch with the foreworldly power of the

soul. Yeats, its greatest poet, always retained a great influence on me.[11]

Roland Holst, who travelled to Ireland in 1913 and later again in 1954, translated fifteen lyrical poems, a dramatic poem and one play by Yeats and, as Theo D'haen has shown, the texts he chose to translate, concentrating on the early to middle Yeats, were motivated by his particular fascination with the ancient Celtic tales and their revival by Yeats and Lady Gregory.[12] From this he developed his own mythical world of what he calls an Elysian longing for an imagined, or remembered, blissful island in the west across the sea, beyond time and the mundane realm of technology-driven modern life and observable reality.[13]

Roland Holst's best known prose text, *Deirdre en de zonen van Usnach* ('Deirdre and the sons of Usnach') is a reworking of the ancient story from the Ulster cycle, first published in 1916 in one of the leading literary journals in the Netherlands, *De Gids*.[14] In 1920 it appeared as a book under the same title and was widely read for decades, and the text is still read regularly in schools (possibly also due to it being relatively short).[15] Roland Holst's other reworkings of ancient Celtic myths/sagas include *De dood van Cuchulainn van Murhevna* ('The death of Cuchulainn of Murhevna') and, interestingly, he also takes up the story of the Brendan voyage in *De zeetocht van Bran zoon van Febal* ('The sea voyage of Bran son of Febal').[16] However, *Deirdre en de zonen van Usnach* remained the most popular of his prose works. The text conveys a captivating sense of brooding atmosphere, with its Ossianic, eerie, wind-swept dark and lonely inhospitable landscape and depictions of extreme weather. It tells a story of inescapable doom; the sombre predictions of the druid at Deirdre's birth warn that her unworldly beauty will lead to the downfall of kings and heroes, indeed of Ireland itself. Roland Holst's awe-inspiring retelling differs from the versions by Yeats and Synge, in that Deirdre, after Noisa's death, is not captured and humiliated by King Concobar but mournfully goes west to the cliffs at the end of the world, to unite herself with the sea and be washed away.[17] The sombre sense of foreboding and of an inescapable fate is, in the end, countered by Deirdre hearing the distant music from the mythical blessed island, presenting a more positive ending.

Marieke Krajenbrink

As the influential Dutch Keltologist Maartje Draak points out, Roland Holst's particular vision of Ireland as a mythical and mysterious island of wonders was, for the Netherlands—where poets traditionally had mainly found their (mythic) inspiration in the east—a new development, as the Ossianic tradition of pre-Romanticism had made relatively little impact in the country.[18] Roland Holst found a number of followers who quite literally followed in his footsteps. One of them, Jan van der Vegt, wrote a biography of Roland Holst and later published an account of his own visit(s) to Ireland.[19] In that work, he celebrates the country and its fascinating landscape and impressive wealth of literature in a similarly high-poetic tone, but also presents Ireland somewhat more realistically, beyond the mythical past.

Historical novels: passionate emotions, colonial oppression and the power of the supernatural

Another important author in our context is the prominent and prolific writer Simon Vestdijk (1889–1971), about whom his personal friend Adriaan Roland Holst coined the famous phrase: 'He writes faster than God can read.'[20] Indeed, the oeuvre produced by Vestdijk includes over fifty novels and demonstrates stupendous productivity and range. He is regarded as the leading Dutch novelist of his generation.[21] His earlier writing was influenced by James Joyce, as evidenced in the use of interior monologue in his first published novel *Meneer Visser's Hellevaart* ('Mr Visser's descent into Hell', which was published in 1936), and he also wrote several essays on the work of Joyce.[22] Vestdijk's later work is formally less innovative but remains highly complex and sophisticated. He published two Irish-themed novels, *Ierse nachten* ('Irish nights', which appeared 1946) and the 1951 work *De vijf roeiers* ('The five rowers'). Both are historical novels, set in late nineteenth-century rural Ireland, and both are concerned with the plight of the rural population of post-famine Ireland. Poverty, suppression, evictions, resistance against the English tyranny, violence, superstition and the supernatural all play a role.[23]

Ierse nachten, written in 1942, is set between 1852 and 1860 in a fictitious estate in Kerry, where increasingly harsh demands by the English absentee landlord lead to tensions and eventually a violent outburst.

The story is told from the perspective of Robert Farfrae, the son of a (Catholic) Irish mother from the locality and a (Protestant) Scottish father, the steward of Billatinny Castle's absentee landlord, Sir Percy Randall. This perspective allows for a nuanced and multi-faceted portrayal of events in which divided loyalties take centre stage. Growing up amidst the country boys, Robert (and with him the reader) gradually gains more insight into the conditions and his own fraught position among his childhood friends. He is torn between his parents. His father obeys the landlord's orders, but also attempts to avoid the violent evictions that are occurring on neighbouring estates (secretly making up for the rent of those unable to pay), yet for the locals he represents the despised agent of 'Saxon' oppression. His mother, a proud Irishwoman, first hopes the local rebel Ulick Mac Carthy can help improve the tenants' lives. When he is killed, she puts her mind to convincing the landlord to return to the estate, believing everything will then be put to rights. Ironically, the landlord's visit brings disaster: Robert's father is killed in a fracas with the angry tenants, and his mother loses her mind after she has tried in vain to put a curse on Sir Percy. For Robert, in the end there is no future but to emigrate to America.

Vestdijk's inspiration for the novel was twofold. On the one hand, an acquaintance told him about the Irish 'otherworld' he had learned about and his fascination for Irish fairies and sagas, while on the other hand his friend, the author Theun de Vries, recalls bringing another side of Ireland to Vestdijk's attention: Ireland as a country of poverty, suppression, famine and absentee landlords.[24] *Ierse nachten* is regarded by many (including the author himself) as the best of Vestdijk's historical novels.[25] The image of Ireland it presents is characterised by passionate emotionality in extreme weather conditions; music; rituals surrounding death (the wake); and, perhaps most notably, superstition and the relation to the supernatural (the 'little people' and their potential threat—curses). The portrayal of Ireland and the Irish is certainly not devoid of stereotyping, but overall the novel is extremely well researched and conveys—despite the fact that Vestdijk never visited Ireland—a remarkable sense of authenticity, further highlighted by a glossary of names, places and terms, as well as historical explanations.[26] As José Lanters has shown very convincingly, the novel is permeated with extraordinary historical detail; for instance, it alludes to specific

Marieke Krajenbrink

events involving conflicts around evictions and the murder of a steward in Donegal.[27] In his own comments on the novel, Vestdijk remarks how *Ierse nachten*, more than any of his other works, is a 'social novel', and he then sheds interesting light on his reasons for choosing an Irish setting for the work by adding that he could have written a social novel situated in the Dutch rural and impoverished province of Drenthe, were it not for the fact that the people there, or so he claims, were so very un-emotional.[28] Another aspect to keep in mind is the time of writing, that is, during the Second World War in the occupied Netherlands. Vestdijk believed that this inevitably brought to the novel a stronger focus on social issues and the portrayal of situations of oppression:

> I was, of course, somewhat handicapped because I wrote this book in *these* times and did not want to rail against England too much. For ... as soon as one goes only a little deeper into the Irish question, into its social, cultural and historical aspects, one is *forced* to take sides against England![29]

Poignantly, the novel was first published in German translation in 1944, in the middle of the war, and this has given rise to vehement criticism and discussion of it in more recent times.[30] Vestdijk's personal circumstances need to be kept in mind though. As one of the most prominent Dutch authors at the time, he was, from May 1942, held hostage by the Gestapo in St Michielsgestel (and later, until February 1943, in the barracks for political prisoners in the *Polizeigefängnis* in Scheveningen). In order to free himself he gave in to the pressure to join the *NS-Kultuurkamer*, an organisation established in 1941 by the occupying Nazi authorities in an attempt to gain control over Dutch cultural life and to more efficiently execute censorship.[31] Writers (like musicians, painters, journalists, film makers, etc.) were forced to join, or could no longer publish their work, but many of them refused (Adriaan Roland Holst very reluctantly joined the *Kultuurkamer*, but protested so vocally and publicly that he had to go into hiding). The original Dutch version of *Ierse nachten* was published in 1946 and was followed by Vestdijk's second Irish novel, *De vijf roeiers*, in 1951. Another historical novel, set in the west of Ireland, this time in 1869, it features a larger cast of characters in a shorter timeframe. Tensions and conflicts between the Irish and their colonial oppressors have aggravated, and the Irish resistance is portrayed more ambivalently.

Intercultural encounters and the shadow of the Second World War

Quite a different category of Dutch writing on Ireland is the novel *Kasteel in Ierland* ('Castle in Ireland') by Jan Gerhard Toonder (1914–92).[32] While Toonder was by no means as renowned (nor as high-brow) a writer as Simon Vestdijk, this book was, nevertheless, successful. It was the *Boekenweekgeschenk* in 1970—the gift book given away with every book purchase during the annual book week—an important award for an author, which obviously also significantly boosts circulation. As in the case of Vestdijk, albeit in very different ways, the concern with Ireland in Toonder's novel becomes at the same time a concern with Nazi Germany and the shadow of the Second World War. This topic is without a doubt the most important and most prevalent theme in Dutch literature, and it is interesting how Ireland becomes an arena in which issues associated with the war, including Dutch collaboration during the German occupation, are explored. It is also important to mention that the author's brother was Marten Toonder, the celebrated comic strip writer and creator of the highly successful *Tom Poes en Heer Bommel* series, who had emigrated to Ireland in 1966, therefore providing a personal connection between the author and the country. Furthermore, both Jan Gerhard and Marten Toonder had been active in the Dutch resistance. *Kasteel in Ierland* can be read as a mild satire by Jan Gerhard on the highly romanticised image of the mysterious emerald island with its storytelling tradition and its perceived close proximity to the magic world of fairies and nature spirits that his brother Marten had encountered.[33]

The novel is set contemporaneously in the mid-1960, and it tells the story of how a middle-aged German, Dr Franz Krause, and his Dutch wife Hilda emigrate to Ireland from Germany. Prompted by an article in their local newspaper lauding the business success of international entrepreneur Ernst Gottlieb (who, unbeknownst to everyone else, is a former SS comrade of Krause), now the proud owner of a factory in Ireland, old acquaintances are renewed. Hilda, who has heard Ireland to be a most beautiful, quiet and green country, encourages Franz to visit his old mentor Gottlieb. Blackmail ensues, with Krause hinting that he has not forgotten anything about Gottlieb and their stay in the (fictitious) Dutch town of Aardenbosch during the last years of the war. Gottlieb subsequently helps the Krauses to buy a castle in Ireland, which they intend to turn into a cosy hotel. In strong contrast to Hilda's romantic view of Ireland, Franz Krause sees his new neighbours with wariness: 'The Irish! Drunkards and liars they were, everyone knew that ...'.[34] Toonder uses the prism of Franz to present old and mostly negative stereotypes of the Irish: 'the singing, annoying policeman, the unreliable workers of that drinking estate agent, the scarecrow of a farmer who stole his land, the smooth-talking priest'.[35]

The novel's play with stereotypes of both the Germans and the Irish leads to hilarious situations, predicated on Franz Krause's love of rationality, order and punctuality, and the gregarious stereotypically unreliable Irish builders revelling in the opposite of all that. Others are bursting into ballad-singing at every possible opportunity and display a logic completely of their own when it comes to land use and building regulations (and everything else for that matter). But the novel has a much more sinister side, and from the outset ominously shrieking black birds surrounding the castle's tower signal a dark secret. Krause's war record as an SS-officer increasingly haunts him, whilst for his wife Hilda, who greatly enjoys her new life, Ireland has an emotionally liberating effect:

> And had he not come to this haunted [*doorspookte*] country, dragged over by that damned Gottlieb and pushed (how strange, a conspiracy, perhaps after all?) by Hilda— ah, maybe he would have never thought of it again. But here in this tranquillity, he could reflect on it, now that he needed to, without self-reproach. He was still an honourable man. But he would never be able to prove that to Hilda, that new, witchlike Hilda.[36]

Through the return of Krause's suppressed memories of the Second World War and ongoing revelations of a brutal and sadistic past, Toonder clearly critiques patterns and discourses of suppression and the denial of guilt. For our context, it is particularly interesting how being in Ireland forces Krause to confront his past, as a result of the effects of supernatural influences and curses that he cannot ignore. Also, stylistically it is interesting how Toonder uses Germanicisms in Krause's inner monologues and gives the dialogue of the locals a distinctly Irish-English flavour. Thus, a kind of linguistic exuberance permeates the Dutch used by the different characters. The story gains much by the satirical depiction of the encounters between the Irish and Krause. Whereas the novel does contain criticisms of Ireland (Krause's experiences with petty forms of corruption, nepotism and administrative chaos), these all remain fairly innocuous, and on the whole the Irish are portrayed very sympathetically indeed. The destitution and oppression we find in earlier portrayals of Ireland have made way for relative prosperity. Tourism has become an important source of income and the Irish are portrayed as endlessly creative—also in exploiting the tourists' romantic notions of Ireland. In fact, we already find this motif in the work of Vestdijk—one of his characters makes 'prehistoric' arrows and also produces other allegedly ancient objects to sell to credulous and gullible tourists.

Tristan and Iseult revisited or Perspectives on the Troubles and impossible love

Leon de Winter's *Zoeken naar Eileen W.* ('Looking for Eileen W.', published in 1981) is a much more serious and critical portrayal, with a strong focus on the 'Troubles' in Northern Ireland.[37] Central elements in this complex narrative are the sectarian divisions within Northern Irish society, the suppression of sexuality, the position of women, and the destruction of people's lives by these circumstances. The narrator here is a Dutch bookseller in London, but much of the narrative is also conveyed through the hypothetical perspective of Eileen, as the narrator imagines her story to possibly have been. The novel starts with Eileen and Kevin secretly travelling to Dublin to have sex for the first time; a love story begins, which, arising as it does against the backdrop of the Troubles, is doomed to fail. Eileen, a seventeen-year-old Catholic from B., becomes pregnant. As abortion is not an option for her and as her Protestant boyfriend Kevin has seemingly disappeared, she turns instead to Mark, Kevin's older Catholic neighbour and employer, with whom Kevin has lived after his parents were killed in an IRA attack. When Eileen disappears, the Dutch antiquarian, who met her and her baby in his London shop where she was looking for a copy of the story of Tristan and Iseult, tries to reconstruct what has happened. His search is aided by (possibly imagined) letters that he found in her vacated lodgings and by his meetings with Mark.

Through intertextual references, Irish literature comes into play: Eileen's friend Ann is reading Edna O'Brien, 'her favourite author', who at that time in Ireland was perceived as scandalous.[38] O'Brien's inclusion points to a longing for escape from the claustrophobic social control in a (Northern) Irish small town, and from the social conservatism, entrenched sectarianism and secrecy that characterise ordinary life in the town as de Winter portrays it. Northern Ireland is described as a place 'where individual behaviour had a much wider political impact than, for instance, in England or the Netherlands'. Every individual could disturb the balance and, therefore, everyone became a politician or diplomat: 'If a truth existed, one was not allowed to speak it... There aren't that many countries in Europe where the madness, which rules every country, shows its face so blatantly'.[39] But the novel goes beyond the portrayal of Northern Ireland and also presents the urban-rural contrasts of the republic: Dublin is portrayed as dirty, gritty, rainy, but also offering Eileen the anonymity she is looking for to be able to consummate her love for Kevin, and this is contrasted with the rugged beauty of remote Lough Mask in Mayo (where Eileen hides and which is depicted with paradisiacal overtones). London, on the other hand, stands for freedom and liberation, but also for danger, for losing yourself and getting lost; it is here that Eileen discovers that Kevin has died of a heroin overdose and here that her own trace vanishes.

The novel, which in 1987 was made into a successful film under the title *Zoeken naar Eileen* ('Looking for Eileen'), was very well received and highly praised for its sophisticated exploration of processes of imagination and representation and their relation to reality in the form of a captivating story.[40] It marked the author's breakthrough to a wider public and continues to be a popular text in secondary-school reading. Leon de Winter has since become one of the Netherlands' best known and most successful writers, both nationally and internationally (and particularly in Germany). His later writing is characterised by a more easily accessible style and a thematic focus on his Jewish background and questions of Jewish identity. In that respect it is interesting that de Winter, when commenting on *Zoeken naar Eileen W.*, stated that he wanted to write about a forbidden and impossible love story and felt he had the choice between a Palestinian–Israeli couple or a romance across the Catholic–Protestant divide in Northern Ireland.[41] The decision for selecting the (Northern-) Irish setting is no doubt, to a significant extent, due to the link with the Tristan and Iseult legend (with its many different European versions). In the Dutch reception of the novel, this aspect of the story plays an important role and is quite strongly identified with Ireland. This medieval story, with its antecedents in Irish mythology, is the central point of reference underpinning the novel, and it functions almost as a curse: a tragic love-triangle that the contemporary characters seem doomed to repeat. For Kevin, the unwitting repetition of the old patterns he and Eileen find themselves entangled in shows the inescapable stranglehold of the past, not only of legends, but also of the troubled Irish history from which they as individuals cannot liberate themselves.

Haunted houses and ghostly islands: feminist and postfeminist rewritings of the Gothic novel

The 'fairy tale' of Tristan and Iseult is also briefly referred to in a novel by one of the Netherlands' best-known feminist writers—Renate Dorrestein's *Een sterke man* ('A strong man').[42] The main focus here, however, is quite different from that in de Winter's novel; Dorrestein brings in new elements in her portrayal of Ireland. In *Een sterke man*, Dutch sculptor Barbara Vrijmoed is, much to her surprise, invited to spend six weeks in the exclusive artist colony Kerrimagannagh, located in a secluded and haunted country house in Ireland. It is famed for the extraordinary creative processes brought about there through group dynamics, facilitated and overseen by the colony's founder—the charismatic and manipulative Stephen O'Shaugenessy [*sic*]. The narrative is structured as a series of accounts by Barbara and other Irish women characters in the novel, prompted by a police investigation into a murder, which, from the outset, raises the question of who has been killed and

Marieke Krajenbrink

who is to blame. In a reversal of the traditional romantic and tourist views of the Irish landscape presented in novels, Barbara, a modern city dweller, has no affinity whatsoever with the Irish countryside:

> I had never been in Ireland before. To be honest, I always had a vague aversion against it. All that boundless green, and everywhere those picturesque cliffs with wild foaming water underneath. I imagined turf fires and deserted villages, and endless varieties on the theme of smoked fish—it seemed an uncomfortable country with far too much nature and an overdose of superstition and sentimentality.[43]

The culture/nature opposition is a key theme in this narrative, which revolves around the sharply and wittily observed interaction among the often eccentric artists and their backgrounds.[44] Life in Ireland is portrayed using typical elements, such as the importance of religion, foggy weather, pub visits, eccentric characters, a lack of infrastructure and—in an indication of the gothic element of the novel—the local hearse doubling as a taxi.[45] The outsider's perspective provided by the Dutch narrator opens the novel; this perspective is then supplemented with the insider perspectives offered by the Irish and Northern Irish women who act as narrators in the subsequent chapters. Thus, a range of women's voices and their experiences is brought into play, including pertinent memories from one character of being sexually abused by IRA fighters who were given shelter in her family home; expectations of being the carer for elderly parents; incest and the shame of teenage pregnancy; and family members being killed in Northern Ireland by the Ulster Freedom Fighters. Through their stories we not only hear about the artistic activities and rivalries in Kerrimagannagh, but we also learn about women's experiences in Ireland, largely characterised by patriarchal suppression, not least within the family.

These all concern experiences from the past, but contemporary conditions in Ireland too are presented as being much more socially conservative than in Barbara's home country, all of which feeds into the auto- and hetero-image of the liberal Netherlands. The critical depiction of Ireland thus develops the idea of liberal and progressive Dutchness, in particular with regard to women's rights. Conversely, the Irish perspective on the Netherlands also casts such perceived liberalism in an ironic and sometimes critical light, most notably in terms of a rather hackneyed notion of sexual liberatedness. In this way, mutual stereotypes are pitted against each other, often to comic effect. Examples of this are the issue of abortion, which is not seen as something positive by the Irish characters, and the perception of those characters that possibly all Dutch people are bi-sexual.[46] Barbara tries to introduce more nuances by referring to Dutch cultural heritage and the artist Vincent van Gogh, but finds this is of little interest to the other women.

For the gothic elements, which abound in the novel, the remote Irish country house provides a very apt setting. Full of uncanny noises at night, it is a labyrinthine building with hidden corridors and traitorous stairs and a closed narrow chamber (a Bluebeard motif) in which the ghost of an English nanny, and the 'soul' of the house, is said to dwell.[47] But these dark elements are not limited to the world of the fantastic and supernatural, as some of them, of course, have their foundation in actual events. Other gothic motifs include the story of one of the Northern Irish women who recalls wandering through Belfast with the dead body of her murdered daughter.[48] The fear of being incarcerated in the dark also finds a realistic basis here in traumatic childhood memories from an orphanage. As one of the male characters says, 'reality is often much more gruesome than all fictions put together'.[49] Arguably, the traditional ingredients of the Gothic novel, including the cruel, even sadistic treatment of women and children and dark experiences—presented in this novel in the context of the Catholic Church—often appear in Ireland to be all too real. It is important to note, however, that the kind of gothic excess with which this is presented is typical of Dorrestein's writing and can also be found in her other novels, many of which are set in the Netherlands and Scotland. Furthermore, among other elements associated with Ireland in the novel are the more positive, perhaps (stereo)typical, characteristics of creativity, spontaneity, ebullience and humour.[50]

Dorrestein's interest in the tradition of the Gothic novel and her use of the genre to explore issues of feminism and the conflict between tradition and modernisation is shared by the author Vonne van der Meer in her *Spookliefde* ('Ghost love'), subtitled *Een Iers verhaal* ('An Irish tale') and published just one year after *Een sterke man*, in 1995.[51] The

Marieke Krajenbrink

subtitle *Een Iers verhaal* immediately draws attention to the setting on a nameless island off the western shore of Ireland. Opening with the lighting of two candles in a church as a narrative hook, Vonne van der Meer's highly atmospheric novella depicts a tragic love triangle, with the added complication of twin brothers, culminating in a violent crime of passion. In a frame story full of doubles and mirror images, the main protagonist, Phil, tells of how she arrived on the remote island in the 1960s as a young girl from the USA. After having difficulties settling in to this entirely different and archaic life— the local priest is the only person with a telephone—she is entranced by the local music and her homesickness gives way to falling in love with Seamus, a local boy, who is a poet, schoolteacher and bookseller. He turns out to have a twin brother, Michael, who is mentally retarded and hardly able to speak, but who opens Phil's eyes to the beauty and spirituality of the island. Complications ensue and the poet/schoolteacher kills his twin brother when he surprises Michael and Phil in what seems to be a compromising situation. Phil is nevertheless soon drawn back to the island and takes over Seamus's bookshop and his position as schoolteacher; he goes to jail and after his release and return to the island never speaks again.

Both *Een sterke man* and *Spookliefde* contain a more-or-less similar structure, as the journalist and critic Mariette Hermans points out: a female stranger comes to Ireland, disturbs the prevailing balance between nature and culture, and this results in an 'accidentally committed' murder.[52] She argues that both authors draw on 'the common image of Ireland as a country of nature and violence' in order to explore the relations between nature and culture, and therefore that it is 'by all means significant that their stories are set in Ireland rather than anywhere else'.[53] Most unusual is the unconventional sexually active role that Phil takes on; her background in American youth culture clashes with the values of the island and thus she is 'transgressing the boundaries of convention'.[54]

From this angle, the literary critic Agnes Andeweg reads *Spookliefde* as a variation on the Gothic novel, which here, however, does not take the anti-Catholic position traditionally inherent in the genre.[55] On the contrary, Andeweg argues convincingly that the Irish setting in van der Meer serves to provide a realistic Catholic context for what she sees as the depiction of religious rituals as a form of empowerment, and for an exploration of the conflict between sexual and religious longing, which questions the values of secularised modernity. The timelessness of the archaic island, which has hardly changed in hundreds of years and where the characters lose all sense of time, initially appears as a threat to the young American Phil, who at first only sees how everything there is rusting and that the island itself is caving into the sea. She is soon enthralled by the island's mysterious spell, however, and at the very end of the novella refers to it as a place to which everyone returns. This reminds us of Adriaan Roland Holst's vision of the mythical island beyond Ireland's western shores and brings us full circle in terms of the enduring fascination among Dutch authors with the unfathomable Atlantic seaboard and the realm even beyond the west of Ireland.

Dutch literary representations of Ireland: fascination and ambivalence

While there is not a vast literature in the Netherlands concerned with Ireland, the six novels by well-established authors explored in this chapter demonstrate that the range of themes and modes in the literature is quite significant. All the writers bring their own preoccupations to Ireland and have different reasons to be interested in Ireland. They see the place as different and harness that potential to explore their literary and social themes. One of the most interesting points to note from this literature is that Ireland is in many instances not viewed in isolation, but instead is contrasted and confronted with images of Germany, England and America. The perspective shown is often that of an outsider, and the image of Ireland is not necessarily very positive. Often, there seems to be a sense of an Ireland untainted by modernity, and the different authors respond to that in different ways; using gothic-feminist, parodist, post-modern, historical and mythic perspectives. Frequently, elements of the supernatural are combined with an awareness of social and historical ills, including British colonial oppression; in other cases, in works from a feminist perspective, the problem is patriarchal oppression, notably, but not exclusively, embodied by the Catholic church and its institutions and often expressed in violence against women and children. The superstitious/supernatural can (see Vestdijk's writing, for example) work as resistance, a kind of rebellion against oppression, whereas in van der Meer's work the Irish Catholic

Marieke Krajenbrink

setting can be seen as a fitting backdrop to explore the unconventional emergence of religious sensitivity.

In recent years there has been a decline in Dutch literary fiction located in Ireland. With the secularising of Ireland, the increasing domestication of its spatial, social and cultural landscape and its more open and multi-cultural society that appears to be moving away from a traditional Irish identity towards a European identity, the attractions of Ireland for Dutch writers seem to have diminished. The particularity of the scenery, the heritage and the history still remain as an inspiration for writers, but the modernisation of the country has diminished the Dutch appetite for all things Irish, with the result that there has been a shift to popular literature and light entertainment in which formulaic narratives (possibly often closer to lived social reality in contemporary Ireland) fulfil reader expectations through stock characters and well-worn ingredients (landscape, music, history, passion, affinity with the supernatural).[56] Accordingly, in the genre of popular romance (marketed as 'chick-lit') there are a number of novels that look at (the clichés of) modern Irish society, but some that now also include more contested issues, such as the Magdalene Laundries. Examples are Afra Beemsterboer's *Een Iers sprookje* ('An Irish fairy-tale', published in 2003), its 2007 sequel *Als alle anderen* ('Like all others'), and Wilma Hollander's *Dans der liefde* ('Dance of love', published in 2010).[57] The general formula in this type of book tends to be a Dutch woman falling in love with an Irishman, beautiful nature, and (family) complications that have to be overcome before the happy end.

The interest in Ireland is, however, also still strong with regard to travel literature. This continues to flourish in, for instance, the work of internationally acclaimed author Cees Nooteboom, who writes a chapter about his visit to the Aran Islands in *Nootebooms Hotel*, originally published in 2002 and in translation in 2006 as *Nomad's hotel. Travels in time and space*.[58] In his book *Mijn Ierland*, Gerrit Jan Zwiers presents a commented collection of excerpts from his favourite travel narratives (mainly Dutch, although Heinrich Böll is also included) alongside his own impressions about Ireland, thereby offering an idea of the range and multitude of examples of the form. In his preface he observes that, although there are some harsh counter-voices, the majority of authors and most of the works in his collection give a clear sense of an intensely romantic attitude towards Ireland, and he wonders whether this is all 'longing for a past world that is first and foremost fed by fantasy? Is this just the projection of romantic feelings onto a different country and people?'. Nevertheless, he hastens to add that he would not want to do without the enraptured prose about 'magical Ireland'.[59]

Overall, the image of Ireland in literature in the Netherlands is clearly a very diverse one. Now that Ireland is much more homogenised with the rest of Europe, not least through cheap travel, it has both spatially and culturally come much closer to the continent, and there has been a corresponding drop in literary Dutch authors locating their narratives in Ireland. While Dutch literary authors might now have to look elsewhere for their creative landscapes, there is, nevertheless, still a market for established images of Ireland in formulaic popular romances and mysteries; more challenging literary endeavours have, or so it would seem, little to profit any more from setting their narratives in Ireland. The question that now arises is whether—in the dynamics of globalisation, whereby the 'European foreign' has become domesticised—Dutch authors will, when their own environment may appear more unfamiliar, turn back to domestic Dutch settings for inspiration or seek pastures new.

Notes

[1] See, for example, the work of the Centre for Irish-German Studies. The centre's publications are listed in its 20-year brochure, which is available on the following website: https://issuu.com/centreforirish-germanstudies/docs/broschure_208_ef_80_a217_20final_20 (28 February 2018).

[2] Jérôme aan de Wiel, 'The Netherlands', in Mervyn O'Driscoll, Dermot Keogh and Jérôme aan de Wiel (eds), *Ireland through European eyes. Western Europe, the EEC and Ireland, 1945–1973* (Cork University Press; Cork, 2013), 190–244.

[3] See, for instance, aan de Wiel, 'The Netherlands', 191; Frank van der Pol, 'De Kerstening van het Noorden', in Herman Selderhuis (ed.), *Handboek Nederlandse Kerkgeschiedenis* (Kampen: Kok, 2006), 42–59. Willibrord and his Irish connections also features among the fifty windows on the canon of Dutch history instituted by the Minister of Education and led by Frits van Oostrum; see online at: https://www.entoen.nu/nl/utrecht/stad/willibrord/verdieping/de-jeugd-van-willibrord (28 February 2018).

[4] Interestingly, while William of Orange is of huge symbolic significance on the Irish side in the context of the Battle of the Boyne, in the Netherlands the way he is perceived in Ireland and his links to that country are hardly known.

Marieke Krajenbrink

[5] See, Gerrit Jan Zwiers, *Mijn Ierland* ('My Ireland') (Atlas; Amsterdam and Antwerpen, 2007), 217.

[6] Adolf Melchior, *Ierland is anders* ('Ireland is different') (De Spaarnestad; Haarlem, 1959).

[7] See, for instance, Dolf Jansen and Margriet Jeninga, *Waar het gras altijd groener is. Ierland, ons tweede moederland* ('Where the grass is always greener. Ireland, our second motherland') (Thomas Rap; Amsterdam, 2013).

[8] See, for instance, Geert Buelens, who also points out important differences with regard to the language issue in Ireland and Belgium: 'Flanders and Ireland seem to have a lot in common: both have a rich medieval tradition, both are (or in the case of Flanders: used to be) mainly Catholic, both consider themselves (post)colonial regions. As a result, nationalist politics play a dominant role in the world of arts and letters. But a major, and for literature crucial, difference lies in the importance of the national language as a cultural language. Despite efforts to promote the use of Irish, the language is only used by a small minority in Ireland even today. In Flanders French was the official language since Belgium became an independent nation in 1830, but unlike Gaelic, Dutch was never completely effaced.' See, Geert Buelens, 'An excessive, Catholic heretic from a nation in danger: James Joyce in Flemish literature', in Geert Lernout and Wim van Mierlo (eds), *The reception of James Joyce in Europe* (2 vols, Continuum; London, 2004), vol. 1, 150–61: 150.

[9] See, Reinder P. Meijer, *Literature of the Low Countries. A short history of Dutch literature in the Netherlands and Belgium* (Martinus Nijhoff; The Hague and Boston, MA 1978), 9. New editions with parallel translations into modern Dutch appeared in 1949 and 1994: Maartje Draak and Bertus Aafjes (eds), *De reis van Sinte Brandaan* (J.M. Meulenhoff; Amsterdam, 1949); Willem Wilmink and W.P. Gerritsen (eds), *De reis van Sint Brandaan. Een reisverhaal uit de twaalfde eeuw* (Uitgeverij Prometheus/Bert Bakker; Amsterdam, 1994). The well-known Dutch author of children's literature Paul Biegel published a novel for young readers based on the Brendan story under the title *Anderland: een Brandaan mythe* (Uitgeverij Holland; Haarlem 1990).

[10] See, for instance, the following website: http://literatuurmuseum.nl/overzichten/activiteiten-tentoonstellingen/pantheon/adriaan-roland-holst (28 February 2018).

[11] Adriaan Roland Holst in his essay 'Eigen achtergronden: Inleiding tot een voordracht uit eigen werk', as cited in and translated by Theo D'haen, 'Yeats in the Dutch-language Low Countries', in Klaus Peter Jochum (ed.), *The reception of W.B. Yeats in Europe* (Continuum; London and New York, 2006), 12–24: 14–5.

[12] D'haen, 'Yeats in the Dutch-language Low Countries'. See also, Roselinde Supheert, *Yeats in Holland: the reception of the work of W.B. Yeats in the Netherlands before World War Two* (Rodopi; Amsterdam, 1995).

[13] See, Adriaan Roland Holst, *Het Elysisch verlangen: Een beschouwing gevolgd door een Iersche sage, De zeetocht van Bran zoon van Febal* (The Halcyon Press, A.A.M. Stols; The Hague and Maastricht, 1928). This view of the west follows a familiar pattern. As Joep Leerssen in a more general context remarks, 'it is here, along the Atlantic coast, that the "mystical" pole of the Irish image is focused', see Manfred Beller and Joep Leerssen (eds), *Imagology: the cultural construction and literary representation of national character. A critical survey* (Rodopi; Amsterdam and New York, 2007), 193.

[14] Adriaan Roland Holst, 'Deirdre en de zonen van Usnach' ('Deirdre and the sons of Usnach'), *De Gids* 80(2) (1916a), 302–432.

[15] Adriaan Roland Holst, *Deirdre en de zonen van Usnach* (Palladium, Hijman, Stenfert Kroese en Van der Zande; Arnhem, 1920).

[16] Adriaan Roland Holst, 'De dood van Cuchulainn van Murhevna' ('The death of Cuchulainn of Murhevna'). It was first published, remarkably enough, in the year of the Easter Rising, *De Gids* 80(1) (1916b), 360–71. Later it was published as a book by Stichting, 'De Roos' (Utrecht, 1951); a second edition was published by De Bezige Bij, Amsterdam, in 1954 as the first in the *Robijnenboekjes* series.

[17] See, Maartje Draak, 'De gecompliceerde bronnen van Holst's Ierse prozaverhalen. (Het werk van de filoloog)', *De Nieuwe Taalgids* 68 (1975), 31–45.

[18] Maartje Draak, 'In memoriam Adrianus Roland Holst', *Jaarboek van de Maatschappij der Nederlandse Letterkunde* (1977), 25–32: 26.

[19] Jan van der Vegt, *A. Roland Holst: biografie* (De Prom; Baarn, 2000) and *Naar Ierland varen* (Nijgh en Van Ditmar; The Hague, 1976).

[20] In a poem on the occasion of Vestdijk's fiftieth birthday, 17 October 1948, 'O Gij, die sneller schrijft dan God kan lezen', published in the literary journal *Podium's* special issue on Vestdijk. Cited in Wim Hazeu, 'Hermans en Vestdijk', *De Gids* 168(11–12) (2005), 949–58: 950; and see also Bert Bakker, Gerrit Borgers, Jan Hulsker, Jurriaan Schrofer and Ellen Warmond, *S. Vestdijk* [Schrijversprentenboek 2] (De Bezige Bij; Amsterdam, 1958), 30; also available online at: http://www.dbnl.org/tekst/bakk002sves01_01/ bakk002sves01_01_0002.php?q=Podium Vestdijknummer#hl2, fig. 46 (21 March 2018).

[21] In addition to the fifty novels, he wrote seven volumes of short stories, twenty-two volumes of poetry, eighteen collections of essays and criticism. 'He was a unique phenomenon in Dutch literature, and it is unlikely that there are many other literatures that can boast a writer of his calibre and versatility. His production was staggering', see, Meijer, *Literature of the Low Countries*, 343.

[22] See, Eric Montague Beekman, *The verbal empires of Simon Vestdijk and James Joyce* (Rodopi; Amsterdam, 1983). Simon Vestdijk's most important essays on Joyce are 'Hoofdstukken over Ulysses' (written in 1934), in *Lier en Lancet* (Nijgh en Van Ditmar; Rotterdam, 1939), 90–125; and 'Afscheid van Joyce' (written in 1941), in *De Poolsche Ruiter* (F.G. Kroonder; Bussum, 1946), 46–52. See, Joris Duytschaever, 'James Joyce's impact on Simon Vestdijk's early fiction', in Pierre Brachin, Jan Goossens, P.K. King and J. de Rooij (eds), *Dutch Studies: an annual review of the language, literature and life of the Low Countries*, vol. 2 (Martinus Nijhoff; The Hague, 1976), 48–74: 52. See also, Geert Lernout and Wim van Mierlo (eds), *The reception of James Joyce in Europe* (2 vols, Continuum; London, 2004), vol. 1, 143.

[23] Simon Vestdijk, *Ierse nachten* (Nijgh en Van Ditmar; Rotterdam, 1946) and *De vijf roeiers* (Nijgh en Van Ditmar; Rotterdam, 1951). British colonial rule is also portrayed very critically in Vestdijk's earlier novel *Rumeiland: uit de papieren van Richard Beckford behelzende het relaas van zijn lotgevallen op Jamaica 1737–1738* (Nijgh en Van Ditmar; Rotterdam, 1940), set in eighteenth-century Jamaica, the German translation of which, *Die Fahrt nach Jamaica* (Rohrer Verlag; Brünn, 1941, transl. by G.K. Schauer) was also very successful. See, S.A.J. van Faassen, 'Vestdijk en zijn Duitse vertalingen, 1937–1949: De correspondentie tussen S. Vestdijk, G.K. Schauer en de Rudolf M. Rohrer Verlag', *Vestdijkkroniek* 87 (1995), 1–74. The novel was later also translated into English as *Rum Island* (John Calder; London, 1963, transl. by B.K. Bowes).

[24] See, José Lanters, 'Simon Vestdijk and the Irish literary tradition', *Études irlandaises* 14 (1) (1989), 105–15: 105–6. Vestdijk pointed out that *Ierse nachten* was not based

on his reading of Joyce: 'For the typically Irish atmosphere, Joyce can be neglected. He is far too ironic and moreover, he only knows Dublin.', quoted in Theun de Vries (ed.), *S. Vestdijk, Brieven uit de oorlogsjaren aan Theun de Vries* (Nederlands Letterkundig Museum en Documentatiecentrum; The Hague, 1968), 78.

[25] See, Hugo Brandt Corstius, 'Wat is Iers? Wat is hysterisch?', *NRC Handelsblad*, 29 April 1994, 24.

[26] Extensive discussions on the Irish elements in these novels ensued; see, for instance, P. Kralt, *Door nacht en ontijd: de Ierse romans van S. Vestdijk* (Huis aan de Drie Grachten; Amsterdam, 1983) and Rudy Cornets de Groot, 'Hendrik Cramers verhaal', *Ladders in de leegte* (Uitgeverij Nijgh & Van Ditmar; The Hague, 1981), 47–56, which is also available online, at: http://www.cornetsdegroot.com/ladders-in-de-leegte-81/hendrik-cramers-verhaal/ (28 February 2018).

[27] Lanters, 'Simon Vestdijk and the Irish literary tradition', 108–9.

[28] Vestdijk: 'Dit brengt mij op Iersche nachten. Inderdaad is het uitgangspunt voor deze roman niet voor mij geweest de Iersche *kwestie*, maar het Iersche *bijgeloof*, dat mij eerlijk gezegd veel méér interesseert, en dat mij ook een gunstiger aanknoopingspunt schijnt voor een roman. Een sociale roman zou je ook heel goed over Drente kunnen schrijven, maar deze lieden zijn zoo verdomd onemotioneel.' He wrote this in a letter dated 17 July 1943; see de Vries (ed.), *S. Vestdijk, Brieven uit de oorlogsjaren aan Theun de Vries*, 77.

[29] As cited in Lanters, 'Simon Vestdijk and the Irish literary tradition', 133. For the original, see Vestdijk's letter from 17 July 1943, in which he wrote 'Verder was ik uiteraard eenigszins gehandicapt doordat ik dit boek in déze tijd schreef en niet al te veel tegen Engeland te keer wou gaan. Want, dat zul je wel met mij eens zijn, zoodra men zich ook maar íets dieper gaat begeven in de Iersche kwestie, in haar sociale, cultureele en historische aspecten, is men gedwongen partij te kiezen tegen Engeland!'; published in de Vries (ed.), *S. Vestdijk, Brieven uit de oorlogsjaren aan Theun de Vries*, 77.

[30] Adriaan Venema reproaches Vestdijk for having played into the hands of Nazi propaganda by seeking this German translation of *Irish nights* and thereby emphasising the anti-British tendency of the novel; see Adriaan Venema, *Schrijvers, uitgevers en hun collaboratie*, IIIb, *S. Vestdijk* (De Arbeiderspers; Amsterdam, 1991). For a critical review, see, for instance, Jan Bank, 'Literatuur en Duitse bezetting, 1940–1945', *BMGN: Low Countries Historical Review* 110 (2) (1995), 224–37.

[31] See, Vestdijk's letter from 28 February 1943. Like his colleagues outside the *Kultuurkamer* he refrained from publishing anything during the Nazi Occupation, but he allowed translations of his work in Germany, and had already sent the manuscript of *Ierse nachten* to the publishing house of Rudolf M. Rohrer Verlag, Brünn, Wien and Leipzig. See, de Vries (ed.), *S. Vestdijk, Brieven uit de oorlogsjaren aan Theun de Vries*, 63–9.

[32] Jan Gerhard Toonder, *Kasteel in Ierland* (Commissie voor de Collectieve Propaganda van het Nederlandse Boek; Amsterdam, 1970).

[33] See, for instance, Marten Toonder, 'De Keltische schemering', in Adriaan van Dis (ed.), *Ierland. Verhalen van een land* (Bibliotheek voor de literaire reiziger) (Meulenhoff; Amsterdam, 1983), 7–15: 15, where he describes his experiences with the supernatural, 'the Shee' and writes that despite changes brought about by Ireland's joining the EEC, Ireland 'is still a great, quiet fairy-tale land of mountains, lakes, rivers and empty beaches and daily rain showers and long twilights. And that is the true life ..., as we in

the Netherlands do not know it'. See also, Marten Toonder, *Autobiografie* (De Bezige Bij; Amsterdam, 2010).

[34] Toonder, *Kasteel in Ierland*, 23. Unless otherwise indicated, translations are the author's own.

[35] Toonder, *Kasteel in Ierland*, 134.

[36] Toonder, *Kasteel in Ierland*, 150.

[37] Leon de Winter, *Zoeken naar Eileen W.* (Wolters-Noordhoff; Groningen, 1996); series Grote Lijsters Nr. 4 (literaire reeks voor scholieren).

[38] de Winter, *Zoeken naar Eileen W.*, 8.

[39] de Winter, *Zoeken naar Eileen W.*, 87.

[40] See, for instance, Jaak de Maere, 'Leon de Winter: op zoek naar Eileen W.', *Dietsche Warande en Belfort* 126 (1981), 701–4. For a discussion of the novel's reception in newspaper reviews, see, Tonny van Winssen's afterword, 'Leon de Winter', in the novel's edition for use in schools cited above, de Winter, *Zoeken naar Eileen W.*, 185–90: 188–90.

[41] See, comments on: https://www.moviemeter.nl/film/2403/info/ (28 February 2018): 'Tijdens een filmavond in Eindhoven in 1988 vertelde Leon de Winter een boek te hebben willen schrijven over een onmogelijke liefde. De keuze was: een verhaal over een Palestijns/Israëlisch koppel, of een verhouding tussen een katholiek en een protestants persoon uit Ierland. Dit laatste is het geworden, en de in het boek meer aanwezige Eileen (=Isolde) en Kevin (=Tristan) overkomt zo goed als volledig datgene dat het genoemde liefdesverhaal Tristan en Isolde behelst.'

[42] Renate Dorrestein, *Een sterke man* (Uitgeverij Contact; Amsterdam, 1994), 243, but here from the critical feminist point of view of Belle, the eponymous strong man's wife, who feels cheated in her subservient role as housekeeper and identifies with Tristan's jealous wife, Iseult of the White Hands.

[43] Dorrestein, *Een sterke man*, 9.

[44] See, Mariette Hermans, 'Een per ongeluk gepleegde moord. Het beeld van Ierland in twee moderne Nederlandse romans', *Surplus* 10 (5) (1996), 10–11.

[45] See, Rosemarie Buikema and Lies Wesseling, *Het heilige huis: De gotieke vertelling in de Nederlandse literatuur* (Amsterdam University Press; Amsterdam, 2006); see, in particular, the chapter on Renate Dorrestein's 'violent women' (89–102).

[46] Dorrestein, *Een sterke man*, 183 and 124.

[47] Dorrestein, *Een sterke man*, 121.

[48] Dorrestein, *Een sterke man*, 157f.

[49] Dorrestein, *Een sterke man*, 181.

[50] See, Joep Leerssen's discussion of images of the Irish in Beller and Leerssen (eds), *Imagology*, 191–4.

[51] Vonne van der Meer, *Spookliefde: een Iers verhaal* (De Bezige Bij: Amsterdam, 1995).

[52] Hermans, 'Een per ongeluk gepleegde moord', 10.

[53] Hermans, 'Een per ongeluk gepleegde moord', 11.

[54] Agnes Andeweg, 'Time and again: anarchronism and the gothic in Vonne van der Meer's *Spookliefde*', *Journal of Dutch Literature* 3 (2) (2012), 68–84: 70.

[55] Andeweg, 'Time and again', 78. Andeweg points out that van der Meer converted to Catholicism, which became public knowledge in 1996, raising many eyebrows and often negatively colouring the reception of her work in the secularised Netherlands. See also, Agnes Andeweg, *Griezelig gewoon: Gotieke verschijningen in Nederlandse romans*,

1980–1995 (Amsterdam University Press; Amsterdam, 2011); see, in particular, the chapter 'Het verlangen naar verlangen: *Spookliefde* van Vonne van der Meer', 133–56.

[56] Leerssen points out that '[e]gregious recent examples of national clichés, or nationally stereotyped characters, can be found more easily in trivial genres ... than in "serious" recent and contemporary literature', see Beller and Leerssen (eds), *Imagology*, 354.

[57] Afra Beemsterboer, *Een Iers sprookje* (Uitgeverij Westfriesland; Hoorn, 2003), *Als alle anderen* (Uitgeverij Westfriesland; Hoorn, 2007); and Wilma Hollander *Dans der liefde* (Uitgeverij Cupido; Soest, 2010). My special thanks to Dorli Krajenbrink-Fässler for her summaries and critical comments of these novels.

[58] See Cees Nooteboom, *Nootebooms Hotel* (Atlas; Amsterdam, 2002), translated as *Nomad's hotel. Travels in time and space* (Harvill Secker; London, 2006; transl. by Ann Kelland). Another example is the prominent author J.J. (Johan Jacob) Voskuil, who includes a section on his cycle tour in Ireland in his travelogue *Gaandeweg. Voettochten 1983–1992* (Van Oorschot; Amsterdam, 2006). Voskuil describes Ireland as a country that once must have been magically beautiful but is now completely spoiled by cars, bungalows and litter.

[59] Zwiers, *Mijn Ierland*, 11.

PART II b   Literary Representations
in Comparative
Perspectives

Irish literature in Italy and in German-speaking countries

Fiorenzo Fantaccini and
Anna Fattori

The aim of this chapter is to present a concise, comparative overview of the reception of Irish culture in Italy and German-speaking countries.[1] Where possible, similarities and differences in the reception of Irish culture in the two different contexts will be highlighted. The chapter will first take a cursory glance at Italy's and Germany's perception of Ireland from the seventeenth to the nineteenth century and it will then concentrate on some major issues relating to Irish–Italian and Irish–German cultural inter-relations in the twentieth century.

When exploring the relationship between the Emerald Isle and Germany over the centuries, it is clear that, on the one hand, they considered each other as being related in some manner, not because of a shared Roman Catholicism (as was the case for Ireland and Italy), but because they both often considered England, especially in the twentieth century, the common 'enemy', and this produced a sort of 'mirror effect'. On the other hand, along with consciousness of this analogy, awareness of Ireland's alterity, especially in terms of its Celtic background, has always been a cause for curiosity among Germans. The field of Celtic Studies was founded by Johann Kaspar Zeuss (1806–1856) who, in 1847, was appointed professor of history at the University of Munich. The first studies about the dialect of the Aran Islanders, which was considered the last repository of Gaelic and therefore the key to the exploration of the Celtic language, were written by German scholars who visited the islands, some of them before the author J.M. Synge did; again, awareness of the connection between the Celtic and Indo-Germanic languages was a result of German scholarship.[2]

FROM THE ORIGINS TO 1800

Before 1700, contacts between Irish, German and Italian cultures mainly involved Irish monks on the continent, who had a notable influence on the development of European culture of the pre-modern age.[3] In 614, St Columbanus, who was the first of a number of missionaries who visited or settled in Italy,[4] founded Bobbio Abbey, one of the most important and powerful monastic and cultural centres in Europe in the Middle Ages. He established a 'Scriptorium', a copying library, holding more than 700 codices, which contributed to the reception of Irish hagiography in Italy: Dante could not have conceived his idea of the Otherworld without knowing *Purgatorium Sancti Patricii* (dating from *c.* 1190), a text that was pivotal in establishing the stereotypical image of a 'fabulous'[5] Ireland in Italian Medieval, Renaissance and Baroque literature. Accounts of the *Purgatorium* provided an interesting point of reference for the German *Volksbuch* (chapbook) *Fortunatus* (produced in 1509) too.

After the Flight of the Earls, many Irishmen (monks and students) left their country and sought their fortunes in various Catholic nations

Fiorenzo Fantaccini and Anna Fattori

on the continent. Many of them decided to settle in Prague, one of the main towns of the German empire. Here in 1629 they founded a Franciscan college, which in the course of time became the most notable centre of diffusion of Irish culture in Central Europe. The Irish college in Rome was established in 1628 and was governed by the Jesuits from 1635 to 1772.

The role of Irish literature in the making of modern German literature

If, up to the eighteenth century, there was a perception of Ireland as distinct from England and Scotland, it was only in the idea of the Emerald Isle as the land of saints and scholars, of legends and myths. In eighteenth-century Germany the need for a national consciousness and a culture with peculiar national features was very strong; a new German literature was beginning to develop, trying to find its own identity. After the appearance of Sterne's, Goldsmith's and Swift's narratives, Irish literature played a significant role in the 'teutonisation of German literature'.[6] In a way, from the very beginning Irish literature gave a decisive impulse to German literature. According to the *fable convenue*, the German word *empfindsam*, which refers to 'new' literature (*empfindsame Literatur, Empfindsamkeit*) that was moving away from French Classicism and looking with interest at Britain, was suggested by Lessing in 1768 to Sterne's translator, Johann Bode, as the translation for the English word 'sentimental' in the German version of the *Sentimental journey*.[7] Recent scholarship has found that the adjective *empfindsam* had wrongly been considered a coinage by Bode, since it already existed before he used it.[8] Nevertheless, it is unquestionable that the mood pervading Sterne's 'unnatural narrative' left its characteristic mark on some German novels of the second half of the eighteenth century.[9] The same can be said of other Irish writers of the eighteenth century, such as Oliver Goldsmith and Jonathan Swift. It would be inconceivable to imagine Goethe's representation of nature in *Die Leiden des jungen Werther* without Goldsmith's *Vicar of Wakefield*, a novel Goethe had read and appreciated. Furthermore, the young Goethe had translated Goldsmith's poem 'The deserted village' and had been affected by its melancholic tone, caused by the consciousness that civilisation would destroy the rural way of life. This was a topic peculiar to his *Werther* as well, in which we find some very emotional verses from the 'Songs of Selma' from the Ossianic poems edited by MacPherson.[10] During Goethe's Weimar period, some Irish scholars visited the acclaimed author to discuss their translations, for instance Charles Des Vœux, who was translating Goethe's *Tasso*, and Charles Knox, who was preparing the English version of the first part of his *Faust*. They made the patriarch and the *Weimarer Kreis* familiar with Irish culture and issues.[11] In addition to the above mentioned Ossianic poetry, a pivotal role in stimulating interest in Gaelic culture in Germany, and also in creating the field of Celtic Studies, was played by the debate over the authenticity of the texts collected by MacPherson. A special place in this debate was occupied by Johann Gottfried Herder, who wrote several essays in favour of the authenticity argument.

Ireland and Italy as 'twin-countries': Catholicism, Goldsmith, Berchet and Manzoni

Between the sixteenth and eighteenth century in Italy, Ireland was essentially perceived of as a Catholic 'companion'; this attitude was reinforced by the diffusion of numerous writings about the 'counter reformation' and of polemical essays dealing with the persecution of Irish Catholics. There were, though, a few exceptions. The debate surrounding Ossian poetry was intense and passionate: in 1763 Melchiorre Cesarotti produced a much-acclaimed and popular translation of part of the poems, much appreciated by Ugo Foscolo, Vincenzo Monti and Vittorio Alfieri. Cesarotti's work initiated a controversy about the authenticity of the poems that, as happened in Germany, aroused deep interest in things Celtic. In 1764 Camillo Zampieri and Giambatista Roberti came out against the authenticity of the poems, but, in spite of this, their popularity did not diminish, and in 1772 Cesarotti published a revised and enlarged version of his translations. Together with Cesarotti, Giovanni Berchet occupies a pivotal position in the development of Romantic aesthetics in Italy: he is the author of the 1816 Italian Romantic manifesto, the *Lettera semiseria di Grisostomo al suo figliolo* ('Semi-serious letter of Chrysostom to his son'), in which he foregrounds the positive aspects of the new Romantic movement by means of the example of two ballads by the German poet G.A. Burger. The letter is an important

Fiorenzo Fantaccini and Anna Fattori

chapter in the history of European Romanticism. Berchet translated German poetry into Italian, but in 1810 he produced a version of Oliver Goldsmith's *The vicar of Wakefield*,[12] which allowed him 'to experiment with his own poetic style'.[13] He claimed that the study of modern foreign literatures, the rejection of academic language and the model provided by classics were essential in the creation of a new literature inspired by national and popular feelings and expressed in simple language: in his opinion Goldsmith represented a good example of this. In Alessandro Manzoni's novel *I promessi sposi* (first published in 1827; published in English in 1834 as *The betrothed*), the notion of 'Providence'—the rational order governing the manifestation of God's will in human history in general and in the lives of individuals—owes much to the quixotic faith in human virtue and integrity of Goldsmith's Vicar Primrose; both novels share a complicated interwoven plot centred on recurring misfortunes and a prevailing religious theme.[14]

The echo of eighteenth-century Irish novelists in Germany and Italy

With reference to the influence of Irish literature on German prose in the eighteenth century, it is worth focusing briefly on the rather neglected German writer Jean Paul (pseudonym of Johann Paul Friedrich Richter, 1763–1825). He wrote his humorous digressive novels under the spell of Sterne, and his satirical texts—*Essigfabrik* ('Vinegar factory'), as he calls them—under the influence of Swift. In his *Vorschule der Ästhetik* ('Introduction to aesthetics') he considers Sterne among all 'British' authors as the only one who, 'thanks to his cheerfulness, light-heartedness confining to superficiality and thanks to his gift of producing a moving and spontaneous prose', can be placed next to Goethe, though in a completely different literary landscape.[15] Jean Paul's novels, in particular his bestseller *Hesperus* (published in 1795), display some of the qualities that he attributes to Sterne and that particularly affected his early work.[16] Although he refers quite often to Sterne and Swift and some other Irish authors, it seems that in the *Vorschule* he mentions the Emerald Isle just once, namely in the passage where he speaks of 'gloomy Ireland', which has produced notable comic writers (Sterne, Swift and Hamilton), who in many cases had a 'very quiet and serious life'.[17] Jean Paul was a voracious reader and his interest in Swift, Sterne and others

must be considered as a part of his regard for English-language literature. In spite of the fact that he probably had only a vague awareness of
the Irishness of Swift and Sterne, Irish authors nevertheless left a notable
mark on his narrative. Novels such as *Die unsichtbare Loge* ('The invisible lodge') and *Hesperus* would not be the same without his 'dearest
digressions' and without the whimsical Sternian figures it features.[18]

Although Swift's *Gulliver's travels* exerted a limited impact on
eighteenth-century Italian literature, two notable examples are worth
mentioning here: Pietro Chiari's sentimental-adventurous novel published in 1760, *Uomo di un altro mondo* ('Man from another world'), and
the Venetian-Armenian writer Zaccaria Seriman's 1749 novel *I viaggi
di Enrico Wanton ai regni delle scimie e dei cinocefali* ('Enrico Wanton's
travels to the kingdoms of the monkeys and of the dogheaded').[19] The
Swiftian influence in Chiari's work is detectable in the general hatred
of humanity expressed by the main character, who resolves to live
'far from the madding crowd' and sets up a utopian community on
an island off the Japanese coast (where the islands visited by Gulliver
on his third journey were also situated). The debt owed by Seriman's
Enrico Wanton to Swift is much more substantial, since the first-
person narration follows the scheme of *Gulliver's travels*, especially the
Lilliput and Brobdingnag sections; the monkeys ('*scimie*') of the novel
are directly inspired by Swift's 'yahoos', and like Swift, Seriman satirises
the corruption of Venetian government, society, science and religion.

In Italy, Sterne found in Ugo Foscolo one of his greatest admirers.
Foscolo passionately translated his *Sentimental journey* and its style left
a notable mark on some of his texts. Likewise, Manzoni in *I promessi
sposi* was fascinated by Sterne's digressive way of narrating. Starting
from these premises, it is rather surprising that the first comprehensive book in Italy about Sterne and Italian culture was only published
as late as 1990, while in Germany, a ground-breaking and illuminating book—*Laurence Sterne und der deutsche Roman des 18 Jahrhunderts*
by Paul Michelsen—had appeared nearly 20 years earlier, in 1972.[20] In
more recent years the paradoxical, humorous and digressive Shandean
narrative style can be observed in the work of Carlo Emilio Gadda and
Alberto Arbasino. Gadda's linguistic invention owes much to Sterne's
influence, whereas the fragmentation and dissociative approach to
the narrative structure of a text is shared by both writers, who often

Fiorenzo Fantaccini and Anna Fattori

prefer a disordered, rambling and meandering process of narration. In Arbasino's words, his own books 'should not be read from beginning to end; they can be read in any direction'.[21]

NINETEENTH TO TWENTY-FIRST CENTURY

Travel literature

In the nineteenth century, travelogues and travel literature proved central in consolidating Irish-German cultural relations and in increasing reciprocal insight across the two different contexts. Up to the end of the eighteenth century, most of the German travellers who crossed the English Channel remained in southern England; if they moved farther, they rarely went beyond the border between England and Scotland, let alone crossing the Irish Sea, but this situation was soon due to change. Eoin Bourke has edited an anthology of 29 short pieces of reportage by German visitors to Ireland from the 1780s to the 1860s.[22] This remarkable collection of writings shows that several German travellers who enjoyed England did visit Ireland too, looking for romantic landscapes and Ossianic atmospheres. As they thought that Ireland would be similar to the democratic, idyllic England they had already seen, they were bitterly taken aback, if not shocked, by the poverty of the country and the harshness of everyday life. They could hardly believe in such a miserable, deplorable gap between the two societies and tended to assume that England and the landlord-tenant system were responsible for the pitiable conditions in Ireland.

The two most popular German accounts written in the nineteenth century were Prince Hermann von Pückler-Muskau's 1830 work, *Briefe eines Verstorbenen* ('Letters of a dead man') and Johann Georg Kohl's mammoth work *Reisen in Irland* ('Travels in Ireland', published in 1843).[23] For many years, these non-fictional volumes were regarded as the reference books for people interested in the Emerald Isle. Visiting German-speaking countries was obviously quite easy for an Irish traveller who might be touring the continent. Maria Edgeworth was one of the most important Irish travellers to German-speaking countries; through her accounts of her stay in Switzerland, she contributed to creating the ambivalent image of the Alps in Ireland.[24]

In addition to the exchanges and links that long existed between Ireland and Italy as the centre of Roman Catholicism (students for the priesthood were sent to Rome to complete their studies), in the nineteenth century Italian art also attracted a great number of architects, painters and sculptors from Ireland, some of whom often lived in the country for a long time.[25] In regard to the Irish gaze on Italy, Lady Morgan is the name to mention: her *Italy* (published in 1821) is a celebrated travelogue based on her sojourn in Italy between 1819 and 1820.[26] The book had a great impact on English-speaking readers as a result of her radical views on Italian politics and her support of Italy's aspirations to unity and independence. The book included outspoken criticism of the Papacy and Italian politics, and support for Italian republicanism. Her negative views on Italian women, whom she accused of being immoral and lacking a maternal instinct and education, was the cause of controversy among Italian literati.

On the Italian side, interest in Ireland was not so profound, as the country was a far-away destination and one that was difficult to reach. The only contribution worth mentioning here is *Diario del soggiorno in Inghilterra e Irlanda 1796–1801*, by the eighteenth-century writer Giuseppe Acerbi: his notes deal with monuments and attractions in Dublin and County Wicklow, but also bear witness to a deep interest in the social and political situation of Ireland and to Acerbi's support for Henry Grattan and the Irish cause.[27]

A new perspective: the two-sidedness of Ireland abroad

Beginning in the nineteenth-century, a perceived two-sidedness to Ireland becomes clearer and clearer in German literature. On the one hand, the image of Ireland as an exotic island, as the country of myths and legends, is kept alive, thanks, for example, to Grimm's translation of Thomas Crofton Croker's fairy tales, the German version of which was published in 1826 and contributed to the *Biedermeierisierung* (domestication) of Irish legends and of the Celtic setting. On the other hand, concern for Ireland now was not so much for its literature as its social history; there was a growing awareness of political oppression, landlordism and induced famine. There was 'sympathy for Ireland's woes', as O'Neill argues.[28] Some of the poems of the committed literature

Fiorenzo Fantaccini and Anna Fattori

of Young Germany revolve around Ireland and express indignation at the miserable conditions and injustice evident in the country.[29] In Georg Weerth's poem 'Deutsche und Ire' ('German and Irishman'), we find evidence of awareness by both the Irishman and the German of their common, sad condition of exile in the cold night of inhospitable England, where they feel they are 'companions ... in joy / and sorrow— for both of them after all were / nothing but poor devils'.[30]

Ireland's literary impact on Germany and Italy in the first decades of twentieth century: the three 'Giants' and the case of Brecht–Synge

Even though in the nineteenth century there were, as we have seen, some texts showing interest in Ireland, it was not until the beginning of the twentieth century that Irish literature began to have a serious and continuous impact on German and Italian writers. Starting from this period, Ireland is not merely perceived as 'the island behind the island', but, thanks to the translations of texts by Wilde, Shaw, Yeats, Synge, Beckett and Joyce, it is considered a country with its own culture, literature and *Weltanschauung.*

Of the three Irish literary giants of the beginning of the twentieth century—Wilde, Shaw and Yeats—it was Wilde who had an immediate success in German-speaking countries. He seemed to represent the anti-realistic concerns of the George-Kreis, a circle of writers who gathered around Stephan George (1868–1933) and who were very close to French symbolism. Shaw's plays were successfully produced in German theatres by the Austrian director Max Reinhardt, and the Irish playwright became for a period the 'king of the German stage'.[31] Yeats was initially somewhat ignored, probably in part because of the bad quality of the translations of his work and maybe, as Kosok argues, because German culture already had its own 'German' Yeats in the figure of Rilke.[32] He was then enthusiastically rediscovered in the 1970s.

Paradoxically, the German reception of poets such as Thomas Moore and W.B. Yeats, whose Irishness in setting, themes and topics is immediately evident, was much slower and less straightforward when compared with the immediate resonance of Wilde and Shaw.

Of course, a prominent author of plays such as J.M. Synge could not be overlooked by a *Dramaturg* like Bertolt Brecht; he not only chose

The playboy of the Western world as one of the European classics to be performed by the *Berliner Ensemble*, but he also drew inspiration from Synge's plays for his own theatre.[33] Thus, Synge's plays, which seem so rooted in the socio-cultural and geographical context of the west of Ireland, and therefore difficult to comprehend outside Ireland, achieved wide-spread European recognition. It was to Brecht's merit that he realised that Synge's theatre could be 'Europeanised' and re-forged to express the current affairs of other nations on the continent. When, in 1936, the German *Dramaturg* was asked to write a play about the Spanish civil war, he produced *Die Gewehre der Frau Carrar* ('Señora Carrar's rifles', which appeared in 1937) using as a model Synge's 1903 work *Riders to the sea*, which he had read in a German translation of 1935; he retained the one-act form and several features of Synge's style that he had already been able to appreciate in the original language.

About fifteen years before, he had read Synge in English and had been fascinated by his unusual style, deriving from his ability to reproduce in English the language patterns of Gaelic. The German playwright was impressed by the dynamism arising from Synge's distinctive usage and positioning of verbs. In an illuminating essay on Synge, Kuno Raeber and Brecht, Anthony Roche observes very rightly that 'Brecht's attention to the matter [placement of verbs in Synge's work] indicates that he is more interested in a subtlety and range of verbal action in his domestic practice than he is often credited with'.[34]

Frau Carrar is not a translation but an adaptation of *Riders*. In Brecht's play the set is shifted from the Aran Islands to 1930s Spain; the eponymous protagonist, after losing her children in the war, changes her position and decides to fight against Franco. Although Maurya and Carrar move in two opposite directions, producing two different if not antithetic endings (passivity and resignation in Synge, activity and revolution in Brecht), in the two plays it is possible to find a similar beginning, parallel scenes, suffering women, and social concern, though Brecht's purpose was of a much more immediate nature. He intended his play to be a stimulus to recruit volunteers to fight for the Republicans against Fascism. Both Maurya and Carrar are archetypical Mother figures who struggle against overwhelming forces (the sea, war). A very similar protagonist appears in Brecht's 1939 work *Mutter Courage und ihre Kinder* ('Mother courage and her children'), which should be seen in relation to *Frau Carrar* and which is indebted to Synge to an even greater extent. Brecht must have clearly perceived that Yeats's characterisation of Synge as a 'pure artist' who 'seemed by nature unfitted to think a political thought' was misleading.[35] His adaptation of *Riders* can be considered the earliest, very convincing recognition of Synge's political commitment.[36] In the second half of the twentieth century, the politicised Synge also appealed to some playwrights of East Germany; in 1956 Peter Hacks translated and staged *The playboy of the Western world* in the Berliner Ensemble, depicting the main figure as a political rebel.[37]

In 1914 *Tragedie irlandesi di William Butler Yeats* ('Irish tragedies by W.B. Yeats') appeared, translated and introduced by Carlo Linati.[38] The latter—an author of impressionistic novels, essays and travelogues—has a unique place in the reconstruction of Italo-Irish literary relationships. He was the first to devote his energies to the diffusion in Italy of the new voices of Irish literature, translating not only Yeats's plays, but also works by J.M. Synge, Lady Gregory and James Joyce.[39] His love for Ireland and its literature originated by pure chance: around 1910 the musician Franco Leoni asked him to translate *Riders to the sea*, a play he intended to set to music.

Synge's tragedy prompted Linati to read Yeats's plays, and he decided to translate them into Italian. To do this he went to London, where he met Yeats. He describes the poet as 'very much taken with a scenic mysticism, to those refined questions of light, darkness and mystery that were fashionable in Italy too, but many years later'.[40] He then read Synge's and Lady Gregory's plays and decided to translate them too. It was not an easy task. Linati's rendering of Yeats's, Synge's and Lady Gregory's language into Italian is not without faults; his taste for imposing Tuscan idioms and erudite nuances on the originals is somewhat disconcerting. Linati revised all his translations accurately in the following years, and the result was less inventive and more faithful to the source texts. As a consequence of his translating Irish writers, Linati came into contact with James Joyce, who asked him to translate *Ulysses* into Italian and offered him an elaborate scheme of the novel's plot 'a sort of summary—key—skeleton—... (for home use only)', to facilitate Linati's work on the text.[41] Only a few short excerpts of Linati's attempts appeared, in 1929, but the scheme has since had a pivotal role in the interpretation of Joyce's masterpiece.[42] Linati's translations from Irish writers are still in print and have contributed to the popularity of Irish literature in Italy.

Due to the fact that Ireland had not imposed economic sanctions against Italy in the Italian–Ethiopian colonial conflict in 1934–35, and that in 1939 it declared its neutrality in international relations, from the mid-1930s Irish writers in Italy enjoyed a vast popularity, since they were not considered part of the expression of an enemy culture, as British writers were. A number of translations were published in the war years, especially of plays (by, for instance, Paul Vincent Carroll, Lennox Robinson, Sean O'Casey, Lord Dunsany, Joyce); these were also successfully produced on Italian stages.

Joyce in Germany and in Italy

If Joyce and Beckett were the Irish authors who probably exerted the greatest impact on European literature of the twentieth century, even though Irishness was perhaps less evident in their writing than in that of Synge or Yeats, who often made use of elements of folklore, this is due to the fact that they represented the human condition *par excellence*.[43] In German-speaking countries—as well as in Italy, together with Yeats—James Joyce can be regarded as the most influential Irish writer of the twentieth century.

Joyce's impact on both Italian and German-speaking culture is grounded in his biography. During his stay in Trieste he befriended Italo Svevo, who wrote an unfinished essay on him and whose narrative was inspired by Joyce's technique. In a parallel manner, Joyce contributed to the diffusion of Svevo's 1923 novel *La coscienza di Zeno* ('Zeno's conscience') in France. Joyce certainly inspired renowned Italian writers such as Gadda who, in his 1957 work *Quer pasticciaccio brutto de via Merulana* ('The awful mess on Via Merulana'), made extensive use of Roman dialect.[44] Nonetheless, the impact of the Irish writer in the Italian context can hardly be compared to his enormous influence on German literature. Finding a novelist in post-war Germany who was *not* indebted to Joyce is not easy. His link to German-speaking countries was multifaceted, and his stay in Zurich played an important role in enhancing his ties to German culture.[45]

As John Banville has noted, 'the figure of Joyce towers behind us, a great looming Easter Island effigy of the Father'.[46] This is especially true in the case of German and Italian literature. As early as 1928—the first German translation had appeared in 1927—Brecht stated that *Ulysses* was the book of the year.[47] It really seems that German writers and the German readership still take a special interest in this novel; in 2012, *Ulysses* was declared the best audio-book of the year.[48] Outstanding authors such as Hermann Broch, Alfred Döblin, Arno Schmidt, Wolfgang Koeppen and Wolfgang Hildesheimer were deeply influenced in their narrative by Joyce's innovative prose, both in terms of form and content. Even in very recent times, some authors have declared that the experience of reading *Ulysses* was a milestone in their perception of literature, as Joyce had already achieved what they intended to do. In this respect, statements by renowned authors are very clear, as in the case of Eimear McBride, winner of the 2014 Bailey's Women's Prize for Fiction: 'I started reading the book ... and just thought: that's it. Everything I have written before is rubbish and today is the beginning of something else.'[49] A similar, but more radical, statement is to be found in a letter the Austrian author Hermann Broch wrote in 1931:

> I see in Ulysses a perfect realisation of everything which it
> is possible to express in a novel. That goal which I had in my
> mind in my work, 'to get beneath the skin' in my writing, I
> find completely fulfilled in Joyce, and I am convinced that
> literature, insofar as it remains an expression of modern life,
> will come more and more under the Joycean influence.[50]

The lecture Hermann Broch delivered in 1932 at the Wiener *Volkshochschule, Joyce und die Gegenwart* ('Joyce and the present time') was a full-scale literary and philosophical comment on *Ulysses*.[51] Broch made special reference to the author's ability to capture and illustrate the *Zeitgeist* through an innovative technique, which Broch himself would later use in his *Der Tod des Vergil.* The article by the Austrian writer can be considered one of the earliest stylistic analyses of *Ulysses.* It even contains an accurate calculation of the relationship between *erzählte Zeit* ('narrated time') and *Erzähl Zeit* ('narration time'): '16 hours in 1200 pages makes 75 pages per hour, that means more than one page per minute, nearly one line per second'.[52] Broch's publisher Rheinverlag was also Joyce's German publisher; hence, the two authors kept in close contact for several years. When, in 1938, after the *Anschluss,* Broch was imprisoned, Joyce and other authors petitioned for his release, thus enabling him to leave Austria.

Unlike Broch, who openly acknowledged his debt to Joyce, Alfred Döblin was rather reluctant in expanding on Joyce's influence on his work:

> Joyce is a magnificent writer, a pioneer of style, and thus also of narrative technique. I myself am not able to analyze whether and which Joycean influences are demonstrable in my last book. I do know, however, that Joyce has nothing to do with the essential parts of my work; only peripheral similarities are concerned.[53]

Actually, analogies are not as 'peripheral' as Döblin observes; not all the points of contact between *Ulysses* and Döblin's *Berlin Alexanderplatz* can be attributed to the *Zeitgeist,* although the *Großstadtroman* was a common genre in expressionism and in the *Neue Sachlichkeit.* On the basis of the original manuscript of the German author, scholars have argued that Döblin had revised the opening lines of the novel and expanded the use of interior monologues after reading Joyce.[54] Indeed, Joyce possibly influenced Döblin's extensive use of certain narrative techniques; moreover, reading the Irish author prompted him to delve into taboo and disturbing issues.

Arno Schmidt was also another fervent admirer of Joyce who is worth mentioning. In his *Zettel's Traum* ('Zettel's dream', published in 1970), a 'monstrous but fascinating book, ... an attempt to outjoyce Joyce', he drove the style of *Finnegans wake* to its extreme.[55]

Before the 1950s, interest in Joyce in Italy was limited to short, critical contributions and attempts at translation. Even though Giulio De Angelis completed his still unsurpassed translation of *Ulysses* in 1950, it still took ten years to see it published due to copyright reasons.[56] The final version was revised and edited by Giorgio Melchiori. His intense and productive research activity on Joyce started in 1951 with the essay 'Joyce and the eighteenth century novelists', and continued for more

Fiorenzo Fantaccini and Anna Fattori

than fifty years.[57] Melchiori's numerous and seminal contributions make him the central figure of Joycean studies in Italy.[58] In the 1980s he set up a research group in Rome, organised many initiatives and promoted many publications, including the *Joyce Studies in Italy* series started in 1984. Between 1982 and 1983 he coordinated the publication of an annotated translation of the *Telemachia* and the first four chapters of *Finnegans wake*.[59]

We can only speak of Joyce's influence on Italian writers from the mid-1950s. The novelist Antonio Pizzuto and the poet Amelia Rosselli should be mentioned as the writers who more than any others fell under the spell of Joyce. For his use of fragmented time and his lexical inventiveness, which encompasses multiple languages and cultures, Pizzuto was called 'the Sicilian Joyce'. Amelia Rosselli considered *Ulysses* 'the Bible of [her] twenties' (*la bibbia dei suoi vent'anni*).[60] Joyce's daring linguistic techniques fascinated her; her poetry and prose books are a 'testament to a unique, multiform sincerity and to a fiendishly restless mind, synthesizing a literary tradition', which included the Joycean example.[61] Joyce's narrative techniques (stream-of-consciousness, interior monologue) also cast a spell on Dino Buzzati and Giuseppe Berto, but most of all on Raffaele La Capria, whose use of overlapping time sequences in the complex, polyphonic structure of his second novel, *Ferito a morte* ('The mortal wound', published in 1961), testifies to the Joycean lesson in narrative form.[62] Last but not least, the name of Umberto Eco should be mentioned; Eco is the author of *Le poetiche di Joyce* ('The middle ages of Joyce: the aesthetics of Chaosmos', as titled in a 1989 translation).[63] This is one of the most consistent and systematic readings of Joyce's works, and in particular of *Ulysses* and *Finnegans wake*, two texts that include the history of all contemporary poetics, but that also enlighten their scholastic-medieval matrix. *Finnegans wake* in particular combines the aesthetics of Thomas Aquinas with the Italian humanist-historicist tradition of Vico and Giordano Bruno and is considered a fluctuating textual machine, the exemplary 'open work'.[64]

Yeats, Beckett and Heaney in Italy

It is well known that Montale, the 1975 Nobel Prize winner for literature, loved poetry in English: he translated works by Shakespeare, Blake,

Hardy, Joyce and Eliot, among many others, but Yeats occupies a particular place in Montale's work. He is the poet Montale liked most.[65] He met the Irish poet once, at Ezra Pound's villa in Rapallo, and his memory of Yeats is of a man with a prophet-like aura. Whatever his view of Yeats as a person, Montale's judgements of his work, scattered throughout his critical writings, are celebratory: Yeats is the greatest poet in the English language, he is a genius of verse, a poet in 'C major'. Most of all, Montale appreciates Yeats's formal elegance, his verse technique, the musicality of his poetry and the rigour of its formal structure: all of Yeats's poems are perfect 'objects', and for this reason they are almost untranslatable. In spite of this, Montale included four of Yeats's poems in his *Quaderno di traduzioni* ('Translation notebook').[66] Montale's translations are remarkable: he chooses a different versification with the obliteration of end rhymes, which he recreates through complex chains of internal alliterations, assonances and rhymes; he attempts to render the prevailing English monosyllabism by means of an extensive use of monosyllabic or disyllabic Italian words. Montale not only appreciates Yeats's perfect 'compromise between sound and meaning', the coincidence of 'form and substance' in Yeats's poetry, but feels a connection with the Irish poet for biographical reasons: they were both elected to the senate of their respective country and had a public political role, and their poems share a recurring theme—namely, aging and old age.

Through the example of Yeats, and thanks to his translation activity, Montale was able to free Italian poetry from its provincialism, inaugurating a new season for Italian poetry. Lucio Piccolo was 'discovered' by Montale; the two poets shared an interest in Yeats.[67] Piccolo corresponded with the Irish poet; the extant replies by Yeats—Piccolo's missives have not surfaced yet—focus on mystical philosophy and on the terminology used in *A vision*. Yeats's influence on Piccolo's poetry is vast and deep. Piccolo shares with Yeats an interest in mystical-esoteric themes and symbolism. Piccolo's poem 'La torre' ('The tower') is very close to Yeats's 'The tower' in its description of the building as a symbol of the artist's individuality, of an elitist idea of poetry, and of a mind musing on the chaos of the world. They also share the image of stairs, which is symbolic of spiritual ascent. Piccolo's collection *Gioco a nascondere* ('Hide-and-seek', which appeared in 1967) opens with a wandering through the rooms of an ancestral house at twilight, and with the image

Fiorenzo Fantaccini and Anna Fattori

of the recurring cycles of time producing a gyre-like movement along the stairs of the building. The clash between a lofty and unforgettable past and a confused and violent present to be forgotten can be connected to similar images in Yeats's 'Meditations in time of war'.

If Yeats's and Joyce's presence in Italy has always been solid and fruitful, 'the history of Beckett's reception in Italy can be read as the history of the inability to react promptly to an oeuvre which was revolutionizing literary canons in two languages'.[68] The early reactions to Beckett's work attest a sort of 'embarrassment' by Italian writers and critics: Beckett's prose and poems remained little known before 1968, and, whereas Joyce was considered an example by the *neoavanguardia* writers, Beckett's name was controversial. Early reviews were generally dismissive, considering Beckett a rhetorical nihilist, a writer with no style and a negative model for Italian literati. In spite of this, several Italian authors (Giorgio Manganelli, Gabriele Frasca, Ermanno Cavazzoni, Gianni Celati and Edoardo Sanguineti) were fascinated by Beckett's style and used Beckettian narrative devices in their own works (the use of basic but significant objects; the Dantean paradigm and example; the 'mutism' of characters; a certain obsession with physical decadence; and the 'investigation of a fragmented self through a language which strives to be simple'[69]). As Aldo Tagliaferri, the author of the first monographic study published in Italy on Beckett (*Beckett e l'iperdeterminazione letteraria*, 'Beckett and literary hyperdetermination', printed in 1967), maintains, the few positive responses focused on Beckett's 'spirituality', and his philosophical, meditative theological attitude.[70]

One of the reasons for this 'embarrassment' is to be attributed to the poor quality of the first translations; they were generally inaccurate, with the original texts often rendered in a simplified and softened language. We owe much to Franco Quadri, Aldo Tagliaferri, Carlo Fruttero, Franco Lucentini and Gabriele Frasca for producing excellent, rigorous Italian versions of Beckett's prose, plays and poetry; they contributed to a new phase of Beckett's reception in Italy, which started in the mid-1980s, characterised by full appreciation of his aesthetics and language. Over the last 30 years, the Italian contribution to Beckett's scholarship has been significant. The monographs by Carla Locatelli, Daniela Caselli, Annamaria Cascetta and Frasca are excellent examples of critical rigour.

On the other hand, Beckett's drama, from the early 1950s on, has constituted a reference point for Italian theatre practitioners. In 1953 the original edition by Roger Blin of *Godot* was staged in Milan, with mild reactions and reviews, but the following year the first Italian production was successfully staged in Rome. Since then Beckett has been a constant presence on Italian stages, both in conservative, traditional circuits and also in 'manipulative', experimental, avant-garde ones, thus endowing Beckett with the status of a contemporary classic.

For Seamus Heaney, Italian culture represented a fundamental source of inspiration. Starting from the mid-1980s, he produced translations from Virgil, Dante, and in his later years from Giovanni Pascoli.[71] Heaney's deep love for Italy has been reciprocated. Since the early 1990s Heaney's poems and prose writings have been translated in periodicals, anthologies and collections, with huge success: all his poetry collections published so far are still in print. Heaney's role as the most appreciated and read poet in the English language in Italy was celebrated in 2016 with a 1,200-page annotated anthology entitled *Poesie scelte e raccolte dall'autore* ('Poems: selected and arranged by the author') in the prestigious Mondadori series 'I Meridiani'.[72] Interestingly, most of the translations of Heaney's poems have been made by poets (Franco Buffoni, Franco Fortini, Roberto Mussapi, Gilberto Sacerdoti, Roberto Sanesi, among others), and this undoubtedly demonstrates how important Heaney is today for Italian culture.

Heinrich Böll and post-war German literature

In the twentieth century, probably no European book could compete with Heinrich Böll's 1957 work *Irisches Tagebuch* (translated as *Irish journal* in 1967) in spreading interest for Ireland and its culture.[73] His *Journal* was perceived not just as a literary text, but as an evocative guide to 'the island behind the island', and it propelled a wave of enthusiasm for Ireland. Of course, for Böll, the book was not conceived of as a means to stimulate the *Reiselust* of the Germans, but as an individual account of his experience of travelling in Ireland. On the one hand, the sketches of the *Irisches Tagebuch* should be considered in the context of post-war Germany, that is as an account written from the point of view of a citizen coming to Ireland from a problematic, war-stressed country that was trying to quickly re-build its industry and economy and trying to cope with the problem of guilt. As Böll stated in one of his last interviews, at that time 'it was far from pleasant being German'.[74] On the other hand, as recent scholarship has pointed out, his *Tagebuch* should not be considered from this perspective only: in fact, Böll can be seen as one of the many authors who expressed their criticism of materialistic industrial society by fleeing to the partially self-constructed idyll of the Emerald Isle.[75] His attempt to travel as far as possible in space to escape from time, that is from German history, took him and his family to one of the most untouched and remote parts of Ireland. If this book still retains much of its allure, it is because Ireland is described as a Never-Never Land outside history and outside time, a sort of Thule where every individual can find shelter. The reason why Böll's legacy is still very much alive is because he refers to, confirms and partially creates significant aspects of Ireland *im Bild,* that is of the imagological complex linked to Ireland, showing that the romantic island which is the setting of myths and legends still exists: you just have to cross the English Channel and the Irish Sea to get there, and the farther you go from continental Europe, the more genuine the context is.[76] Of course, the 'iconic quality' of this apparently simple but actually 'sophisticated' text was and still is of central importance for its appeal to a German readership.[77] Böll's book has also been translated into Italian.[78] Although it cannot be said to be as successful as in Germany where it sold over a million copies, it is often included in the reading lists for Italian students of *Germanistik.*

Böll's view of Ireland has been referred to, broadened, quoted and in some cases criticised and corrected by a number of writers. Nearly 40 years after the appearance of the original book, the German-Jewish-Italian author Ralph Giordano published *Mein irisches Tagebuch* ('My Irish journal', 1996), which refers, not only in the title, to Böll's travel account. Though Giordano claims in the opening pages that his book does not depend on Böll's *Irish journal* ('My *Irish journal* [is] an independent work which is based on my own sources, my observations my experiences'), one can feel Böll's presence on every page.[79] Giordano himself is firmly convinced that the author of the *Irisches Tagebuch* would 'literally subscribe' to some of his descriptions.[80] The approach of the Irish-German Hugo Hamilton is quite different. In his 2007 publication *Die redselige Insel: Irisches Tagebuch* ('The isle of talking'), which displays formal analogies with the *Irisches Tagebuch*, he retraces Böll's travels across Ireland and describes the Irish landscapes and people in a fresh and literarily convincing way.[81] As stated by Gisela Holfter, 'the legacy picked up by Hamilton is the literary approach, the transformation of reality into a poetic truth'.[82] He takes single elements from Böll's sketches and proposes them back to us from the point of view of an insider, on the basis of his first-hand knowledge of the Irish context, including of current issues and problems.

Böll's influence is far from being exhausted; it seems that he has stimulated German writers to explore Ireland from the perspective of the 'outsider' and form their own opinions about it.[83] Heinrich Böll, 'the doyen of modern German hibernophiles', can, as the title of an article by Eda Sagarra reads, be considered the father of German tourism in Ireland. She observes that 'he can be regarded as having been a long-serving if unofficial expert and adviser to Bord Fáilte'.[84] It seems that this point of view is widely shared outside of literary circles too. When in 1992 Mary Robinson, the then president of Ireland, welcomed the former German president Richard von Weizsäcker, she said that Heinrich Böll could be a candidate for national saint, if Ireland did not already have St Patrick.[85] As Holfter very rightly observes, Böll is still the frame of reference for German authors writing on Ireland, but their approach is now broader, more nuanced and multifaceted, even if they find that the green 'island behind the island' is still the hideaway they long for.[86]

In the last few decades, Swiss-German authors have shown a keen interest in Ireland. Probably they are attracted by the Emerald Isle because of the liminal position of the two countries, both being 'marginal' voices within the context of a broader linguistic and cultural sphere; but they are perhaps also interested because of the peculiar insularity—geographical, in the case of Ireland, political, in the case of Switzerland—of the two nations.[87] Following in the steps of Böll's *Journal*, Claudia Storz, Gerold Späth, Margit Baur, Hansjörg Schertenleib and Rolf Lappert have written novels that depict Ireland as a green, friendly and magical island. From the point of view of imagology, they often reproduce established *clichés* about Ireland, contrasting its variety of landscapes with the dullness of Swiss everyday life (*Schweizer Enge*).[88] In many of these texts, one of the most frequent

Fiorenzo Fantaccini and Anna Fattori

motives in Swiss-German literature, the *Sehnsucht* of the sea, is used as a reminder of the positive otherness of the foreign country.[89] Another Swiss author whose fiction displays interest in Irish culture is Thomas Hürlimann. His novella *Fräulein Stark* ('Miss Stark', published in 2001) is set in the 1960s in the Stiftsbibliothek St. Gallen, which is indebted to Irish monks and which hosts one of the largest collections of old Irish manuscripts on the continent.[90] In an indirect way, in this subtle and well-wrought text Hürlimann evokes a period of shared Swiss and Irish cultural and religious history.

Probably due to the Böll-*Effekt* combined with the success of crime stories, Ireland has also recently inspired detective novels by German authors who sometimes write under a pseudonym (for instance Hanna O'Brien for Hannelore Hippe), perhaps in order to convey the impression that the book has been written by someone who is familiar with the Irish context. Of course, this increases the (fictional) reliability of the narrative as well as of the numerous landscape descriptions. Strangely enough, in these books the role played by nature goes beyond the function of creating an atmosphere, as normally happens in detective novels. The wild Irish landscape, with its rugged coasts, high cliffs, romantic seascapes, mysterious dolmens and Gothic architectures (some of these elements are even featured on book covers), is much more than a setting: it plays an active role in the plot, inasmuch as the characters often seem to mingle with elements of the landscape and share its fate.

Ireland—Germany—Italy. Irish Studies from a transcultural/comparative perspective: scholarship, translations, contacts among writers

Given the pivotal role of the German *Keltologie* in continental Europe, it is not surprising that in the twentieth and twenty-first century Germany is the nation that probably has the largest number of specialists of Irish Studies outside of Britain and Ireland, although the serious gap between the lack of institutional visibility of the field and the wide range of publications on Irish themes should be highlighted. It is worth noting that in Germany—as in several other countries—the field which in Ireland is called 'Irish Studies' is a weirdly distributed topic, as there are two different academic fields related to the subject. On the one hand there is the above mentioned *Keltologie* (Celtic Studies, structured in a similar way to 'Classic Philology'), which includes the study of Ireland's ancient history, historical linguistics, philology and archeology; on the other hand, there is 'Irish Studies', which deals with Anglo-Irish literature, culture and history. Due to the reduction in the number of academic chairs in the subject, the only German universities in which it is possible to study *Keltologie* are now Bonn, where one can take a BA degree in this subject, and Marburg, which offers both BA and MA courses.[91] In Vienna there is an MA in 'comparative Indo-European linguistics and Celtic Studies (*Keltologie*)' on the basis of there being a BA in 'related' fields (ancient history, classical archeology, linguistics).[92] In accordance with what in Germany has been the general policy over the years, the curriculum of *Keltologie* in Marburg concentrates on the history, culture and literature of the Middle Ages and does not deal with modern Irish literature or issues of politics, history, etc., in present day Ireland. In Bonn, *Keltologie* is studied in the 'Institut für Anglistik, Amerikanistik und Keltologie', and in Marburg in the 'Institut für klassische Sprachen und Literaturen'. In Germany 'Irish Studies' is usually to be found in English Departments and sometimes not even under the label of 'Irish Studies' or 'Postcolonial Literatures', but as a part of English-language literatures (which include American literature, too). At present, in German-speaking countries there are three main centres of Irish Studies: Wuppertal, Mainz and Zurich.

In Italy the situation is even worse: only a few universities (Florence, Roma III, Sassari, Turin and, up to a few years ago, also Verona) offer courses in Irish culture and literature, but no chairs of Irish Studies have been established. Most of the published works of Irish interest printed in Italy are now merely the result of the specific commitment of individual scholars. Two exceptions are worth mentioning here, both bearing witness to the deep interest in Irish culture in Italy: *Studi celtici*, the first scholarly journal of Celtic studies in Italy, established in 2002 at Bologna University and published once a year, covering important issues in history, literature and linguistics related to Celtic countries and cultures; and *Studi irlandesi. A Journal of Irish Studies*, an annual, open-access interdisciplinary periodical founded in 2011 and sponsored by the University of Florence, promoting and contributing to the interdisciplinary debate on themes and research issues pertaining to all aspects of Irish culture and society.[93] No chairs of Celtic studies have been created in Italy so far, but there are courses in Celtic philology in Macerata, Pisa and Pavia.

In Germany, Irish writers have been published by notable publishing houses and have often been translated by acclaimed writers: Hildesheimer translated passages from *Finnegans wake*; Böll translated (with his wife Annemarie who did, as he acknowledged, most of the work) G.B. Shaw, J.M. Synge, Flann O'Brien, Brendan Behan and others; Richard Pietraß translated Seamus Heaney. In some cases, German translations have themselves become bestsellers. Probably no translator of the twentieth century has contributed more to the diffusion of Irish literature in Germany than Elisabeth Schnack. She has translated classical authors and collections of short stories, providing German readers interested in Irish literature with a representative selection of names and often introducing new authors to readers (among them Frank O'Connor, Sean O'Faolain, John McGahern).[94]

In German-speaking countries, many books and essays on Irish culture have been published in the last few decades; a large number are devoted to the relationship between Irish and German-speaking culture.[95] It is also worth mentioning that the Dublin press Coiscéim, which specialises in books in Irish, publishes a series of trilingual (German-English-Gaelic) literary texts.

Italy is a country in which large portions of the international book market are being translated, and since the mid-1980s Ireland has become one of the favourite sources for the Italian book industry, boosting the demand for translations from Irish literature. Several publishers have now specialised in things Irish: the Parma based Guanda, for example, publishes fiction by Roddy Doyle, John Banville, William Trevor, Joseph O'Connor and Catherine Dunne, and poetry by Paul Muldoon and Seamus Heaney, with excellent results in terms of sales and critical acclaim. The catalogues of smaller publishing houses such as Trauben, in Turin, or Kolibris, in Bologna, include anthologies of Irish poetry and translations from popular contemporary poets such as Theo Dorgan, Derek Mahon, Desmond Egan, Thomas Kinsella and John F. Deane, to less well-known ones such as Eva Bourke, Pat Boran and Ray Givans, amongst others. Ireland as a 'cultural entity' is now a guarantee for the Italian publishing world. Carlo Linati, the pioneer of Irish Studies in Italy, wrote in the late 1920s that, in spite of being different in their 'places and customs', many affinities were detectable between the Italian and Irish peoples; he asserted that they were akin for the 'common decades of servitude' from which the two countries were 'freed through odysseys of sorrows and sacrifices'.[96] The popularity and availability of Irish literature in Italy testifies to Linati's early recognition of the special relationship existing between the two countries.

If German-speaking authors are fascinated by Irish culture, it is also the case that contemporary Irish writers, such as John Banville and the German-Irish Hugo Hamilton, display a particular interest in German literature. Texts such as *The Newton letter, Mephisto* and 'The Broken Jug' by Banville, and *The speckled people* and *Die redselige Insel* by Hamilton have already drawn the attention of scholars of Irish-German Studies.[97] Indisputably, these and other similar books will provide stimulating material for further analysis over the next few years from the trans-cultural point of view.

In the last few decades a lot has indeed been achieved in the fields of Italian-Irish and German-Irish studies: pioneering critical contributions and stimulating anthologies have been published; intercultural institutions such as the Centre for Irish-German Studies in Limerick, the James Joyce Stiftung in Zürich, and the Trieste Joyce School have been created; and important journals focusing on the exciting and deep cultural inter-relationships among the three countries, such as *Studi irlandesi. A Journal of Irish Studies* in Italy, the journal and book series *Irish-German Studies* in Ireland and *Angermion. Yearbook for Anglo-German Literary Criticism* in England, have become internationally renowned forums in which the fruitful interaction within Irish, German and Italian cultures are brought to light.

The richness and intensity of the exchanges that have marked the relationships among Ireland, Germany and Italy find a symbolic example in the intense friendship between Claudio Magris, a celebrated novelist and one of the doyens of German Studies in Italy, and John Banville. The deep appreciation of each other's work, their mutual interest in German literature (for example a shared concern for Hofmannsthal—in particular for the problem of the ineffability of human experience we find in 'Ein Brief', 'A letter'), and their love for their own literary traditions, represent the best way to illustrate how transcultural connections can be enriching and fruitful.

Fiorenzo Fantaccini and Anna Fattori

Notes

1 Irish literature in German-speaking countries is dealt with by Anna Fattori. Fiorenzo Fantaccini examines the Italian context.

2 Notable names in these fields were Kuno Meyer, Heinrich Zimmer, Julius Pokorny.

3 See, Patrick O'Neill, *Ireland and Germany. A study in literary relations* (Lang; Frankfurt a. Main, New York, Bern, 1985), 29, and Helmut Flachenecker, 'The contribution of Irish scholars and monks to the religious landscape in Germany in the Late Middle Ages and early Modern Period', in Claire O'Reilly and Veronica O'Regan (eds), *Ireland and the Irish in Germany. Reception and perception* (Nomos Verlagsgesellschaft; Baden Baden, 2014), 13–25.

4 See, A.M. Tommasini, *Irish saints in Italy* (Sands and Company; London, 1937). See also C.M. Pellizzi, '"Hibernia fabulosa": per una storia delle immagini dell'Irlanda in Italia', *Studi irlandesi. A Journal of Irish Studies* 1 (2011), 29–119.

5 Ludovico Ariosto, *Orlando furioso* (1516, Ferrara) (Mondadori; Milano, 1976), canto X, 92.

6 Fritz Strich, *Goethe and world literature*, translated by C.A.M. Sym (Greenwood; Westport, Connecticut, 1971), 87. (Originally published as *Goethe und die Weltliteratur* (A. Francke Verlag; Tübingen, 1945. First English edition, Routledge and Kegan Paul; London, 1949).)

7 See, Johann Joachim Christoph Bode, 'Der Übersetzer an den Leser', in Laurence Sterne, *Yoricks empfindsame Reise durch Frankreich und Italien*, aus dem Englischen von Johann Joachim Christoph Bode (S. Fischer Verlag; Frankfurt a. Main, 2008; first German edn Cramer Verlag; Hamburg and Bremen, 1768), 7–15: 7–8.

8 See, Georg Jäger, *Empfindsamkeit und Roman. Wortgeschichte, Theorie und Kritik im 18. und frühen 19. Jahrhundert* (Kohlhammer; Stuttgart, Berlin, 1969), 77–8.

9 On the issue of 'unnatural narrative', see Brian Richardson,'What is unnatural narrative theory?', in Jan Alber and Rüdiger Heinze (eds), *Unnatural narratives—unnatural narratology* (de Gruyter; Berlin and Boston, 2001), 23–40. Regarding the German novels of the latter half of the eighteenth century, see, Peter Michelsen, *Laurence Sterne und der deutsche Roman des 18. Jahrhunderts* (Vandenhoeck & Ruprecht; Göttingen, 1962). On Goethe and Sterne specifically, see, W.R.R. Pinger, *Laurence Sterne and Goethe* (University of California Press; Berkeley, 1920).

10 See, John Hennig, 'Goethe's translations of Ossian's "Songs of Selma"', in John Hennig, *Goethe and the English speaking world* (Lang; Bern, Frankfurt a. Main, 1988a), 152–62. On Goethe and Irish literature, see, in the above-mentioned book by Hennig, 'Goethe's personal relations with Ireland', (1988b), 123–34; and Nicholas Boyle and John Guthrie (eds), *Goethe and the English speaking world. Essays from the Cambridge symposium for his 250th anniversary* (Camden House; Rochester NY, Woodbridge Suffolk, 2002). About Goethe's role in Irish-German studies, see, Eda Sagarra, 'Goethe and Irish German studies', in Boyle and Guthrie (eds), *Goethe and the English speaking world*, 227–42.

11 See, Karl S. Guthke, '"Destination Goethe": travelling Englishmen in Weimar', in Boyle and Guthrie (eds), *Goethe and the English speaking world*, 116–42.

12 Oliver Goldsmith, *Il vicario di Wakefield*, transl. by Giovanni Berchet (Giuseppe Destefanis; Milano, 1810).

13 Piero Garofalo, 'Giovanni Berchet and Early Italian Romanticism', *Rivista di studi italiani* 2 (2011), 107–31: 109.

14 Alessandro Manzoni, *I promessi sposi* (Tipografia Guglielmini e Radelli; Milano, 1827; 2nd edn 1842). See, Adriano Bozzoli, 'Manzoni e Goldsmith', *Aevum* 45 (1–2) (1971), 46–56.

[15] Jean Paul (Johann Paul Friedrich Richter), *Vorschule der Ästhetik*, in Jean Paul, *Werke*, ed. by Norbert Miller, 6 Bände, (Hanser; München, 1963a), Bd. 5, 470 ('durch seine Heiterkeit, Leichtigkeit bis zu Nachlässigkeiten und durch seine Gabe der Rührung und Naturkunst').

[16] Jean Paul, *Hesperus oder 45 Hundsposttage. Eine Biographie* (Matzdorff; Berlin, 1795).

[17] Jean Paul, *Vorschule der Ästhetik*, 118 ('das trübe Irland'; 'so still und ernst im Leben').

[18] Jean Paul, *Blumen, Frucht- und Dornenstücke oder Ehestand, Tod und Hochzeit des Armenadvokaten F. St. Siebenkäs*, in Jean Paul, *Werke* (1963b), Bd. 2, 26 ('liebste Abschweifungen').

[19] Pietro Chiari, *Uomo di un altro mondo* (Carmignani; Parma, 1760; 2nd edn 1768); Zaccaria Seriman, *I viaggi di Enrico Wanton ai Regni delle scimie e dei cinocefali* (Tipografia di Alvisopoli; Venezia, 1749; further editions 1750, 1764).

[20] Giancarlo Mazzacurati, *Effetto Sterne: la narrazione umoristica in Italia da Foscolo a Pirandello* (Nistri-Lischi; Pisa, 1990). See also: Francesca Testa, *'Tristram Shandy' in Italia* (Bulzoni; Roma, 1999). Peter Michelsen, *Laurence Sterne und der deutsche Roman des 18. Jahrhunderts* (Vandenhoeck & Ruprecht; Göttingen, 1972).

[21] Alberto Arbasino, *Certi romanzi* (Einaudi; Torino, 1977), 60–1.

[22] See, Eoin Bourke, *'Poor Green Erin'. German travel writers' narratives on Ireland from before the 1798 rising to after the great famine*. Texts edited, translated and annotated by Eoin Bourke (Lang; Frankfurt a. Main, Berlin, Bern, 2012). See also Andreas Oehlke (ed.), *Fahrten zur Smaragdinsel. Irland in den deutschen Reisebescheibungen des 19. Jahrhunderts* (Peperkorn; Göttingen, 1993).

[23] Hermann von Pückler-Muskau, *Briefe eines Verstorbenen: Reisetagebuch aus Deutschland, Holland, England, Wales, Irland und Frankreich* (Franckh und Hallberger; Stuttgart, 1830); Johann Georg Kohl, *Reisen in Irland* (Arnoldische Buchhandlung; Dresden and Leipzig, 1843).

[24] See the letters written from Switzerland in Christian Colvin (ed.), *Maria Edgeworth in France and Switzerland: selections from the Edgeworth family letters* (Clarendon Press; Oxford, 1979).

[25] See, Donatella Abbate Badin and Anne O'Connor (eds), 'Italia Mia: transnational Ireland in the nineteenth century', Special section of *Studi irlandesi. A Journal of Irish Studies* 6 (2016), 17–189.

[26] Lady Morgan (Sydney Owenson), *Italy* (Henry Colburn & Co.; London, 1821).

[27] Giuseppe Acerbi, *Diario del soggiorno in Inghilterra e Irlanda*, ed. by Simona Cappellari (Fiorini; Verona, 2012).

[28] O'Neill, *Ireland and Germany*, 174.

[29] See, O'Neill, *Ireland and Germany*, 172–7.

[30] Georg Weerth, translated by O'Neill, see, *Ireland and Germany*, 177 ('Genossen in Freud und Leide— / Denn arme Teufel waren sie beide').

[31] O'Neill, *Ireland and Germany*, 168–9.

[32] Heinz Kosok, 'Yeats in Germany', in Heinz Kosok, *Plays and playwrights from Ireland in international perspective* (Wissenschaftlicher Verlag Trier; Trier 1995), 117–30.

[33] See, Ben Levitas, 'J. M. Synge: European encounters', in P. J. Mathews (ed.), *The Cambridge companion to J. M. Synge* (Cambridge University Press; Cambridge, 2009), 77–91: 87.

[34] Anthony Roche, 'Synge, Brecht, and the Hiberno-German connection', *Hungarian Journal of English and American Studies* 10 (1–2) (2004), 9–32: 26. See also Michael Morley, 'Brecht and the strange case of Mr. L.', *German Quarterly* 46 (4) (November 1973), 540–7.

[35] W.B. Yeats, 'J.M. Synge and the Ireland of his time', in W.B. Yeats, *Essays and introductions* (Macmillan; London, 1961) 311–41: 323, 319.

[36] Cf., O'Neill, *Ireland and Germany*, 274

[37] See, Klaus Völker, *Irish theatre I: Yeats and Synge* (Friedrich; Hannover, 1967).

[38] W.B. Yeats, *Tragedie irlandesi*, transl. and intr. by Carlo Linati (Studio Editoriale Lombardo; Milano, 1914).

[39] On Carlo Linati, see Arturo della Torre, *Carlo Linati* (Piero Cairoli; Como, 1972).

[40] Carlo Linati, *Memorie a zig-zag* (Buratti; Torino, 1929), 23.

[41] James Joyce, *Selected letters*, ed. by Richard Ellman (Viking; New York, 1975).

[42] See, Giorgio Guzzetta, 'Linati between Ireland, Milan and Europe', in Giorgio Guzzetta, *Nation and narration. British Modernism in Italy in the first half of the 20th century* (Longo; Ravenna, 2004), 99–135; and Maurizio Pasquero, '"Mi par di trovarmi di fronte a un fatto nuovo letterario": Carlo Linati alla scoperta di James Joyce', *Studi irlandesi. A Journal of Irish Studies* 2 (2012), 199–254.

[43] For similar reasons Kafka, who wrote novels with neuter and unspecified settings using a language with no local colour, was the German-speaking author who had the most serious impact on European literatures. In the Irish context, he was very much admired by Beckett.

[44] See, Loredana di Martino, 'Gadda-Joyce', *Edinburgh Journal of Gadda Studies* 4 (2004); available online at: https://www.gadda.ed.ac.uk/Pages/resources/walks/pge/joycedimarti.php (12 December 2017); and Loredana Di Martino, *Il caleidoscopio della scrittura: James Joyce, Carlo Emilio Gadda e il romanzo modernista* (Edizioni Scientifiche Italiane; Napoli, 2009).

[45] In 1985 the James Joyce Stiftung Zurich was founded. This archive, run by Fritz Senn, contains one of the most significant and comprehensive collections of Joyciana outside of Ireland. It regularly hosts scholars from all over the world.

[46] John Banville, 'Survivors of Joyce', in Augustine Martin (ed.), *James Joyce: the artist and the labyrinth* (Ryan Publishing; London, 1990), 73–4.

[47] Bertolt Brecht, *Schriften zur Literatur und Kunst*, Bd. 1 (Suhrkamp; Frankfurt a. Main 1967), 82. He considered *Ulysses* 'an indispensable reference work for writers' (*ein unentbehrliches Nachschlagewerk für Schriftsteller*).

[48] See, *Die Zeit*, 21 November 2012; available at: http://zeit.de/news/2012-11/21/medium-ulysses-zum-hoerbuch-des-jahres-gewaehlt-2114484 (15 October 2017).

[49] Eimear McBride, 'My hero: Eimear McBride on James Joyce', *The Guardian*, 6 June 2015, 15.

[50] Hermann Broch, *Gesammelte Werke* (Rhein Verlag; Zurich 1952–61), 10 B.de, Bd. 10, 330 ('... ich [sehe] im *Ulysses* ein vollkommenes Realisat dessen ..., was im Roman überhaupt ausdrückbar ist. Dasjenige, was mir bei meinen Büchern vorgeschwebt ist: "unter der Haut" zu schreiben, das finde ich bei Joyce restlos erfüllt und ich bin überzeugt, dass die Literatur, so weit sie überhaupt Ausdruck des modernen Lebens bleiben wird, sich immer mehr unter den Joyceschen Einfluss begeben wird'). English translation by Breon Mitchell, *James Joyce and the German novel 1922–1933* (Ohio University Press; Athens, Ohio 1976), 154.

[51] Hermann Broch, 'James Joyce und die Gegenwart. Rede zu Joyces 50. Geburtstag', in Hermann Broch, *Schriften zur Literatur I. Kritik*, Bd. 9/1 Kommentierte Werkausgabe, ed. by Paul Michael Lützeler (Surhkamp; Frankfurt a. Main, 1975), 63–94.

[52] Broch, 'James Joyce und die Gegenwart',70 ('Wenn sechzehn Lebensstunden auf 1200 Seiten beschrieben werden, das ist 75 Seiten pro Stunde, mehr als eine Seite für jede Minute, nahezu eine Zeile für jede Sekunde.').

[53] Alfred Döblin, typescript of a lecture before the 'Lesezirkel Hottingen' in Zurich, 1932, quoted in English translation in Mitchell, *James Joyce and the German novel*, 145 ('Joyce ist ein grossartiger Schriftsteller, ein Pionier im Stilistischen und darum auch in der Darstellungsweise. Ich vermag selbst nicht zu analysieren, ob und welche Einflüsse von Joyce bei meinem letzten Buch nachweisbar sind. Ich weiss aber [sic!] dass mit wesentlichen Bestandteilen meiner Arbeit Joyce nicht zu tun hat, es kann sich nur um periphere Ähnlichkeiten handeln', Mitchell, *James Joyce and the German Novel*, 149–50, footnote 28).

[54] Mitchell has convincingly elucidated that Döblin's and Joyce's styles had become increasingly similar as far as the 'hybrid' quality of the narrative is concerned; see, Mitchell, *James Joyce and the German novel*, 131–50. They both shared the use of dialect, of newspaper articles and advertisements, the tendency to say 'everything, *but* everything'—as Tucholski observes (in Kurt Tucholski, 'Ulysses', *Die Weltbühne* 23 (November 1927), 792, 'Hier ist tatsächlich alles, aber auch alles, gesagt'), and the widespread use of techniques aimed at reproducing the characters' subconscious thoughts in an immediate and effective way.

[55] Mitchell, *James Joyce and the German novel*, 297. See Arno Schmidt, *Zettels Traum* (Goverts Kruger Stahlberg; Stuttgart, 1970).

[56] James Joyce, *Ulisse*, transl. by Giulio De Angelis, intro. by Giorgio Melchiori (Mondadori; Milano, 1960). Reprinted in various formats.

[57] Giorgio Melchiori, 'Joyce and eighteenth century novelists', *English Miscellany* II (1951), 227–45.

[58] In 1994 Melchiori published *Joyce: il mestiere dello scrittore* (Einaudi; Torino), and in 1995 *James Joyce's feast of languages. Seven essays and ten notes*, edited by Franca Ruggieri, Joyce Studies in Italy, 4 (Bulzoni; Roma). His last contribution to Joyce studies is *Joyce Barocco/Baroque Joyce*, edited by Franca Ruggieri, English transl. by Barbara Arnett (Bulzoni; Roma, 2007), the first volume in a new series called Piccola Biblioteca Joyciana.

[59] James Joyce, *Ulisse: Telemachia: episodi 1–3*; traduzione di Giulio De Angelis, a cura di Giorgio Melchiori, commento di Carlo Bigazzi, Carla de Petris, Miranda Melchiori (Mondadori; Milano, 1983). James Joyce, *Finnegans wake: H. C. E.*; transl. and annotated by Luigi Schenoni, introduction by Giorgio Melchiori (Mondadori; Milano, 1982).

[60] See, *La Repubblica*, 22 February 1999; available online at: http://ricerca.repubblica. it/repubblica/archivio/repubblica/1992/02/22/amelia-rosselli-sulle-palafitte.html (December 2017).

[61] Jennifer Scappettone, 'Stanza as "homicilie": the poetry of Amelia Rosselli', in Amelia Rosselli, *Locomotrix. Selected poetry and prose of Amelia Rosselli*, ed. by Jennifer Scappettone (University of Chicago Press; Chicago and London, 2012), 1.

[62] Raffaele La Capria, *Ferito a morte* (Bompiani; Milano, 1961).

[63] Umberto Eco, *Le poetiche di Joyce* (Bompiani; Milano, 1966).

[64] For an assessment of the critical fortune and reception of Joyce in Italy, see, Giovanni Cianci, *La fortuna di Joyce in Italia (1917–1972)* (Adriatica; Bari, 1974); Serenella Zanotti, 'James Joyce among the Italian writers', in Geert Lernout and Wim van Mierlo (eds), *The reception of James Joyce in Europe* (Continuum; London 2004a), 329–61; Serenella Zanotti, *Joyce in Italy. L'italiano in Joyce* (Aracne; Roma, 2004b).

[65] See, Fiorenzo Fantaccini, 'Quattro poeti italiani e Yeats', *W.B. Yeats e la cultura italiana* (Firenze University Press; Firenze, 2009), 113–64.

[66] Montale, *Quaderno di traduzioni* (Mondadori; Milano, 1975).

[67] See, Fiorenzo Fantaccini, 'Montale, Lucio Piccolo e l'opera di William Butler Yeats', in Francesco Marroni, Mariaconcetta Costantini, Renzo D'Agnillo (eds), *Percorsi di poesia irlandese* (Tracce; Pescara, 1998a), 63–92.

[68] Daniela Caselli, 'Thinking of a "Rhyme for Euganean": Beckett in Italy', in Mark Nixon and Matthew Feldman (eds), *The international reception of Samuel Beckett* (Continuum; London, 2009), 209–33. On Beckett in Italy, see also: Luca Scarlini, *Un altro giorno felice. La fortuna dell'opera teatrale di Samuel Beckett in Italia 1953–1996* (Maschietto & Musolino; Siena, 1996), and Gianfranco Alfano, Andrea Cortellessa (eds), *Tegole dal Cielo. L'"effetto Beckett" nella cultura italiana* (2 vols, EDUP; Rome, 2006).

[69] Caselli, 'Thinking of a "Rhyme for Euganean": Beckett in Italy', 211.

[70] Aldo Tagliaferri, *Beckett e l'iperdeterminazione letteraria* (Feltrinelli; Milano, 1967).

[71] Gabriella Morisco, 'Two poets and a kite: Seamus Heaney and Giovanni Pascoli', *Linguæ* 1 (2013), 37.

[72] Marco Sonzogni (ed.), *Poesie scelte e raccolte dall'autore: Seamus Heaney*, I Meridiani series (Mondadori; Milano, 2016).

[73] Heinrich Böll, *Irish journey*, transl. by Leila Vennewitz (McGraw-Hill Book Company; New York, Toronto, 1967).

[74] Heinrich Böll's interview with Margarete Limberg, 11 June 1985, quoted in Gisela Holfter, *Heinrich Böll and Ireland*, with a Foreword by Hugo Hamilton (Cambridge Scholars Publishing; Newcastle upon Tyne, 2012a), 75.

[75] See, Holfter, *Heinrich Böll and Ireland*, 2–5, and Steve Brewer, 'Ireland as a religious Utopia. Böll, Ireland and *Irisches Tagebuch*', in Joachim Fischer, Gisela Holfter and Eoin Bourke (eds), *Deutsch-Irische Verbindungen. Geschichte—Literatur—Übersetzung/ Irish-German Connections. History—Literature—Translation.* Akten der 1. Limericker Konferenz für deutsch-irische Studien 2.–4. September 1997 (Wissenschaftlicher Verlag Trier; Trier, 1998), 123–31.

[76] The most comprehensive work on Böll's relationship to Ireland is the above-mentioned book by Holfter, *Heinrich Böll and Ireland*. By the same author, see also *Erlebnis Irland. Deutsche Reiseberichte über Irland im zwanzigsten Jahrhundert* (Wissenschaftlicher Verlag Trier; Trier 1996).

[77] On the 'iconic quality' of Böll's work, see Eda Sagarra, 'Heinrich Böll, father of German tourism in Ireland', in Gisela Holfter (ed.), *Heinrich Böll's 'Irisches Tagebuch' in context* (Wissenschaftlicher Verlag Trier; Trier, 2010; Irish-German Studies 5), 13–7: 16; and see page 15 of Sagarra's work in relation to the 'sophisticated' nature of the text. On the complexity of Böll's text, see, Thorsten M. Päplow, 'New perspectives: Heinrich Böll's *Irish Journal* as Intertext', in Holfter (ed.), *Heinrich Böll's 'Irisches Tagebuch' in context*, 63–75.

[78] Heinrich Böll, *Diario d'Irlanda*, tansl. by Marianello Marianelli, intr. by Italo Alighiero Chiusano (Mondadori; Milano 1967, several reprints).

[79] Ralph Giordano, *Mein irisches Tagebuch* (Kiepenheuer & Witsch; Köln, 1996), 21: ('Mein *Irisches Tagebuch* [ist] eine selbständige Arbeit ..., geschöpft aus eigenen Quellen, eigenen Beobachtungen, Erfahrungen und Beziehungen').

[80] Giordano, *Mein irisches Tagebuch*, 216 ('wortwörtlich unterschreiben').

[81] Hugo Hamilton, *Die redselige Insel: Irisches Tagebuch* (Luchterhand; München, 2007).

[82] Gisela Holfter, 'After the *Irisches Tagebuch*: Changes and continuities in the German image of Ireland 1961–2011', in Joachim Fischer and Rolf Stehle (eds),*Contemporary German-Irish cultural relations in a European perspective. Exploring issues in cultural policy and practice* (Wissenschaftlicher Verlag Trier; Trier, 2012b), 159–71: 167.

[83] Patrick O'Neill, '"Kennst Du das Land?" Ireland and the German literary imagination', in Holfter (ed.), *Heinrich Böll's 'Irisches Tagebuch' in context*, 79–87: 86.

[84] Sagarra, 'Heinrich Böll, father of German tourism in Ireland', 14.

[85] This episode is reported in Holfter, *Heinrich Böll and Ireland*, 175.

[86] Holfter, 'After the *Irisches Tagebuch*', 171.

[87] About Ireland and Switzerland, see, Lorena Silos Ribas, 'Introduction', in Lorena Silos Ribas (ed.), *Britannia/Helvetia* (figurationen gender literaturkultur, 11. Jg., 2010, H. 1; Böhlau Verlag; Wien, Köln and Weimar, 2010), 7–14: 12–14.

[88] See, Jürgen Barkhoff, 'Kulturkontakt im Zeichen von Traum und Trost. Hansjörg Schertenleibs Irlandromane', in Silos Ribas (ed.), *Britannia/Helvetia*, 93–112; Valerie Heffernan, 'Swimming against the current? Rolf Lappert's *Nach Hause schwimmen*', both in Silos Ribas (ed.), *Britannia/Helvetia*, 113–127; Anna Fattori, 'Ireland as a "better elsewhere" in Heinrich Böll's *Irisches Tagebuch* and in Margrit Baur's *Alle Herrlichkeit*', in Holfter (ed.), *Heinrich Böll's 'Irisches Tagebuch' in context*, 99–113.

[89] See, Heffernan, 'Swimming against the current?', 122–3.

[90] Thomas Hürlimann, *Fräulein Stark. Novelle* (Ammann; Zürich, 2001).

[91] Further details are available on the various university websites, see: https://www. uni-marburg.de/fb10/iksl/sprachwissenschaft/ma-keltologie/index_html (20 December 2017); https://www.uni-marburg.de/fb10/iksl/sprachwissenschaft/fachgebiet/keltologie (20 December 2017); https://www.uni-bonn.de/studium/vor-dem-studium/faecher/kelt-ologie/keltologie-bachelor-of-arts (20 December 2017).

[92] See the university website, at: https://linguistik.univie.ac.at/studium/ids-keltologie (20 December 2017).

[93] Further information is available at: http://www.fupress.net/index.php/bsfm-sijis (25 April 2018).

[94] See, O'Neill, *Ireland and Germany*, 289–91.

[95] The creation of the Centre for Irish-German Studies at the University of Limerick in 1997 stimulated a lot of academic papers on this topic and has given a great impulse to this field, through the organisation of conferences and the coordination of research projects.

[96] Carlo Linati, *Sull'orme di Renzo e altre prose lombarde* (Treves; Milano 1927), 20–21.

[97] See, Joseph Swann, 'Banville's Faust: *Doctor Copernicus, Kepler, The Newton letter* and *Mefisto* as stories of the European mind', in Donald E. Morse, Csilla Bertha and István Pálffy (eds), *A small nation's contribution to the world. Essays on Anglo-Irish literature and language* (Colin Smythe; Gerrards Cross, 1993), 148–60; Elke d'Hoker, 'Negative aesthetics in Hugo von Hofmannsthal's *Ein Brief* and John Banville's *The Newton letter*', in Karen Vandevelde (ed.), *New voices in Irish criticism 3* (Four Courts Press; Dublin, 2002), 36–43; Anna Fattori, '"A genuinely funny German farce" turns into a very Irish play: *The broken jug* (1994), John Banville's adaptation of Heinrich von Kleist's' *Der zerbrochene Krug* (1807)', *ANGERMION. Yearbook for Anglo-German Literary Criticism, Intellectual History and Cultural Transfers / Jahrbuch für britisch-deutsche Kulturbeziehungen* 4 (2011), 75–94, and Thomas Eoin Bourke, '"The birthmark of Germanness". Hugo Hamilton and the question of belonging', in Joachim Fischer and Gisela Holfter (eds), *Creative influences. Selected Irish-German biographies* (Wissenschaftlicher Verlag Trier; Trier, 2009), 179–94.

At the brink of Europe: Nordic encounters with Irish literature

Anne Karhio

Irish, Nordic and 'European' literatures

In one of his last works before his death, *Euroopan Reuna* ('Brink of Europe'), the Finnish modernist author Pentti Saarikoski, also a translator of both Homer's *Odyssey* and Joyce's *Ulysses*, told the story of his journey across Europe, and from Finland to Ireland.[1] In Ireland, Saarikoski stayed in Dublin, the city of Joyce that he had come to know intimately as the setting for *Ulysses*. He wrote:

> The journey ends here, as I sit in a hotel room in the Ormond in Dublin and watch Anna Livia,

the seagulls circling above the water, and the row of buildings on the opposite shore. Or, the journey doesn't really end, only I've sat here before, watching, as I do now. No city planner conceived that row of houses, it is so disorderly that when you have watched it for some time, and then return to the scene, this is my fourth time, the disorder becomes order and then beauty, which is memory.[2]

Due to his detailed familiarity with *Ulysses*, the Dublin of Saarikoski was not only his, not even in his private musings, but would always be partially filtered through the encounters with Joyce's novel. A similar process characterises the Swedish Erik Andersson's 2012 volume *Dag ut och dag in med en dag i Dublin* ('Day out and day in with one day in Dublin'), an account of Andersson's four-year-long undertaking of translating *Ulysses*. It is told within the Swedish setting but also the temporal framework of a single day, the novel's date, 16 June 1904.

I come in, hang up my coat, unlace my boots, turn on the kettle, put on my sandals, go to the kitchen, run the water, walk back, take off the sandals, turn off the water, measure the coffee grounds, turn on the fluorescent light, turn on the phone, pick up the cigarettes, turn on the computer, wonder where my USB memory stick is, and check the place for chocolate.

It is now February, with raw and harsh weather, but in Dublin it is still 16 June 1904, and the time is ten o'clock in the morning and we enter right into a history lesson that Stephen Dedalus is giving at a private boys' school a short way down the coast from the tower in Sandycove.[3]

The Irish capital, and Joyce's close encounters with and narratives of its people and places, has become a part of the European heritage and literary cartography in a manner that extends well beyond the specific geographical coordinates of its most famous literary rendition. European authors and translators have made Joyce's Dublin their own, and also transported the city to their various home countries, including the Nordic region. As the above examples demonstrate, Joyce, in particular, has left his mark on Nordic literature in a way that goes well beyond translation, prompting creative encounters with Dublin and beyond that are Joycean, while not remaining solely within the framework of *Ulysses*. Similarly, Joyce's Ireland finds its way, in various direct and indirect ways, into the Nordic settings of numerous authors; Jacob Greve and Steen Klitgård Povlsen, for example, suggest that the young Friedrich on the beach of the Danish island of Rømø is 'a distant relative of Stephen on Sandymount Strand'.[4]

Such a negotiation between home and elsewhere, or familiarity and strangeness, also characterises Nordic authors' and audiences' encounters with Irish literature more widely, and illustrates the complexities involved in the question of how Ireland and its literature have been considered by Nordic readers, or how they have left a mark on Nordic literary texts and discourses. The significance of the Irish context in particular is also unevenly recognised. The international standing of authors such as Yeats, Joyce and Beckett gives their texts a canonical status as *world* literature rather than situating these figures as *Irish* authors. While their works tend to be included as required reading in the curricula of the English departments of Nordic universities, they are frequently discussed through their alignment with other, non-Irish texts that are now considered as part of the Western cultural and literary heritage. At the same time, a more specific historical and geographical focus has informed the reception of contemporary Northern Irish poetry during and after the 'Troubles' among Nordic scholars, writers or readers. And, even more recently, Irish fiction, and women's popular fiction in particular, has gained considerable audiences in all Nordic countries, again bypassing the question of Irish cultural setting in favour of issues related to gender in the middle-class Western experience. In literary encounters with Ireland and its culture, travel literature and related personal accounts stand out; the Finnish writer Hanna Tuuri, for example, examines the intricacies and quirks of life in County Mayo through Finnish eyes in *Irlantilainen aamiainen* ('An Irish breakfast'), and sections of the Swedish author Gösta Oswald's autobiographical *Breven till Ranveig* ('Letter to Ranveig') draw on his travel in the west and south of Ireland.[5]

In the case of the more canonical twentieth-century writers, even a superficial glance at the volume *European and Nordic modernisms* well illustrates the manner in which Irish authors have made their way into twentieth century Nordic writing, while doing so first and foremost as key figures in the cross-currents of European modernist writing.[6] The collection of essays emerged from a project between the universities of Leeds and Oslo, entitled 'Anglo-Scandinavian Cross-Currents 1870–1914' and a related conference on 'Joyce and the Nordic Countries'. The editors saw a need to 'continue the work by extending this kind of comparative study beyond one, albeit exceptionally important author'.[7] Joyce, nevertheless, remains a constant presence throughout the volume, as do Yeats and Beckett, who are repeatedly mentioned as key figures in European modernism, rather than contextualised within twentieth-century Irish literature and culture. Cultural and/or biographical context mainly become relevant in as much as they also support arguments related to literary themes and aesthetics that transcend cultural and national concerns: Joyce and Beckett, who wrote most of their best-known works abroad, are seen to represent the phenomenon of modernist exile, and Yeats's Thoor Ballylee is considered alongside other examples of the tower as a literary symbol in European and in Nordic writing, before and during the modernist period.[8]

This kind of identification of Ireland's perhaps most highly regarded modern writers as 'European' challenges the frequent differentiation between 'Irish' versus 'European' traditions and cultures in the Irish context. 'European' in many accounts is something that characterises cultural production on the European continent, as opposed to the British-Irish archipelago. The European continent's other geographical and cultural margins have, however, similarly considered their own position as something that should be considered in *relation*, or even opposition to, rather than simply as an integral *part* of, the multi-faceted formation that we call Europe (this present volume being another case in point). While this may in some cases result in a sense of shared historical experience, distance often tends to blur difference, and, viewed from the opposite edge of Northern Europe, the cluster of countries, languages and various (and often conflicting) historical narratives that constitutes the Nordic region may appear deceptively coherent. The same, of course, applies to perceptions of Ireland in the Nordic eye(s): a no less simplified view of Ireland's cultural specificity (particularly in relation to its bigger neighbour) from a distance frequently depicts the present and the past of the island as misleadingly homogenous and idealised. In other words, if Irish representations of Finnish, Swedish, Norwegian, Danish or Icelandic cultures, at times, fail to do justice to the diversity between and within these nation states, Nordic perceptions of Ireland are no less in danger of veering towards romanticised images of the green island of bardic poetry and song. Titles such as the Norwegian *Grøne dikt* ('Green poems'), the 2005 anthology of modern Irish poetry, or *Bardernas Irland* ('Ireland of the bards') the 1993 Swedish-language volume, are good examples.[9] Regardless of authors', scholars' and translators' approaches, publishers may reach out to audiences by drawing their attention to recognisable markers of Irishness. The opposite tendency is to present Irish writing in anthologies of 'English and American' literature, as in the case of Asplund and Silfverstolpe's older poetry anthology *Vers från väster: Modern engelsk och amerikansk lyrik* ('Verse from the west: modern English and American poetry'), which includes translations of Oscar Wilde's and W.B. Yeats's poetry.[10]

The biggest challenge for the task of mapping Irish literature's presence in Nordic culture and cultural production is the sheer size and diversity of the geographical and cultural region covered, from Denmark's southern border to the Norwegian coastline at the Arctic Sea, and from the non-Scandinavian Finland in the east to the north-western edges of Iceland. And while Danish, Norwegian and Swedish languages are sufficiently related to communicate across linguistic borders, the same does not quite apply to their more distant Scandinavian cousin Icelandic. The Finno-Ugric Finnish has less in common with any of these languages than Irish has with modern Swedish or Russian, though it is related to the Sami languages of northern Finland and Scandinavia. Thus, the sheer variety of ways in which Ireland's literature has been encountered in the region would make it challenging to do justice to the topic of Irish presence in the Nordic region even in a full-length monograph, let alone in a short chapter.

A considerable number of translations exists of works by Beckett, Joyce and Yeats; there are theatrical productions of the works of Synge, Shaw and more contemporary authors, including Marina Carr, Brian Friel, Marie Jones, Conor McPherson or Enda Walsh (to mention but a few); numerous translations of and literary engagements with contemporary poets and novelists including Seamus Heaney, Paul Muldoon,

Roddy Doyle, Anne Enright, Colm Tóibín, John McGahern or Marian Keyes can be found. An even bigger challenge is the charting of Irish literary presence and influence that may go beyond explicit literary reference or repurposing of Irish literary texts. Works that *do* acknowledge their Irish antecedents include, for example, the Norwegian Tomas Espedal's 2013 novel *Bergeners* (translated into English in 2017 by James Anderson), which openly acknowledges the influence of the portraits of Joyce's *Dubliners* in its portrayal of the people of Norway's second biggest city (and this is anything but downplayed in the marketing material by the volume's Norwegian publisher Gyldendal).[11] In Finland, Jyrki Vainonen's translations of Irish poetry, particularly focusing on the work of Seamus Heaney and Paul Muldoon, have been accompanied by his own work in narrative fiction, for example the 2011 novel *Swiftin Ovella* ('At Swift's door'). The novel tells the story of a man called Lennart Beren who time-travels back to eighteenth-century Dublin to become Watt, Swift's servant, though he fails to become an observer of the great author's daily life in the manner he had initially planned.[12] Encounters with Ireland may also be filtered through other European perspectives; the best known example is probably Heinrich Böll's 1957 *Irisches Tagebuch*, which has been translated into all major Nordic languages, as *Irsk dagbog* (Danish), *Irsk dagbok* (Norwegian), *Irländsk dagbok* (Swedish), *Úr írskri dagbók* (translated section only, Icelandic) and *Päiväkirja vihreältä saarelta* (Finnish).[13]

What Bjørn Tysdahl has noted in the context of Joyce's presence in modern Norwegian writing applies to Nordic–Irish literary exchanges more widely: the question of influence is 'a slippery one'.[14] And Tysdahl's comments on the literary engagement with Joyce's writing in Norway are also applicable to the question of creative literary dialogues generally:

> The main reason for [the challenge of mapping these engagements] is found in the nature of international influences in a shrinking world. A creative writer may be in a position in which she or he knows something, though not necessarily a lot, about very many contemporary or near-contemporary writers. Even authors that the creative writer barely knows can be an inspiration.[15]

Anne Karhio

Ulrika Maude similarly acknowledges the complexities related to tracing Beckett's presence in Nordic literature, as 'Beckett is ever the shape-shifter'.[16] His minimalist style and the scarcity of explicit cultural or intertextual reference in many of his texts may make his work more adaptable to new contexts and languages, but this also leaves more room for uncertainty when it comes to establishing connections between the Irish author and those who draw on his work in other languages.

Despite the challenges involved in tracing the roots and routes of literary influence, it is nevertheless possible to suggest some starting points for further, more detailed discussions. In the following pages there is more focus on fiction and poetry than on drama, as discussing theatrical performances and translations poses its own additional demands. Engagement with original texts, translations and scholarly works in different Nordic languages would also require a considerable degree of detailed consideration of these languages, as would a discussion of Irish-language literature and literary culture. The latter is therefore given less attention than it would deserve, and is thus left for another occasion, even though Nordic scholars have made some notable contributions to the study of Irish-language literary and folk tradition, perhaps the best known example being the Swedish folklorist Bo Almqvist. The translation of Máirtín Ó Cadhain's *Cré na cille* into Danish (by Ole Munch-Pedersen in 2000) and Norwegian (by Jan Erik Rekdal in 1995) before its first publication in English would certainly also merit further attention.[17] The historical period covered in this discussion is mostly limited to the twentieth and twenty-first century, and thus excludes the vast amount of scholarship and hundreds of years of cultural exchange between Scandinavia and Ireland before and during the modern period.[18] And, finally, the limiting of the discussion to literary texts and engagements in national majority languages excludes examination of the possible exchanges between Irish literary texts and minority languages, like the different varieties of Sami, Faroese, Romani or the numerous languages of immigrant communities in the Nordic region.[19]

Revivals and recognitions

One of the contexts in which Nordic or Scandinavian literature already made an impact on the Irish literary imagination prior to the twentieth century was that of the Irish cultural revival, and literature of this same period written by self-identified non-revivalists, most importantly James Joyce. The connections that emerged were, to no small degree, a result of the perceived similarity of experiences between Ireland and those Nordic countries that were also striving for national sovereignty, or had done so in recent decades. As John Wilson Foster has noted in the context of Finland, for example, 'the Finnish experience of cultural revival … largely preceded the Irish experience' as the country sought to define its self-image during the nineteenth century, 'under Swedish and later under Russian administration, like the Irish under English'.[20]

The role of the Norwegian plays of Ibsen, the editing of folk literature by the Finnish philologist Elias Lönnrot (the compiler of the national epic *Kalevala*), or the cultural significance of the Sagas, were a frequent point of reference for Yeats, for example, who in 'The Celtic element in literature' presented various Nordic examples to support his ideas on the role that Ireland's folk literature and cultural tradition could play in building the nation's future.[21] In the later essay 'The bounty of Sweden', Yeats's account of his visit to Sweden to receive his Nobel Prize in literature in 1923, the poet's views on Irish society were contextualised through Nordic points of comparison, and were also presented through comments made by his fellow passengers en route to Sweden, via Denmark.[22] While the kingdom of Denmark itself was understandably less preoccupied with urgent questions of nation-building, the most eastern of the Nordic countries was presented as undergoing a struggle not unlike that of Ireland:

> … when I am asked about Ireland I answer always that if the British Empire becomes a voluntary Federation of Free Nations, all will be well, but if it remains as in the past, a domination of one, the Irish question is not settled. That done with, I can talk of the work of my generation in Ireland, the creation of a literature to express national character and feeling but with no deliberate political aim. A journalist who has lived in Finland says, 'Finland has had to struggle with Russian influence to preserve its national culture'.[23]

Anne Karhio

The reference is brief and remains somewhat isolated; no other mention of Finland's historical situation is made in the essay, and the Norwegian national character is similarly described by a fellow passenger in one single instance as 'rough'.[24] Yeats does describe his attempts to find out more about Swedish literature by unsuccessfully trying to purchase 'some history of Sweden, or of Swedish literature' in Dublin before his trip; the poet also makes several references to Ibsen, Swedenborg and Strindberg.[25] Nordic cultures and traditions thus had a certain impact on Yeats's own work, but even more importantly for the topic of this essay, the Nobel Prize and the journey to Sweden also had a lasting influence on Yeats's role in Swedish literary culture (I will return to this in the context of literary translation below).

For reasons that go beyond the scope of this chapter, the Nordic countries that gained national sovereignty in the early twentieth century—Finland, Iceland and Norway—have not as frequently been examined through the frameworks of the 'colonial' or 'post-colonial' condition, in popular discourse or in scholarly discussion, as Ireland has in recent years. This applies to the societies' own cultural self-perception, which does not focus on them as subjects of colonial rule *per se*, as well as to a mixed response to the idea of their own participation in, or complicity with, the European colonial project.[26] In addressing the situation of Finland and Norway, Hans Hauge raises the question of whether the term 'post-colonial' can be applied to these countries and societies at all, and stresses that in as much as it is applicable, it should be considered in an expanded sense of the term 'colonial'.[27] (The borders of Nordic nation states also mask more extreme cases of colonial marginalisation *within* these states, perhaps most notably in the experience of the Sami cultures in Finnish, Swedish and Norwegian Lapland.) Hauge draws on Toril Moi, and points out that 'post-colonial' in the case of a society like Norway does not mean that the country would have been a colony in the strictest sense of the word, but that it was, for a large part of its history, not an independent, sovereign nation.[28]

According to Moi, suitable parallels for understanding an author like Henrik Ibsen can be found in Ireland in the figures of George Bernard Shaw, Oscar Wilde and James Joyce, and the connections between Ibsen, Joyce and Yeats and Nordic cultures have been studied in detail by a number of scholars.[29] Yet in the case of Ibsen, the exchange was largely, if not entirely, one-sided, not least because Ibsen's reputation was established well before Joyce's, or even Yeats's.

While one should thus remain wary of any straightforward adoption of the post-colonial framework in the Nordic context, it may, nevertheless, be useful for a tentative consideration of the possible reasons for the different emphases in the reception of Irish authors in the region. In addition to outlining Ibsen's impact on the Irish Revival and the work of Joyce, Bjørn Tysdahl, for example, has argued that Joyce received more early scholarly and literary attention in Norway than elsewhere in the Nordic countries—with the 'possible exception of Finland'—and he sees that this can at least partially be explained by 'the similarities between Ireland and Norway', as 'both were poor countries on the outskirts of Western Europe', and had a complicated relationship with their bigger neighbours.[30] The first translator of Joyce's *Ulysses* into Swedish, Thomas Warburton, was a (Swedish-speaking) Finn, though it should be noted that Hannu Riikonen's discussion of Joyce's Finnish and Swedish reception is more restrained in drawing conclusions regarding shared *cultural* experience in various public figures' interest in Joyce's writing.[31] Interestingly, according to Greve and Povlsen, the initial responses to Joyce's writing in the neighbouring Denmark were reserved, yet the first Danish translations of his work were published during the German occupation of World War Two, and the political Left, especially, read Joyce as a 'European' and an 'innovator'.[32] They also note that the wider interest in European symbolism had its impact on the partial marginalisation of Joyce in Danish modernism.[33] In the kingdom of Sweden, itself a colonial power historically, a sense of national/cultural marginalisation did not offer points of identification, and was replaced by other emphases. For example, Beckett's Nobel Prize award, like Yeats's, raised awareness of his work, despite (or perhaps also because of) the author's rather adverse reaction of exclaiming '*Quelle catastrophe!*' at first hearing about the award.[34]

But comments echoing Tysdahl's observations have also been made in discussions of other Irish writers' Nordic reception, including reaction to Beckett's work. Ulrika Maude, for example, argues that the shared historical experiences between Finland and Ireland can help illustrate why Finland was the first to stage Beckett's theatrical work, and why the author appealed to Finnish cultural practitioners. According to

Anne Karhio

Maude, '[the] author's awkward, off-kilter characters have appealed to the Finnish imagination, perhaps, for obvious historical reasons ... The similarities with Irish history are obvious'. These include the strive for national sovereignty and independence in the nineteenth and twentieth century, the focus on the indigenous language, the search for cultural self-definition, and a sense of linguistic and cultural otherness under a foreign ruler.[35] She similarly considers Beckett's reception in Norway through such a historical perspective (also referencing Moi's views expressed in the context of Ibsen), though with an awareness of the specific circumstances of the literary cultures of each country. She underlines, for example, the Finnish sense of cultural difference in the Nordic region as a non-Scandinavian country bordering the Russian empire, and Norway's shared experience with Ireland due to them both being North-Atlantic coastal communities with an overwhelmingly rural society.[36] Such connections are, of course, highly generalised, and establishing links between historical circumstances and literary aesthetics or reception remains, by necessity, somewhat speculative and in need of much more detailed research.

In other words, the relationship between cultural and national specificity, (expanded) post-colonialism, historical parallels, and literary cross-currents between different countries, is at best a complicated issue. The extent of the challenge is well demonstrated by the fact that even in the context of English-language literary studies, the Nordic connections of key literary figures like Beckett, Joyce and Yeats alone have been outlined in numerous scholarly studies, and even more research has been published in Nordic languages, and in the context of individual Nordic authors' works.[37] The different responses to the texts of these twentieth-century authors in Finland, Sweden, Norway or Denmark, however, seem to suggest that the reception and influence of these key figures of Irish and European literature was, at least partially, informed by the ways in which they offered moments of shared experience and recognition to the literary audiences in different Nordic countries, or enabled authors and audiences to address issues closer to home through the perspectives offered by literary figures from elsewhere.

Translation: language and culture

Within a region of five nation states and languages, and numerous minority languages, the work of translators plays a key role in making literature from other countries and linguistic traditions accessible to reading audiences.[38] And while a considerable percentage of the Nordic population is fluent enough in English to be able to read English-language texts in the original, the significance of translation goes beyond simple access. Any act of translation requires an intimacy between the translator and the literary text that encourages further creative engagement, and as translators are also often scholars or literary authors themselves, such intimacy is likely to leave a lasting mark on their own writing. Furthermore, in addition to the questions relating to the subtleties of literary expression and the challenges they pose to linguistic as well as cultural translation, the choice of who translates, what, and when is related to the complex processes of literary readership, cross-cultural communication, education, and the economic frameworks guiding literary dissemination and publishers' decision-making. The above section's discussion on historical experiences of cultural self-determination and definition is only a small part of this process.

Irish literature has found a route into the original literary works of its Nordic translators, published in these translators' native languages, in various ways. In Finland, the radically modernist writing of Pentti Saarikoski drew on his detailed reading of Joyce during his translation work and can be detected, for example, in the 1964 novel *Ovat muistojemme lehdet kuolleet* ('Dead are the leaves of our memories'), and the autobiographical prose volume *Kirje vaimolleni* ('A letter to my wife').[39] The novel, as Hannu Riikonen observes, uses the Joycean technique of narrative collage, and its perambulations in the city of Helsinki bear a close resemblance to the 'Wandering rocks' episode of *Ulysses. Kirje vaimolleni* presents Saarikoski wandering around the city of Dublin, which he has already encountered in Joyce's texts, and imagining how he would show the Irish capital to his wife.[40] Tysdahl similarly detects Joyce's presence in the Norwegian Sigurd Christiansen's trilogy *Drømmen og livet* ('The dream and the life'), *Det ensomme hjerte* ('The lonely heart') and *Menneskenes lod* ('The people's lot').[41] In Iceland, the Nobel-winning author Halldór Laxness's encounters with Joyce have

Anne Karhio

been seen to have had a profound impact on the (somewhat belated) rise of the novel within the country's literary culture, though the Irish writer otherwise long remained a somewhat marginal presence in Icelandic literary culture.[42]

In his reading of Jørgen Sonnes's and Mogens Boisen's Danish translations of *Ulysses*, Ida Klitgård emphasises different approaches to linguistic, as well as cultural translations by adopting the framework of Lawrence Venutis's translation theory and the concepts of 'domestication' and 'foreignisation'. Sonnes seeks to make the translated text as accessible as possible to the reader in the target language, and foregrounds the new ethnic/cultural home of the translated work. By contrast, Boisen foregrounds the unfamiliar and foreign elements of the text, thus seeking to draw the reader into the world of the literary work he or she encounters, and away from the familiar ground of his/her own ethnic and cultural context.[43] These approaches can also be useful in addressing the issues related to the less than clear-cut distinction between translation and the creation of a new, original literary text. Andersson's account of his translation of Joyce in *Dag in och dag ut med en dag i Dublin*, for example, can be seen as a balancing act between 'domestication' and 'foreignisation', as a *mélange* of autobiographical and literary engagement with translation.

The presence of Yeats in the Nordic region is perhaps somewhat more limited than Joyce's (though there are considerable differences between approaches in different countries), and there are likely to be a variety of reasons for this (including the historical/cultural perceptions regarding his Anglo-Irish background, and the more limited overall interest in lyric poetry versus prose fiction). As Klaus Peter Jochum suggests, the Swedish engagements with Yeats's writing have perhaps been most numerous, not least because of the 1923 Nobel Prize award and Yeats's visit to Stockholm to retrieve it.[44] The attention given to Yeats's work in Scandinavia and the Baltic region, however, mostly in the form of translation, has received little attention and is only summarised in a couple of short pages in Jochum's *The reception of W.B. Yeats in Europe*. To date, no book-length translation of Yeats's work has appeared in Norwegian, for example, although there have been some performances of his plays, and the Norwegian responses and early translations of Yeats were earlier than those of other Nordic countries.

Furthermore, at the time of the publication of Jochum's volume, there was only one anthology of Yeats's selected poems translated into Finnish, published by Aale Tynni in 1966; Jyrki Vainonen has, however, since published another volume of translations.[45] Two book-length translations have appeared in Denmark: *Drømmerier over barneår og ungdom* (*Reveries over childhood and youth*) and *Blæsten mellem sivene* (*The wind among the reeds*).[46] At present, however, Jochum's overview is in need of updating, as interest in Yeats's work has surged in recent years. In Sweden, the most extensive selection of Yeats's poems to date was published in Ann-Kristin Åklint's translation in 2012, with the title *Ett kristalliskt rop: dikter i urval* ('A crystalline cry: selection of poems'), and the same year also saw the publication of *Tornet* (*The tower*), translated by Thomas Sjöswärd Bromberg. Yet another selection of poems, *Valda dikter* ('Selected poems') by Gunnar Artéus appeared in 2014.[47] Publishers and translators tend to respond to significant dates relating to well-known authors' biographies, and the 150th-anniversary of Yeats's birth also sparked a renewed interest in the poet's work in all Nordic countries, as well as in Ireland and internationally. In addition to numerous talks, seminars and other scholarly gatherings, several volumes and news articles offering new translations of Yeats's work were published all over the Nordic region. In Finland, the Irish poet's anniversary also coincided with the 150th-anniversary of the composer Jean Sibelius, who, in many ways, holds a similar position in the Finnish cultural imagination as Yeats does in Ireland. Indeed, Vainonen opened his introduction to *Torni ja kierreportaat* ('The tower and the winding stair') by pointing out the parallels between the biographies of these two cultural figures.[48]

Gender: reception of high and popular Irish literature

While the above discussion on Irish presences in Nordic literature is, by necessity, merely a cursory overview of some of the authors and themes that characterise the overall topic, what particularly stands out in much of the scholarly material addressing Nordic encounters with Irish literature in the twentieth century is the strong gender bias that can be detected among authors who have been most frequently discussed and who are most influential in translation, in scholarship, and in creative production. It would be misleading to say that Irish women authors have remained entirely unregistered in the Nordic countries, of course. In Norway, Radioteatret has staged plays by Lady Gregory, for example, and Marina Carr's *The bog of cats* was performed in Norwegian as *Ved kattemyra* at *Den Nationale Scene* in Bergen in 2004. Elizabeth Bowen's *Huset i Paris* (*House in Paris*, 1947), and *Lykken og de høstlige jordene* (*The demon lover and other stories*, 1949) precede Norwegian translations of novels by Anne Enright and Deirdre Madden. The work of Eavan Boland and Eva Bourke appears alongside Heaney, Muldoon, Montague and others in the 2005 anthology *Grøne dikt* ('Green poems'), edited by Knut Ødegård and Jostein Sæbøe. Elizabeth Bowen's work has also appeared in Danish, Swedish and Finnish, as has Anne Enright's and Edna O'Brien's. Book-length translations of Irish women's poetry have only been published in Denmark, where a selection of Medbh McGuckian's verse was translated by Peter Laugersen as *Det sprog Fergus taler i drømme, udvalgte digte* ('The dream-language of Fergus'), and a selection of Nuala Ní Dhomhnaill's was translated as *Ellefolk, udvalgte digte* ('Fairies: selected poems') by Ole Munch-Pedersen and Peter Nielsen.[49] This list is far from complete, but it is nevertheless safe to say that even a more detailed account would pale in comparison with the various translations of poetry and fiction by established contemporary male authors. The discrepancy is particularly noticeable in the translation of contemporary Irish poetry: numerous volumes by Paul Muldoon and Seamus Heaney have appeared in all Nordic countries, and there are also several volumes of translations of the work of Michael Longley, Derek Mahon and Ciaran Carson.

It is in the area of popular narrative fiction, however, that Irish women authors have gained more ground, as some of the examples mentioned above already suggest. In addition to established authors who have attracted much scholarly attention, including for example Bowen, Enright, Madden and O'Brien, by far the most prominent Irish literary presence in the Nordic countries today is the work of Irish women writers of popular prose fiction. While popular male authors such as Roddy Doyle and Frank McCourt have been translated widely into different Nordic languages, the popularity of their work pales in comparison to the number of translated volumes by women novelists such as Cecilia Ahern, Maeve Binchy and Marian Keyes, whose writing is available in all Nordic languages. The work of these authors is discussed less in scholarly papers or literary publications than it is in blog posts and magazines, and the English term 'chick-lit' is in wide use in Nordic countries, too. It can be argued, however, that Irish popular fiction by women contests and highlights, more than any other area of Irish literature available in Nordic countries today, the established emphases on high modernist writing in scholarly discourse. Such fiction also steers clear of the romanticised perceptions and narratives of Irish cultural nationalism (with their focus on rural landscapes and various forms of folk tradition), still often repeated in the reception and analysis of Irish literary culture. If Yeats, Joyce and Beckett have become a part of the high literary canon in a manner that transcends the Irish context, the work of contemporary female Irish authors of chick-lit also frequently moves beyond specific frameworks of Irishness. Instead, it is often considered, in popular media and scholarship, in the context of gender, society and literary reception more widely.[50] No term similar to 'chick-lit' has emerged to describe popular fiction by men, and the responses to popular fiction by women, with a largely female audience, are frequently marked by a considerable degree of 'snobbery' as one Danish literary blog describes it.[51]

While the aesthetic complexity of popular fiction may indeed be more limited and may merit an approach that differs from that applied to more formally and philosophically ambitious literary works, this does not explain the difference between responses to popular fiction by women and men. In other words, the international reach of Irish chick-lit writers is hardly less extensive than is the case with the established figures of Irish literary modernism and beyond, and the reasons for the scholarly dismissal of much of the former goes beyond a simple division between 'high' and 'popular' literature. The phenomenon has been discussed in more detail by Sorcha Gunne, for example, who adopts the perspectives of world literature and global capitalism to consider the economic and socio-political contexts of women's popular fiction from Ireland, and its circulation. Importantly, Gunne stresses that despite the frequent focus on Western, highly educated, middle-class women across national/cultural boundaries, chick-lit is 'not the same everywhere'.[52] Irish chick-lit, too, becomes something different as it is received in the Nordic countries. The focus on the historical and social context of Irish women's place and status in society, as stressed by Gunne, for example,

Anne Karhio

or the impact of the Irish constitution's statement that the place of women (as mothers) is in the domestic sphere, gets little attention in Nordic discussions of Irish chick-lit. Instead, many readers, including scholars and students, focus more on issues of gender and agency in general, or consider Irish chick-lit in the context of the literature of the whole English-speaking world; Cecelia Ahern and Helen Fielding are considered equal representatives of the chick-lit phenomenon in the Anglo-American cultural sphere.

Conclusion

The above examples, while limited in scope and depth, demonstrate the highly diverse ways in which artistic and literary communities in different Nordic countries have responded to Irish literary encounters from their own specific cultural and historical coordinates. As Edna Longley has stressed in the context of Northern Irish poetry and 'internationalism', 'any poet seizes the familiar in the foreign' in an act of translation.[53] The same applies to genres other than poetry, as well as other forms of literary circulation, and is no less the case with prose writers, playwrights, scholars or literary audiences, in academia and beyond. Longley quotes Pierre Bourdieu, who pointed out that when

> texts circulate without their context ... they don't bring with them the field of production of which they are a product, and the fact that the recipients, who are themselves in a different field of production, re-interpret the texts in accordance with the structure of the field of reception.[54]

Thus, in the case of Irish drama in Finland, for example, Sirkku Aaltonen has, in a similar manner, argued that performances of Irish plays in Finnish theatres should be examined primarily as cases of *Finnish* literary production.[55]

Whether one focuses on Irish literature or the cultural distinctiveness of Finland, Sweden, Norway, Denmark or Iceland, this chapter has sought to highlight, through specific examples and some tentative suggestions, that understanding the impact of Irish literature on Nordic culture and literary production resists easy generalisations related to national or cultural character, or geographical context, but is, never-theless, unavoidably linked to such contexts. More than anything, the aim has been to draw attention to differences, gaps, and uncharted ter-ritories in these literary exchanges, and to highlight a demand for more detailed studies on individual authors' works, and new translations of authors whose work is yet to be recognised in Europe's north.

Notes

[1] Here and elsewhere in this chapter, I use quotation marks for my English translations of the original titles in Nordic languages, in cases where no published English language title exists. In cases where I refer to a published title of an English-language (or Irish-language) original, I use italics.

[2] Pentti Saarikoski, *Euroopan reuna: kineettinen kuva* (1983), quoted in Yrjö Hosiaisluoma, *Euroopan reunalla, kosken korvalla—Jumalten narri Pentti Saarikoski* (Like; Helsinki, 1998), 341. Author's translation from Finnish original: 'Matka päättyy tähän, kun istun Ormondin hotellihuoneessa Dublinissa ja katselen Anna Liviaa, veden yllä kaartelevia lokkeja, ja taloriviä vastapäisellä rannalla. Tai ei matka pääty, minä vain olen istunut tässä ennenkin, ja tällä tavalla katsellut. Tuota taloriviä ei mikään kaupunkisuunnitte-lija ole ajatellut, epäjärjestys siinä on niin suuri että kun sitä aikansa on katsellut, ja sitten palaa katselemaan, tämä on minulle neljäs kerta, epäjärjestys muuttuu järjestyk-seksi ja kauneudeksi, joka on muisto.'

[3] Author's translation, from Erik Andersson, *Dag in och dag ut med en dag i Dublin* (Albert Bonniers Förlag; Stockholm, 2012), 19. Swedish original: 'Jag kommer in, hänger av mig, snörar upp kängorna, hämtar vattenkokaren, tar på sandalerna, går bort till pentryt, spolar upp vatten, går tillbaka, tar av sandalerna, sätter på vattnet, mäter upp kaffepulver, tänder lysröret, sätter på mobilen, plockar fram cigarretterna, slår på datorn, undrar var usb-minnet är, ser efter om det finns choklad. Det har hunnit bli Februari, småruskigt, härdande väder, men i Dublin ör det fortfarande den 16 Juni 1904, klockan är tio på morgonen och vi kommer rakt in i en historielektion som Stephen Dedalus håller i en privatskola för pojkar i Dalkei en bit ner längs kusten frå tornet i Sandycove.'

[4] Jacob Greve and Steen Klitgård Povlsen, 'The reception of James Joyce in Denmark', in Geer Lernout and Wim Van Mierlo (eds), *The reception of James Joyce in Europe*. Vol. 1: *Germany, Northern and Eastern Central Europe* (Continuum; London and New York, 2004), 111–28: 121.

[5] Hanna Tuuri, *Irlantilainen aamiainen: kertomuksia vihreältä saarelta* (Otava; Helsinki, 2013); Gösta Oswald, *Breven till Ranveig* (Bokförlaget Atlantis; Stockholm, 1995).

[6] Mats Jansson, Jacob Lothe and Hannu Riikonen (eds), *European and Nordic modern-isms* (Norvik Press; London, 2004).

[7] Jansson, Lothe and Riikonen, *European and Nordic modernisms*, 12.

[8] See, Anders Olsson, 'Exile and literary modernism', and Peter Fjågesund, 'The modern-ist tower: a many-faceted symbol', in Mats Jansson, Jacob Lothe and Hannu Riikonen (eds), *European and Nordic modernisms* (Norvik Press; London, 2004), 37–50 and 233–51.

Anne Karhio

[9] Jostein Sæbøe and Knut Ødegård (eds), *Grøne dikt: 9 moderne irske lyrikarar* (Cappelen Damm; Oslo, 2005), and Ingeborg Nilsson and Jan Östergren, *Bardernas Irland* (Symposion; Stockholm, 1993).

[10] Karl Asplund and Gunnar M. Silfverstolpe (eds), *Vers från väster. Modern engelsk och amerikansk lyrik* (Bonnier; Stockholm, 1922).

[11] Thomas Espedal, *Bergeners* (Gyldendal; Oslo, 2014).

[12] See, Jyrki Vainonen, *Swiftin Ovella* (Tammi; Helsinki, 2011).

[13] Heinrich Böll, *Irsk dagbog*, transl. Herbert Steinthal (Grafisk; Copenhagen, 1965); *Irsk dagbok*, transl. Morten Ringard (Gyldendal; Oslo, 1973); *Irländsk dagbok*, transl. Karin Franke (Aldus; Stockholm, 1972); *Úr írskri dagbók*, transl. I. Grein (Lesbók Morgunblaðsins; Reykjavik, 1973), 14; and *Päiväkirja vihreältä saarelta*, transl. Kai Kaila (Otava; Helsinki, 1975).

[14] Bjørn Tysdahl, 'The reception of James Joyce in Norway', in Geert Lernout and Wim Van Mierlo (eds), *The reception of James Joyce in Europe*. Vol. 1: *Germany, Northern and Eastern Central Europe* (Continuum; London and New York, 2004), 103–10: 110.

[15] Tysdahl, 'Joyce in Norway', 110.

[16] Ulrika Maude, 'Beckett's Nordic reception', in Mark Nixon and Matthew Feldman (eds), *The international reception of Samuel Beckett* (Continuum; London and New York, 2009), 234–50: 249.

[17] Ole Munch-Pedersen (transl.), *Kirkegårdsjord: genfortælling i ti mellemspil* (Husets Forlag; Århus, 2000) and Jan Erik Rekdal (transl.), *Kirkegårdsjord: gjenfortellinger i ti mellomspill* (Gyldendal Norsk Forlag; Oslo, 1995).

[18] For research and scholarship on historical connections between Irish and Scandinavian folklore and literary traditions, see, for example, Bo Almqvist, 'Scandinavian and Celtic folklore contacts in the earldom of Orkney', *Saga-Book* 20 (1978–81), 80–105, and 'Waterhorse legends (MLSIT 4086 and 4086B): the case for and against a connection between Irish and Nordic tradition', *Béaloideas* 59 (1991), 107–20; Gísli Sigurðsson, *Gaelic influence in Iceland: historical and literary contacts: a survey of research* (Bókaútgáfa Menningarsjóðs; Reyjkavik, 1988).

[19] For an overview on minority cultures and literatures in the Nordic region, see, Eila Rantonen and Matti Savolainen, 'Postcolonial and ethnic studies in the context of Nordic minority literatures', in Satu Gröndahl (ed.), *Invandrar- och minoritetslitteratur i nordiskt perspektiv* (Uppsala Multiethnic Papers 24, Uppsala Universitet; Uppsala, 2002), 71–94.

[20] John Wilson Foster, *Fictions of the Irish literary revival: a changeling art* (Syracuse University Press; Syracuse, NY, 1987), 20.

[21] W.B. Yeats, 'The Celtic element in literature', in *Essays and introductions* (The Macmillan Press; London and Basingstoke, 1961a), 173–88.

[22] W.B. Yeats, 'The bounty of Sweden', in *Autobiographies: the collected works of W.B. Yeats, Volume 3* (Scribner; New York, 1999), 389–409.

[23] W.B. Yeats, *Autobiographies* (Macmillan; London, 1961c), 536.

[24] Yeats, *Autobiographies*, 535.

[25] Yeats, *Autobiographies*, 533.

[26] Joel Kuortti, Mikko Lehtonen and Olli Löytty in their recent volume of essays *Kolonialismin jäljet* ('The traces of colonialism'; Gaudeamus; Helsinki, 2007), for example, state that their work is one of the few to examine Finnish history as colonial, and modern Finland as a postcolonial society. On colonialism, post-colonialism and

colonial complicity in the Nordic context, see also Salla Tuori, Sari Irni, Suvi Keskinen and Diana Mulinari (eds), *Complying with colonialism: gender, race and ethnicity in the Nordic region* (Ashgate; Aldershot, 2009).

[27] Hans Hauge, 'Norsk litteratur som post-kolonial?', *Passage* 23 (59) (2008), 19–32:19.

[28] Hauge, 'Norsk litteratur', 25.

[29] See, for example, Irina Ruppo Malone, *Ibsen and the Irish revival* (Palgrave Macmillan; Houndmills, Basingstoke, 2010) and Tore Rem, 'Nationalism or internationalism? The early Irish reception of Ibsen', *Ibsen Studies* 7 (2) (2007), 188–202.

[30] Tysdahl, 'Joyce in Norway', 103–10.

[31] Hannu Riikonen, 'Blooms of the north: the translations of *Ulysses* in Finland and Sweden', in Geert Lernout and Wim Van Mierlo (eds), *The reception of James Joyce in Europe*. Vol. 1: *Germany, Northern and Eastern Central Europe* (Continuum; London and New York, 2004), 129–39.

[32] Greve and Povlsen, 'Joyce in Denmark', 114.

[33] Greve and Povlsen, 'Joyce in Denmark', 111.

[34] Maude, 'Beckett's Nordic reception', 234.

[35] Maude, 'Beckett's Nordic reception', 234.

[36] Maude, 'Beckett's Nordic reception', 234.

[37] In the case of Joyce, see, for example, Tommy Olofsson, 'James Joyce och den sekulära uppenbarelsen', *Svenska Dagbladet*, 23 July 2011, 4; Hannu Riikonen, '*Ulysses*—tekstin ja tulkinnan odysseiat', *Niin & Näin: filosofinen aikakauslehti* 3 (2012b), 122–5; Linnea Wenell, *Den engelska ing-formen i nyöversättning: en komparativ grammatisk studie av två svenska översättningar av James Joyces Ulysses* (Uppsala Universitet; Uppsala, 2015).

[38] See, for example, Hannu Riikonen, 'Klassikot: käännöksiä ja uusintakäännöksiä', *Kiiltomato.net* 7 (June 2012a), available online at: http://www.kiiltomato.net/klassikot-kaannoksia-ja-uusintakaannoksia/ (6 January 2018); Yvonne Lindqvist, *Högt och lågt i skönlitterär översättning till svenska* (Hallgren och Fallgren; Stockholm, 2005).

[39] Pentti Saarikoski, *Ovat muistojemme lehdet kuolleet* (Otava; Helsinki, 1964) and *Kirje vaimolleni* (Otava; Helsinki, 1968).

[40] See Riikonen, 'Blooms in the north', 137.

[41] Tysdahl, 'Joyce in Norway', 110; Sigurd Christiansen, *Drømmen og livet* (Gyldendal; Oslo, 2013 [1935]); *Det ensomme hjerte* (Gyldendal; Oslo, 2012a [1938]); *Menneskenes lod* (Gyldendal; Oslo, 2012b [1945]).

[42] Astadur Eysteinsson, 'Late arrivals: James Joyce in Iceland', in Geer Lernout and Wim Van Mierlo (eds), *The reception of James Joyce in Europe*. Vol. 1: *Germany, Northern and Eastern Central Europe* (Continuum; London and New York, 2004), 89–102: 90–3.

[43] Ida Klitgård, 'Hjemliggørelse og fremmegørelse: *Ulysses* på dansk ved Jørgen Sonne og Mogens Boisen', *Tijdschrift voor Skandinavistiek* 33 (1) (2012), 5–13.

[44] Klaus Peter Jochum, 'Epilogue: Yeats from Iceland to Turkey', in Klaus Peter Jochum (ed.), *The reception of W. B. Yeats in Europe* (Continuum; London and New York, 2006), 255–66: 256.

[45] W. B. Yeats, *William Butler Yeats: Runoja*, transl. Aale Tynni (WSOY; Helsinki, 1966) and W.B. Yeats, *Torni ja kierreportaat: valikoima W.B. Yeatsin runoja*, transl. Jyrki Vainonen (Basam Books; Helsinki 2015).

[46] W.B. Yeats, *Blæsten mellem sivene: digte og skuespil*, transl. Valdemar Rørdam (B. Haase og søns forlag; Copenhagen, 1924a); *Drømmerier over Barneår og Ungdom*, transl. Valdemar Rørdam (B. Haase og søns forlag; Copenhagen, 1924b).

Anne Karhio

[47] W.B. Yeats, *Ett kristalliskt rop: dikter i urval,* transl. Ann-Kristin Åklint (Lund; Elleströms, 2012a); W.B. Yeats, *Tornet,* transl. Thomas Sjöswärd (Bromberg; Stockholm, 2012b), W.B. Yeats, *Valda Dikter,* transl. Gunnar Artéus (Nacka; Sköna konster förlag, 2014).

[48] Jyrki Vainonen, 'Elämästä syntyy järkyttävä kauneus—W.B. Yeats istä ja hänen runoudestaan', in *Torni ja kierreportaat: valikoima W.B. Yeatsin runoja,* transl. Jyrki Vainonen (Basam Books; Helsinki, 2015), 5–22: 5.

[49] Medbh McGuckian, *Det sprog Fergus taler i drømme: udvalgte digte,* transl. Peter Laugesen (Husets Forlag; Stockholm, 1996) and Nuala Ní Dhomhnaill, *Ellefolk: udvalgte digte af Nuala Ní Dhomhnaill,* transl. Ole Munch-Pederson and Peter Nielsen (Husets Forlag; Stockholm, 1996).

[50] For examples on Nordic responses to chick-lit, including Irish authors see Emilie Boyd, *Chick lit and existentialismen: en undersökning kring chick lit—hjältinnan* (Högskolan i Halmstad, 2010); Charlotte Jørgensen, 'Kvindelighedens snubletråde: chicklit i et nordisk perspektiv', in *The history of Nordic women's literature* (28 September 2016), available online at: https://nordicwomensliterature.net/da/2016/09/28/kvindelighedens-snubletraade-chicklit-i-et-nordisk-perspektiv/ (9 January 2018); Laura Lahtinen, *Chick lit -kirjallisuus Suomen yleisissä kirjastoissa - maakuntakirjastojen tarkastelua,* Pro Gradu thesis (SeAMK; Seinäjoki, 2017); Charlotta Lindell, 'Chick lit litteraturen som fyller tomrummet', *Sydsvenskan* (22 June 2003), available online at: https://www.sydsvenskan.se/2003-06-22/chick-lit-litteraturen-som-fyller-tomrummet (9 January 2018).

[51] Birgitte Tindbæk, 'Irske Stemmer i Litteraturen—Januar/Februar 2009', available online at: https://litteratursiden.dk/temaer/irske-stemmer-i-litteraturen-januarfebruar-2009 (12 December 2017).

[52] See, Sorcha Gunne, 'World-literature, world-systems and Irish chick lit', in Jernej Habjan and Fabienne Imlinger (eds), *Globalizing literary genres: literature, history, modernity* (Routledge; New York and London, 2016), 241–53: 245.

[53] Edna Longley, 'Irish poetry and "internationalism": variations on a critical theme', *Irish Review* 30 (Spring–Summer, 2003), 48–61: 53.

[54] Pierre Bourdieu, 'The social conditions of the international circulation of ideas', quoted in Longley, 'Irish poetry and "internationalism"', 53.

[55] Sirkku Aaltonen, 'Rewriting representations of the foreign: the Ireland of Finnish realist drama', *TTR: traduction, terminologie, redaction* 9 (2) (1996), 103–22.

Irish-language literature in Europe: a survey of translations and reception patterns in continental countries

Joachim Fischer
and Éamon Ó Ciosáin

Introduction

This chapter aims to provide an overview of translations from Irish into the various continental European languages. It may very well be the first time that this has been attempted, and our work should be seen as an exploratory investigation into a complex and diverse situation that covers more than fifteen national literary cultures. The aim cannot be a full and exhaustive treatment of the subject; rather it is a first attempt at identifying popular texts, common themes, transmission patterns, translators, receptions and book markets—and indeed, whether there are any general patterns at all, considering the sometimes very different relationships, both cultural and political, that European countries may have with Ireland and Irish culture. We have chosen to cover translations in book form only at this stage of research, as a full survey of texts in periodicals and other formats would be a much larger project.

We are not in a position to evaluate all the translations critically, nor to examine their reception in detail, limited as it may be in many instances in any case, except in languages we are familiar with. We have, however, the advantage of being practitioners in the field and have, thus, first-hand insights into the issues and difficulties that can arise when a lesser-used language is translated into a world language such as French or German. These, however, can be of a different nature when it comes to translations into 'smaller' European languages such as Czech, and different again with minority languages such as Breton.

In our survey there will be a particular focus on the reception and translation of Irish-language texts in the French- and German-speaking countries. This is not the result of the linguistic background of the authors. It is often forgotten, given the predominance of English in international discourse, that German is, after all, the most widely spoken vernacular in the European Union, followed by French. It is a fair assumption that the most extensive readership for literature translated from Irish will come from these two language communities. Interestingly, these substantial potential readerships do not necessarily coincide with the variety and number of works translated from Irish published in book form. In fact, smaller language communities, such as Romanian and Czech, form a surprisingly substantial part of our corpus. In many countries, translations exist because of a very small number of either academics with an interest in Ireland or admirers of Irish-language culture, who have sometimes single-handedly created a considerable interest in writings in Irish.

A good proportion of the texts we are dealing with here were translated either wholly from published English translations, have been assisted by such translations, or were done by means of a crib. This, however, should not lead to the exclusion of such material from consideration, as in most cases their Irish-language provenance is explicitly stated and is an important factor in their reception. At the same time, there are also just as many examples of direct translations by writers who had an adequate command of both the source and the target language to enable them to produce translations.

Most of the countries covered here are now member states of the European Union, and the bulk of our texts are post-1973, when Ireland became a member of what was then the European Economic Community. We will, however, also make reference to countries outside the union, such as Russia, Norway and Switzerland. Outside the very limited and occasional EU schemes for translation that have supported and encouraged translation activity, membership of the European Union appears to have had little significant impact on the reception of literature in Irish on the continent: the admittedly sporadic interest in Irish literature in Croatia, for example, long preceded the entry of the latter into the European Union.

Compilation of the list of translations we have established was greatly facilitated by Literature Ireland (known as Irish Literature Exchange until 2016), which has generously made its database available to us. The ILE/LI has, since its foundation in 1994, financially supported the translation of over 1,750 works of Irish literature into languages other than English, and it has approximately 90 works in Irish in its lists. Not only has the organisation played a key role in fostering the dissemination of literature in Irish, both in Europe and further afield, it has also supported translations into Turkish, Arabic and Japanese. Considering the small niche that publishing in Irish occupies in its home country, its activities may in some countries have led to a situation whereby works translated from the Irish language occasionally rivalled Irish literary works in English in terms of public attention.

Historical background

It was James MacPherson's *Ossian*, which was translated into all major European languages, that provided the initial impetus for an exploration of Celtic cultures and languages, with a particular focus on Ireland. Subsequent translation activity from the Celtic languages was closely

Joachim Fischer and Éamon Ó Ciosáin

connected to the development of Celtic Studies in various European countries, with Germany/Austria, France, Italy and the Scandinavian countries playing prominent roles. From the middle of the nineteenth century onwards, the interest in Irish nationalism, underpinned by a Europe-wide reception of Herder's cultural nationalism, generated a renewed interest in the Irish language; this was intensified in the twentieth century by the foundation of the Irish Free State and its decision to make Irish the first language of the state.

The translations of modern Irish literature we are dealing with here were aimed at the general reading public. These were, however, by no means the only texts in Irish to have been translated into continental vernaculars; in terms of sales figures, it is perfectly possible that Irish folk literature, in particular folk- and fairy-tales, may constitute a larger corpus of translations. This was, for a time at least, the case in Germany, where from the 1980s until his early death in 2006 translations by Hans-Christian Kirsch, under his pen-name Frederik Hetmann, achieved exceptionally high sales—more than any of the other books we are dealing with here—both in their first hard-cover versions and then via the Fischer pocket book series.[1] Titles like *Irischer Zaubergarten* ('The Irish magic garden') or *Die Reise in die Anderswelt* ('The journey to the other world') highlight the tendency of these works to affirm prevailing romantic images of Ireland while diverting attention away from the contemporary 'real' world—and from literature that dealt with real-world issues.

These publications should also be distinguished from another type of translations from Irish: scholarly translations usually of Old and Middle Irish texts in book-length editions for an exclusively academic readership of Celtic scholars and medievalists. These have a long tradition, in both French and German, both historically established academic languages that only very recently have had to consider their survival against the overwhelming dominance of English as the medium of international scholarship. On the German side, scholarly translations are associated with the names of famous German Celtic scholars such as Kuno Meyer, Ludwig Christian Stern, Rudolf Thurneysen and Julius Pokorny.[2] In France, the scholar of note is Georges Dottin. There have been fewer scholarly translations into European languages recently. Wolfgang Meid's *Die Romanze von Froech und Findabair: Táin bó Froích,* first published in German in 1970 and in a revised edition in 2009, was eventually brought out in English translation in 2015, in response to the demands of international scholarship.[3]

In the early decades of the twentieth century, the interest in modern literature in Irish had political roots and focused in particular on the writings of the nationalist hero Patrick Pearse. In 1922 Julius Pokorny published *Die Seele Irlands*, which contained short stories and poems by Pearse, Pádraig Ó Conaire and Pádraig Ó Siochfhradha, otherwise known as An Seabhac.[4] Only a year later Pearse featured again in Hans Trausil's *Ein Zweig von Schlehdorn*, another collection containing poems originally written in Irish, which for many years remained the only German translation of poetry in Irish, extended and republished in 1957 and reprinted in 1983 as *Irische Harfe*.[5]

The German-speaking countries

As we have seen, Irish literature has been popular with German-speaking audiences since before the post-World-War II period, which is our primary concern. While James Joyce, Flann O'Brien, Sean O'Casey, Liam O'Flaherty *et al.* have become household names in Germany, largely through the translations in paperback editions of the Zurich-based Diogenes Verlag, in more recent years Roddy Doyle, Maeve Binchy and especially Cecilia Ahern have reached popular audiences, and in Ahern's case even climbed to the top of the bestseller lists. Fergal Lenehan's recently published survey of German perceptions of Ireland between 1946 and 2010 based on two key weeklies has shown that Ireland has remained a constant presence in the German media.[6] Generally, the image of Ireland among Germans, while perhaps stereotypical and cliché-ridden, has been favourable; the bad news coming from the Green Isle between 2008 and 2010 did not impact negatively on it.[7] In the conclusion to her 2012 exploration of the changes and continuities in the German image of Ireland, Gisela Holfter is probably correct in stating the current situation: '... the picture has broadened. ... Ireland is still the island where everything is possible, but the German perspective has become a far more ambivalent one, though arguably still overwhelmingly positive.'[8] This creates a positive reception environment for any cultural product coming from the *Grüne Insel*.

It is probably fair to say that while awareness of the 'other' language tradition is widespread in Germany, and indeed adds to Ireland's attraction, its literary dimension is still known in Germany only to the most devoted Hibernophiles. Before the flowering of translation activity in the 1990s there were a handful of book-length texts in Irish, which came into German invariably through their English translations. Muiris Ó Suilleabháin's Blasket autobiography *Fiche bliain ag fás* was translated by Elisabeth Aman in 1956; Annemarie and Heinrich Böll added their translation of Tomás Ó Criomhthain's *An tOileánach* four years later.[9] More recently, in 1996, Hans-Christian Oeser completed the trilogy with his translation of *Peig*. In that instance we have a rare case of a hybrid translation: while the prose text was translated from English, the songs and poems were translated from the Irish to better retain their original flavour.[10]

To the Blasket trilogy we could add the various short stories by Liam O'Flaherty that have an Irish original.[11] Brendan Behan's *Die Geisel* (*An Giall*) is a further example.[12] *Die Geisel* has also been performed, but in either form few would have been aware of the (somewhat different) Irish-language original of 1958.[13] Myles na gCopaleen's *An béal bocht*, or rather, the actual source text *The poor mouth*, translated by Harry Rowohlt and published as *Irischer Lebenslauf* by Suhrkamp, exploded some German myths about the nature of Gaelic or Celtic literature and the image of Ireland as a backward superstitious country full of bogs, sheep, boreens and poor but God-fearing peasants, a country untouched by the vices of modern civilisation.[14] Whether many German readers actually fully grasped the satire and tongue-in-cheek style of *An béal bocht*, is an open question, although those readers of Böll's translation of Ó Criomhthain's text might at least have been aware of the satirical dimension.

Mention should be made of the German Democratic Republic (1949–89). While there was a small core of Celtic scholars active in the Humboldt University of East Berlin around Martin Rockel, the only major translation of a text in Irish in the GDR had more to do with the author than with Celtic Studies. Breandán Ó hEithir was one of the few Irish writers who were officially invited to the GDR; his statements criticising capitalism as well as his membership of the Ireland-GDR Friendship Society had endeared him to the regime. Ó hEithir financed his later visits out of the royalties for the German translation of his novel, *Lig sinn i gcathú*, which appeared in 1985.[15] The translator, Sigrid Wicht, explicitly stated that her work was based on the English translation *Lead us into temptation* (1976); her annotations made sure the readership understood who was on the right side of history and who was not. A few years earlier, Hans Petersen edited an Irish issue of the Volk und Welt book series *Erkundungen,* which since 1966 had brought several volumes presenting mostly prose writers from different countries to GDR audiences. The volume with Irish texts was first published in 1979 and contained short stories by Tomás Mac Síomóin, Colbert Ó Cearnaigh and Seán Mac Mathúna translated from English versions prepared by the authors.[16]

In 1988, just before unification, translations of modern literature in Irish had started to appear in West Germany when one of the leading literary magazines, *die horen*, in a special issue on Ireland edited by Barbara Freitag and Hans-Christian Oeser, set out to acquaint German audiences with contemporary (1980s) Irish literature.[17] Probably due to Freitag's background in Celtic Studies, this included works in the Irish language. Freitag translated three Old Irish poems, Gabriel Rosenstock in collaboration with Oeser supplied translations of poems by Rosenstock, while Joachim Fischer and Gabriele Haefs presented German versions of a few selected poems by Nuala Ní Dhomhnaill, Liam Ó Muirthile, Michael Davitt and Cathal Ó Searcaigh. Haefs, of whom more later, has since become the main translator of literature in Irish in the German-speaking countries. The Irish-language section of the publication was influenced by contemporary interests and dealt with feminist perspectives, generational conflict and political issues, such as the Israeli-Palestinian conflict in a translation of Michael Davitt's poem 'Ó mo bheirt Phailistíneach'. Altogether, the section focusing on the Irish language made up one-fifth of the book, with the bulk taken up by a passage from Brian Friel's *Translations*. The actual amount of direct translations from Irish was 12 pages in a 230-page volume.

The idea of translating from Irish had been planted. It took another few years until, in 1993, a more ambitious project developed. In the 1990s two publications consciously set out to further familiarise German audiences with literature in Irish. They were both products of Druckhaus Galrev, one of several new publishing ventures set up

Joachim Fischer and Éamon Ó Ciosáin

in the former East Germany after unification. Druckhaus Galrev had an internationalist, left-wing orientation and Jürgen Schneider's 1993 edition *Irrlandt—Ireland—Irland* fitted this interest.[18] The Irish-language element makes up the first third of the book, and Schneider, in placing the Irish-language material ahead of that translated from Ireland's 'second', English, language tradition made a not-too-subtle political point. In an introduction to the Irish section, Liam Mac Cóil picked up on the programme the publishing house continued to pursue in the new unified Germany:

> Is writing in a lesser-used language such as Irish subversive? Can the monolithic centralised imperialistic cultures of the major languages be undermined with it? Has the oldest literature in Western Europe a subversive meaning? ...Is literature in the lesser used languages the last refuge of human values? Or is writing in a lesser-used language just a bit of fun, should everything—including Wittgenstein, deconstruction and classic works—just be reduced to fun?[19]

In the volume translations from Irish are functionalised to support an anti-imperialist cause; small and oppressed linguistic cultures are the harbinger of a more humane world beyond the centralising and levelling forces of capitalism about to go global, though Mac Cóil also offers a divergent reading. The Irish language becomes an argument in a struggle by the losers in the ideological battle in Germany against the overwhelming capitalist might of the West.

The 21 poets represented in the collection comprised all major figures in contemporary Irish-language poetry. Many of the translations had been presented at a major literary event in Berlin when, in November 1991, the Literaturwerkstatt Berlin organised the 'Tage der irischen Literatur'. The bulk of the translations were supplied by Andrea McTigue, then senior lecturer in German at St Patrick's College Maynooth; as was the case in the Foreword of the *horen* volume the editor emphasised that the translations were directly from the original, *ohne Umweg übers Englische*, 'without a detour via English'. McTigue edited another volume three years later, also published by Galrev, in which she placed literature in Irish in a less political, pan-Celtic context.

Und suchte meine Zunge ab nach Worten ... presented love poetry from the four extant Celtic languages.[20] The Irish side is represented by a larger number (26) of poets than before, from the older generation of Máire Mhac an tSaoi to the then rising star Cathal Ó Searcaigh.

The book appeared just in time for the 1996 Frankfurt Book Fair, at which Ireland was the featured country. Marianne Gerold/Kurd Windels's *Gedichte des gälischen Irlands* ('Poems from Gaelic Ireland') also appeared that year, and both books were launched at the fair.[21] A pupil of Rockel's, Sabine Asmus née Heinz, taking her cue from McTigue's earlier venture, brought out *Keltische Sprachinseln*, an anthology of contemporary Celtic literatures, in which writing in Irish is once again placed alongside examples of Scottish-Gaelic, Welsh and Breton literature.[22] In that volume we find translations of poems by Mícheál Ó Conghaile, Ré Ó Laighléis and Nuala Ní Dhomhnaill. In the anthology *Das Zweimaleins des Steins* edited by Gregor Laschen, a volume in the series *Poesie der Nachbarn* ('Poetry of our neighbours'), poetry in Irish (by MacSíomóin, Ní Dhomhnaill and Ó Searcaigh), Irish poetry in English and their respective German translations are placed in a consciously European context. In a perceptive postscript, Hans-Christian Oeser highlights the language-political power of such foreign anthologies to symbolically redress imbalances at home: the three poets in Irish featured in the collection perfectly balance their three colleagues in English.[23]

Poetry had thus been firmly established as the most vibrant and prominent aspect of writing in Irish, and literary festivals have provided useful platforms to cement its position. *Das Zweimaleins* was the result of such a literary event, as was *VERSschmuggel—VÉARSaistear* edited by Aurélie Maurin and Thomas Wohlfahrt and published in 2006.[24] The latter is a collection of Irish and German poetry and it came about as a result of a project during the Berlin Poetry Festival of 2004, which paired six German poets with six Irish-language poets in order to translate each other's work. Interestingly, the pairs often transcended gender: Nuala Ní Dhomhnaill was paired with Mirko Bonné; Gréagóir Ó Dúill with Monika Rinck; and Michael Davitt with Barbara Köhler. The book contains original versions of the poems with facing translations and includes two CDs recorded during the festival. This format began to move literature and translation into the era of digital media. In

Joachim Fischer and Éamon Ó Ciosáin

more recent years the internet has become more prominent as a forum for poetry and translation, as the poetry platform lyrikline.org proves. Several Irish poets feature on this website in translation. The website includes recordings of the Irish originals.[25] As with all internet publications, however, the loss of the quality control traditionally supplied by publishing houses remains an unresolved issue.

The tiny number of those capable of translating Irish into German can result in both bursts of publication and silences. For many years Gabriele Haefs devoted her energies to Scandinavian literature; she made a name for herself as the German translator of *Sophie's world*, the phenomenal success of which in Germany prompted the English translation. Nevertheless, she did find time to produce *Das Vieh*, a German translation of Pádraig Standún's children's classic *An tAinmhí*.[26] That there are so few such translators may be related to the decline of both Irish and Celtic Studies in German universities; this is occurring for a multiplicity of reasons which we cannot go into here, including the inability of the discipline of *Keltologie* to make modern Celtic languages and contemporary concerns a key area of scholarly interest.

Haefs was the only choice when the Kröner Verlag was looking for a translator of Máirtín Ó Cadhain's *Cré na cille*, of which more in the concluding section. The ground for the German version of the Irish classic was carefully laid by another German translation of Ó Cadhain's work, *Der Schlüssel*, a translation of the author's 1967 novella *The key/An eochair*, which had come out in a bilingual edition in 2015.[27] The German translation of Ó Cadhain's satire of bureaucracy appeared in 2016 and was automatically linked to the centenary of the Easter Rising, which reviewers were aware of, but it also fitted into contemporary discourses about an interfering state. Paula Böndel sees the novella as 'a testimony of the revolt against a repressive state and its institutions at a time of individualising tendencies'.[28] Increasingly, contemporary concerns have come to replace nostalgic longings as the dominating reception disposition for Irish-language texts. The particular status of Irish as a minority language may have prompted Haefs's translation of Peadar Ó hUallaigh's poems for the small poetry journal *Krautgarten* for the (minority) German-language community in Belgium.[29]

Northern Europe

Given the long-established connection with the German context and a common tradition of Celtic Studies—with the towering figures of Holger Pedersen, Carl Marstrander, Alf Somerfelt and Carl Hjalmar Borgström—it is not surprising that a few major translations of Irish works were published in Scandinavia. The Danish translator Ole Munch-Pedersen had edited Holger Pedersen's original papers from his sojourn in the Aran Islands.[30] He then directed his attention to translating contemporary Irish-language literature, such as Nuala Ní Dhomhnaill, Tomás Ó Criomhthain (1996), *Deoraíocht* by Padraig Ó Conaire (1999) and Máirtín Ó Cadhain's *Cré na cille* (2000).[31]

The other prominent Scandinavian translator is a Celtic scholar, Jan Erik Rekdal, professor of Medieval Studies at Oslo University. Rekdal published *Kirkegårdsfjord*, the first publicly available translation of *Cré na cille* in any language, in 1995, some twenty years before the English translations came out.[32] Rekdal has also published on his experience of translating *Cré na cille*. He details the linguistic problem of choosing between the two forms of Norwegian and also discusses cultural references that caused difficulties, or were impossible to translate and had to be replaced by equivalents.[33] Curiously, Haefs, who is also a major translator from Norwegian, in a recent interview appeared unaware of Rekdal's work.[34] That Haefs had missed an important potential aid for her own translation is as much an indication of the extent to which translators work in isolation as it is evidence of the effort required to find the sometimes obscure and out-of-print publications of works translated from Irish. In any case, there is clearly no international 'community' of translators from Irish on the European continent.

France, Belgium, Switzerland, Brittany

French translations of Irish literature prior to the 1980s tended to be focused on major names such as Yeats, Joyce, Wilde, Synge and some earlier writers in English, and on translations of medieval Irish tales by academics and non-academic writers. Although Celtic languages were taught in Paris, the methodology was philological, and no language course in Modern Irish was provided at university level. Modern Irish

Joachim Fischer and Éamon Ó Ciosáin

was taught as an optional subject in Lille, Rennes and Brest universities, but not to a level that would equip a translator to work from Irish. In the course of the twentieth century, collections of mythological stories were translated from medieval Irish, as were a small number of folk-tales. Georges Dottin (1863–1928) was the leading figure in translating both types of tale; his command of Irish and his French translations were both excellent. Little was known among French readers of Irish literature in English about Ireland's other modern literature, although one work did make its way into French: Muiris Ó Súilleabháin's auto-biography, translated in 1936—from the English version—by Raymond Queneau as *Vingt ans de jeunesse*.[35]

Translations of modern literature in Irish began to appear in the mid-1980s, thanks to individual initiatives: 1984 saw an anthology by Éamon Ó Ciosáin of modern poetry by six poets, titled *Une île et d'autres îles*, and a translation of Tomás Ó Criomhthain's *An tOileánach* appeared in 1989.[36] Both works had a collaborative aspect, whereby an Irish speaker worked on the originals with native speakers of French. In the case of *L'homme des îles*, as the translation of Ó Criomhthain was called, the Swiss writer and personality Jean Bühler joined Una Murphy. Their translation has gone through a number of reprints.[37] The title of the poetry anthol-ogy referred both to an important poem by Seán Ó Ríordáin and to the idea that there were islands/Irelands other than English-speaking Ireland with whose literature a French-speaking public would be familiar.

As in Germany, poetry has remained the mainstay of translations from Irish to French: 1996 was the year of the Imaginaire Irlandais fes-tival throughout France, in the same year as the Frankfurt Book Fair referred to above; that year can therefore be regarded as a highpoint of continental awareness of Irish literature. Two volumes containing poetry translated directly from Irish were published that year in France: numerous twentieth-century Irish-language poems appeared in the sub-stantial *Anthologie de la poésie irlandaise au XXe siècle* and a volume of translations of Cathal Ó Searcaigh's poetry by A.J. Hughes was pub-lished.[38] Further selections of poetry were translated in subsequent years, notably Breandán Ó Doibhlin's translations of poems by Patrick Pearse in the monumental *Patrimoine littéraire européen*, and an anthol-ogy of Pearse Hutchinson's poetry by Pádraig Ó Gormaile with Clíona Ní Ríordáin.[39] Ní Ríordáin also edited an anthology of Irish women poets in 2013, which included a minority representation of Irish-language writers; the work was a collaborative venture by ten translators.[40] An outlier text in this period is Jean Le Dû's *Une vie irlandaise: du Connemara à Rath Chairn: histoire de la vie de Micil Chonraí*, a translation of the autobiography of Micil Chonraí from the Irish-speaking area of Rath Cairn, a story of Gaeltacht life and migration, which can be classified alongside the Blasket autobiographies.[41] Theatre did get one look in: Alan Titley's *Tagann Godot* was adapted and published in 2006 as *Voilà Godot: Tragédie comique en deux actes* and no doubt benefited from the connection to Beckett's masterpiece, whose plot it extends.[42]

Most of the authors of these French translations were Irish academics fluent in French and French academics well-versed in Irish; one of the translators of Myles na gCopaleen's *An béal bocht*, André Verrier, was a member of the Celtic seminar at the Sorbonne and also published French translations of earlier poetry on the Fianna.[43] While a few other translators have participated in this activity, the absence of courses in Irish at an advanced level in France means that the pool of workers is small. Translations from Irish have been dwarfed by the upsurge in translations (or versions) of Irish English-language writers since L'Imaginaire Irlandais. The choice of texts to be translated has, until now, been made by the translators, not publishers or other agents. Creative prose in Irish is notably absent. The prominence of poetry reflects both the prestige of the form among Irish-language *literati* and the promotion of Irish-language poets over prose writers by the official bodies that select writers to represent Irish literature abroad (such as Culture Ireland, the Arts Council). This is unfortunate, as poetry has long become an élite, if not esoteric, form and practice in France, and translations focused on poetry are likely to have limited impact. Irish literature in English, on the other hand, is well represented in literary publishers' catalogues in France and consists mainly of novels, arguably the dominant form in French language literature, thus ensuring the main language of Ireland maintains its dominance in the eyes of the French reading public. The few works of modern Irish prose translated via English are from the early twentieth century, namely two works of Blasket literature and Pearse's short stories.[44] All three major Blasket autobiographies are available in French, but no novel or short stories post-1916 have been translated from Irish to French.

Joachim Fischer and Éamon Ó Ciosáin

More balance is visible in the small number of texts translated to Breton. While individual texts in translation had appeared in reviews since the modernising and pan-Celtic Gwalarn movement of the 1920s–30s, the first full book from Irish was one of short stories by Patrick Pearse, whose name had a particular resonance among Breton nationalists looking to Ireland for inspiration. Loeiz Andouard's *Isagan* (published in 1979) was not Andouard's first translation from Irish, and the work was translated directly from the original.[45] An anthology of twentieth-century poets by Ó Ciosáin and others followed in 1983, and two short stories by Séamus Mac Annaidh appeared as booklets, one in French and one in Breton, as part of the Breton contribution to Imaginaire activity.[46] A.J. Hughes was among those who authored versions of Nuala Ní Dhomhnaill's poetry in a selection of her poems titled *Ar Gwele Seiz*.[47] To conclude, reception of poetry is more favourable in Breton, and the major figures of Pearse and Ní Dhomhnaill are evident in translated works available in Brittany as in other countries.

Southern Europe

Even though there has been some activity in Celtic Studies in recent decades in Spain, Portugal, Italy and Greece, there has been little scholarship or university teaching in the field of Gaelic languages. The few texts translated to Spanish do not originate in university departments: Antonio Rivero Taravillo, a respected and widely-published literary translator and critic, authored Spanish versions of Myles na gCopaleen's *An béal bocht* and of Liam Ó Flaithearta's short story collection in Irish *Dúil*, published as *Deseo*.[48] Rivero Taravillo's original training was in Scottish Gaelic and he translated works from Gaelic to Spanish in collaboration. He subsequently studied Irish and chose to translate texts by writers whose reputation rests on their English-language works, including other works by Flann O'Brien. His interest in Irish literature is also manifest in his 2001 edition of translations from Old Irish poetry, *Antiguas poemas irlandeses*.[49] A second Iberian translation of *An béal bocht*, by Isaac Fernández Fernández in 2016, is available in Galician.[50] The prominent poet Tomás Mac Síomóin self-translated 21 of his poems into Spanish and Catalan in a trilingual edition published in Dublin in 2010.[51] This translation activity is relatively recent, and the small number of texts translated means that, in Spanish terms, the corpus is probably not substantial enough to appear autonomous from Irish English-language literature.

A more substantial number of books are available in Italian, mainly due to the commitment of Bari literature professor and translator Rosangela Barone, a frequent visitor to Ireland who learned Irish, having studied for her doctorate at Dublin City University. Her earliest translations were of poetry, and poetry dominates her output. She published a small trilingual (Irish, English, Italian) volume of Caitlín Maude's work in 1985.[52] The first of her four translations of Pádraig Ó Snodaigh (well-known also as director of the prolific publishing house Coiscéim) was his poetry collection *Solitudine e Compagnia* (*Cumha agus Cumann*), which also appeared in 1985. There followed *Linda* (1997), *Len* and *Mal* (1999); a further work by Ó Snodaigh, *Parnell a Queenie* (2010) was translated by Laura Sanna. Barone also translated, in 1998 with Melita Cataldi, an anthology, *Venti e una poesia* ('Twenty-one poems').[53] Authors range from eighteenth-century satirist Brian Merriman to Pearse Hutchinson, Cathal Ó Searcaigh and Nuala Ní Dhomhnaill. That work had been preceded in 1996 by another anthology of contemporary Irish language poetry, *Bollirà la Rugiada: Poesia irlandese contemporea*, by Fabbri, Giosa and Montevecchi, about whose grounding in the Irish language we are not certain.[54] Rosangela Barone also translated modernist works such as Titley's sequel to Beckett's *Godot* (*Arriva Godot*), and Eoghan Ó Tuairisc's poetic 'Mass for the dead at Hiroshima', *Aifreann na Marbh* (*Messa di Defunti*), also translated into French by Ó Ciosáin.[55] Barone's work as director of the Italian Institute in Dublin brought her into frequent contact with literary circles in both languages, especially the group associated with Coiscéim publishers— the most active publisher of translations from non-English language literatures into Irish.

Research thus far has identified only one translation in Greek originating from Irish: Pádraic Ó Conaire's novel *Deoraíocht*, translated by Persefoni Koumoutsi as *Tha klápsei kaueís yia tou Máikel*.[56] The reasons for this choice may be similar to those that prompted interest in *Deoraíocht* in Eastern European countries.

Eastern Europe

In 1997 Ranko Matasovic and Hrovoje Bozicevic, in collaboration with Mícheál Ó Conghaile of Cló Iar-Chonnacht (CIC), edited in Croat a collection of short stories in Irish: *Koje je Vrijeme? Suvremena Irska Pripovijetka*.[57] The collection contains stories by Ó Conghaile himself, Pádraic Breathnach, Dara Ó Conaola and Alan Titley. This publication appears to mark the beginning of a steady reception of literature in Irish in the post-communist countries that joined the EU from 2004 onwards. In a foreword later published in English, Ranko Matasovic emphasises the Irish tradition in the short story as one impetus for the collection, but he also makes an important point about the minority language status of Irish. In Slavonic fashion he does not mince his words:

> One should not be deluded: although the Irish Constitution states that Ireland is a bilingual country, the people who speak Irish as their mother tongue could fill nothing but a Dublin or Zagreb suburb, while exclusively Irish-speaking people are almost extinct. Literature in Irish today is written only for a limited audience, for the persistent and embittered, for those educated in the language of the uneducated, for those who still care for forgotten values. In the graveyard of languages that Europe is about to become, the aforementioned fact warns that the readers of Irish stories are the guardians of one of the oldest standard languages of western culture.[58]

This somewhat dispiriting view from Croatia twenty years ago sees the Irish language, and indeed all other smaller languages, as important carriers of cultural memory, but also as being past-oriented. Possibly influenced by the political situation in his country at the time, Matasovic regarded the future as bleak, mono-cultural and conformist. He saw a particular affinity between a less-developed country such as Croatia was then and the west of Ireland as perhaps traditionally perceived: 'One can identify [*sic*] the people from Zagorje or Istria with the peasants quarrelling about field boundaries ... while the dialect spoken on the Aran Islands could be translated into local Croatian dialects.'[59]

The parallel Matasovic highlights may help to explain the popularity of Ó Conaire in particular, whose work, as well as being a vehicle for the author's culture-critical perspectives, deals with the clash between traditional cultures and modernity and the alienation of man in the modern world.

Micheál Ó Conghaile recognised a burgeoning interest in Irish-language writing in Eastern Europe, and promotional work by CIC as much as by the ILE has led to many translation ventures there. The majority of translations published in the region date from about the turn of the twenty-first century. In the former Eastern bloc countries they are more evenly weighted between poetry and prose translations than is the case in the major languages of German and French. Two countries stand out in terms of activity since the beginning of the century. Between 1998 and 2010, Romanian writer and academic Christian Tămas translated the extraordinary number of 21 poetry collections by contemporary writers in Irish into his native language. Publisher Ars Longa's catalogue is relatively cosmopolitan, including as it does texts drawn from various European languages. Its webpage 'Literatura Irlandeza Contemporaneă' presents nineteen translations, only three of which are of English-language originals, thus reversing the customary proportion of works in the two languages in catalogues.[60] Ars Longa's series is focused on living poets, with a noticeable gender balance (Bríd Ní Mhóráin, Dairena Ní Chinnéide, Nuala Ní Dhomhnaill, Áine Ní Ghlinn and Celia de Fréine are the women writers published). Whatever about the 'faithfulness' of Tămas's translations, which we are not in a position to judge and, in the case of poetry, is a highly contentious concept in any case, it is no doubt a welcome feature that readers in the EU periphery of Iaşi on the Moldovan border are acquainted with poetry produced by writers from the extreme west of the European continent; a remarkable example of the cultural exchange the European Union aims to foster. Irish prose is represented in Romanian by a translation of Pádraig Standún's novel *An t-Ainmhí.*[61]

The second major area of activity after eastern Romania is in the Czech Republic. A group of translators centred on the Irish literature section of the Department of Anglophone Cultures and Literatures at Charles University, Prague, have been prolific, focusing on modernist fiction from Irish. Under the benevolent guidance of Anglo-Irish

Joachim Fischer and Éamon Ó Ciosáin

literature professor Ondřej Pilný, Irish language tuition, literary criticism and translation from Irish have flourished. Daniela Theinová pioneered this work with her translation of Ó Conaire's modernist novel *Deoraíocht* (a popular choice for translation in Eastern Europe), published as *Vyhnanství* in 2004.[62] The translation was very successful; it was adapted and broadcast on Czech national radio the following year. A second modernist novel appeared in 2007, Eoghan Ó Tuairisc's treatment of the 1798 rebellion *L'Attaque*, translated by Radvan Markus.[63] Markus has been very active since that time, translating Ó Conaire's *Scothscéalta* in 2013 and also an anthology of short stories by modern authors in Irish.[64] His very recent version of Ó Cadhain's 1949 masterpiece *Cré na cille*, *Hřbitovní hlína*, marks a major contribution to the field in the Czech language. It received a major award shortly after publication.[65] Ivana Peroutková translated Pádraig Ó Snodaigh's poetry collection *Ó Pharnell go Queenie*.[66] The publisher of this book lists poetry collections by other Irish writers in English in its programme and slotted Ó Snodaigh into this category.

Two novels by Pádraig Standún, Liam Mac Cóil's novel *An litir* and de Fréine's *Faoi chabáistí is ríonacha* are available in Bulgarian.[67] The collection of short stories by four contemporary authors in Croatian mentioned at the outset of this section was also translated into Albanian and Polish, which indicates a certain level of interchange between Eastern European countries fostered by Cló Iar-Chonnacht and Literature Ireland. Prose dominates recent Polish translations.[68] A remarkable five novels by Standún, short stories by Pearse and Pádraic Ó Conaire's *Deoraíocht* are available.[69] Standún and Ó Conaire were translated by Barbara Sławomirska, who usually translated from English versions; several novels by Standún have been published in English by publishers in Ireland. The choice of Standún for translation to Polish is no doubt down to his readable contemporary prose but may also be related to the fact that he is a Catholic priest, writing about the full range of modern life. Prior to the twenty-first century, the few existing translations were largely due to the work of Ernest Bryll and Małgorzata Goraj-Bryll, who between 1978 and 1986 edited two volumes of poetry from the sixth to the nineteenth century as well as Ó Suilleabháin's *Fiche bliain ag fás*, invariably from their English translations.[70] Ernest Bryll's translation work impacted on his professional career: between 1991 and 1995 he was the first Polish ambassador to Ireland. In 2008 the then PhD student Anna Paluch developed an interest in Pearse, whose writings she found particularly congenial to a Polish audience. Rather than the modernist impulse, which may have drawn others to Ó Conaire, Ó Tuairisc and Ó Cadhain, for her

> [t]he stories are so similar to Polish stories, and when I learned they were from the 20th century I was completely surprised... They're stories about the countryside, stories about children, and similar to works by some Polish authors.[71]

Traditionalism, thus, can also impact on the reception of writing in Irish. Paluch's translation of Pearse's stories into Polish appeared in 2008.[72] Of an entirely different nature again is Jerzy Jarniewicz's recent anthology of six Irish women poets, which included nineteen poems by Nuala Ní Dhomhnaill.[73]

Lastly, a brief look at Russia. Tatyana Mikhailova, professor of Celtic at Moscow State University, began learning Irish in the 1970s and wrote her doctoral thesis on the medieval tale *Buile Suibhne* ('Sweeney's madness'). In addition to her scholarly publications on Old Irish literature, Mikhailova contributed Russian translations of works from modern Irish to various publications. *Words of Ireland: voice of Erin* contained her translation of Ó Conaire's *Deoraíocht*.[74] She also translated some Irish poems by Pearse and Mairtín Ó Direáin in the book *Irish poetry*.[75] Her Russian versions of Alan Titley's *Tagann Godot* and his novel for young readers *Amach* appeared in 2002 and 2006 respectively.[76] The modernist leaning of translations from Irish to Russian is also evident in that Séamas Mac Annaidh's major novel *Cuaifeach mo londubh buí* was translated into Russian in 1989 and reportedly sold well. A Russian version of *An béal bocht* was published in 2003, using the Irish original.[77]

Patterns — Trends — Transmission

In cataloguing translations and assessing tendencies, a distinction between Western and Eastern European countries is noticeable. We propose to classify the texts in three periods or chronological categories:

Joachim Fischer and Éamon Ó Ciosáin

the early twentieth century (Pearse and Ó Conaire); the Blasket books of the mid-century and their parody *An béal bocht* (as well as some poetry); and contemporary works from the 1980s onwards. There are clear breaks in the transmission of translations of works in Irish between these periods. The three categories are represented in quite variable proportions in countries on either side of the old Iron Curtain. The presence of the discipline of Celtic Studies in countries such as Denmark, France and Germany has meant that the early and mid-century are well represented by classics in Irish language literature, whereas modern prose and poetry is much less in evidence in that part of the continent (poetry is, however, well-represented in German). The choice of the Blasket texts may be in keeping with the romantic and *passéiste* leaning of much of Celtic Studies, as well as with an attraction to an exotic view of Ireland in some countries. It is true that modernist works such as *Deoraíocht* and *Cré na cille* have been translated into Scandinavian languages, but these are rare texts, and indeed an argument could be made as to the attractiveness of the latter book for Celtic Studies in terms of its linguistic qualities. The absence of modern creative prose translations in France, and until more recently in Germany, indicates that poetry is seen as the principal form of literary expression in Irish, to the detriment perhaps of the image of the language as a medium for modern life. The reception of Irish-language works in these countries could also be viewed as confirmation of the romantic European idea of the Celts' predilection for lyricism and imagination, as opposed to Ó Cadhain's manifesto stating that prose, as opposed to poetry is 'the substance, the concrete, the masonry of life'.[78]

We can detect a noticeable increase of translation activity, especially without the intermediary of English, from the 1980s onwards. This may have been the result of Europe-wide interest in regionalism and minority cultures during the 1980s and 1990s—particularly strong in Germany—which for a while helped to generate a new market and readership for translations from works in the Irish language. The EU's European Bureau for Lesser-Used Languages was an expression of this particular aspect of the *zeitgeist*.

Eastern European translators tend to be less interested in the romantic and the 'backward look' (Frank O'Connor's expression) and focus instead on the immediate contemporary in terms of poetry, and novels in terms of prose, with some attention being paid to the short story. Thus, we see translations of the modern-day novels of Pádraig Standún into several languages and an interest in Ó Conaire's *Deoraíocht* which, although it dates from the beginnings of modern literature in Irish, appears to appeal to a Central/Eastern European aesthetic given its almost expressionistic style, its choice of protagonist, and its Kafkaesque or absurd view of life. Ó Conaire's limpid style may also have been an attraction for translators. Eoghan Ó Tuairisc (in Czech), Séamas Mac Annaidh (in Russian) and Liam Mac Cóil (in Bulgarian) are in line with this modernist trend. None of these three texts was available in an English version.[79] The Blasket autobiographies are noticeably absent from publications in the Eastern half of Europe. One could speculate that the very recent beginnings of translation from Irish in Eastern Europe mean that the activity does not carry the romantic baggage and exotic leaning of the vision of Ireland that all too often appears in France and Germany, nor is it subject to the influence of Celtic Studies and 'Celticism' in general. Historical factors may also operate here, as visits to Ireland were rare before the fall of the Iron Curtain in 1989, and the Irish tourist board has not been active in those countries as long as it has in the West.

In terms of reception and perception among the literary publics in Europe, writing in Irish is often perceived as part of Irish literature in general. In certain countries, and more so in Western Europe, name recognition is an important factor in drawing attention to texts in Irish. This appears to be the case in Spanish and Galician, where there are translations of writers whose international reputation rests on their work in English. The explicit reference to Beckett's *Godot* in the title of Alan Titley's play no doubt sparked interest in translating it in various countries. Mention of Máirtín Ó Cadhain as being comparable to James Joyce, or as being the 'Joyce of the Irish language', drew attention to his work, as did the unusual publication of two English-language versions of *Cré na cille* in close succession by Yale University Press. Occasionally, the names and reputations of the translators (Queneau in French, Böll in German) could impact positively on the reception of literature in Irish.

The list of texts we have established shows that there is a noticeable preponderance of poetry and novels. There are very few dramas among the texts we have located. This of course mirrors the state of contemporary literature in Irish, where poetry occupies a dominant position. Poetry also offers the greatest degree of liberty to the translator, and 'versions' rather than actual translations are readily accepted. There may also be a very practical reason for the preponderance of poetry collections, as dual-language editions in particular very quickly reach the size of an acceptable publication in book-form.

The widespread popularity of translations of Nuala Ní Dhomhnaill's poetry may well be the result of a combination of factors. A substantial part of her work has been translated into English. The translators have been prominent English-language poets in their own right, and this has no doubt smoothed the way. It is noticeable that Ní Dhomhnaill appears at times as the sole Irish-language writer in anthologies of Irish writers, and it could be said that her work 'travels' as part of a pan-Irish group. Indeed, her own physical travels to read her works worldwide also explains her popularity throughout Europe. No doubt her reputation as a feminist writer also plays a significant role; the rather rare instance of re-prints of translations into German can be taken as proof of this: only those of her poems with an explicitly female or feminist viewpoint have been selected.[80]

Frequently, literary festivals provide the impetus for later publications, but this is not always the case. For the Irish authors themselves, encounters at such festivals with translations in languages they do not understand can be an enriching and liberating experience since it sidelines English, as Dairena Ní Chinnéide explains:

> I have travelled throughout Europe singing my poems, first in Irish and then in English translation. One of my most enjoyable experiences was at a festival in Slovenia where I stood onstage reading in Irish and the audience read a translation projected onto a screen behind me. This way I could sing my song in the language in which it was meant to be sung. The audience shared and enjoyed the music of the language.[81]

Still, one of the most important factors for the selection of Irish language texts for translation on the continent is the availability of

English translations. There are numerous examples where translations into other languages are translations of the English versions. The recent upsurge in translations of *Cré na cille* (see below) indicates that even where the translations are evidently from the original, translators are more likely to undertake the task if an English version, or in this case two, by competent translators is also available. The Irish text of *Cré na cille*, after all, had been available since 1949. The reading public would mostly be unaware of the many problems that can result from translating an intermediary text. This at times can extend to the translator: Heinrich and Annemarie Böll would have been surprised if they had known how much Robin Flower actually left out in his translation of *An tOileánach*, which they used as the basis for their translation to German. It is only in the last two decades that the value of translations directly from the original is widely acknowledged.

Thus, translators broadly fall into two categories: those with a scholarly Celtic Studies background who have publications to prove their academic credibility, such as Haefs, Markus, Munch-Pedersen and Mikhailova; and then established literary translators and others who, as far as we can ascertain, are largely if not entirely relying on cribs or full English translations (as is the case in Polish). This is by no means a problematic procedure, once it is openly stated. Gerold and the Brylls emphasise that they would not have been able to translate the Irish texts if it had not been for the availability of English translations. In any case, it is quite common for translators to use all available resources and aids; those who are competent in more than two languages will occasionally consult translations of the same book into other languages they are familiar with to check on their solutions to difficult issues. Most credible translators will also regularly consult with native speakers (usually via English), no matter how solid their knowledge of Irish, or indeed any language that is not their mother tongue. Many of the translations listed here are the result of collaborative work between speakers/readers of Irish and users of other languages. These tend to result in the best outcomes, all the more so if the collaboration is well-established and well-honed over many years, as it is in the case of the Oeser/Rosenstock collaboration.[82] Any criticism from a scholarly or purist perspective of using an intermediate English text should be balanced against the positive aspects of such translations in generating interest in Ireland's Irish-language tradition.

Provision of notes, explanations and cribs by Irish-language authors or publishers (or indeed other persons) is clearly involved in some translations. This was the case in Italian, where the Irish publishing house Coiscéim supported the work of Rosangela Barone; some support may well also have been given to Christian Tămaş in Romania. A step further in this direction has been taken by Cló Iar-Chonnacht in providing unpublished English versions of some works in its catalogue for the attention of publishers and translators on the European continent and elsewhere. The active role of publishers should be noted: Mícheál Ó Conghaile of CIC has directed his efforts in recent years at increasing the translation of literature in Irish, and it is this that has provided the impulse for translations of *Cré na cille*. It remains to be seen if literature in Irish breaks through into publishing as a separate entity and if publishers and translators are attracted to it. For the moment, translations from Irish across Europe are published by smaller publishing houses, with a few exceptions, which tend to be publishers known for their foreign language lists/collections.

Cré na cille — Grabgeflüster — Whisperings from the grave

We will conclude our survey with one very important, recent and exceptional case of a continental European reception of an Irish language text. After the English language translations of *Cré na cille* finally appeared, in quick succession in 2015 as *The dirty dust* by Alan Titley and a year later in a more literal version, *Graveyard clay*, by Liam Mac Con Iomaire and Tim Robinson, translators in several countries set to work on it.[83] Rarely have translators into European languages had such assistance in their work. The two translations offer two different strategies to translate Ó Cadhain's text, a freer one by Titley and a more faithful and literal one by Mac Con Iomaire and Robinson. This makes the efforts by earlier translators such as Jan Erik Rekdal into Norwegian (1995) and Ole Munch-Pedersen into Danish (2000) all the more praiseworthy, though even in their case an early unpublished US doctoral thesis by Joan Trodden Keefe may have been of assistance.[84]

The German and Czech translations published most recently, it is reported, will be followed by over ten others, including by Alex Hijmans into Dutch, which will no doubt be another interesting piece of work by a competent translator.

The arrival of Ó Cadhain's classic on several European literary scenes is a major and possibly unique event for Irish-language literature. The background and (early) reception of the German translation is (for now) the best documented, and in fact represents the only occasion on which the response to a text in Irish can be studied in a little more detail. Its origin was a chance encounter. Gabriele Haefs' *Grabgeflüster* was surprisingly published by the classic, well-established but somewhat traditionalist, '*verstaubt*' ('dusty') Albert Kröner publishing house, which added to the exceptionality of the event and to the aura surrounding the book.[85] A literary editor from Kröner on holidays in the west of Ireland came across the English translation, probably the earlier one by Titley, in a Galway bookshop. She was fascinated by the text as much as by the complete obscurity of its author outside Ireland. She persuaded her employer to pursue the project, and through Ó Conghaile's good offices she was put in contact with, effectively, the only person in Germany with a track record in translating Irish. As part of an elaborate strategy to prepare the market, a smaller Ó Cadhain text was published first. *Der Schlüssel* (see above) was reasonably well received and reviewed in important fora, while the publisher emphasised that this was only the taster for bigger things to come.

The book, with the clever title *Grabgeflüster* ('Whispers from the grave') was finally launched on the carefully chosen date of St Patrick's Day 2017. The publication of the book was bolstered by several readings, most importantly perhaps at the Leipzig Bookfair, where Micheál Ó Conghaile of Cló Iar-Chonnacht was present. The literary sections of all major German papers picked it up. It was precisely its Irish-language provenance that contributed to the attention it was accorded. While the parallels to Joyce were foregrounded, it was the exoticism of a hidden culture in a country that everybody thought they knew well that underpinned the invariably positive response to the book. The text was also read as a social satire, a genre that modern continental reading audiences, faced with the absurdities, hypocrisies and lies of contemporary real life and politics, are more

than ready for. Apart from usual Joyce-associations, the '*glanzvolle ...*
Durcheinander' ('splendid chaos') of the novel reminded Rainer Wild
more of Beckett's absurd theatre than of Joyce.[86] It also resonates
in Sylvia Staudte's admiration for the dark humour inherent in 'the
densely poetic passages about the seriousness of the situation once
we are dead and buried'.[87]

The attractive exoticism of the text is extended to the language, both
of the original and the translation. Curiously, there is unanimity about
the quality of the translation, by critics who would hardly be in a position to judge it. Jan Wilms commends the translator and recommends
reading the text aloud, well aware of the clash this creates with the
title.[88] The 'strangeness' of the language here works for the translators.
Gabriele Haefs was explicitly complimented for some peculiar phrases
and odd constructions. Equally taken with the 'brilliant German translation', Sylvia Staudte in the *Frankfurter Rundschau*, a newspaper with
a long-standing interest in Ireland, was fascinated by the German versions of 'highly original' curses.[89]

While translators of texts from the little-known world of Irish-
speaking Ireland, as we have seen, had been busy unlocking its secrets
for decades, with this text Irish-language literature is now, in the
German-language literary world at least, making an appearance in the
mainstream literary-critical discourse. *Cré na cille* will provide proof for
the reading public in several European countries that there is life in the
'old corpse' of Irish yet. The reviews of *Cré na cille*, certainly as far as
Germany is concerned, seem to indicate that the interest in literature in
Irish is still there, as it always is for undiscovered gems. Still, whether
or not this almost frenetic translation activity occasioned by the
appearance of the English translations indicates a renaissance of Irish-
language literature on the continent, only the future will tell. Perhaps
the publication of translations of *Cré na cille* will attract translators and
readers to other works in the language and act as catalysts for a surge
of translations from Irish, similar to what happened for Irish writers in
English in France following the year of the Imaginaire Irlandais.

For many years there was a reluctance among Irish-language *literati*
to allow their works to be translated into English in particular, as it was
feared that the specificity of Irish-language literature would be diluted
and lost. Dual-language editions, as practised in the kindred language

of Scottish Gaelic, were also viewed with distrust and seen as giving in to the dominance of English. However, bilingual anthologies such as *The bright wave* (1986) and translations of Nuala Ní Dhomhnaill's poetry in parallel format marked a departure from this ideological position. Authors such as Ó Cadhain and Biddy Jenkinson, who explicitly refused to translate their work or have it translated to English, were nevertheless open to being translated into other languages not perceived as a threat to the survival of Irish. The problem of course has always been the paucity of translators. It is ironic that English-language versions and English-language references, such as to Godot (in the case of Titley's play), have helped to pull aside the curtain behind which literature in Irish had been hidden from the European-wide audience it now enjoys.

Notes

[1] Published from 1979 onwards by the traditionally conservative Diederichs Verlag, a long-established publisher specialising in mythological and folk literature from around the world. Diederichs has had a long-standing interest in Celtic cultures alongside a more problematic relationship with 'Nordic' cultures during the Third Reich.

[2] For more details relating to the German-speaking countries, see, Brian Ó Catháin (ed.), *Saothrú an Léinn Cheiltigh ag scoláirí thíortha na Gearmáinise* (An Sagart; Maynooth, 2013).

[3] Wolfgang Meid (ed.), *The romance of Froech and Findabair or The driving of Froech's Cattle*. Táin Bo Fróich: Old Irish text, with introduction, translation, commentary and glossary. English-language version based on the original German-language edition prepared with the assistance of Albert Bock, Benjamin Bruch and Aaron Griffith (Institut für Sprachen und Literaturen der Universität Innsbruck; Innsbruck, 2015). Gisbert Hemprich, *Rí Érenn, 'König von Irland'* (2 vols; Curach bhán; Berlin, 2015), which also contains texts and translations, shows that German as a language of Old Irish scholarship has not been abandoned entirely.

[4] Julius Pokorny, *Die Seele Irlands: Novellen und Gedichte aus dem Irisch-Gälischen des Patrick Henry Pearse und anderer (Padraic Ó Conaire, Padraic Ó Siochfhradha)* (Max Niemeyer; Halle, 1922).

[5] Hans Trausil (ed. and transl.), *Ein Zweig vom Schlehdorn* (Roland Verlag; Munich, 1928) and *Irische Harfe: Gedichte vom 8. Jahrhundert bis zur Gegenwart* (Langewiesche-Brandt; Ebenhausen, 1957); new edn Langewiesche-Brandt; Ebenhausen, 1983.

[6] Fergal Lenehan, *Stereotypes, ideology and foreign correspondents: German media representations of Ireland, 1946–2010* (Lang; Oxford, 2016).

[7] See also Gisela Holfter, 'After the *Irisches Tagebuch*: changes and continuities in the German image of Ireland, 1961–2011', in Joachim Fischer and Rolf Stehle (eds), *Contemporary German-Irish cultural relations in a European perspective: exploring issues in cultural policy and practice* (Irish-German Studies 6, WVT; Trier, 2012), 159–71: 165. Derek Scally may well be right in suggesting that Irish financial difficulties re-enforced earlier more romantic stereotypes, which had only been temporarily lost during the materialist and consumerist Celtic Tiger years; see, Derek Scally, 'Germans can't get enough of Ireland and they can't get enough of Cecilia Ahern', *Irish Times*, 25 June 2016.

[8] Holfter, 'After the *Irisches Tagebuch*', 171.

[9] Maurice O'Sullivan, *Inselheimat* transl. by Elisabeth Aman (Manesse; Zurich, 1956); Tomás O'Crohan, *Die Boote fahren nicht mehr aus* transl. by Annemarie and Heinrich Böll (Walter; Olten, Freiburg i. Br., 1960).

[10] Peig Sayers, *So irisch wie ich: Eine Fischersfrau erzählt ihr Leben* transl. by Hans-Christian Oeser; songs and poems transl. by Joachim Fischer (Lamuv; Göttingen, 1996).

[11] In Liam O'Flaherty, *Silbervogel und andere Meistererzählungen* transl. by Elisabeth Schnack (Diogenes; Zurich, 1961; new edn 2008).

[12] In Brendan Behan, *Stücke fürs Theater* transl. by Annemarie and Heinrich Böll (Luchterhand; Neuwied, 1962).

[13] The reception of Behan was arguably more enthusiastic in the GDR: Joachim Krehayn (ed.), *Englische Dramen* (Volk und Welt; Berlin, 1966) also contained *Die Geisel.*

[14] Earlier edition with the title *Das Barmen* (Suhrkamp; Frankfurt am Main, 1977), later editions as *Irischer Lebenslauf* (Suhrkamp; Frankfurt am Main, 1984).

[15] Brendán Ó hEithir, *Führe uns in Versuchung* transl. by Sigrid Wicht (Gustav Kiepenheuer; Leipzig and Berlin, 1985). See Jerôme aan de Wiel, *East German intelligence and Ireland, 1949–90: espionage, terrorism and diplomacy* (Manchester University Press; Manchester, 2015), 55–6; on Ó hEithir and Germany, see also Joachim Fischer, '"... 'thar lear' chomh hiomlán is chomh haoibhinn...": Aspekte des Deutschlandbildes in der zeitgenössischen irischsprachigen Literatur Irlands', in M.G. Schmidt and W. Bisang (eds), *Philologica et linguistica: historia, pluralitas, universitas* (WVT; Trier, 2001), 385–411: 389–90.

[16] Hans Petersen (ed.), *Erkundungen: 30 irische Erzähler* (Volk und Welt; Berlin, 1979), 131–3.

[17] Barbara Freitag and Hans-Christian Oeser (eds), 'Irland: Glaube, Liebe, Hoffnung—Armut, Qual, Buße: Irische Augenblicke', *die horen* 33 (3) (1988).

[18] Jürgen Schneider (ed.), *Irrland—Ireland—Irland* (Galrev; Berlin, 1993).

[19] Back-translated from the German translation of the English original by the authors. 'Ist Schreiben in einer weniger gebräuchlichen Sprache wie dem Irischen subversiv? Können mit ihr die monolithischen zentralisierten, imperialistischen Kulturen der Hauptsprachen untergraben werden? Ist im permanenten Kampf mit dem englischen Imperialismus die älteste Literatur Westeuropas von subversiver Bedeutung? ... Ist Literatur in den weniger gebräuchlichen Sprachen das letzte Refugium menschlicher Werte? Oder ist das Schreiben in einer weniger gebräuchlichen Sprache nur Spaß, sollte es alles—einschließlich Wittgenstein, Dekonstruktion und der Klassiker der Sprache—auf Spaß reduzieren?'; Liam Mac Cóil, 'Literatur in irischer Sprache heute', in Jürgen Schneider (ed.), *Irrland—Ireland—Irland* (Galrev; Berlin, 1993), 15–21: 21.

[20] Andrea McTigue (ed.), *Und suchte meine Zunge ab nach Worten: Liebesgedichte der Gegenwart aus vier keltischen Sprachen* (Galrev; Berlin, 1996).

[21] Marianne Gerold and Kurd Windels (eds), *Gedichte des gälischen Irlands* (WVT; Trier, 1996). For the broader context, see, Claire O'Reilly and Gisela Holfter, 'Changes and developments in German-Irish relations since 1989 with special regard to media, literary and diplomatic aspects: best of friends or rocky relationship?', in Niamh O'Mahony and Claire O'Reilly (eds), *Societies in transition: Ireland, Germany and Irish–German relations in business and society since 1989* (Nomos; Wiesbaden, 2009), 169–84.

[22] Sabine Asmus, *Keltische Sprachinseln* (Berlin: Frieling, 2001).

[23] Hans-Christian Oeser, 'Ein Land, zwei Sprachen, sechs Dichter', in Gregor Laschen (ed.), *Das Zweimaleins des Steins: Poesie aus Irland* (Wirtschaftsverlag NW; Bremerhaven, 1998), 174–8; 174.

[24] Aurélie Maurin and Thomas Wohlfahrt (eds), *VERSschmuggel—VÉARSaistear* (Cló Iar-Chonnacht/Das Wunderhorn; Galway and Heidelberg, 2006).

[25] The site can be accessed at: https://www.lyrikline.org/de/gedichte/ (18 January 2018).

[26] Pádraig Standún, *Das Vieh* transl. by Gabriele Haefs (Pendragon; Bielefeld, 1999).

[27] Máirtín Ó Cadhain, *The key / An Eochair* transl. by Louis de Paor and Lochlann Ó Tuairisg (Dalkey Archive Press; Champaign, IL, 2015).

[28] Paula Böndel, 'Die Logik des Widersinnigen'; available at: http://literaturkritik.de/o-cadhain-der-schluessel-die-logik-des-widersinnigen,23006.html (16 December 2017).

[29] Five poems from *Tír Tairngire* (Coiscéim; Dublin, 2009) and one from *Soilse an chroí* (Coiscéim; Dublin, 2011), see, *Krautgarten* (63) (November 2013), 44–7.

[30] Ole Munch-Pedersen (ed.), *Scéalta Mháirtín Neile: bailiúchán scéalta ó Árainn,* transcr. by Holger Pedersen (Four Courts Press; Dublin, 1994).

[31] Nuala Ní Dhomhnaill, *Ellefolk: utvalgte digte* transl. by Ole Munch-Pedersen and Peter Nielsen (Husets Forlag; Århus, 1996), Tomás Ó Criomhthain, *Manden på øen* transl. by Ole Munch-Pedersen (Husets Forlag; Århus, 1996), Pádraig Ó Conaire, *Emigrantliv* transl. by Ole Munch-Pedersen (Husets Forlag; Århus, 1999) and Máirtín Ó Cadhain, *Kirkegårdsjord: genfortælling i ti mellemspil* transl. by Ole Munch-Pedersen (Husets Forlag; Århus, 2000).

[32] Máirtín Ó Cadhain, *Kirkegårdsfjord* transl. by Jan Erik Rekdal (Gyldendal; Oslo, 1995).

[33] Jan Erik Rekdal, 'Ioruais a chur ar *Cré na Cille*', in Cathal Ó Háinle (ed.), *Criostalú: aistí ar shaothar Mháirtín Uí Chadhain* (Coiscéim; Dublin, 1998), 105–19.

[34] Gabriele Haefs, 'Ich habe noch einen Klassiker übersetzt ... Máirtín Ó Cadhain, Grabgeflüster'; available online at: https://www.schwarzaufweiss-internet.de/gabriele-haefs-klassiker-uebersetzt-mairtin-o-cadhain (16 December 2016).

[35] Maurice O'Sullivan, *Vingt ans de jeunesse* transl. by Raymond Queneau (Gallimard; Paris, 1936). See Anne Gallagher's chapter in this volume for a more detailed treatment of Queneau and Ireland.

[36] Éamon Ó Ciosáin (ed.), *Une île et d'autres îles* transl. by Éamon Ó Ciosáin (Calligrammes; Quimper, 1984); Tomás O'Crohan, *L'homme des îles* transl. by Jean Bühler with Una Murphy (Favre; Lausanne, Paris, 1989, 1994; Payot et Rivage; Paris, 2003).

[37] Favre; Lausanne, Paris, 1989, 1994; Payot et Rivage; Paris, 2003.

[38] Jean-Yves Masson (ed.), *Anthologie de la poésie irlandaise au XXe siècle* transl. by Éamon Ó Ciosáin and Pierre-Yves Lambert (Verdier; Paris, 1996); A.J. Hughes (ed.), *Le chemin du retour—Pilleadh an deoraí* (La Barbacane; Paris, 1996).

[39] Jean-Claude Polet (ed.), *Patrimoine littéraire européen* (De Boeck Supérieur; Louvain La Neuve, 2000), see vol. 12. B. Escarbelt and P. Ó Gormaile (eds), *Poèmes* (Presses Universitaires du Septentrion; Villeneuve d'Ascq, 2008).

[40] Clíona Ní Ríordáin (ed.), *Femmes d'Irlande en poésie 1972–2013* (Editions Caractères; Paris, 2013).

[41] Micil Chonraí, *Une vie irlandaise: du Connemara à Rath Chairn: histoire de la vie de Micil Chonraí* transl, by Jean Le Dû (Editions Terre de Brume/Presses Universitaires de Rennes; Rennes, 2010).

[42] Alan Titley, *Voilà Godot: tragédie comique en deux actes* transl. by L. Ó Baoill (Forsai Publications; Paris, 2006).

[43] André Verrier, *Ossianiques* (Orphée La Différence; Paris, 1989).

[44] Maurice O'Sullivan, *Vingt ans de jeunesse*, see above, and Peig Sayers, *Autobiographie d'une grande conteuse d'Irlande* transl. from English by Joelle Gac (An Here; Relecq-Kerhuon, 1999; 2nd edn 2000). Patrick Pearse, *Gens du Connemara* transl. from English by Frédéric Collemare (Editions Terre de Brume; Rennes, 2016).

[45] Padraig Mac Piarais (Patrick Pearse), *Isagan* transl. by Loeiz Andouard (Imbourc'h; Questembert, 1979).

[46] Éamon Ó Ciosáin, *et al.*, *Barzhonegoù Iwerzhonek* (Skrid; Douarnenez, 1983). The short stories by Mac Annaidh that were translated were 'Fuath' from *Féirín: scéalta agus eile* (1992) transl. by Ó Ciosáin as 'La Haine', and 'Misteach Bhaile Átha Cliath' transl. by Alan Heussaff as 'Kevrinad Dulenn' (both Institut Culturel de Bretagne; Rennes, 1996).

[47] Nuala Ní Dhomhnaill, *Ar gwele seiz: un dibab barzhonegoù gant Nuala Ní Dhomhnaill* transl. by H. Ar Bihan, A. Botrel, G. Denez, A. J. Hughes (Mouladurioù Hor Yezh; Lesneven, 2000).

[48] Myles na gCopaleen, *La boca pobre* transl. by Antonio Rivero Taravillo (Nordica Libros; Madrid, 1989; reprint 2008); Liam O'Flaherty, *Deseo* (Nordica Libros; Madrid, 2012).

[49] Antonio Rivero Taravillo (ed.), *Antiguas poemas irlandeses* (Editorial Gredos; Madrid, 2001).

[50] Myles na gCopaleen, *A boca pobre* transl. by Isaac Fernández Fernández (Rinoceronte Editora; Cangas, 2016).

[51] Tomás Mac Síomóin, *21 dán poemes poemas* (Coiscéim; Dublin, 2010).

[52] Caitlín Maude, *File. Poet. Poeta* transl. by Rosangela Barone (Edizioni del Sud; Bari, 1985).

[53] Pádraig Ó Snodaigh, *Solitudine e Compagnia* transl. Rosangela Barone and G. Lendaro Camiless (Edizione des Sud; Bari, 1986); *Linda* transl. Rosangela Barone (Mobydick Edizioni; Faenza, 1997), *Len* transl. Rosangela Barone (Mobydick Edizioni; Faenza, 1999), *Mal* transl. Rosangela Barone (Mobydick Edizioni; Faenza, 1999), *Parnell a Queenie* transl Laura Sanna (Mobydick Edizioni; Faenza, 2010); R. Barone and Melita Cataldi, *Venti e una poesia traduzione dall'irlandese* (La Vallisa; Bari, 1998).

[54] A. Fabbri, M. Giosa and M. Montevecchi, *Bollirà la Rugiada: poesia irlandese contemporea* (Mobydick Edizioni; Faenza, 1996).

[55] Alan Titley, *Arriva Godot: tragicommedia in due atti* transl. by Rosangela Barone (Mobydick Edizioni; Faenza, 1999); Eoghan Ó Tuairisc, *Messa di Defunti* transl. by Rosangela Barone (Trauben; Torino, 2004); Éamon Ó Ciosáin, French version, see notes 36 and 39.

[56] Pádraig Ó Conaire, *Tha klápsei kaueís yia tou Máikel* transl. by Persefoni Koumoutsi (Empeiria Ekdotikē; Athens, 1999).

[57] Ranko Matasovic, Hrovoje Bozicevic and Mícheál Ó Conghaile, *Koje je Vrijeme? Suvremena Irska Pripovijetka* (Nakladi zavod Matice hrvatske; Zagreb, 1997).

[58] Ranko Matasovic, 'The contemporary short story in Irish: a view from Croatia', *Translation Ireland* 11 (4) (December 1997), 3–5: 3.

[59] Matasovic, 'The contemporary short story in Irish', 3.

[60] The catalogue can be accessed online at: http://www.arslonga.ro/ (11 December 2018). Nearly all the translations from Irish are of writers published by CIC, with a predominance of poetry. Publisher Mícheál Ó Conghaile confirms that these resulted from contacts on his part and visits by Tămas to Ireland, and states that the translations were directly from Irish (Mícheál Ó Conghaile, Pers. Comm., 4 December 2017).

[61] Pádraig Standún, *Strigoiul Anvy* transl. by Gabriela Lucia Sabau (Editura Pandora; Bucharest, 2002).

[62] Pádraig Ó Conaire, *Vyhnanství* transl. by Daniela Theinová (Fraktály; Prague, 2004).

[63] Eoghan Ó Tuairisc, *L'Attaque* transl. by Radvan Markus (Baronet; Prague, 2007).

[64] *Muž, který vybouchl: výbor povídek přeložených z irštiny* (Jitro; Prague, 2016). It includes texts by Ó Cadhain, Ó Grianna, Mac Mathúna, Ó Conghaile, etc.; various translators.

[65] Máirtín Ó Cadhain, *Hřbitovní hlína* transl. by Radvan Markus (Argo; Prague, 2017). Magnesia Litera best translation award, April 2018. Markus read passages of his Ó Cadhain translation at the Imram Irish language and literature festival in October 2016; the reading can be viewed online, at: http://www.thejournal.ie/whats-on-imram-2016-3012009-Oct2016/ (16 December 2016).

[66] Pádraig Ó Snodaigh, *Parnell královničce* transl. by Ivana Peroutková (Artur; Prague, 2012).

[67] Pádraig Standún, *Súil le breith* (Zhar Publishers; Sofia, 2010) and *An t-ainmhí — Anvi* (Zhar Publishers; Sofia, 2011); Liam Mac Cóil, *Pismoto (An litir)* transl. by Emil Minchev (Perseus; Sofia, 2015) from an unpublished English translation, information from Liam Mac Cóil to the authors; and Celia de Fréine, *Вucoku Етажи (Faoi chabáistí is ríonacha)* transl. by Vergil Nemchev (Orpheus; Sofia, 2003).

[68] As regards Poland, a rare piece of relevant research to rely on is, Patrycja Lewków, 'The rocky road to Polish: an overview of Irish-language literature in Polish translation', in Robert Looby (ed.), Polish/Irish issues in translation *Translation Ireland* special issue 19 (2) (2014), 49–58.

[69] Pádraig Standún, transl. Barbara Sławomirska in all cases, *Straszydło* (Sagittarius; Kraków, 2005) from *The Anvy*; *Umrzeć z miłości* (Sagittarius; Kraków, 2006); *Miłość kobiety* (Sagittarius; Kraków, 2006) from *Cion mná/A woman's love*; *Kochankowie* (Sagittarius; Kraków, 2006) from *Lovers*; *Stygmaty* from *Stigmata*. Pádraig Ó Conaire, *Deoraíocht/Exile* transl. by Barbara Sławomirska (Sagittarius; Kraków, 2004).

[70] Ernest Bryll and Małgorzata Goraj-Bryll (eds), *Miodopój. Wybór wierszy irlandzkich (Wiek VI–XII)* ('The honey well: a selection of Irish poetry (6th–12th centuries)') (Instytut Wydawniczy PAX; Warszawa, 1978); Ernest Bryll and Małgorzata Goraj-Bryll (eds), *Irlandzki tancerz: Wybór wierszy irlandzkich (Wiek XIII–XIX)* ('The Irish dancer: a selection of Irish poetry (13th–19th centuries)') (Instytut Wydawniczy PAX; Warszawa, 1981); Maurice O'Sullivan, *Dwadzieścia lat dorastania (Twenty years a-growing / Fiche bliain ag fás)* transl. by Ernest Bryll and Małgorzata Goraj-Bryll (Państwowa Spółdzielnia Wydawnicza; Warszawa, 1986). They also translated *Táin czyli uprowadzenie stad z Cuailnge* ('The cattle raid of Cooley / Táin bó Cuailgne') transl. by Ernest Bryll and Małgorzata Goraj-Bryll (Ludowa Spółdzielnia Wydawnicza; Warszawa. 1986). All of these are considered by Lewków in her article (see note 68).

[71] Jason O'Brien, 'Pieces of Pearse are translated into Polish', *Irish Independent*, 18 November 2008.

[72] Pádraig Pearse, *Opowiadania* (Norbertinum; Lublin, 2008).

[73] Jerzy Jarniewicz (ed.), *Sześć poetek irlandzkich* ('Six Irish women poets') transl. by Jerzy Jarniewicz (Biuro Literackie; Wrocław, 2012).

[74] Михайлова Т. А., Анненкова К. В. Слово об Ирландии: голос Эрина (составление). (Молодая гвардия; Москва, 1986).

[75] Tatyana Mikhailova, Голос Эрина: Слово об Ирландии ('The voice of Ireland') Moscow, 1986.

[76] Details on Titley in Russian are available at: http://magazines.russ.ru/inostran/2006/6/avt18.html accessed (17 December 2017).

[77] Séamas Mac Annaidh, Мой Рыжий Дрозд transl. by Tatyana Mikhailova (Moscow; Molodaya Gvardiya, 1989) from *Cuaifeach mo londubh buí* (Coiscéim; Dublin, 1983); information on the sales of the Russian translation is available in the 2005 Imram literary festival programme. Flann O'Brien, Поющие Лазаря, или На редкость бедные люди transl. by Anne Korosteleva (Saint Petersburg; Symposium, 2003). The Russian title translates as 'Singing of Lazarus, or of very poor people'. The authors are grateful to Dr Mark Ó Fionnáin, Lublin University and to Dr Maxim Fomin, University of Ulster, for information on these titles for notes 74, 75, 77.

[78] ''Sé an pros tathán, coincréad, clocha saoirsinne an tsaoil'; see Máirtín Ó Cadhain, *Páipéir bhána agus páipéir bhreaca* (Clóchomhar Teo.; Dublin, 1969), 37.

[79] At the time of translation at least. Gearailt Mac Eoin's English translation of *Deoraíocht* was first published in 1994 (reprints 1999, 2009) and may have influenced several of the continental translations of the novel.

[80] Two poems from the *horen* anthology were republished in *ad libitum: Sammlung Zerstreuung*, no. 21 (Volk und Welt; Berlin, 1991), 131–3.

[81] Dairena Ní Chinnéide, 'Crisis of translation in minority languages', *Poetry Ireland News* (July/August 2010); available online at: http://www.poetryireland.ie/writers/articles/crisis-of-translation-in-minority-languages (16 December 2016).

[82] Gabriel Rosenstock, *Ein Archivar großer Taten* transl. by H.-C. Oeser (Edition Rugerup; Hörby, 2007).

[83] Máirtín Ó Cadhain, *The dirty dust* transl. by Alan Titley (Yale University Press; New Haven and London, 2015), and *Graveyard clay: Cré na cille* transl. by Liam Mac Con Iomaire and Tim Robinson (Yale University Press; New Haven and London, 2016).

[84] Joan Trodden Keefe, "Churchyard Clay": a translation of "Cré na Cille" by Máirtín Ó Cadhain, with introduction and notes. Unpublished PhD thesis (University of California, Berkeley, 1984).

[85] Rainer Moritz, 'Irre irisch', *Die Welt*, 2 July 2017.

[86] Moritz, 'Irre irisch'.

[87] Sylvia Staudte, 'Unter Schilling-Leichen', *Frankfurter Rundschau*, 1 July 2017. Transl. by the authors.

[88] Jan Wilm, 'Gräber haben Ohren', *Frankfurter Allgemeine Zeitung*, 21 June 2017; also available online at: https://www.buecher.de/shop/schwarzer-humor/grabgefluester/-cadhain-mirtn/products_products/detail/prod_id/47157479/#reviews (16 December 2017).

[89] Staudte, 'Unter Schilling-Leichen'.

PART III   Irish Art, Architecture,
Film and Music in
European Discourses

A cabin and not a cottage: the architectural embodiment of the Irish nation

Finola O'Kane

In 1779 Arthur Young prepared his plate of 'An Irish Cabbin' for his seminal publication *A tour in Ireland 1776–1779* (see Plate I). The small decrepit construction, described as a 'weedy dung-hill', was chosen to represent Ireland—not an image of an Irish city, street, public building or great house. This preference for small, vernacular buildings set in rural environments has dogged the representation of Irish architecture, and of Ireland, ever since. Irish tour guides have tended to favour Ireland's rivers, lakes, seasides, mountains, hills and roads whilst avoiding any architecture that could not be subsumed into the setting. The visual representation of the country, externally perceived as a land devoid of great cities and industries, continued to presume a rural setting, and Irish architecture, and architects, continued to be un-represented in the European eye. The one dominant exception has been the prevalence of printed quayside views, in which the border between land and sea provided an acceptable landscape setting for Dublin and Cork's great eighteenth-century public buildings. This chapter will examine representations of Ireland in the tourist literature, and the relative weighting of landscape and architecture that they describe. It will also examine characterisations of Ireland in the profession-al nineteenth-century building journals of Britain and France, while touching briefly on how this legacy continues to affect the position and perception of Irish architecture, landscape design and planning.

Arthur Young's 'Irish cabbin'

During his tour, Young was very eager to document how Ireland's poorest inhabitants lived. He 'made many enquiries concerning the state of the lower classes' and 'found that in some respects they were in good circumstances, in others indifferent'. Most of them 'had a cow, and some two', while all of them had 'a pig, and numbers of poultry' and in general 'the complete family of cows, calves, hogs, poultry, and children, pig[ged] together in the cabbin.'[1] His description of the typical 'Irish cabbin' corresponds closely with its printed image (Plate I, opposite):

> The cottages of the Irish, which are all called cabbins, are the most miserable looking hovels that can well be con-ceived: They generally consist of only one room: mud kneaded with straw is the common material of the walls; these are rarely above seven feet high, and not always above five or six; they are about two feet thick, and have only a door, which lets in light instead of a window, and should let the smoke out instead of a chimney, but they had rather keep it in especially when the cabbin is not built

Finola O'Kane

Plate I—Plate of 'An Irish Cabbin', frontispiece in Arthur Young, *A tour in Ireland...1776–1779*, vol. 1/1, London 4to, 1780.

with regular walls, but supported on one, or perhaps on both sides by the banks of a broad dry ditch.[2]

Despite his evident dismay with most cabins, in some parts of Ireland Young was more positive about the small structures. When travelling through Summerhill, Co. Meath he did 'not hesitate' to pronounce one cabin's inhabitants 'as well off as most English cottagers' because the cabin was 'built of mud 18 inches or 2 feet thick, and well thatched' and this was 'far warmer than the thin clay walls in England'.[3]

The influence of Arthur Young on external perceptions of Ireland was not slight. His originality in plotting an entire country's improvement in *A tour in Ireland* led him to correspond with some of the most powerful men of the eighteenth-century world, among them George Washington and the Duc de la Rochefoucauld who turned to him for advice on agriculture and landscape design. His writings were widely translated, and a complete French edition of his travel and agricultural works was published by order of the French Directory in 1801.[4] His 'various agricultural tours, translated almost immediately into a range of different languages ... fed German armchair travellers' interest in the foreign' and 'contributed to the growing corpus of British literature of farming in German translation'.[5] His posthumous influence was also considerable, with his son, the less talented Rev. Arthur Young, invited to visit Russia in 1815 and asked to pronounce on possible improvements to Russian agriculture.

As William Williams has observed, it was not the beggar but the ubiquitous cabin that became the focus of attention for tourists and analysts of Irish poverty, and Young's book and frontispiece reinforced this perception.[6] Few tourists who followed in Young's wake avoided the topic of Ireland's housing and its attendant social and cultural effects, and while Ireland's tour guides continued, in the main, to be written, illustrated and published by inhabitants of the British Isles, there were some notable exceptions.[7] Visiting Connacht, the 'wild part of Ireland, seldom visited by natives, never by foreigners', in 1828, the German tourist Hermann von Pückler-Muskau found 'the cabins of the inhabitants are beyond description wretched, and the appearance of all the flat country extremely poor'.[8] In Wicklow, which was 'awfully void, lonely, and monotonous', he remarked on 'one single wretched cabin ... but in ruins, and uninhabited; and a white footpath wind[ing] along toilfully through the brown heather, like a huge worm'.[9] Cabins drew the foreigner's gaze, particularly the long strings of cabins that stretched along the approach roads to every Irish town and village. One of the earliest descriptions of an Irish 'Cabbin', in fact, is to be found in James Farewell's 1689 poem 'The Irish Hudibras; or Fingallian Prince':

> Built without either Brick or Stone,
> Or Couples to lay Roof upon:
> With Wattlets unto Wattles ty'd,
> (Fixt in the ground on either side)
> Did like a shaded Arbour show,
> With Seats of Sods, and Roof of Straw.
> The Floor beneath with Rushes laid, stead
> of Tapestry; no Bed nor Bedstead;
> No Posts, nor Bolts, nor Hinges in door,
> No Chimney, Kitchin, Hall, or Windor [Window];

But narrow Dormants stopt with Hay
All night, and open in the day.
On either side there was a door
Extent from Roof unto the floor,
Which they, like Hedg-hogs, stop with straw,
Or open, as the Wind does blow:

In this so rich and stately Cabbin,
To lie in state came this Sea-Crab in,
Dy'd for the nonce in liquid Sable,
And laid him underneath the Table;
Where in one end the parted Brother
Was laid to rest, the Cows in t'other...[10]

Surprisingly technical, the poem described what Young then drew some ninety years later. Young's cabin also had no chimney or window and its scale was such that no hall or kitchen could possibly be expected to lie within. Both Farewell and Young's cabin doors stretched from the eaves to the bare rough ground, with no threshold, lintel, hinge or latch to seal the inside from the elements. The Irish cabins were inhabited by people and animals together, and this commingling of humans and their chattel upset many commentators. Both cabins are examples of what the later 1841 Census of Ireland would define as fourth-class housing, or 'mud cabins having only one room'; a third-class house was a 'better description of a cottage, still built of mud but varying from two to four rooms and windows'.[11]

Irish cabins versus English cottages

Young's print was derived from a pen and wash illustration (Plate II, overleaf). The characteristic inhabitants of the cabin—the people, pigs, poultry, cows, calves and other animals—were, however, omitted from the printed version, together with their potatoes (see Plate I). The late eighteenth-century predilection for cottage paintings, and for landscape designs animated by cottages, was familiar to Young.[12] Visiting Innisfallen, Killarney in 1776, he was enchanted by the small island's potential as a 'delicious retreat', if provided with 'a cottage, a few cows,

Plate II—Pen and wash drawing of 'An Irish Cabbin', from Arthur Young's own extra-illustrated edition of *A tour in Ireland...1776–1779*, vol. 1/1, London 4to, 1780. NLI LO10203, courtesy of the National Library of Ireland.

and a swarm of poultry'.[13] Young was not a gifted artist but he was familiar with movements in contemporary art and landscape design.[14] He took Thomas Roberts's paintings of Lough Erne as inspiration for his own pen and wash views of the same lake prospects, if not very successfully.[15] Only three of the many illustrations Young planned to use in *A tour in Ireland* were eventually printed. One of these was 'The Irish Cabbin' (Plate II), the other two were of Powerscourt Waterfall in County Wicklow and Mary's Island, Lough Erne (see Plate III, opposite, for the latter). While the inclusion of Powerscourt is not surprising, given the fame of the waterfall as a tourist site by 1780, the reproduction of Lady E. Forster's amateur pencil drawing of Lough Erne with its 'cabbin for a poultryman, a covered bench' and 'a spot marked out for a cottage' appears to have been selected as a textbook example of a picturesque view.[16] The tripartite division of Forster's drawing into a foreground of lake, middle ground of island and a distant view through

Plate III—'A view of Mary's Island, Innisfandra & Carlat, a distant view of Knockniny Lord Ross' Park, on Lough Erne', from Arthur Young's own extra-illustrated edition of *A tour in Ireland... 1776–1779*, vol. 1/1, London 4to edition, 1780. NLI LO10203, courtesy of the National Library of Ireland.

to another lake was composed to exact picturesque conventions. The inclusion of a cottage gave the composition scale.

Eighteenth-century English landscape painters, notably Gainsborough, painted many scenes of happy fecund families at the cottage door. These 'fantasies of rural England or "Happy Britannia" that never was' have been discussed by John Barrell, amongst others.[17] The Georgic illusion—that cottages personified a simpler, idyllic and harmonious way of life—was hard to uphold in Ireland. Young's figures are neither at work nor at play; neither in a Georgic or a Pastoral, but held in a state of apathetic stasis. If Gainsborough placed the hunched and careworn woodcutter in the pen and grey ink preparatory sketch 'Wooded landscape with figures outside a cottage door' (Plate IV, overleaf) in opposition to the relaxed and well-cared for female inhabitants of the cottage and its doorway, so as 'to hint at a balanced life in which repose is properly only the reward of industry', no such work/life balance can be inferred from Young's view, in which men, women and children are locked in poverty together.[18] Work *and* leisure are equally unimaginable in such a setting and the precise gender relations that Ann Bermingham has found between the exterior and the interior in Gainsborough's cottage paintings are absent from Young's amateur drawing, where everyone is outside and at the mercy of the weather. Gainsborough's cottages are invariably whole and inhabited, with glazed windows and doors that possess frames and hinges. His cottages have stone steps that lead up to thresholds at which women sit suckling fat and contented children. Young's cottage has no happy peasants beside the cabin door. His children are not suckled at the breast but fend for themselves in the dirt. Dog and horse are shackled, and the lamb is tied up.

If, as Ann Bermingham remarks, 'neither poverty nor frippery had any place in the genuine "British Cottage"', then Young's cabin was very clearly Irish and not British. If such views of English cottages invited the positive interpretation of 'the cottage family as the embodiment of the nation', what was Young implying with his gaping cabin door bereft of any family to inhabit it? Bermingham also asks what it

Plate IV—Thomas Gainsborough RA (1727–1788), 'Wooded landscape with figures outside a cottage door', Gray wash with pen and gray ink. The Yale Center for British Art, Paul Mellon Collection.

Finola O'Kane

means 'to conceive of the nation in private terms as a cottage family, or to conceive of the cottage family in public terms as the nation?', both in respect of Gainsborough's cottage door paintings and of British late eighteenth-century architectural culture.[19] This culture had adopted cottages as the building type most suited to demonstrating both social altruism and professional competence. Countless manuals, guidance documents and other publications were produced at the turn of the nineteenth century to advise on the design of workers' housing.[20] Some of these were then reproduced in Irish publications with little or no revision for the Irish context.[21] Young, by making his drawing the frontispiece to *A tour in Ireland 1776–1779*, conceives of Ireland in private terms as a cabin family and the cabin family in public terms as the nation. This is a harsh critique of Britain's governance of Ireland, as only a government with no interest in the security and wellbeing of the peasantry could countenance Young's 'Irish Cabbin' (see Plates I and II). Could a cabin be an example of 'workers' housing' when the essential contract between work and some degree of material reward in the form of environmental protection was so clearly lacking?

The Irish cabin and the architectural profession

What did the personification of Ireland as cabin mean for the architectural profession that sought to adopt the cottage as a building that could enhance its prospects? How could architecture advance in a country populated overwhelmingly with cabins? The principal nineteenth century British architectural periodical was *The Builder, An Illustrated Weekly Magazine for the Drawing-room, the Studio, the Office, the Workshop and the Cottage.*[22] It was described by Nikolaus Pevsner as 'the most important professional journal of the early and High Victorian decades ... the years in which architecture became a profession'.[23] Joseph Aloysius Hansom and Alfred Bartholomew founded the journal in 1842; George Godwin replaced them both as editor in 1844. He transformed *The Builder* into the 'most important and successful professional paper of its kind with a readership well beyond the architectural and building world', and Godwin was 'reputed to have written much of each issue himself'. *The Builder* was particularly 'known for its campaigns for health and housing reform', which were initiated by Godwin. [24]

In 1845 *The Builder*'s growing professional focus was evident in its revised description as 'An illustrated weekly magazine for the architect, engineer, opperative, and artist'. Neither volume one of 1842/3 or volume two of 1844 contained any index entry for Ireland, but volume two did contain articles on 'Clonatton Church, Ireland' and the 'Schools at Gorey', along with some published correspondence that touched on Irish matters.[25] Volume three of 1845 did have a specific index entry for Ireland and also contained articles of an antiquarian character on the architecture of Galway, St Canice's Cathedral in Kilkenny and the perennially popular topic of Irish round towers. Volume four listed the major public works projects in Ireland, but this coverage lapsed in the subsequent two volumes. Volume four also included entries under Ireland for 'ecclesiastical architecture, leases, marble, wages' and the 'waste of water power'.[26] Volume five contained an article on 'The state of architecture in Ireland' describing how a body of men from the Royal Institute of Architects of Ireland (RIAI) had met with the lord lieutenant, who had found it 'strange' that 'architecture should not be esteemed in Dublin, one of the most picturesque cities in her Majesty's dominions' and remarked on 'how little care has hitherto been bestowed upon the dwellings of the humbler classes of our fellow-subjects'.[27]

An article in the succeeding issue pressed home the RIAI's real grievance—the appointment of an Englishman (George Wilkinson) to design and construct the workhouses of Ireland. This had resulted in 'the erection of a class of buildings wholly at variance with common architectural propriety, and unsuited to the purposes of their construction, as well as to the character of the country'.[28] The formation of the RIAI, partly as a consequence of this agitation concerning the workhouse building programme, is not perhaps the most felicitous of beginnings for a professional body. Neither volume six nor seven had any entries under Ireland in the index, but matters changed in 1850 when volume eight included a slew of entries to document not only the building programme for the workhouses but also entries such as 'Building notes from Ireland', which contained descriptions of such major works projects as the Youghal Embankment.[29] Nevertheless, the focus on workhouses continued, together with its connection to the RIAI, as a running example of the Irish architectural profession's lack of national power and identity. Acting as a euphemism for the 'calamity' that had overwhelmed the country, Irish workhouses continued to animate *The Builder*'s Irish reports, creating a generally negative impression of Ireland's own 'workers' housing' and implied connected levels of architectural competence.

The image of Ireland portrayed by *The Builder* was piecemeal, inconsistent, reactionary and defensive. Sometimes, with contributions such as 'Building notes from Ireland' or 'Architecture and building in Ireland', the coverage, rather than being included in the 'Notes from the Provinces' section like the remainder of Great Britain, approached giving Ireland the status of a separate island, if not a nation state.[30] The buildings most consistently documented were workhouses, and to a lesser degree churches. Strange projects for Ireland's general improvement were sometimes published, such as one on 'The Irish Amelioration Society', which had been 'established by royal charter, for the employment of the Irish peasantry in the manufacture of peat charcoal as a substitute for wood charcoal in all its purposes, but particularly for deodorisation of manure'. The society's inauguration ceremony took place 'at one of the society's stations, in a wild and remote part of the bog of Allen' at Derrymullen, County Kildare.[31]

Although we may deduce that *The Builder* influenced the perception of Ireland and Irish architecture from within the British empire, it is difficult to estimate how widely it was read in Europe. The comparable French nineteenth-century building periodical was the *Revue Générale de l'Architecture*, whose editor was César Daly, his name implying some Irish ancestry.[32] The *Revue* did contain many entries under 'Angleterre', but I have found no specific references to *The Builder* by searching the *Revue*'s online archive. The growing body of research into nineteenth-century architectural print culture does not yet include the analysis of French perceptions of British architecture or British perceptions of the French architecture.[33] César Daly did refer openly to Irish architecture and to the famine in an article from the 1845–6 edition recording the construction of a round tower/house for Father Matthew, founder of the Irish Temperance movement:

> Irish architecture. The English possess originality; the French spirit; the Irish have a bit of both. Although the famine has desolated Ireland, with her inhabitants dying of inanition and misery, their dreams however are of banquets and festivities rather than abnegation and asceticism. Look how the members of the Temperance Society of Cork have

Plate V—Henry Mark Anthony (1817–86), A view of the Lower Lake, purchased by Prince Albert in 1845. Royal Collections Trust /© Her Majesty Queen Elizabeth II 2019.

built a house in their city for Father Matthew, the apostle of the temperance movement and the enemy of alcoholic drinks. This house, according to the Irish newspapers, is in the form of a tower.[34]

The letter pages of the same issue included a letter from 'Guillaume, capitaine du génie', which chastised the larger island of Great Britain as 'this despotic island that hypocritically employs the right to board and inspect for negroes yet tramples on its sister Ireland?'[35] A degree of Anglo-French animosity coupled with some religious overtones

and the common comparison of Irish peasants and slaves is evident in these instances. French writers touring Ireland continued to reinforce a poor perception of Irish housing, connecting it with famine: 'Misery is Ireland's permanent condition. It is no exaggeration to say that, since its forced union with England, Ireland had been in want of food, clothing and housing. Ireland is the classic famine country.'[36]

Irish cabins 1845–1900

As Ireland moved towards the cataclysm of the famine of 1845–9, cabins were rarely represented in Irish landscape paintings, and even less so in its aftermath. Some landscape paintings, such as Henry Mark Anthony's painting of the Lower Lake, Killarney (bought by Prince Albert in 1845 and now in the Royal Collection), reiterated Young's characterisation of Ireland: a bowl of potatoes, seated peasants, a ruined structure—in this case the chapel of Aghadoe—and a mountainous rear ground, but it contained little evidence of a changing landscape (Plate V, previous page). Notable exceptions include the works of George Washington Brownlow, Francis W. Topham and William Evans of Eton, who all documented the realities of life in the fourth-class cabin.[37] George Petrie's watercolours and printed views, which served to illustrate many tour guides, rarely depicted cabins, with the exception of those he drew stretching along the approach roads to Lusk, Drogheda, Kildare, Kells, Cashel and Kilmallock, although most of these had windows and chimneys.[38] Medieval ruins continued to be preferred to cabins or cottages in most visual images of Ireland. Yet the cabin or fourth-class house 'constituted 37% of all Irish houses' in pre-famine Ireland and in the west of Ireland parishes of 'the Burren, Loop Head, the Dingle, Beara, Sheep Head and the Mizen peninsulas over 85% of all houses were of this class'.[39] The potato's failure led inexorably to a mass failure of Irish housing and to a landscape denuded of both people and houses.

By 1851 a 'total of 271,000 dwelling houses had disappeared, of which 72.4% were in the fourth-class category'.[40] Willie Smyth finds 'the correlation coefficient' of 0.81 'between the percentage of fourth-class houses and levels of population loss' indicative of 'a massive interconnection between the two conditions.'[41] Few visual images depicted what must have been a dramatically changing landscape and none as eloquently as the housebook of Griffith's Valuation of 1847 for the mountain townland of Boolkennedy in Co. Tipperary. On page 59 every house, barn, porch and office listed, with the one exception of Michael Carey's '3B' class house, was harshly redacted in thick lines of black ink and renamed 'Ruins' in blue (Plate VI, opposite).[42] The lithographs produced by artists during the famine period for *The Illustrated London News*, often featuring 'roofless dwellings and deserted villages', are generally considered to be less sentimental and more representative of the actual state of Ireland's landscape and housing than many of the more formal oil paintings of the period.[43] The stark representation of the ruined village of Moveen (Plate VII, overleaf, top) seems to record the reality of the Irish western landscape in 1849 more accurately than the paintings of artists such as Daniel Mc Donald, who tend to foreground dramatic and emotional

Finola O'Kane

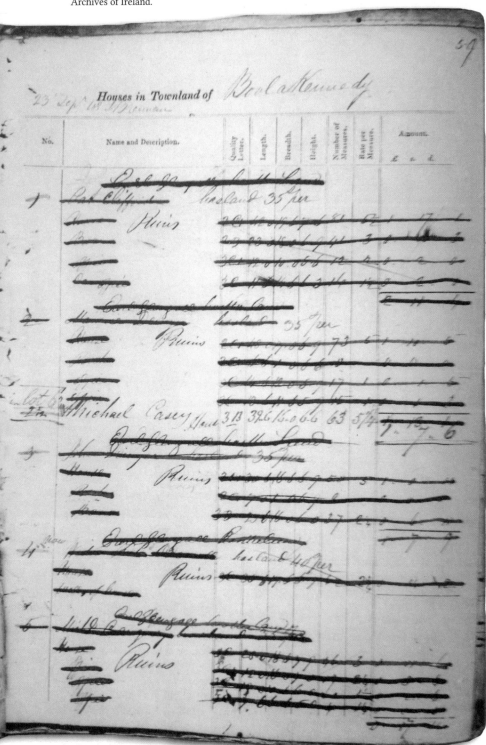

VILLAGE OF MOVEEN.

EVICTION KILRUSH. 4918. W.L.

Above: Plate IX—'At Gweedore, Co. Donegal', Robert French, photographer; NLI L-ROY-01365, courtesy of the National Library of Ireland.
Opposite, top: Plate VII—'The village of Moveen', *Illustrated London News*, 15 December 1849.
Opposite, bottom: Plate VIII—'Eviction, Kilrush' *c.* 1886: Mathias Magrath's house, Moyasta, Co. Clare after destruction by the Battering Ram', Vandaleur Estate, Co. Clare. Robert French, photographer; NLI L-CAB-04918, courtesy of the National Library of Ireland.

human events. Part of the power of Young's 'An Irish Cabbin' and of the 'Village of Moveen' images lies in this absence of people; both illustrations present landscapes of broken houses with no people to live in them.

If the incidence of fourth-class housing or cabins in Ireland had declined dramatically by 1850, the violent destruction of housing by the eviction process, with the attendant bailiffs and soldiers involving the official organs of the state, began to complicate the image of housing, and architecture's role in providing it. With writers and architects preoccupied in improving the condition of the rural poor, how was this to be reconciled with the destruction of substantial and clearly 'improved' housing during evictions? The 'Eviction' photographs contained in the National Library of Ireland's (NLI) William Lawrence photographic collection generally record the destruction of substantial cottages with

windows and chimneys (Plate VIII, p. 274, bottom). Destroying visibly 'improved' housing, when many organisations were campaigning elsewhere (particularly in urban contexts) for its construction, points to a profound disconnection between landlords and tenants, country and city, state and society. Robert French's photographs of Gweedore, Co. Donegal include one of a family in front of a cottage entitled 'At Gweedore, Co. Donegal' (Plate IX, p. 275), and another of nearly the same family group posed in front of a 'Labourer's Hut, Gweedore' (Plate X, opposite, top). The titles do not reveal the family's spatial progress, and the move from cottage to cabin can only be deduced from the fact that the same father, mother and two of the family's three children inhabit both settings. Nor is it certain that these people lived in either setting in reality, rather than serving as actors in the staged perspective of the photograph. The eldest daughter and all the furniture have either disappeared en route between the two locations or are now inside the peat 'labourer's hut' with its ramshackle window (Plate X).

Novel contemporary solutions for rehousing the evicted are suggested by some of the photographs, notably one that seems to draw heavily

Opposite, top: Plate X—'Labourer's Hut, Gweedore', Robert French, photographer; Lawrence Photographic Collection, NLI L-ROY-01366, courtesy of the National Library of Ireland.

Opposite, bottom: Plate XI—'Evicted', Robert French, photographer; Lawrence Photographic Collection, NLI L-ROY-02648, courtesy of the National Library of Ireland.

Below: Plate XII—'Mountain Stage Cabin, Glenbeigh, Co. Kerry', Robert French, photographer; Lawrence Photographic Collection, NLI L-ROY-08290 courtesy of the National Library of Ireland.

Plate XIII—'Evicted, Clongorey', Robert French, photographer; Lawrence Photographic Collection, NLI L-ROY-02158, courtesy of the National Library of Ireland.

from the contemporary construction techniques for railway carriages and signal cabins (Plate XI, p. 276, bottom). The eviction of tenants from fourth-class housing was but rarely photographed, despite the fact that such accommodation could reasonably be classified as uninhabitable and therefore deserving of destruction. Fourth-class cabins that were photographed were generally situated in particularly bleak locations, such as 'Mountain Stage Cabin, Glenbeigh, Co. Kerry' (Plate XII, previous page), or belonged to such notables as Widow Quirke at Coomasahan or Mick McQuaid in Conemara.[44] Some photographs of mass village evictions are reminiscent of the earlier newspaper lithographs and also reveal the known predominance of cabins over cottages (Plate XIII, above).

Conclusion

Much of Ireland is still depopulated and dotted with the ruins and walls of the countless houses, hovels, homes and homesteads that once inhabited the landscape. The disappearances at an individual building level were predominantly those of fourth-class cabins, but where such homes were clustered together into clachans, or where they formed substantial portions of Irish town suburbs, these also disappeared. Unlike the people who inhabited them, the buildings themselves were not quite cleared but slowly subsumed into the landscape. Architecture subsumed by landscape usually indicates a tragic history. Landscape subsumed by architecture usually does not. It remained as challenging as it had been for Arthur Young to resolve any sentimental image of cottage life with the harsh reality of the Irish cabin's form and wider setting. Discussion of the impact of the disappearance of much Irish architecture (and I use the word without any implicit professional involvement but to indicate all types of manmade roofed enclosure), is not very evident in the historiography.[45] There are many reasons why this might be so. Architecture is fundamentally a constructive, positive discipline, not given to writing histories of its destruction. Yet

Plate XIV—Paul Henry, 'The road through the village'. Private collection.

the unmaking of these many, many cabins, cottages, streets, clachans and villages is part of Irish architectural history, and also an implicit critique of its most fundamental purpose: to shelter and to house. Irish architecture had to position itself against this landscape, one containing so much evidence of building failure. The visual dominance of small buildings, invariably falling into decay, fought against any positive projection of Irish architecture. Ireland's visualisation continued to presume a rural, ruined, landscape setting; a legacy of the country's complex relationship with cabins, cottages and their representation.[46] The strength of the depopulated rural landscape (sometimes with a lone cottage and not a cabin) as the personification of Ireland continues to endure (Plate XIV, previous page).

Notes

[1] Arthur Young, *A tour in Ireland 1776–1779* (2 vols., vol. 1; T. Cadell and J. Dodsley; London, 1780), 59.

[2] Young, *A tour in Ireland*, 25–6.

[3] Young, *A tour in Ireland*, 21.

[4] François de La Rochefoucauld and Norman Scarfe (eds), *A Frenchman's year in Suffolk: French impressions of Suffolk life in 1784* (Boydell Press; Suffolk, 1988), xx. See also, Peter Michael Jones, 'Translations into French of Arthur Young's *Travels in France* (1791–1801)', *La Révolution française* [En ligne], December 2017, mis en ligne le 15 septembre 2017; available at: http://journals.openedition.org/lrf/1739; DOI: 10.4000/lrf.1739 (25 January 2018). 'The work was finally published in the course of the *an IX* 1800–1, with the truncated version of the *Travels* consigned to volume seventeen.'

[5] Alison E. Martin, 'Paeans to progress: Arthur Young's travel accounts in German translation', in Stefanie Stockhorst (ed.), *Cultural transfer through translation; the circulation of Enlightenment thought in Europe by means of translation* (Rodopi Editions; Amsterdam and New York, 2010), 297–314: 303. See also, Ina Ferris, 'The question of ideological form: Arthur Young, the agricultural tour, and Ireland', in David E. Richter (ed.), *Ideology and form in eighteenth-century literature* (Texas Tech University Press; Lubbock, TX, 1999), 129–45.

[6] William H.A. Williams, *Creating Irish tourism: the first century, 1750–1850* (Anthem Press; London, 2010), 178–9.

[7] See John McVeagh, *Irish travel writing: a bibliography* (Wolfhound Press; Dublin, 1996). I have counted twenty-two travel books dealing wholly or partly with Ireland, that were published in France before 1850 and with identified authors, in this helpful bibliography. In comparison, only ten books published in Germany are listed and one each from Hungary and Italy.

[8] Hermann von Pückler-Muskau, *Tour in England, Ireland, and France in the years 1826, 1828, and 1829 ... In a series of letters* (Carey, Lea and Blanchard; Philadelphia, PA, 1833), 345–6.

[9] von Pückler-Muskau, *Tour in England, Ireland, and France*, 435.

[10] James Farewell, *The Irish Hudibras; or Fingallian Prince, Taken from the sixth book of Virgil's Aeneaids, and adapted to the present times* (Richard Balwin; London, 1689),

32–4. See also, Andrew Carpenter (ed.), *Verse in English from Tudor and Stuart Ireland* (Cork University Press; Cork, 2003), 516–17.

[11] *Census of Ireland 1841* (Government Publications; Dublin, 1843), xiv.

[12] For cottages in eighteenth-century landscape design, and women's role in their design, see, Finola O'Kane, 'Design and rule: the feminine amateur and the picturesque', in *Ireland and the picturesque, design, landscape painting and tourism 1700–1840* (Yale University Press; New Haven and London, 2013), 174–80.

[13] Arthur Young, *A tour in Ireland*, 359.

[14] See, Finola O'Kane, 'Arthur Young's study of landscape gardens and parks for his publication "A tour in Ireland 1776–1779"', *Journal of Scottish Thought* 9 (2017), 110–23: 112.

[15] See, Finola O'Kane, 'Arthur Young's published and unpublished illustrations for "A tour in Ireland, 1776–1779"', *Irish Architectural and Decorative Studies, The Journal of the Irish Georgian Society* 19 (2016), 118–60.

[16] Young, *A tour in Ireland*, 70.

[17] Ann Bermingham 'The simple life: cottages and Gainsborough's cottage doors', in Peter de Bolla, Nigel Leask and David Simpson (eds), *Land, nation and culture, 1740–1840: thinking the republic of taste* (Palgrave Macmillan; Hampshire and New York, 2005), 37–62: 56. See, John Barrell, *The dark side of the landscape: the rural poor in English painting, 1730–1840* (Cambridge University Press; Cambridge, 2009).

[18] See, Barrell, *The dark side of the landscape*, 71. I am grateful to Michael Rosenthal for alerting me to the existence of this sketch.

[19] Bermingham, 'The simple life', 56.

[20] Examples taken from Ann Bermingham's extensive bibliography include: John Wood, *A series of plans for cottages or habitations of the labourer* (J. Taylor; London, 1806; 1st edn 1781); James Malton, *An essay on British cottage architecture* (Hookham and Carpenter; London, 1798); Edmund Bartell, *Hints for picturesque improvements in ornamental cottages and their scenery: including some observations on the labourer and his cottage. In three essays* (J. Taylor; London, 1800 and 1804); and William Atkinson, *Cottage architecture, including perspective views and plans of labourers cottages, and small farm houses* (J. Barfield; London, 1805).

[21] Robert Beatson, 'On cottages', in John Hamilton, *Irish agricultural magazine* (T.M. Bates; Dublin, 1798), 138–48.

[22] This full title was given on the frontispiece page to the first two volumes of 1843 and 1844.

[23] Nicklaus Pevsner, *Some architectural writers of the nineteenth century* (Oxford University Press; Oxford, 1972), 79. See also, Michael Brooks, 'The Builder in the 1840's: the making of a magazine, the shaping of a profession', *Victorian Periodicals Review* 14 (3) (Fall 1981), 86–93, and Anthony King, 'Architectural journalism and the profession: the early years of George Godwin', *Architectural History* 19 (1976), 32–53.

[24] *Oxford Dictionary of National Biography*: 'George Godwin 1813–1888'; available online at: http://www.oxforddnb.com (15 December 2017). See also, Anthony King, 'Another blow for life: George Godwin and the reform of working class housing', *Architectural Review* 86 (1964), 448–52.

[25] I have used the Bodley library's digitised volumes 1–10. These are available online at: http://www.bodley.ox.ac.uk/cgi-bin/ilej/pbrowse.pl?item=title&id=ILEJ.6.&title=The+ Builder (1 November 2017 to 20 January 2018).

[26] *The Builder*, vol. 4, 1846: Index.

[27] *The Builder*, vol. 5, 25 September 1847, 460.

[28] *The Builder*, vol. 5, 2 October 1847, 469.

[29] *The Builder*, vol. 8, 5 October 1850, 473. The full list of 'Irish' articles from the 1850 volume is as follows:
- 89 'How they build workhouses in Ireland'
- 403 'Building works in Ireland'
- 416 'Architecture and building in Ireland'
- 424 'Notes of building works in Ireland...workhouse at Glyn'
- 436–7 'Position of architects in Ireland'
- 466 'The Irish Amelioration Society'
- 473 'Building notes in Ireland'
- 478 'Youghal embankment'
- 488–9 'Engineering and architectural works in Ireland'
- 501 'The ruins of Glendalough'
- 568–9 'Architectural and railway matters in Ireland, [Workhouse, Thomastown, Kilkenny]
- 569 'Neglect of antiquities in Ireland' RRB
- 605 'Engineering and architectural doings in Ireland... [workhouses in Berehaven, Castlecomer]'.

[30] 'Building notes from Ireland', *The Builder*, vol. 8, 5 October 1850, 473; 'Architecture and building from Ireland', vol. 8, 31 August 1850, 416.

[31] *The Builder*, vol. 8, 28 September 1850, 466.

[32] Further information on this periodical is available online on the website of the Sorbonne; see: http://elec.enc.sorbonne.fr/architectes/147 (21 December 2017).

[33] Richard Wittman, 'Print culture and French architecture in the eighteenth and nineteenth centuries: a survey of recent scholarship', in *Perspective, actualité en historie de l'art*; available at: http://journals.openedition.org/perspective/5806?lang=en (19 December 2017). Wittman cites the following in his article:
- Marc Saboya, *Presse et architecture au xixe siècle: César Daly et la Revue générale de l'architecture et des travaux publics* (Picard; Paris, 1991).
- Marc Saboya, 'Remarques préliminaires à une étude du travail sur l'image dans la presse architecturale française du xixe siècle', in Béatrice Bouvier and Jean-Michel Leniaud, *Les périodiques d'architecture, xviiie-xxe siècle: recherche d'une méthode critique d'analyse* (L'école nationale des chartes; Paris, 2001), 67–79.
- Marc Saboya, 'Les medias au service de l'architecture: la presse architecturale française entre 1800 et 1871', in Giuliana Ricci, Giovanna D'Amia, Francesco Cherubini (eds), *La cultura architettonica nell'età della Restaurazione* (Mimesis; Milano, 2002), 329–34.

[34] *Revue générale de l'architecture et des travaux publiques* ... vol. 6 (1845–6), 557; the periodical is available online at: https://babel.hathitrust.org/cgi/pt?id=mdp.39015024232210;view=1up;seq=293 (25 January 2018). I have translated the extract from the following original: *Architecture irlandaise. Les Anglais ont de l'originalité; les Francais, de l'esprit; les Irlandais tiennent un peu aux uns et aux autres. Tandis que la famine désole l'Irlande, que ses habitants meurent d'inanition et de misère, que dans leurs rêves doivent figurer plus de banquets et de festins que d'anégation e' d'ascétisme, voici que les membres de la Société de tempérance de Cork viennent de faire bâtir dans leur cité une maison pour le révérand pére Mathieu, l'apôtre de la tempérance et l'ennemi des boissons spiriteuses. Cette maison, d'aprés les journaux irlandais, est en forme de tour.*

[35] *Revue générale de l'architecture et des travaux publiques*, vol. 6 (1845–6), 115; available at: https://babel.hathitrust.org/cgi/pt?id=mdp.39015024232210; view=1up;seq=72 (25 January 2018): *cette île despote qui fait l'hypocrite avec son droit de visite pour les nègres, et foule aux pieds l'Irlande sa soeur* (The boarding of French vessels by the British navy and vice versa, was legally permitted if they were considered to be illegally continuing the transatlantic slave trade, by then abolished by both Britain and France. The naval captain Guillaume evidently believes this *droit de visite* to have been be exploited so as to force French-owned slaves to work as indentured servants in British colonies). See also: https://www.histoire-image.org/etudes/traite-illegale (9 January 2018).

[36] Louis Blanc, 'Une scène en Irlande', *Lettres sur L'Angleterre (1862)* 2 (2) (1866–7), 344; available at: http://gallica.bnf.fr/ark:/12148/bpt6k4906t/f346.item.r=de%20la%20faim (25 January 2018). I have translated the following: *Le misère, on le sait, est l'état permanent de l'Irlande. On pourrait affirmer sans exagération que, depuis son union forcée avec l'Angleterre, l'Irlande n'a cessé d'être en peine de sa nourriture, de son vêtement et de son gîte. L'Irlande est le pays classique de la faim.*

[37] Claudia Kinmonth, 'Rural life through artists' eyes: an interdisciplinary approach', in *Whipping the herring; survival and celebration in nineteenth-century Irish art*, Crawford Art Gallery exhibition catalogue (Crawford Art Gallery; Cork, 2006), 40. See also, Tom Dunne, 'The dark side of the Irish landscape: depictions of the rural poor, 1760–1850', in *Whipping the herring*, 46–62.

[38] *George Petrie (1790–1866), The rediscovery of Ireland's past*, Crawford Art Gallery exhibition catalogue (Crawford Art Gallery; Cork, 2004).

39 William J. Smyth, '"Variations in vulnerability": understanding where and why the people died', in John Crowley, William J. Smyth and Mike Murphy (eds), *Atlas of the Great Irish Famine* (Cork University Press; Cork, 2012), 180–99:187.

[40] William J. Smyth, '"Variations in vulnerability"', 190.

[41] William J. Smyth, '"Variations in vulnerability"', 187–8.

[42] William J. Smyth, 'The famine in the County Tipperary parish of Shanrahan', in John Crowley, William J. Smyth and Mike Murphy (eds), *Atlas of the Great Irish Famine* (Cork University Press; Cork, 2012), 385–98: 388.

[43] L. Perry Curtis Jr., *The depiction of eviction in Ireland* (UCD Press; Dublin, 2011), 48.

[44] National Library of Ireland, William Lawrence Photographic Collection, Robert French, photographer, L_ROY_06805, EB 2658 and L_ROY_06805.

[45] This history has generally been approached more by geographers than architectural historians. See, for example, Kevin B. Whelan, 'Reading the ruins: the presence of absence in the Irish landscape', in Howard B. Clarke, Jacinta Prunty and Mark Hennessy (eds), *Surveying Ireland's past: multidisciplinary essays in honour of Anngret Simms* (Geography Publications; Dublin, 2004), 297–328. The recent Royal Irish Academy/Yale University Press *Architecture* volume in the five-volume *Art and Architecture of Ireland* series contains thirteen entries for the Great Famine in the index, and an article by Nessa Roche on 'Cabins', in Rolf Loeber, Hugh Campbell, Livia Hurley, John Montague and Ellen Rowley (eds), *Art and Architecture of Ireland, volume 4: Architecture 1600–2000* (Yale University Press; New Haven and London, 2015), 332.

[46] For a discussion on the impact Ireland's monastic and castle ruins had on perceptions of Ireland, see, Finola O'Kane, 'Ruins: a case study', in Rolf Loeber, Hugh Campbell, Livia Hurley, John Montague and Ellen Rowley (eds), *Art and Architecture of Ireland, volume 4: Architecture 1600–2000* (Yale University Press; New Haven and London, 2015), 508–9.

Irish contemporary art in European eyes

Caoimhín Mac Giolla Léith

IRELAND: the green island at the extreme limit of northwest Europe. What exactly do we know about that country? What images does the word 'Ireland' evoke in our minds? In addition to dark beer and golden whiskey there is certainly the tradition of folk music. Maybe the names of a few successful rock bands come to mind. When we tax our brains a little harder perhaps we can recall the names of famous writers or the titles of certain contemporary films. According to our stereotypical mental picture of 'Irishness', an Irishman is a jovial red-haired fellow in possession of sharp wit. But what do the words 'Irish contemporary art' conjure up in our minds? And is it possible to talk about contemporary art in the same framework as 'nationality'? [1]

This is the opening paragraph of an essay by Maija Koskinenen, director of the Turku Art Museum, introducing 'Something else', an exhibition of Irish contemporary art that opened there in September 2002 and subsequently travelled to several other venues around Finland. Unsubtle though the rhetoric of her opening gambit may be, it is not unusual. Six years earlier in Denmark the Århus Kunstbygning, in collaboration with the Kulturhus Århus, had organised a festival of Irish art under the banner 'Kelterne kommer/The Celts are coming', incidentally showing scant consideration for distinctions between the very different categories of Celtic, Gaelic and Irish. Music featured prominently in a programme that also included performances and readings alongside painting, sculpture and photography. Of particular note was a flagship collaborative project described by the curators as 'a direct artistic meeting between Ireland and Denmark', in which two Irish artists, Brian Bourke and Helen Farrell, joined two Danes, Hans Oldayu Krull and Tine Hand, in exploring the continuing resonance of a classic medieval Irish story.[2] The tale of 'The madness of Sweeney' (*Buile Shuibhne*), the archetypal artist-outsider, had long fascinated Bourke in particular, as it has many other artists and writers, both in Ireland and abroad. An accursed king, fallen from grace, Sweeney was doomed to haunt the peripheries of civilised life, yet in his mouth, by way of compensation, was put some of the most treasured nature poetry in the Irish language. The implied subordination of the visual to the verbal, and the concentration on land and landscape, reflected by this project's prominence was both telling and typical.[3]

'Kelterne kommer' included twelve Irish artists, whereas 'Something else' accommodated exactly twice that number. That these showcases had only two artists in common, Elizabeth Magill and Nigel Rolfe, indicates that neither was beholden to a well-established canon. Also noteworthy are the radically disparate backgrounds and practices of the two artists in question. Elizabeth Magill is a painter who was born in Canada, grew up in County Antrim and went to study in the early 1980s at the Slade School of Art in London, the city in which she has lived and worked ever since. At the time of the earlier exhibition her protean, if not capricious, art practice owed much to the shifting sands of American post-modern painting of the 1980s and little to any native soil. By the end of the 1990s, however, an unexpected turn to the time-honoured genre of landscape-painting—though reconceived from a contemporary perspective—had also entailed a return to the land of her youth as a favoured, though far from exclusive, image source. This change of tack has proved enduring. Nigel Rolfe, on the other hand, is a performance artist, born and raised in England, who is of the same generation as such 1970s pioneers of the form as the Serbian Marina Abramović and the American Chris Burden. In his mid-twenties Rolfe moved to Dublin, where he has now been based for over 40 years. During this time he has presented performances in more than 30 coun-tries world-wide, in North and South America and the Far-East, as well as across much of Europe, notably in the Eastern Bloc countries during the 1970s and 1980s. Throughout these turbulent times, in the history of Northern Ireland in particular, 'the matter of Ireland' was a recurring aspect of his work's symbology.

While the two Nordic exhibitions just cited might seem arbitrarily chosen, a cursory survey of other such presentations of contemporary Irish art in recent times in mainland Europe confirms the sense of het-erogeneity they evince. Unlike comparable accounts and presentations of artists working in Scotland or in England since, say, the fall of the Berlin wall—the so-called 'Glasgow miracle' or the London-based 'yBas' (young British artists) spring to mind—such exhibitions have shown little evidence of a tight-knit, generation-bound artistic community with shared concerns, a similar sensibility and comparable practices born of their experience of the same geo-political moment and context.[4] For reasons that should be obvious, this is less true of art made north of the border during the course of the Northern Irish 'Troubles', a point to which we shall return. For instance, the curator Catherine Hemelryk readily acknowledged the diversity of the group of Irish artists whose work she presented in a programme of events titled 'An exhibition in five chapters' at the Contemporary Art Centre in Vilnius over the

Caoimhín Mac Giolla Léith

course of 2007; though ironically, in retrospect, this was on the eve of a financial crash that would render much of what she had to say about contemporary Irish–Lithuanian links redundant.

> Recently, Ireland has become prominent in Lithuanian life; as one of the most popular destinations for Lithuanians wishing to work abroad, talk of entire families, or villages even, upping and moving to Ireland are commonplace. Ireland has become almost legendary; a land of plenty, like the America of the 19th and early 20th centuries for the Irish ... Ireland's cultural life, particularly its literary heritage, is internationally renowned. 'An Exhibition in Five Chapters' brings five elements of the Irish contemporary art world to Vilnius in a series of diverse events taking place throughout 2007. Participants will range from established international artists to those in their mid career and young emerging practitioners. Weaving throughout the programme are ideas of narrative and aspects of fiction, storytelling, and a sense of place or time—presenting a snippet of the concerns of artists in Ireland that so many Lithuanians are now experiencing.[5]

So, once again, what Hemelryk suggests as a binding agent for her presentation of the diffuse field of contemporary Irish art is a cluster of 'ideas of narrative and aspects of fiction, storytelling, and a sense of place or time'.[6]

It is worth noting at this point that any attempt to assess European perceptions of Irish art must contend not only with exhibitions selected by continental curators but also with those selected by Irish curators to be presented on the European stage. In her compendious account of twentieth-century Irish art, *Modern art in Ireland*, the critic Dorothy Walker singled out 1980 as a milestone year for the international appreciation of Irish art. She did so on two accounts: (i) the inclusion that autumn of three Irish artists representing the Republic of Ireland in the Paris Biennale des Jeunes, alongside two artists from Northern Ireland, and (ii) the impact made by the sprawling festival 'A sense of Ireland', spread across numerous London venues earlier in the year. Presented as a celebration of the Irish arts, the latter was also perceived, as Walker notes, as an attempt 'to counteract the images of violence emanating from Northern Ireland'.[7] In addition to various ancillary shows presented in private galleries, 'A sense of Ireland' included three main exhibitions of Irish art: *The delighted eye: Irish painting and sculpture of the seventies*, curated by the art historian Frances Ruane; *The international connection*, a show of abstract paintings in a modernist idiom, curated by Cyril Barrett, an authority on Op Art; and *Without the walls*, an exhibition of installation and performance organised by Walker herself. Several works in the last of these shows explicitly addressed the historically fraught relationship between Ireland and Great Britain in light of the conflict that continued to convulse Northern Ireland and would lead the following year to one of the era's most traumatic events, the 1981 republican hunger strike. Given the complex nature of Ireland's relationship with Britain, British perceptions of Irish art are necessarily of a different order from those elsewhere in Europe. The existence of a substantial Irish diaspora in Britain—this is equally true of the US, of course—also complicates matters to such a degree that the remainder of this chapter will largely confine itself to the presentation and reception of Irish art on the continent.

The only project in recent times of comparable ambition to 'A sense of Ireland' in which Irish contemporary art was presented *in extenso* to a foreign public was 'L'imaginaire irlandais'. Unfolding over the course of 1996, this was a 'mammoth festival of Irish culture in France ... initiated at the joint suggestion of Presidents Mitterand of France and Robinson of Ireland'.[8] One novel aspect of the festival, which distinguished it from the frontal assault of 'A sense of Ireland', was the organisation of numerous temporary residencies for Irish visual artists in institutions throughout France. According to a phrase used repeatedly at the time by Declan McGonagle, director of the then newly established Irish Museum of Modern Art (IMMA), the long-term aim was 'to enter into the bloodstream of French culture', a somewhat optimistic ambition, it must be said in retrospect. Meanwhile the festival's main exhibitions were located in the capital: solo shows at the Musée d'Art Moderne de la Ville de Paris by Willie Doherty and Nigel Rolfe and one by James Coleman at the Centre Georges Pompidou, as well as a group show of sixteen artists presented at l'École national supérieure des Beax-Arts

Caoimhín Mac Giolla Léith

de Paris. Introducing the last of these in the catalogue accompanying 'L'imaginaire irlandais', the French critic Philippe Cyroulnik discerned three broad tendencies among the artists exhibited:

> *Un premier ensemble d'artistes prende en compte le context politique et social: Shane Cullen, Willie Doherty, John Kindness, Locky Morris, Mike [recte Mick] O'Kelly, Philip Napier et Paul Seawright ... Francis Hegarty, Alice Maher et Alanna O'Kelly constituent un second groupe qui aborde plus precisément les problèmes d'origine et d'identité, en particulier les questions de statut et d'identité sexuelle feminine ... Enfin John Aiken, Ciaran Lennon, Fionnualla Ni Chiosain [recte Fionnuala Ní Chiosáin], Sean Scully, Sean Shanahan et Anne Tallentire travaillent dans des problématiques issus de l'expérience des avant-gardes (moderniste, minimaliste et conceptuelle) et s'insérant dans le courant artistique international ...*

'A first group of artists takes account of the political and social context: Shane Cullen, Willie Doherty, John Kindness, Locky Morris, Mick O'Kelly, Philip Napier and Paul Seawright ... Francis Hegarty, Alice Maher, and Alanna O'Kelly form a second group, which focuses more specifically on issues of origin and identity, in particular questions of status and of female sexual identity ... Finally, John Aiken, Ciaran Lennon, Fionnuala Ní Chiosáin, Sean Scully, Sean Shanahan and Anne Tallentire address problems arising from the experience of the avant-gardes (modernist, minimalist and conceptual) and fit into the mainstream of international art ...'[9]

As it happens, this tracking by a French critic of general trends and inclinations within Irish art chimed with perceptions closer to home. In 1990 and 1991 the Douglas Hyde Gallery in Dublin mounted a series of five exhibitions, collectively titled *A new tradition*, surveying Irish art of the 1980s and presented under specific rubrics. Anticipating Cyroulnik's categorisation, these included 'Politics and polemics',

'Sexuality and gender', and 'Abstraction'.[10] (The Dublin shows and the French critic's analysis were also alike in their somewhat reductive suggestion that in Ireland, by and large, sexuality was what women made art about whereas politics was what (male) Northerners made art about.) Cyroulnik also noted that a significant point of intersection between members of all three of the groups he outlined—including Doherty, O'Kelly, Hegarty, Aiken and Tallentire—was a concern with the landscape, 'la question du paysage'.[11] This had long been a core concern in the work of Willie Doherty, especially, who also featured in the most prominent of the ancillary exhibitions on the programme of L'imaginaire irlandais, *Langage, cartographie et pouvoir/*'Language, mapping and power', a group show curated by Liam Kelly, director of Derry's Orchard gallery, at Galerie Nikki Diana Marquaerdt, in Paris.[12]

The European reception of the work of Willie Doherty merits consideration at some length, given that he is one of Ireland's most widely exhibited artists, having been included in a steady succession of large-scale international exhibitions since the early 1990s. The two most prestigious of such events in an increasingly crowded art calendar are the Venice Biennale and Documenta, which takes place every five years in Kassel, a small town in the centre of Germany. Ireland had sporadically participated at Venice between 1950 and 1960, but the country's involvement was allowed to lapse in the early 1960s. It was not renewed until 1993. Setting the tone for some time to come, the selection that year judiciously balanced gender and provenance by pairing Willie Doherty (born and based in Derry), who works with photography and film-installation, with Dorothy Cross (born in Cork, but based at the time in Dublin), a sculptor whose practice has since expanded to include other media. Both were in their mid-thirties when Venice beckoned.

Doherty's work is renowned for its persistent exploration of themes of memory and place in a landscape inscribed by territorial division and haunted by dark secrets.[13] It is thus in keeping with Hemelryk's invocation of 'ideas of narrative and aspects of fiction, storytelling, and a sense of place or time' in characterising Irish art in general. His 2002 retrospective at IMMA was aptly described as follows: 'Closely keyed to his native city of Derry and the Northern Ireland "Troubles", Doherty's work reveals a complex and shifting range of relationships between places, events and the images by which they come to be represented and recalled.'[14] Yet despite, or perhaps even because of this localised grounding, Doherty is in the unique position of having represented Ireland at the 1993 Venice Biennale, the United Kingdom at the 2002 Bienal de São Paolo and Northern Ireland at the 2007 Venice Biennale.[15] When questioned on one occasion about the potential incompatibility of these various representative roles, he replied:

> I think that for many artists the identification of their art with an often simplistic idea of national identity is highly problematic. In general, I find it frustrating when my work is only considered within the context of nationality or place. So, to participate in any show that maps an idea of nationality onto the work has to be considered very carefully. I try to look at these occasions as an opportunity to disrupt an easy reading of Britishness or Irishness or whatever ... I come from a place where how one positions oneself is always extremely layered ... So I am always happy to look at each exhibiting context for opportunities to expand how my work can be seen and understood.[16]

In fact, it seems that Doherty's capacity to generate a universally resonant set of concerns from an engagement with the particularly charged situation of Northern Ireland has been one of the principal attractions of his work to European curators. For instance, the Portuguese curator Isabel Carlos introduced Doherty's 2016 solo exhibition at the Centro de arte moderna Gulbenkian in Lisbon as follows:

> Geography counts, the place where we live counts, carrying its own world view. In a context such as Portugal in which the question of post-colonialism has always been examined within the tension between Europe and Africa, between whites and blacks, we gaze at this work, which forces us to reflect on another post-colonial situation amongst whites in central [sic] Europe, where a native language was also repressed and religious choice became the origin for conflict, not unlike what is happening more broadly now, as we well know, in many parts of the world.[17]

Ten years earlier, in 2006, a solo exhibition by Doherty was jointly mounted by the Kunstverein in Hamburg and the Städische Galerie im Lenbachhaus und Kunstbau München, which was described in the accompanying publication as 'the first large-scale solo exhibition of its kind, dedicated to exploring the underlying continuities and quality of his slide and video work'.[18] Some indication of the level of commitment to the artist on the curators' part is indicated by the fact that the publication contained 'an exhaustive oeuvre catalogue of all Doherty's films and slide installations' and was presented as 'both an exhibition catalogue and a reference tool' in the hope that it 'might also inspire a similarly exhaustive treatment of the photographic works.'[19] Here again, the capacity of Doherty's art to transcend the local and speak to a wider audience is stressed:

> Doherty's works have a remarkable ability to reach out beyond the specifically Northern Irish conflict and deal at a sophisticated level with general topics such as the surveillance of public space, mechanisms of exclusion and inclusion, and national and religious conflicts. Between the opposing poles of authenticity and fiction, his videos explore the possibilities and conditions of the filmic apparatus, drawing on genres as various as action film, *Autorenfilm*, and documentary ... It is precisely this productive ambiguity that implicates the viewer at a level that is not only emotional but also intellectual, and reveals that those fears of possible violence and the paranoiac projections vis-à-vis the supposedly strange and unfamiliar are by no means confined to Northern Ireland.[20]

A similar extrapolation from the specific to the general was suggested by Ulrich Loock, writing in the catalogue for a presentation of Doherty's work at the Kunsthalle Bern, in Switzerland, ten years earlier again, in 1996:

> In a general sense Willie Doherty's work has its place in the outlined field of the works of this century that set writing and picture, vision and concept against one another. More

particularly, however, he deconstructs procedures of the fixing of meaning in the relationship between photography and writing. In later works this structure is transferred to the relationship between video and voice. Doherty's interest in this is twofold: the object of deconstruction lies not only in specific attributions of meaning (connected with the conflict in Northern Ireland), but the fixing of meaning in general.[21]

In light of this generative dynamic between the local and the universal, not to mention the dialectics of word and image, it is also worth recalling the most successful of the Irish presentations at the Venice Biennale to date, at least in terms of official recognition. In 1995 Kathy Prendergast—a near contemporary of Doherty's, though born in Dublin and based in London since she attended art school there—was awarded the coveted *Premio Duemila*, the prize for the best young artist in the Biennale. The work that gained her this accolade, *City drawings, 1992–8*, derived its considerable power from a comparable shuttling between geographic specifics and a global perspective, and from the relationship between the verbal and the visual, though unlike many of the artist's related 'map works', language is notable here for its absence. In 1992 Prendergast embarked on a series of small pencil drawings of all of the world's capital cities that, at the time, were about 180 in number. By the time of their Biennale presentation she had completed over 80 of these exquisitely realised maps, minutely detailed but entirely free of the verbal annotation that would ordinarily anchor them in the known world. While the individual cities are recognisable to those familiar with their contours, most of the disparities in scale, importance and power between them were occluded by their all being depicted at roughly the same size. Declared complete as an artwork in 1998, Prendergast's *City drawings* could nonetheless have been continued indefinitely, given the constant appearance and disappearance of capital cities as new nation states emerge and old ones are dissolved. This aspect of the work was poignantly underscored by the fact that her six years' labour on the work coincided more or less with the violent breakup of Yugoslavia

As it happens, two years after Prendergast declared the *City drawings* complete the city of Ljubljana, capital of Slovenia, which had achieved independence from Yugoslavia the year the series was begun, hosted Manifesta 3. This was the third iteration of a European Biennial set up in the mid-1990s in explicit opposition to what many viewed as the outdated Venetian model of national representation. Produced by a quartet of curators from Italy, the Netherlands, Slovakia and Austria, the exhibition was titled *Borderline syndrome*, a term borrowed from psychology but clearly meant also to be read geo-politically. The show's subtitle, *Energies of defence* was intended, according to a subsequent account, as 'an effort to shield culture from political, economic and cultural homogenization, an additional theme addressed in local discussions', as well as an attempt to 'interrogate the social and political ambiguities of territory for global culture at large and, in particular, artistic production in light of the transformation in Europe.'[22] Unsurprisingly, perhaps, given Ireland's notoriously contested border, the exhibition included no less than four artists who were based in Northern Ireland at the time. Ironically, though, given the emphasis on local engagement, it appears that the curator taxed with exploring the Irish scene neglected to venture south of the border; and there was also some disgruntlement among natives that none of the four artists chosen were born or raised in Ireland. Indeed, two of them would shortly depart again for other shores.

By way of contrast with the account of European perspectives on Willie Doherty's work offered earlier, let us examine, in conclusion, a very different case in which the manifestly 'Irish' aspects of the work of an internationally acclaimed artist have been a source of some critical contention. Judged by the standards of European visibility already proposed—inclusion in prestigious showcases such as the Venice Biennale and Documenta, and solo exhibitions in major continental museums and art institutions—the single most successful Irish artist of the past fifty years has undoubtedly been James Coleman, whose inclusion in five successive editions of Documenta from 1987 to 2007 remains a unique achievement for any artist. And yet, on the occasion of a major 2009 retrospective—spread across the Irish Museum of Modern Art, the Project Arts Centre and the Royal Hibernian Academy in Dublin— IMMA Director Enrique Juncosa felt compelled to point out that, in spite of Coleman's international prominence, the Irish art public had had little opportunity to see his work over the previous two decades.

Caoimhín Mac Giolla Léith

While there are a few artists, mostly painters, who have become almost household names in Ireland during the course of Coleman's career, he has remained relatively unknown outside the confines of the professional Irish art world, despite his international eminence.

In an illuminating essay published in a special Irish issue of the British journal *Third Text* in 2005, Gavin Murphy argued that two strands may be discerned in Irish art-critical discourse concerning the relationship between contemporary Irish artworks and 'the wider international circuits of which they are part'.[23] The first of these argues for the uniqueness of Irish art, often emphasising art that has 'recourse to a latent Celtic mythology (the Irish as poetic, oblique sensual etc.), [as] ... a means by which to resist colonial and metropolitan discourse', while the second favours 'art that articulates the cultural and historical complexities of local circumstance as a means to invigorate wider [i.e. international] art discourse on matters of place, identity and conflict'.[24] Murphy notes that, despite their differences, in both trains of critical thought 'the discourse of Irishness continues to dominate the evaluation of art deemed significant'.[25] He further notes that there is an implicit assumption that such evaluation is best undertaken by those with an intimate knowledge of the Irish context, rather than those approaching it from afar. But what, he then proceeds to ask, of the situation 'where an artist from Ireland makes it on the grand stage where Irishness does not appear to be a dominating feature of how his or her work is perceived?'[26]

The case he has in mind is that of James Coleman, whose work has attracted a substantial body of critical exegesis by leading international art historians, as confirmed by his inclusion in a series of monographic essay collections devoted by the influential American journal *October* to what its editors consider to be the world's most significant contemporary artists. As Murphy points out, Coleman's assumption into this pantheon has sometimes involved attempts to disengage his work from the discourse of Irishness and to resist its subsumption into general debates about post-colonialism. The fiercest such resistance is offered by the American art historian Rosalind Krauss, who argues that his importance lies in his having effectively invented a 'new medium'—sequential slide-projection—and that any consideration of the Irish aspect of his work is consequently little more than a distraction. Her *October* co-editor Benjamin H. Buchloh, however, has been more amenable to mediating between localised and universalising appreciations of Coleman's importance. In an analysis of Coleman's 1977 installation *Box (ahhareturnabout)*, which incorporates footage of the famous fight in 1927 between world champion Gene Tunney and the favoured challenger Jack Dempsey, Buchloh acknowledges that

> one could argue that within the general project of reconstituting a historically specific body to the universalist abstraction of phenomenology, Coleman insists on a sociopolitically specific body, structured by the discourse on national identity (in this case by presenting the Irish fighter Gene Tunney as the struggling protagonist who tries to save his boxing championship as much as his sociopolitical identity as an Irishman).[27]

A comparable point is made by the French film theorist Raymond Bellour when describing how Coleman's work has gradually 'opened itself out ... to all the major issues of the day while still finding a part of its strength in the dimension of local memory'.[28]

> He was trained abroad, in France and Italy, where he worked for a long time before returning to Ireland. Coleman seems to owe the force of his work to the contradiction that makes of him an eternal exile in his own country as well as a nomad who carries this country with him wherever he exhibits and develops his art.[29]

And yet, once again, even such an eminent film critic finds it necessary to invoke Ireland's *literary* reputation in assessing the work of the country's most internationally acclaimed visual artist, relating the exemplary recalcitrance of Coleman's work to Gilles Deleuze and Félix Guattari's concept of 'minor literature', a contrary form of writing emanating from the margins of a major world literature:

> The good fortune of Irish literature has always been
> that it is 'minor literature', divided in its language and

pushing the language of its colonizer, now its own, to
points of rupture ... The good fortune of the Irish artist is
perhaps to confront a similar situation with the particularity proper to a culture constructed in opposition to a
realism of the image ... There is such a thing as an Irish
iconoclasm that finds a way to use words to the detriment
of images, even as it treats words as the images of words
in order to extract from them the symbolic weight of the
local, archaic, and territorial attachments that tempt all
'minor' cultures.[30]

Of course there are other Irish artists who have achieved considerable international prominence in recent years according to the criteria
already proposed—the Dublin-based artist Gerard Byrne is merely the
most obvious example—whose work is neither as clearly informed
by 'the discourse on national identity' as all commentators on Willie
Doherty would agree, nor as resistant to it as some readings of James
Coleman would maintain. In any case, the time is past when a simple
local/global dialectic might have seemed adequate to the assessment of
art of any degree of seriousness or sophistication within the European
context. Nuit Banai has argued that the founding of such institutional framing devices as Documenta (1955) and the Paris Biennale (1959)
played a role in fortifying the sovereign status of individual nation-states
(West Germany and France in those instances) as a prerequisite to their
integration into a new Europe. In contrast, the founding of Manifesta
(1995) four decades later recognises that 'the problematic of borders is
one of the most pressing issues that courses through the contemporary
imagination of Europe'.[31] On the evidence to date, there is no reason to
suppose that Irish artists will not continue to make valuable contributions to the debate on this and other pressing issues.

Notes

[1] Maija Koskinen, 'Something else from somewhere else', in *Something else: Irlantilaista nykytaidetta/Irish contemporary art/Irländsk nutidskonst* (Turun taidemuseo/Turku Art Museum/Åbo konstmuseum; Turku, 2002), 17–22: 17.

[2] *Kelterne kommer/The Celts are coming* (Århus Kunstbygning af 1847; Århus, 1996).

[3] See, for example, the curator's introduction to 'A way a lone a last a loved a long the', a presentation of four Irish artists at Zagreb's Museum of Contemporary Art in 2000: 'I am deliberately avoiding naming the exhibition project ... as "contemporary Irish art". Instead, I have decided to borrow, in a function of a title [*sic*], the "sentence" which ends *Finnegan's Wake* [*sic*], a famous book by an even more famous Irish writer', Leonida Kovač, 'A way a lone a last a loved a long the' (Muzei Suvremene Umjetnosti; Zagreb, 2000), 6.

[4] 'The Glasgow miracle' was a phrase first used by Swiss curator Hans Ulrich Obrist in 1996 to describe the remarkable vitality of the young art scene in that city, whereas the acronym yBa was coined the same year in *Art Monthly*.

[5] Catherine Hemelryk, 'An exhibition in five chapters'; the text of the exhibition catalogue is available online at: www.cac.lt/en/exhibitions/past/07/1355 (26 April 2018).

[6] Hemelryk, 'An exhibition in five chapters'.

[7] Dorothy Walker, *Modern art in Ireland* (Lilliput Press; Dublin, 1997).

[8] Walker, *Modern art in Ireland*, 213.

[9] Philippe Cyroulnik, '16 artistes irlandais à l'École nationale supérieure des Beaux-Arts de Paris', in Pascal Bonafoux (ed.), *L'imaginaire irlandais* (Fernand Hazan; Vanves, 1996), 86–7: 87. The English language translation is the author's own.

[10] The other two categories were 'Nature and culture' and 'Myth and mystification'. See, *A new tradition: Irish art of the eighties* (The Douglas Hyde Gallery; Dublin, 1990).

[11] Cyroulnik, '16 artistes irlandais', 87.

[12] Liam Kelly, *Langage, cartographie et pouvoir/Language, mapping and power* (Orchard Gallery; Derry, 1996).

[13] See, for instance, Carolyn Christov-Bakargiev and Caoimhín Mac Giolla Léith, *Willie Doherty: false memory* (Irish Museum of Modern Art/Merrell; Dublin and London, 2002). See also, Charles Wylie and Erin K. Murphy, *Willie Doherty: requisite distance—Ghost story and landscape* (Dallas Museum of Art/Yale University Press; New Haven and London, 2009).

[14] For more information on Doherty's 2002 exhibition at IMMA, titled 'False memory', see, https://imma.ie/whats-on/willie-doherty-false-memory/ and http://www.kerlingallery.com/publications/willie-doherty-false-memory (4 December 2018).

[15] In 2003, 2005 and 2007 Northern Ireland was represented at the Venice Biennale by an exhibition separate from the British Pavilion, as were Wales and Scotland. The Welsh and Scots have continued this practice.

[16] Yilmaz Dziewor and Matthas Mühling (eds), *Willie Doherty: Anthologie zeitbasierter Arbeiten/anthology of time-based works* (Kunstverein in Hamburg and Städtische Galerie im Lenbachhaus und Kunstbau München; Hamburg and Munich, 2006), 40.

[17] Isabel Carlos, 'Again and again', in *Willie Doherty: again and again/uma e outra vez* (Centro de arte moderna Gulbenkian; Lisbon, 2016), 137–9: 138–9.

[18] Dziewor and Mühling, *Willie Doherty*, 9.

[19] Dziewor and Mühling, *Willie Doherty*, 9.

[20] Dziewor and Mühling, *Willie Doherty*, 9–10.

[21] Ulrich Loock, "'This is not a work of art' (Marcel Broodthaers)—Willie Doherty', in Carolyn Christov-Bakargiev (ed.), *In the dark. Projected works/Im Dunkeln Projizierte Arbeiten* (Kunsthalle Bern; Bern, 1996), 5–8: 7.

[22] Barbara Vanderlinden and Elena Filipovic (eds.), *The Manifesta decade: debates on contemporary art exhibitions and biennials in post-Wall Europe* (The MIT Press; Cambridge MA, 2006), 269.

[23] Gavin Murphy, '"Tonguetied sons of bastards' ghosts": postconceptual and postcolonial appraisals of the work of James Coleman', *Third Text* 19 (5) (2005), 499–510: 499.

[24] Murphy, '"Tonguetied sons of bastards' ghosts"', 499.

[25] Murphy, '"Tonguetied sons of bastards' ghosts"', 500.

[26] Murphy, '"Tonguetied sons of bastards' ghosts"', 500.

[27] Benjamin H.D. Buchloh, 'Memory lessons and history tableaux: James Coleman's archaeology of spectacle', in George Baker (ed.), *James Coleman: October files 5* (MIT Press; Cambridge, MA and London, 2003), 83–112; 99.

[28] Raymond Bellour, 'The living dead (Living and presumed dead)', in George Baker (ed.), *James Coleman: October files 5* (MIT Press; Cambridge, MA and London, 2003) 57–72; 58.

[29] Raymond Bellour, 'The living dead', 58.

[30] Raymond Bellour, 'The living dead', 58–9.

[31] Nuit Banai, 'From nation state to border state', *Third Text* 27 (4) (2013), 456–69: 468.

The diffusion of a Celtic artistic aesthetic in the art and architecture of continental Europe in the Early Middle Ages

Lynda Mulvin

Introduction

'Ireland in Europe' conjures up images capturing a sense of tranquillity and timelessness extending from Ireland to Europe, evoking a sense of place and an ideal of romantic longing. It is bound up with ideas of the magical mystery of the remote island at the Celtic fringes of Europe, as determined by an appreciation of history. Ireland remains etched in continental Europe's eye as an idealised sanctuary elsewhere. It exists as a distant remote space inhabited by local tribes and chieftains, ruled over by the High King of Ireland invested on the great Hill of Tara. It is an ancient rugged landscape, 'beyond the borders of the Roman Empire', as described by Heinrich Böll, winner of the Nobel Prize for literature 1972, who was enchanted by the Ireland of 1950s and who, when he visited, referred to Irish missionaries who made Ireland 'the glowing heart of Europe'.[1]

Ireland's relationship with Europe was profoundly active during the early middle ages when the migration of Irish scholars and wandering monks, also known as *peregini*, or pilgrims, to Europe created an impact of overlapping connections of literacy, learning and artistic contributions. This is manifest in the presence nowadays of many Hiberno-Latin manuscripts from the seventh to twelfth century among the holdings of European libraries, collected over time from various Irish monastic foundations in continental Europe; a Europe that once teemed with Irish missionaries during a zenith of learning. Furthermore, the presence of traces of early Christian ecclesiastical sites in the European built environment and the survival of Irish medieval ecclesiastical artefacts stem from the impetus of insular art. When taken together, this evidence exerts a considerable influence on early medieval taste, form and meaning, in terms of what it meant being Irish in Europe.

Innovative scholarly research today emphasises a focus on issues of transmission from the western margins of Ireland directly to the heart of Europe. This relates to the Hiberno–Scottish mission, and questions the transfer of religious art from Ireland, Scotland and England to the Frankish empire of the seventh to the tenth century AD.[2] With this objective in mind, we have to ask how concepts and objects are translated into new contexts to investigate narratives linked to the notion of Irishness. The exploration of the cultural 'entanglement' of the Atlantic Isles changes our perception and understanding of early medieval art and its processes. It shapes our current understanding of what it means to be Irish in Europe. This involves an appraisal of the legacy of the golden age of Irish art.[3] The question arises as to what is specific about Irish artistic traditions, and how this informs perceptions of Ireland and Irishness that have emerged over the years of Ireland's engagement in Europe. More difficult to evaluate is the production of knowledge from Ireland, and the concept of knowledge transfer to Europe in terms of transmission of language, learning and literacy. Therefore, the contribution to the scholarship, culture and faith of medieval Europe is considered as the embodiment of Irishness at this stage. There is an underlying value and quality assurance to consider, which relates to the eminence of Irish scholarship that emerges at the beginning of the early middle ages. This is combined with artistic endeavour in monastic culture, as connections between the continent and Ireland are formed.

The measure of the achievements of the Celtic artistic aesthetic is acknowledged in terms of the reception of insular art and its dissemination from more remote parts of Europe and the Atlantic Isles; the Hiberno–Scottish Mission travelled from Ireland, Scotland and England to continental Europe. This represents a transmission of artistic ideas, which enabled a substantial contribution to be made in relation to art and architecture and evolving ornament and figural decoration, to core areas in Europe during the early middle ages, most notably during the Frankish, Carolingian and Ottonian kingdoms of the Holy Roman Empire.

The golden age of Irish art

The golden age of Irish art, which occurred from the seventh to the tenth century, is considered as having arisen out of the Celtic monastic movement. It is characterised as Insular art.[4] It involves a highly ornate and decorative style, utilised, for example, in manuscript illumination, sculpture carvings and metalwork decorating artworks from ecclesiastical centres in Ireland and Britain, from to Iona to Lindisfarne, Northumbria and beyond. The *Book of Kells*, for example, is one such item typifying Insular art. It is associated with the Columban churches, and was transported from Iona to Kells. It was once protected with a decorated cover, long since lost, and represents a level of maturity attained in 'High' Insular art. It is unique, with full-page portraits and illuminations: the Virgin and Child is one of the earliest representations of this scene in Western art and refers to Byzantine sources (Plate I, opposite). There is a recognised legacy

Plate I—Mother and Child from the Book of Kells (Copy 1991; private collection). Photo by Muiris Moynihan.

Lynda Mulvin

of Roman and Byzantine artistic imagery maintained during the medieval period through memory of Rome and recurring images featuring Roman motifs.[5] The iconic Ardagh Chalice is hailed as one of the great treasures of Insular metalwork, bearing decorative detailing that fuses different decorative strands of interlace, geometric patterning, Anglo-Saxon and Germanic zoomorphic detailing and Celtic *La Tène* artistic style. Equally significant are other church artefacts, such as crosiers, bells, brooches and reliquaries. House-shaped reliquaries (vessels that were designed to be portable and that contained a holy relic of a saint, seen to hold miraculous powers) and ornamental ecclesiastical objects found at monastic sites and in various European locations point to collective production. This is evident in terms of stylistic input and is an indication of the transmission of Celtic design. Such objects are entangled with new meaning in their new locations and are models for ecclesiastical architectural forms.[6]

Fundamental issues pertaining to the Irish in Europe addressed in this chapter assess the impact of the Hiberno–Scottish mission to Europe, as measured through the dissemination of artistic language and the spread of literacy, intimated by the sheer volume of Insular texts and manuscripts safeguarded in Europe. Common elements identified in the layout of monastic centres in Europe—transmitted from monastic sites such as Armagh to Luxeuil, from Reichenau to Bobbio—are also considered, as is the survival of portable objects, such as the already mentioned house-shaped reliquaries and other ecclesiastical treasures associated with these great centres of learning.

This Insular Christian mission develops as a migration to Europe. This cultural movement infuses the Carolingian Renaissance and is perceived as a genuine contribution to European knowledge: an Irish achievement within Western Europe. The spread of knowledge, as a concept, is difficult to define, yet it is the most significant factor of the Irish presence in Europe, as Irish scholarship crystallises and knowledge emerges from *Insula sanctorum et doctorum*, the 'Island of saints and scholars'. The reputation of Irish scholarship, therefore, emerges as a building block of the golden age of European learning, providing a platform for significant developments in art and architecture.[7]

Lynda Mulvin

The Hiberno–Scottish mission in Europe

The early Christian church is a stimulating force in terms of the international dynamics of Western Europe in the early middle ages. The mobility of Irish pilgrims contributes much to this dynamic.[8] Latin is preserved as the language of the book and transported to continental Europe. The Venerable Bede makes reference to the spread of Christianity throughout Ireland from the fifth century.[9] This impetus leads to an Insular mission spreading out from monastic complexes that arose in Ireland. St Columba established Derry and Durrow in the sixth century AD and is credited with spreading Christianity to sites in Scotland from a base at Iona in AD 560—one of the greatest Irish monastic and cultural foundations of the early middle ages.[10] Iona is the mother house of a great monastic federation that stretched from Lindisfarne where Aiden, a follower of St Columba, settled (as recorded in *Vita Columbae* written by Adomnán).[11] St Columba (Latin) or Columcille (Irish) is honoured during the Early Middle Ages, along with Patrick and Brigid, as one of the three patron saints of Ireland.

The cult of saints is a catalyst for the creation of ecclesiastical objects, from manuscripts to metalwork and sculpture.[12] Movement is seen as a means of disseminating the Celtic artistic aesthetic to Europe via missionary migration. For example, the characteristics of the three aforementioned main saints of Ireland, St Patrick, St Brigid and St Columcille, are emphasised as Adomnán's manuscript *Vita Columba*, written in Ireland, arrives on the continent via northern France, reaching *Augia Dives*, Reichenau, Lake Constance by AD 841, enshrining the life of Columba and establishing the Cult of Saints as a new medium for veneration. In this way, the existing maritime, trade and pilgrimage routes across Europe are used for the diffusion of new ideas and artistic currents.

Another strand of influence penetrates Europe through the actions of St Columbanus, the founder of a monastery at Bangor, County Down, who left Irish shores with twelve disciples, one of them St Gall, to establish a continental network of monastic houses, from Annegray in the Vosges mountains to Luxeuil-le-Bains (*c.* AD 585–90). Other Irish disciples also established houses in the region: St Fiachra (AD 670) of Breuil and Meaux and St Feuillen of Belgium (AD 652). St Gall founded a house on the shores of Lake Constance, Switzerland (AD 630), and St Pirmin at Reichenau (AD 720).[13] St Killian of Würzburg (AD 689) and St Fergail, Virgilius of Salzburg, (AD 784) were founders of *Scottus* monasteries in Germany and Austria respectively. Across the Alps on the pilgrimage route to Rome, St Columbanus, founder and abbot at Bobbio, Italy, later died there in AD 615.[14]

There is a recurrence of references to Irish *peregrini* during the sixth to the eighth century; these represent the first phase of *peregrination*, bringing a unique conception of monastic culture to Europe.[15] They are part of the initial wave of missionary migrants to Europe who impart monastic tradition with its origins in existing Gallic monasticism.[16] The exchange process became centred on literacy and the dissemination of artistic influences, and subsequently on art objects and design ideas.

In 1887 Margaret Stokes wrote about Irish scribes and scholars in Europe. She gathered invaluable information about the survival of manuscripts in various monastic libraries and town repositories across Europe.[17] The survival of manuscripts in such locations is a further testament to the spiritual attainments of early Irish Christian culture. Some of the earliest references are found at the monastery of Echternach, Luxembourg, founded AD 699 by Pippin II for Willibrod. The Echternach Gospel, now in Paris, for instance, is an Insular manuscript with artistic parallels to the book of Durrow. One of the oldest secular texts, a system of canon law, *Collectio Canonum Hibernensis,* was created in Iona *c.* AD 700 and entered the continent through Brittany.[18] This is a gateway to Europe for other insular texts, such as Gildas's *De excidio Britanniae,* also connected to the Carolingian sphere.

Another manuscript from *Augia Dives,* Reichenau, the *Vita Columbae,* later deposited in Schaffhausen, Switzerland (see Plate II, opposite), is a perfectly preserved, almost complete biography of the life of St Columba dating to AD 700.[19] It is the oldest extant manuscript linked

Plate II—Schaffhausen, Generalia 1 Adomnan, Vita Columba. Courtesy of Stadt Bibliothek Schaffhausen Switzerland.
Following pages:
Plate III—St Gallen, Codex Sang. 51, Gospel of Mark. Courtesy of Abbey Library St. Gallen, Switzerland
Plate IV—MS 363, Burgbibliothek Bern, folio 87v Ovid Metamorphoses. Courtesy of Burgerbibliothek Bern, Switzerland.

enarrauerat · qui eam biam
natam ab one ipriuf uin
gnoui abbatir & a uinculifui
ab eo in quantū potuit uipam
audicbat ·⁊ſſ ⁊ſ̄

Ya tradbn nocte quidā
clefnatnib: col ʒiur no
mine filiur aido dnaiʒ miche
de nepotib: ꝑech neſ · cuiuſ in
primo ꝑecimur mbrtionbn car
ru ad ianuā ecleʒiæ aliiſ don
mibrtib: deubirc · ibidbn q̇ ali
quandiu ꝑtanſ onabat · tum
pro inde ſubito totā uidb
eelhiā eelhti luce nꝑhlbn
quæ ꝑaliceꝰ fulʒonaliſ lu_ce
dicto ertiuſ ab eiuſ neceſſit
oculiſ · Scm ū colū bā houa
eadbn intrua eelhiam onanū
iʒnonabat · ꝑ quē talbn ſubi
tā luminiſ apparationbn
ualde pꝭtqmſebiſ domū ne
uhꝭtaiu · ꝑorchiadie ſeſ
illū ad uocanſ arꝑhiuſ obluī
ʒauit in quibiſ · de cehtio ꝑ

caueto deb̄ ſilii nequaꝑi ex
plonator eelhtē lumbi q̇tibi
non ÷ donaiū in ꝑpiehꝭ confuiſ
quia te effuʒibꝰ & ne alicui
in meiſ ehebꝰ: quod uidiꝑti ⁊
nanniſ ·⁊ ··

Yo tradbn intrbn pone
uin beatuſ cuidā ſuo ꝑa
pibrtiam diꝑehrti alumno
nomine behichano cuiuſ coʒno
mbriū merlobi non mediocri
th̄ quadā dehuntiauit die in
quibir · caueto ſilii ne hac ſe
qubiti nocte iuxta tuā ſbnꝑ
con ſuetu dinbn ad meū apꝓno
pin quiſ horpriciolū qui ii au
dibiſ contria intehidiciū ad
domū beati uiui in noc tiſ ʒi
tbrtio aliuſ quiſ ehrtibꝰ: ac
ehſrit · callideꝰ q̇ ex plonanſ
oculoꝑ enhrione ad clauium
ſonamina porruit · eſtiꝷ
nꝑ ſaliceꝰ ut nꝑ pnobauit
aliquam intuſ eelhtbn ui
rionbn ꝑeo manipehtaiu.

In noua fert animus mutatas dicere formas
corpora. di coeptis nam uos mutastis et illas
aspirate meis primaque ab origine mundi
ad mea perpetuum deducite tempora carmen.

Ante mare et terras et quod tegit omnia caelum
unus erat toto naturae uultus in orbe
quem dixere chaos rudis indigestaque moles
nec quicquam nisi pondus iners congestaque eodem
non bene iunctarum discordia semina rerum.

[Body text in heavily abbreviated medieval Latin minuscule; Ovid, Metamorphoses, Book I — largely illegible in reproduction] to a scribe, Dorbhéne, abbot of Iona, who had personal knowledge of Adomnán (who died in AD 704). Adomnán had many achievements; for instance, it was he who prepared *De locis sanctis*, one of the earliest descriptions of a pilgrimage to the Holy Land. This work includes a plan of the church of the Holy Sepulchre.[20]

According to the ninth century AD hagiographies, St Gall (*c.* AD 550–646), a student of Bangor Abbey, Co. Down, was one of twelve companions of St Columbanus on a mission to the continent and founder of the St Gall monastery in AD 612. The St Gall Stiftsbibliothek holds spectacular insular manuscripts from the eighth century, such as *St Gall Gospels Con Sang 51*, a copy of the gospels in Latin divided into lessons and verses.[21] The beginnings of the lessons are marked in illuminated initials.[22] Written in Irish semi-uncial script and dated to AD 750, this set of New Testament Gospels is illustrated with twelve decorated pages that were written and illuminated by Irish monks.[23] The image of St Mark has strong stylistic and visual connections to the Book of Durrow in the centre panels (Plate III, p. 308). Illustrated books such as this demonstrate the arrival on the continent of the literacy skills brought by many pilgrims.[24]

Early medieval Irish scholarship is also characterised by a passionate interest in classical mythology. The *Bern Manuscript 363* contains one of the earliest surviving tracts on Ovid's Metamorphoses (see Plate IV, previous page). It also holds copies of classical treatises, including six different tracts and a copy of Servius's commentary on Virgil, which is remarkable for its extensive marginal notes naming numerous Irish scholars of the ninth century. It includes the signature of a scribe, Godescalc, whose name is also a reference to an insular monk (Plate V, opposite).

In Bavaria, southern Germany, Irish manuscripts such as MS Cogitosus *Vita St Brigid* and a copy of Adomnán's *De locis sanctis* are found in Ingolstadt. The Latin Bible of St Kilian (who is still celebrated today) is preserved at Würzburg, and Regensburg (Ratisbon) also has associations with Hiberno-Scottish monasteries.[25] In Vienna, a manuscript written by Sedulius Scottus, *Vita Columba*—in two columns with red

---

Opposite: Plate V—MS 363, Burgerbibliothek Bern, folio 10v, signature of Godescalc. Courtesy of Burgerbibliothek Bern, Switzerland.

Pulchrius in celo nil est sole sereno Qd dea cert isab est non

asimile & q de q unicuiq cleur q colir sumz uidec ut. siuie de
ij custoz sci sacratz apollo ut apolline &equauit loui
cuit cepit ordo sit talis. me 7phoebz amat itz 7plus dicat Nec
ioui uideac apolline coparare... Sua munera. ipsi gratd. id lau
dz 7ladcinthz. Na scimz ut dafnin ladonis flumin arcadie filia
dilecta. ab apolline baire miseracione i laur uersa... & ladcinthu
amatu tam ab oue qd ab apolline qui e mgr apollinis
amore letante dū exercet disco abirato borea. eodem disco
& it tempz 7mutati iflorem nois sui... An uideri... ang lare
lo... Offert ultro istc plur dc lige Amoebei carminis
Delia nris... Delia alii amica bore uolunt... Alii diand
que e a delo &canibz nota pzar uenamur. q dc deaue
nacionis... Na si ad amica priferat hoc dc sic ad me freqint
7pata pparata. me uenem me amice... deuies der q
colorir... egissere. mdificauere... Aurea mala. x. miss...
plur dc. Nam cu ille duissec re et msur. iste id missise 7
to allegoria et ad augustū. de. x. eglozis q supfluū
que it necessitas hoc loco allegorie... Diuit piferatur
hur digna sint uba... Animo nsefuit. id liberassime habet
& e Litotes ffigura. pz munera nec serno. & multa
hc locu allegoricos accipiunt. ut uideac augusto dre
qd pz q me diligir si ad capiendos hostis pzenir socio me
relinquis... Ariturisq sequi uoluisse augustū re amoru
ad docile bella pparante... Retia seruo q res inuentione
minz possidet uoluptis... Amintā uocā zz... A sciendū
sed noa i dz &euuiid su crescant su norescant. ize
tituo uocati. z. d. mittet ut. Eneadr. Enee. o. enea.
Pallas antis. o. palla ut. Kth o palla dederat pmisra pd
penti Phyllida mittem... Amica comune. Caura natalis
diei inqr tm sacrificio licebit. uoluptatibz opt dare. Natalis

fabula narratur mutato nomine de te...

PBATIO penno Godescalo.

initial letters—is reported, as is as a copy of Adomnán's *De locis sanctis*. Furthermore, the cult of St Columcille has also been traced through calendars and martyologies as far south as Bavaria and south Tyrol. The evidence of the *Karlsruhe calendar* (Karlsruhe Landesbibliothek), a manuscript glossed by an Irish monk, originating in ninth-century-AD Ireland at either the monastery of Clonmacnoise or Glendalough, was later brought to Reichenau.[26] The library at Bobbio is a significant repository of manuscripts from Ireland.[27] Among the works it holds is *The Bangor Antiphony*, a short manuscript that resembles a similar *Mass in Hexameters* document from Reichenau.[28]

Such innovation and energy in producing manuscripts stands as a testament to the impact of Irish knowledge transfer to European monastic centres.[29] This confirms an impression that during the period of the seventh to the tenth century many of the Irish on the continent were monks, scholars and scribes in differing status of exile who were actively producing manuscripts. It is from these centres of learning that the Irish reputation for scholarship emerged in continental Europe.[30]

The architectural layout of early Irish monasteries

The impact of artistic connections in Europe from late antiquity to the early middle ages stems, in part, from the legacy of the layout of Columban and post-Columban abbeys in continental Europe. An early written description of the organisation of an Irish monastery is found in the *Collectio Canonum Hibernensis*.[31] This reaches the continent as a manuscript by the mid-eighth century. It is thought this it was used at Corbie, Picardie, in AD 740.[32] It is interpreted as describing early Irish church oval-form layout:

> There ought to be two or three termini around a holy place: the first in which we allow no one at all to enter except priests, because laymen do not come near it, nor women unless they are clerics; the second, into the streets the crowds of common people, not much given to wickedness, we allow to enter; the third, in which men who have been guilty of homicide, adulterers and prostitutes, with permission and according to custom, we do not prevent

Lynda Mulvin

from going within. Whence they are called, the first *sanctissimus*, the second *sanctior*, the third *sanctus*, bearing honour according to their difference.[33]

This creates an image that defines the early Irish monastery as having enclosures with three separate, well-defined areas for different activities: *sanctissimus, sanctior* and *sanctus*. The main church was at the core, with oratories and the smaller chapels in other *sectors*. Initially, these consisted of timber huts and shelters hastily erected in forests and in secluded areas; in time, stone architecture replaced the earlier more ephemeral timber buildings.[34] The *Liber Angeli* describes the layout of the Patrician churches, with each composed of an enclosure, a house with a kitchen, an oratory, and cloisters; and inside the rath, were two churches, a south church in which bishops and priests and anchorites worshipped, and a north church for virgins, penitents and those serving the church.[35]

Traces of early Christian church oval-form layout are known in Ireland from Devenish to Clonmacnoise, Kells and Glendalough. In each, the enclosure wall surrounds a round tower and a main church, with two or more aligned smaller, single-celled churches arranged in different quarters of the monastery. The 1601 Bartlett map of Armagh (Plate VI, overleaf) is a visual depiction of the monastic settlement of St Patrick. This evolved from a simple enclosure with single-celled, aligned, churches arranged in an organic way, as at Kells, Glendalough, and that at Rathmichael in south Dublin, associated with St Comhgall, teacher of St Columba (Plate VII and Plate VIII, p. 315).[36] The majority of sites had a burial ground; some had a round tower, with an inner enclosure and external boundary walls; while some others were adorned with High Crosses.[37] The interior of churches exhibited tapestry hangings, a church plate, chalices, bells, manuscripts, processional crosses and reliquaries.[38]

Such monastic layouts and their associated practices were then transmitted to Europe by the travelling monks. The monasteries in Iona, Lindisfarne, Luxeuil, Honau, Saint-Gallen, Bobbio, Reichenau, as well as the *Scottus*-monasteries in Germany and Austria, share these simple common attributes. They consist of clusters of small stone structures, defined in the *Collectio Canonensis Hibernensis*, as arranged in

Plate VI—Bartlett Map of Armagh City, *c.* 1601. Courtesy of National Library of Ireland.

Plate VII—Round Tower, Rathmichael, South Dublin. Photo by Muiris Moynihan.
Plate VIII—High Cross, Rathmichael, South Dublin. Photo by Muiris Moynihan.

St Columba's foundations from Durrow to Derry to Iona. The Insular mission is associated with an evolving network of knowledge-exchange linked to these monastic complexes. The ascetic practice of missionary monks is reflected in their retirement from the world by retreating to small oratories such as found at these early church sites.

The mission spread further afield to Luxeuil (c. AD 585–90), which was also founded by St Columba; recent excavations have unearthed a small-scale rectangular church building with a chevet, constructed during AD 670.[39] Another example of this type of building is the church of Saint Martin reconstructed in the ninth century by abbot Anségise (AD 817–33).[40] The monastic plan of the settlement has traces of these early Irish origins, such as a circular enclosure and three aligned churches.[41] While it is estimated that some fifty houses are associated with these early Irish foundations, these Irish footprints and traces often now exist only in local place names and appear as little more than a small chapel with a link to the main church.[42]

The survival of the settlement pattern is seen at the holy island monastery of Reichenau, Bodensee. Here, the influence of the Irish Celtic pre-Benedictine plan, perceptible in overview, is suggested by a circular enclosure and several aligned churches and small lay huts. The 1649 map of Reichenau should be compared to Bartlett's Map of Armagh (see Plate VI above). It depicts an imprint of the early monastic layout of three churches: Mittelzell at the centre of the sacred enclosure, and Oberzell and Niederzell, two outlying churches with associated service buildings. Other oratories and chapels have not survived the passage of time.

Pirmin, an Irish-Franconian bishop at Meaux, founded Reichenau in AD 724 in honour of Mary and the apostles Peter and Paul, on the order of Charles Martell. The founding legend bears close similarity to that of St Patrick, who rid Ireland of the snakes. According to *Vita Pirmin*, that saint rid the island of Reichenau of serpents and wormlike creatures by 'for three days and three nights creating an area in a clearing' and building 'a lovely house for the living and true God and shared lodging for his disciples'.[43] Reichenau gained an exalted position at the educational heart of the Carolingian court and became one of the greatest monasteries of Europe, with a school, library and scriptorium. It produced some well-known monks, such as Wetti, Walahfrid, Waldo (AD 786–806) and Heito. The church of the Mittelzell is dedicated to

Plate IX—Mittellzell, Reichenau. Photo by Lynda Mulvin.

St Mary and Mark and is at the core of the monastic complex, dating from AD 816 (Plate IX, above). The church of St George (Plate Xa, p. 318, top) has exceptional wall paintings, depicting scenes from Christ's life with an emphasis on biblical tales of the Resurrection (see Plate Xb, p. 318, middle). The church of Saints Peter and Paul at Niederzell has the earliest depiction of the *Maiestas* surviving north of the Alps, and constitutes scene-painting on a large scale, relatively unknown for this time (see Plate Xc, p. 318, bottom). The underlying structure of this monastery is also similar to the Irish monastic layout.

This continental network is connected further at the site of St Gall, Switzerland (AD 630), as referred to by abbot Notkar Balbulus.[44] Although only few traces remain on the ground, there is evidence of similarities with the original monastic layout of early Irish churches —a simple church at the centre surrounded by cell-like structures of an Irish planning type—throughout the continent. Such structures, derived from Celtic traditions and the rule of St Columba, can be found at Bobbio (AD 615), where there is a central church and outlying chapels dedicated to San Lorenzo, San Policaro and San Nicola.[45]

Plate XI—House shrine, Monymusk, Glenmorangie. Courtesy of National Museums Scotland.
Opposite page:
Plate Xa—Oberzell, Reichenau. Photo by Lynda Mulvin.
Plate Xb—Oberzell Wall Painting, Reichenau. Photo by Lynda Mulvin.
Plate Xc—Seventeenth-century Reichenau Insel. Photo by Lynda Mulvin.

The Insular mission is fundamental to the stimulus of knowledge transfer in Europe. Thus, as the Irish church developed in association with the Cult of Saints, the first wave of Irish missionary migrants to Europe brought with them literacy and the study of manuscripts.[46] In addition, the impetus is associated with the development of monastic complexes emerging from the Columban network in several European centres, and it reflects the connective context of Irish monasticism from the seventh to the tenth century AD and the transmission of the Irish monastic plan to these continental centres of learning. At the same time there was, in these monastic centres, a crystallising of the reputation of Irish scholarship on the mainland of Europe.

Portable antiquities, house shrines and monastic sites

The discovery of several Insular reliquaries at monastic sites in Europe is further evidence of the dissemination of artistic creation in Europe.[47] Reliquaries are portable containers designed to hold relics, and themselves believed to have the healing power of the relics inside. They are also ecclesiastical objects, brought to Europe by pilgrims for matters of the church.[48] The simplicity of many reliquaries conceals the precious nature of the ecclesiastical objects that accompanied *peregrini*. Reliquaries in the form of miniature chapel buildings, similar to the temple of Jerusalem depicted in the *Book of Kells*, are seen as models of church architecture.[49] These are indicators of collective production and design associated with continental monastic houses. The house-like shrine at Monymusk, Scotland (Plate XI, p. 319), for example, is modelled on the small chapel structures such as St Kevin's Glendalough. Similarly, the Clonmore shrine, Co. Kilkenny can be compared to the Bobbio house shrine; both are enamelled and carry animal ornament in a more developed form of Insular art.[50]

There are nine surviving house shrines from Scotland, Denmark, France and Italy and further afield. These have been accorded different functions as reliquaries and chrismals of the Holy Host.[51] In each case the metalwork is stylistically connected to Insular examples; the shrines reflect Christ, the eternal temple and tabernacle.[52] Other reliquaries symbolic of portable high-status ecclesiastical objects, such as the Irish Horn-Reliquary of Tongres/Tongeren, Belgium, are metalwork products of Irish craftsmanship made for export.[53] Portable church antiquities have also been found in other continental contexts, such as the shrine mount from St Germain-en-Laye, an object with decorative Insular spiral motifs.[54]

The Viking incursions and the Irish impact on Carolingian renaissance and learning

The various Viking incursions to Ireland—from the eighth century AD—forced many to flee their homeland and subsequently led to a new wave of migration to Europe from Ireland.[55] Dicuil, an Irish cleric and geographer of the ninth century, describes in *Liber de Mensuna Orbis Terrae* Irish clerics living as ascetics on remote northern isles

Plate XII—Viking Grave Slab, Rathmichael, South Dublin. Photo by Muiris Moynihan.

The diffusion of a Celtic artistic aesthetic

who disappear with the arrival of the Vikings. [56] Scholarly renewal, however, also began in earnest after the Viking invasions, which heralded a programme of revival and religious revitalisation in Ireland in terms of cultural synthesis.[57] In a significant development, evidenced for example at Rathmichael, south Dublin, a combination of Viking and early Christian grave slabs are present, with a stone cross featured beside grave slabs decorated with cup marks and herringbone markings that can be traced back to Viking motifs (see Plate XII, p. 321).[58] The ecclesiastical site at Rathmichael has early and long associations with Comhgall of Bangor, and within its monastic enclosure features a chapel and a round tower. It is evidence of the widespread adoption of Christianity in the region after AD 980.

From the ninth century, Viking incursions contributed to changing patterns of trade, exchange and knowledge-production, transforming aspects of design, as exemplified in those found in the artistic ornament of the grave slabs of Vikings who converted to Christianity, and resulting in a new artistic form. Furthermore, by creating a new wave of Irish 'diaspora' to continental Europe, the stimulus of the Viking presence in Ireland played a role in generating a second wave of learning in which Ireland was again accorded a special place in the Western, post-Roman world.

Viking incursions in Ireland reflect a change in stylistic focus in terms of the production of artistic objects, manuscripts and ecclesiastical artefacts. The second wave of migration to Europe caused by the arrival of the Vikings in Ireland contributed to an expanding pool of learning and provided a significant platform for new developments in art and architecture.[59] The intellectual impact of the Irish scholars is apparent at the court of Charlemagne and is one of the factors contributing to the Carolingian renaissance. As an element of this regeneration, Columban monastic rules were written down as part of Carolingian church reform.[60] Irishness is a thus a link to scholarly excellence; the international scene in the Carolingian courts reflects Charlemagne's appreciation of education. Einhard's biography, *Life of Charlemagne*, describes the revival of Latin learning and reveals that by AD 800 the Irish scholar, Dungal of Pavia, is charged by Charlemagne to assist in the organisation of education throughout Italy.[61] In this way, the cultural contribution of the Irish abroad in Europe as a result of successive waves of migration becomes apparent.

Lynda Mulvin

The court of Charlemagne and Irish scholarly presence

The characteristic of 'Irishness' as a sort of synonym for scholarly excellence within the international scene at the time is reflected throughout Charlemagne's Carolingian Court. Alcuin from Northumberland is dominant at the court at Aachen and in the School of Charlemagne from AD 790.[62] At the imperial abbey of Reichenau, one monastic scribe, Walahfrid Strabo (d. AD 849), conjures up an image of the continent being full of Irish pilgrims when he observes that 'custom to travel had become almost second nature'.[63] Knowledge is imported as Sedulius Scottus leaves Ireland for the Carolingian court at Liège in AD 840, to serve as a dignitary.[64] Sedulius Scottus was a ninth-century author of political thought, who examined the relationship between spiritual and secular power in his *De rectoribus Christianis* (Bremen Staats und Universitätsbibliothek).[65] The presence of John Scottus Eriugena is also recorded at the Palace School of Charles the Bald.[66] He was a prolific scholar, and this is reflected in his wide-ranging *De rerum natura*, written in AD 860.[67]

A later wave of *peregrini* was connected to Otto I (AD 912–73), among them the Irish abbot Fingen, who succeeded St Cadroe as abbot of St Felix, alias St Clement, at Metz *c.* AD 976.[68] In the period from the sixth to the eighth century AD, the Irish pilgrims created their own unique concept of monastic culture, and set in motion a type of monastic institution, with Irish origins, venerating the memory of Irish founders.[69] As recorded by Adomnán in *De locis sanctis*, as travel began to fuel a desire for pilgrimage as a means of salvation—from Ireland to Rome and Jerusalem—so these early Irish foundations became centres hosting transient communities, bound together as families of nations. Furthermore, these communities gained knowledge of geographical territories and garnered interest in nationhood and observable differences. Of note are references, as featured in Einhard's *Vita Caroli Magni*, to tribes beyond Christian lands as non-believing and having different rules of ancient law.[70]

Artworks associated with the Carolingian imperial court were also produced, reflecting steadfast rulers such as Henry I (AD 919–36) and Otto the Great (AD 936–73). These works suggest the presence of highly skilled craftsmen in Germanic courts.[71] The decoration of the

Oberzell and Niederzell churches at Reichenau, for example, developed different iconographic themes from the tenth century onward. Principally, the theme of resurrection evident in the fresco cycle in the church at Oberzell (see Plate Xb) is a constant reminder of the Irish founders and their connections to the Celtic Christian and Insular past. Monumentality arrives in the form of the more structured St Gall monastic plan, at Reichenau, which clearly differs from the Irish model and survives as a Carolingian blueprint for an ideal monastery, shaping the natural environment with a framework connected to Rome.[72] Such evidence in combination with the Insular ecclesiastical artefacts and manuscripts that have survived, collectively demonstrates the dominance of Irish material as a key part of the content and make-up of early medieval European art and architecture.[73]

Conclusion

From the sixth to the tenth century AD, wandering Irish monks arrive in successive phases to Europe and create their own unique concept of monastic culture. Columbanus ignites a new monastic tradition, bringing a simpler form of monasticism to Europe. While not laying the foundations for Gallic monasticism, his contribution is related to a type of ecclesiastical institution with Irish origins. The abbeys of St Gall, Reichenau and Bobbio, and other *Scottus*-monasteries in Germany and Austria, keep Insular manuscripts.[74] The significance of the Irish cultural achievement is evident during the Carolingian era. Notker Balbulus, writing in the 890s, clearly knew of the cult of Columba, presenting it as a testimonial to the cultural contribution of the Irish abroad in Europe. The Irish connections to Latin literacy are significant, as Latin is the language of the Holy Scriptures. Missionaries influential in the early Church history of Reichenau, Konstanz, Würzburg, Vienna and Regensburg are referred to as being from *Schottenklöster*, 'Scotti monasteries', the lasting name applied to the monastic houses of Irish missionaries. The extent to which their writings are disseminated can be understood in the way that Adomnán's *De locis sanctis* makes a lasting impression in *exegesis*; it was used by the Venerable Bede and was later found at the core of Sedulius Scottus's teachings.[75] The *St Gallen Manuscript 51* is a further example of the enduring connections to early Insular gospels and, as with the manuscript *Bern 363*, is indicative of the preservation of classical texts. The survival on the continent of key Irish manuscripts from the seventh to twelfth century is the result of the long-lasting presence of the Irish monastic centres. Gospel books devoted to the saints, from both home and abroad, are guarded by hereditary keepers in European libraries.[76]

It is helpful to visualise medieval communities with shared connections, and with the Irish pilgrims making a contribution as an embodiment of unity, cultural identity and connective tradition. In other words, what can be appreciated as our common European cultural heritage is rooted in art, architecture, literature, philosophy and music as it originates from the European perspective to determine what is binding in terms of cultural characteristics.[77]

Furthermore, knowledge transfer can be regarded as a phenomenon of the migration of Irish *peregrini* in a European context. The resulting impression is one of a lasting social and cultural exchange, conditioned by an understanding of the past. Thus, major overarching themes of connectivity and diversity emerge during the early middle ages and give shape to individual elements such as the memory of the ancient Roman empire, the effects of travel and the impact of the connection of knowledge and faith, all of which reflect the cohesive nature of Europe, with Irish art an essential element at the core. This points to what is specific about Irish artistic traditions as a major contributor to the production and transfer of knowledge that underlies cultural heritage and faith in medieval Europe. The shared idea of the quality and value of Irish learning is viewed as a major legacy in European terms, as Irish scholarship emerges at the beginning of the medieval period and endures in terms of artistic endeavour in monastic culture. This develops in a comprehensive manner as connections between the continent and Ireland continue to be made; scholars bring ideas with them, informing our perceptions of Ireland and Irishness as it evolves into a pan-European narrative.[78]

Notes

[1] For further details, see, Heinrich Böll, *Irisches Tagebuch* (Melville House; Brooklyn, NY, 2011), 8.

[2] The Hiberno-Scottish mission is a title given to a series of recorded excursions and missions by Irish scholars and clerics from Ireland to Scotland and to continental Europe for religious purposes. It is not recognised as a coordinated mission, but there are accounts of pilgrims (*peregrini*) and wandering monks organised by Irish clerics who travelled as part of this movement. See, Elva Johnston, 'Exiles for the edge? The Irish contexts of *Peregrinatio*', in Roy Flechner and Sven Meeder (eds), *The Irish in Medieval Europe, identity culture and religion* (New York; Palgrave, 2016), 38–52.

[3] John Hennig, 'Irish saints in the liturgical and artistic tradition of central Europe', *Irish Ecclesiastical Record* 61 (1943), 181–92, outlines the presence of persistent traditions of Irish culture in Europe, for example in festivals and music, such as the presence of the Irish *bodhrán* in Galician music. See also Lynda Mulvin, 'Ireland and Europe: transmission of Celtic aesthetic in the early Middle Ages', in Wim Huppertz, Lynda Mulvin and Michael Schmauder (eds), *Crossroads: travelling in the Early Middle Ages* (W Books; Amsterdam, 2017a), 78–86.

[4] Peter Harbison, *The golden age of Irish art: the medieval achievement, 600–1200* (Yale University Press; New Haven, CT and London, 2001), 2–15, and Rachael Moss 'Introduction: the Irishness of Medieval Irish art and architecture', in Rachel Moss (ed.), *Art and Architecture of Ireland* vol. 1, *Medieval, c.400 – c.1600* (5 vols, Yale University Press for Royal Irish Academy; New Haven, CT, London and Dublin, 2014), 1–8: 6–7.

[5] Ian M. Ferris, *Enemies of Rome: Barbarians through Roman eyes* (Sutton Publishing; Stroud, 2000), 125–7.

[6] For general reading, see Rachel Moss, 'Influences and impacts': 'Pilgrimage' and 'Irish art and artists abroad', in Moss (ed.), *Art and Architecture of Ireland* vol. 1, 9–38: 7–20 and 20–2.

[7] See, Lynda Mulvin, 'Identity and shifting attitudes', in Wim Huppertz, Lynda Mulvin and Michael Schmauder (eds), *Crossroads: travelling in the Early Middle Ages* (W Books; Amsterdam, 2017b), 174–81, and more generally, see, Edel Bhreathnach, *Ireland and the Medieval world 400–100: landscape kingship and religion* (Four Courts Press; Dublin, 2014), 1–35.

[8] Christopher Loveluck and Aidan O'Sullivan, 'Travel, transport and communication to and from Ireland, c. 400–1100', in Roy Flechner and Sven Meeder (eds), *The Irish in Early Medieval Europe, identity culture and religion* (Palgrave; New York, 2016), 19–38.

[9] The Venerable Bede; see, Bertram Colgrave and Roger A.B. Mynors (eds), *The ecclesiastical history of the English people*, Oxford Medieval Texts 1 (5 books, Clarendon Press; Oxford, 1969), chapter xiii.

[10] Damian Bracken and Eric Graff, *The Schaffhausen Adomnán* (Cork University Press; Cork, 2015), 135–6; Jean Michel Picard, 'Notker Balbulus Adomnán's *Vita Columbae* and the cult of Colum Cille in continental Europe', *Proceedings of the Royal Irish Academy* 98C(1) (1998), 1–23; Jean Michel Picard, 'The Schaffhausen Adomnán: a unique witness to Hiberno-Latin', *Peritia* 1 (1982), 216–49; Jean Michel Picard, 'The cult of Columba in Lotharingia (9th–11th centuries): the manuscript evidence', in John Carey, Máire Herbert and Pádraig Ó Riain (eds), *Studies in Irish hagiography: saints and scholars* (Four Courts Press; Dublin, 2001), 221–36; and Jean-Michel Picard, 'Early contact between Ireland and Normandy: the cult of Irish saints in Normandy before

the conquest', in Michael Richter and Jean Michel Picard (eds), *Ogma: essays in Celtic Studies in honour of Próinséas Ní Chatháin* (Four Courts Press; Dublin, 2002), 85–93.

[11] *Quies Aedain episcopi Saxonum*, Aiden dies in AD 651. See, Séan Mac Airt and Gearóid Mac Niocaill (eds), *The Annals of Ulster (to A.D. 1131)* (Dublin Institute for Advanced Studies; Dublin, 1983), 126.

[12] The 'Cult of saints', focusing on devotion to certain saints, evolved in the early middle ages. As an Irish religious trend, the focus related mainly to St Columba, St Patrick and St Brigid. See, Donald A. Bullough, 'The missions to the English and Picts and their Heritata (to *c.* 800)', in Heinz Löwe (ed.) *Die Iren und Europa im früheren Mittelalter* (2 vols, Klett-Cotta; Stuttgart, 1982), vol. 1, 80–97, and Arnold Angenendt, 'Die irische *Peregrinatio* und ihre Auswirkungen auf dem Kontinent vor dem Jahre 800', in Heinz Löwe (ed.), *Die Iren und Europa im früheren Mittelalter* (2 vols, Klett-Cotta; Stuttgart, 1982), vol. 1, 52–79.

[13] Pádraig A. Breathnach, 'Irish churchmen in pre-Carolingian Europe', *Cumann Seanchais Ard Mhacha/Journal of the Armagh Diocesan Historical Society* 11 (2) (1985), 319–30.

[14] For more on these, see, *Jonas of Bobbio, Life of Columbanus, Life of John of Réomé, and Life of Vedast, Translated with commentary by Alexander O'Hara and Ian Wood* (Liverpool University Press; Liverpool, 2017).

[15] Yaniv Fox, *Power and religion in Merovingian Gaul, Columbanian monasticism and the Frankish elites* (Cambridge University Press; Cambridge, 2014), 2–6. Ralf W.Mathisen, 'The ideology of monastic and aristocratic community in Late Roman Gaul', *Revista de ideas y formas políticas de la Antigüedad Clásica* 6 (1994), 203–20.

[16] Margaret Stokes, *Early Christian art in Ireland* (South Kensington Museum; London; 1887), 30–52. In terms of Irish rule, the Irish monasteries adhered to Old Testament teachings and observed a Celtic date for Easter, which was in violation of canon law referred to by Bede, as later determined in the Council of Whitby AD 664. See, Michele Tosi, 'Il governo abbaziale di Gerberto a Bobbio', *Archivum Bobiense* 2 (1985), 195–223.

[17] See also, Ludwig Bieler, *Ireland, harbinger of the Middle Ages* (Oxford University Press; London, Oxford, New York and Toronto, 1963). For ongoing research regarding Insular manuscripts on the continent, see the CODices project at University College Galway, which can be accessed online at: http://foundationsirishculture.ie/catalogue/ (25 April 2018). In addition, see the British Library and Bodleian Library, Oxford, collections of Anglo-Saxon manuscripts.

[18] See, Roy Flechner, 'Aspects of the Breton transmission of the Hibernensis', *Pecia* 12 (2008), 27–44.

[19] Judith Herrin, *The formation of Christendom* (Princeton University Press; Princeton, NJ, 1987), 481–7; Wolfgang Erdmann, *Die Reichenau im Bodensee Geschichte und Kunst* (Karl Robert Langewiesche; Königstein, 1979); and Julius von Pflugk-Harttung, 'The Old Irish on the continent', *Transactions of the Royal Historical Society* 5 (1891), 75–102.

[20] Ludwig Bieler, 'Adamnani de locis sanctis libri tres', in Denis Meehan (ed.), *Adamnan's De locis sanctis*, Scriptores Latini Hiberniae 3 (1958), 36–120.

[21] Georg L. Micheli, 'Recherches sur les manuscrits Irlandais décorés de Saint-Gall et de Reichenau', *Revue Archéologique*, Sixième Série, T. 7 (1936),189–223.

[22] Gustav Scherrer, 'Commemoration of Columba in Lotharingia, Metz', *Verzeichnis der Handschriften der Stiftsbibliothek von St. Gallen* (Verlag der Buchhandlung des Waisenhauses; Halle, 1875), 22–3.

[23] Dábhí Ó Cróinín, *Early Medieval Ireland, 400–1200* (2nd edn; Routledge; London and New York, 2016), 252–4.

[24] The presence of the comparative *Clavium*, resurrection and *maestas* suggest that these ideas were already in the liturgical repertoire, indicating a widespread desire to express images with common roots; see Roger Stalley, 'European art and the Irish high crosses', *Proceedings of the Royal Irish Academy* 90C (1990), 135–58.

[25] Thomas O'Loughlin, 'The diffusion of Adomnán's "*De locis sanctis*" in the Medieval Period', *Ériu* 51 (2000), 93–106.

[26] Elizabeth Duncan, 'The Irish and their books', in Roy Flechner and Sven Meeder (eds), *The Irish in Early Medieval Europe: identity, culture and religion* (Palgrave Macmillan; London, 2016), 214–30.

[27] Other Irish manuscripts can be found in Italy at the Ambrosian Library, Milan and the University Library, Turin. At Bobbio: 'a coffin, chalice and holy stick or crosier of St Columbanus are still preserved'; see Thomas Moore, *The history of Ireland* (4 vols, Longman, Orme, Brown, Green; London, 1835), vol. 1, 265–6.

[28] The text image is appended in *Reichenau Primer*. The manuscript is in St Paul in Lavathal Carinthia, Austria. See, Dáibhí Ó Cróinín, 'The Irish as mediators of antique culture on the continent', in Paul L. Butzer and Dietrich Lohrmann (eds), *Science in Western and Eastern civilization in Carolingian times* (Birkhäuser Verlag; Basel, Boston and Berlin, 1993), 41–52.

[29] Thomas O'Loughlin, 'Perceiving Palestine in Early Christian Ireland: martyrium, exegetical key, relic and liturgical space', *Ériu* 54 (2004), 125–37.

[30] Brigitta M. Bedos-Rezak 'Medieval identity: a sign and a concept', *American Historical Review* 105 (5) (2000), 1489–533.

[31] Rob Meens, 'The oldest manuscript witness of the *Collectio Canonum Hibernensis*', *Peritia* 14 (2000), 1–19.

[32] Roger E. Reynolds, 'The transmission of *The Hibernensis* in Italy: tenth to twelfth century', *Peritia* 14 (2000), 20–50.

[33] Roger E. Reynolds, 'Unity and diversity in Carolingian Canon law collections: the case of the *Collectio Canonum Hibernensis* and its derivatives', in Ute-Renata Blumenthal (ed.), *Andrew W. Mellon lectures in Early Christian studies, Carolingian essays* (Catholic University of America Press; Washington, D.C., 1983), 99–135.

[34] Tomás Ó Carragáin, 'Skeuomorphs and spolia: the presence of the past in Irish pre-Romanesque architecture', in Rachael Moss (ed.), *Making and meaning in Insular Art* (Four Courts Press; Dublin, 2007), 95–109.

[35] According to St Patrick's biographer, Tíreachán; see, Jonathan J.G. Alexander, *A survey of manuscripts illuminated in the British Isles* (6 vols, Harvey Miller; London, 1978), vol. 1: *Insular manuscripts, sixth to the ninth century*, 76–7. The basic work on the Book of Armagh is John Gwynn, *Liber Ardmachanus* (Hodges Figgis and Co.; Dublin, 1913), especially: xii–xvi, lxxix–xcii, and ci–xxxiv.

[36] See, John Smith, *The Life of St. Columba: the apostle and patron saint of the ancient Scots* (J. Mundell and Son; Edinburgh, 1798), and Ó Cróinín, *Early Medieval Ireland*, 158. Michael Charles-Edwards, *Early Christian Ireland* (Cambridge University Press; Cambridge, 2000), 421–8.

[37] There are references to a round tower at St Columba's church, and to an abbot's house, kitchen, guest house, library, numerous houses and high cross at St Brigid's church Kildare, in *Vita Brigita, Cogitosus*; see, Ó Cróinín, *Early Medieval Ireland*, 125.

[38] Françoise Henri, *Irish Art during the Viking Invasions 800–1000 AD* (Methuen; London, 1967), Fig 2.

[39] Further information on these excavations and what they have uncovered to date is available at: http://www.amisaintcolomban.org/ARCHEO-LUXEUIL.html (10 April 2018).

[40] Sébastian Bully, 'Luxeuil-les-Bains (Haute-Saône), ancienne église Saint-Martin', *Bulletin du Centre d'études médiévales* 10 (2006), 89–92.

[41] Associated manuscripts more likely produced at Honau on the Rhine, which is known for an intervention from Charlemagne: 'Charles by the Grace of God King of the Franks gives orders the king of the Franks have given freedom to all Irish Pilgrims to the end that no one shall carry off anything of their property and that no generation except their generation shall occupy their churches'. Dr Rev William Reeves, 'On the Irish Abbey of Honau on the Rhine,' *Proceedings of the Royal Irish Academy (1836–69)* 6 (1853), 452–61.

[42] Louis Gougaud, 'Achievement and influence of Irish monks', *Studies: an Irish Quarterly Review* 20 (78) (1931), 195–208. Mathias Untermann, *Klosterinsel Reichenau im Bodensee: UNESCO Weltkulturerbe* (vol. 8 of Arbeitsheft/Landesdenkmalamt Baden-Württemberg, Konrad Theiss Verlag; Stuttgart, 2001), 157–71.

[43] *Vita Pirmium* 9, 75. See, Timo John, *The monastery island of Reichenau in Lake Constance. Cradle of Western Culture* (UNESCO World Heritage; Freiburg, 2006), 13.

[44] Notker Balbulus, *Martyrologium*, 9 June, cols 1101–3: *In Scotia insula Hybernia deposition sancti Columbae, cognomento apud suos Columb-Killi, eo quod multarum cellarum id est monasterium uel ecclesiarum instititutor fundator et rector existerit... beattisimi Columbani magistri domini et patris nostril Galli, virtutatum ac meritaorum suiru quasi unicum*, Heinrich Canisius (ed.), *Lectiones Antiquae, VI* (Ingolstadt, 1604); reproduced in Jacques Paul Migne (ed.), *Patrologia Latina* (221 vols, Garnier; Paris, 1844–65), vol. 131, 1015–164. See also, Picard, 'Notker Balbulus Adomnán's "Vita Columbae"', 1–23.

[45] Michele Tosi, *Bobbio: Guida storica artistica e ambientale della città e dintorni* (Archivi Storici Bobiensi; Bobbio, 1978).

[46] See, Mulvin, 'Ireland and Europe', in *Crossroads*, 78–86.

[47] See, Rachel Moss, 'Art of worship and devotion: reliquaries', in Moss (ed.), *Art and Architecture of Ireland* vol. 1, 225–327: 282–97.

[48] Michael Ryan, 'Decorated metalwork in the Museo Dell'Abbazia, Bobbio, Italy', *Journal of the Royal Society of Antiquaries of Ireland* 120 (1990), 102–11.

[49] Pádraig A. Breathnach, 'Irish churchmen in pre-Carolingian Europe', *Cumann Seanchais Ard Mhacha/Journal of the Armagh Diocesan Historical Society* 11 (2) (1985), 319–30.

[50] Cormac Bourke, 'Further notes on the Clonmore Shrine', *Cumann Seanchais Ard Mhacha/Journal of the Armagh Diocesan Historical Society*, 16 (2) (1995), 27–32, and also, on Early Irish Church architecture generally, see, Tómas Ó Carragáin, *Churches in Early Medieval Ireland: architecture, ritual and memory* (Yale University Press; New Haven, CT and London, 2006).

[51] Jan Soderberg, 'A lost cultural exchange: reconsidering the Bologna Shrine's origin and use', *Proceedings of the Harvard Celtic Colloquium* 13 (1993), 156–65.

[52] Peter Harbison, *Pilgrimage in Ireland. The monuments and the people* (Syracuse University Press; Syracuse, NY, 1998), 163–5.

[53] Elizabeth James, 'Ireland and Western Gaul in the Merovingian period', in Dorothy Whitelock, Rosamund Mc Kitterick and Dorothy N. Dumville (eds), *Ireland in Early Medieval Europe. Studies in memory of Kathleen Hughes* (Cambridge University Press; Cambridge, 1982), 362–6. See also, Donnchadh Ó Corráin, 'Irish law and Canon law', in Proinseas Ní Chatháin and Micael Richter (eds), *Irland und Europa. Die Kirche im Frühmittelalter* (Four Courts Press; Dublin, 2002), 157–66, and Michael Ryan 'The Irish

horn-reliquary of Tongres/Tongeren, Belgium', in G. Mac Niocaill and P. Wallace (eds), *Keimelia: studies in Medieval archaeology and history in memory of Tom Delany* (Galway University Press, 1988), 127–42.

[54] For the shrine mount, see Francois Vallet, 'Trésors de Irlande', in *Catalogue de L'Exposition* (Association Française d'Action Artistique; Paris, 1982), Inv. Man 52748.01-02. This information is kindly provided by Professor Laurent Olivier, curator-in-chief of the department of Celtic and Gallic archaeology at the National Museum of Archaeology in Saint-Germain-en-Laye, France. Many thanks to both Laurent Olivier and to the curator, Ms Christine Lorre, for providing further inventory information.

[55] For further reading on Viking incursions into Ireland, see, Howard B. Clarke, Maire Ní Mhaonaigh and Raghnall Ó Floinn (eds), *Ireland and Scandinavia in the Early Viking Age* (Four Courts Press; Dublin, 1998).

[56] For a detailed translation of Columbanus's 'Life' by Jonas of Susa, see, Dana C. Munro, *Life of St Columban by the monk Jonas* (Miracles Publisher; Philadelphia, 1993; reprint of 1895 edition).

[57] Máire T. Herbert, 'Crossing historical and literary boundaries: Irish written culture around the year 1000', in Patrick Sims-Williams and George A. Williams (eds), *Croesi Ffiniau: Trafodion Y 12fed Gyngres Astudiaethau Celtaidd Ryngwladol 24–30 Awst 2003, Prifysgol Cymru, Aberystwyth / Crossing boundaries: Proceedings of the 12th International Congress of Celtic Studies, 24–30 August 2003, University of Wales, Aberystwyth.* Cambrian Medieval Celtic Studies 53–4 (CMCS Publications; Aberystwyth, 2007), 87–101. See also, Máire T. Herbert, *Iona, Kells, and Derry: the history and hagiography of the monastic familia of Columba* (Clarendon Press; Oxford, 1988), and Máire T. Herbert and Pádraig Ó Riain, *Betha Adamnáin: the Irish Life of Adamnán*, Irish Texts Society 54 (Irish Texts Society; London, 1988).

[58] Christiaan Corlett, 'The Rathdown slabs—Vikings and Christianity', *Archaeology Ireland* 17 (4) (2003), 28–30.

[59] Stalley, 'European art and the Irish high crosses', 135–58.

[60] Carolingian reformer Benedict of Aniane (d. AD 821) produced a collection of monastic rules in *Vita Benedicti Anianensis.* The earliest examples pertain to textual reference in the teaching of the church of St Columban as absorbed by the new orders.

[61] Widukind Von Corvey, *Res Gestae Saxonicae* edited by Ekkehart Rotter and Bernd Schneidmüller (Reclam; Stuttgart, 1981), and Rosamund Mc Kitterick, *The resources of the past in Early Medieval Europe* (Cambridge University Press; Cambridge, 2001).

[62] Stefan Allot, *Alcuin of York* (William Sessions Ltd; York, 1984), 83–112.

[63] *De natione Scotorum quibus consuetudo peregrinandi iam paene in naturam conuensa est;* see, Bruno Krusch (ed.), *Walahfrid Strabo, Vita S. Galli Confessoris,* Monumenta Germaniae Historica, Scriptores rerum merovingicarum [4] (Bibliopolii Hahniani; Hanover, 1902), 280–337.

[64] Ó Cróinín, 'The Irish as mediators of antique culture on the continent', 50–1.

[65] The *Reichenau Primer* manuscript is in St Paul in Lavathal Carinthia, Austria. Sedulius Scottus is also associated with a poem about his white cat, Pangur Bán, in which he compares the cat's hunting skills to his own scholarly pursuits.

[66] The ninth-century AD Irish philosopher John Scottus Eriugena referred to the angelic hierarchy as determined by his translation of Dionysius the Areopagite; see, Anton. J. Gurevich, *Categories of medieval culture* transl. by George L. Campbell (Routledge; London, 1972), 220–42.

[67] The papal librarian Anastasius remarked: 'it is a wonderful thing how that barbarian, living at the ends of the earth who might be supposed to be as far removed from the knowledge of this other language, as he is from familiar use of it, has been able to comprehend such ideas and translate them into another tongue: I refer to John Scottigena whom I have learned by report to be in all things a holy man'; see, Gurevich, *Categories of medieval culture*, 240.

[68] John Lanigan, *Ecclesiastical history of Ireland* (Graisberry; Dublin, 1822), 402, and Aubrey Gwynn 'Irish monks and the Cluniac reform', *Studies: an Irish Quarterly Review* 29 (115) (1940), 409–30.

[69] Yaniv Fox, 'The political context of Irish monasticism in seventh century Francia: another look at sources', in Roy Flechner and Sven Meeder (eds), *The Irish in Early Medieval Europe* (Palgrave; New York, 2016), 53–67.

[70] Einhard, *Vita Karoli Magni (Das Leben Karls des Großen)* (Reclam; Ditzingen, 1986).

[71] Henry Mayr-Hartung, *An historical study, Ottonian book illumination* (2nd revised edn; Harvey Miller; London, 1999), 63–5: The Egbert Psalter.

[72] Victor Czumalo, 'Architecture and identity, genius loci', *Autoportet* 36 (2012), 47.

[73] Margaret Stokes, *Three months in the forests of France: a pilgrimage in search of vestiges of Irish saints in France* (George Bell and Sons; London, 1895).

[74] Marcia L. Colker, '*Die Regensburger Schottenlegende:* Libellus de fundacione ecclesie Consecrati Petri. P.A. Breatnach', *Speculum* 54 (3) (1979), 548–50.

[75] Robert Hoyland and Sarah Waidler, 'Adomnán's *De locis sanctis* and the seventh-century Near East', *English Historical Review* 129 (539) (2014), 787–807.

[76] Brád O' Doherty, 'Alsace and Ireland: medieval links', *Cumann Seanchais Ard Mhacha/ Journal of the Armagh Diocesan Historical Society* 14 (2) (1991), 161–78.

[77] Huppertz, Mulvin and Schmauder (eds), 'Introduction', *Crossroads*, 1–3.

[78] Ó Carragáin, *Churches in Early Medieval Ireland*, 287–91.

From film noir to scientific-pastoralism: depictions of Ireland in British, German and French cinema, 1938–2014

Fergal Lenehan

Irish film studies and the cinema of other countries

Film historian Ruth Barton, in a 2017 article, has written of a crisis in Irish film scholarship, whereby 'Irish cinema, an *arriviste* art form with little history, may have slipped down the priority list' of international publishers.[1] Irish film scholarship itself was, of course, 'virtually non-existent' before the 1980s, and the co-authored 1987 volume *Cinema and Ireland* by Kevin Rockett, Luke Gibbons and John Hill may rightly be seen as the founding text of an academic Irish film studies.[2] Rockett *et al.* chart the sporadic history of Irish cinematic production; the dominant emphasis, however, is given to depictions of Ireland within movies emanating from the American and British film industries.

Images of green pastoralism and political violence were established in *Cinema and Ireland* as the dominating paradigms for the examination of Ireland on screen. Building on the ideas of German art historian Erwin Panofsky, Gibbons argues that Irish filmic pastoralism may be divided into an idyllic or nostalgic 'soft primitivism', characteristic of US productions such as *Finian's rainbow* (1968) or *The quiet man* (1952), and a romantic but harsh and often violent 'hard primitivism', seen in British productions such as Robert Flaherty's *Man of Aran* (1934) or David Lean's *Ryan's daughter* (1970).[3] This soft–hard US–British dichotomy is also to be seen—if not quite nearly as neatly—in relation to the topic of violence in depictions of Ireland; at least according to John Hill in the same volume. While violence in US genre movies may often have cathartic elements, British cinema, with Britain's legacy of direct military involvement in Ireland, has usually, Hill believes, preferred a darker and largely de-contextualised vision of Ireland; he argues British cinema has tended to blame the Irish themselves for the violence the country has experienced.[4]

Pastoralism and violence have indeed remained the dominant paradigms for the study of Anglo-American cinematic images of Ireland, with Martin McCloone, for example, in 2000 also writing of a filmic 'benign primitivism' and representations of Ireland as a society in which 'a proclivity to violence was seen as a tragic flaw of the Irish themselves'.[5] Thus, screen images of Ireland that have 'emerged out of the national industries of other countries' have remained a significant element of Irish film studies.[6] The 'national industries of other countries', however, have largely been Anglo-American. There is a need, thus, to include further contexts in order to acquire a wider perspective of how Ireland has been viewed on screen; an argument this author has made elsewhere.[7]

Yet, as Ruth Barton also notes, even the study of the Irish in British cinema remains a 'still underdeveloped area'.[8] This chapter thus seeks to extend this discussion by juxtaposing some Irish elements of British cinema with Irish elements of German and French cinema. The British–Irish filmic relationship has undoubtedly been of a symbiotic nature, with many Irish people actively involved in the British cinema industry in a variety of artistic roles. This representational relationship has often had, of course, an uneven power relation rooted in the problematic colonial, or quasi-colonial, Irish–British relationship. German and French representations of Ireland have had a more culturally detached perspective, usually with very little or no direct Irish participation within the production of the multi-agent filmic texts.

This chapter is approached in two distinct—but intertwined—ways. One perspective takes a generic approach and examines specific Irish-themed genre movies from a British, German and French context. A second, wider, perspective looks to provide an overview of some Irish elements within these national cinemas. What should be noted here is how 'green pastoralism' and violence have remained important themes within depictions of Ireland in Britain, Germany and France; these elements are also innovatively drawn upon and may undoubtedly be seen to have evolved, especially in later periods. This chapter is not exhaustive and more may be written on this topic—not least in relation to the French context.

Ireland and World War Two

Irish characters' positioning and Ireland's neutrality in relation to World War Two has featured historically in both British and German cinematic depictions of Ireland. The nature of these representations has also frequently changed, according to contemporary needs. During the period of World War Two itself, Anglo-Irish conflict was utilised directly in two German propaganda vehicles directed by Max W. Kimmich, *Der Fuchs von Glenarvon* ('The fox of Glenarvon'; 1939–40) and *Mein Leben für Irland* ('My life for Ireland'; 1940–1); the aim here was to incite hatred of 'England' as a repressor of smaller nations. The anti-Semitic propaganda film *Die Rothschilds* (Erich Waschneck, 1940) also retained an anti-British Irish character who communicates to the audience the

Fergal Lenehan

message that Jewish and English are basically the same thing; a facet of Nazi anti-British propaganda sought at this time to represent the British as the Jews among the so-called Aryans.[9] In British war movies made during World War Two, on the other hand, the Irish were called on to love the British and 'to commit themselves to the cause of the allies'; however, the Irish had to 'draw on their own rebel identities as true fighting Irishmen, not on their allegiance to Britain'.[10] This is seen, for example, in Belfast-born director Brian Desmond Hurst's *Dangerous moonlight* (1941), while in Basil Dearden's *Halfway house* (1944) the Irishman Terence initially defends Irish neutrality and is reluctant to take sides, but with German bombs raining down, he changes his mind and asks: 'is this a private fight or can anyone join in?'[11]

As Barton notes, post-war British cinema took a much darker view of Irish neutrality 'producing a slew of films that suggested that the Irish were spying on behalf of the Germans', such as *Nightboat to Dublin* (Lawrence Huntington, 1946), *I see a dark stranger* (Frank Launder, 1946), *Against the wind* (Charles Crichton, 1948) and *The man who never was* (Ronald Neame, 1956).[12] *The lost people* (Muriel Box and Bernard Knowles, 1949), set in Germany among displaced persons, stars Siobhan McKenna as a Franco-Irish communist and 'anti-British troublemaker'.[13] The Irish countryside was now more usually seen as a 'dark, malevolent space', drawing on the Gothic rather than a benign pastoralism, with Barton seeing Irish 'diabolism and irrationality' reaching its 'discursive apogee' in the movie *Daughter of darkness* (Lance Comfort, 1948), starring Siobhan McKenna again as a violent and unhinged Irish servant in Yorkshire.[14] Even by 1960 and Tay Garnett's *A terrible beauty*, Irish collaboration with Nazi Germany is a central theme, as a British-based IRA grouping splits between those who wish to collaborate with the Nazis and those who do not. Depictions of Irish disloyalty and ambiguity in relations during World War Two may be seen as helping to bolster a British self-image of ceaseless heroism.

The German movie *Ein Tag, der nie zu Ende geht* ('A day that will never end'; Franz Peter Wirth, 1959) is also set in Ireland during World War Two. At the centre of the movie is an unlikely love triangle between Galway shopkeeper Maureen, stranded German U-Boot commander Robert, who initially poses as a Swiss national, and Bill, an American pilot based in Belfast. Shot in Technicolor and prominently featuring the landscape of County Galway, the film may undoubtedly be seen as marked by an idyllic, soft primitivism; menacing gothic elements are nowhere here to be seen. In neutral Ireland, the movie makes clear, the Germans were not automatically perceived as enemies; nor, however, were they automatically seen as allies. An initial voiceover emphasises the neutrality of the 'Republic of Ireland' [sic], which was, the narrator tells us, 'as neutral as Switzerland, Sweden and Portugal'.[15] This is contrasted with Northern Ireland, from where 'British and American aeroplanes attacked German U-Boots'.[16] It is also implied that both the German Robert and the American Bill would be interned if found by the *Gardaí*, the Irish police force, and at one stage both characters hide together from them. World War Two is seen here, thus, from a humanistic perspective, and the film may be viewed as part of a post-war German societal process that looked to downplay distinct German war guilt.[17] The film's setting in neutral Ireland partly facilitates this.

By the late 1960s, war films had fallen out of vogue somewhat in British cinema. Those that were now made often tackled the conventions of the genre head-on. *The eagle has landed* (John Sturges, 1977) breaks so many taboos, according to Murphy, 'that it becomes more than a simple adventure story', while Donald Sutherland's portrayal of an Irishman helping a small group of German soldiers in an attempt to assassinate Winston Churchill 'makes IRA support for the German cause look fair and reasonable'.[18] Yet, Sutherland's character of Liam Devlin should be seen in a rather more ambivalent and ironic light, even if the portrayal of an IRA man working with German soldiers is now undoubtedly sympathetic. Devlin teaches literature at Berlin University and is an IRA operative. Yet, he belittles both the IRA and Nazi Germany, explaining that he has left the British-based IRA, as 'I don't like soft-target hits', while his reaction to the idea of Germany winning the war is: 'Pigs might fly one day, Colonel, but I doubt it'.[19] At one stage Devlin is asked whether he has any motive for his actions at all, to which he replies 'regrettably no', agreeing that if someone wanted to kidnap Adolf Hitler, he would probably join them. Thus, Devlin is portrayed as an ideological sceptic and devoid of hate. He appears, rather, to be consciously and ironically playing a game of adventure—without actually giving very much thought to the ethics of his stance.

Fergal Lenehan

British director Terence Ryan's *The Brylcreem boys* (1998) fully embraces irony in its sending up of the prisoner-of-war film genre; this is done by basing the film at the Curragh Camp in Ireland during World War Two, where British and German soldiers are interned together. Unlike the harsh regime portrayed in earlier prisoner-of-war movies, the Curragh Camp, as depicted here, is ruled in an easy-going manner, from which most of the movie's humour springs; prisoners are allowed out on day passes once they promise to return. Thus, the prisoners regularly go to the races, while both German and Allied barrack-rooms retain their own well-stocked bars. Camp-leader O'Brien, played by Gabriel Byrne, explains that 'the best way to keep people in is to let them out'. Similarly to *Ein Tag, der nie zu Ende geht*, an Irish-Canadian-German love triangle ensues. While the closing credits of the German movie imply the death of the German sailor Robert, an explanation before the closing credits of *The Brylcreem boys* tells the viewer that the Canadian pilot later dies, while the German pilot marries the Irishwoman after the war. Thus, the principal German character in this instance gets to live in a more collaborative, post-war Europe.

Irish-themed film noir? *Odd Man Out* (1947), *Mein Leben für Irland* ('My life for Ireland'; 1940–1) and *Le Puritain* ('The puritan'; 1938)

As James Naremore has noted, film noir was first discussed in relation to Hollywood cinema in France in 1946, and should be seen as an analytical category for movies, belonging to 'the history of ideas as much as the history of cinema'.[20] Paul Schrader writes of film noir in terms of tone and mood, and a number of recurrent characteristics: scenes lit for night; vertical lines preferred to horizontal lines; faces covered by shadow; water and rain; a claustrophobic atmosphere and a romantic narration in which there is 'no hope for the future: one can only take pleasure in reliving a doomed past'.[21] Carol Reed's *Odd man out*, Kimmich's *Mein Leben für Irland* and Jeff Musso's *Le puritain* are all marked by the hopelessness of central characters. Johnnie in *Odd man out* wanders Belfast dying from gunshot wounds after a failed robbery, mentally reliving aspects of his past as his consciousness dwindles; Patrick O'Connor becomes a double-agent for revolutionary Irish nationalists in *Mein Leben für Irland*, his situation becoming increasingly difficult until he ultimately sacrifices his life for Ireland (communicating a propagandistic message of sacrifice in the process); while in the French movie *Le puritain*—a relatively faithful adaptation of Liam O'Flaherty's novel *The puritan*, with O'Flaherty also credited as one of four scriptwriters—the troubled journalist Ferriter murders his prostitute neighbour in an act driven partly by his very extreme Catholic faith.[22] Ferriter then wanders throughout Dublin pondering his actions and meeting various people, shadowed by the police, until he completely loses his sanity in the concluding scene in a prison cell. A claustrophobic, dark, urban location is central to both *Odd man out* and *Le puritain* and such a setting reflects the central characters' hopelessness, while Dublin in *Mein Leben für Irland* is at times rural, at times urban, shifting to serve propagandistic purpose. *Odd man out* has long been recognised as a fine example of British film noir.[23] *Le puritain* is a work of 1930s French poetic realism, which is also seen, similarly to German Expressionist cinema, as an influence upon Hollywood film noir.[24] *Mein Leben für Irland* is stylistically unsophisticated in comparison.

All of these movies are also culturally non-realist in terms of their representation of Ireland. This is most obviously true for the movies in which French and German only are spoken—but it is also linguistically true for the Belfast of *Odd man out*, in which all characters, except for locally recruited children, speak with a soft southern Irish accent rather than in Belfast tones. The Albert Memorial Clock Tower dominates the filmic landscape of Belfast in *Odd man* out; it is visible, it would appear, from virtually every part of the city. Belfast is depicted as a gritty and complex urban space: a space of industry, automobiles and dancing, as well as poverty and ambivalent political violence. *Mein Leben für Irland* is marked by a rebel trench-coat aesthetic, while the depiction of Dublin is dominated by what looks like Dublin Castle, which remains visible in numerous scenes; this seat of British power is then stormed and taken over by Irish rebels. The internal spaces that mark the portrayal of Dublin in *Le puritain* probably owe more to the aesthetics of French urban living than 1930s Dublin; this cultural confusion is most evident in the concluding bar scenes, complete with French button accordion music and Ferriter dancing drunkenly with a Spanish dancer, who plays the castanets. Ireland, in all three films, is distinctly urban; and laced with violence.

Depicting Anglo-Irish conflict: *Shake hands with the Devil* (1959), *Meines Vaters Pferde* ('My father's horses'; 1953) and *Le jeune folle* ('Desperate decision'; 1952)

Depictions of political violence have often dominated the image of Ireland in Anglo-American cinema, as already noted. The 1950s saw a number of movies centring on Anglo-Irish conflict being made also outside of the English-speaking world. The French film *Le jeune folle*, ('Desperate decision') directed by Yves Allégret and partly shot on location in Dublin, utilises Anglo-Irish conflict as the background for a gangster genre piece, set largely among a self-contained world of what the movie calls 'Republicans' in Dublin. Central to the film is Catherine, a servant at a convent in Dundrum, where she is, largely, bullied and harassed by the nuns—the filmmakers here, perhaps, making a prescient comment on the situation of vulnerable women in early-twentieth-century Ireland. Catherine has a vision of her brother being shot in Dublin. She goes to the city to find out how he is and falls in love with the volunteer Kevin, who has indeed murdered her brother—in a visually striking beach scene—as a traitor to the Republicans. The movie concludes with Catherine shooting Kevin. She then experiences a number of more visions and promptly appears to lose her sanity. Ireland here is largely a dark, urban and violent Dublin; casual drunkenness is also commonplace, with rail workers at Dundrum railway station seen drinking heavily—while working—as Catherine gets the train to the city.

Meines Vaters Pferde ('My father's horses'), directed by Gerhard Lamprecht, is actually a riding film, shot in Germany and County Wicklow and set partly in the 'south of Ireland', where in 1902 a German former soldier (and talented horse-rider) visits his friend who had also served in the German army. The friend is an Irish aristocrat called Sir John Fitzpatrick St. Ives, Baronet of Eryllgobragh [*sic*], known as Pat. The film is a melodramatic love triangle: the German visitor spends time riding with Pat's wife Nicoline, while Pat exhibits brooding emotional intensity as he balances his secret activities as a leader of an Irish nationalist rebel grouping with his married life. A hard, primitive pastoral aesthetic is evident here; the Irish landscape is frequently wracked by violent storms, reflecting also the nature of the Irish characters. Pat is also a fervent whiskey-drinker, while the Catholic chaplain of the Eryllgobragh estate, Fr Quentin, neatly combines extreme Irish nationalism with Catholicism; he chides Pat for serving 'English' (actually Scottish) rather than Irish whiskey, while he sarcastically feels sorry for the 'British police' outside in one of the many storms.

Marcia Landy sees Michael Anderson's *Shake hands with the Devil* as containing the 'familiar myth of the Irish as worshipping death', while 'the effects of colonialism are thus seen to be traceable to the attitudes of the colonised and not their colonisers'.[25] Hill includes *Shake hands with the Devil* among British films that de-contextualise Irish political violence. Yet the movie also depicts the Black and Tans beating a man, in what is 'one of the few, albeit individualised, examples of English, and not just simply Irish, malevolence'.[26] One of the characters, Kitty, refers to 'talk of taking life' as 'what men in Ireland, over tea, talk about'.[27] Irish violence is here also individualised in the psychopathic character of the IRA leader and pathological abuser of women, Lenihan, played by James Cagney. When a truce is offered, all of the Irish volunteers are eager to stop fighting; except for Lenihan who wants to go to the west of Ireland to build a new army and to fight on. Similarly, the Black and Tan Colonel Smithson—who had earlier beaten the Irish prisoner, but whose character is less developed than Lenihan—does not appear to be liked or respected by the other British officers. They stare uncomprehendingly at him as he states that violence is 'the only language these people [the Irish] understand'.[28] The movie's initial voiceover explains that 'often in its turbulent history the men of Ireland had risen to fight for their freedom'.[29] Thus, Irish violence, apart from the character of Lenihan, is actually portrayed here as a response to a colonial situation.

Ireland in British, German and French cinema: some trends from 1960 to 2014

A small number of German productions from the early 1960s depict Ireland in terms of a 'benign pastoralism' or idyllic 'soft primitivism'. The comedies *Das schwarze Schaf* ('The black sheep'; Helmut Ashley and Axel von Ambesser, 1960) and *Er kann's nicht lassen* ('He just can't stop'; von Ambesser, 1962) are versions of G.K. Chesterton's Father Brown stories; but set, and partly filmed, in Ireland rather than England. *...nur der Wind* ('Only the wind'; Fritz Umgelter, 1961) is a musical and adventure story, set partly in a gangster milieu, that makes very good use of

Fergal Lenehan

location shooting from both the Aran Islands and Dublin, drawing on idyllic primitive, as well as urban, Irish imagery.

British movies dealing with Ireland in the 1960s and 1970s centred largely on violent narratives. In John Ford and Jack Cardiff's *Young Cassidy* (1965), which deals with the life of Sean O'Casey, the title character rejects the mob violence of Irish life in what is seen by Hill to be, again, the 'de-contextualisation of Irish history'.[30] David Lean's *Ryan's daughter* (1970) famously engages in an extreme type of 'hard primitivism', while also offering a narrative of political violence. As Barton notes, Lean's movie is 'not interested in trying to understand the causes and consequences of Irish historical events but reproduces them as signifiers of incomprehensible otherness'; Irish natives are largely depicted as an 'ignorant rabble' with a 'malevolent and uncontrollable energy'.[31] *Hennessy* (Don Sharp, 1975) and *The long Good Friday* (John Mackenzie, 1979) are gangster movies that incorporate the Provisional IRA, but remain devoid of politics. Both are notable for marking somewhat of a shift in terms of the depiction of violence; in the first film British soldiers are responsible for the deaths of innocent bystanders, while in the second movie the British police are as brutal as the IRA (but not nearly as efficient).[32] Political-historical context remains virtually non-existent, while violent agency is now more widely spread.

French director Yves Boissset's *Un taxi mauve* ('The purple taxi'; 1977), filmed extensively in Ireland, centres on a number of ex-pats (French, American and probably Russian) living in a small village in the west of Ireland. Retaining little in terms of actual narrative, the film consists of numerous extended scenes in the wild Irish countryside—shooting, riding, walking and driving. The movie is, however, a tour-de-force of violent hard primitivism, in which the native Irish characters are largely alcohol-sodden, and pub violence reigns. A number of bar scenes deteriorate into drunken brawling; the natives do not take this very seriously however, and, after the final violent outbreak in the pub, the guests simply return to playing music and *ceilidh* dancing. According to Roderick Flynn and Patrick Brereton, the film was a box-office hit in France, while they believe that 'for many French tourists the film's representation of Ireland as a primitive paradise untouched by the trappings of modernity (albeit peopled by brawling and savage locals) is a key factor in encouraging them to visit'.[33] The best-known Irish element within 1980s German cinema is the character of Brian Sweeny Fitzgerald in Werner Herzog's *Fitzcarraldo*—an opera fanatic of Irish origin who dreams of building an opera house deep in the South American jungle. Fitzgerald/Fitzcarraldo is a dreamer and an eccentric; indeed his unusual Irish roots accentuate his very eccentricity among the Spanish elites. He is also, of course, complicit in South American colonialism. Mary Lawlor believes that Herzog looks to take 'advantage of the Irishman's ostensive non-implication in Europe's imperial projects' and, thus, 'attempts to distinguish Fitzcarraldo as historically innocent'.[34] Forcing large numbers of native South Americans to haul a steamship over a mountainside reveals the character, however, to be anything but historically innocent; the character's Irishness does not disentangle him successfully from colonial power relations.

A little-seen short film by French director Dominique Boccarossa, *Grève au pays des nègres blancs* ('Strike in the country of white negroes'; 1983), engages directly with Northern Ireland.[35] Shot in a disjointed, gallery film-art style, the piece is also extraordinarily naïve in its explicit pro-Provisional IRA politics. The film centres on an unnamed man who drives from Dublin to Belfast, gets taken away by men in army uniform from a derelict-looking apartment block, is then viciously tortured and dies on hunger strike. Images of the man being beaten and brutalised (at one stage a syringe is injected into his penis), and of the physical realities of imprisonment and hunger strike—the film shows the man defecating and becoming thinner and thinner—are interspersed with what is meant to be explanatory text. The movie concludes with pictures and short biographies of the actual IRA hunger strikers. The interposed text tells the viewer about the deaths in the famine of the nineteenth century while Ireland still exported food, quotes Friedrich Engels on Ireland's exploitation by Britain, and, rather astonishingly, compares British forces in Northern Ireland to Nazis and the Dublin government to the World War Two Vichy regime. The film fails to mention the distinct reality of Northern Irish unionist communities with British identities, the fact that the H-Block prisoners were themselves violent and murderous terrorists, or that the IRA systematically assassinated prison officers.

By the 1990s British movies dealing with Ireland often centred on a nostalgic green pastoralism—the tone of these British depictions of

Ireland, which Ruth Barton terms 'heritage films', had undoubtedly changed. Heritage films share a 'nostalgic edenic view of Ireland'; while many are set in the 1950s, the genre also includes 'an Ireland of the present distinguishable by its "pastness"'.[36] Barton writes that 'the Irish of the heritage films have no axe to grind with the British'; furthermore, the Irish landscape had now been 're-tamed, its gothic threat removed' in heritage movies such as Mike Newell's *Into the west* (1992) and John Roberts's *War of the buttons* (1994).[37] A more benign British view of the island needs to be seen in relation to the diminishing of conflict in Northern Ireland. Barton believes that the 'excessive use of stereotypes' in heritage movies such as Peter Chelsom's *Hear my song* (1991) and Kirk Jones's *Waking Ned* (1999) 'invite an ironic reading'.[38] Martin McLoone, on the other hand, argues that *Waking Ned*—shot on the Isle of Man—'lacks any degree of self-consciousness', as the rural village stands for 'an authentic organic community that outfoxes the po-faced representative of urban modernity'. The movie sets up a tradition-versus-modernity opposition, but without any 'ironic self-subversion', he believes.[39] Thus, here British cinema can now be undoubtedly seen as engaging in an idyllic 'soft primitivism'.

Yet British cinema, in the early 2000s, also began to make serious-minded Irish-themed movies with a degree of societal significance. Shot solely in Scotland by Scottish director Peter Mullan, *The Magdalene sisters* performs a public function by helping to enable its viewership 'to work through the legacy of Irish history in its more traumatic formulations'; yet it, in addition, reinforces the idea of Ireland as a country absorbed by its history and reproduces 'the signifiers of Irishness that outside audiences expect from Irish fictions'.[40] The all-pervasive signifier of Catholicism indeed remains significant here. As James M. Smith writes, however, the movie 'indicts familial culpability as well as a wider patriarchal social politics', while it also targets state and communal collaboration in the imprisonment of young, vulnerable and innocent women.[41] Stephen Frears's *Philomena* (2013) would later continue this discussion about Ireland's traumatic past, albeit in a more light-hearted manner.

British cinema has continued to retain Irish and/or Irish-British characters, sometimes signified solely by name, accent or Catholicism. Although most of his work is set within working-class communities of England and Scotland, director Ken Loach's movies have contained numerous Irish and Irish-British characters, not least Catholic priests. According to John Hill, Irish-Catholic elements of British working-class experience reinforce the sense of authenticity and 'working-class disadvantage' in Loach's work, while tropes of Irishness also complicate conventional understandings of Britishness, reinforcing the complexity of identity.[42] For Bronwen Walter, 'Irish presences' in 'apparently "English" films' with 'no Irish content', such as Gurinder Chadha's *Bend it like Beckham* (2002), Richard Eyre's *Notes on a scandal* (2007) and Mike Leigh's *Happy-go-lucky* (2007), '[reinforce] the Englishness' of the movies, bolstering the English setting.[43] Cillian Murphy's Irish character in Danny Boyle's *28 days later* (2002), however, does not fit with either of these explanations. Murphy plays an Irish cycling courier in London who wakes up after an accident to find the city absolutely deserted—except, that is, for swarms of zombies. Murphy's Irishness, which plays no narrative role, nevertheless enhances his sense of isolation. He is isolated in a two-fold manner: by the abandoned, post-apocalyptic atmosphere he suddenly finds himself in, and also culturally by being, at core, an outsider in the British capital.

Changes must also be noted in relation to depictions of violence in Irish-themed cinema emanating from Britain during this recent period. Paul Greengrass's graphic documentary-style drama *Bloody Sunday* (2002) examines the murder of thirteen civil rights campaigners by British army paratroopers on the streets of Derry in 1972—British malevolence now takes centre-stage. According to Ellen E. Sweeney, Greengrass had an 'idealistic motivation...to produce British acknowledgement for their role in Irish suffering'.[44] Indeed, Ken Loach's War of Independence movie *The wind that shakes the barley* (2006) was criticised by prominent Irish historian Roy Foster for what he sees as its historically misleading depiction of violence; of British violence, however, not Irish violence. According to Foster, by beginning the film in 1920 Loach de-contextualises Black and Tan brutality, which was a reaction to the activities of the IRA and not the other way around. Instead, 'the impression created by this film is that Black and Tan rule was the general state of things in Ireland before independence, fully authorised and sanctioned by the authorities—which was not the case'.[45] Foster also critiques the portrayal of IRA men as 'clean-cut, handsome heroes with soft voices' while their opponents 'resemble Nazi storm troopers with Yorkshire and Geordie accents'.[46] Cultural commentator Fintan O'Toole has also criticised British director Steve McQueen's IRA hunger strike film *Hunger* (2008) for being, implicitly, supportive of the Provisional IRA. O'Toole sees McQueen as politically naïve for seeking to engage with the hunger strikes as an 'aesthetic event' and for looking to give them 'a neutral political treatment', as the point of the strikes was to tap into a Christ-like imagery that simplified and distorted a complex political truth, eradicating 'the reality that the prisoners were killers'. By repeating this aesthetic process and de-contextualising the political act of starving oneself to death, the movie simply repeats this mode of IRA propaganda.[47]

Ken Loach's latest directly Irish-themed movie *Jimmy's hall* (2014) centres on the story of Leitrim-man Jimmy Gralton; a socialist organiser who established a cultural centre for dancing and education outside of the control of the Catholic Church in post-independence Ireland, that was subsequently shut down, while Gralton, who had taken American citizenship, was deported. In a 2016 article, Ruth Barton interestingly sees the film as breaking down the binary of Irish-themed movies that deal with either a traumatic past and depict Ireland as a 'traumatic space', or heritage films that depict Ireland as an idyllic, green, pastoral space of soft primitivism. Instead, *Jimmy's hall* reorganises 'heritage principles to produce a narrative that allows for utopian moments to appear within an otherwise conventionally tragic retelling of Irish history'. According to Barton the film also reflects 'a very specific left wing view of Irish history (as a textbook case of the terrible consequences of the imperial endeavour)'.[48] Thus, British depictions of Ireland have come full circle; from representations that downplay colonialism and that situate responsibility for violence in Ireland with the Irish themselves, to more contemporary narratives centring directly on British colonialism, its mechanics and consequences, and that depict Ireland more in terms of traumatic victimhood.

It is perhaps apposite to conclude this discussion with the sole recent German cinematic work to be set partly in Ireland, namely Oskar Roehler's *Elementarteilchen* ('Elementary particles'; 2006)—a film adaptation of Michel Houellebecq's 1999 novel *Les particules elémentaires* (translated into English as *Atomised* in the British edition and *The elementary particles* in the US)—set now, however, in Germany rather than France.[49] While Ireland does not play a central role, its depiction is still significant when seen within the context of Irish film history. The movie deals with two (half-) brothers who react in different ways to their mother's liberal sexuality; one brother becomes a troubled sex obsessive, while the other brother, Michael, is completely asexual but also a scientific genius who dedicates his life to the study of sexless reproduction. Ireland appears here in the manner of a unique scientific-pastoralism; the Irish landscape is depicted as intertwined with innovative science, and Ireland is portrayed as a space in which modern scientific thought merges effortlessly with an idyllic soft primitivism.

Michael leaves his uninteresting job at a research centre in Berlin to return to Ireland, where he had worked at an international research centre and where he had written the 'Clifden Notes'—an unpublished theoretical genetic code from which every species may be reproduced, including people. Thus, Ireland appears here initially as a space of scientific freedom, to which Michael escapes. Next, we see Michael driving along a green Irish landscape bordering the sea, the camera dwelling on the luscious scenery. His final destination, however, beside the sea and placed within this landscape, is what looks like a highly modern research centre. Michael's Irish boss welcomes him back—unlike the earlier German movies, the film changes here into English—and also tells him that he has tested his 'Clifden Notes' and that they are, in fact, correct. In a further scene Michael and his Irish boss are filmed according to typical Irish tropes, namely in front of a green field gazing upon cattle. It becomes apparent, however, that these cattle have been cloned at the research centre, using Michael's genetic code.

In one of the few other Irish scenes the camera focuses on two stereotypical red-haired 'Irish colleens'—these are, however, lab-coated scientist Irish colleens, listening to a paper on genetics. Thus, typical Irish signifiers, such as Catholicism, alcohol and political violence are here nowhere to be seen. Instead, luscious green Irish pastoralism and 'Irish types' merge with a modern European scientific rationality, in what is an unusual Irish scientific-pastoralism. Ireland is here depicted as a modern European space that successfully merges elements of tradition and modernity.

Fergal Lenehan

Conclusion

Pastoralism and violence have, thus, remained central to depictions of Ireland in the cinemas of Britain, Germany and France. Yet, as has been shown, Ireland has more recently been portrayed in a multi-faceted manner. Some directors have actively engaged creatively with the imagery of Irish pastoralism and now look to photograph the Irish landscape in a manner that does not necessarily suggest either an exclusive soft or hard primitivism, while (historical) narratives centring on violence are more likely now to concentrate on British agency and responsibility than inherent Irish culpability. It is hoped that new Irish societal realities of multi-culturalism and emerging secularism may also feature in future filmic narratives.

Indeed, recent international co-productions filmed in Ireland, such as Polish director Urszula Antoniak's mediation on loneliness, *Nothing personal* (2009), and Greek director Yorgos Lanthimos's absurdist dystopian comedy *The lobster* (2015), have utilised Irish settings in ways that go well beyond the narrow confines of social realism. While the integration and analysis of filmic outside perspectives on Irish experience from beyond the English-speaking world remains most welcome, Irish film scholarship should, however, not become overly preoccupied and entrenched within a narrow paradigm of cultural verisimilitude; the filmic text constitutes its own world, its own reality.

Notes

[1] Ruth Barton, 'Introduction: Irish film and media studies publications', *Estudios Irlandeses* 12 (2017), 241–51: 241.

[2] John Hill and Kevin Rockett, 'Introduction', in Kevin Rockett and John Hill (eds), *National cinema and beyond* (Four Courts Press; Dublin and Portland, Oregon, 2004), 9–18: 9.

[3] Luke Gibbons, 'Romanticism, realism and Irish cinema', in Kevin Rockett, Luke Gibbons and John Hill, *Cinema and Ireland* (Routledge; Guildford, 1987), 194–257: 198–202.

[4] John Hill, 'Images of violence', in Kevin Rockett, Luke Gibbons and John Hill, *Cinema and Ireland*, 147–193: 147–9 and 176–7.

[5] Martin McLoone, *Irish film: the emergence of a contemporary cinema* (British Film Institute; London, 2000), 34.

[6] Ruth Barton, *Irish national cinema* (Routledge; London and New York, 2004), 4.

[7] Fergal Lenehan, 'A land and a people of extremes: Ireland and the Irish in German cinema', *Irish Studies Review* 20 (1) (2012), 25–47.

[8] Ruth Barton, 'Screening the Irish in Britain: introduction', *Irish Studies Review* 19 (1) (2011), 1–4: 3.

[9] Lenehan, 'A land and a people of extremes: Ireland and the Irish in German cinema', 27–31.

[10] Barton, 'Screening the Irish in Britain: introduction', 2.

[11] Basil Deardon, *Halfway house* (Ealing Studios; UK, 1944).

[12] Barton, *Irish national cinema*, 80.

[13] Robert Murphy, *British cinema and the Second World War* (Continuum; London and New York, 2000), 181.

[14] Barton, *Irish national cinema*, 80.

[15] Franz Peter Wirth, *Ein Tag, der nie zu Ende geht* (Divina-Film; Germany, 1959).

[16] Wirth, *Ein Tag, der nie zu Ende geht.*

[17] Jens Thiele, 'Die große Versöhnung—Ruth Leuweriks vermittelnde Frauenrollen', in Peter Mänz and Nils Warnecke (eds), *Die ideale Frau: Ruth Leuwerik und das Kino der fünfziger Jahre* (Henschel; Berlin, 2004), 33–40: 38.

[18] Murphy, *British cinema and the Second World War*, 256.

[19] John Sturges, *The eagle has landed* (Associated Films; UK, 1977).

[20] James Naremore, 'American film noir: the history of an idea', *Film Quarterly* 49 (2) (1996), 12–28: 14.

[21] Paul Schrader, 'Notes in film noir', in Barry Keith Grant (ed.), *Film genre reader III* (University of Texas Press; Austin, 2005), 229–43: 235–6, 236.

[22] Liam O'Flaherty, *The puritan* (Jonathan Cape; London, 1932).

[23] Michael F. Kenny, *British film noir guide* (McFarland; Jefferson, North Carolina, 2008), 142–4.

[24] Edward Dimendberg, 'Down these mean streets a man must go: Siegfried Krakauer's "Hollywood's terror films" and the spatiality of film noir', *New German Critique* 89 (2003), 113–43: 117.

[25] Marcia Landy, *British genres: cinema and society, 1930–1960* (Princeton University Press; Princeton, 1991), 119.

[26] Hill, 'Images of violence', 165.

[27] Michael Anderson, *Shake hands with the Devil* (Pennebaker Productions; UK and USA, 1959).

[28] Anderson, *Shake hands with the Devil.*

[29] Anderson, *Shake hands with the Devil.*

[30] Hill, 'Images of violence', 176.

[31] Barton, *Irish national cinema*, 134.

[32] Hill, 'Images of violence', 172.

[33] Roderick Flynn and Patrick Brereton, 'The purple taxi (1977)', in Roderick Flynn and Patrick Brereton, *Historical dictionary of Irish cinema: Historical dictionaries of literature and the arts, no. 17* (Scarecrow Press; Lanham, MD, Toronto and Plymouth, UK), 300.

[34] Mary Lawlor, 'Fitzcarraoldo, Irish explorer', in Ruth Barton (ed.), *Screening Irish-America: representing Irish-America in film and television* (Irish Academic Press; Dublin and Portland, Oregon, 2009), 249–60: 259.

[35] The film played at the Clermont short film festival in 1984, see www.clermont-film-fest.com/ (22 May 2017), and is now also available to view online: www.youtube.com/

watch?v=50FkxFNgvaE&t=47s (14 August 2017). Dominique Boccarossa, in addition to directing short and feature films, has also worked as a set designer and painter. See, Philppe Rège, *Encyclopaedia of French film directors* (2 vols), vol. 1. (A–M). (Scarecrow Press; Lanham, MD, Toronto and Plymouth, UK, 2009), 113.

[36] Barton, *Irish national cinema*, 148.

[37] Barton, *Irish national cinema*, 153.

[38] Barton, *Irish national cinema*, 153.

[39] McLoone, *Irish film*, 59.

[40] Barton, *Irish national cinema*, 131.

[41] James M. Smith, '*The Magdalene sisters*: evidence, testimony ... action?', *Signs: Journal of women in culture and society* 32 (2) (2007), 431–58: 439: 441.

[42] John Hill, 'Routes Irish: "Irishness", "authenticity" and the working class in the films of Ken Loach', *Irish Studies Review* 19 (1) (2011), 99–109: 101, 107.

[43] Bronwen Walter, 'Including the Irish: taken-for-granted characters in English films', *Irish Studies Review* 19 (1) (2011), 5–18: 9.

[44] Ellen E. Sweeney, 'Revisioning vision in the Bloody Sunday films', in John Hill and Kevin Rockett (eds), *Film history and national cinema* (Four Courts Press; Dublin and Portland, Oregon, 2005), 154–64: 161.

[45] Roy Foster, 'The red and the green', in Brenden Barrington (ed.), *The Dublin Review reader* (Dublin Review Books; Dublin, 2007), 151–58: 154.

[46] Foster, 'The red and the green', 153.

[47] Fintan O'Toole, '*Hunger* fails to wrest the narrative from the hunger strikers', *Irish Times*, 28 November 2008; available online at: www.irishtimes.com/news/hunger-fails-to-wrest-the-narrative-from-the-hunger-strikes-1.913725 (27 May 2017).

[48] Ruth Barton, '*Jimmy's hall*, Irish cinema and the telling of history', *Review of Irish Studies in Europe* 1 (1) (2016), 93–106: 93.

[49] Having previously examined this movie in an overly dismissive manner (see, Lenehan, 'A land and a people of extremes', 41), the author thinks it now necessary to reassess this film.

Das Land ohne Musik? Ireland in the European ear

Harry White

In an article headed 'Germany wants more Irish culture. Why can't we deliver?' published in *The Irish Times* on 23 October 2010, Derek Scally begins:

> If the bust of Felix Mendelssohn had feet they would have been tapping along with the music echoing through the vaulted hall below the Irish Embassy in Berlin. In the old home of the Mendelssohn Bank, the new traditional Irish music group

Cirrus give it their all and soon even the German junior minister in row two is jiggling his foot in time with the music.

The evening is a welcome distraction from the doom and gloom about Ireland in the German media, but it's not quite what it seems…

Government agencies do tremendous work promoting Ireland abroad but, looking in from outside, there appears to be a worrying gap between the reality and the lip service the State pays to promoting what makes Ireland uniquely Irish.[1]

Scally goes on to explore the contrast between traditional Irish music in Germany, 'where the hunger for Irish culture is almost insatiable', and the 'apathy' of Irish government initiatives at home in the enterprise of promoting and indeed selling traditional music for a ready market abroad. He makes a persuasive case for traditional music as a commodity whose commercial potential has been underdeveloped in Europe (and above all in Germany), notwithstanding a more general assent to trad as a flagship of Irish culture, so that the music itself, as a living expression of Irish culture and history, remains under-resourced as a means of attracting European tourists to Ireland. At the end of his piece, Scally quotes the traditional musician (and former member of Clannad), Moya Brennan, in ardent support of this reading: 'We have a bank in Ireland called culture, so rich that other countries would dearly love to be able to draw on it. It's a treasure chest that hasn't been opened yet.'[2]

This projection of Irish music as a tourist commodity, as a commercial resource akin to natural spring water or Irish butter (both of which loom large in the export economy between Ireland and Germany), could hardly be said to dismay those whose business it is to exploit Ireland as a tourist destination for continental Europeans. Nevertheless, the equation drawn by Scally and Brennan between Irish music and economic enrichment is worth a moment's further scruple. It rests on the authority and prestige of traditional music as an immensely popular source of entertainment in Germany that is, in turn, underwritten by a concept of cultural authenticity that lends the music itself a status unavailable to (or unattained by) any other kind of Irish musical practice. For many Europeans (to look no further afield), the sound of Ireland *is* its traditional music. The Irish language has long been in abeyance as an easily communicated signature of Irish identity: Irish music, by contrast, enjoys an international currency rivalled by few other agents of Irish culture, with the sovereign exception of Irish writing in English. W.B. Yeats, in an address on the formation of the National Theatre Society published in 1905, blithely exempted 'the peasant, who has his folk-songs and his music' from the more general charge of artistic life 'indentured to a cause'.[3] It is not difficult to see that what might once have appeared a peremptory dismissal of Irish musical culture and its political resonances must now be read otherwise. We can justifiably argue that Yeats—however inadvertently—was uncannily right, and on a scale he could never have envisaged. That is because the unprecedented expansion of popular entertainment in post-war Europe has been strikingly receptive to the growth of an Irish musical tradition (or certain aspects of that tradition) predicated upon music as a recreational alternative to and distraction from the high seriousness of other art forms. In such terms, Irish traditional music is also 'a welcome distraction from doom and gloom', to invoke Scally's own formulation. In this very narrow but very powerful sense, it is an 'other', a soothing refuge from the grave preoccupations of European history itself. Small wonder, perhaps, that it captivates the German popular imagination to the extent that it unmistakably does. In this sense too, traditional music partakes of a neo-romantic version of Ireland (leaving all Irish matters of sombre concern decorously to one side), which the tourist industry cannot but acclaim. This remains the case even when—as Scally argues— much remains to be achieved in the enterprise of exploiting this balm commercially.

In this chapter, my intention is to explore the history of European musical ideas that underlies this state of affairs, if only because the reception of Irish music in Europe is not perhaps as uncomplicated as its present condition appears to suggest. To this end, there are three agents whose influence on the transmission of Irish music in Europe in the nineteenth century helps to explain the consolidation and conventional understanding of the present moment, which is to say that in Europe (and especially in Germany) Irish music is traditional music, and that traditional music is authentic music. These agents are respectively: (1) the circulation and influence of Thomas Moore's writings in Europe, (2) the relationship between Beethoven's Irish folksong settings and German musical idealism, and (3) the intransitive condition of Irish music (including certain of Moore's own songs) in the aftermath of German musical romanticism. All three agents contribute to the equations between Irishness, tradition and cultural authenticity proposed in this chapter. But these equations in turn have eclipsed other modes of Irish musical practice, and most especially Ireland's claim to participate (not least as a nation state) in the discourse of European art music. In attempting to distinguish between this claim, which for many people remains unwarranted and unexamined, and the conventional reception of Irish music in Europe (that is, as a natural resource of great beauty, which gives relief to the careworn travails of the continent itself), I briefly enlist a comparatively recent counter-argument about the nature of Irish musical discourse and its partial eclipse. This alternative reading, as it transpires, also originates in Germany. In this respect, the abiding perception of a 'borrowed musical culture' (in relation to Ireland's aspirations and achievements other than in the domain of popular and traditional modes) is acutely relevant to the problems of reception-history discussed here.

Irish music and European culture: the Moore paradox

Derek Scally may be forgiven for imagining that Felix Mendelssohn's feet would have tapped along to the music heard during the Irish 'Tradfest' in Berlin in 2010, but the truth might well have been otherwise: In a letter of 25 August 1829 to his sister Fanny Hensel, the composer commented on the musical impressions he received during his tour of Scotland and Wales:

> No national music for me! Ten thousand devils take all folkishness! A harper in the hall of every reputed inn playing incessantly so-called folk melodies; that is: infamous, vulgar, out-of-tune trash, with a hurdy-gurdy going at the same time! Anyone, who, like myself, cannot endure

Beethoven's national songs, should come here and listen to them bellowed out by rough, nasal voices, and accompanied with awkward, bungling fingers, and not grumble.[4]

It would be hard not to conclude from such an outburst that for Mendelssohn at least, these sentiments marked the end of German enchantment with the great 'other' of folk music, an 'other' that Mendelssohn himself axiomatically designates as 'national music' in unruly contrast to the supreme condition of *Kunstmusik* ('art music'), notwithstanding his own apotheosis of modality in such works as *Fingal's cave* and the *Scottish* Symphony. The disillusion and contempt that characterise Mendelssohn's apprehension of peasant musical culture in this passage throw into sharp relief the romance and rapture of Germany's earlier engagement with the Bardic ideal in literature and music. As Matthew Gelbart has argued, Mendelssohn's disdain is expressive of a belief not only in the superiority of German art music, but also in its universal condition.[5] Indeed, the centre–periphery model of musical thought that Gelbart locates in the romantic generation of German composers (Mendelssohn and Schumann in particular) entails a drastic relegation of folk music from its idealised status as an originary and universal substratum of European art, to an expression of national culture, in which the marginal or local claim inevitably defers to the universal strength of the German musical imagination. One thinks, for example, of Schumann's reception of Chopin, in which the German composer conceded the presence of a Polish 'physiognomy' in Chopin's earlier works, which would (for Schumann at least) happily disappear into the melting pot of the great tradition of German art music.[6]

Mendelssohn's disavowal of 'national music' in his 1829 letter would seem to belie a long-standing German preoccupation with 'folkishness' that originates in the enthusiastic reception afforded to the Ossianic forgeries of James MacPherson in German literary circles during the 1770s and 1780s. Even if MacPherson's 'translations' from the Gaelic substituted Scottish names and myths for their original Irish prototypes (to the extent that 'Ireland' and 'Scotland' were effectively interchangeable designations in late eighteenth-century Germany, as they had often been previously), this did not attenuate the impact of Gaelic culture in German letters as a proto-romantic stimulus. The rage for Ossian (and the impulse to assimilate Ossian himself as a 'German' bard) shaped German literary idealism for over half a century. From Herder to Goethe, the Ossianic lay represented a degree of poetic emancipation and imaginative regeneration of unrivalled importance in the enterprise of creating a specifically German literature. It was inevitable that such a sea-change in German letters would soon elicit a corresponding echo in German music. By the turn of the nineteenth century, the *ossianische Gesang* was a stable presence in the German musical imagination. German settings of MacPherson's poetry and of verse written in emulation of its Bardic content became commonplace. Beethoven, Schubert and Schumann—the great architects of German musical romanticism—cultivated a radically stylised musical diction answerable to what they perceived as the purity, originality and naturalness of Ossianic poetry. The very concept of 'folksong', adapted from Herder's own essentially linguistic understanding of this phenomenon, came into being as a domesticated German art form. In this process, German music *imagined* Gaelic folksong. When Schubert and Schumann set Ossianic verse, their melodic and harmonic contrivances, as well as their strophic dependencies, were nevertheless self-made. They were not setting Scottish folksongs. They were not arranging Scottish or Irish melodies, as Haydn and Beethoven had done (and only then for a foreign market). On the contrary: German music, in its engagement with the very idea of 'folksong' halted at the borders of its own lyric genius, as if to distinguish between an originary ideal and its imaginative afterlife. Gaelic music (Irish music, Scottish music) remained decisively at one remove.

The publication and dissemination of Thomas Moore's *Irish melodies* between 1808 and 1834 entered a rival claim to this German assimilation of idealised Gaelic prototypes. It is not only that Moore's *Melodies* were wildly popular on the continent: their success (controversial as this was in the British Isles) transcended the exotic condition of European romanticism by representing Irish music not as an ideal but as a sounding form. At one stroke Moore reversed the normative condition of European song by engaging Irish music as the express precondition for his own verse, a process that confounded the 'words first' (*prima le parole*) convention of vocal music on the continent. Moore declared that his avowed intention in publishing the *Melodies* was to 'interpret in verse the touching language of my country's music' (an avocation that inevitably politicised Irish music as an expression of dispossession and loss).[7] The passage from (Irish) music into (English) poetry that resulted from this process would entail fateful (and often fruitful) consequences for the reception of music in Ireland, but in Europe, Moore's verse and the music that inspired it often thereafter led separate lives.[8] In this connection, we are bound to acknowledge what amounts to the paradox of Moore's influence in Europe. Whereas it was Irish music that inspired the poetry of the *Irish melodies*, it was Moore's verse, and not the airs themselves that inspired Hector Berlioz, Robert Schumann, Frederic Chopin and a host of lesser composers throughout Europe in their re-generation of vocal-instrumental music. Julian Rushton has observed in this regard that 'we must count Moore at this time a literary and musical influence on the level of Goethe and Shakespeare'.[9] Beyond the *Melodies*, Moore's *Lalla Rookh* (1817) was no less influential as a catalyst in the development of vocal-dramatic European music. Schumann believed that Moore's epic poem 'was intended for music from the start', a conviction that undoubtedly inspired his own break-through as a dramatic composer, namely his setting (in close German translation) of 'Paradise and the Peri' (*Das Paradies und die Peri*, op. 50 [1843]), the second part of *Lalla Rookh*. In all such enterprises, the German reception of Moore was a literary one, however greatly this impacted upon the music written by German composers themselves. The musical afterlife of the Irish airs versed by Moore was to remain a separate matter.[10]

Works without an opus number: Beethoven's Irish interventions

[S]ince art music established itself as a strong origin-based category, even folkish melody itself needed to be passed through the filter of original genius...if it was to be part of a true masterpiece. As this idea of organic musical high art spread outward from Germany, the German reception tropes that greeted Beethoven's most 'quotational' folkish work at one end, and his most 'original-internalizing' folkish work at the other, also spread and entrenched themselves internationally. ...even in the newest *New Grove* [2001], Beethoven's large corpus of folk song settings comes at the very bottom of the works list—even below the spurious works![11]

It is notable that Beethoven composed more folksong settings than any other genre, and that more of them are Irish than any other nationality.[12]

Ludwig van Beethoven made 71 settings of Irish airs (eight of which are duplicate settings) supplied to him by the Scottish publisher George Thomson between 1809 and 1815, all but seven of which were completed by 1813. Notwithstanding Barry Cooper's critical comprehension of these songs in the mid-1990s and their (very) recent rehabilitation in a series of CDs produced by the DIT Conservatory of Music and Drama, it is fair to remark that these settings were eclipsed from the outset by the success of Moore's *Irish melodies*, to say little of their muted reception-history ever since.[13] They are undoubtedly an important episode in the narrative of German responses to Irish music (of which more below), but they illustrate by contrast not only the success enjoyed by Moore's settings (until his own songs went into decline) but more especially—as I would wish to argue here—the organic idealism that animated Beethoven's imagination through the agency of generic models that privileged (and radically re-shaped) instrumental music. Beethoven's later contemporaries or near-contemporaries (as in the case of Mendelssohn) axiomatically distinguished between the *Kunstmusik* (or 'higher music') of his symphonies, string quartets, piano sonatas and chamber music (carefully retrieved and catalogued as a sequence of highly significant and hugely influential opus numbers), and the routine commissions represented by his folksong arrangements (which, for Beethoven and his editors, did not warrant the privilege of an opus number).[14]

We might press this distinction between Beethoven's own regard for his original compositions and his folksong arrangements further by noting that his Irish settings were written for foreign (that is, British) consumption, and not intended to form part of the organic unfolding of his genius. This is not to suggest that Beethoven was indifferent to these settings, but it is to argue that in the end, his own conception of 'folk music', vitally re-imagined in the 'Ode to joy' that crowns the ninth symphony, was a romantic invention, which took precedence over his encounter with the airs supplied to him by Thomson. When Beethoven dramatically reunited words and music in this work, which effectively brought his contribution to the genre to a utopian end, he turned to Schiller and his own imaginative reliances. Once again, a German composer had idealised the music of the 'folk' rather than have recourse to the real thing. In this process, the marginal condition of Beethoven's Irish folksongs became more extreme than ever. Despite the magnitude of the composer's influence in German musical affairs throughout the nineteenth century (and ever since), his own engagement with Irish music had very little impact on its reception in Europe. And when we consider this engagement afresh (as in the recent recordings issued by the DIT Conservatory of Music and Drama), we stumble upon a degree of incompatibility between Beethoven's musical discourse and the airs themselves, which was there from the start.

In this regard, Barry Cooper has cited correspondence between Beethoven and his publisher, which arose when Thomson requested him to revise the original settings Beethoven had sent him. An early setting of 'Tis but in vain' (1810), for example, elicited the following exchange between publisher and composer (Thomson first):

> Here the ritornellos for the piano, though fine, are much too brilliant. The roulade should be replaced, for the song is of a tender and plaintive character. Allow me then, to ask you for ritornellos in a simple, flowing and cantabile style.

To which, Beethoven responded (in French):

> I am not accustomed to retouching my compositions; I have never done so, thoroughly convinced that any partial change alters the character of the composition. I am sorry that you are the loser, but you cannot blame me, since it

was up to you to make me better acquainted with the taste of your country and the meagre facility of your performers. Now, armed with your information, I have composed them entirely anew and I hope, in a manner that answers your expectations.[15]

Whatever concessions Beethoven may have made to the 'character' of the airs communicated to him by Thomson, it is hard to supervene the disconnect between the composer's technique and the original melodies, which all too readily manifests itself when we listen to these songs now, two centuries after they first appeared. One musical constituent invariably impedes the other, a problem exacerbated by the purity and/or simplicity of diction these airs have enjoyed (in Germany as well as elsewhere) in the interim. Beethoven's settings, to coin a phrase, are Irish music conveyed through the inadvertence of a pronounced German accent.[16]

In an intransitive mood: German variations on an Irish air

If Beethoven drew Irish music too closely to the template of his own art, European composers in his wake did otherwise. In fact, German and Italian composers who had settled in Ireland since the early eighteenth century had been long accustomed to arranging Irish airs for various combinations of instrumental ensemble (the earliest extant collection of 'the most celebrated Irish airs' for violin, oboe and continuo was published in Dublin in 1724). Nevertheless, the romance and refuge of the Irish air in the long nineteenth century (and in the immediate aftermath of German sovereignty in the domain of instrumental music) comprises a special category of European composition in relation to Irish music, which has only recently received the (scholarly) attention it deserves. Given the evidence that this research suggests, it is not too much to add that European composers in general (and German composers in particular) formed the habit of 'listening' to Irish music through the simple expedient of writing idiomatic variations (especially for piano) on traditional Irish airs, which were first presented as the theme on which the remainder of such compositions explicitly depended.

An early example of this theme-and-variations approach to Irish music by the composer Frederic Hoffmann was published in Dublin c. 1810. Hoffmann's composition is entitled 'Les fruits de loisir or The groves of Blarney' and it predates by three years Thomas Moore's setting of the same melody as 'The last rose of summer' in the fifth volume of the Irish melodies (1813).[17] What strikes the ear as well as the eye throughout Hoffmann's variations is the intransitive condition of the Irish tune in apposition with the (then) contemporary idiom of the piano writing. For all the ebullience and versatility of the keyboard figuration, the tune remains intact throughout. It is adorned but not developed. Rather it is fully formed, a definitive version (as it were) that remained constant in the hundreds of settings it would subsequently attract from European composers for a century afterwards.

The relations between this air and the variations it inspired can help to gloss the term 'intransitive' as one that describes a stable feature of the traditional repertory. 'The last rose of summer' is the title of Moore's lyric verse; 'The groves of Blarney' is the title under which the tune appeared in an early print from the collector, publisher and composer Smollett Holden, c. 1803; 'The young man's dream' is the title of the earliest printed source for the tune, namely Edward Bunting's Ancient music of Ireland, in which the tune first appears in a (rudimentary) arrangement for piano (1796–97). It was Bunting who transcribed the air from the harper Denis Hempson during the Belfast Harp Festival of 1792, even if this transcription—insofar as it is reflected in Bunting's 1796–97 version—differs in significant detail but not in essence from the version popularised by Holden and Moore.[18]

This miniature source-study illustrates a general principle of Irish traditional music that can scarcely be overlooked if we are to understand its reception-history after 1800, namely, that once a tune entered general circulation through the agency of music notation, its transmission thereafter was consolidated and exact. This principle occluded the oral transmission of the repertory to a decisive degree, at least to judge by the fixed forms it assumed in the wake of Bunting's publications. As a compelling witness to this stability, one can summon 'The last rose of summer' itself, unchanged in its musical morphology between 1810 (at the latest) and the present day. (By instructive contrast, almost any tune from Bunting's collections adapted by Moore—including this one—underwent significant alterations from source to song, a process that more narrowly reflects the oral tradition itself).[19]

But there are two other aspects to the term 'intransitive' that apply to this representation of Irish music in nineteenth-century Europe. The first of these concerns a centre–periphery reading of musical experience fomented by the organic idealism and sovereignty of German instrumental music across the continent between 1800 and 1918. The prestige attached to 'art music' (or 'higher music') in Germany during the nineteenth century required (or entailed) a corresponding relief from the serious business of original composition when it came to arranging or varying Irish airs. (As a public figure, the political and social significance of the artist-as-hero embodied by Beethoven would ultimately and unerringly extend to Richard Wagner).[20] Art music was the domain of public consciousness, psychological insight and historical interpretation. 'Folk music' was the refuge of innocence. In this binary pairing, the present tense of European musical discourse could represent and act upon 'folk music' as a sounding icon of romantic otherness. Folk music, and in particular Irish music, became a musical object, engaged in a dialectical relationship with the storm and stress of the German musical imagination. Small wonder, perhaps, that its beguiling signatures of modal purity were so carefully preserved. And when the European composer encountered the Irish air (so to speak), he did so through the medium of a musical compromise, namely the salon show piece or expressive reminiscence. On such occasions, the serious business of original composition was not in play.

The other intransitive aspect of Irish traditional music, which its European circulation helped to confirm, was (and is) its organic intransigence. Traditional Irish music bears and promotes repetition (to a degree that attests its early eighteenth-century origins, especially in relation to fixed dance forms), but it does not accommodate development. Its signatures are too well-formed and complete to facilitate such a compositional impulse. But even if one were to dispute this completeness (or this limitation, depending on one's point of view), one could scarcely mistake or underestimate the evidence of European musical history that—as in the case of 'The last rose of summer'—loudly confirms the *a priori* condition of Irish music in the context of its European afterlife. This condition, as Axel Klein has recently demonstrated in a magisterial survey and catalogue of European settings of 'The last rose of summer', encouraged a sub-genre of composition (frequently marketed under such titles as *Souvenir d'Irlande* or *Erinnerungen an Irland*) in which the 'domestic' technique of the composer played host to his 'recollection' of Ireland through the agency of variations on an Irish air.[21]

In the case of 'The last rose of summer', Klein catalogues 205 works by various composers from 1810 until 1913 (most, although not all, of which are based on the air itself) and attributes its remarkable popularity in the second half of the nineteenth century to the song's appearance in Friedrich von Flotow's (German) opera, *Martha* (1847).[22] *Martha* appears to have acted as a unique stimulus, to judge by the number of instrumental variations on the air published in Germany and France in the aftermath of the opera's great success, but before and after *Martha* it is the melody itself that calls attention to the in-transitive nature of 'the Irish air', even in those settings in which the composer's technique completely departs the morphology of the tune. Thus, in Mendelssohn's piano fantasia on 'The last rose of summer' (1827), the air periodically reoccurs in its original guise and tempo as a reassurance against the florid (and often athematic) 'variations' that adjoin it.

An inaudible art: Irish musical identity in Europe

> Irish folk-song and the bardic music of the seventeenth and eighteenth centuries seems to have fixed itself on the popular imagination, lending to this country a reputation for musical culture that it does not yet possess. Nicely-turned phrases, such as 'our music-loving people' and 'our heritage of music' have made this legend a household word. Nobody likes to hear that *this* is the land without music, a land that is literally music-starved (Aloys Fleischmann in 1936).[23]

> What remains is the sad fact that Ireland is possibly one of the very few countries in which the people are deprived of their own classical musical heritage. To put it more plainly,

whereas virtually every other Western country can listen
to its own musical past, Ireland—apart from its ethnic traditions—cannot (Axel Klein in 2005).[24]

The identity formation that Irish music achieved in Europe during the
long nineteenth century would not count for much if its cultural authority solely depended on a handful of Moore songs and other airs
scattered through the annals of German and French salon music as the
century wore on. But this authority deepened in the second half of the
twentieth century. The romantic otherness and refuge of Irish music in
Europe became a principle of reception exclusively located within the
tradition itself as a re-imagined and reanimated alternative to the rival
claims of popular culture and the collapse of German musical sovereignty (other than as an abiding and vigorous expression of museum
culture). Although the popularity of Irish traditional music in Germany
today appears as a *donnée* (as in the excerpts from Derek Scally's *Irish
Times* piece cited at the outset of this chapter), the cultural significance
of this popularity remains unresearched to a significant degree. The
neo-romantic condition of Irish traditional music (as a recreational
distraction from the [di]stress of urban culture) exerts an appeal that
is virtually self-evident, to judge by its enormous (if under-exploited)
success as an export commodity, but the commercial potential of Irish
music leaves something to be desired if we seek an explanation for this
success in other terms.

Such an explanation would invariably engage the culture of folk
music revival across Europe and the US from the early 1960s onwards,
and it would likewise seek to comprehend the practical reinvention
of Irish traditional music as an ensemble art through the agency (and
sheer musical prowess) of bands such as The Chieftains, Planxty and
Clannad (as well as individual musicians including Donal Lunny,
Christy Moore, Bill Whelan and Moya Brennan, among very many
others) during the same period.[25] But this narrative would also require
an answering echo from the continent, beyond the existential (and
manifest) appeal of Irish traditional music as an auditory image of
Ireland itself. If 'Ireland in the European ear' is traditional music (or
neo-traditional music, given its newfound absorption of other musical
genres, notably rock music, as well as its decisively and stylishly

expanded instrumental palette, drawn in some instances from the continent itself), we can hardly maintain Fleischmann's impassioned insistence back in 1936 that Ireland was (or is) the 'country without music' (*Das Land ohne Musik*). But we might be prompted (following Axel Klein in 2005), to propose instead that Ireland—at least in terms of European reception-history—remains 'the country without *art* music' (*Das Land ohne Kunstmusik*).

Klein's work over the past twenty years affords another vital gloss on the phrase 'Ireland in the European ear' (and in the European mind, for that matter), because it probes—initially from the vantage point of a German and German-trained musicologist—the hidden history of Irish musical discourse *other than as an assent to the romantic sovereignty of the tradition itself.* Although Klein is assuredly no longer alone in this enterprise, his monographs and catalogues on Irish art music in the twentieth century and on Irish classical recordings, his biographical studies of Irish composers in Europe, together with a steady stream of articles, essays, lexical entries and reviews, comprise a formidable (and patiently achieved) dissolution of the axiomatic equation as yet obtaining between Irish music and Irish traditional music.[26] 'As things stand', Klein writes in a recently published (2016) essay entitled 'No state for music', 'we must find an explanation as to why the majority of Irish people seem to think they have no history of classical music'.[27]

I would not wish to soften this imperative or diminish its importance at the close of a chapter preoccupied by the reception of Irish music in Europe, but I would argue that the pervasive domestic indifference to Irish art music (that is, Ireland's historic and contemporary engagement with classical European genres) is complicated and even ratified by the European reception-history I have outlined here. In Germany, 'where the hunger for Irish culture is almost insatiable' (Scally), and throughout Europe, the Irish musical soundscape remains a traditional soundscape, at least insofar as any national representation worth the name continues to be relevant. This abiding European enchantment with the musical 'other' is unlikely to be displaced, however much we might deplore its apparently restrictive influence at home.

Notes

[1] See, Derek Scally, 'Germany wants more Irish culture', *The Irish Times*, 23 October 2010; available online at: www.irishtimes.com/news/germany-wants-more-irish-culture-why-can-t-we-deliver (7 November 2017).

[2] See, Scally, 'Germany wants more Irish culture', np.

[3] See, W.B. Yeats, 'Samhain: 1903', in Mary Fitzgerald and Richard J. Finneran (eds), *W.B. Yeats. The Irish dramatic movement* (Scribner; New York and London, 2005), 20–6: 23.

[4] Cited in Matthew Gelbart, *The invention of 'folk music' and 'art music'. Emerging categories from Ossian to Wagner* (Cambridge University Press; Cambridge, 2007), 248.

[5] Gelbart remarks that in such passages Mendelssohn 'had come to use "national music" (and even "folk" in this particular context) as inherently local and coarse, directly opposed to the absolute art music history he cared so much about'. See, Gelbart, *The invention of 'folk music' and 'art music'*, 248.

[6] See, Robert Schumann, *Gesammelte Schriften über Musik und Musiker* ed. H. Simon, Leipzig, 1888, vol. I, 188, cited in Carl Dahlhaus, *Between romanticism and modernism: four studies in music of the later nineteenth century*, transl. Mary Whittall (University of California Press; Berkeley CA, 1984), 84.

[7] Cited in the preface to the second edition of *Moore's Irish melodies. With symphonies and accompaniments for the pianoforte by Michael William Balfe* (London: Novello, Ewer and Co., 1865), v.

[8] For a reading of Moore's literary and musical influence in Europe, see, Harry White, *Music and the Irish literary imagination* (Oxford University Press; New York and Oxford, 2008), 35–78. On Moore's songs and their musical and literary sources, see, Una Hunt, *Sources and style in Moore's Irish melodies* (Routledge: New York, 2017).

[9] See, Julian Rushton, 'Berlioz and Irlande: from romance to mélodie', in Patrick F. Devine and Harry White (eds), *The Maynooth international musicological conference 1995, selected proceedings: part two* Irish Musical Studies, vol. 5 (Four Court Press; Dublin, 1996), 224–40: 240. It is relevant to add that the term *Mélodie* has been used in France to designate art songs following the composition in 1829 of Berlioz's short song cycle (*Irlande*), which comprises nine settings of Moore's verse (from the *Irish melodies*) translated by Thomas Gounet.

[10] On Moore's literary influence in Germany, see, White, *Music and the Irish literary imagination*, 57–67.

[11] Gelbart, *The invention of 'folk music' and 'art music'*, 224.

[12] See, Barry Cooper, 'Beethoven's folksong settings as sources of Irish folk music', in Devine and White (eds), *The Maynooth international musicological conference 1995, selected proceedings: part two*, 65–81: 65.

[13] For information on the Beethoven recordings issued by the DIT in 2014, see, www.beethovensirishsongs.ie (7 November 2017). Beethoven's settings were originally published by Thomson in 1814 and 1816.

[14] For a discussion of this distinction between 'higher music' and 'folk music', see, Gelbart, *The invention of 'folk music' and 'art music'*, 234–5.

[15] Cited in Cooper, 'Beethoven's folksong settings', 69–70.

[16] It is obviously difficult to develop this reading here, but my own impression of the Beethoven songs in performance (on the occasion of the launch of the DIT recordings in April 2014) was one in which the incompatibility between the airs and their stilted representation at Beethoven's hands was emphasised. ('Beethoven at his best' was the sardonic response of one Beethoven expert present on this occasion).

[17] A copy of Hoffmann's variations is held in the National Library of Ireland (call number Add Mus 6171); the NLI catalogue records that it was published by Paul Alday in Dublin in 1810. This copy is available online (in PDF format) from the National Archive of Irish Composers, and can be accessed at the following link: https://arrow.dit.ie/cgi/viewcontent.cgi?referer=https://www.google.ie/&httpsredir=1&article=1021&context=naiccomp (9 September 2018).

[18] For further details of the source relationship between Bunting, Holden and Moore, see, Hunt, *Sources and style in Moore's Irish melodies*, and Veronica Ní Chinnéide, 'The sources of Moore's melodies', *Journal of the Royal Society of Antiquaries in Ireland* 89 (2) (1959), 109–34.

[19] Moore's alterations to the tempo and character of the airs as he found them in Bunting were much to Bunting's chagrin.

[20] For a classic reading of the composer's public status in Germany and throughout Europe, see, Scott Burnham, *Beethoven Hero* (Princeton University Press; Princeton NJ, 1995). Wagner's vast influence in the development of music, poetry, fiction and the spoken drama in France and Germany would have been inconceivable were it not for the prominence afforded to the composer in European cultural affairs throughout the nineteenth century.

[21] See Axel Klein, '"All her lovely companions are faded and gone". How "The last rose of summer" became Europe's favourite Irish melody', in Brian Carraher and Sarah McCleave (eds), *Thomas Moore and romantic inspiration* (Routledge; New York, 2017), 132–45. On the sub-genre of musical 'recollections' or 'souvenirs' of Ireland, Klein writes as follows: 'If, however, a foreign composer used an Irish traditional melody in the nineteenth century, this could have two possible meanings: either the composer wanted to add an "exotic" element to his music or he/she was also a travelling performer and intended to greet his audience in Ireland with a kind gesture of acknowledgement—while later providing his audience back home with a "souvenir piece" of his travels. Some composers like Ferdinand Ries, François-Joseph Dizi, Louis Spohr, and Frédéric Kalkbrenner wrote pieces inspired by Irish traditional music after visits to or short-term residences in England, and they did not confuse English with Irish music... [T]here are souvenir pieces that aren't souvenirs at all, such as Carl Czerny's Reminiscences of Ireland Opus 675 for piano in 1842, written by the composer without his ever having set foot on Irish soil', 129.

[22] See, Klein, 'Appendix 1', in Carraher and McCleave (eds), *Thomas Moore and romantic inspiration*.

[23] Aloys Fleischmann, 'Ars nova', *Ireland Today* 1 (July 1936), 41–8: 41.

[24] Axel Klein, 'Stage-Irish, or the national in Irish opera, 1780–1925', *The Opera Quarterly* 21 (1) (2005), 27–67.

[25] Harry White and Barra Boydell (eds), *The encyclopaedia of music in Ireland* (University College Dublin Press; Dublin, 2013), contains extensive entries on the ensembles and musicians named here, as well as comprehensive surveys of traditional

music from its original recension in the late seventeenth century to the present day.
[26] A complete list of the author's publications, in addition to information about his current research, is available at: www.axelklein.de (9 September 2018).
[27] See, Axel Klein, 'No state for music', in Michael Dervan (ed.), *The invisible art: a century of music in Ireland, 1916–2016* (New Island Press; Dublin, 2016), 47–68: 48.

PART IV

European Studies, Tourism and Journalism

European Studies in Irish universities

Edward Moxon-Browne

At the outset, it is worth reminding ourselves of the origins and principal characteristics of the academic field known as European Studies. Its essential multidisciplinarity has been based in the firm conviction that the patterns and processes of European integration are only properly understood if the contribution made to them by a range of traditional academic disciplines is fully acknowledged. This in turn stems from the nature of the European integration process itself, which is rooted in the neo-functionalist belief that economic forces can bring about political change that, in turn, creates new social realities in terms of loyalties, expectations and new power relationships. In addition, these processes are influenced by historical experiences, expressed in new geographical configurations, and defined by new legal structures. Thus, subjects most commonly involved in European Studies have been, *inter alia*, politics, economics, history, sociology, law, geography, literature and languages. There are, however, few limits to what European Studies may encompass in view of its role in preparing graduates for life and work in the European Union or in countries affected by its existence.[1] Thus, academic fields as disparate as women's studies, finance, agriculture, security studies, or public administration may plausibly, and beneficially, be included in a European Studies degree. So, from its beginnings in Ireland in 1974, European Studies was to be based on a multidimensional interpretation of contemporary European reality. Inevitably, over time, the emphases of this multifaceted characteristic varied and evolved. Nevertheless, it is possible to identify a consistent model involving a language (or languages) as core subjects and a varying number of ancillary subjects attached to them.[2]

The story of European Studies in Irish universities since 1974 mirrors, to some extent, the experience of Irish membership of the European Union. We can detect an early phase of enthusiasm linked to a strongly perceived need to prepare graduates for living and working with, and within, the countries of the EU. This entailed a focus on policy-making, on understanding how the EU institutions operated, and on the best ways to derive benefits from new trading opportunities offered by the increasing consolidation of the European single market. Since about 2008, however, a number of factors have combined to dilute and diversify the hitherto strict attention to the 'mechanics' of membership and transform European Studies (especially at the graduate level) into something more reflective, but also more specialised, in the sense that formerly multidisciplinary degrees have been replaced by programmes focusing on discrete disciplinary themes, such as law or regional development.

Among factors contributing to this dilution have been, first, the success of Irish membership of the EU, and the concomitant 'Celtic Tiger' phenomenon that created a certain complacency that found expression in negative referendum results and a somewhat arrogant belief that 'they' (that is other EU countries and especially the new East European member-states) had much more to learn from Ireland's success than Ireland did from them. Second, and more recently, the bracing experience of supervision by the 'Troika' (comprising the European Central Bank, International Monetary Fund and European Commission) caused public opinion to doubt if the EU was any longer an undisputed 'good thing'; with students, anecdotally at least, beginning to question why they needed to study something that had apparently failed to cement the prosperity generated by the boom of the Tiger years. Ironically, at a time when it was (is) arguably more important than ever to understand the implications of Ireland's EU membership, and especially the permanent and beneficial sharing of sovereignty involved therein, the focus of university curricula on matters European has tended to be somewhat dissipated. To be fair, Ireland's tendency to accord less priority to its EU membership has not been helped by severe budgetary constraints in the higher-education sector, nor by the development of new curricular themes that seemingly offered a welcome relief from the tedious troubles of a turbulent Eurozone: themes such as the environment and climate change, human rights, the developing world, and new perspectives on global peace and security. As we shall see below, the evolution of university postgraduate curricula, in particular from 2008 onwards, has reflected these wider developments.

Resource constraints have also discouraged risking the relatively greater costs that interdisciplinary programmes inevitably incur; they have also contributed to a disciplinary 'siege mentality', whereby academics tend to hold on to what they do they best (teach their own subjects) instead of following the more perilous path of trans-disciplinary cooperation that lies at the heart of any credible European Studies programme. Budgetary retrenchment in the age of austerity has also led to a general decline in the international standing of Irish universities in widely publicised league tables. While one may quibble with one or other of these 'objective' indicators, collectively they tell a rather depressing story. To mention them is not to argue for their infallibility: but any serious assessment of European Studies education in Ireland today needs to take into account this rather gloomy context. Third, as we live in an international market-place, and if students cannot find what they are looking for in Ireland, there are thriving postgraduate European Studies degrees abroad in third-level institutions such as the ZEI in Bonn, Germany, the University of Lund, Sweden, the College of Europe in Bruges, Belgium, and the European University Institute in Florence, Italy.[3]

Postgraduate courses

Postgraduate courses in European Studies in Ireland have tended to evolve more incrementally than undergraduate programmes, in which, as we shall see, there is considerable continuity. One reason for the more fluid evolution of postgraduate programmes has been a perception that these programmes need to be more 'relevant' to the needs of the labour market. This supposition is based on the assumption that students proceed to a postgraduate degree to prepare themselves for a particular career choice, for which the undergraduate degree has been too broad and insufficiently focussed. As noted at the outset, we can see a process whereby postgraduate programmes in European Studies have generally moved away from being specifically attuned to the needs of the EU institutions in the context of EU membership, and towards either more 'academic' approaches, or being more sharply focussed on a particular discipline. Thus, at University College Dublin (UCD), Trinity College Dublin (TCD) and the University of Limerick (UL), until recently, postgraduate programmes were geared to bridging the gap between academe and the demands of the EU institutions. For example, an early MSc Econ degree run jointly by TCD and UCD routinely included civil servants among its student body.

This joint degree was superseded by one at UCD entitled MEconSc in European Economic and Public Affairs. It included a tight focus on the policy-making processes of the EU; it provided two study trips (one to the European University Institute (EUI) in Florence, and one to Brussels) thus giving students an opportunity to make early and fruitful contacts with policy-makers, among whom many would eventually be working. This link with 'real world' exigencies was cemented by a series of scholarships, provided to UCD by the Irish government, to enable young high-fliers from the 'accession countries' to benefit from relevant training in Dublin. This process ran in parallel with visits by East European civil servants to government departments in Dublin, and missions by Irish policy-makers to help accession countries prepare for membership. This was a time when the Irish economy was displaying precocious growth and allowing Ireland to be seen as a template for emerging economies.

A number of factors changed the status of postgraduate programmes in European Studies in Ireland, however. The demise of the Celtic

Tiger took the shine off Ireland as a role-model; cutbacks in financing for higher education generally made it more difficult to support programmes at the same level; public opinion was turning against the EU, partly as a result of Ireland no longer being a net beneficiary from the EU structural funds, and partly from a misplaced popular scepticism that underestimated the value of the EU to Ireland. One reaction to the dilution of European Studies programmes was the attempt to recoup student numbers by offering alternative programmes: Peace and Development Studies at UL; Development Studies at UCC, European Regional and Minority Cultures at UCD, a bifurcation of the UCD programme into an MA/MSc offering two alternative 'tracks'; and European Employment Studies at TCD. One apparent exception to the apparent splintering and dissipation of postgraduate programmes in European Studies was a new MPhil degree at TCD (discussed below).

Today (2019) there remain four European Studies programmes at the postgraduate level that merit consideration. The MA in European Politics and Policy at UCD is a 90-credit taught degree normally taken in one academic year. The aims of the programme are to recruit students for careers in which a deep and comprehensive knowledge of European and EU politics is essential.[4] In addition, graduates are trained to appraise critically events and developments in European integration. The course provides a well-grounded knowledge of the issues facing European governments, and of how European political systems address challenges in an increasingly Europeanised and globalised world. In the first semester, students take three 10-credit modules and one 5-credit module on 'dissertation design'. In the second semester, students take three 10-credit modules and write a dissertation (worth 25 credits), making a total of 90 credits for the two semesters. Among the many optional modules available are: comparative European politics; EU foreign and security policy; international political theory; political violence; the geopolitics of Brexit; and the law and governance of the EU. Instead of writing a dissertation, students may opt for an internship over the summer months at a host organisation approved by UCD.

At Dublin City University (DCU), the MA in European Law and Policy (MELP) is a 90-credit programme that aims to integrate legal and policy analysis and to equip students with skills across both fields. The syllabus is designed to make sure that students have a grounding in EU law and policy analysis but allows for some specialisation in one field, or the other, through optional modules offered and the dissertation topic selected. In the first semester, three core modules are required, covering EU law, public policy analysis and research methods in both fields. In the second semester, students choose three optional modules from a range of eight, including, for example, environmental law and policy; EU employment law; EU migration and asylum law; politics of the euro; and EU foreign and security policy. A dissertation module worth 30 credits contributes to the total of 90 credits for the year.[5]

At UL, the MA in European Politics and Governance is a one-year, full-time programme and consists of seven components taken over three semesters. In the first semester, students take two core modules (institutions and policies in the EU and research methods), and one elective module. In the second semester, students take four modules: two core modules—European governance and research methods—and two electives from a range that includes *inter alia*: multi-level governance; comparative politics; peace building; external relations of the EU; foreign aid and development; representative democracy in Europe; and international political economy. In the summer semester, a dissertation of about 15,000 words is written under the direction of an appropriately qualified supervisor. The MA provides students with advanced understanding of how European societies are governed through the complex interaction between public and private actors at different levels of government. The ability of national governments to determine domestic policy is increasingly limited by the interdependence with local and European levels of government. Moreover, the distinction between governmental and non-governmental actors is now more blurred, with the implementation of policy relying more heavily on the cooperation of private actors.[6]

The MPhil at TCD is a 90-credit, full-time programme lasting one academic year. It is built around a substantial core module (20 credits) that extends over both semesters and is entitled 'Europe and its Others'. The purpose of this core module is to explore various aspects of the construction of 'Europe' as an idea, a utopia, and a political project, as well as a form of identity. The main theme of this course is the construction of Europe, as opposed to an imagined Other, seen in cultural, geographic, ethnic and racial terms in different periods through history. The course

Edward Moxon-Browne

aims to present the dynamics of exclusion and inclusion in practice, and to investigate the way such practices shape the development of the idea and portrayal of Europe in European culture. In addition to this core module, students follow four optional modules (two in each semester) from a range linked to the central theme of identity. Among these quite varied optional modules are: figurations of European national identities; memory and identity in central Europe; Spain's European identity; EU–Russia relations; and cultural representations of the Mafia. In addition, some approved options in other schools are available to students, such as: modern literature in East Central Europe; Classics and European identity; and gender, war and peace. In addition to this coursework, a dissertation (30 credits) of 15,000 to 20,000 words is also required.[7]

Undergraduate courses

At the time of writing (2019), there are four BA European Studies degrees in Irish universities: Limerick, TCD, Cork and Maynooth. These programmes share some features regarding both structure and content. All four include a compulsory language element; all four are multidisciplinary; and all four require students to spend some time abroad. It is, however, worth discussing in more detail the differences between these degrees, because each has its own distinctive emphasis.

The BA degree at Limerick is the longest-established European Studies programme still extant in Europe, having been established in 1974. Six semesters are spent on campus and two are spent off-campus on language study in a foreign country and in a work placement. The degree is built around a core European Studies module stream, and a language stream in which one language (French, German, Spanish) is paired with a choice of three disciplines chosen from history, sociology, law or economics. Alternatively, students can choose to follow two languages, one of which can be Irish, and just two disciplinary subjects. For their language study abroad, students normally participate in the Erasmus programme, and for the work experience semester, students may choose to visit a country outside the European Union where the relevant language is spoken (for example Colombia is an option for students of Spanish). In the final year, the student writes a project on a suitably European theme and, in addition to a language module, a wide selection of disciplinary modules can be selected, such as history, politics. sociology, cultural studies, or teaching English as a foreign language.[8]

The BA at Trinity College Dublin requires students to select two languages from among French, Spanish, German or Italian, and these are pursued throughout the four-year programme, although one language is designated as the 'major' language from year two onwards. In the first year, students follow three compulsory disciplinary modules: Europe 1500 to 1800, introduction to social science, and introduction to the history of ideas. In year two, language study continues alongside two compulsory modules (Making modernity 1752–1820 and modern European history), plus a choice from a series of modules such as Europe and the world 1860–1970, comparative politics, international relations, the Hundred Years War, and gender, work and family. The third year is spent studying abroad at a partner institution in the country of the major language. The year abroad is seen as a key component in the European Studies degree, since competency is provided in the chosen language as well as in the ability to adapt to a new educational and cultural environment. In the final year, study of the major and minor languages continues. In addition, students take one compulsory module: Modernity and society, ideas and culture in Europe since 1850, and one or two optional modules from a wide range of topics, including, for example, Germany from democracy to dictatorship 1918–39; Art, gender and the body in mediaeval and Renaissance Italy; European Union politics; French cinema; madness and literature; contemporary international relations; Islam and gender; and monsters and metamorphosis in German literature.[9]

At UCC, the four-year European Studies degree is anchored in the School of History, although geography, law, business and development are also involved. In the first year, students explore the processes and consequences of political, diplomatic, administrative, socio-economic and environmental decision-making in Europe. In year two, the core modules are methodologies, data study and research, and the model EU. Year two electives include a range of topics such as the EU and the international system, comparative European politics, Mediterranean politics, the 1989 revolutions, political and economic Europe, geography and tourism, contemporary European migration, and economic

Edward Moxon-Browne

and rural development. In year three, students spend their time at a foreign university relevant to their choice of language. In year four, students write a dissertation and choose two electives, for example Ireland and international relations, European foreign policy, regional and local planning, Northern Ireland, international relations, and the law of the European Union.[10]

The BA in European Studies at Maynooth is built around a language stream (a choice from French, German or Spanish) and a number of electives extending across subjects as disparate as anthropology, classics, history, geography and sociology. In the first year, students take the following core modules: introduction to European Studies, and big ideas in European Studies. As in other European Studies programmes, time is spent abroad on language study, but a distinctive feature of the Maynooth degree is a field trip to the EU institutions in Brussels. This enables students to make early, and potentially fruitful, contacts with politicians and policymakers among whom graduates may eventually be employed.[11]

This brief survey of some of the major BA European Studies programmes inevitably raises the question as to what students are seeking when they embark on such a degree programme. What all these degrees have in common is the acquisition of fluency in one (or two) European languages, linked to a study of the political, cultural and economic contexts in which these languages might be used: international finance, tourism, banking, commerce, and any public authority that has dealings with its European counterparts, such as county councils, universities and semi-state bodies. For anyone wishing to work in, or around, or in a direct relationship with, the EU institutions in Brussels, a European Studies degree is often seen as an ideal preparation. Interestingly, however, the Central Applications Office (CAO) entry points for European Studies degrees seem to suggest that curricular content relevant to an understanding of 'how Brussels works' is not a key factor in guiding student choice. The TCD curriculum, which has no required study of the European Union, commanded a 520-point CAO entry level in 2017, while UL (at 370 points) and Maynooth (at 340 points), both include much more EU-specific content. What this suggests is that 'employability' may not (despite what is often assumed) be the key factor in guiding student choice. If not, it may be the oft-quoted 'student experience' or the perceived 'reputation' of the university that guides students in their choice of university.[12]

In view of the requirement that students should travel abroad for language study, it is not surprising that a key component of undergraduate education in European Studies has been the Erasmus programme. Over three million students have benefited from the Erasmus mobility exchanges since they were established in 1987. Since then, the numbers of students and countries involved has risen steadily, from just over 3,000 students and eleven countries in 1987 to over 250,000 annually today, with 33 countries involved (the 28 EU member-states plus Iceland, Liechenstein, Norway, Switzerland and Turkey). Another feature of the programme, since 2007, has been the support for work placements—now accounting for about one in six of all Erasmus exchanges. The programme can be seen, therefore, as partly an attempt to enhance EU labour mobility by familiarising young graduates with foreign labour markets, but partly (although intangibly) as an effort to create a 'transnational society' that is less conscious of the limitations of national borders. EU Education Commissioner Androulla Vassiliou touched on these themes in alluding to the various benefits of Erasmus:

> By enabling students to spend a period studying or working abroad, Erasmus provides them with more than what is for many the experience of a lifetime. It teaches them a foreign language, it hones their communication skills, it improves their interpersonal and intercultural abilities.[13]

Not only are young people given the confidence and ability to work in other countries where the right jobs may be available, rather than being trapped by a geographic mismatch, but they are also likely to form permanent personal partnerships across national borders. Thirty-three percent of Erasmus students have life partners of a different nationality (compared to 13 per cent of non-Erasmus students), with the result that one million babies are reckoned to have been born to transnational Erasmus parents since 1987.[14]

Despite its size, Ireland has been a conspicuously active participant in the Erasmus programme. Since 1987, about 60,000 students from Ireland have participated in Erasmus, while 100,000 students from the

EU have come to Ireland. The countries most involved in the inward and outward flows have been France, Germany and Spain. In the year 2015–16, 3,173 Irish students went abroad for study or work placement, while almost twice as many (7,579) Erasmus students came to Ireland from abroad.[15] This almost certainly reflects a high demand for competence in English among continental European countries. What impact has the Erasmus programme had on Irish universities, and on national higher education policy? Internationalisation did not play a significant role in higher education policy-making until the mid-1990s. The 1991 OECD report on Ireland's national education policy did not mention internationalisation issues at all.[16] Nor did the 1995 report of the steering committee on the future of higher education in Ireland.[17] That said, it is not wise to assume that Irish universities were unaffected by international issues. On the contrary, they were attracted early by funding opportunities (from the EU Social Fund) and by the Erasmus programme itself, which forced universities to adopt credit-transfer schemes that guaranteed the equivalence of courses undertaken by mobility students.

In some respects, we can argue that the higher-education sector was the 'tail that wagged the dog' in the evolution of a more internationally focussed higher-education system, notwithstanding the demands of the harmonising Bologna Process (which provided a short burst of energy to fuel the more long-term, 'slow-burn' benefits of the Erasmus programme). In the late 1990s, government policy also tried to encourage the development of Ireland as a centre of educational excellence. In tandem with this initiative, bodies were set up to monitor and maintain the credibility of educational qualifications, partly with a view to matching equivalent standards in countries to which, and from which, students might be expected to travel. Partly for financial reasons, universities began more energetically to recruit students from non-EU countries, but these ventures, even where they were educationally desirable, ran into opposition on the grounds that 'home' (that is EU) students already place a strain on increasingly scarce resources. Moreover, Ireland is in competition for students with many other 'educational destinations', a challenge that is all the more daunting in the context of a relative decline of all Irish universities in global league tables.

The impact of Erasmus on universities is difficult to calibrate precisely, but what is clearly visible is developments such as the establishment of international offices; orientation programmes for EU students; firmly established credit-transfer schemes; the standardised Europass CV; 'semesterisation' of the academic year to align with other EU countries; curricular adaptations to cater for a more cosmopolitan clientele; and an increase in teaching exchanges and research collaboration. Universities have become increasingly aware of the European environment in which they operate. Erasmus has helped to raise this consciousness, but it cannot be said to be totally responsible for it. Despite funding constraints, Irish universities are still relatively autonomous in the sphere of teaching and research: a desire for self-preservation, in the teeth of a more managerial culture being imposed from above, has, if nothing else, driven the academy towards cooperation in Europe, and beyond.[18]

European languages

Given that languages play an essential role in European Studies degrees, the fate of language teaching at secondary level in Ireland is of more than passing interest. The concern about this extends far beyond the universities, however. Recent analysis of job market vacancies in Ireland highlights the need of employers for graduates with language skills. Not only are multinationals being compelled to import graduates from outside Ireland to fill vacancies in which linguistic skills are essential, but even at the level of small and medium-sized enterprises whose export activities are crucial to their viability, there is a need to do business in the language of their foreign customers. Due to an anachronistic attachment to French in Irish schools, it is by far the most popular language for secondary students, even though France is not a major trade partner for Ireland and French is not one of the ten most widely spoken languages in the world. On the other hand, very few students take German despite the growing influence of Germany in Europe and the still-untapped opportunities for Irish experts in the German market.

Overall, only eight per cent of Irish secondary school students learn two or more foreign languages, compared with a European average of 60 per cent. It is significant that Ireland is the *only* country in Europe where a foreign language is not compulsory at any stage in the school curriculum. Google's former European CEO, John Herlihy, says that there is a shortage of job applicants for vacancies in his Portuguese, Hungarian and Swedish customer-service teams:

> There is a huge opportunity for Ireland if we can adapt our education system to allow for the studying of more languages. Indeed, we need to do so if we are to be a truly open economy operating in the global economy.[19]

The recent emphasis on incentivising mathematics, whatever its merits may be, has tended to elbow languages out of the classroom. It is also true that the 1,500 hours spent learning Irish could put pressure on timetable availability for foreign languages. Behind the complacency regarding foreign language learning lies the easy assumption that, in a globalised world, English is the universal *lingua franca*. However, 75 per cent of the world's population cannot speak English, and only 9 per cent have it as their first language; and to research one's market thoroughly, and to appreciate cultural nuances in the target market, knowledge of a foreign language gives the exporter a valuable edge over the competition.

Finally, the health or otherwise of European Studies in Ireland depends in part on the existence of an active and vibrant professional association dedicated to promoting and protecting European Studies. The record so far in this regard has been rather patchy. Again, we can perceive a period of 'missionary zeal' in the 1970s and early 1980s when the Irish Association for Contemporary European Studies (IACES), and, more latterly, the European Studies Specialist Group (ESSG) of the Political Studies Association of Ireland (PSAI) have provided an Irish 'home' for scholars of European integration. To be fair, such associations have been hampered by at least three factors: lack of funding; poor public transport links within Ireland that made Dublin the inevitable hub for such activities; and, most importantly, the process of 'satellisation', whereby Irish organisations were overshadowed by broader associations, for example the University Association for Contemporary European Studies (UACES) in the UK, the European Consortium for Political Research (ECPR) in Europe, and the European Union Studies Association (EUSA) in the United States. Some Irish academics in

European Studies often meet each other more frequently at these international gatherings than in their home country! Recently, the revival of IACES under the rejuvenated Jean Monnet Chairs at Maynooth and Cork is already providing a welcome boost to European Studies across the country. What any new professional organisation will need to do besides stimulating research and conferences, is (a) defend the discipline in its own institutions; (b) provide a talent-bank for policy-makers; and (c) help to shape opinion in civil society.[20]

A natural home for European Studies

There are several reasons why Ireland provides a natural 'home' for European Studies. First, public opinion has remained strongly supportive of EU membership ever since 1973, when over 80 per cent of the population voted in favour of entry into the European Economic Community.[21] Second, the political party system reflects and leads this positive sentiment towards European integration. In strong contrast to the United Kingdom, where pro-European policies can be politically risky, political parties in Ireland compete with each other in their enthusiasm for EU membership. Moreover, and again in contrast with the UK, national identity in Ireland is perceived as congruent with an attachment to a European identity.[22] Likewise, EU citizenship is interpreted as an extension of Irish citizenship, whereas in the UK, European citizenship is seen as either vacuous or vaguely menacing. Third, perceptions of Ireland within European Studies have tended to flatter its international profile and have been shaped primarily by key factors related to the country's history, geography, and political evolution. The country has been independent for less than a century and is therefore younger than many other EU member states. Its neutral status, coupled with its past as a colonised territory, also mark it off from most other European countries. Its geographical location on the western periphery of Europe, as an 'island behind an island', and its relatively underdeveloped economy have rendered all the more significant its political and economic progress as a member state of the European Union. Fourth, within European Studies, Ireland is frequently cited as an example of how the integration process enables a small member state to punch above its weight within a transnational institutional framework that

Edward Moxon-Browne

both recognises the formal equality of member states and also makes provision for actual inequalities in economic status and political influence. Lastly, from a foreign policy viewpoint, Ireland's neutrality, its relatively small size, and its lack of a colonising legacy, make it disproportionately competent as an honest broker in resolving diplomatic disputes between member states; while its skill in exploiting the potential of EU redistributive development programmes has often provided a template for newer member states to emulate. In short, European Studies rests comfortably within the Irish academic community because its subject matter resonates easily with the nation's view of itself.

Notes

[1] Elaine Larkin, 'European studies proving a global attraction', *The Irish Times*, 15 May 2001.

[2] Edward Moxon-Browne, 'The grin of the Cheshire Cat: European Studies in Irish universities 1974–2014', *Journal of Contemporary European Research* 11 (4), 359–69.

[3] Moxon-Browne, 'The grin of the Cheshire Cat', 360.

[4] For further information on this degree programme, see the UCD website: https://sisweb.ucd.ie/usis/!W_HU_MENU.P_PUBLISH?p_tag=PROG&MAJR=W346 (2 September 2018).

[5] Details of this degree programme are available at: https://www.dcu.ie/courses/Postgraduate/law_and_government/MA_European_Law_and_Policy.shtml (2 September 2018).

[6] Further information is available on the UL website, at: https://www.ul.ie/graduate-school/courses/european-politics-governance-ma (2 September 2018).

[7] For more details on this programme, see the TCD website: www.tcd.ie/courses/postgraduate/az/course.php?id=DPTAH-EURS-1F09 (2 September 2018).

[8] For further information, see: https://www.ul.ie/courses/bachelor-arts-european-studies (2 September 2018).

[9] Details of this programme can be accessed at: www.tcd.ie/courses/undergraduate/az/course.php?id=DUBEU-EURS-1F09 (4 September 2018).

[10] For further information on this degree programme, see: https://www.ucc.ie/en/ck101/eurostudies (2 September 2018).

[11] For further information, see: www.maynoothuniversity.ie/study-maynooth/undergraduate-studies/course/ba-european-studies (4 September 2018).

[12] Moxon-Browne, 'The grin of the Cheshire Cat', 363.

[13] Androulla Vassiliou, 'Commissioner Vassiliou speech in Copenhagen', Press release, 9 May 2012, available online at: http://europa.eu/rapid/press-release_SPEECH-12-345_en.htm (4 September 2018).

[14] For further information, see: http://ec.europa.eu/education/tools/statistics.en.htm (2 September 2018).

[15] For further details on the Irish involvement with the Erasmus programme, see: http://eurireland.ie/programmes/erasmusplus/ (4 September 2018).

[16] Organisation for Economic Cooperation and Development, *Review of national education policies: Ireland* (Paris; OECD, 1991).

[17] Higher Education Authority, *Report of the steering committee on the future development of higher education* (HEA; Dublin; 1995).

[18] Moxon-Browne, 'The grin of the Cheshire Cat', 367.

[19] 'Irish students lost in translation', *The Irish Times*, 8 November 2011.

[20] Moxon-Browne, 'The grin of the Cheshire Cat', 367.

[21] Brigid Laffan, *Ireland and the European Union* (Palgrave; Basingstoke, 2008), 124–5.

[22] John Coakley, 'Public opinion and the European Communities', in David Coombes (ed.), *Ireland and the European Communities* (Dublin; Gill and Macmillan, 1983), 43–67.

(Re)imagining communities: *cara* magazine and the negotiation of Irish identity, 1997–2017

Linda King

> The airline...has a product so intangible that it cannot be displayed or inspected before purchase, and in any case the retailer holds no stock. The airline has to reach the consumer directly, and... one of the few stimulants to sales an airline has, is the conduct of advertising.[1]

Introduction

In January 1968, Aer Lingus introduced its in-flight magazine, *cara*. Inspired by the success of *Clipper travel*—the ground-breaking promotional tool of industry leader, Pan American Airlines (Pan Am)—it was conceived as a mechanism to promote both Ireland as a tourist destination and the airline's services. The previous decade had been defined by exceptional growth for international commercial airlines; thus, effective advertising strategies became a central concern for all tourism and tourism-related agents. Aer Lingus was established in 1936 but it wasn't until the 1940s that it developed any significant marketing policies. The 1950s witnessed a huge push to expand Irish tourism for international markets, and in the absence of clear leadership from the state-supported Irish tourism bodies, Aer Lingus became a *de facto* tourist authority and continued in this role for many decades. Consequently, it became a principal voice of Irish tourism promotion, establishing patterns of representation and strategies of communication that became the bedrock of the industry.[2]

Over the past fifty years, *cara* has become more than a means of disseminating Irish tourism publicity and recording the reach of the airline: it has become a tangible measure of travel patterns between Ireland, Europe and North America and of how Irish identity has been commodified for international and indigenous audiences. In so doing, *cara* has had to maintain three distinct audiences—local, European and North American—and has had to establish over-arching marketing policies that are inclusive of all potential tourists. In exploring this argument, this chapter analyses *cara* over twenty years (1997–2017), a period marked by unprecedented change within the international and national aviation industries. It has been suggested that tourism is a 'seduction process', through which travellers are 'enticed to particular cultures ... through visual culture and the agencies of the tourism industry', and it is argued here that *cara* is one such important 'agent'.[3] Touristic relationships are fuelled by images; travellers have long been expected to 'see the sights', appreciate the 'picture-postcard' or notice the 'eye-catching'. While most visual research about destinations now takes place on-line, in-flight magazines still have an important role in establishing or confirming what the tourist should engage with and consume. As the sociologist John Urry once remarked, '[tourists] have to learn how, when and where to "gaze". Clear markers have to be provided'.[4] As such, an in-flight magazine can be described as a tourist 'marker', that is, a visual and/or textual means of conveying information about specific attractions; as contemporary life becomes increasingly dominated by images these are instrumental in establishing where the tourist's gaze should be directed.

Yet, within extant literature there is scant research that prioritises popular tourist images to be 'read' as primary 'texts'. One exception—in an Irish context—is Barbara O'Connor's pioneering essay 'Myths and mirrors: tourist images and national identity', which examined historical patterns of how Ireland was represented and commodified up to the early 1990s.[5] This chapter seeks to compliment that research through focusing on a selection of *cara*'s front covers, chosen as being emblematic of how the emphasis and intent of each issue is visually synopsised.[6] It also reflects on how Ireland has related to international markets, particularly Europe, in terms of touristic relationships—and thus economic exchange—and on the commodification of Irish culture more broadly.

The controlled environment of air travel ensures a captive audience that is willing to be distracted and entertained. The cover of an in-flight magazine is the principle means of engaging the traveller with the publication, ensuring that, at the very least, the magazine will be picked up and leafed through. Customers do not choose these publications but are presented with them; the need to reach as broad a target market as possible ensures that their content needs to be entertaining, not controversial, and must generally provide a feel-good factor that all can enjoy. Ultimately, such publications are extended advertisements for a company; feature articles are presented alongside information on the airline's routes, on products available through on-board shopping, and on service provision. Unlike with other publications, the demographic for in-flight magazines is particularly diverse, and airlines need to be mindful of attracting the attention of all travellers regardless of their destination, age, or cultural background; therefore, content cannot be too specific in its orientation.

Common to all audiences, however, is the expectation that tourism publicity provides some articulation of national identity as a badge of distinction, and thus appeal, regardless of whether the publication is focused on the possibilities of inward or outward tourism. It is proposed here that for much of its existence, *cara* has focused on expressing Irish national identity for external audiences. In the 1990s, *cara* typically emphasised inward tourism by routinely presenting conventional images of Ireland, including through architecture (castles, Georgian architecture), scenery (stone walls, green landscape), and ethnicity (red-headed women). These tropes had a proven track record of appealing to multiple external audiences for a variety of reasons, including exotic appeal, connections to the diaspora, and escaping modernity. These highly successful strategies have dominated Irish tourism publicity since the 1950s, and Aer Lingus was instrumental in the establishment and dissemination of such mythologies.

During the 2000s, this emphasis shifted as the Irish national airline was reinvented as a low-cost carrier and *cara* became more focused on outward tourism as Irish people began travelling abroad in greater numbers. In recent years *cara* has again been repackaged as a 'glossy' magazine with a distinct focus on celebrities, lifestyle, food and drink; this is reflective of an increased globalisation of, and confidence in, Irish culture. In returning to a focus on Irish identity, Aer Lingus is acknowledging how this is still a powerful draw for many tourists who have a real (through familial connections) or imagined (through a general sense of kinship) connection to Ireland and its culture. In his 1983 work *Imagined communities*, the political scientist and historian Benedict Anderson famously suggested that a distinct sense of national identity gives rise to a sense of camaraderie between people, but that 'all communities larger than primordial villages of face-to-face contact ... are imagined'.[7] He states that nation is:

> imagined because the members of even the smallest nation will never know most of their fellow-members, meet them, or even hear of them, yet in the minds of each lives the image of their communion ... it is imagined as a community, because, regardless of the actual inequality and exploitation that may prevail in each, the nation is always conceived as a deep, horizontal comradeship.[8]

Linda King

It is proposed here that such solidarity has been routinely promoted by *cara* and is keenly felt in the current iteration of the publication, particularly when its front covers are evaluated. The sociologist Daniel Miller once stated that the study of popular visual and material culture demonstrates that 'human values' are captured in 'cultural forms'.[9] This chapter offers *cara* as an example of one such cultural form and argues that because of their short circulation span, examples of printed ephemera, including magazines—and in this case in-flight magazines—have a unique ability to harness and reflect the *zeitgeist* and therefore to record societal concerns at particular moments. In essence, they provide an important record of cultural history at a fundamental and instinctual level.[10] By examining covers of *cara* over a specific twenty-year period, it is possible to explore these concepts through charting the trajectory of Irish tourism specifically, and Irish culture and society more broadly, as the country moved from economic boom to bust and back again. The sheer quantity of tourism ephemera available (both print and screen-based) typically makes the analysis of any tourism-related subject difficult. This chapter suggests, however, that by focusing exclusively on *cara*—as a distinct and autonomous voice amongst Irish tourism agents—a methodological appraisal can be made of Ireland's shifting relationship with international markets and of how Irish identity has been, and continues to be, commodified.

'Fly the friendly airline': national ambition, economic pragmatism and the commodification of Irish culture

Aer Lingus was established by Seán Lemass as minister for Industry and Commerce, and, from the outset, was a bold statement of Irish sovereignty. This was originally conveyed through the company's name—a neologism of modified words from the Irish language (broadly translating as 'air fleet')—and by means of a tricolour painted on the tailfin of each plane, to emphasise the company's 'flag carrier' status. This was replaced in the 1960s by the shamrock, a conventional (and learned) symbol of Irish identity.[11] As the economic historian Simon Bennett suggests: 'A flag carrier is national ambition made tangible. It is *a political instrument*', and these choices demonstrate such intent.[12] From the 1950s onwards, Aer Lingus became a valuable contributor to

Ireland's tourism revenue, and in this respect it was unusual amongst other national airlines in continental Europe in that its long-term economic viability was reliant on attracting visitors to Ireland, as most Irish people could not afford the luxury of airline travel. Indeed, an international economic appraisal of the importance of airline advertising published in 1962 contended that:

> For many countries, particularly those least industrialized, the promotion of tourism is important in earning foreign currency, and a strong national airline is seen as a major exporter both directly as a carrier and indirectly as a contributor to tourism.[13]

From the outset, Aer Lingus was an extremely ambitious project for a newly independent, economically impoverished state. It was established with a single route to Bristol, and by the time *cara* was launched in 1968 had expanded this modest provision of services to 53 routes, operating out of three national airports: Dublin, Shannon and Cork. In the immediate post-World War II climate of aviation expansion, Aer Lingus evolved a particularly sophisticated and forward-thinking development plan that was highly conscious of the power of marketing strategies, including an astute awareness of the importance of advertising in a sector that does not sell a tangible commodity. Its passenger numbers increased fifty-fold, from 4,401 in 1944 to 180,057 in 1948 partly due to the Irish government securing—an often controversial—bilateral agreement with the USA in 1945.[14] This ensured that all American flights travelling through Irish airspace had to land in Ireland, thus giving Aer Lingus the option of transporting trans-Atlantic passengers onwards to Europe.[15]

By 1948, the airline was advertising in the international edition of *Time* magazine with a degree of regularity that was only eclipsed by industry leaders Pan Am, Trans World Airlines (TWA) and Royal Dutch Airlines (KLM). Writing in 1949, Garret FitzGerald—an Aer Lingus employee at the time—commented that, by 1947, the airline had grown from an 'insignificant feeder airline to an air transport system of European standing'.[16] Aer Lingus's proactive contribution to Irish tourism development continued throughout the next two decades. By the time *cara* was launched on foot of a suggestion made by Neil McIvor, Aer Lingus's head of publicity, the airline was carrying over 1.3 million passengers per annum.[17] Thus when Chief Executive Michael Dargan stated on the occasion of its launch that 'CARA in its content and its production will reflect the high international standard which we [Aer Lingus] set ourselves in all our endeavours', he was confident in a proven track-record of high achievement.[18]

Early Aer Lingus in-flight reading material comprised *Ireland of the welcomes*, the magazine produced by Bord Fáilte Éireann, the national body for the promotion of tourism.[19] The inclusion of that publication on Aer Lingus flights indicates the blurring of boundaries between the tourism authorities and the airline that persisted at this time. *Ireland of the welcomes* was first published in 1952 (Plate I, below), it focused

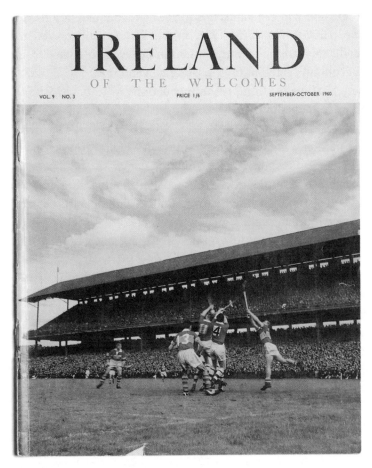

Plate I—Front cover: *Ireland of the welcomes*, September/October 1960. (Magazine from author's own collection.)

on inward tourism and was art-directed by Dutch designer Jan de Fouw, who was also designing tourist bureaux posters for Aer Lingus at the time. De Fouw was one of a number of Dutch graphic designers recruited from the publicity department of KLM to work on the Aer Lingus account throughout the 1950s, and these men were pivotal in establishing and disseminating images of Irishness throughout the Irish tourism industry.[20] *Ireland of the welcomes* focused on promoting the indigenous beauty of the landscape and those aspects of Irish culture that were distinctly 'pre-modern', including activities such as hare-coursing; Irish crafts, for example lace manufacturing; and early Christian monuments; all of which emphasised Irish cultural difference when compared to continental Europe or the USA. This emphasis on Ireland as 'other' within Europe had crystallised on foot of recommendations made by the *Christenberry Report* of 1951, in which tourism experts from the USA had analysed the extant tourism industry with a view to increasing its economic contribution to the Irish economy.[21]

The report made strong recommendations as to how Irish publicity strategies could be improved through the adoption of more modern advertising practices (such as magazine advertising) and an emphasis on specific markers, including the friendliness of the people, indigenous architecture (for example castles, churches and shrines), scenery, and the availability of outdoor activities (such as fishing, hunting, shooting and golf). The report, while focusing on the 'dollar tourist potential' of Ireland as a tourism destination, acknowledged that such strategies and tropes would also appeal to continental Europeans, a point with which the Dutch designers concurred. By the late 1950s target markets comprised Britain, Italy, France, Spain, Portugal, Germany, the Netherlands, Switzerland and Denmark. Aer Lingus was particularly interested in capitalising on the German market due to popularity of Heinrich Böll's *Irisches Tagebuch* (*Irish journal*, published in 1957); however, the airline avoided the extreme emphases of the book, specifically the romanticisation of poverty and the strong Catholic influence.[22] By the mid-1960s the traffic from continental Europe had increased, with German tourists comprising the largest demographic group of visitors.[23]

In the early 1960s Aer Lingus passengers were offered a 'flight pack', comprising a route map, airsickness bag, a list of what was available from the bar and various pieces of 'promotional literature'. This rather disparate collection of ephemera reflected international industry standards established in the 1940s, that were now being replaced by magazine formats. From the mid-twentieth century onwards, in-flight magazines were purposely employed to distract and entertain travellers, complementing on-board provisions that already comprised food, alcohol and in-flight movies and broadcasts. Therefore, in commissioning an in-flight magazine for the Irish airline, McIvor capitalised on the opportunity to bring these fragments of information together, thus mirroring international industry norms in addition to 'promoting both Ireland and the airline'.[24]

cara means 'friend' in the Irish language and the choice of this name for the in-flight magazine encompassed two strategies. First, it referenced the use of the Irish language as a badge of cultural distinction for an external audience or consumer. Second, it was an attempt to humanise the air travel experience by using a strategy of personalisation—between a company and its potential audience—that pre-empted the marketing techniques now familiar within a contemporary globalised economy.[25] *cara*'s systematic use of lower case typography for its masthead reinforced this informality and, working in tandem with the name, provided the consumer with the illusion of intimacy and personal connection. These choices have provided a masthead that is distinct amongst those of competitor airlines, which routinely choose literal and Anglicised titles, including *Magazine* (Air France), *Let's go* (Ryanair), *High life* (British Airways) and *Sky* (Delta), in addition to providing an extension of the airline's most well-known slogan, 'Fly the friendly airline'. This strategy was introduced after the *Christenberry Report* recommended 'genuine friendliness' as a defining 'selling point' for Irish tourism expansion, and, in line with industry norms of the period that 'feminised' the service provision of all airlines, it was extended through the motif of the air-hostess.[26] This personification is still promoted in the company's publicity today, albeit now conveyed by all cabin crew regardless of gender.

'Bringing Ireland to the world': legacy and nostalgia (1997–2001)

It is outside the remit of this chapter to provide a complete appraisal of *cara* magazine since it was first published, but the broad strategies of defining Ireland's difference for potential tourists as established in the 1950s continued to be evident in the publication during the 1990s. This decade comprised a huge period of change for the international aviation industry: the Gulf War (1990) created global economic uncertainty and greatly inflated fuel prices, contributing to the demise of the market leader Pan Am in 1991; the establishment of the Single European Market in 1993 presented opportunities for a more liberal aviation climate; while an alliance based on greater co-operation between European and American airlines, called *Oneworld*, was established in 1999, with Aer Lingus as a member. During this period *cara* continued to utilise decades-old, and thus, well-worn advertising strategies.[27] From the mid-twentieth century Aer Lingus became primarily focused on attracting inward tourism, and in this regard the magazine foregrounded the Irish landscape and its indigenous flora, fauna and wildlife; Ireland's relative lack of industrialisation by comparison to other developed countries; indigenous architecture; ethnographic difference; and a personable population; tropes that had long provided the visual canon for promoting a distinct Irish identity. Whereas American visitors were often attracted by the landscape—particularly that of the west of Ireland—and the discourse of 'tradition' as a means of connecting with their diasporic history, Europeans were also drawn to these motifs as exemplars of a pre-modern environment that had escaped the ravages of two world wars, excessive industrialisation, and by extension, modernisation.

Examining the covers of *cara* from the mid-1990s through to the millennial turn demonstrates the clear longevity of such mid-century strategies: an image of a red-headed woman in a rustic knit against the backdrop of west of Ireland stone walls was clearly understood to be so familiar as to not warrant a qualifying headline (March/April 1998); 'Ireland: Selling the dream' was accompanied by the iconic Paul Henry painting of Mount Errigal (September/October 1999); 'Irish Art: the golden age' (November/December 1999) featured a page from the Book of Kells; and 'A stout tradition: the story of James' Gate' (March/April 2001; see Plate II, opposite) celebrated the opening of the Guinness Storehouse with an archival photo of Guinness barges on the Liffey transporting barrels past the Four Courts.

The covers of the magazine throughout this period are peppered with references to feature articles on Irish individuals and places,

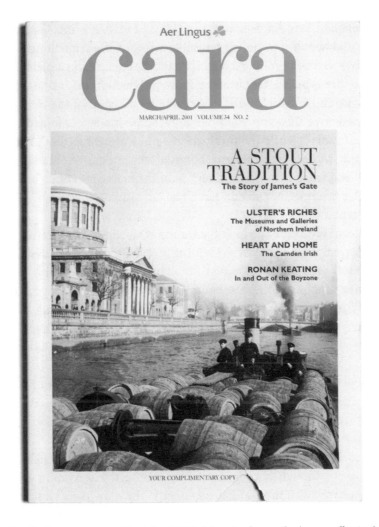

Plate II—Front cover: *cara*, March/April 2001. (Magazine from author's own collection.)

including: Patrick McCabe, Jonathan Swift, Mick McCarthy, Ronan Keating, Derry, Christchurch Cathedral, and 'The Camden Irish'. The inclusion of articles such as these demonstrates an emphasis on Irish celebrities and individuals from within the arts, cultural endeavours, and the diaspora, but these are subordinate to the established visual tropes of Irish tourism that pictorially dominate the magazine's covers. When *cara*'s covers did prioritise foreign destinations, the imagery included a detail of a Roman fountain (November/December 1997) and a sun-drenched Los Angeles balcony (May/June 1999), images that are obtuse and would not be recognisable without their qualifying head-lines. The covers all follow a distinct pattern, comprising a masthead in Bodoni—the typeface favoured by high-end fashion magazines includ-ing *Vogue* and *Harper's Bazaar*—a discrete inclusion of the company's logotype above this, and a large photographic image contained within a white frame.[28] While the production values of *cara* at this time were high, the rather disparate—as opposed to integrated—arrangement of text and image suggests 'trade' publication as opposed to a com-mercial magazine that would have had to compete for attention on a newsagent's shelf.

Collectively, there is a tangible thread of nostalgia permeating these covers, a palpable sense of presenting Ireland's past to contemporary travellers based on an assumed familiarity with pre-existing stereo-types that emphasise the 'authenticity' of Ireland when compared with visitors' own cultures. Sociologist Dean MacCannell, writing in 1976, proposed that tourists seek out what they believe to be 'authentic' as a response to the fragmentation and displacement of modern living:

> For moderns, reality and authenticity are thought to be elsewhere: in other historical periods and in other cul-tures, in purer, simpler lifestyles...the concern of moderns for 'naturalness', their nostalgia and their search for authenticity are not merely casual and somewhat dec-adent, though harmless, attachments to the souvenirs of destroyed cultures and dead epochs. They are also compo-nents of the conquering spirit of modernity—the grounds of its unifying consciousness.[29]

Irish tourism has a long history of capitalising on an ability to empha-sise such qualities, yet, the Ireland of the 1990s and early 2000s was encountering a period of intense social change and modernisation. The issues *cara* identified here emerged at the height of the 'Celtic Tiger' years: a time when many Irish people had more disposable income than ever before, when air travel was becoming increasingly more affordable for Irish citizens, and Ireland was evolving into a multi-cul-tural society that would challenge contemporary pre-conceptions of

Linda King

Irish identity. These seismic shifts were not reflected by *cara* during this period, but this is understandable because, within the context of tourism publicity, most tourists do not expect to be confronted with challenges to their pre-conceptions about a destination unless it is to heighten extant expectations.

Cumulatively, the magazine's covers reflect a palpable nostalgia for an Ireland that either no longer exists (for example, the Guinness cover) or is rooted in past achievements (for example, The Book of Kells). Literary theorist Svetlana Boym has proposed that nostalgia is a defining feature of contemporary life, stating that:

> The twentieth century began with utopia and ended with nostalgia... a longing for a home that no longer exists or has never existed. Nostalgia is a sentiment of loss and displacement, but it is also a romance with one's own fantasy.[30]

She suggests that nostalgia, while it is accepting of modernity, rebels against it and embodies a desire to escape from the speed of societal change and to take life at a slower pace.[31] She proposes that this has particular resonance with those displaced from their homelands, as the emigrant/immigrant experience challenges the romanticised views of home and country.[32] The images of Irishness promoted by *cara* at this time can be seen as symptomatic of this condition and may be interpreted as feeding an indigenous nostalgia for an Ireland that was rapidly disappearing, an international nostalgia for a slower pace of life, and a nostalgia fuelled by the experiences of the diaspora. In this sense, *cara* in the 1990s reflects an Ireland and an airline that, while proud of their historical achievements, were experiencing accelerated societal shifts and facing an uncertain future.

'Low fares. Way better': crisis, expansion, competition (2002–11)

The first decade of the new millennium was a volatile period for all airlines. The aviation industry, already affected by a global recession beginning in 2000 and lasting three years, was radically altered by the attacks on the World Trade Centre in New York on 11 September 2001. In the direct aftermath of those attacks, numerous international airlines declared bankruptcy: fifteen domestic USA airlines—including the market pioneer TWA—disappeared altogether, and the European flag carriers Swissair (established in 1931) and Sabena (established in 1923) also collapsed. In 2003 Air France and British Airways retired their Concorde fleet due to a global decline in passenger numbers and an inability to recover consumer confidence in the wake of an Air France crash in 2000 that killed all 109 passengers and crew. Many airlines restructured their operations following of years of global financial losses and a wavering consumer confidence.[33] In tandem with these events, Willie Walsh, a former Aer Lingus pilot, became the company's chief executive officer in 2001. In a climate that saw a drastic reduction in global tourism revenue, coupled with a slowdown in the Irish economy, Aer Lingus was in great financial difficulty, and Walsh pared back the company's staff and stock and began to reconfigure it as a low-cost airline in the mould of Ryanair. Ryanair had launched its website and on-line, self-service booking facility in 2000; this has since proved revolutionary within the industry. In trying to focus the consumer on its new on-line service, Walsh downplayed Aer Lingus's flag carrier status, side-lined the shamrock logotype, and introduced a new text-based, single-word, lower-case 'channel mark' in red and green.

The 'aerlingus.com' mark was a crude attempt at over-emphasising the company's web presence—hence the visual exaggeration of the red dot in '.com'. It distanced the airline from its image as a conduit of national identity and followed the design lead of other low-cost airlines of the period, including Easyjet, Buzz and Go. The company's shamrock logotype continued to exist on the tailfin of most of the air fleet—as it would have been hugely costly to repaint these—but was, nevertheless, removed from much publicity material. A new slogan—'Low fares. Way better'—was also introduced to emphasise the new direction the airline was moving in, while rumours abounded that the shamrock logo would be completely retired and a whole new, less obviously 'Irish' corporate identity would be launched.[34] In parallel, the apparatus of Irish tourism was also under review, as an all-Ireland strategy for the promotion of inward tourism had been identified as part of the Good Friday Agreement of 1998.[35] This led to the North–South Ministerial Council being charged with developing co-operation between Northern Ireland and the republic. As a direct consequence, a new company called

Tourism Ireland was established in 2002 to manage the promotion of tourism on both sides of the border, replacing the roles previously occupied by Bord Fáilte Éireann and the Northern Ireland Tourist Board. Bord Fáilte Éireann remained responsible for marketing and for the development of tourism infrastructure across the island until it was replaced by a new organisation, Fáilte Ireland, in 2003.

cara in 2002 reflects this period of indecision and flux (Plate III, below). The magazine was radically reduced in size, down to a standard 100 pages (from anything up to 158 pages in 2001) and was published less

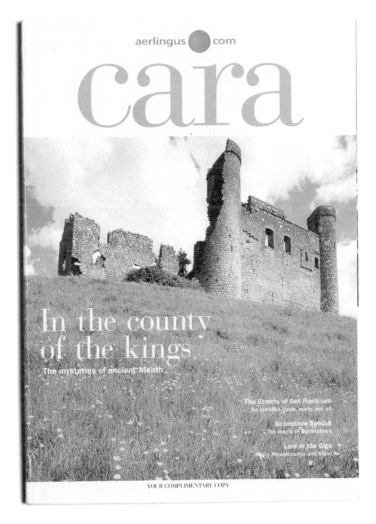

Plate III—Front cover: *cara*, August 2002. (Magazine from author's own collection.)

Plate IV—Front cover: *cara*, December 2002. (Magazine from author's own collection.)

frequently, at six issues per year. A new editor oversaw these changes, and a variety of design strategies were tested, but these lacked clarity or cohesion.[36] By September 2002, months of experimentation resulted in a new magazine format, including a crudely stretched Helvetica masthead, a larger channel mark, a full-bleed photograph of (mostly) European destinations, and feature articles that similarly focused on travel abroad. 'Czeching it out: a weekend in Prague' (the December 2002 issue; see Plate IV above) is an example of this focus and is reflective of Aer Lingus opening new routes into Eastern Europe in the wake of EU expansion and a significant decline in North American tourism.

Plate V—Front cover: *cara*, August 2003. (Magazine from author's own collection.)

Easily recognisable touristic markers—here the St Charles Bridge—occupied the front covers, and the overall aesthetic of the magazine reflected the company's reinvention as budget airline: cheap, functional and—unless examined closely—indistinct from the plethora of international airline ephemera.

The Irish economy began to recover in 2003, ensuring that outbound travellers had greater expendable income, and *cara* was further redesigned to take account of this development. A new masthead was contained within a cropped circle, clumsily mimicking the dot in the channel mark, and this was reinterpreted in a new typeface. 'Eyeless in

Plate VI—Front cover: *cara*, April/May 2009. (Magazine from author's own collection.)

Palma: Mallorca's magnificent capital' (August 2003; see Plate V, previous page), 'Warsaw: Eastern promise (February/March 2004) and 'Dubai high: Aer Lingus opens the door to the city of gold' (December/January 2006), represent typical covers from this period, continuing a pattern of promoting travel from Ireland through established routes and recognisable touristic markers (specifically, the Mediterranean coastline and the Burj Al Arab hotel). New Aer Lingus destinations including Berlin, Valencia, Zurich, Warsaw and Copenhagen—all launched during a period of unprecedented expansion by Ryanair, particularly into Eastern Europe and the new EU accession countries—offered new opportunities for different emblematic photos and feature articles. In 2004, the international aviation industry began to recover from the aftermath of the 11 September 2001 attacks and, coupled with Irish economic growth, the number of plane journeys from Ireland rose from over 8.2 million in 2000 to a peak of over 14.6 million in 2008, demonstrating the growth in outward tourism and Aer Lingus's resilience during a period of huge change and uncertainty. In addition, the national carrier successfully fought off a takeover bid by Ryanair in 2006, before the Irish government decided to sell 60% of its 80% share in the company.

Aer Lingus's focus on external routes proved to be an astute one, as Irish tourism had been experiencing difficulties in an increasingly globalised and homogenised economy. As Irish cities became more visually similar to those in Britain due to the spread of popular retail outlets, Tourism Ireland discovered that tourists were disappointed that 'Ireland was not unique enough', which further orientated European tourist traffic towards the East of the continent.[37] Just as the aviation industry was back in profit, however, the worst global recession since the 1930s began in 2007, adversely affecting inward tourism; a year later, Ireland began plummeting towards financial crisis. Aer Lingus was haemorrhaging money, which led to the introduction of two consecutive cost savings plans, while Ryanair launched another take-over bid that was again repelled. Against this backdrop, *cara* was redesigned once more, under a new editor, designer and publisher.[38] The redesign included another new masthead and typeface integrated with the cover image, a reinstating of the shamrock logotype, and an increase in the number of pages to 112 (see Plate VI, opposite). Yet, these changes were moderate, and the magazine's pattern of prioritising international destinations continued.

'Smart flies Aer Lingus': Irish exceptionalism (2011–2017)

As the Irish economy continued to nose-dive, tourism to Ireland began to show signs of moderate growth in 2011. Fáilte Ireland noted that by the end of the year the Irish tourism industry had experienced:

> gradual but solid progress towards some stabilisation following two or three years of free-fall. Indeed, it was a year

Plate VII—Front cover: *cara*, August 2017. (Magazine from author's own collection.)

when visitor numbers eventually climbed back upwards although revenues still remained significantly down on their boom time peak.[39]

cara found a new publisher in Image Publications, which produces Ireland's highest-end women's glossy magazine in addition to a number of lifestyle-focused publications.[40] In employing a publishing company that states it reaches 'over three million female consumers' and is 'a power brand for the modern Irish woman', indications were that *cara* was going to be put through a radical re-haul in terms of both design and

Linda King

direction.⁴¹ The first issue produced by Image revealed a new visual approach, incorporating a new, bespoke, larger masthead integrated with a full-bleed photograph of an Irish celebrity or personality (Plate VII, opposite). This mimicked the layouts typical of high-end fashion publications, and the tone of the magazine's content, also under a new editor, demonstrated a radical shift from a focus on European destinations back to a focus on Ireland. This time, however, the narrative of Irishness was played out through the lens of indigenous industries (typically sport and entertainment) and notable personalities attached to those.

The first cover featured apprentice jockey Gary Carroll standing in front of a racing track, accompanied by the slogan 'The Turf Club: meet Ireland's racing sets', presenting Carroll as an Irish personality to those familiar with his work, or a synecdoche for Irish racing more broadly for those who are not. The surrounding feature articles, 'Cork for gourmets: follow the foodie trail', and 'Sebastian Barry: on the writer's life', extended the emphasis on the attractions of Ireland. The following issue, 'Surf's up: catch the best Irish waves' (September 2011), followed a similar trajectory: a photograph of the surfer Lee Wood on a beach in Donegal was surrounded by feature article headlines, evenly split between Irish subjects and international destinations. One month later, the focus shifted from the use of 'a personality' to the foregrounding of 'celebrity' with 'Hitting the high note: meet singer Lisa Hannigan and Ireland's new music makers' (October/November 2011). The principal difference here was that Hannigan was specifically named, placing the focus on her as opposed to the industry she represents. With the exception of a small number of non-celebrity-focused covers, including 'Saddle up: on the trail in Florida' (February/March 2012), or commemorative illustrative covers, for example 'Brave new world: Ireland tackles the 2023 Rugby World Cup bid' (September 2017), cara settled into a pattern of foregrounding Irish celebrities and their achievements.

This roll-call is split between actors, sportspeople and musicians who are of international influence. To date these have included: Aidan Gillen, Charlene McKenna, Cillian Murphy (twice), Jamie Dornan, Annalise Murphy, Ruth Negga, Graham Norton, Roy Keane, Dara O'Briain, Gabriel Byrne, Saoirse Ronan (twice), Graham McDowell (twice), Hozier, Imelda May, Colin Farrell, Bernard Brogan and Johnny

Sexton (twice). The collective emphasis is one of talent and achievement that promotes the discourse of celebrities as 'stars'—that is, respected for their skills within their chosen professions—by comparison to many contemporary celebrities whose notoriety reflects a prowess for self-promotion, regardless of specific talent. The feature articles have been more-or-less evenly split between those of an Irish and those of an international focus but, overall, with the emphasis firmly placed on a new confidence in a contemporary Irish identity, albeit an identity that is predominantly young and Caucasian and, consequently, not particularly reflective of Ireland's current multi-culturalism.

This new approach can be interpreted as promoting what cultural historian Michael Cronin identifies as Irish 'exceptionalism'. When previous tourism strategies directed the tourist's gaze towards Irish people, they were, as O'Connor has noted, typically indistinct, sublimated to the landscape or presented as synechdoches for an entire population. Cronin points out that when the Anglo-Irish writer Arland Ussher sought to explain what distinguished the Irish people from their British or continental European counterparts in the 1950s, he focused on the exceptional qualities of the Irish psyche.[42] Thus, *cara*'s recent emphasis on skilled celebrities to promote contemporary Ireland is an alternative to the historical visual patterns that defined Ireland for decades: landscape, architecture, artefacts and monuments. This new strategy follows a long-established, USA-devised tactic of celebrity product endorsement (here, for both Aer Lingus and Ireland) that has existed since the late nineteenth century, but that has become increasingly popular in the era of social media.[43] Utilising celebrity validation has proved to be a highly successful marketing strategy for innumerable products, ensuring heightened levels of 'brand recall' and an inflated sense of 'value'.[44]

In his analysis of the Hollywood system, the film historian Richard Dyer examines the 'economic importance' of stars, stating that: 'Stars are made for profit...stars sell newspapers and magazines...and almost anything else'.[45] He notes that a star's attraction centres on having charisma and therefore on embodying qualities that are understood to be 'exceptional', setting the star 'apart from ordinary men'.[46] The current *cara* design supports this agenda through the promotion of Irish exceptionalism, thus Charlene McKenna is a 'Roaring success', Aidan Gillen 'Strikes gold' and Colin Farrell is a 'Local hero'. This new direction places focus on the diaspora (including Farrell, Byrne, O'Briain and May), re-flecting a discourse that began with the election of Mary Robinson as president of Ireland in 1990, when she famously placed a 'candle in the window' of Áras an Uachtaráin—the official presidential residence—to welcome back the would-be returning emigrant.

The successes of the Irish diaspora are potently attractive for a broad number of audiences—indigenous and international, young and old. At the same time, these exceptional members of the diaspora challenge conventional nostalgic views of Irish identity and its pre-occupations with the successes of the past. As Boym has suggested:

> In the twenty-first century millions of people find them-selves displaced from their place of birth, living in voluntary or involuntary exile. Immigrants' stories are the best narratives of nostalgia—not only because they suffer through nostalgia, but also because they challenge it.[47]

In the wake of the economic downturn of 2007 and the subsequent years of austerity, Ireland's tourism sector has placed an increased importance on the Irish diaspora and its economic potential. This is part of a wider government-supported agenda, which culminated in The Gathering in 2013. This year-long festival of events was designed to attract back to Ireland emigrants or those of Irish descent, and it bore more than a passing resemblance to *an Tóstal*, a festival held between 1953 and 1958, which was conceived along similar lines to The Gathering and in a similar climate of economic difficulties.

An increased focus by Irish governments on the Irish diaspora over the past two decades has included the establishment, in 2002, of a task force on policy regarding Irish emigrants and, in 2004, of the Irish Abroad Unit by the Department of Foreign Affairs. The post of a Minister of State for the Diaspora was created in 2014, and the report *Global Irish*, on Ireland's diaspora policy, was published in 2015.[48] In 2013 Fáilte Ireland was commissioned by Shane Ross—as the minister for Transport, Tourism and Sport—to examine the feasibility of estab-lishing 'a National Diaspora Centre'. The terms of reference included an examination of Irish influence on world culture—with a particular em-phasis on the arts, including music and acting—in an effort to determine how this demographic group might function as a unique selling point for Irish tourism. The project proposed that:

> The National Diaspora Centre could help to recast the relationship between Ireland and its diaspora...It has the potential to enhance the image and appeal of Ireland, both at home and abroad, not just for the benefit of tourism but also for economic, academic and socio-cultural benefit.[49]

The centre's global reach was estimated to be between 60 and 65 million people, who had either been born in Ireland, were carrying Irish passports, or identified as being of Irish descent. The centre did not go ahead, but a version of the idea, Epic Ireland, was privately initiated in Dublin's International Financial Services' Centre by Northern Ireland-born, former Coca-Cola CEO, Neville Isdell in 2016.

Conclusion

In *Imagined communities* Anderson noted how expressions of national identity and solidarity were made concrete by the development and expansion of print capitalism. In an era of digital communication and dissemination, however, print can no longer be regarded as the sole arbiter of how national identity is visualised. Nevertheless, in the context of in-flight publications in cases where the parent airline is constructed or perceived as a flag carrier, or a representative of the country of origin, printed material remains a powerful conduit for such ideas. In *cara*, the in-flight magazine of Aer Lingus, the imagined community of Irishness has, for the last eight years, been personified by talented Irish people who have made distinct contributions to Irish culture, albeit with an emphasis on youth. Whether or not this continues as a marketing strategy remains to be determined. In 2015 Aer Lingus was privatised and bought over by the International Aviation Group (IAG), the parent company of Iberia and British Airways. In January 2019 Aer Lingus 'refreshed' its livery, providing the first substantial change in the company's corporate identity system since 1996. In totality this new look modifies the expression of the airline's Irish connections: the shamrock has been retained but adapted, however, the aircraft are no longer painted green and white. *cara* has reflected the change with a new masthead, but the magazine's pattern of promoting the Irish diaspora via its front covers continues.

Both the Irish economy and the Irish tourism industry are currently experiencing a period of growth: the total number of overseas visitors to Ireland grew by 3% to 7.7 million up to September 2017—with visitors from North America representing the biggest increase at 19%, and the number of tourists from continental Europe growing by 3%—while the number of trips Irish people made abroad was up 10.7% for the same period.[50] The Fáilte Ireland tourism statistics for 2016 reveal that, in descending order, the largest numbers of tourists to Ireland came from Britain, Germany, France, Spain, Italy and the Netherlands and their spending contributed €6.6 billion to the Irish economy. The Fáilte Ireland statistics also demonstrate that tourist experiences exceeded expectations—with friendliness, scenery and culture, still being the dominant attractions—and that the majority of tourists were at least 45 years old and from professional and clerical backgrounds.[51] Aer Lingus has also experienced a period of growth, as passenger revenue and numbers increased in 2016 by 4.9% and 2.9% respectively. The airline remains a pivotal Irish tourism agent and an important interface between Ireland and its continental European and North American markets.[52] It has been suggested that 'tourists travel in order to collect images, and these images are both objective and material (postcards, snapshots, videos) as well as subjective and immaterial (hopes, dreams, visions)'.[53] *cara* magazine's strategy of promoting Irish culture through celebrities speaks to a newly found confidence in Irish achievement and an alternative approach to Irish tourism promotion. Should this continue, it remains a highly effective marketing strategy that neatly circumvents the need to target specific demographics, given that, in our contemporary society, the pervasiveness and attraction of celebrity culture is something to which all ages and nationalities can relate.

Acknowledgements

With sincere thanks to Andrew Woodcock (for photography), and to Aer Lingus and *Ireland of the welcomes* (for image permissions).

Notes

[1] A.J. Burkart 'Advertising and marketing in the airline industry', *Journal of Industrial Economics* 11 (1) (November 1962), 18–32: 27.

[2] For further analysis of this and Aer Lingus's advertising strategies in the mid-twentieth century, see, Linda King, '(De)Constructing the tourist gaze: Dutch influences on Aer Lingus tourism posters, 1951–61', in Linda King and Elaine Sisson (eds), *Ireland, design and visual culture: negotiating modernity 1922–1992* (Cork University Press; Cork, 2011a), 164–87, and Linda King 'Aer Lingus summer timetable, by Guus Melai', in Fintan O'Toole (ed.), *Modern Ireland in 100 artworks* (Royal Irish Academy; Dublin, 2016), 118–20.

[3] David Crouch and Nina Lübbren, 'Introduction', in David Crouch and Nina Lübbren (eds), *Visual culture and tourism* (Berg; Oxford and New York, 2003), 1–12: 8.

[4] John Urry, *The tourist gaze: leisure and travel in contemporary societies* (Sage; London, 1990), 9.

[5] Barbara O'Connor, 'Myths and mirrors: tourist images and national identity', in Barbara O'Connor and Michael Cronin (eds), *Tourism in Ireland: a critical analysis* (Cork University Press; Cork, 1993), 68–85. For broader histories of Irish tourism, see Irene Furlong, *Irish Tourism, 1880–1980* (Irish Academic Press; Dublin, 2009) and Eric G.E. Zuelow, *Making Ireland Irish: tourism and national identity since the Irish civil war* (Syracuse University Press; Syracuse, NY, 2009) are useful references.

[6] The author is not including commemorative copies of the publication in this analysis (for example, April/May 2008, which celebrated 50 years of the transatlantic route, and April/May 2011, which celebrated 75 years of the airline), as these are atypical.

[7] Benedict Anderson, *Imagined communities: reflections on the origin and spread of nationalism* (Verso; London, 1996, 2nd edn), 6.

[8] Anderson, *Imagined communities*, 6–7.

[9] Daniel Miller, 'Why some things matter', in Daniel Miller (ed.), *Material cultures: why some things matter* (University College London; London, 1998), 3–21: 19.

[10] For further analysis of this point as applied to Aer Lingus's advertising strategies in the mid-twentieth century, see, King, '(De)Constructing the tourist gaze', 164–87.

[11] For further discussion on this, see, Linda King, 'Saints, shamrocks and signifying practices: Aer Lingus and the materialization of Irish identity', *Éire-Ireland* 46 (1–2) (2011b), 128–51.

[12] Simon Bennett, *Victims of hubris? The decline and fall of Pan Am and Swissair* (University of Leicester; Leicester, 2002), 7–9.

[13] Burkart, 'Advertising and marketing in the airline industry', 22.

[14] Garret FitzGerald, 'Aer Lingus', *Irish Monthly* 77 (917) (November 1949), 499–504: 499.

[15] Brendan O'Regan invented the Duty Free concept at Shannon airport in 1946 as a consequence of this opportunity.

[16] Garret FitzGerald, 'Aer Lingus', 499.

[17] Bernard Share, *The flight of the Iolar: the Aer Lingus experience, 1936–1986* (Gill and Macmillan; Dublin, 1986), 286.

[18] Dargan occupied this position from 1967 to 1974: Share, *The flight of the Iolar*, 222.

[19] Share, *The flight of the Iolar*, 222. Michael Cronin has written about *Ireland of the welcomes* from the perspective of its literary content, see Cronin, 'Next to being there: Ireland of the welcomes and tourism of the word', in Michael Cronin and Barbara

O'Connor (eds), *Irish tourism: image, culture, and identity* (Channel View Publications; Clevedon, UK, 2003), 179–95.

[20] King, '(De)Constructing the tourist gaze', 164–87.

[21] Department of Industry and Commerce, *Synthesis of reports on tourism 1950–51* (Stationery Office: Dublin, 1951). This was referred to as the *Christenberry Report* after Robert K. Christenberry, the Astor Hotel president who led the USA delegation of tourism experts to Ireland in July/August 1950, under the auspices of a Technical Assistance Programme, as part of Ireland's Marshall Aid plan.

[22] Heinrich Böll, *Irisches Tagebuch* (Kiepenheuer and Witsch; Köln, 1957).

[23] German tourists have continued to be a significant source of Irish tourism revenue, comprising the largest target market in Europe from 1995 to 2001. See, Tourism Policy Review Group, *New horizons for Irish tourism: an agenda for action* (Tourism Policy Review Group; Dublin, 2003), x. As other authors have demonstrated in this volume, literature of and about Ireland is still a very powerful draw for overseas tourists.

[24] Share, *The flight of the Iolar*, 222.

[25] Slogans including 'l'Oreal: because you're worth it' or 'Your M&S' are typical of contemporary advertising strategies that attempt to provide the illusion of personal connection between companies and consumers.

[26] Department of Industry and Commerce, *Synthesis of reports on tourism 1950–51*, 27.

[27] These were under the direction of the American-born editor and journalist Vincent de Veau. Paul Whittington became editor at the end of 2001, with de Veau remaining as 'editor-in-chief' and later 'editorial director'.

[28] This was under the art direction of Kevin Gurry. The publisher was Smurfit Communications (renamed Harmonia after a management buyout in 2004), a company specialising in producing women's and niche magazines, including *U, Irish Tatler, Woman's Way, Food and Wine* and *Auto Ireland*.

[29] Dean MacCannell, *The tourist: a new theory of the leisure class* (University of California Press; Berkeley, 1999), 3.

[30] Svetlana Boym, 'Nostalgia and its discontents', *Hedgehog Review* 9 (2) (Summer, 2007), 7–18: 7.

[31] Boym, 'Nostalgia and its discontents', 8.

[32] Boym, 'Nostalgia and its discontents', 16.

[33] The International Air Transport Association (IATA), *The impact of September 11 2001 on aviation* (IATA; Montreal, 2011), np.

[34] The author is grateful to a former cabin crew member (who asked to remain anonymous) for this information.

[35] The Good Friday Agreement was passed by two referenda—in Northern Ireland and Ireland—in May 1998. It officially marked the end of 'The Troubles' in Northern Ireland and paved the way for the decommissioning of weapons by paramilitary organisations. It acknowledged the aspiration to a united Ireland, but only if desired by the majority population of Northern Ireland, and provided a framework for future governance and increased north-south and Irish-British co-operation.

[36] Paul Whittington was the editor at this point, and Gurry continued as art director.

[37] Michael Cronin, 'Small worlds and weak ties: Ireland in the new century', *Journal of Irish Studies* 22 (2007), 63–73: 64.

[38] The editor was the music journalist Tony Clayton-Lea, who continues to write for the publication. Lisa Meagher edited the magazine in 2005. The designer was Garret Whelan and the new publisher, Maxmedia.

[39] Redmond O'Donoghue, in *Fáilte Ireland annual report* (Fáilte Ireland; Dublin, 2011), 3.

[40] Image Publications was founded in 1975 and its titular magazine is *Image*. It began publishing *cara* in August of that year and also publishes *Image Brides, Image Interiors & Living* and *Garden Heaven*.

[41] Information sourced from the Image website, at:<https://www.image.ie/advertise (14 December 2017). This change was under the art direction of Clare Meredith and editor Frances Power. Power was previously travel and features editor at *Image* magazine. Jessie Collins took over as editor in 2015 and Lucy White in 2016. At the time of writing, the art director is Niamh Richardson.

[42] Michael Cronin, 'Small worlds and weak ties', 63.

[43] For example, in 1870 US Congregationalist preacher Reverend Henry Ward Beecher endorsed Waltham watches by appearing in an advertisement for the product in the magazine *Harper's Weekly*; see, C. Robert Clark and Ignatius J. Horstmann, 'A model of advertising format competition: on the use of celebrities in ads', *Canadian Journal of Economics* 46 (4) (November 2013), 1606–30: 1606.

[44] Clark and Horstmann, 'A model of advertising format competition', 1609.

[45] Richard Dyer, 'Heavenly bodies', in Sean Redmond and Su Holmes (eds), *Stardom and celebrity: a reader* (Sage; London, 2007a), 85–9: 86.

[46] Richard Dyer, 'Stars', in Sean Redmond and Su Holmes (eds), *Stardom and celebrity: a reader* (2007b), 78–84: 82.

[47] Boym, 'Nostalgia and its discontents', 16.

[48] 'Global Irish' is now also a service operated by the Department of Foreign Affairs and Trade to help 'Irish people and people of Irish descent maintain their connections to Ireland and each other'; for further details see the Global Irish website, at: https://www. dfa.ie/global-irish/ (6 December 2018).

[49] Fáilte Ireland, *National diaspora feasibilty study* (Fáilte Ireland; Dublin, 2013), 3.

[50] These statistics were sourced from the website of Fáilte Ireland, at: http://www.failteireland.ie/Utility/News-Library/Overseas-Tourism-January-to-September-2017.aspx, and the Central Statistics Office, at: http://www.cso.ie/en/releasesandpublications/er/tt/tourismandtravelquarter32017 (12 December 2017).

[51] Fáilte Ireland, *Tourism facts 2016* (Fáilte Ireland; Dublin, 2016), 1–8.

[52] Aer Lingus, *Annual report* (Aer Lingus; Dublin, 2016), 6.

[53] Crouch and Lübbren, *Visual culture and tourism*, 5.

Irish media discourse on Europe: the search for a wider horizon

Paul Gillespie

Introduction

European discourses in Irish media come in several periods, from the beginning of the twentieth century to the contemporary setting of Brexit and the future of European integration. This chapter examines selected issues emerging from that historical retrospect. Europe has been a constant theme in Ireland's journey from dependence to independence to interdependence with Britain over this time, holding out the promise of a relief from Anglo-centricity in a wider political identity; but representations of Europe in the Irish media have differed from period to period.[1] Common patterns explored here concentrate on structure, including the sourcing of news about European developments by Irish media in agencies, among syndication services and by correspondents, and on how they organised and edited that coverage internally.

A lot changed in the sphere of media discourse on Europe as in others during the 1960s and after Ireland's accession to the EEC from the 1970s, but understanding that editorial structure is essential for an informed discussion of how media handle these issues. The chapter concentrates on editorial structures and European coverage in *The Irish Times*, where the author worked as a journalist editing and covering international and European affairs in those decades. It argues that more research is needed on the actual coverage of Europe across all Ireland's media to establish the extent to which that newspaper's reputation as the editorial and market leader in this field is justified and, if so, how differentiated it was in the quantity and quality of its coverage.[2]

Media are diverse and in Ireland's case legally relatively free. Newspapers, periodicals, broadcasting and the newer social media serve different audiences with specific interests, political affiliations and socio-cultural characteristics. They are owned by powerful yet competing groups, but are subject to similar controlling norms and ideologies despite that diversity. In media studies, a pluralist model assumes power is dispersed in public opinion and the media, whereas an elite model assumes it is concentrated within groups capable of dominating society and politics.[3] Such contrasting explanatory frameworks complicate how public opinion and media coverage should be understood. News content is an imperfect indicator of public opinion; while it may frame the subject matter of public debate it is not determining.[4] The public sphere is a deliberative political space between government and civil society in which media are central players.[5] Research on the role of the public sphere in European integration has grown with the realisation that politicisation and contestation of its end goals and methods is now part and parcel of national and transnational political processes in the continent.[6] Good journalism shares professional, craft and ethical skills across these changing domains of contemporary European politics, but standards vary in application and commitment.[7] Hence real world heterogeneity should caution against generalisations on how 'the media' treat this or that subject or cover particular European developments. Mediation is a central feature of Ireland's international engagement.[8] Only detailed empirical research, however, can establish whether coverage is uniform and standardised or diverse and contested in any particular period or domain.

Ireland's self-perceptions also developed in the transitions from one period to another. From the 1970s, compared to the era of Ireland's previous Anglo-centricity, EEC membership was seen by official nationalism and more broadly by civil society as an opportunity for development through economic and social transfers and as a broadening horizon. In the 1980s and 1990s Ireland's peripherality compared to older and more central powers' comparative development was another central theme of political and media debate. That changed in the 2000s when a new prosperity gave rise to fresh dependence on the English-speaking world and a relative loss of European affinities.

This latter period provided opportunities for public and media deliberation in the four referendums held on the Nice and Lisbon treaties in 2001, 2002 and 2009 and 2010 and in the cross-party Forum on Europe at that time; whether media optimally took up that challenge to better inform public opinion in a lasting way is doubtful. The experience of financial crisis requiring a European bailout from 2008 to 2014 reoriented Irish policy and attitudes back towards Europe, a cast of mind that was reinforced by the UK's decision in June 2016 to leave the European Union. Brexit poses a fundamental challenge to an Ireland that wishes to stay in the EU but will now be without its close UK ally there and must find closer European cultural and political anchors to sustain that path. Media too are challenged to help develop such a new narrative.[9]

The chapter concludes with reflections on how media coverage of the crisis around Brexit and its likely consequences for Ireland's engagement in the future of Europe should be framed theoretically in terms of the state's several continuing peripheralities.

Media structures for international coverage

Irish national newspapers did not have international correspondents resident in the main countries or theatres of conflict in the 1920s and

1930s, with the exception of their London offices—a clear indication of continuing media dependence on the former ruling power. They relied on news agencies and syndicated services for their international coverage and on their own editorial staff to select, edit, present and comment.[10] Some of the difficulties involved were addressed by Frank Gallagher, editor-in-chief of the *Irish Press*, who advised his sub-editors when the paper was starting to 'give the Irish angle in the headlines' and be on their guard 'against the habits of British and foreign news agencies who look at the world mainly through imperialist eyes'. The editorial in the first edition of the *Irish Press* on 5 September 1931 stated:

> In foreign news truth may not be so easy to discover, for like all papers the *Irish Press* must rely for accounts of certain foreign happenings on agencies which see international events from their own angles. We shall, however, never consciously use this journal to mislead our friends or to misrepresent those who oppose us.

In a letter to the news distributor of United Press based in London, Gallagher outlined the kinds of international stories the paper would be interested in receiving:

> Movements for national independence anywhere, particularly those in the British empire ... Irish groups in other countries ... Political situations in all big nations with particular reference to foreign comments on British policy abroad ... Events in Catholic nations, European and South American ... Definite news from Russia (facts rather than propaganda) ... The progress of Gandhi's movement in India ... the national movement in Palestine ... and also all secessionist movements in Canada, Australia and South Africa.[11]

Gallagher makes it clear there is substantial scope to vary international coverage even while relying on agencies. A great deal depends on how the material is selected and angled by editors and sub-editors. In domestic coverage this editorial nexus is created by the dialogue between news editors and reporters, and in better-resourced media providing international news by a similar dialogue between foreign desks and correspondents. Lacking that facility Irish media have therefore relied on internal selection to provide their distinctive international coverage. The skills, knowledge and specialism of those making that selection matter for the quality of the coverage. In the 1930s the *Irish Press* foreign desk was staffed mainly by Geoffrey Coulter and Brian O'Neill, two left-wing republicans who endeavoured to follow Gallagher's norms.

Occasionally in that period special correspondents were sent to cover stories or commissioned for particular reports. The most notable conflict to receive such treatment in Ireland during the inter-war years was the Spanish civil war of 1936–39. It was seen by the three national newspapers published in Dublin variously as a fundamental clash between communism and Catholicism or a struggle between an elected government and a military intent on overthrowing it in the pattern of the 30 or so nineteenth-century Spanish coups.[12] Since these were some of the major European discourses of the twentieth century with strong resonances in Ireland it is illuminating to understand how Irish media handled them. Doing so reveals how newspapers' internal structures determine their coverage of international affairs; this is helped by the detailed research historians have devoted to this episode, which is unusual even in such major crises.[13] Contrasting that experience with subsequent developments in post-war years gives a benchmark for further analysis of European themes in Irish media— including those in Spain.

The *Irish Independent* had used red-scare tactics about the prospect of communist style rule under a Fianna Fáil government ahead of the 1932 general election. The *Press* denied these charges, saying Fianna Fáil promises were in line with Pope Pius XI's encyclical *Quadragesimo Anno*, which attacked the reduction of society to slavery at the hands of capitalism.[14] These themes were resurrected nationally in 1936 as the country responded to the unfolding Spanish civil war. Within weeks of Franco's attempted coup, the *Irish Independent* had hailed the war as 'a struggle to the death between Christianity and Communism', while *The Irish Times* denounced it as a conflict between 'a Fascist junta ... and a population which has tasted, for the first time, some of the sweets of democracy'.[15]

The civil war was framed in a sensational way by the then dominant *Irish Independent*, which ran a daily half-page section entitled 'In war torn Spain', concentrating on persecution of the Catholic church and atrocities against priests and nuns and on the communist role in the republican side of the war in favour of the Spanish government. It devoted a large amount of space to Irish responses to the war, including several big demonstrations organised by pro-Franco forces and clerical groups. Letters, photographs, features and many editorials supplemented this news coverage. The *Irish Press*, by then the second national daily selling largely into the Fianna Fáil electorate, gave as much news coverage to the war, but very little domestic response and fewer editorials, in line with the Fianna Fáil government's policy of neutrality between the contending Spanish forces. In *The Irish Times*, selling many fewer papers to a mainly Protestant and minority readership, there was comparatively twice as much news coverage, half as many editorials, and substantially fewer features and letters, and less domestic coverage than in the *Independent*.[16]

Lionel Fleming, a young reporter with *The Irish Times*, was commissioned by its editor Bertie Smyllie to cover the war from the republican side in Barcelona after saying he was going there on holiday, and was told only to be honest in reaching his conclusions. His ten-part series ran from late August to mid-September 1936, giving a rounded picture of the war based on the main premise that it was a legitimate struggle by an elected government against a fascist movement backed by the powerful Catholic church. The atrocities on both sides were reported on and contextualised historically and politically by the paper in what the historian John Bowyer Bell described as 'some of the most factual, balanced editorial analyses to be found in Europe'.[17] In response, a campaign to withdraw Catholic school advertising from the paper was mounted by Catholic activists, which saw its revenues decline but did not affect its coverage. A very different series was published by the *Irish Independent* in February and March 1937 by Gertrude Gaffney, its women's editor. Her reports came from the nationalist side, including on the Irish brigade commanded by Eoin O'Duffy and were an uncritical account of the war from that perspective, without an effort to explain its origins.[18] The *Irish Press* despatched an undercover reporter with O'Duffy's brigade and ran only one report from him, which was denounced by its subject and then disowned by the paper.

Historians conclude that the Irish newspapers framed the Spanish civil war very much in terms of the conflicts in Irish society—many of which were at play in Europe as well.[19] Similarly one can say that any assessment of European discourses in Irish media should take account of the overall structures of editorial control and policy in the different media; they do not depend only on the role of foreign or special correspondents, however much these enrich coverage. That conclusion stands for later periods as well. As mentioned before, the Spanish example is unusual in Irish media analysis for the detailed attention given to the actual content of international reportage and commentary; it was unusual too for the strongly opposing viewpoints within Irish media on an international question. The extent to which that was so needs to be established by research on other periods and themes if we are to draw more rounded conclusions about how Irish media treat European issues.[20] The Vietnam war from the mid-1960s to the mid-1970s and the United States-led invasion of Iraq in 2003 both provoked protest movements and public demonstrations, but were they as polarised in media coverage? Similarly, Ireland's series of referendums on EU treaties give an opportunity to examine whether media coverage converged or was contested as much as voters were.

The next section describes how one newspaper, *The Irish Times*, developed its foreign coverage from the 1960s to the present time and how that has affected its treatment of European themes. The author was directly involved in that process as a sub-editor, editor, editorial writer, columnist and correspondent. The period coincided with the paper's expansion in circulation and enlargement of vision and positioning in the media market when it became the leading newspaper of the Irish middle class and a more central voice in the country's political and social system.[21] Enhanced international and European coverage from an Irish point of view broadened the horizons of this readership and became a definite source of attraction for them.[22] Editors argued that the costs involved were justified, would be repaid in sales and revenues, and that in a more open Ireland subject to globalised and European influences there is no longer as much of a boundary between home and international news as before.[23] EU referendum coverage illustrates these points and could usefully be supplemented by research on how media in general reported and commented on them.

International and European coverage in *The Irish Times*

Lionel Fleming's subsequent career included distinguished service for the BBC as diplomatic correspondent. Towards its end he returned to *The Irish Times* as foreign editor in 1964. That involved selecting news from agencies and syndication services, determining the relative importance of international news, commissioning special articles when needed, and advising the paper's editor on editorials and on when to send staff reporters to international events. The Press Association provided British news and a selection of international stories from Reuters and the Associated Press.[24] In the 1960s and 1970s the paper also took the American United Press International service and syndicated foreign coverage from the London *Times*. Later *Washington Post, Los Angeles Times* and *New York Times* services were added. Coinciding with Ireland's accession to the EEC in 1973 the Agence France-Presse news service in English was included to provide an alternative French perspective.[25] For a period after that the paper ran daily items in French from *Le Monde* and provided free French lessons for interested journalists.

In the 1980s the paper substituted the London *Independent* service for that of the *Times* and later added the *Financial Times* and *Guardian* syndication services after the Irish Independent group bought the London *Independent* in the 1990s. These services from British and United States papers added range and depth to agency coverage and allowed stories to be by-lined and sourced for readers' benefit. *The Irish Times* could afford to hire foreign correspondents in major European and international capitals whose reporting was more personalised, analytical and better written than agency copy. Using them still involved paying attention to the strictures expressed about agency and syndicated material originating in Anglo-America by Gallagher to *Irish Press* journalists, suitably adjusted to the culture and policy of a different news agenda.

This agenda was set by Fleming and his successors in charge of *The Irish Times*'s foreign desk in the 1960s and following decades, including Andrew Whittaker, James Downey, Peter Froestrup, Paul Gillespie, Pat Comerford, Patrick Smyth, Seamus Martin, Peter Murtagh, Denis Staunton and now Chris Dooley. These editors were senior journalists in the paper and usually had been competitively appointed through an interview system; they circulated into other reporting, executive and international correspondent roles as well as these editing and sub-editing ones. From the 1960s a gradual specialisation occurred, which saw more sub-editors allocated permanently to the foreign desk, giving it greater continuity and expertise. Along with that came more dedicated space for international news and features when resources permitted—at best three news pages compared to seven or eight for home news. When Ireland joined the EEC in 1973 that space was sub-divided until the 1980s into World, European and British sections to ensure a proportionate coverage of European affairs. This was in addition to international stories appearing on the front page of the newspaper and Irish-related international stories in home and business news pages.

By then *The Irish Times* had more than doubled in circulation under Douglas Gageby's dynamic editorship in the 1960s.[26] International and European coverage was part of that transformation as the paper anticipated Ireland joining the EEC. The London office was centrally involved, and Anglo-Irish and Northern Ireland coverage was a focus.[27] Fergus Pyle was appointed Paris correspondent in 1968 after serving in Belfast, giving the paper its first continental staff position. He moved to Brussels in 1971 before Ireland joined the EEC two years later, providing extensive coverage of the new policy setting and contextualising it in regular weekly features. The paper strongly supported Ireland's accession on the basis that it would widen horizons, and reduce dependency on the UK: 'For too long we have been hypnotised by Britain. Entry to the EEC is an opportunity to break out of that hypnotic state'.[28] EEC membership would also help prepare the path to Ireland's reunification. These links were made by Gageby, his close associate, the political columnist John Healy, and columnists such as Garret FitzGerald.[29]

Part of the paper's international profile came from coverage of Irish foreign policy by its diplomatic correspondents. They reported on the diplomatic beat in Dublin as part of the political team, with direct access to political decision-makers, their senior officials and those who lobbied them. In 1969 Dennis Kennedy, a northern journalist who had worked in the *Belfast Telegraph* and then in Ethiopia, became diplomatic correspondent, replacing Wesley Boyd. He travelled to the United Nations for General Assembly sessions and to South Africa to report on apartheid ahead of the national rugby team's trip to Ireland. He was given the title of European editor in the early 1970s to track EEC accession talks, which involved close coverage of Irish ministers and policy-makers negotiating with Brussels and other European capitals alongside EEC correspondents from other newspapers and RTÉ.

Reporters like Frank Darcy and Raymond Smyth from the *Irish Independent*, Joe Carroll and Julian de Kassel from the *Irish Press*, Val Dorgan from the *Cork Examiner*, John Cooney and later Andy Sheppard from RTÉ and their contacts and colleagues in the Association of European Journalists were important mediators of the early and middle years of Ireland's EEC membership.[30] Kennedy was also involved in editorial writing on European affairs in Gageby's office. There he joined the other principal international leader writer, Bruce Williamson, who was also deputy editor and letters editor.[31] Kennedy and James Downey became assistant editors to Pyle when he replaced Gageby as editor in 1974. European affairs were given prominence in that period, including by Pyle's successors as Brussels correspondent in the following decades—Walter Ellis, John Cooney, Colm Boland, Sean Flynn, Patrick Smyth, Denis Staunton, Jamie Smyth, Arthur Beesley, Suzanne Lynch and Patrick Smyth again from 2017.

These staff-correspondent and editorial-writing layers of European and international coverage in *The Irish Times* were gradually supplemented in the late 1970s and substantially from the 1980s by freelance and then more staff correspondents in other European and world capitals. Ian Gibson, Brian Trench, Geraldine Mitchell, Jane Walker, Paddy Woodworth and now Guy Hedgecoe in Madrid, Barcelona and Bilboa; Norman Crosland and Tony Paterson in Bonn; and later Fergus Pyle, Denis Staunton and Derek Scally in Berlin; Anne Sington, Kathryn Hone and then Lara Marlowe in Paris; Alessandro Silj and later Paddy Agnew in Rome; Judy Dempsey and Daniel McLoughlin covering Central and Eastern Europe; these and more occasional 'stringers' in other European capitals built up a profile and personality for the paper and deepened its European coverage. Individual correspondents brought their own interests to the work and operated within a common approach to news and feature coverage.

That required the creation of a larger contributors' budget for the foreign desk. It brought into greater play a key determinant of good international coverage: the daily nexus between editors and

Paul Gillespie

correspondents in agreeing the subject matter and treatment of particular stories for a predominantly Irish readership. Language proficiency and established contacts and access to official and Irish sources were standard requirements for these jobs, in addition to journalistic ability. The positions usually went to Irish journalists or those with a deep knowledge of this country, in recognition that the nexus between the national and the European requires sensitive mediation.

More staff correspondent appointments, including most prominently Conor O'Clery in Moscow, Lara Marlowe in Paris, Denis Staunton and later Derek Scally in Berlin, set the scene for a consolidation of the new regime of European and international coverage in the 1990s. The paper had by then built up a series of bureaux in London, Brussels, Paris, Berlin, Washington, New York and Beijing, supplemented by freelancers retained in other world centres and regions that enhanced its international coverage and reputation. Conor Brady, editor of the paper from 1986 to 2002, defined its foreign coverage as 'the single most significant area of editorial development' in that period. He resolved to continue the commitment to EEC and later EU membership and 'to expand the range of editorial services to support it'. That would also commit the paper 'to provide regular space for viewpoints on Europe that were contrary to our official line'—a commitment that came fully into play during the successive referendums on treaty changes.[32] Even though these appointments were often seen as mould-breaking in the context of Irish journalism at the time, Brady points out that '[i]n reality *The Irish Times* was following the path of its counterpart newspapers elsewhere in Europe'. It never involved having more than five or six staff correspondents working abroad at any one time, unlike the *Berlingske Tidenda* in Denmark or *Diario* in Lisbon, which would have had twice or more that number. 'Stringers' and 'parachute' journalists made up the difference.

Reader research confirmed there was

> an appetite and an appreciation among our readers for accurate, balanced and Irish-mediated news from beyond our own shores ... It gave a valuable service to decision-makers and key figures in politics, the administration and business.[33]

Smyth reinforces this point about the appeal of international and European coverage:

> [C]ore readers saw foreign coverage as a key, authoritative dimension of the paper, a strengthening of interest in such coverage associated with events like the fall of communism, and a conviction that a significant subset of the readers had a developed expertise and sophisticated interest in foreign issues. There is in Ireland a substantial NGO/public service/business academic engagement with a range of issues, from development to EU policy, which needs specialist servicing. Polling also suggested strong readership identification with correspondents like O'Clery and, latterly, Lara Marlowe.[34]

Diplomatic or foreign affairs and development correspondents, including Colm Boland, Renagh Holohan, Mark Brennock, Deaglán de Bréadún, Mary FitzGerald, Ruadhán Mac Cormaic and Simon Carswell continued to cover the diplomatic beat and other foreign policy and development issues in Ireland and abroad. A weekly column, World View, by foreign editor and then foreign policy editor Paul Gillespie appeared in the Saturday foreign pages and later the op-ed pages from 1991; after 2009 Patrick Smyth and Ruadhán Mac Cormaic joined Gillespie as contributors to World View. The column contextualised the international and European news and linked the paper's coverage to the developing policy and academic involvement of foreign-policy experts in Ireland. These journalists were responsible for the paper's European and international editorial writing, with Williamson and Pyle after Kennedy's departure in 1986. Editorials are an important and influential part of the paper's persona on European and international as well as national affairs, as Brown's history testifies and Brady's memoir strongly confirms.[35] Features, Weekend and Arts pages' content and contributors interacted increasingly with this more internationalised news coverage. There was substantial demand for it from readers, as evidenced by the fact that Ireland was declared the most globalised state in the world by *Foreign Policy* magazine in 2004.[36]

As part of that consolidation the paper joined media networks with papers such as *Le Monde, Le Soir, Libération, La Repubblica, To Vima,* and *Der Standaard* in the 1990s, producing international supplements on a joint basis. National special report supplements were produced on Baltic, Central and Eastern European states as well as on the main Western European ones, giving an opportunity to deepen coverage by and travel opportunities for staff ahead of anticipated EU enlargements in 1995 and 2004. An exchange scheme, *Journalistes en Europe,* operated in the 1970s and 1980s for young journalists to work abroad for a year. Conor Brady was prominently involved with the European Journalism Centre at Maastricht University and with The World Editors' Forum, another valuable source of international networking. The paper was an associate member of Eurozine, a network of European cultural journals, from 2004. From 2012 the paper has run a weekly online podcast, 'World View' on international affairs, with regular European features.

This summary profile of one newspaper's developing coverage as it moved progressively closer to the centre of the country's life from its marginal position as a minority paper in the first four decades of independence explains the setting in which European media discourses are produced. The paper's policy to broaden and deepen its European coverage was driven by a conviction that this was necessary as Ireland took up and grew into membership of the EEC/EU, to service readers who would need to know as much about the other member-states as about the Brussels policy beltway. Nor was coverage confined to fellow member-states, as extensive direct reportage from Russia, Turkey and the Balkans testified. The focus was continental rather than simply EEC/EU oriented. High policy making had a new Irish angle, which should be reported on directly. Brady quotes a revealing observation made to him by then Taoiseach Charles Haughey:

> It's necessary for Ireland to engage on the world stage and it's important that Irish people understand why we're doing it so much. *The Irish Times* is always there whenever an Irish minister goes abroad. That's very good. It allows Irish people to see world events through Irish eyes.[37]

Research on foreign correspondents finds that US, German and UK officials and ministers put interpretive reportage by authoritative newspapers and experienced correspondents ahead of or on a par with intelligence or embassy reports as conflicts develop.[38] The experience of *The Irish Times* bears that out. Smyth's account of how Irish correspondents in Brussels have privileged access to leading officials and political decision-makers, enabling them to contextualise and interpret the news for an Irish readership or audience, reinforces this.[39]

Brady makes the point that coverage was not restricted to only the political news, but that writing, for example by Conor O'Clery from Moscow, on everyday life—on shopping, going to the cinema and trying to maintain hope and dignity in a collapsing social order—also captured readers' imaginations and became talking points in Ireland, helping to raise the paper's profile in other media as well.[40] Brown gives several further examples of O'Clery's reporting on queuing, buying alcohol, artistic freedoms and atheism in retreat in the late 1980s to illustrate how the paper contextualised the momentous changes that were to happen in Europe when the Berlin Wall collapsed in November 1989, and with it the Cold War that had framed so much of popular understanding of Europe up to those historic moments.[41] O'Clery's recollections as a foreign correspondent illustrate the diversity of styles and subject matter he brought to this work.[42] Other correspondents such as Lara Marlowe and Seamus Martin were as versatile in covering a range of topics in their respective assignments, including cultural and everyday issues, as their collections and memoirs make clear.[43]

European correspondents like Fergus Pyle, Denis Staunton and later Derek Scally in Germany were given similar briefs to range beyond high politics and responded skilfully and in depth, drawing on their knowledge of German language and culture. Such a running narrative of another culture accumulates in readers' minds and generates a following, as research on and by *The Irish Times* has established. The European discourses built up by the work of these journalists and that of the other correspondents mentioned here should be judged as an orchestration of national discourses gradually becoming entangled in a European Union that became more integrated in the 1990s and 2000s. Europeanisation happens more through national involvement and engagement than top-down from Brussels, as integration specialists dealing with emerging European identities and public spheres argue.[44] Politicisation of the integration discourse from the 2000s, and especially through the financial and Brexit crises, made such discourse more contentious between cosmopolitan liberals and populists concentrating on national and sovereigntist solutions.[45]

The Irish Times's case has been relatively well documented in memoirs and by historians, but it is only one strand in the wider Irish picture.[46] Research on internal staffing and organisation, staff and freelance correspondents and the proportion of their coverage devoted to European and international affairs in other media is needed. Broadcasting especially became much more prominent from the 1960s.[47] It did not, however, become as internationalised as *The Irish Times*, notwithstanding RTÉ's longstanding resident correspondents in London, Brussels and Washington, its regular sending of staff to big news stories, and its use of syndicated international news services.[48] RTÉ's reportage from Brussels with correspondents Sean Whelan and then Tony Connelly since 2001 has been authoritative and often innovative, particularly from 2015 on Brexit issues. Connelly's book on Brexit broke new ground by contextualising and documenting the impact of Britain's departure from the EU on Ireland.[49] The other national newspapers did not seek to compete with *The Irish Times*'s international and European coverage; having gradually scaled down their bureaux in London and Brussels, the *Irish Independent* and *Irish Examiner* relied on wire services and British syndication services for cost reasons and because they saw no large reader demand for increased coverage. The strong Sunday newspaper market was similarly constrained, although the Sunday papers have used once-off European correspondents more.[50]

British media continue to circulate and be viewed in Ireland. This affects and constrains their European discourse, however much the more middle-market and tabloid newspapers needed to editionalise for an Irish market with different political preferences, as we see clearly with Brexit. Some of the demand for British media arises from Irish readers' and viewers' desire for more international news and larger or different perspectives than are available from Irish-based daily or Sunday media. The London *Times*'s daily Irish edition and the Irish edition of the *Sunday Times* aim to meet both expectations.

Online media have added to this picture from the 2000s and should be examined from a similar perspective. In due course the online sphere has opened up a greater space for online public commentary and analysis by foreign policy experts and academics. The following reflections on European discourses in Irish media draw on the experience of *The Irish Times* and on other media accounts in an exploratory way. The themes selected are by no means exhaustive and arise in part from wider policy and academic discourses echoed or amplified in media.

Reflections on media discourse

Ireland's nationalism found resonance and vindication in a wider European setting when the state joined the EEC in 1973 along with the UK. This allowed Ireland escape the economic dependence and political fixation on its former ruling power that had continued from formal independence in the 1920s until the 1970s. Broader horizons flowing from EEC membership were bolstered by transfers from cohesion funds and by the adoption of legislation that had a decisive impact on legal rights for women and on citizenship.[51] These developments indirectly but substantially affected Ireland's relations with Britain. They helped create a more complex interdependence between the two states and peoples—within a wider setting in which European policies on open markets, corporate taxation, EU enlargement, and completion of the single market also converged.[52]

Such developments have been chronicled by historians and political scientists and recur in political arguments about Ireland's future trajectory in the European Union after Brexit.[53] They draw on media reportage and representations of that long transition in the relations between Ireland and the UK within the new European setting, as well as on many other sources. There are several platforms for this media discourse—in direct reportage, journalistic commentary, feature articles, editorials or guest columns from political figures, academics and intellectuals; but it is difficult, given media diversity, to impute unity to the discourse on Europe, including on Ireland's changing relations with the UK in Europe.

By the 2000s national journalists as a group had emerged as a relatively highly educated and predominantly middle-class group, in which popular political preferences for Fianna Fáil and Fine Gael were radically under-represented and for the Labour Party over-represented, even though most proclaimed political neutrality in the name of journalistic objectivity.[54] How social factors like these affected their coverage of European and other issues is a matter for detailed research. The same point applies to the distributional side of Irish media, as *The Irish Times* has had at most a 15 per cent share of the market, compared to a much larger proportion for the Independent newspaper group and the broadcaster RTÉ.[55]

With such qualifications in mind, one can explore selected dimensions of Ireland's European discourse as expressed in media. In his column in *The Irish Times* two days after the accession referendum on 12 May 1972, Garret FitzGerald, future minister for foreign affairs and taoiseach argued that

> The Anglo-centricity of Irish life, so carefully fostered by Britain after the end the 18th century (starting with the Government grant to Maynooth College designed to cut Irish educational contacts with the Continent), will be weakened, and the rich and diverse culture of the Continent will become more accessible to us...[56]

Many more examples of such a sentiment can be found in media articles over subsequent decades, as this became one of the key tropes of Ireland's official nationalism. Hayward points out that such official discourse about Irish membership was conducted in the belief that the EEC would revive the vitality of Irish national culture 'by not only being an alternative to Anglo-American influence, but by strengthening Irish distinctiveness itself'.[57] That theme has recurred right through the various periods of Ireland's engagement with the EEC/EU since the 1970s. It was regularly taken up by intellectuals concerned with Ireland's identity in Europe, often in newspapers and broadcasting media. Among them the critic and writer Desmond Fennell argued that the real effect of such efforts by the 1980s amounted not to the sense of liberation experienced by Irish political elites in the wider European setting of policy-making and relations with the UK, but to a new provincialist consumer liberalism inspired by London and Washington, disparaging Irish parties and institutions compared to preferred metropolitan ones.[58] He saw *The Irish Times* and RTÉ as particularly responsible in what 'began to be called "the mass media" or simply the "media"':

> Financed and made important by the economic boom, and particularly by the expanding advertising industry, this amalgum [*sic*] of television, radio and the printed word emerged as a new, evangelising force in Irish politics. The evangel was 'liberalism', and the media gradually found therein a common cause. They became more autonomous from the political parties, more mentally uniform, and much more a separate interest group, than the mere 'press' had ever been in Ireland.[59]

Fennell's distinctive voice in such debates and his perspective, expressed in media such as the *Sunday Press* and *Irish Times* as well as in books and periodicals, is not representative, but is unusually acute. While *The Irish Times* had a left, its editorial line was at most liberal radical, not socialist.

Other critical discussions about Irish identity and Europeanisation in the 1980s and 1990s paid relatively little heed to media coverage. Joseph Lee's bravura survey of Ireland's intellectual capacity and failings in 1989 ranges over all the social science disciplines and government departments and bemoans 'the incapacity of the Irish mind to think through the implications of independence for national development', tracing this incapacity to

> the dependency syndrome that had wormed its way into the Irish psyche during the long centuries of foreign dominance. The Irish mind was enveloped in, and to some extent suffocated by, an English mental embrace. This was quite natural. A small occupied country, with an alien ruling class, culturally penetrated by the language and many of the thought processes of the coloniser, was bound in large measure to imitate the example of the powerful and prosperous ... England was the only model the Irish were familiar with for several centuries.[60]

Arguing that smaller states need to deploy their intelligence smartly and strategically, he compared Ireland unfavourably to Sweden, Finland and Denmark; in Ireland the dependency syndrome kept England rather than Europe as the usual reference group. In the 1950s he argues that the fine international journalism and commentary carried in the weekly *Leader* magazine edited by the historian Desmond Williams could not be long sustained by a newspaper, because it would run ahead of its readers and would soon become defunct.[61] He does allow that *The Irish Times* later became a newspaper of genuine quality, if not of penetrating social analysis, when the popular market expanded and mentions a number of influential columnists in media; he reserves his main criticism for intellectual elites not able or willing to write for a wider public through the media, rather than the media for not seeking them out.

Lee's 1984 paper examining Ireland's role in the EEC similarly criticised the civil service for not taking civic culture and strategic interests seriously, rather than media for not holding them to account.[62] The European Movement's own retrospect on Ireland's 25-year membership does not deal with media coverage, nor does the comprehensive survey edited by Patrick Keatinge (other than as part of the EU's culture policy), and neither does that of the Institute of European Affairs.[63]

The latter volume does, however, contain Tom Garvin's stimulating essay arguing that 'Europe symbolises the end of empire and, therefore, the obsolescence of the ancient English-Irish quarrel' and concluding that the eventual cultural consequences of this Europeanisation will be profound.[64] If that is so, the habituation to European national and integration narratives for Irish citizens, civil society and policy-makers provided by the media discussed here surely deserves more attention from historians and social scientists. Mark O'Brien's history of journalism in twentieth-century Ireland criticises historians for neglecting the professional and organisational aspects of journalism and their contribution to the evolution of modern Ireland. He points out that the word 'journalism' is remarkable for its absence in the indexes of Irish historiography.[65]

If the nexus between Ireland and Europe is mediated, that process was found wanting in the referendums Ireland held on successive European treaties in 1987, 1993, 1997, 2001, 2002, 2008, 2009 and 2012. The cross-party National Forum on Europe was deliberately set up to examine and discuss Ireland's place in the EU between the first Nice and the first Lisbon referendums and received 'disappointlingly patchy' coverage, according to Laffan and O'Mahony, 'reflecting the inadequacy of the reporting of European issues among the Irish media outside of referendum campaigns and European Parliament elections'.[66] Such criticism has more force for domestic than international reportage of the running narrative from Brussels for those media that take the EU seriously. That reflects the division of labour in most newsrooms between home and foreign desks and reporters, in which those journalists more exposed to European coverage are more knowledgeable about it; press and broadcasting companies should reasonably be expected to coordinate them when they perceive a public interest, but they find it difficult to spread that knowledge around when the European becomes domestic. As a result, expertise can be dissipated, especially when the inevitably more technical aspects of European integration issues are perceived as boring and uninteresting for domestic readers and audiences by home news desks. Such perceptions overlook the diversity of groups with a real interest in detailed EU coverage.

In *The Irish Times* Brexit coverage was more fully incorporated from 2017, with a conscious effort having been made to equalise expertise, and coverage appears mainly in the home news pages. The key to this issue was identified by Laffan in a Thomas Davis lecture broadcast on RTÉ 1 radio in 2003 as part of a series devoted to Ireland's first 30 years of EU membership (again none of the lectures dealt with media):

> ... much of the debate on the democratic deficit [in the EU] missed the point that you cannot have democracy without politics. All of the discourse on European citizenship and a European identity fails to acknowledge that political identity will openly develop if there are opportunities to participate in politics. Without politics there cannot be a European public space ... Quite simply Europe and Ireland's engagement with it cannot come alive without politicisation and contestation.[67]

Ireland is ahead of other EU member-states in its experience of referendums, and its experiences in this regard display a definite development in the electorate's capacity to handle the politics and contests involved.

Paul Gillespie

That requires a real effort from political and official elites as well as by media; it is wrong to expect media to create a public sphere aside from that wider effort.

Research from Eurobarometer and special Irish polling showed Irish public opinion about the EU relatively under-informed in the 1990s and 2000s, notwithstanding engagement in referendums and positive perceptions of the organisation overall. Low levels of knowledge are closely affected by social class and education, as are general attitudes: the greater the levels of knowledge and engagement, the higher the levels of approval of the EU tend to be.[68] Most people rely on television rather than newspapers for information on the EU.[69] The link between media coverage and knowledge should take account of the need for politicisation and contestation to generate the public interest that animates politics and media in similar ways.

Public interest became open to Eurosceptic influence from a more populist British media having an impact on Ireland according to a European Commission study after the 2008 Lisbon referendum was rejected.[70] Movements of Irish public opinion tend to track the intensity and credibility of political campaigning.[71] Irish experience supports the proposition that media framing of issues sets agendas, including those during EU referendum campaigns. One study of EU referendums argues that fringe activists used the McKenna and Coughlan judgments about balance in broadcasting coverage to capture important footholds in the media during the 2008 Lisbon campaign, affecting the result and leading to the treaty being rejected.[72]

Journalists are aware of this tension between strict quantitative balance and a more supple fairness of coverage that does not artificially distort the actual shape of public opinion. How much this is applied varies across different media. Referendum campaigns polarise attitudes towards European integration, introducing arguments about federalism versus inter-governmentalism and about encroaching European bureaucracy that are not discussed in normal politics. As Ireland emerged from the recession and Europe dealt with the continuing crises over eurozone governance and migration, theorists of European integration argued over the new populism and how it relates to political practice and the public sphere, while journalists suggested ways that such linkages can be made.[73]

Conclusion: beyond peripherality, which cores?

The traumatic experience of austerity and direct involvement by Brussels in domestic economic management when Ireland's banking system crashed and had to be rescued in 2008–14 reintroduced to Irish discourse a sense of peripherality in relation to cores in Germany, the UK, Europe and the International Monetary Fund. That resurrected the earlier discourse about underdevelopment vis-à-vis London and Brussels that had been superseded in the Celtic Tiger years. Media played an increasingly influential role here. Social science theorising can help media understand how Ireland's dependencies on such cores relate to one another and what is required to negotiate and mediate a way through them in the Brexit crisis and the debate about the future of Europe currently unfolding in the EU.

Colonial and post-colonial dependence on the British core pre-occupied the first generations of political and media elites in Ireland as they sought to develop an independent polity and culture more in keeping with Ireland's history and ethos. The new relationship with Europe promised by EEC accession, and which came with the Common Agricultural Policy, cohesion and structural funds, and economic diversification in the 1970s, 1980s and 1990s, seemed to confirm an escape from simple peripherality. This trend was reinforced by the globalisation originating in the United States in the 1990s and 2000s, and the associated development of digital and online technology, which liberated media from distance and geography. These are central themes in Morash's history of Irish media.[74]

Joseph Ruane suggests the Celtic Tiger and globalisation discourses challenged the previous focus on simple peripherality. These discourses substituted 'catch-up with' and 'convergence on' the London and Brussels cores for 'peripherality', and 'interdependence' for 'dependence' as a more appropriate way to talk about Ireland's relations with Britain and the EU. But that new narrative collapsed in 2008, leaving the Irish public angry and bewildered—and the political class, officialdom and media lamenting loss of the capacity and autonomy they had so recently realised. Ruane proposes a different multiple model of peripherality to account for this triple Irish relationship with the EU, the UK and the US. He draws on Stein Rokkan's concept of an 'interface periphery', referring to territories located historically in the zones of overlap between different political and cultural regions that looked outwards to both.[75] Ireland is now a 'multiple interface periphery' between these three cores, he argues, and must negotiate its way through the choices posed by each of them. That certainly requires skill, capacity and autonomy to identify opportunities and resist policy capture, recalling Lee's critique from the 1980s. Ruane says these attributes were lost in the years of the 2000s boom to vested interests and over-reliance on the Anglo-American economic model.

Public opinion and media, though critical of how the financial and austerity crises were conducted by the government and Brussels, tended to trust the latter more, resisted exclusion from the EU system, and became more engaged and politicised through the crisis. Media reportage intensified during these years and was frequently critical of EU policy—and yet remained uncritical of the neoliberal policy framework within which solutions were sought, according to Julian Mercille, who studied domestic reportage and analysis of the crisis using an elite model or propaganda framework.[76] Mercille's methodologies use databases generated from online searches of *The Irish Times*, *Sunday Times*, *Irish Independent*, *Sunday Independent* and *Sunday Business Post*, and could be replicated in other studies of European discourses in Irish media. Other methodologies of media analysis dealing with the sociolinguistic aspects of sub-editing and editing, the framing of stories, and visual design and composition could also be used to build a more comprehensive picture of how Irish media discourses on Europe are constructed and communicated.[77]

For Irish media and the society they service, a 'multiple interface periphery' model has profound implications. Negotiating such a complex relationship towards a new equilibrium requires accurate information and first-class reportage on the state of play from each of the cores and on the balance between their internal and external aspects. It equally requires that political and official elites have the capacity and autonomy to tread their way through the choices involved—and that they are publicly accountable for that. These are fundamental tasks for a well-functioning media.

Official Ireland has had substantial success in negotiating and charting its way out of the financial crisis with the EU and US cores and back towards a buoyant economic growth and nearly full employment, although political and expert opinion differs on how sustainable that is.[78] A similar skill is acknowledged in the official handling of the first phase of the Brexit negotiations, which puts at stake future relations with Ireland's still-closest neighbour and economic interlocutor.[79] Beyond that, choices on the future of Europe involving deeper political, economic, fiscal and security integration pose again the 'Boston or Berlin' debate of 2001–03, which signalled a fateful tilt towards the Anglo-American world during the boom years, leading to collapse in 2008. Ireland will have to adjust and choose between sharply different models of political economy and society, and it needs a better functioning media scene to chart that way.[80] In doing so it must heed the advice of seasoned journalist Sean Whelan not to see the future of Europe only through a Brexit lens, as if to confirm the old dependency.[81]

Notes

[1] Paul Gillespie, 'The complexity of British–Irish interdependence', *Irish Political Studies* 29 (1) (2014), 37–57.

[2] Conor Brady, *Up with the Times* (Gill and Macmillan; Dublin, 2005); Paddy Smyth, 'Feeding in the peripatetic press tent: on being an Irish foreign correspondent', *Studies* 93 (369) (2004), 79–90.

[3] Paul Gillespie, 'Civil society and Irish foreign policy', in Ben Tonra, Michael Kennedy, John Doyle and Noel Dorr (eds), *Irish foreign policy* (Gill and Macmillan; Dublin, 2012), 99–114: 104.

[4] Gillespie, 'Civil society and Irish foreign policy', 105.

[5] Thomas Risse (ed.), *European public spheres: politics is back* (Cambridge University Press; Cambridge, 2015); Giovanni Barbieri, Donatella Campus, Marco Mazzoni, 'How the EU member states' press represented the Euro Crisis', *Journalism* 19 (2) (2018), 1–21.

[6] Paul Gillespie, 'News media as actors in European foreign-policymaking', in Knud Erik Jørgensen, Åsne Kalland Aarstad, Edith Drieskens, Katie Laatikainen and Ben Tonra (eds), *The SAGE handbook of European foreign policy* (Sage; London, 2015), vol. 1, 413–28: 416–17; see also, Risse (ed.), *European public spheres.*

[7] Pieter de Wilde, Anna Leupold and Henning Schmidtke, 'Introduction: the differentiated politicisation of European governance', *West European Politics* 39 (1) (2015), 3–22.

[8] Christopher Morash, *A history of the media in Ireland* (Cambridge University Press; Cambridge, 2010), 225.

[9] Joachim Fischer, 'Life after Brexit', RTÉ blog, 5 January 2018, available at: https://www.rte.ie/eile/brainstorm/2017/1123/922301-life-after-brexit/ (15 April 2018). Fischer makes the argument that '[w]hile the first language of communication within the EU will continue to be English, the native tongue of around one percent of the EU's citizenship will hardly be the language in which key political and cultural debates determining the present and future of the EU will develop their full complexity. There is no indication so far that the Department of Education and Skills has even begun to grasp the cultural and linguistic consequences of Brexit and the quantum leap that is required in the teaching

of EU languages ... Much can be gained from this shift. The narrowness and intellectual poverty of Irish EU debates contrasts starkly with that in other EU member states.'

[10] Mark O'Brien, *De Valera, Fianna Fáil and the Irish Press: the truth in the news?* (Irish Academic Press; Dublin and Portland, 2001), 30.

[11] O'Brien, *De Valera, Fianna Fáil*, 31.

[12] John Bowyer Bell, 'Ireland and the Spanish Civil War, 1936–1939', *Studia Hibernica* 9 (1969), 137–63.

[13] This account draws on: Bowyer Bell, 'Ireland and the Spanish civil war'; Fearghal McGarry, 'Irish newspapers and the Spanish civil war', *Irish Historical Studies* 33 (129) (2002), 68–90; Mark O'Brien, '"In war-torn Spain": the politics of Irish press coverage of the Spanish civil war', *Media, War and Conflict* 10 (3) (2017a), 345–58; and John Horgan and Roddy Flynn, *Irish media: a critical history* (Four Court Press; Dublin and Portland; 2nd edn, 2017).

[14] O'Brien, *De Valera, Fianna Fáil*, 47–8.

[15] McGarry, 'Irish newspapers', 69.

[16] McGarry, 'Irish newspapers', 75.

[17] Bowyer Bell, 'Ireland and the Spanish civil war', 152; Mark O'Brien, *Fourth estate: journalism in twentieth-century Ireland* (Oxford University Press; Oxford, 2017b), 350–1.

[18] O'Brien, *De Valera, Fianna Fáil*, 351–2.

[19] Bowyer Bell, 'Ireland and the Spanish'.

[20] For example, the journalism of the 1930s to the 1950s is defended from charges of insularity, provincialism and uninformed comment by Brian Fallon, *An age of innocence: Irish culture 1930–1960* (Gill and Macmillan; Dublin, 1998), 230, as follows: 'There was, of course, a great deal of flatness, provincialism and dullness, but apart from the fact that Irish newspapers of the period gave a good proportion of the features space to specialists of all kinds and even to intellectuals, a glance at old yellowed copies will often reveal a quite surprising awareness of the outside world.'

[21] Bowyer Bell, 'Ireland and the Spanish'; O'Brien, *Fourth estate*.

[22] Brady, *Up with the Times*, 63–75.

[23] Smyth, 'Feeding in the peripatetic press tent', 83–4.

[24] Smyth, 'Feeding in the peripatetic press tent', 82.

[25] Smyth, 'Feeding in the peripatetic press tent', 82–3

[26] Terence Brown, *The Irish Times: 150 years of influence* (Bloomsbury; London and New York, 2015), 253; Mark O'Brien, *The Irish Times: a history* (Four Courts Press; Dublin and Portland, 2008), 177.

[27] James Downey, *In my own time: inside Irish politics and society* (Gill and Macmillan; Dublin, 2009), chapter 6: 'The Irish question': 112–52.

[28] Editorial, *The Irish Times*, 3 May 1972.

[29] Brown, *The Irish Times: 150 years*, 279.

[30] Dennis Kennedy, *Square peg: the life and times of a northern newspaperman south of the border* (Nonesuch Publishing; Dublin, 2009), 109–17.

[31] Kennedy, *Square peg*, 45, 86–94.

[32] Brady, *Up with the Times*, 67.

[33] Brady, *Up with the Times*, 70.

[34] Smyth, 'Feeding in the peripatetic press tent', 84.

[35] Brown, *The Irish Times: 150 years*; Brady, *Up with the Times*, 90–2.

[36] 'Measuring globalisation', *Foreign Policy* (March–April 2006), 54–60.

[37] Brady, *Up with the Times*, 70.

[38] Florian Otto, Christoph O. Meyer, 'Missing the story? Changes in foreign news reporting and their implications for conflict prevention', *Media, war and conflict* 5 (3) (2010), 205–21: 207.

[39] Smyth, 'Feeding in the peripatetic press tent', 88–9.

[40] Brady, *Up with the Times*, 68.

[41] Brown, *The Irish Times: 150 years*, 343–6.

[42] Conor O'Clery, *May you live in interesting times* (Poolbeg; Dublin, 2008).

[43] Lara Marlowe, *The things I've seen* (Dublin; Liberties Press, 2010); Seamus Martin, *Good times and bad* (Cork; Mercier Press, 2008).

[44] Thomas Risse, *A community of Europeans? Transnational identities and public spheres* (Cornell University Press; Ithaca and London, 2010), 127–56.

[45] Edgar Grande and Hanspeter Kriesi, 'The restructuring of political conflict in Europe and the politicisation of European integration', in Thomas Risse (ed.), *European public spheres: politics is back*, 190–226.

[46] Brady, *Up with the Times*; Downey, *In my own time*; Kennedy, *Square peg*; Smyth, 'Feeding in the peripatetic press tent'; Brown, *The Irish Times: 150 Years*; O'Brien, *The Irish Times: a history*.

[47] Horgan and Flynn, 'Broadcasting, 1957–73', in *Irish Media*, 78–104.

[48] Smyth, 'Feeding in the peripatetic press tent', 85.

[49] Tony Connelly, *Brexit and Ireland, the dangers, the opportunities, and the inside story of the Irish response* (Penguin Ireland; Dublin, 2017a).

[50] Smyth, 'Feeding in the Peripatetic Press Tent', 83.

[51] Jane O'Mahony and Brigid Laffan, *Ireland and the European Union* (Palgrave Macmillan; Basingstoke, 2008), 35–42.

[52] Paul Gillespie, 'The complexity of British–Irish interdependence', *Irish Political Studies* 29/1 (2014), 37–57; Paul Gillespie (2018a), 'Brexit rudely interrupts Irish-British reconciliation', in Adrian Guelke and Paul Gillespie 2018, *Ireland-UK Relations and Norther Ireland after Brexit*, 13, LSE Ideas (London School of Economics; London, 2018); available online at: https://lseideas.atavist.com/ireland-uk (15 April 2018).

[53] Brigid Laffan and Ben Tonra, 'Europe and the international dimension', in John Coakley and Michael Gallagher (eds), *Politics in the Republic of Ireland* (Routledge; London and New York, 2017, 6th edn), 349–70.

[54] Mary P. Corcoran, 'The political preferences and value orientations of Irish journalists', *Irish Journal of Sociology* 13 (2) (2004), 23–42.

[55] Kevin Rafter, 'The media and politics', in John Coakley and Michael Gallagher (eds), *Politics in the Republic of Ireland* (Routledge; London and New York, 2017, 6th edn), 295–320.

[56] Brown, *The Irish Times: 150 years*, 279.

[57] Katy Hayward, *Irish nationalism and European integration: the official redefinition of the island of Ireland* (Manchester University Press; Manchester, 2009), 131.

[58] Desmond Fennell, *Beyond nationalism: the struggle against provinciality in the modern world* (Ward River Press; Dublin, 1985), 37–40.

[59] Fennell, *Beyond nationalism*, 37.

[60] J.J. Lee, *Ireland 1912–1985* (Cambridge University Press; Cambridge, 1989), 627–28.

[61] Lee, *Ireland 1912–1985*, 607.

[62] Joseph Lee, *Reflections on Ireland in the E.E.C.* (Irish Council of the European Movement; Dublin, 1984).

[63] Jim Dooge and Ruth Barrington (eds), *A vital national interest: Ireland in Europe 1973– 1998* (Institute of Public Adminstration; Dublin, 1999); Patrick Keatinge (ed.), *Ireland*

and EC membership evaluated (Pinter; London, 1991); Rory O'Donnell (ed.), *Europe: the Irish experience* (Institute of European Affairs; Dublin, 2000).

[64] Tom Garvin, 'The French are on the sea', in O'Donnell (ed.), *Europe: the Irish experience* 35–43: 43

[65] O'Brien, *The fourth estate*, 2.

[66] Brigid Laffan and Jane O'Mahony, *Ireland and the European Union* (Palgrave Macmillan; Basingstoke and New York, 2008), 131.

[67] Brigid Laffan, 'Irish politics and European politics', in Jim Hourihane (ed.), *Ireland and the European Union* (Lilliput Press; Dublin, 2004), 54–66: 66.

[68] Richard Sinnott, *Knowledge of the European Union in Irish public opinion: sources and implications* (Institute of European Affairs; Dublin, 1995); Laffan and O'Mahony. *Ireland and the European Union*, 128–31.

[69] Rafter, 'The media and politics', 307.

[70] Mark Hennessy, 'Irish media now more Eurosceptic warns EC report', *The Irish Times*, 2 September 2008, 6.

[71] John Coakley, 'Irish public opinion and the new Europe', in Michael Holmes (ed.), *Ireland and the European Union: Nice, enlargement and the future of Europe* (Manchester University Press; Manchester, 2005), 94–113.

[72] Jane O'Mahony, 'Ireland's EU referendum experience', in Katy Hayward and Mary C. Murphy (eds), *The Europeanisation of party politics in Ireland, north and south* (Manchester University Press; Manchester, 2010), 31–50, 24; Rafter, 'The media and politics', 307.

[73] Liesbet Hooghe, Brigid Laffan and Gary Marks, 'Introduction to theory meets crisis collection', *Journal of European Public Policy* 25 (1) (2017), 1–6; Paul Gillespie (2018b), 'Public debate about Europe has shifted', *The Irish Times*, 17 February 2018, 13.

[74] Morash, *A history of the media*, 225.

[75] Joseph Ruane, 'Ireland's multiple interface-periphery development model: achievements and limits', in Michael Bøss (ed.) *The nation-state in transformation: the governance, growth and cohesion of small states under globalisation* (Århus University Press; Århus, 2010), 213–32; Joseph Ruane, 'Modelling Ireland's crises', in Niall Ó Dochartaigh, Katy Hayward and Elizabeth Meehan (eds), *Dynamics of political change in Ireland: making and breaking a divided island* (Routledge; London, 2017), 93–109.

[76] Julian Mercille, *The political economy and media coverage of the European economic crisis: the case of Ireland* (Routledge; London, 2015).

[77] Colleen Cotter, *News talk: investigating the language of journalism* (Cambridge University Press; Cambridge, 2010); Robert M. Entman, *Projections of power: framing news, public opinion, and U.S. foreign policy* (University of Chicago Press; Chicago, 2010); Ruth Wodak and Michael Meyer (eds), *Methods of critical discourse analysis* (Sage; London, 2010; 2nd edn). The author thanks Joe Breen for suggesting these references.

[78] Donal Donovan and Antoin E. Murphy, *The fall of the Celtic Tiger: Ireland and the Euro debt crisis* (Oxford University Press; Oxford, 2013).

[79] Tony Connelly, 'The Brexit veto: how and why Ireland raised the stakes', RTÉ blog, 19 November 2017b; available at: https://www.rte.ie/news/analysis-and-comment/2017/1117/920981-long-read-brexit/ (15 April 2018). Connelly, *Brexit and Ireland*.

[80] Derek Scally, 'Ireland's days of hiding behind the UK are over', *The Irish Times*, 13 September 2017, 12.

[81] Sean Whelan, 'If you are not British, the UK Supreme Court case is irrelevant', RTÉ News, 25 January 2018; available at: https://www.rte.ie/news/2017/0124/847466-brexit-blog/ (15 April 2018).

Bibliography

Aaltonen, S., 1996 'Rewriting representations of the foreign: the Ireland of Finnish Realist drama', *TTR: traduction, terminologie, redaction* 9 (2), 103–22.

aan de Wiel, J., 2013a 'Luxembourg', in M. O'Driscoll, D. Keogh, and J. aan de Wiel (eds), *Ireland through European eyes: Western Europe, the EEC and Ireland, 1945–1973*, 291–313. Cork. Cork University Press.

aan de Wiel, J., 2013b 'Belgium', in M. O'Driscoll, D. Keogh, and J. aan de Wiel (eds), *Ireland through European eyes: Western Europe, the EEC and Ireland, 1945–1973*, 245–90. Cork. Cork University Press.

aan de Wiel, J., 2013c 'The Netherlands', in M. O'Driscoll, D. Keogh, and J. aan de Wiel (eds), *Ireland through European eyes: Western Europe, the EEC and Ireland, 1945–1973*, 190–244. Cork. Cork University Press.

aan de Wiel, J., 2013d 'The Commission, the Council and the Irish application for the EEC, 1961–73', in M. O'Driscoll, D. Keogh, and J. aan de Wiel (eds), *Ireland through European eyes: Western Europe, the EEC and Ireland, 1945–1973*, 314–82. Cork. Cork University Press.

aan de Wiel, J., 2014 'The trouble with Frank Ryan: "corpse diplomacy" between Ireland and East Germany, 1966–1980', *Irish Studies in International Affairs* 25, 203–20.

aan de Wiel, J., 2015 *East German intelligence and Ireland, 1949–90: espionage, diplomacy and terrorism*. Manchester. Manchester University Press.

aan de Wiel, J., 2017 'Ireland's war and the Easter Rising in European context', in J. Crowley, D. Ó Drisceoil, M. Murphy and J. Borgonovo (eds), *Atlas of the Irish Revolution*, 227–39. Cork. Cork University Press.

Abalain, H., 2000 *Histoire de la langue bretonne*. Plouédern. Éditions Gisselot.

Abbate Badin, D. and O'Connor, A. (eds), 2016 'Italia Mia: transnational Ireland in the nineteenth century', Special section of *Studi irlandesi. A Journal of Irish Studies* 6, 17–189.

ad libitum: Sammlung Zerstreuung, 1991 Nr. 21. Berlin. Volk und Welt.

Aer Lingus, 2016 *Annual Report*. Dublin. Aer Lingus.

Aldecoa, I., 1957 *Gran Sol*. Barcelona. Noguer.

Alexander, J.J.G., 1978 *A survey of manuscripts illuminated in the British Isles* (6 vols), vol. 1: *Insular manuscripts, sixth to the ninth century.* London. Harvey Miller.

Alfano, G. and Cortellessa, A. (eds), 2006 *Tegole dal Cielo. L'"effetto Beckett" nella cultura italiana* (2 vols). Rome. Edup.

Allot, S., 1984 *Alcuin of York.* York. William Sessions Ltd.

Almqvist, B., 1978–81 'Scandinavian and Celtic folklore contacts in the Earldom of Orkney', *Saga-Book* 20, 80–105.

Almqvist, B., 1991 'Waterhorse Legends (MLSIT 4086 and 4086B): the case for and against a connection between Irish and Nordic tradition', *Béaloideas* 59, 107–20.

Anderson, B., 1996 *Imagined communities: reflections on the origin and spread of nationalism* (2nd edn). London. Verso.

Anderson, M., 1959 *Shake hands with the devil.* UK and USA. Pennebaker Productions.

Anderson, W.S., 1997 *Ovid's Metamorphoses Books 1–5.* Oklahoma. University of Oklahoma Press.

Andersson, E., 2012 *Dag in och dag ut med en dag i Dublin.* Stockholm. Albert Bonniers Förlag.

Andeweg, A., 2011 *Griezelig gewoon: Gotieke verschijningen in Nederlandse romans, 1980–1995.* Amsterdam. Amsterdam University Press.

Andeweg, A., 2012 'Time and again: anarchronism and the gothic in Vonne van der Meer's *Spookliefde*', *Journal of Dutch Literature* 3 (2), 68–84.

Angenendt, A., 1982 'Die irische Peregrinatio und ihre Auswirkungen auf dem Kontinent vor dem Jahre 800', in Heinz Löwe (ed.), *Die Iren und Europa im früheren Mittelalter* (2 vols), vol. 1, 52–79. Stuttgart. Klett-Cotta.

Antiguas poemas irlandeses, 2001 Transl. by A.R. Taravillo. Madrid. Editorial Gredos.

Arbasino, A., 1977 *Certi romanzi.* Turin. Einaudi.

Ariosto, L., 1976 *Orlando furioso.* Milan. Mondadori. (Originally printed 1516, Ferrara. Giovanni Mazzocco dal Bondeno).

Asmus, S., 2001 *Keltische Sprachinseln.* Berlin. Frieling.

Asplund, K. and Gunnar M.S. (eds), 1922 *Vers från väster. Modern engelsk och amerikansk lyrik.* Stockholm. Bonnier.

Author unknown, 2003 'Measuring globalization: who's up, who's down?', *Foreign Policy,* 134, 60–72.

Author unknown, 2005 'Measuring globalization', *Foreign Policy,* 148, 52–60.

Baeza, R., 2010 *La isla de los santos: itinerario en Irlanda.* Montblanc (Tarragona). Igitur/Piedras Vivas. (Originally printed 1930, Madrid. Renacimiento.)

Balfe, M.W. (ed.), 1865 *Moore's Irish melodies. With symphonies and accompaniments for the pianoforte by M.W. Balfe.* London. Novello, Ewer and Co.

Bakker, B., Borgers, G., Hulsker, J., Schrofer, S and Warmond, E., 1958 *S. Vestdijk.* (Schrijversprentenboek 2). Amsterdam. De Bezige Bij. Available online:

http://www.dbnl.org/tekst/bakk002sves01_01/bakk002sves01_01_0002. php?q=Podium Vestdijknummer#hl2. Accessed 21 March 2018.

Banai, N., 2013 'From nation state to border state', *Third Text* 27 (4), 456–69.

Bank, J., 1995 'Literatuur en Duitse bezetting, 1940–1945', *BMGN: Low Countries Historical Review* 110 (2), 224–37.

Banville, J., 1990 'Survivors of Joyce', in A. Martin (ed.), *James Joyce: the artist and the labyrinth*, 73–4. London. Ryan Publishing.

Barbieri, G., Campus, D. and Mazzoni, M., 2018 'How the EU member states' press represented the Euro Crisis', *Journalism* 19 (2), 1–21.

Barjavel, R. and de Veer O., 1974 *Les Dames à la licorne*. Paris. Presses de la Cité.

Barkhoff, J., 2010 'Kulturkontakt im Zeichen von Traum und Trost. Hansjörg Schertenleibs Irlandromane', in L. Silos Ribas (ed.), *Britannia/Helvetia*, (figurationen gender literatur kultur), 11. Jg., H. 1, 93–112. Wien, Köln and Weimar. Böhlau Verlag.

Barone, R. and Cataldi, M. (ed. and transl.), 1998 *Dán is scór / Venti e una poesia traduzione dall'irlandese*. Bari. La Vallisa.

Barrell, J., 2009 *The dark side of the landscape: the rural poor in English painting, 1730–1840*. Cambridge. Cambridge University Press. (Originally printed 1980, Cambridge, Cambridge University Press.)

Barrett, C., 1976 'The visual arts and society, 1921–84', in J.R. Hill (ed.), *A new history of Ireland*, 587–620. Oxford. Oxford University Press.

Bartlett, T. and Jeffery, K., 1996 *A military history of Ireland*. Cambridge. Cambridge University Press.

Barton, R., 2004 *Irish national cinema*. London and New York. Routledge.

Barton, R., 2011 'Screening the Irish in Britain: introduction', *Irish Studies Review* 19 (1), 1–4.

Barton, R., 2016 '*Jimmy's hall*, Irish cinema and the telling of history', *Review of Irish Studies in Europe* 1 (1), 93–106.

Barton, R., 2017 'Introduction: Irish film and media studies publications', *Estudios Irlandeses*, 12, 241–51.

Beatson, R., 1798 'On Cottages', in John Hamilton, *Irish Agricultural Magazine*, 138–48. Dublin. T.M. Bates.

Bedos-Rezak, B.M., 2000 'Medieval identity: a sign and a concept', *American Historical Review* 105 (5), 1489–533.

Beekman, E.M., 1983 *The verbal empires of Simon Vestdijk and James Joyce*. Amsterdam. Rodopi.

Beemsterboer, A., 2003 *Een Iers sprookje*. Hoorn. Uitgeverij Westfriesland.

Beemsterboer, A., 2007 *Als alle anderen*. Hoorn. Uitgeverij Westfriesland.

Behan, B., 1962 *Stücke fürs Theater*. Transl. by A. and H. Böll. Neuwied. Luchterhand.

Beller, M. and Leerssen, J. (eds), 2007 *Imagology: the cultural construction and literary representation of national character. A critical survey*. Amsterdam and New York. Rodopi.

Bellour, R., 2003 'The living dead (Living and presumed dead)', in G. Baker (ed.), *James Coleman: October Files 5*, 57–72. Cambridge, MA and London. The MIT Press.

Bennet, M., 2018 'Late Medieval Ireland in a wider world', in B. Smith (ed.), *The Cambridge history of Ireland*: vol. i, *600–1550*, 329–52. Cambridge. Cambridge University Press.

Bennett, S., 2002 *Victims of hubris? The decline and fall of Pan Am and Swissair*. Leicester. University of Leicester.

Bermingham, A., 2005 'The simple life: cottages and Gainsborough's cottage doors', in P. de Bolla, N. Leask and D. Simpson (eds), *Land, nation and culture, 1740–1840: thinking the republic of taste*, 37–62. Hampshire and New York. Palgrave Macmillan.

Bhreathnach, E., 2014 *Ireland and the Medieval world 400–1000: landscape, kingship and religion*. Dublin. Four Courts Press.

Biegel, P., 1990 *Anderland: een Brandaan mythe*. Haarlem. Uitgeverij Holland.

Bielenberg, A., 2002 *The Shannon scheme and the electrification of the Irish Free State*. Dublin. Lilliput Press.

Bielenberg, A. and Ryan, R., 2013 *An economic history of Ireland since independence*. Abingdon. Routledge.

Bieler, L., 1958 'Adamnani de locis sanctis libri tres', in D. Meehan (ed.), *Adamnan's De locis sanctis, Scriptores Latini Hiberniae 3*, 36–120. Dublin. Dublin Institute for Advanced Studies.

Bieler, L., 1963, *Ireland: harbinger of the Middle Ages*. London, Oxford, New York and Toronto. Oxford University Press.

Blanc, L., 1866–7 *Lettres sur L'Angleterre (1862)* (2 vols). Paris. Librairie internationale.

Blanchard, J., 1958 *Le droit ecclésiastique contemporain d'Irlande*. Paris. Librairie générale de droit et de jurisprudence.

Bode, J.J.C., 2008 'Der Übersetzer an den Leser', in L. Sterne, *Yoricks empfindsame Reise durch Frankreich und Italien*, 7–15, aus dem Englischen von Johann Joachim Christoph Bode. Frankfurt a. Main. S. Fischer Verlag. (Originally printed 1768, Hamburg and Bremen. Cramer Verlag.)

Böll, H., 1957 *Irisches Tagebuch*. Köln-Berlin. Kiepenheuer and Witsch.

Böll, H., 1965 *Irsk dagbog*. Transl. by H. Steinthal. Copenhagen. Grafisk.

Böll, H., 1967a *Diario d'Irlanda*. Transl. by M. Marianelli, with an introduction by I.A. Chiusano. Milano. Mondadori.

Böll, H., 1967b, *Irish journal*. Transl. by L. Vennewitz. New York, Toronto. McGraw–Hill Book Company.

Böll, H., 1972 *Irländsk dagbok*. Transl. by K. Franke. Stockholm. Aldus.

Böll, H., 1973a *Irsk dagbok*. Transl. by M. Ringard. Oslo. Gyldendal.

Böll, H., 1973b *Úr írskri dagbók*. Transl. by I. Grein. Reykjavik. Lesbók Morgunblaðsins, 14.

Böll, H., 1975 *Päiväkirja vihreältä saarelta*. Transl. by K. Kaila. Helsinki. Otava.

Böll, H., 2011 *Irish journal*. Transl. by L. Vennewitz. Melville House. New York.

Böndel, P., 2017 'Die Logik des Widersinnigen', available online: http://literaturkritik.de/o-cadhain-der-schluessel-die-logik-des-widersinnigen,23006. html. Accessed 16 December 2017.

Bolufer Peruga, M., 2008 *La vida y la escritura en el siglo XVIII: Inés Joyes: Apología de las Mujeres*. València. Universitat de València.

Borkowski, T., 2010 *Irlandia Jones poszukiwany*. Wrocław. Gajt.

Bourke, C., 1995 'Further notes on the Clonmore Shrine', *Seanchas Ardmhacha/ Journal of the Armagh Diocesan Historical Society* 16 (2), 27–32.

Bourke, E. and Farago, B. (eds), 2010 *Landing places: immigrant poets in Ireland*. Dublin. Dedalus Press.

Bourke, E. (ed., transl. and annot.), 2012 *'Poor Green Erin'. German travel writers' narratives on Ireland from before the 1978 Rising to after the Great Famine*. Frankfurt a. Main, Berlin and Bern. Peter Lang.

Bourke, T.E., 2009, '"The birthmark of Germanness". Hugo Hamilton and the question of belonging', in J. Fischer and G. Holfter (eds), *Creative influences. Selected Irish-German biographies*, 179–93. Trier. Wissenschaftlicher Verlag Trier.

Bowyer Bell, J., 1969 'Ireland and the Spanish Civil War, 1936–1939', *Studia Hibernica* 9, 137–63.

Boyd, E., 2010 Chick Lit and Existentialismen: en undersökning kring Chick Lit–hjältinnan. Unpublished undergraduate thesis. Högskolan i Halmstad.

Boyle, N, and Guthrie, J. (eds), 2002 *Goethe and the English speaking world. Essays from the Cambridge symposium for his 250th anniversary*. Rochester, NY and Woodbridge Suffolk. Camden House.

Boym, S., 2007 'Nostalgia and its discontents', *Hedgehog Review* 9 (2), Summer, 7–18.

Bozzoli, A., 1971 'Manzoni e Goldsmith', *Aevum* 45 (1)–2, 46–56.

Bracken, D. and Graff, E., 2015 *The Schaffhausen Adomnán*. Cork. Cork University Press.

Brady, C., 2005 *Up with the Times*. Dublin. Gill and Macmillan.

Brady, J., 1944 'Father Christopher Cusack and the Irish college of Douai 1594–1624', in S. O'Sullivan (ed.), *Measgra Mhichíl Uí Chléirigh*, 98–107. Dublin. Assisi Press.

Brandt Corstius, H., 1994 'Wat is Iers? Wat is hysterisch?', *NRC Handelsblad:* 24. 29 April.

Breathnach, P.A., 1985 'Irish churchmen in pre-Carolingian Europe', *Cumann Seanchais Ard Mhacha/Armagh Diocesan Historical Society* and *Seanchas Ardmhacha / Journal of the Armagh Diocesan Historical Society* 11 (2), 319–30.

Brecht, B., 1967 *Schriften zur Literatur und Kunst*, Bd. 1. Frankfurt am Main. Suhrkamp.

Brewer, S., 1998 'Ireland as a religious utopia. Böll, Ireland and *Irisches Tagebuch*', in J. Fischer, G. Holfter and E. Bourke (eds), *Deutsch-Irische Verbindungen. Geschichte – Literatur – Übersetzung / Irish German connections. History – Literature – Translation*, 123–31. Akten der 1. Limericker Konferenz für deutsch-irische Studien, 2–4. September 1997. Trier. Wissenschaftlicher Verlag Trier.

Broch, H., 1975 'James Joyce und die Gegenwart. Rede zu Joyces 50. Geburtstag', in H. Broch, *Schriften zur Literatur I. Kritik*, Bd. 9 (1), 63–94, Kommentierte Werkausgabe, P.M. Lützeler (ed.), Frankfurt a. Main. Suhrkamp.

Brockliss, L.W.B. and Ferté, P., 1987 'Irish clerics in France in the seventeenth and eighteenth centuries: a statistical survey', *Proceedings of the Royal Irish Academy* 87C, 527–72.

Brockliss, L.W.B., and Ferté, P., 2004 'Prosopography of Irish clerics in the universities of Paris and Toulouse, 1573–1792', *Archivium Hibernicum* 58, 1–166.

Brooks, M., 1981 '*The Builder* in the 1840s: the making of a magazine, the shaping of a profession', *Victorian Periodicals Review* 14 (3) (Fall), 86–93.

Brown, T., 2015 *The Irish Times: 150 years of influence.* London and New York. Bloomsbury.

Bryll, E. and Goraj-Bryll, M. (eds), 1978 *Miodopój. Wybór wierszy irlandzkich (Wiek VI–XII)* ('The honey well: a selection of Irish poetry (6th–12th century)'). Warszawa. Instytut Wydawniczy PAX.

Bryll, E. and Goraj-Bryll, M. (eds), 1981 *Irlandzki tancerz: Wybór wierszy irlandzkich (Wiek XIII – XIX)* ('The Irish dancer: a selection of Irish poetry (13th–19th century)'). Warszawa. Instytut Wydawniczy PAX.

Bryll, E. and Goraj-Bryll, M., 2010 *Irlandia. Celtycki splot.* Poznań. Zysk i Sk-a.

Brzezińska, G., 2010 *Irlandzki koktajl.* Warszawa. Wydawnictwo Bliskie.

Buchloh, B.H.D., 2003 'Memory lessons and history tableaux: James Coleman's archaeology of spectacle', in G. Baker, *James Coleman*, 83–112. Cambridge, MA and London. The MIT Press.

Buelens, G., 2004 'An excessive, Catholic heretic from a nation in danger: James Joyce in Flemish literature', in G. Lernout and W. van Mierlo (eds), *The reception of James Joyce in Europe* (2 vols), vol. 1, 150–61. London. Continuum.

Buikema, R. and Wesseling, L., 2006 *Het heilige huis. De gotieke vertelling in de Nederlandse literatuur.* Amsterdam. Amsterdam University Press.

Bullough, D.A., 1982 'The missions to the English and Picts and their Heritata (to *c.* 800)', in H. Löwe (ed.), *Die Iren und Europa im früheren Mittelalter* (2 vols), vol. 1, 80–97. Stuttgart. Klett-Cotta

Bully, S., 2006 'Luxeuil-les-Bains (Haute-Saône), ancienne église Saint-Martin', *Bulletin du Centre d'études médiévales* 10, 89–92.

Burkart, A.J., 1962 'Advertising and marketing in the airline industry', *Journal of Industrial Economics* 11 (1), November, 18–32.

Burnham, S., 1995 *Beethoven Hero.* Princeton NJ. Princeton University Press.

Caillet, M., 1991 'La bibliothèque du collège des Irlandais et son fonds des livres anciens', *Mélanges de la bibliothèque de la Sorbonne*, 2, 151–63.

Canny, N. (ed.), 1994 *Europeans on the move: studies on European migration 1500–1800.* Oxford. Clarendon Press.

Carlos, I., 2016 'Again and again', in *Willie Doherty: again and again/ uma e outra vez,* 137–9. Lisbon. Centro de arte moderna Gulbenkian.

Carnicer, C., 2008 *La cruz de Borgoña.* Madrid. La esfera de los libros.

Carpenter, A. (ed.), 2003 *Verse in English from Tudor and Stuart Ireland.* Cork. Cork University Press.

Casway, J., 1991 'Irish women overseas, 1500–1800', in M. MacCurtain and M. O'Dowd (eds), *Women in early modern Ireland,* 112–32. Edinburgh. Edinburgh University Press.

Centre for Irish-German Studies, 2017 'Centre for Irish-German Studies: the first 20 years 1997–2017'; available online: https://issuu.com/centreforirish-germanstudies/docs/broschure_208_ef_80_a217_20final_20. Accessed 28 February 2018.

Chalandon, S., 2008 *Mon traître.* Paris. Éditions Grasset et Fasquelle.

Chalandon, S., 2011 *My traitor.* Transl. by F. McCann and K. Lyddon. Dublin. Lilliput Press.

Chalandon, S., 2011 *Retour à Killybegs.* Paris. Éditions Grasset et Fasquelle.

Chalandon, S., 2013 *Return to Killybegs.* Transl. by U. Meany Scott. Dublin. Lilliput Press.

Charles-Edwards, M., 2000 *Early Christian Ireland.* Cambridge. Cambridge University Press.

Chonraí, M., 2010 *Une vie irlandaise: du Connemara à Rath Chairn: histoire de la vie de Micil Chonraí.* Transl. by J. Le Dû. Rennes. Editions Terre de Brume/ Presses Universitaires de Rennes.

Christiansen, S., 2012a *Det ensomme hjerte.* Oslo. Gyldendal. (Originally published 1938.)

Christiansen, S., 2012b *Menneskenes lod.* Oslo. Gyldendal. (Originally published 1945.)

Christiansen, S., 2013 *Drømmen og livet.* Oslo. Gyldendal. (Originally published 1935.)

Christov-Bakargiev, C., Mac Giolla Léith, C. and Doherty, W., 2002 *Willie Doherty: false memory.* Dublin and London. Irish Museum of Modern Art/Merrell.

Cianci, G., 1974 *La fortuna di Joyce in Italia (1917–1972).* Bari. Adriatica.

Clark, C.R. and Horstmann, I.J., 2013 'A model of advertising format competition: on the use of celebrities in ads', *Canadian Journal of Economics* 46 (4), November, 1606–30.

Clarke, H.B., Ní Mhaonaigh, M. and Ó Floinn, R. (eds), 1998 *Ireland and Scandinavia in the Early Viking Age.* Dublin. Four Courts Press.

Coakley, J., 1983 'Public opinion and the European Communities', in D. Coombes (ed.) *Ireland and the European Communities,* 43–67. Dublin. Gill and Macmillan.

Coakley, J., 2005 'Irish public opinion and the new Europe', in M. Holmes (ed.), *Ireland and the European Union: Nice, enlargement and the future of Europe,* 94–113. Manchester. Manchester University Press.

Cole, R., 2006 *Propaganda, censorship and Irish neutrality in the Second World War*. Edinburgh. Edinburgh University Press.

Colgrave B. and Mynors, R.A.B. (eds), 1969 *The ecclesiastical history of the English people* (Oxford Medieval Texts, 5 books; book 1). Oxford. Clarendon Press.

Colker, M.L., 1979 'Die Regensburger Schottenlegende: Libellus de fundacione ecclesie Consecrati Petri. P.A. Breathnach', *Speculum* 54 (3), 548–50.

Connelly, T., 2017a 'The Brexit veto: how and why Ireland raised the stakes', RTÉ blog, 19 November. Available online: https://www.rte.ie/news/analysis-and-comment/2017/1117/920981-long-read-brexit/. Accessed on 15 April 2018.

Connelly, T., 2017b *Brexit and Ireland: the dangers, the opportunities, and the inside story of the Irish response*. Dublin. Penguin Ireland.

Connolly, S.J., 2007 *Contested island: Ireland 1460–1630*. Oxford. Clarendon Press.

Connolly, S.J., 2008 *Divided kingdom: Ireland 1630–1800*. Oxford. Clarendon Press.

Connor, B., 1698 *The history of Poland; In several letters to persons of quality*. London. 2 vols.

Cooper, B., 1995 'Beethoven's folksong settings as sources of Irish folk music', in P. Devine and H. White (eds), *The Maynooth international musicological conference 1995, selected proceedings: part two*, 65–81, Irish musical studies vol. 5. Dublin. Four Courts Press.

Corcoran, M.P., 2004 'The political preferences and value orientations of Irish journalists', *Irish Journal of Sociology* 13 (2), 23–42.

Corlett, C., 2003 'The Rathdown slabs—Vikings and Christianity', *Archaeology Ireland* 17 (4), 28–30.

Cornets de Groot, R.A., 1981 'Hendrik Cramers verhaal', *Ladders in de leegte*. The Hague. Nijgh & Van Ditmar.

Cotter, C., 2010 *News talk: investigating the language of Journalism*. Cambridge. Cambridge University Press.

Cronin, M., 2003 'Next to being there: *Ireland of the welcomes* and tourism of the word', in M. Cronin and B. O'Connor (eds) *Irish tourism: image, culture, and identity*, 179–95. Clevedon. Channel View Publications.

Cronin, M., 2007 'Small worlds and weak ties: Ireland in the new century', *Journal of Irish Studies* 22, 63–73.

Crouch, D, and Lübbren, N., 2003 *Visual culture and tourism*. Oxford/New York. Berg.

Cruz, J., 2010 'Entrevista Enrique Vila-Matas', *El País*, 13 March. Available online: https://elpais.com/diario/2010/03/13/babelia/1268442746_850215.html. Accessed 12 April 2017.

Cullen, L., 1994 'The Irish diaspora', in N. Canny (ed.), *Europeans on the move: studies on European migration 1500–1800*, 113–49. Oxford. Oxford University Press.

Cunqueiro, A., 1986 *Viajes imaginarios y reales*. Barcelona. Tusquets.

Curtis Jr., L.P., 2011 *The depiction of eviction in Ireland*. Dublin. University College Dublin Press.

Cyroulnik, P., 1996 '16 artistes irlandais à l'École nationale supérieure des Beaux-Arts de Paris', in P. Bonafoux (ed.), *L'imaginaire irlandais,* 86–7. Vanves. Fernand Hazan.

Czartoryska, W.T. (ed.), 2011 *Wyfruneli. Nowa emigracja o sobie.* Łomża. Oficyna Wydawnicza Stopka.

Czerwiński, P., 2009 *Przebiegum życiae.* Warszawa. Świat Książki.

Czerwiński, P., 2017 *Zespół ojca.* Warszawa. Wielka Litera.

Czumalo, V., 2012 'Architecture and identity, genius loci', *Autoportet* 36, 47.

D'haen, T., 2006 'Yeats in the Dutch-language Low Countries', in K.P. Jochum (ed.), *The reception of W.B. Yeats in Europe,* 12–24. London and New York. Continuum.

D'Hoker, E., 2002, 'Negative aesthetics in Hugo von Hofmannsthal's *Ein Brief* and John Banville's *The Newton letter*', in Karen Vandevelde (ed.), *New voices in Irish criticism 3,* 36–43. Dublin. Four Courts Press.

Da Conceiçao, P., 1970 *Portugal e Irlanda: laços duma civilizaçao Atlântica na bruma dos séculos.* Lisbon. Sociedad da língua Portuguesa.

Daly, M., 2018 'Migration since 1914', in Thomas Bartlett (ed.), *The Cambridge history of Ireland:* vol. iv *1880 to the present,* 527–552. Cambridge. Cambridge University Press.

Davis, V., 2000 'Irish clergy in late medieval England', *Irish Historical Studies* 32, 145–60.

Davis, V., 2002 'Material relating to Irish clergy in England in the late middle ages', *Archivium Hibernicum* 56, 7–50.

de Fréine, C., 2003 *Bucoku Етажи (Faoi chabáistí is ríonacha).* Transl. by V. Nemchev. Sofia. Orpheus.

De La Rochefoucauld, F. and Scarfe, N. (eds), 1988 *A Frenchman's year in Suffolk: French impressions of Suffolk Life in 1784.* Suffolk. Boydell Press.

De Maere, J., 1981 'Leon de Winter: op zoek naar Eileen W.', *Dietsche Warande en Belfort* 126, 701–4.

De Mesa, E., 2014 *The Irish in the Spanish armies in the seventeenth century.* Woodbridge, Suffolk. Boydell Press.

De Toro, S., 2010 *O país da brétema.* Madrid. Aguilar.

De Toro Santos, A.R., 2007 *La literatura irlandesa en España.* Corunna. Netbiblo.

de Valera, S., 2000 'Minister for the Arts, Culture, Gaeltacht and the Islands, address to Boston College', 18 September. Dublin. Department of Arts, Culture, Gaeltacht and the Islands.

De Vries, T. (ed.), 1968 *S. Vestdijk, Brieven uit de oorlogsjaren aan Theun de Vries.* The Hague. Nederlands Letterkundig Museum en Documentatiecentrum.

De Wilde, P., Leupold, A. and Schmidtke, H., 2015 'Introduction: the differentiated politicisation of European governance', *West European Politics* 39 (1), 3–22.

De Winter, L., 1996 *Zoeken naar Eileen W.* (Series Grote Lijsters Nr 4). Groningen. Wolters-Noordhoff. (Originally printed 1981. Amsterdam. In de Knipscheer).

Del Carmen Lario de Oñate, M., 2000 *La colonia mercantile Británica e Irlandesa en Cádiz a finales del siglo XVIII.* Cádiz. Servicio de Publicaciones Universidad de Cádiz.

Della Torre, A., 1972 *Carlo Linati.* Como. Piero Cairoli.

Deardon, B., 1944 *Halfway House.* United Kingdom. Ealing Studios.

Denez, P., 1971 'Modern Breton literature', in J.E.C. Williams (ed.), *Literature in Celtic Countries*, 124–5. Cardiff. University of Wales Press.

Déon, M., 1970 *Les poneys sauvages.* Paris. Éditions Gallimard.

Déon, M., 1973 *Un taxi mauve.* Paris. Éditions Gallimard.

Déon, M., 1982 'Insaisissable Irlande', in P. Rafroidi and P. Joannon (eds), *Études Irlandaises* VII, 13–15. Lille. Université de Lille III.

Déon, M., 2005 *Cavalier, passe ton chemin!.* Paris. Éditions Gallimard.

Déon, M., 2016 *Horseman, pass by!: Irish pages.* Transl. by C. Ní Ríordáin. Dublin. Lilliput Press.

Department of Industry and Commerce, 1951 *Synthesis of reports on tourism 1950–51.* Dublin. Stationery Office.

Di Martino, L., 2004 'Gadda-Joyce', *Edinburgh Journal of Gadda Studies* 4. Available online: https://www.gadda.ed.ac.uk/Pages/resources/walks/pge/joycedimarti.php. Accessed 12 December 2017.

Di Martino, L., 2009 *Il caleidoscopio della scrittura: James Joyce, Carlo Emilio Gadda e il romanzo modernista.* Naples. Edizioni Scientifiche Italiane.

Dickel, H., 1983 *Die deutsche Aussenpolitik und die Irische Frage von 1932 bis 1944.* Wiesbaden. Franz Steiner Verlag.

Dimendberg, E., 2003 'Down these mean streets a man must go: Siegfried Krakauer's "Hollywood's terror films" and the spatiality of film noir', *New German Critique* 89, 113–43.

Donovan D. and Murphy, A.E., 2013 *The fall of the Celtic Tiger: Ireland and the Euro debt crisis.* Oxford. Oxford University Press.

Dooge, J. and Barrington, R. (eds), 1999 *A vital national interest: Ireland in Europe 1973–1998.* Dublin. Institute of Public Adminstration.

Doorley, C., Bolger D. and Phelan, C. (eds), 2012 *Yet to be told.* Dublin. Fighting Words.

Doorley, M., 2005 *Irish–American diaspora nationalism: the friends of Irish freedom, 1916–35.* Dublin. Four Courts Press.

Dorrestein, R., 1994. *Een sterke man.* Amsterdam. Uitgeverij Contact.

Downey, J., 2009 *In my own time: inside Irish politics and society.* Dublin. Gill and Macmillan.

Draak, M., 1975 'De gecompliceerde bronnen van Holst's Ierse prozaverhalen. (Het werk van de filoloog)', *De Nieuwe Taalgids* 68, 31–45.

Draak, M., 1977 'In memoriam Adrianus Roland Holst', *Jaarboek van de Maatschappij der Nederlandse Letterkunde* , 25–32.

Draak, M. and Aafjes, B. (eds), 1949 *De reis van Sinte Brandaan.* Amsterdam. J.M. Meulenhoff.

Draghi, M., 2015 'Letter to Matt Carthy MEP', 17 February. Available online: https://www.ecb.europa.eu/pub/pdf/other/150218letter_carthy.en.pdf. Accessed 17 March 2018.

Duncan, E., 2016 'The Irish and their books', in Roy Flechner and Sven Meeder (eds), *The Irish in Early Medieval Europe: identity, culture and religion*, 214–30. London. Palgrave Macmillan.

Dunne, T., 2006 'The dark side of the Irish landscape: depictions of the rural poor, 1760–1850', in *Whipping the herring: survival and celebration in nineteenth-century Irish art*, 46–62. Cork. Crawford Art Gallery (exhibition catalogue).

Dunning, C.S.L. and Hudson, D.R.C., 2013 'The transportation of Irish swordsmen to Sweden and Russia and the plantation in Ulster (1609–13)', *Archivium Hibernicum* 57, 422–53.

Durozoi, G., 1971 *Le Surréalisme*. Paris. Larousse.

Duytschaever, J., 1976 'James Joyce's impact on Simon Vestdijk's early fiction', in P. Brachin, J. Goossens, P.K. King and J. de Rooij (eds), *Dutch Studies: an annual review of the language, literature and life of the Low Countries*, vol. 2, 48–74. The Hague. Martinus Nijhoff.

Dyer, R., 2007a 'Heavenly bodies', in S. Redmond and S. Holmes (eds), *Stardom and celebrity: a reader*, 85–9. London. Sage.

Dyer, R., 2007b 'Stars', in S. Redmond and S. Holmes (eds), *Stardom and celebrity: a reader*, 78–84. London. Sage.

Dziewor, Y. and Mühling, M. (eds), 2006 *Willie Doherty: Anthologie zeitbasierter Arbeiten/Anthology of time-based works*. Hamburg and Munich. Kunstverein in Hamburg and Städische Galerie im Lenbachhaus und Kunstbau München.

Einhard, 1986 *Vita Karoli Magni (Das Leben Karls des Großen)*. Ditzingen. Reclam.

Entman, R.M., 2010 *Projections of power: framing news, public opinion, and U.S. foreign policy*. Chicago. University of Chicago Press.

Erdmann, W., 1979 *Die Reichenau Im Bodensee Geschichte Und Kunst*. Königstein. Karl Robert Langewiesche.

Espedal, T., 2014 *Bergeners*. Oslo. Gyldendal.

European Union, 2017 *Guiding principles for the dialogue on Ireland/Northern Ireland*, 21 September. Available online: https://ec.europa.eu/commission/publications/guiding-principles-dialogue-ireland-northern-ireland_en. Accessed 17 March 2018.

Everett Green, M.A (ed.), 1869 *Calendar of state papers, domestic series, of the reign of Elizabeth, 1598–1601*. London. Longmans, Green, and Co.

Eysteinsson, A., 2004 'Late arrivals: James Joyce in Iceland', in G: Lernout and W. Van Mierlo (eds), *The reception of James Joyce in Europe* vol. 1: *Germany, Northern and Eastern Central Europe*, 89–102. London and New York. Continuum.

Fabbri, A., Giosa, M. and Montevecchi, M., 1996 *Bollirà la Rugiada: poesia irlandese contemporea*. Faenza. Mobydick Edizioni.

Fagan, G., 2017 Opening statement by Gabriel Fagan, Chief Economist, Central Bank of Ireland at the Seanad Committee on Brexit, 4 May. Available online: https://www.centralbank.ie/news/article/opening-statement-by-gabriel-fagan-at-the-seanad-committee-on-brexit. Accessed 17 March 2018.

Fáilte Ireland, 2011 *Annual report.* Dublin. Fáilte Ireland.

Fáilte Ireland, 2013 *National diaspora feasibilty study.* Dublin. Fáilte Ireland.

Fáilte Ireland, 2016 *Tourism facts 2016.* Dublin. Fáilte Ireland.

Fallon, B., 1998 *An age of innocence: Irish culture 1930–1960.* Dublin. Gill and Macmillan.

Fannin, S., 2011 'Documents of Irish interest in the Archivo de la Diputación Foral de Bizkaia', *Archivium Hibernicum* 64, 170–93.

Fantaccini, F., 1998 'Montale, Lucio Piccolo e l'opera di William Butler Yeats', in F. Marroni, M. Costantini and R. D'Agnillo (eds), *Percorsi di poesia irlandese,* 63–92. Pescara. Tracce.

Fantaccini, F., 1999 'Italian contributions to the study of Irish culture: a select bibliography', in C. de Petris, J.M. Ellis D'Alessandro and F. Fantaccini (eds), *The cracked lookingglass. Contributions to the study of Irish literature,* 253–91. Roma. Bulzoni Editori.

Fantaccini, F., 2003 'La letteratura irlandese in Italia', *Quaderni del premio letterario Giuseppe Acerbi* 4/anno 4, 168–74.

Fantaccini, F., 2009 'Quattro poeti italiani e Yeats', *W.B. Yeats e la cultura italiana,* 113–64. Florence. Firenze University Press.

Farewell, J., 1689, *The Irish Hudibras; or Fingallian prince, taken from the sixth book of Virgil's Aenaeids, and adapted to the present times.* London. Richard Balwin.

Fattori, A., 2010 'Ireland as a "better elsewhere", in Heinrich Böll's *Irisches Tagebuch* and in Margrit Baur's *Alle Herrlichkeit'*, in Gisela Holfter (ed.), *Heinrich Böll's 'Irisches Tagebuch' in context,* 99–113. Trier. Wissenschaftlicher Verlag Trier.

Fattori, A., 2011 '"A genuinely funny German farce" turns into a very Irish play: *The broken jug* (1994), John Banville's adaptation of Heinrich von Kleist's *Der zerbrochene Krug* (1807)', *Angermion. Yearbook for Anglo-German literary criticism, intellectual history and cultural transfers / Jahrbuch für britisch-deutsche Kulturbeziehungen* 4, 75–94.

Fennell, D., 1985 *Beyond nationalism: the struggle against provinciality in the modern world.* Dublin. Ward River Press.

Fenning, H., 2005 'Irishmen ordained at Rome, 1572–1697', *Archivium Hibernicum* 59, 1–36.

Fenning, H., 2009 'Students at the Irish college at Salamanca, 1592–1638', *Archivium Hibernicum,* 62, 7–36.

Fernández Duro, C., 2009 *Naufragios de la armada española: Relación histórica formada con presencia de los documentos oficiales que existen en el archivo del Ministerio de Marina.* Seville. Renacimiento Isla de Tortuga. (Originally printed 1867, Madrid, Tipográfico de Estrada, Díaz y López.)

Ferreiro, C.E., 1967 *Longa noite de pedra*. Barcelona. El Bardo.

Ferris, I., 1999 'The question of ideological form: Arthur Young, the agricultural tour, and Ireland', in D.E. Richter (ed.), *Ideology and form in eighteenth-century literature*, 129–45. Lubbock, TX. Texas Technical University Press.

Ferris, I.M., 2000 *Enemies of Rome: Barbarians through Roman eyes*. Stroud. Sutton Publishing.

Fischer, J., 2001 '"… 'thar lear' chomh hiomlán is chomh haoibhinn…": Aspekte des Deutschlandbildes in der zeitgenössischen irischsprachigen Literatur Irlands', in M. G. Schmidt and W. Bisang (eds), *Philologica et linguistica: historia, pluralitas, universitas*, 385–411. Trier. Wissenschaftlicher Verlag Trier.

Fischer, J., 2018 'Life after Brexit', RTÉ blog, 5 January. Available online: https://www.rte.ie/eile/brainstorm/2017/1123/922301-life-after-brexit/. Accessed 15 April 2018.

FitzGerald, G., 1949 'Aer Lingus', *Irish Monthly* 77 (917), November, 499–504.

FitzGerald, G., 1975 'Irish foreign policy within the context of the EEC', text of address given by the Irish Minister for Foreign Affairs, Dr Garret FitzGerald TD, to the Royal Irish Academy, 10 November. Available online: http://aei.pitt.edu/8545/. Accessed 17 March 2018.

FitzGerald, M., 2000 *Protectionism to liberalisation: Ireland and the EEC, 1957 to 1966*. Aldershot. Ashgate.

FitzGerald, M., 2005 'The "mainstreaming" of Irish foreign policy', in B. Girvin and G. Murphy (eds), *The Lemass era: politics and society in the Ireland of Seán Lemass*, 82–98 Dublin. University College Dublin Press.

Fitzgerald, P. and Lambkin, B., 2008 *Migration in Irish history 1607–2007*. London. Palgrave.

Fjågesund, P., 2004 'The Modernist tower: a many-faceted symbol', in M. Jansson, J. Lothe and H. Riikonen (eds), *European and Nordic Modernisms*, 233–51. London. Norvik Press.

Flachenecker, H., 2014 'The contribution of Irish scholars and monks to the religious landscape in Germany in the Late Middle Ages and early Modern Period', in C. O'Reilly and V. O'Regan (eds), *Ireland and the Irish in Germany. Reception and perception*, 13–25. Baden Baden. Nomos Verlagsgesellschaft.

Flanagan, C., 2015 'Speech delivered by the Irish Minister for Foreign Affairs, Charles Flanagan, TD, Leinster House, 25 March 2015 at the launch of the book *Britain in Europe: the end game—an Irish perspective*. Available online: https://www.dfa.ie/news-and-media/press-releases/press-release-archive/2015/march/minister-launches-iiea-book/. Accessed 17 March 2018.

Flanagan, C., 2016 'Statement by the Irish Minister for Foreign Affairs, Charles Flanagan, TD, to the Dáil on the UK–EU Referendum outcome, 27 June 2016'. Available online: https://www.dfa.ie/news-and-media/speeches/speeches-archive/2016/june/uk-exit-from-eu-mfat-dail-statement/. Accessed 17 March 2018.

Flechner, R., 2008 'Aspects of the Breton transmission of the Hibernensis', *Pecia* 12, 27–44.

Flechner, R. and Meeder, S., 2016 (eds), *The Irish in early medieval Europe: identity, culture and religion*. London. Palgrave.

Fleischmann, A., 1936 'Ars nova', *Ireland Today* 1, 41–8.

Fleuriot, L., 1987 'Le Récit de navigation', in J. Balcou and Y. Le Gallo (eds), *L'Histoire littéraire et culturelle de la Bretagne* (3 livres), livre 1, 131–64. Paris et Genève. Éditions Champion-Slatkine.

Flynn, R., and Brereton, P., 2007 'The purple taxi (1977)', in R. Flynn and P. Brereton, *Historical dictionary of Irish cinema*. Historical Dictionaries of Literature and the Arts, no. 17, 300. Lanham, MD, Toronto and Plymouth, UK. Scarecrow Press.

Freitag, B. and Oeser, H-C. (eds), 1988 *Irland: Glaube, Liebe, Hoffnung— Armut, Qual, Buße: Irische Augenblicke* (*die horen* 33/3). Bremerhaven. Wirtschaftsverlag NW.

Foster, J.W., 1987 *Fictions of the Irish literary revival: a changeling art.* Syracuse NY. Syracuse University Press.

Foster, R., 2007 'The red and the green', in B. Barrington (ed.), *The Dublin Review reader*, 151–8. Dublin. Dublin Review of Books.

Fox, Y., 2014 *Power and religion in Merovingian Gaul, Columbanian monasticism and the Frankish elites.* Cambridge. Cambridge University Press.

Fox, Y., 2016 'The political context of Irish monasticism in seventh century Francia: another look at sources', in R. Flechner and S. Meeder (eds), *The Irish in Early Medieval Europe*, 53–67. New York. Palgrave.

Furlong, G., 1962 *Misiones y sus pueblos de Guaranies, 1610–1813.* Buenos Aires. Ediciones Teoria.

Furlong. G. (ed.), 1971 *Tomas Fields S.J. y su 'Carta al preposito general 1601'.* Buenos Aires. Casa Pardo.

Furlong, I., 2009 *Irish tourism, 1880–1980.* Dublin. Irish Academic Press.

García García, B.J. and Recio Morales, Ó. (eds), 2014 *Las corporaciones de nación en la monarquía hispánica (1580–1750).* Madrid. Fundación Carlos Amberes.

García Hernan, E., 2008 'Clérigos irlandeses en el corte de Madrid', in Declan M. Downey and Julio Crespo MacLennan (eds), *Spanish–Irish relations through the ages* 49–71. Dublin. Four Courts Press.

Garofalo, P., 2011 'Giovanni Berchet and Early Italian Romanticism', *Rivista di studi italiani* 2, 107–30.

Garvin, T., 2000 'The French are on the sea', in R. O'Donnell (ed.), *Europe: the Irish experience*, 35–43. Dublin. Institute of European Affairs.

Geary, M.J., 2009 *An inconvenient wait: Ireland's quest for membership of the EEC, 1957–73.* Dublin. Institute of Public Administration.

Gelbart, M., 2007 *The invention of 'folk music' and 'art music'. Emerging categories from Ossian to Wagner.* Cambridge. Cambridge University Press.

Genet-Rouffiac, N., 2007 *Le Grand Exil: les Jacobites en France, 1688–1715.* Paris. Service Historique de la Défense.

Gerold, M. and Windels, K. (eds), 1996 *Gedichte des gälischen Irlands.* Trier. WVT.

Gibbons, L., 1987 'Romanticism, realism and Irish cinema', in K. Rockett, L. Gibbons and J. Hill, *Cinema and Ireland*, 194–257. Guildford. Routledge.

Gil Soto, J.L., 2008 *La colina de las piedras blancas*. Barcelona. Styria.

Gillespie, P., 2012 'Civil society and Irish foreign policy', in B. Tonra, M. Kennedy, J. Doyle and N. Dorr (eds), *Irish foreign policy*, 99–114. Dublin. Gill and Macmillan.

Gillespie, P., 2014, 'The complexity of British–Irish interdependence', *Irish Political Studies* 29 (1), 37–57.

Gillespie, P., 2015 'News media as actors in European foreign-policymaking', in K.E. Jørgensen, Å.K. Aarstad, E. Drieskens, K. Laatikainen and B. Tonra (eds), *The SAGE handbook of European foreign policy*, vol. 1, 413–28. London. Sage.

Gillespie, P., 2018a 'Brexit rudely interrupts Irish-British reconciliation', in A. Guelke and P. Gillespie, *Ireland-UK relations and Northern Ireland after Brexit*, 12–21. London. LSE Ideas/London School of Economics. Available online: https://lseideas.atavist.com/ireland-uk. Accessed 15 April 2018.

Gillespie, P., 2018b 'Public debate about Europe has shifted', *The Irish Times*, 17 February, 13.

Gillespie, R. and Ó hUiginn, R. (eds), 2013 *Irish Europe 1600–50: writing and learning*. Dublin. Four Courts Press.

Gillissen, C., 2008 'Ireland, France and the question of Algeria at the United Nations, 1955–62', *Irish Studies in International Affairs* 19, 151–67.

Gillissen, C., 2013 'France', in M. O'Driscoll, D. Keogh and J. aan de Wiel (eds), *Ireland through European eyes: Western Europe, the EEC and Ireland, 1945–1973*, 75–127. Cork. Cork University Press.

Giordano, R., 1996 *Mein irisches Tagebuch*. Köln. Kiepenheuer & Witsch.

Gironella, J.M., 1946 *Un hombre*. Barcelona. Destino.

Gironella, J.M., 1953 *Los cipreses creen en dios*. Barcelona. Planeta.

Goldsmith, O., 1810 *Il vicario di Wakefield*. Transl. by G. Brechet. Milan. De Stefanis.

Gonçalves Da Costa, M. (ed.), 1981 *Fontes inéditas Portuguesas para a história de Irlanda*. Braga. Oficinas Gráficas de Barbosa & Xavier.

González de Matauco, J., 2009 *En el purgatorio de Irlanda: crónicas de un penitente*. Barcelona. Niberta.

Gougaud, L., 1931 'Achievement and influence of Irish monks', *Studies: an Irish Quarterly Review* 20 (78), 195–208.

Gourval, A., 1977 'Poem', in C. Le Mercier d'Erm (ed.), *Les bardes et poètes nationaux de la Bretagne Armoricaine: anthologie contemporaine des XIXe-XXe siècles, etc.*, 321.Guipavas. Kelenn. (Originally published 1919. Rennes. Plihon et Hommay.)

Government of Ireland, 1843 *Census of Ireland 1841*. London. Her Majesty's Stationery Office.

Government of Ireland, 2016 *Report of the Joint Committee of Inquiry into the Banking Crisis*. Available online: https://inquiries.oireachtas.ie/banking/. Accessed 17 March 2018.

Goździkowski, A., 2007 *Lenie*. Warszawa. Lampa i Iskra Boża.

Grande, E. and Kriesi, H., 2015 'The restructuring of political conflict in Europe and the politicisation of European integration', in T. Risse (ed.), *European public spheres: politics is back*, 190–226. Cambridge. Cambridge University Press.

Grall, X., 1977 *Le Cheval couché*. Paris. Hachette.

Greene, G., 1981 *The lawless roads*. London. Penguin Books.

Greve, J. and Povlsen, S.T., 2004 'The reception of James Joyce in Denmark', in G. Lernout and W. Van Mierlo (eds), *The reception of James Joyce in Europe* – vol. 1: *Germany, Northern and Eastern Central Europe*, 111–28. London and New York. Continuum.

Grogan, G.F., 1991a 'Daniel O'Connell and European Catholic thought', *Studies: an Irish Quarterly Review* 80 (137), 56–64.

Grogan, G.F., 1991b *The noblest agitator: Daniel O'Connell and the German Catholic movement, 1830–50*. Dublin. Veritas.

Grosjean, A., and Murdoch, S., 2005 *Scottish communities abroad in the early modern period*. Leiden. Brill.

Gruchawka, R.A., 2007 *Buty emigranta*. Warszawa. Exlibris.

Guerrero, M., 2013 *La mujer que llegó del mar*. Madrid. Random.

Gunne, S., 2016 'World-literature, world-systems and Irish chick lit', in J. Habjan, and F. Imlinger (eds), *Globalizing literary genres: literature, history, modernity,* 241–53. New York and London. Routledge.

Gurevich, A.J., 1972 *Categories of medieval culture*. Transl. into English by G.L. Campbell. London. Routledge.

Guthke, K.S., 2002 '"Destination Goethe": travelling Englishmen in Weimar', in N. Boyle and J. Guthrie, J. (eds), *Goethe and the English speaking world, essays from the Cambridge symposium for his 250th anniversary,* 116–42. Rochester, NY and Woodbridge Suffolk. Camden House.

Guzzetta, G., 2004 'Linati between Ireland, Milan and Europe', in G. Guzzetta, *Nation and narration. British Modernism in Italy in the first half of the 20th century,* 99–135. Ravenna. Longo.

Gwynn, A., 1940 'Irish monks and the Cluniac reform', *Studies: an Irish Quarterly Review* 29 (115), 409–30.

Gwynn, J., 1913 *Liber Ardmachanus*. Dublin. Hodges Figgis and Co.

Harbison, P., 1998 *Pilgrimage in Ireland: the monuments and the people*. Syracuse, NY. Syracuse University Press.

Harbison, P., 2001 *The Golden Age of Irish art, the medieval achievement, 600–1200*. New Haven and London. Yale University Press.

Harney, M., 2000 'Address by the Tánaiste (Deputy Prime Minister) Mary Harney, TD, to a meeting of the American Bar Association, Dublin, 21 July'. Dublin. Government Information Service.

Hauge, H., 2008 'Norsk litteratur som post-kolonial?', *Passage* 23 (59), 19–32.

Haugh, D., 2016, 'Ireland's economy: still riding the globalisation wave', *OECD Observer* 305/January. Available online: http://oecdobserver.org/news/

fullstory.php/aid/5456/Ireland_92s_economy:_Still_riding_the_globalisation_wave.html. Accessed 17 March 2018.

Hayward, K., 2009 *Irish nationalism and European integration: the official re-definition of the island of Ireland*. Manchester. Manchester University Press.

Hazeu, W., 2005 'Hermans en Vestdijk', *De Gids* 168 (11–12), 949–58.

HEA, 1995 *Report of the Steering Committee on the Future Development of Higher Education*. Dublin. HEA.

Heaney, S., 1990 'Alphabets' (from *The haw lantern*), in *New selected poems 1966–1987*, 211–13. London. Faber and Faber.

Heaney, S., 1995 *44 wiersze*. Transl. by Stanisław Barańczak. Kraków. Wydawnictwo Znak.

Heaney, S., 1996 *Ciągnąc dalej. Nowe wiersze 1991-1996*. Transl. by Stanisław Barańczak. Kraków. Wydawnictwo Znak.

Heaney, S., 1998 *Kolejowe dzieci*. Transl. by Piotr Sommer. Legnica. Centrum Sztuki–Teatr Dramatyczny.

Heffernan, V., 2010 'Swimming against the current? Rolf Lappert's *Nach Hause schwimmen*', in L. Silos Ribas (ed.), *Britannia/Helvetia*, (figurationen gender literatur kultur), 11. Jg., H. 1, 113–27. Wien, Köln and Weimar. Böhlau Verlag.

Hélias, P.J., 1975 *Le Cheval d'orgueil*. Paris. Terre Humaine.

Hemprich, G., 2015 *Rí Érenn, 'König von Irland': Fiktion und Wirklichkeit* (2 vols). Berlin. Curach Bhán.

Henchy, M., 1981 'The Irish college at Salamanca', *Studies: an Irish Quarterly Review* 70, 220–7.

Hennessy, M., 2008 'Irish media now more Eurosceptic, warns EC report', *The Irish Times*, 2 September, 6.

Hennig, J., 1943 'Irish saints in the liturgical and artistic tradition of central Europe', *Irish Ecclesiastical Record* 61, 181–92.

Hennig, J., 1988a 'Goethe's translations of Ossian's "Songs of Selma"', in J. Hennig (ed.), *Goethe and the English speaking world*, 152–62. Bern and Frankfurt am Main. Lang.

Hennig, J., 1988b 'Goethe's personal relations with Ireland', in J. Hennig (ed.), *Goethe and the English speaking world*, 123–34. Bern and Frankfurt am Main. Lang.

Henri, F., 1967 *Irish art during the Viking invasions 800–1000 AD*. London. Methuen.

Henry, G., 1992 *The Irish military community in Spanish Flanders, 1586–1621*. Dublin. Four Courts Press

Hetmann, F. (ed. and transl.), 1979 *Irischer Zaubergarten: Märchen, Sagen und Geschichten von der Grünen Insel*. Düsseldorf, Köln. Diederichs.

Hetmann, F., 1981 *Die Reise in die Anderswelt: Feengeschichten und Feenglaube in Irland*. Düsseldorf, Köln. Diederichs.

Herbert, M.T., 1988 *Iona, Kells, and Derry: the history and hagiography of the monastic familia of Columba*. Oxford. Clarendon Press.

Herbert, M.T., 2007 'Crossing historical and literary boundaries: Irish written culture around the year 1000', in P. Sims-Williams and G. A. Williams (eds), *Croesi ffiniau: trafodion Y 12fed Gyngres Astudiaethau Celtaidd Ryngwladol 24–30 Awst 2003, Prifysgol Cymru, Aberystwyth / Crossing boundaries: proceedings of the 12th International Congress of Celtic Studies, 24–30 August 2003, University of Wales, Aberystwyth*. Cambrian Medieval Celtic Studies 53–4, 87–101. Aberystwyth. CMCS Publications.

Herbert M.T. and Ó Riain, P., 1988 'Betha Adamnáin: the Irish Life of Adamnán', *Irish Texts Society* 54. London. Irish Texts Society.

Hermans, M., 1996 'Een per ongeluk gepleegde moord. Het beeld van Ierland in twee moderne Nederlandse romans', *Surplus* 10 (5), 10–11.

Herrin, J., 1987 *The formation of Christendom*. Princeton, NJ. Princeton University Press.

Hersant de la Villemarqué, T., 1959 *Barzaz Breiz: Chants populaires de la Bretagne*. Paris. Perrin.

Hidalgo, N., 2008 *Lo que dure la eternidad*. Barcelona. Ediciones B.

Higgins, M.D., 2017 'Keynote address by the President of Ireland, Michael D. Higgins to the IBEC Conference, 9 March'. Available online: http://www.president.ie/en/diary/details/president-addresses-the-ibec-ceo-conference. Accessed 17 March 2018.

Hill, J., 1987 'Images of violence', in K. Rockett, L. Gibbons and J. Hill, *Cinema and Ireland*, 147–93. Guildford. Routledge.

Hill, J., 2011 'Routes Irish: "Irishness", "authenticity" and the working class in the films of Ken Loach', *Irish Studies Review* 19 (1), 99–109.

Hill, J. and Rockett, K., 2004 'Introduction', in K. Rockett and J. Hill (eds), *National cinema and beyond*, 9–18. Dublin and Portland OR. Four Courts Press.

Hitchcock, W.I., 2003 *The struggle for Europe: the history of the continent since 1945*. London. Profile Books.

Hobson, B., 2003 *Recognition struggles and social movement*. Cambridge. Cambridge University Press.

Holfter, G., 1996 *Erlebnis Irland. Deutsche Reiseberichte über Irland im zwanzigsten Jahrhundert*. Trier. Wissenschaftlicher Verlag Trier.

Holfter, G., 2007 'From bestseller to failure? Heinrich Böll's *Irisches Tagebuch* ('Irish journal') to *Irland und seinere Kinder* ('Children of Eire')', in C. Schönfeld and H. Rasche (eds), *Processes of transposition: German literature and film*, 207–21. Amsterdam. Editions Rodopi.

Holfter, G. (ed.), 2010 *Heinrich Böll's 'Irisches Tagebuch' in context*. Trier. Wissenschaftlicher Verlag Trier.

Holfter, G., 2012a *Heinrich Böll and Ireland*, with a Foreword by Hugo Hamilton. Newcastle upon Tyne. Cambridge Scholars Publishing.

Holfter, G., 2012b 'After the *Irisches Tagebuch*: changes and continuities in the German image of Ireland 1961–2011', in Joachim Fischer and Rolf Stehle (eds), *Contemporary German-Irish cultural relations in a European perspective. Exploring issues in cultural policy and practice,* 159–71. Trier. Wissenschaftlicher Verlag Trier.

Holfter, G. and Dickel, H., 2017 *An Irish sanctuary: German-speaking refugees in Ireland 1933–1945.* Berlin and Boston. De Gruyter.

Holl, K., 1958 *Die irische Frage in der Ära Daniel O'Connells und ihre Beurteilung in der politischen Publizistik des deutschen Vormärz.* Mainz. Johannes-Gutenberg-Universität.

Hollander, W., 2010 *Dans der liefde.* Soest. Uitgeverij Cupido.

Honohan, P., 2010 *The Irish banking crisis: regulatory and financial stability policy 2003–2008. A report to the Minister for Finance by the governor of the Central Bank.* Dublin. Government Publications Office.

Hooghe, L., Laffan B. and Marks, G., 2017 'Introduction to theory meets crisis collection', *Journal of European Public Policy* 25 (1), 1–6.

Horgan, J., 1999 'Irish foreign policy, Northern Ireland, neutrality and the Commonwealth: the historical roots of a current controversy', *Irish Studies in International Affairs* 10, 135–47.

Horgan, J. and Flynn, R., 2017 *Irish media: a critical history.* Dublin. Four Court Press.

Hosiaisluoma, Y., 1998 *Euroopan reunalla, kosken korvalla—Jumalten narri Pentti Saarikoski.* Helsinki. Like.

Hoyland, R.E. and Waidler, S., 2014 'Adomnán's *De locis sanctis* and the seventh-century Near East', *English Historical Review* 129 (539), 787–807.

Hünseler, W., 1978. *Das Deutsche Kaiserreich und die Irische Frage 1900–1914.* Frankfurt am Main. Peter Lang.

Hume, J., 1998 'Nobel Lecture, Oslo, 10 December'. Available online: https://www.nobelprize.org/nobel_prizes/peace/laureates/1998/hume-lecture.html. Accessed 17 March 2018.

Hunt, U., 2017 *Sources and style in Moore's Irish melodies.* London and New York. Routledge.

Huppertz, W., Mulvin, L. and Schmauder, M. (eds), 2017 *Crossroads: travelling in the Early Middle Ages.* Amsterdam. W Books.

Hutcheson, D.S., 2011 'The February 2011 parliamentary election in Ireland', *Working Papers in British-Irish Studies: University College Dublin* 109, 20.

Hutchinson, P., 2008 *Poèmes.* Ed. by B. Escarbelt, transl. by Pádraig Ó Gormaile with Clíona Ní Ríordáin. Villeneuve d'Ascq. Presses Universitaires du Septentrion.

International Air Transport Association (IATA), 2011 *The impact of September 11 2001 on aviation.* Montreal. IATA.

Jäger, G., 1969 *Empfindsamkeit und Roman. Wortgeschichte, Theorie und Kritik im 18. und frühen 19. Jahrhundert.* Stuttgart and Berlin. Kohlhammer.

Jansen, D. and Jeninga, M., 2013 *Waar het gras altijd groener is. Ierland, ons tweede moederland.* Amsterdam. Thomas Rap.

Jansson, M., Lothe, J. and Riikonen, H. (eds), 2004 *European and Nordic modernisms*. London. Norvik Press.

James, E., 1982 'Ireland and Western Gaul in the Merovingian period', in D. Whitelock, R. Mc Kitterick and D.N. Dumville (eds), *Ireland in Early Medieval Europe: studies in memory of Kathleen Hughes*, 362–6. Cambridge. Cambridge University Press.

Jarniewicz, J., 2011 *Heaney. Wiersze pod dotyk*. Kraków. Znak.

Jarniewicz, J. (ed. and transl.), 2012 *Sześć poetek irlandzkich* ('Six Irish women poets'). Wrocław. Biuro Literackie.

Jean Paul (Richter, J.P.F.), 1963a *Vorschule der Ästhetik*, in Jean Paul, *Werke*, N. Miller (ed.), (6 B.de), Bd. 5. München. Karl Hanser Verlag.

Jean Paul (Richter, J.P.F.), 1963b *Blumen, Frucht - und Dornenstücke oder Ehestand, Tod und Hochzeit des Armenadvokaten F. St. Siebenkäs*, in Jean Paul, *Werke*, N. Miller (ed.), (6 B.de), Bd. 2. München. Karl Hanser Verlag.

Joannon, P., 1983 'L'Irlande, mais quelle Irlande?', in A chacun ses Irlandes, *Artus* 15, 15–17.

Joannon, P., 1991 'O'Connell, Montalembert and the birth of Christian democracy in France', in M.R. O'Connell (ed.), *Daniel O'Connell: political pioneer*, 86–109. Dublin. Institute of Public Administration.

Joannon, P. and Whelan, K. (eds), 2017 *Paris—capital of Irish culture: France, Ireland and the republic, 1798–1916*. Dublin. Four Courts Press.

Jochum, K.P., 2006 'Epilogue: Yeats from Iceland to Turkey', in K.P. Jochum (ed.), *The reception of W.B. Yeats in Europe*, 255–66. London and New York. Continuum.

John, T., 2006 *The monastery island of Reichenau in Lake Constance, 'Cradle of Western culture'*. Freiburg. UNESCO World Heritage publication.

Johnston, E., 2016 'Exiles for the edge? The Irish contexts of *Pereginatio*', in R. Flechner and S. Meeder (eds), *The Irish in Medieval Europe: identity, culture and religion*, 38–52. New York. Palgrave.

Jonas of Bobbio, 2017 *Life of Columbanus, Life of John of Réomé, and Life of Vedast*. Transl. with commentary by A. O'Hara and I. Wood. Liverpool. Liverpool University Press.

Jones, P.M., 'Translations into French of Arthur Young's *Travels in France (1791–1801)*', *La Révolution française [En ligne]*. Published online 15 September 2017: http://journals.openedition.org/lrf/1739; DOI: 10.4000/lrf.1739. Accessed 25 January 2018.

Jones, S., 2017 'Nobel winner Mario Vargas Llosa finds perfect protagonist in Roger Casement', *The Guardian*, 18 October 2017. Available online: https://www.theguardian.com/books/2010/oct/18/mario-vargas-llosa-roger-casement. Accessed 24 October 2017.

Jørgensen, C., 2016 'Kvindelighedens snubletråde: chicklit i et nordisk perspektiv', *The history of Nordic women's literature*, 28 September 2016. Available online: https://nordicwomensliterature.net/da/2016/09/28/kvindelighedens-snubletraade-chicklit-i-et-nordisk-perspektiv/. Accessed 9 January 2018.

Joyce, J., 1916 *A portrait of the artist as a young man.* New York. Huebsch.

Joyce, J., 1960 *Ulisse.* Transl. by G. De Angelis, Introduction by G. Melchiori. Milan. Mondadori.

Joyce, J., 1969a *Ulysses.* London. Penguin.

Joyce, J., 1969b *Ulisess.* Warszawa. Państwowy Instytut Wydawniczy.

Joyce, J., 1975 *Selected letters.* R. Ellman (ed.). New York. Viking.

Joyce, J., 1982 *Finnegans wake: H.C.E.* Transl. and annotated by L. Schenoni, Introduction by G. Melchiori. Milan. Mondadori.

Joyce, J., 1983 *Ulisse: Telemachia: episodi 1–3.* Transl. by G. De Angelis. Edited by G. Melchiori, annotated by C. Bigazzi, C. de Petris and M. Melchiori. Milan. Mondadori.

Kaplan, Y. (ed.), 2017 *Early modern ethnic and religious communities in exile.* Newcastle. Cambridge Scholars Publishing.

Keane, B., 2016 *Irish drama in Poland: staging and reception, 1900–2000.* Bristol. Intellect.

Keatinge, P., 1973 *The formulation of Irish foreign policy.* Dublin. Institute of Public Administration.

Keatinge, P. (ed.), 1991 *Ireland and EC membership evaluated.* London. Pinter.

Keefe, J.T., 1984 'Churchyard clay': a translation of *Cré na cille* by Máirtín Ó Cadhain, with introduction and notes. Unpublished PhD thesis. University of California, Berkeley.

Kelly, L., 1996 *Langage, cartographie et pouvoir/Language, mapping and power.* Derry. The Orchard Gallery.

Kennedy, D., 2009 *Square peg: the life and times of a Northern newspaperman south of the border.* Dublin. Nonesuch Publishing.

Kennedy, K.A., Giblin, T. and McHugh, D., 1988 *The economic development of Ireland in the twentieth century.* London. Routledge.

Kennedy, M., 1992 'The Irish Free State and the League of Nations, 1922–32: the wider implications', *Irish Studies in International Affairs* 3 (4), 9–23.

Kennedy, M., 1996 *Ireland and the League of Nations, 1919–1946: international relations, diplomacy and politics.* Blackrock. Irish Academic Press.

Kennedy, M.J. and O'Halpin, E., 2000 *Ireland and the Council of Europe: from isolation towards integration.* Strasbourg. Council of Europe.

Kenny, E., 2016 'Press conference of the Taoiseach (Irish Prime Minister) Enda Kenny, TD, in London with UK Prime Minister David Cameron, 26 January'. Available online: https://www.gov.uk/government/speeches/pm-press-con-ference-with-enda-kenny-january-2016. Accessed 17 March 2018.

Kenny, M.F., 2008 *British film noir guide.* Jefferson, NC. McFarland.

Keogh, A. and Keogh, D., 2013 'Italy and the Holy See', in M. O'Driscoll, D. Keogh, and J. aan de Wiel (eds), *Ireland through European eyes: Western Europe, the EEC and Ireland, 1945–1973,* 128–89. Cork. Cork University Press.

Keogh, D., 1989 'Eamon de Valera and Hitler: an analysis of international reaction to the visit to the German minister, May 1945', *Irish Studies in International Affairs* 3 (1), 69–92.

Keogh, D., 1990 *Ireland and Europe, 1919–1989: a diplomatic and political history.* Dublin. Hibernian University Press.

Keogh, D., 1995 *Ireland and the Vatican: the politics and diplomacy of church–state relations, 1992–1960.* Cork. Cork University Press.

Keogh, D., 1997 'The diplomacy of "dignified calm"—an analysis of Ireland's application for membership of the EEC, 1961-3', *Journal of European Integration History* 3 (1), 81–102.

Keogh, D., 1997 'De Valera, Hitler and the visit of condolence May 1945', *History Ireland* 5 (3), 58–61.

Keogh, D. and Keogh, A., 2009 'Ireland and European integration: from the Treaty of Rome to membership', in Mark Callanan (ed.), *'Foundations of an ever closer union': an Irish perspective on the fifty years since the Treaty of Rome*, 6–50. Dublin. Institute of Public Administration.

Keogh, D. and McCarthy, A., 2005 *Twentieth-century Ireland: revolution and state building.* Revised edn. Dublin. Gill and Macmillan.

Keown, G., 2017 *From strangers to neighbours: encounters between Poland and Ireland* (exhibition of the Embassy of Ireland in Poland). Warszawa. Open-Air Gallery, the Royal Łazienki Museum, 1–30 August.

Kerr, A., 2011, 'Irish students lost in translation', *Irish Times*, 8 November.

King, A., 1964 'Another blow for life: George Godwin and the reform of working class housing', *Architectural Review* 86, 448–52.

King, A., 1976 'Architectural journalism and the profession: the early years of George Godwin', *Architectural History* 19, 32–53.

King, L., 2011a '(De)Constructing the tourist gaze: Dutch influences on Aer Lingus tourism posters, 1951–61', in L. King and E. Sisson (eds), *Ireland, design and visual culture: negotiating modernity 1922-1992*, 164–87. Cork. Cork University Press.

King, L., 2011b 'Saints, shamrocks and signifying practices: Aer Lingus and the materialization of Irish identity', *Éire-Ireland* 46 (1–2), 128–51.

King, L., 2016 'Aer Lingus summer timetable, by Guus Melai', in Fintan O'Toole (ed.) *Modern Ireland in 100 artworks*, 118–20. Dublin. Royal Irish Academy.

Kinmonth, C., 2006 'Rural life through artists' eyes: an interdisciplinary approach', in *Whipping the herring: survival and celebration in nineteenth-century Irish art*, 34–46. Cork. Crawford Art Gallery (exhibition catalogue).

Kirby, P., 2001 'Three tiger sightings, but its stripes are in dispute', *Feasta Review* 1. Available online: http://www.feasta.org/documents/feastareview/kirby.htm. Accessed 18 October 2006.

Kirby, P., 2002 *The Celtic Tiger in distress: growth with inequality in Ireland.* Basingstoke. Palgrave.

Kirby, P. and Murphy, M., 2011 *Towards a second republic.* Dublin. Pluto Press.

Klein, A., 2005 'Stage-Irish, or the national in Irish opera, 1780–1925', *Opera Quarterly* 21 (1), 27–67.

Klein, A., 2016 'No state for music', in M. Dervan (ed.), *The invisible art: a century of music in Ireland*, 47–68. Dublin. New Island Press.

Klein, A., 2017 '"All her lovely companions are faded and gone". How "The last rose of summer" became Europe's favourite Irish melody', in B. Carraher and S. McCleave (eds), *Thomas Moore and romantic inspiration*, 132–45. London and New York. Routledge.

Klitgård, I., 2012 'Hjemliggørelse og fremmegørelse: *Ulysses* på dansk ved Jørgen Sonne og Mogens Boisen', *Tijdschrift voor Skandinavistiek* 33 (1), 5–13.

Kolasiński, P., 2012 *Co mi dała Irlandia?/What I got from Ireland?* Bloomington. Xilbris.

Koskinen, M., 2002 'Something else from somewhere else', in *Something else: Irlantilaista nykytaidetta / Irish contemporary art / Irländsk nutidskonst*, 17–22. Turku. Turun Taidemuseo.

Kosmalska, J. and Rostek, J., 2015 'Irish-Polish cultural interrelations in practice: interviews with Chris Binchy, Piotr Czerwiński, Dermot Bolger and Anna Wolf', *Studi irlandesi. A Journal of Irish Studies* 5, 103–30.

Kosok, H., 1995 'Yeats in Germany', in H. Kosok, *Plays and playwrights from Ireland in international perspective*, 117–30. Trier. Wissenschaftlicher Verlag Trier.

Kovač, L., 2000 *A way a lone a last a loved a long the*. Zagreb. Muzei Suvremene Umjetnosti.

Kralt, P., 1983 *Door nacht en ontijd: de Ierse romans van S. Vestdijk*. Amsterdam. Huis aan de Drie Grachten.

Krehayn, J. (ed.), 1966 *Englische Dramen*. Berlin. Volk und Welt.

Krusch, B. (ed.), 1902 *Walahfrid Strabo, Vita S. Galli Confessoris*. Monumenta Germaniae Historica, Scriptores rerum merovingicarum, 4, 280–337. Hannover. Bibliopolii Hahniani.

Kuortti, J., Lehtonen, M. and Löytty, O. (eds), 2007 *Kolonialismin jäljet*. Helsinki. Gaudeamus.

Laffan, B., 2004 'Irish politics and European politics', in J. Hourihane (ed.), *Ireland and the European Union, the first thirty years, 1973-2002*, 54–66. Dublin. Lilliput Press.

Laffan, B. and O'Mahony, J., 2008 *Ireland and the European Union*. Basingstoke and New York. Palgrave Macmillan.

Laffan, B. and Tonra, B., 2018 'Europe and the international dimension', in J. Coakley and M. Gallagher (eds), *Politics in the Republic of Ireland* (6th edn), 349–69. Abingdon, UK and New York. Routledge.

Lahtinen, L., 2017 *Chick lit -kirjallisuus Suomen yleisissä kirjastoissa—maakuntakirjastojen tarkastelua*, Pro Gradu thesis. Seinäjoki. SeAMK.

Landy, M., 1991 *British genres: cinema and society, 1930-1960*. Princeton NJ. Princeton University Press.

Lanigan, J., 1822, *Ecclesiastical history of Ireland*, Dublin. Graisberry.

Lanters, J., 1989 'Simon Vestdijk and the Irish literary tradition', *Études irlandaises* 14 (1), 105–15.

Larkin, E., 2001 'European studies proving a global attraction', *The Irish Times*, 15 May 2001.

Lasa, L., 2014 *Por el oeste de Irlanda*. Córdoba. Almuzara.

Latocha, A., 2008 *Irlandia, moje ścieżki*. Wrocław. Gajt.

Lawlor, M., 2009 'Fitzcarraldo, Irish explorer', in R. Barton (ed.), *Screening Irish-America: representing Irish-America in film and television*, 249–60. Dublin and Portland OR. Irish Academic Press.

Le Braz, A., 1914 'Impressions d'Irlande', *Bulletin de la Société géographique de Lille*, 3–19. Bibliothèque nationale de France (BnF): 1914/01/25. Available online: http://catalogue.bnf.fr/ark:/12148/cb327240723. Accessed 12 January 2018.

Le Braz, A., 1995 *Excerpt from Démocratie de l'Ouest, 1905*, in Yan-Ber Piriou, *Il était une voix, Anatole Le Braz. Discours et Conférences*, 87. Rennes. Éditions Apogée.

Lee, J., 1984 *Reflections on Ireland in the E.E.C.* Dublin. Irish Council of the European Movement.

Lee, J., 1989 *Ireland 1912–1985*. Cambridge. Cambridge University Press.

Leerssen, J., 2007 'Irish', in M. Beller and J. Leerssen (eds), *Imagology: the cultural construction and literary representation of national character. A critical survey*, 191–4. Amsterdam and New York. Rodopi.

Lenehan, F., 2012 'A land and a people of extremes: Ireland and the Irish in German cinema', *Irish Studies Review* 20 (1), 25–47.

Lenehan, F., 2016 *Stereotypes, ideology and foreign correspondents: German media representations of Ireland, 1946–2010*. Oxford. Peter Lang.

Lernout, G. and Van Mierlo, W. (eds), 2004 *The reception of James Joyce in Europe* (2 vols), vol. 1. London. Continuum.

Levitas, B., 2009 'J.M. Synge: European encounters', in P.J. Mathews (ed.), *The Cambridge companion to J.M. Synge*, 77–91. Cambridge. Cambridge University Press.

Lewków, P., 2014 'The rocky road to Polish: an overview of Irish-language literature in Polish translation', in R. Looby (ed.), Polish/Irish Issues in Translation. *Translation Ireland* special issue 19 (2), 49–58.

Linati, C., 1927 *Sull'orme di Renzo e altre prose lombarde*. Milano. Treves.

Linati, C., 1929 *Memorie a zig-zag*. Torino. Buratti.

Lindell, C., 2003 'Chick lit litteraturen som fyller tomrummet', *Sydsvenskan* 22 June 2003. Available online: https://www.sydsvenskan.se/2003-06-22/chick-lit-litteraturen-som-fyller-tomrummet. Accessed 9 January 2018.

Lindqvist, Y., 2005 *Högt och lågt i skönlitterär översättning till svenska*. Stockholm. Hallgren och Fallgren.

Lisak, M., 2012 *Dwie fale. Przewodnik duchowy emigranta*. Kraków. Homini.

Longley, E., 2003 'Irish poetry and "Internationalism": variations on a critical theme', *Irish Review* 30 (Spring–Summer), 48–61.

Loock, U., 1996 '"This is not a work of art" (Marcel Broodthaers)—Willie Doherty', in C. Christov-Bakargiev (ed.), *In the dark. Projected works / Im Dunkeln Projizierte Arbeiten*, 5–8. Bern. Kunsthalle Bern.

Lotz-Heumann, U., 2009 'Between conflict and coexistence: the Catholic community in Ireland as a visible underground church in the late sixteenth and early seventeenth centuries', in B.J. Kaplan, B. Moore, H. Van Nierop and J. Pollman (eds), *Catholic communities in Protestant states: Britain and the Netherlands c. 1570–1720*, 168–82. Manchester. Manchester University Press.

Loveluck C. and O' Sullivan, A., 2016 'Travel, transport and communication to and from Ireland, c. 400–1100', in R. Flechner and S. Meeder (eds), *The Irish in Early Medieval Europe: identity, culture and religion*, 19–38. New York. Palgrave.

Lyons, M.A. and O'Connor, T., 2008 *Strangers to citizens: the Irish in Europe 1600–1800*. Dublin. National Library of Ireland.

Mac Airt, S. and Mac Niocaill G. (eds), 1983 *The annals of Ulster (to A.D. 1131)*. Dublin. Dublin Institute of Advanced Studies.

Mac Annaidh, S., 1983 *Cuaifeach mo londubh buí*. Dublin. Coiscéim. Dublin.

Mac Annaidh, S., 1989 *Мой Рыжий Дрозд*. Transl. by T. Mikhailova. Moskva. Molodaya Gvardiya.

Mac Annaidh, S., 1996 *La Haine*. Transl. by É. Ó Ciosáin. Rennes. Institut Culturel de Bretagne.

Mac Annaidh, S., 1996 *Kevrinad Dulenn*. Transl. by A. Heussaff. Rennes. Institut Culturel de Bretagne.

Mac Cana, P., 2001 *Collège des Irlandais Paris and Irish studies*. Dublin. Dublin Institute for Advanced Studies.

MacCannell, D., 1999 *The tourist: a new theory of the leisure class*. Berkley CA. University of California Press.

Mac Cóil, L., 1993 'Literatur in irischer Sprache heute', in J. Schneider (ed.), *Irrland – Ireland – Irland*, 15–21. Berlin. Galrev.

Mac Cóil, L,. 2011 *An litir*. Indreabhán. Leabhar Breac.

Mac Cóil, L,. 2011 *Pismoto*. Sofia. Perseus.

Mac Murchaidh, C. 2009 'Text and translation of James Gallagher's "A sermon on the Assumption of Our Blessed Lady" (1736)', *Archivium Hibernicum* 62, 154–82.

Macpherson, J., 1760 *Fragments of ancient poetry collected in the Highlands of Scotland and translated from the Galic or Erse language*. Edinburgh. Hamilton and Balfour.

Mac Síomóin, T., 2010. *21 dán poemes poemas*. Transl. by T. Mac Síomóin. Dublin. Coiscéim.

McBride, E., 2015 'My hero: Eimear McBride on James Joyce', *The Guardian*, 6 June 2015, 15.

McCrohan, J., 2010 'An Irish merchant in late seventeenth century Málaga', in I. Pérez Tostado and E. García Hernan (eds), *Irlanda y el Atlántico Ibérico: movilidad, participación e intercambio cultural*, 23–33. Valencia. Albatross.

McGarry, F., 2002 'Irish newspapers and the Spanish civil war', *Irish Historical Studies* 33 (129), 68–90.

McGuckian. M., 1996 *Det sprog Fergus taler i drømme: udvalgte digte*. Transl. by P. Laugesen. Stockholm. Husets Forlag.

McKitterick, R., 2001 *The resources of the past in Early Medieval Europe*. Cambridge. Cambridge University Press.

McLoone, M., 2000 *Irish film: the emergence of a contemporary cinema*. London. British Film Institute.

McMahon, D., 2005 '"Our mendicant vigil is over": Ireland and the United Nations, 1946–1955', in Michael Kennedy and Deirdre McMahon (eds), *Obligations and responsibilities: Ireland and the United Nations, 1955–2005*, 5–24. Dublin. Institute of Public Administration.

McTigue, A. (ed.), 1996 *Und suchte meine Zunge ab nach Worten: Liebesgedichte der Gegenwart aus vier keltischen Sprachen*. Berlin. Galrev.

McVeagh, J., 1996 *Irish travel writing: a bibliography*. Dublin. Wolfhound Press.

Maddox, M., 2016 'Reconceptualising the Irish monastic town' *Journal of the Royal Society of Antiquaries* 146, 23–8.

Maher, D.J., 1986 *The tortuous path: the course of Ireland's entry into the EEC 1948–73*. Dublin. Institute of Public Administration.

Maher, E. and Maignant, C. (eds), 2012 *Franco-Irish connections in space and time: peregrinations and ruminations*. Bern. Peter Lang.

Maleno, C., 2014 *Mar de Irlanda*. Palma de Mallorca. Sloper.

Marlowe, L., 2010 *The things I've seen*. Dublin. Liberties Press.

Martin, A.E., 2010 'Paeans to progress; Arthur Young's travel accounts in German translation', in Stefanie Stockhorst (ed.), *Cultural transfer through translation: the circulation of Enlightenment thought in Europe by means of translation*, 297–314. Amsterdam and New York. Rodopi Editions.

Martin, S., 2008 *Good times and bad*. Cork. Mercier Press.

Masson, J.-Y. (ed.), 1996 *Anthologie de la poésie irlandaise au XXe siècle*. Transl. from Irish by E. Ó Ciosáin and P.-Y. Lambert. Paris. Verdier.

Mathisen, R.W., 1994 'The ideology of monastic and aristocratic community in Late Roman Gaul', *Revista de ideas y formas políticas de la Antigüedad Clásica* 6, 203–20.

Matasovic, R., 1997 'The contemporary short story in Irish: a view from Croatia', *Translation Ireland* 11 (4), 3–5.

Matasovic, R. and Bozicevic H. (eds), 1997 *Koje je Vrijeme? Suvremena Irska Pripovijetka*. Zagreb. Nakladi zavod Matice hrvatske.

Maude, C., 1985 *File. Poet. Poeta*. Transl. by R. Barone. Bari. Edizioni del Sud.

Maude, U., 2009 'Beckett's Nordic reception', in M. Nixon, and M. Feldman (eds), *The international reception of Samuel Beckett*, 234–50. London and New York. Continuum.

Maurin, A. and Wohlfahrt, T. (eds), 2006 *VERSschmuggel—VÉARSaistear.* Galway and Heidelberg. Cló Iar-Chonnacht/Das Wunderhorn.

Mayr-Hartung, H., 1999 *An historical study, Ottonian book illumination* (2nd revised edn). London. Harvey Miller.

Mazzacurati, G., 1990 *Effetto Sterne: la narrazione umoristica in Italia da Foscolo a Pirandello.* Pisa. Nistri-Lischi.

Meens, R., 2000 'The oldest manuscript witness of the *Collectio Canonum Hibernensis*', *Peritia*, 14, 1–19.

Meid, W. (ed.), 2015 *The romance of Froech and Findabair or The driving of Froech's Cattle.* Táin Bo Fróich: Old Irish text, with introduction, translation, commentary and glossary. Innsbruck. Institut für Sprachen und Literaturen der Universität Innsbruck.

Meijer, R.P., 1978 *Literature of the Low Countries: a short history of Dutch literature in the Netherlands and Belgium.* The Hague and Boston. Martinus Nijhoff.

Melchior, A., 1959 *Ierland is anders.* Haarlem. De Spaarnestad.

Melchiori, G., 1951 'Joyce and eighteenth century novelists', *English Miscellany* II, 227–45.

Melchiori, G., 1994 *Joyce: il mestiere dello scrittore.* Turin. Einaudi.

Melchiori, G., 1995 *James Joyce's feast of languages. Seven essays and ten notes. Joyce Studies in Italy* (F. Ruggieri (ed.)) 4. Rome. Bulzoni Editore.

Melchiori, G., 2007 *Joyce Barocco/Baroque Joyce*, edited by F. Ruggieri. Transl. by B. Arnett. Rome. Bulzoni Editore.

Mercille, J., 2015 *The political economy and media coverage of the European economic crisis: the case of Ireland.* London. Routledge.

Micheli, G.L., 1936 'Recherches sur les manuscrits Irlandais décorés de Saint-Gall et de Reichenau', *Revue Archéologique*, 6 (7), 189–223.

Michelsen, P., 1962 *Laurence Sterne und der deutsche Roman des 18. Jahrhunderts.* Göttingen. Vandenhoeck and Ruprecht.

Migne, J.P. (ed.), (1844–65) *Patrologia Latina* (221 vols), vol. 131. Paris. Garnier.

Mikhailova, T., 1986 Голос Эрина: Слово об Ирландии ('The Voice of Ireland'). Moscow.

Mikulska, B., Wędrychowski, D., Zychla M., Dzik, A., Grzanek A., Osikowicz-Chwaja, A., Brzeska, A., Burling A.K., Hołub M., Kasica M., Machowski R. and Piotrowicz R., 2013 *Transgeniczna Mandarynka.* Sieniawa Żarska. Wydawnictwo Morpho.

Miller, D., 1998 'Why some things matter', in Daniel Miller (ed.), *Material cultures: why some things matter*, 3–21. London. University College London.

Miszczak, S., '"Druga Irlandia", czyli wpadka Donalda Tuska', in *Wirtualna Polska*, 19 December 2007. Available online: https://wiadomosci.wp.pl/druga-irlandia-czyli-wpadka-donalda-tuska-6037410533958785a. Accessed 4 September 2018.

Mitchell, B., 1976 *James Joyce and the German novel 1922–1933.* Athens, OH. Ohio University Press.

Mohrt, M., 1961 *La prison maritime*. Paris. Gallimard.

Mohrt, M., 1975 *Les moyens du bord*. Paris. Gallimard.

Mohrt, M., 1986 *La guerre civile*. Paris. Gallimard.

Montale, E., 1975 *Quaderno di traduzioni*. Milano. Mondadori.

Moore, T., 1835 *The history of Ireland* (4 vols), vol. 1. London. Longman, Orme, Brown, Green and Longmans.

Morand, F., 2004 *Doña María Gretrudis Hore (1742–1801): vivencia de una poetisa gaditana entre el siglo y la clausura*. Alcalá. Ayuntamiento de Alcalá de Henares.

Morash, C., 2010 *A history of the media in Ireland*. Cambridge. Cambridge University Press.

Morley, M., 1973 'Brecht and the strange case of Mr. L.', *German Quarterly* 46 (4) (November), 540–7.

Morley, V. 2018 'Irish Jacobitism, 1691–1790', in James Kelly (ed.), *The Cambridge history of Ireland:* vol. iii *1730–1880*, 23–47. Cambridge. Cambridge University Press,

Moss, R. (ed.), 2014, *Art and architecture of Ireland* (5 vols), vol. 1: *Medieval, c.400–c.1600*. New Haven, CT, London and Dublin. Yale University Press and Royal Irish Academy.

Motin, P., 1875–96 Quoted in P. De L'Estoile, *Mémoires-journaux* (12 vols), vol. xi, 234–6. Paris. A. Lemerre.

Moxon-Browne, E., 2012 'Ireland from prosperity to poverty and back again', in Iva Honová (ed.), *Proceedings of the first international conference on European integration 2012*, 30–7. Ostrava. VŠB – Technical University of Ostrava.

Moxon-Browne, E., 2015 'The grin of the Cheshire cat: European Studies in Irish universities 1974–2014', *Journal of European Research* 11, 359–69.

Mulvin, L., 2017a 'Ireland and Europe: transmission of Celtic aesthetic in the early Middle ages', in W. Huppertz, L. Mulvin and M. Schmauder (eds), *Crossroads: travelling in the Early Middle Ages*, 78–86. Amsterdam. W Books.

Mulvin, L., 2017b 'Identity and shifting attitudes', in W. Huppertz, L. Mulvin and M. Schmauder (eds), *Crossroads: travelling in the Early Middle Ages*, 174–81. Amsterdam. W Books.

Munch-Pedersen, O. (ed.), 1994 *Scéalta Mháirtín Neile: bailiúchán scéalta ó Árainn*. Transcr. by Holger Pedersen. Dublin. Four Courts Press.

Munro, D.C., 1993 *Life of St. Columban by the monk Jonas*. Philadelphia. Miracles Publisher. (Originally printed 1895, Philadelphia, University of Pennsylvania, Department of History.)

Murphy, G., 2005 '"Tonguetied sons of bastards' ghosts": postconceptual and postcolonial appraisals of the work of James Coleman', *Third Text* 19 (5), 499–510.

Murphy, R., 2000 *British cinema and the Second World War*. London and New York. Continuum.

na gCopaleen, M., 2003 *Поющие Лазаря, или Наредкость бедные люди*. Transl. by A. Korosteleva. Saint-Petersburg. Symposium.

Ní Chinnéide, D., 2010 'Crisis of translation in minority languages', *Poetry Ireland News* July/August. Available online: http://www.poetryireland.ie/writers/articles/crisis-of-translation-in-minority-languages. Accessed 16 December 2016.

Ní Chinnéide, V., 1959 'The sources of Moore's melodies', *Journal of the Royal Society of Antiquaries of Ireland* 89 (2), 109–34.

Ní Dhomhnaill, N., 1996 *Ellefolk: udvalgte digte af Nuala Ní Dhomhnaill*. Transl. by O. Munch-Pederson and Peter Nielsen. Stockholm. Husets Forlag.

Ní Dhomhnaill, N., 2000 *Ar gwele seiz: un dibab barzhonegoù gant Nuala Ní Dhomhnaill*. Transl. by H. Ar Bihan, A. Botrel, G. Denez, A. J. Hughes. Lesneven. Mouladurioù Hor Yezh.

Ní Ríordáin, C. (ed.), 2013. *Femmes d'Irlande en poésie 1972–2013*. Paris. Editions Caractères.

Naremore, J., 1996 'American film noir: the history of an idea', *Film Quarterly* 49 (2), 12–28.

Nieto, A.B., 2013 *La huella blanca*. Barcelona. Ediciones B.

Nieto, A.B., 2016 *Los hijos del Nieto*. Barcelona. Ediciones B.

Nilis, J., 2006/7 'Irish students in Leuven', *Archivium Hibernicum* 60, 1–304.

Nilsson, I. and Östergren, J., 1993 *Bardernas Irland*. Stockholm. Symposion.

Nooteboom, C., 2002 *Nootebooms Hotel*. Amsterdam. Atlas.

Nooteboom, C., 2006 *Nomad's Hotel: travels in time and space*. Transl. by A. Kelland. London. Harvill Secker.

Ó Buachalla, B. 1996 *Aisling ghéar: na Stíobartaigh agus an t-aos léinn 1601–1788*. Baile Átha Cliath. An Clóchomhar.

Ó Cadhain, M., 1969 *Páipéir bhána agus páipéir bhreaca*. Dublin. Clóchomhar Teo.

Ó Cadhain, M., 1995 *Kirkegårdsjord*. Transl. by J. E. *Rekdal*. Oslo. Gyldendal.

Ó Cadhain, M., 2000 *Kirkegårdsjord, genfortælling i ti mellemspil*. Transl. by O. Munch-Pedersen. Århus. Husets Forlag.

Ó Cadhain, M., 2015 *The key / An eochair*. Transl. by L. de Paor and L. Ó Tuairisg. Champaign, IL. Dalkey Archive Press.

Ó Cadhain, M., 2015 *The dirty dust*. Transl. by A. Titley. New Haven and London. Yale University Press.

Ó Cadhain, M., 2016 *Graveyard clay: cré na cille*. Transl. by L. Mac Con Iomaire and T. Robinson. New Haven and London. Yale University Press.

Ó Cadhain, M., 2016 *Der Schlüssel: Novelle*. Transl. by G. Haefs. Stuttgart. Kröner.

Ó Cadhain, M., 2017 *Hřbitovní hlína*. Transl. by R. Markus. Prague. Argo.

Ó Cadhain, M. 2017 *Grabgeflüster*. Transl. by G. Haefs. Stuttgart. Kröner.

Ó Carragáin, T., 2006 *Churches in Early Medieval Ireland: architecture, ritual and memory*. New Haven, CT and London. Yale University Press.

Ó Carragáin, T., 2007 'Skeuomorphs and spolia: the presence of the past in Irish pre-Romanesque architecture', in R. Moss (ed.) *Making and meaning in Insular Art*, 95–109. Dublin. Four Courts Press.

Ó Catháin, B. (ed.), 2013 *Saothrú an Léinn Cheiltigh ag scoláirí thíortha na Gearmáinise*. Maynooth. An Sagart.

Ó Ciosáin, É. (ed.), 1984 *Une île et d'autres îles*. Quimper. Calligrammes.

Ó Ciosáin, É., 1997 'Voloumous deamboulare: the Wandering Irish in French literature, 1600–1789', in A. Coulson (ed.), *Exiles and migrants: crossing thresholds in European culture and society*, 32–42. Eastbourne. Sussex Academic Press.

Ó Ciosáin, É. (ed.), 1983. *Barzhonegoù Iwerzhonek*. Douarnenez. Skrid.

Ó Conaire; P., 1986 'Muzhestvo', in T.A. Mikhaĭlov and K.V. Annekova, K. V. (eds), *Slovo ob Irlandii: golos Erina*. Moskva. Molodaya Gvardia.

Ó Conaire, P., 1999a *Emigrantliv*. Transl. by O. Munch-Pedersen. Århus. Husets Forlag.

Ó Conaire, P., 1999b *Tha klápsei kaueís yia tou Máikel*. Transl. by Persefoni Koumoutsi. Athens. Empeiria Ekdotikē.

Ó Conaire, P., 2000. *U progonstvu*. Transl. by S. Drach. Zagreb. Edicije Božičević.

Ó Conaire, P., 2004 *Vyhnanství*. Transl. by D. Theinova. Praha/Prague. Fráktaly.

Ó Conaire, P., 2013 *Biskupova duše*. Transl by R. Markus. Praha/Prague. Jitro.

Ó Corráin, D., 2002 'Irish law and Canon law', in P. Ní Chatháin and M. Richter (eds), *Irland und Europa. Die Kirche im Frühmittelalter*, 157–66. Dublin. Four Courts Press.

Ó Crohan (Ó Criomthain), T., 1960 *Die Boote fahren nicht mehr aus*. Transl. by A. and H. Böll. Olten, Freiburg i. Br. Walter.

Ó Crohan (Ó Criomhthain), T., 1989 *L'homme des îles*. Transl. by J. Bühler and U. Murphy. Lausanne, Paris. Favre. Also Paris. Payot et Rivage.

Ó Crohan (Ó Criomhthain), T., 1996 *Manden på øen*. Transl. by O. Munch-Pedersen. Århus. Husets Forlag.

Ó Cróinín, D., 1993 'The Irish as mediators of antique culture on the continent', in P.L. Butzer and D. Lohrmann (eds), *Science in Western and Eastern civilization in Carolingian times*, 41–52. Basel, Boston and Berlin. Birkhäuser Verlag.

Ó Cróinín, D., 2016 *Early Medieval Ireland, 400–1200* (2nd edn). London and New York. Routledge. (Originally published 1995, London, Longman.)

Ó Dúshláine, T., 1987 *An Eoraip agus litríocht na Gaeilge*. Baile Átha Cliath. An Clóchomhar.

Ó hAnnracháin, T., 2015 *Catholic Europe, 1592–1648: centre and peripheries*. Oxford. Clarendon Press.

Ó hEithir, B., 1985 *Führe uns in Versuchung*. Transl. by S. Wicht. Leipzig, Weimar. Kiepenheuer.

Ó hUallaigh, P., 2009 *Tír tairngire*. Dublin. Coiscéim.

Ó hUallaigh, P., 2011 *Soilse an chroí*. Dublin. Coiscéim.

Ó hUallaigh, P., 2013 'Gedichte', *Krautgarten*, no. 63, November, 44–7.

Ó Muraíle, N. (ed.), 2008 *Mícheál Ó Cléirigh, his assoicates and St Anthony's College, Louvain*. Dublin. Four Courts Press.

Ó Riain, S., 2014 *The rise and fall of Ireland's Celtic Tiger: liberalism, boom and bust*. Cambridge. Cambridge University Press.

Ó Searcaigh, C., 1996 *Le chemin du retour / Pilleadh an deoraí*. Transl. by A.J. Hughes. Paris. La Barbacane.

Ó Snodaigh, P., 1986 *Solitudine e compagnia. Cumha agus cumann*. Transl. by R. Barone. Bari. Edizione dal Sud.

Ó Snodaigh, P., 1997, 1999 *Linda*. Faenza. Mobydick.

Ó Snodaigh, P., 1999 *Len*. Faenza. Mobydick.

Ó Snodaigh, P., 2010 *Parnell a Queenie*. Transl. by L. Sanna. Faenza. Mobydick.

Ó Snodaigh, P., 2012 *Parnell královničce*. Transl. by I. Peroutková. Prague. Artur.

Ó Súilleabháin, M., 1933 *Fiche bliain ag fás*. Baile Átha Cliath. Talbot.

Ó Tuairisc, E., 2004 *Messa di defunti*. Torino. Trauben.

Ó Tuairisc, E., 2007 *L'Attaque*. Translated by R. Markus. Prague. Baronet.

O'Brien, F., 1977 *Das Barmen*. Frankfurt am Main. Suhrkamp; later editions after 1984 as *Irischer Lebenslauf*. Frankfurt am Main. Suhrkamp.

O'Brien, F., 1998 *Le pleure-misère*. Transl. by A. Le Berre, R. Steadman, A. Verrier. Paris. Ombres.

O'Brien, F., 1989 *La boca pobre*. Transl. by A. Rivero Taravillo. Barcelona. Ediciones del Serbal, 1989. 2nd edn. Madrid. Nórdica, 2008.

O'Brien, F., 2016. *A boca pobre*. Transl. by I. Fernández Fernández. Cangas. Rinoceronte Editora.

O'Brien, M., 2001 *De Valera, Fianna Fáil and the Irish Press: the truth in the news?* Dublin and Portland. Irish Academic Press.

O'Brien, M., 2008 *The Irish Times: a history*. Dublin and Portland. Four Courts Press.

O'Brien, M., 2017a 'In war-torn Spain': the politics of Irish press coverage of the Spanish civil war', *Media, War and Conflict* 10 (3), 345–58.

O'Brien, M., 2017b *Fourth Estate: journalism in twentieth-century Ireland*. Oxford. Oxford University Press.

O'Callaghan, J.C. 1969 *History of the Irish Brigades in the service of France*. Shannon. Irish University Press. (Originally printed 1870, Glasgow, Cameron and Ferguson).

O'Clery, C., 2008 *May you live in interesting times*. Dublin. Poolbeg.

O Connell, P., 1997 *The Irish college at Alcalá de Henares*. Dublin. Four Courts Press.

O Connell, P., 2001 *The Irish college in Lisbon*. Dublin. Four Courts Press.

O Connell, P., 2007 *The Irish college at Santiago de Compostela 1605–1769*. Dublin. Four Courts Press.

O'Connor, B., 1993 'Myths and mirrors: tourist images and national identity', in B. O'Connor and M. Cronin (eds), *Tourism in Ireland: a critical analysis*, 68–85 Cork. Cork University Press.

O'Connor, P., 2001 'Irish clerics and Jacobites in early eighteenth-century Paris (1700–30)', in O'Connor, T. (ed.), *The Irish in Europe 1580–1815*, 175–90. Dublin. Four Courts Press.

O'Connor, P., 2006 Irish clerics in the University of Paris 1570–1770. Unpublished PhD thesis. National University of Ireland, Maynooth. Maynooth.

O'Connor, T., 2008 *Irish Jansenists 1600–70: religion and politics in Flanders, France, Ireland and Rome.* Dublin. Four Courts Press.

O'Connor, T., 2016 *Irish voices from the Spanish Inquisition: migrants, converts and brokers in Early Modern Iberia.* London. Palgrave.

O'Connor, T., 2018 'Irish collegians in Spanish service (1560–1803)', in L. Chambers and T. O'Connor (eds), *Forming Catholic communities: Irish, Scots and English College networks in Europe 1568–1918*, 15–38. Leiden. Brill.

O'Connor, T. and Lyons, M.A. (eds), 2010 *The Ulster earls in baroque Europe.* Dublin. Four Courts Press.

O'Doherty, B., 1991 'Alsace and Ireland medieval links', *Seanchas Ardmhacha / Journal of the Armagh Diocesan Historical Society* 14 (2), 161–78.

O'Donnell, R. (ed.), 2000 *Europe: the Irish experience.* Dublin. Institute of European Affairs.

O'Driscoll, M., 1999 'The economic war and Irish foreign trade policy: Irish–German commerce 1932–9', *Irish Studies in International Affairs* 10, 71–89.

O'Driscoll, M., 2010 'Hesitant Europeans, self-defeating irredentists and security free-riders? West German assessments of Irish foreign policy during the early Cold War, 1949–59', *Irish Studies in International Affairs* 21, 89–104.

O'Driscoll, M., 2011 'The "unwanted suitor": West Germany's reception, response and role in Ireland's EEC entry request, 1961–3, *Irish Studies in International Affairs* 22, 163–86.

O'Driscoll, M., 2012 'Multilateralism: from Plato's Cave to European Community, 1945–73', in Tonra, B., Kennedy, M., Doyle, J. and Dorr, N. (eds), *Irish Foreign Policy*, 36–53. Dublin. Gill and Macmillan.

O'Driscoll, M., 2013 'West Germany', in M. O'Driscoll, D. Keogh, and J. aan de Wiel (eds), *Ireland through European eyes: Western Europe, the EEC and Ireland, 1945–1973*, 9–74. Cork. Cork University Press.

O'Driscoll, M., 2016 '"We are trying to do our share": the construction of positive neutrality and Irish post-war relief to Europe', *Irish Studies in International Affairs* 27, 21–38.

O'Driscoll, M., 2017 *Ireland, Germany and the Nazis: politics and diplomacy 1919–39.* Revised edn. Dublin. Four Courts Press.

O'Driscoll, M., 2018 *Ireland, West Germany and the new Europe, 1949–1973: best friend and ally?* Manchester. Manchester University Press.

O'Driscoll, M., Keogh, D. and aan de Wiel, J. (eds), 2013 *Ireland through European eyes: Western Europe, the EEC and Ireland, 1945–1973.* Cork. Cork University Press.

O'Flaherty, K., 1988 'Regards français sur l'Irlande', in *Etudes Irlandaises* 13 (12), 31–43. Available online: https://www.persee.fr/issue/irlan_0183-973x_1988_num_13_2?sectionId=irlan_0183-973x_1988_num_13_2_2813. Accessed 12 August 2018.

O'Flaherty, L., 1932 *The Puritan.* London. Jonathan Cape.

O'Flaherty, L., 2012 *Deseo*. Madrid. Nordica Libros.

O'Flaherty, L., 2008 *Silbervogel und andere Meistererzählungen*. Zürich. Diogenes.

O'Grady, J.P., 1990 'Ireland and the defense of the North Atlantic, 1948–1951: the American view', *Éire-Ireland* 25 (3), 58–78.

O'Halpin, E., 1996 'The army in independent Ireland', in Bartlett, T. and Jeffery, K. (eds), *A military history of Ireland*, 407–30. Cambridge. Cambridge University Press.

O'Halpin, E., 1999 *Defending Ireland: the Irish state and its enemies since 1922*. Oxford. Oxford University Press.

O'Hearn, D., 2000 'Globalization, "New Tigers", and the end of the developmental state? The case of the Celtic Tiger.' *Politics and Society* 28 (1), 67–92.

O'Kane, F., 2013 *Ireland and the picturesque: design, landscape painting and tourism 1700–1840*. New Haven and London. Yale University Press.

O'Kane, F., 2015 'Ruins: a case study', in R. Loeber, H. Cambell, L. Hurley, J. Montague and E. Rowley (eds), *Art and Architecture of Ireland*, vol. 4: *Architecture 1600–2000*, 508–9. New Haven, London and Dublin. Yale University Press and Royal Irish Academy.

O'Kane, F., 2016 'Arthur Young's published and unpublished illustrations for "A Tour in Ireland, 1776–1779"', *Irish Architectural and Decorative Studies, The Journal of the Irish Georgian Society* 19, 118–60.

O'Kane, F., 2017 'Arthur Young's Study of landscape gardens and parks for his publication "A Tour in Ireland 1776–1779"', *Journal of Scottish Thought* 9, 110–23.

O'Keeffe, D., 2017 'Phoenix miracle or Celtic phoenix, Paddy never learns any lessons.', *The Avondhu*, 19 April. Available online: https://avondhupress.ie/phoenix-miracle-celtic-phoenix-paddy-never-learns-lessons/. Accessed 12 February 2018.

O'Loughlin, T., 2000 'The diffusion of Adomnán's *De locis sanctis* in the Medieval period', *Ériu* 51, 93–106.

O'Loughlin, T., 2004 'Perceiving Palestine in Early Christian Ireland: Martyrium, exegetical key, relic and liturgical space', *Ériu* 54, 125–37.

O'Mahony, J., 2010 'Ireland's EU referendum experience', in K. Hayward and M.C. Murphy (eds), *The Europeanisation of party politics in Ireland, north and south*, 31–50. Manchester. Manchester University Press.

O'Mahony, J. and Laffan, B., 2008 *Ireland and the European Union*. Basingstoke. Palgrave Macmillan.

O'Mahony, N. and O'Reilly, C. (eds), 2009 *Societies in transition: Ireland, Germany and Irish–German relations in business and society since 1989*. Wiesbaden. Nomos.

O'Neill, P., 1985 *Ireland and Germany. A study in literary relations*. New York, Bern and Frankfurt am Main. Lang.

O'Neill, P., 2010 '"Kennst Du das Land?" Ireland and the German literary imagination', in G. Holfter (ed.), *Heinrich Böll's 'Irisches Tagebuch' in context*, 79–87. Trier. Wissenschaftlicher Verlag Trier.

O'Reilly, C. and Holfter, G., 2009 'Changes and developments in German-Irish relations since 1989 with special regard to media, literary and diplomatic aspects: best of friends or rocky relationship?', in N. O'Mahony and C. O'Reilly (eds), *Societies in transition: Ireland, Germany and Irish-German relations in business and society since 1989*, 169–84. Wiesbaden. Nomos.

O'Rourke, K., 2017 'Brexit a reminder of how EU has benefited republic', *The Irish Times*, 14 August. Available online: https://www.irishtimes.com/business/economy/brexit-a-reminder-of-how-eu-has-benefited-republic-1.3185625. Accessed 17 March 2018.

O'Scea, C., 2015 *Surviving Kinsale: Irish emigration and identity formation in early modern Spain, 1601–40*. Manchester. Manchester University Press.

O'Sullivan, M., 1936 *Vingt ans de jeunesse*. Transl. by R. Queneau. Paris. Gallimard.

O'Sullivan, M., 1956 *Inselheimat*. Transl. by E. Aman. Zurich. Manesse.

O'Sullivan, M., 1986 *Dwadzieścia lat dorastania (Twenty years a-growing / Fiche bliain ag fás)*. Transl. by E. Bryll and M. Goraj-Bryll. Warszawa. Państwowa Spółdzielnia Wydawnicza.

O'Toole, F., 2008 '*Hunger* fails to wrest the narrative from the hunger strikers', *The Irish Times*, 28 November. Available online: www.irishtimes.com/news/hunger-fails-to-wrest-the-narrative-from-the-hunger-strikes-1.913725. Accessed 27 May 2017.

O'Toole, F., 2010 'The multiple hero', *New Republic*, 12 October. Available online: https://newrepublic.com/article/105658/mario-vargas-llosa-dream-of-celt-fintan-otoole. Accessed 15 September 2016.

OECD, 1991 *Review of national education policies: Ireland*. Paris. OECD.

Oehlke, A. (ed.), 1993 *Fahrten zur Smaragdinsel. Irland in den deutschen Reisebeschreibungen des 19. Jahrhunderts*. Göttingen. Peperkorn.

Oeser, H-C., 1998 'Ein Land, zwei Sprachen, sechs Dichter', in G. Laschen (ed.), *Das Zweimaleins des Steins: Poesie aus Irland*, 174–8. Bremerhaven. Wirtschaftsverlag N. W. Verlag für neue Wissenschaft.

Olofsson, T., 2011 'James Joyce och den sekulära uppenbarelsen', *Svenska Dagbladet* 23 July, 4.

Olsson, A., 2004 'Exile and literary modernism', in M. Jansson, J. Lothe and H. Riikonen (eds), *European and Nordic modernisms*, 37–50. London. Norvik Press.

Olszewska, K., 2010 'Site for sale', in E. Bourke and B. Farago (eds), *Landing places: immigrant poets in Ireland*, 144–7. Dublin. Dedalus Press.

Orzeł, M., 2007 *Dublin, moja polska karma*. Kraków. Skrzat.

Ossianiques, 1989. Transl. by A. Verrier. Paris. Orphée La Différence.

Oswald, G., 1995 *Breven till Ranveig*. Stockholm. Bokförlaget Atlantis.

Otto, F. and Meyer, C.O., 2012 'Missing the story? Changes in foreign news reporting and their implications for conflict prevention', *Media, War and Conflict* 5 (3), 205–21.

Päplow, T.M., 2010 'New perspectives: Heinrich Böll's *Irish journal* as intertext', in G. Holfter (ed.), *Heinrich Böll's 'Irisches Tagebuch' in context*, 63–75. Trier. Wissenschaftlicher Verlag Trier.

Parti National Breton, 1942 *L'exemple de l'Irlande*. Rennes. Éditions du Parti National Breton.

Pasquero, M., 2012 '"Mi par di trovarmi di fronte a un fatto nuovo letterario": Carlo Linati alla scoperta di James Joyce', *Studi irlandesi. A Journal of Irish Studies* 2, 199–254.

Pearse, P., 1979 *Isagan*. Transl. by L. Andouard. Roazhon (Rennes). Imbourc'h.

Pearse, P., 2008 *Opowiadania*. Transl. by A. Paluch. Lublin. Norbertinum.

Pearse, P., 2016 *Gens du Connemara*. Transl. by F. Collemare. Rennes. Editions Terre de Brume.

Pellizzi, C.M., 2011 '"Hibernia fabulosa": per una storia delle immagini dell'Irlanda in Italia', *Studi irlandesi. A Journal of Irish Studies* 1, 29–119.

Petersen, H. (ed.), 1979 *Erkundungen: 30 irische Erzähler*. Berlin. Volk und Welt.

Pevsner, N., 1972, *Some architectural writers of the nineteenth century*. Oxford. Oxford University Press.

Picard, J.-M., 1982 'The Schaffhausen Adomnán: a unique witness to Hiberno-Latin', *Peritia* 1, 216–49.

Picard, J.-M., 1998 'Notker Balbulus, Adomnán's "Vita Columbae" and the cult of Colum Cille in continental Europe', *Proceedings of the Royal Irish Academy* 98C (1), 1–23.

Picard, J.-M., 2001 'The cult of Columba in Lotharingia (9th–11th centuries): the manuscript evidence', in J. Carey, M. Herbert and P. Ó Riain (eds), *Studies in Irish hagiography: saints and scholars*, 221–36. Dublin. Four Courts Press.

Picard, J.-M., 2002 'Early contact between Ireland and Normandy: the cult of Irish saints in Normandy before the conquest', in M. Richter and J.M. Picard (eds), *Ogma: essays in Celtic Studies in honour of Próinséas Ní Chatháin*, 85–93. Dublin. Four Courts Press.

Picard, J.-M. and De Pontfarcy, Y., 1985 *Saint Patrick's Purgatory: a twelfth century tale of a journey to the Other World*. Dublin. Four Courts Press.

Pinger, W.R.R., 1920 *Laurence Sterne and Goethe*. Berkeley. University of California Press.

Pokorny, J., 1922 Die Seele Irlands. *Novellen und Gedichte aus dem Irisch-Gälischen des Patrick Henry Pearse und anderer (Padraic Ó Conaire, Padraic Ó Siochfhradha)*. Halle. Max Niemeyer.

Polet, J.-C., 2000 *Patrimoine littéraire européen*, vol. 12. Louvain La Neuve. De Boeck Supérieur.

Południak, M., 2016 *Mullaghmore*. Szczecin-Bezrzecze. Wydawnictwo Forma.

Południak, M., 2017 *Pierwsze wspomnienie wielkiego głodu*. Szczecin-Bezrzecze. Wydawnictwo Forma.

Pons, A., 1985 *La Villa irlandaise*. Paris. Éditions Grasset.

Pons, A., 1991 *Dark Rosaleen*. Paris. Éditions Grasset.

Puig, V., 1987 *Dublín*. Barcelona. Destino.

Queneau, R., 1962 *Les oeuvres complètes de Sally Mara*. Paris. Éditions Gallimard.

Queneau, R., 1996 *Journaux*. Paris. Éditions Gallimard.

Rafter, K., 2017 'The media and politics', in J. Coakley and M. Gallagher (eds), *Politics in the Republic of Ireland*, 295–319. London and New York. Routledge.

Rantonen, E. and Savolainen, M., 2002 'Postcolonial and ethnic studies in the context of Nordic minority literatures', in S. Gröndahl (ed.), *Invandrar- och minoritetslitteratur i nordiskt perspektiv*, 71–94. Uppsala University. Uppsala Multiethnic Papers 45.

Recio Morales, Ó., 2004 *Irlanda en Alcalá*. Alcalá. Fundación del Rey.

Recio Morales, Ó., 2010 *Ireland and the Spanish Empire: 1600–1825*. Dublin. Four Courts Press.

Recio Morales, Ó. (ed.), 2012 *Redes de nación y espacios de poder: la comunidad irlandesa en España y la América española, 1600–1825*. Valancia. Albatross.

Reeves, Dr. Rev. J., 1853 'On the Irish Abbey of Honau on the Rhine,' *Proceedings of the Royal Irish Academy (1836–69)* 6, 452–61.

Rège, P., 2010 *Encyclopaedia of French film directors* (2 vols), vol. 1. (A–M). Lanham, MD, Toronto and Plymouth, UK. Scarecrow Press.

Regling, K. and Watson, M., 2010 *A preliminary report on the sources of Ireland's banking crisis*. Dublin. Government Publications Office.

Rekdal, J.E., 1995 *Kirkegårdsjord: gjenfortellinger i ti mellomspill*. Oslo. Gyldendal Norsk Forlag.

Rekdal, J.E., 1998 'Ioruais a chur ar *Cré na cille*', in C. Ó Háinle (ed.), *Criostalú: aistí ar shaothar Mháirtín Uí Chadhain,* 105–19. Dublin. Coiscéim.

Rem, T., 2007 'Nationalism or internationalism? The early Irish reception of Ibsen', *Ibsen Studies* 7 (2), 188–202.

Renan, E., 1982 *L'Ame bretonne* (*La poésie des races celtiques*). Maulévrier. Éditions Philippe Camby.

Revelles, D., 2015. *En los confines de Hibernia: Tras la leyenda de la armada invincible en Irlanda*. Barcelona. Editorial de la Universitat Oberta de Catalunya.

Reverte, J., 2014 *Canta Irlanda: un viaje por la isla esmeralda*. Barcelona. Plaza y Janés.

Reynolds, R.E., 1983 'Unity and diversity in Carolingian Canon Law collections: the case of the *Collectio Canonum Hibernensis* and its derivatives', in U.R. Blumenthal (ed.), *Andrew W. Mellon Lectures in Early Christian Studies, Carolingian Essays*, 99–135. Washington, D.C. Catholic University of America Press.

Reynolds, R.E., 2000 'The transmission of *The Hibernensis* in Italy: tenth to twelfth century', *Peritia* 14, 20–50.

Richardson, B., 2001 'What is unnatural narrative theory?', in J. Alber and R. Heinze (eds), *Unnatural narratives—unnatural narratology*, 23–40. Berlin and Boston. De Gruyter.

Riikonen, H., 2004 'Blooms in the north: translations of *Ulysses* in Finland and Sweden', in G. Lernout and W. Van Mierlo (eds), *The reception of James Joyce in Europe* vol. 1: *Germany, Northern and Eastern Central Europe*, 129–39. London and New York. Continuum.

Riikonen, H., 2012a 'Klassikot: käännöksiä ja uusintakäännöksiä', *Kiiltomato. net* 7 June. Available online: http://www.kiiltomato.net/klassikot-kaannoksia-ja-uusintakaannoksia/. Accessed 6 January 2018.

Riikonen, H., 2012b '*Ulysses*—tekstin ja tulkinnan odysseiat', *Niin & Näin: filosofinen aikakauslehti* 3, 122–25.

Risse, T., 2010 *A community of Europeans? Transnational identities and public spheres*. Ithaca, NY and London. Cornell University Press.

Risse, T. (ed.), 2015 *European public spheres: politics is back*. Cambridge. Cambridge University Press.

Roche, A., 2004 'Synge, Brecht, and the Hiberno-German connection', *Hungarian Journal of English and American Studies* 10 (1–2), 9–32.

Roche, N., 2015 'Cabins', in R. Loeber, H. Cambell, L. Hurley, J. Montague and E. Rowley (eds), *Art and Architecture of Ireland*, vol. 4: *Architecture 1600–2000*, 332. New Haven, London and Dublin. Yale University Press and Royal Irish Academy.

Rod, J.J., 2014 *La suerte de los irlandeses*. Barcelona. Ediciones B.

Rodrein, R., 2012 *La herencia de la rosa blanca*. Barcelona. Roca.

Roland Holst, A., 1916a 'Deirdre en de zonen van Usnach', *De Gids* 80 (2), 302–432.

Roland Holst, A., 1916b 'De dood van Cuchulainn van Murhevna', *De Gids* 80 (1), 360–71.

Roland Holst, A., 1920 *Deirdre en de zonen van Usnach*. Arnhem. Palladium, Hijman, Stenfert Kroese en Van der Zande.

Roland Holst, A., 1928 *Het Elysisch verlangen. Een beschouwing gevolgd door een Iersche sage, De zeetocht van Bran zoon van Febal'*. The Hague and Maastricht. Halcyon Press and A.A.M. Stols.

Ruane, J., 2010 'Ireland's multiple interface-periphery development model: achievements and limits', in M. Boss (ed.), *The nation-state in transformation: the governance, growth and cohesion of small states under globalisation*, 213–32. Århus. Århus University Press.

Ruane, J., 2017 'Modelling Ireland's crises', in N. Ó Dochartaigh, K. Hayward and E. Meehan (eds), *Dynamics of political change in Ireland: making and breaking a divided island*, 93–109. London. Routledge.

Ruppo Malone, I., 2010 *Ibsen and the Irish revival*. Houndmills, Basingstoke. Palgrave MacMillan.

Rosenstock, G., O'Muirthile, L., Ní Dhomhnaill N., 1996 *Bollirà la Rugiada: poesia irlandese contemporea*. Transl. by A. Fabbri, M. Giosa and M. Montevecchi. Faenza. Mobydick.

Rosenstock, G., 2007 *Ein Archivar großer Taten*. Transl. by H.-C. Oeser. Hörby. Edition Rugerup.

Rushton, J., 1995 'Berlioz and Irlande: from romance to mélodie', in P. Devine and H. White (eds), *The Maynooth international musicological conference 1995, selected proceedings: part two*, 224–40. Dublin. Four Courts Press.

Ryan, M., 1990 'Decorated metalwork in the Museo Dell'abbazia, Bobbio, Italy', *Journal of the Royal Society of Antiquaries of Ireland* 120, 102–11.

Saarikoski, P., 1964 *Ovat muistojemme lehdet kuolleet*. Helsinki. Otava.

Saarikoski, P., 1968 *Kirje vaimolleni*. Helsinki. Otava.

Saarikoski, P., 1983 *Euroopan Reuna: Kineettinen kuva*. Helsinki. Otava.

Sæbøe, J. and Ødegård, K., 2005 *Grøne dikt: 9 moderne irske lyrikarar*. Oslo. Cappelen Damm.

Sagarra, E., 2002 'Goethe and Irish German Studies', in N. Boyle and J. Guthrie (eds), *Goethe and the English speaking world: essays from the Cambridge symposium for his 250th anniversary*, 227–42. Rochester NY, and Woodbridge Suffolk. Camden House.

Sagarra, E., 2010 'Heinrich Böll, father of German tourism in Ireland', in G. Holfter (ed.), *Heinrich Böll's 'Irisches Tagebuch' in context*, 13–7. Trier. Wissenschaftlicher Verlag Trier.

Sanz Villanueva, S., 2010 'Dublinesca'. Enrique Vila-Matas. *El Cultural*. Available online: http://www.elcultural.com/revista/letras/Dublinesca/26847. Accessed 15 September 2016.

Sayers, P., 1996 *So irisch wie ich: Eine Fischersfrau erzählt ihr Leben*. Transl. by H.-C. Oeser. Göttingen. Lamuv.

Sayers, P., 1999 *Autobiographie d'une grande conteuse d'Irlande*. Transl. by J. Gac. 2nd edn. Relecq-Kerhuon. An Here.

Scally, D., 2010 'Germany wants more Irish culture', *The Irish Times*. Available online: www.irishtimes.com/news/germany-wants-more-irish-culture-why-can-t-we-deliver. Accessed 7 November 2017.

Scally, D., 2017 'Ireland's days of hiding behind the UK are over', *The Irish Times*, 13 September.

Scappettone, J., 2012 'Stanza as "Homicilie": the poetry of Amelia Rosselli', in J. Scappettone (ed.), *Locomotrix: selected poetry and prose of Amelia Rosselli*, 1–49. Chicago and London. University of Chicago Press.

Scarlini, L. 1996 *Un altro giorno felice. La fortuna dell'opera teatrale di Samuel Beckett in Italia 1953–1996*. Siena. Maschietto and Musolino.

Scherrer, G., 1875 'Commemoration of Columba in Lotharingia, Metz', *Verzeichniss der Handschriften der Stiftsbibliothek Von St. Gallen*. Halle. Verlag der Buchhandlung des Waisenhauses.

Schrader, P., 2005 'Notes in film noir', in B.K. Grant (ed.), *Film genre reader III*, 229–43. Austin TX. University of Texas Press.

Schüller, K., 1999 *Die Beziehungen zwischen Spanien und Irland im 16. und 17. Jahrhundert*. Münster. Aschendorff Verlag.

Schumann, R., 1888 *Gesammelte Schriften über Musik und Musiker*, ed. H. Simon, Leipzig, 1888, vol. I, 188; cited in Dahlhaus, C., 1984 *Between romanticism and modernism: four studies in music of the later nineteenth century*, trans. M. Whittall, 84. Berkeley CA. University of California Press.

Seoane, L., 1959, *El irlandés astrólogo*. Buenos Aires. Losange.

Share, B., 1986 *The flight of the Iolar: the Aer Lingus experience, 1936–1986*. Dublin. Gill and Macmillan.

Sigurðsson, G., 1988 *Gaelic influence in Iceland: historical and literary contacts: a survey of research*. Reykjavik. Bókaútgáfa Menningarsjóðs.

Silke, J., 1976 'The Irish abroad, 1534–1691', in T.W. Moody, F.X. Martin and F.J. Byrne (eds), *A new history of Ireland, vol. iii: early modern Ireland 1534–1691*, 587–633. Oxford. Clarendon Press.

Silos Ribas, L., 2010 'Introduction', in L. Silos Ribas (ed.), *Britannia/Helvetia* (figurationen gender literatur kultur), 11. Jg., H. 1, 7–14. Wien, Köln and Weimar. Böhlau Verlag.

Silvestre, M., 2013 *La fuga del naúfrago*. Seville. Barataria.

Sinnott, R., 1995 *Knowledge of the European Union in Irish public opinion: sources and implications*. Dublin. Institute of European Affairs.

Skelly, J.M., 1997 *Irish diplomacy at the United Nations, 1945–1965: national interests and the international order*. Dublin. Irish Academic Press.

Słabuszewska-Krauze, I., 2006 *Hotel Irlandia*. Warszawa. Wydawnictwo Naukowe Semper.

Ślipko, Ł., 2011 *Pokój z widokiem na Dunnes Stores*. Opole. Wydawnictwo RB.

Smith, J., 1798 *The life of St Columba: the apostle and patron saint of the ancient Scots*. Edinburgh. J. Mundell and Son.

Smith, J.M., 2007 'The Magdalene sisters: evidence, testimony … action?', *Signs: Journal of Women in Culture and Society* 32 (2), 431–58.

Smyth, P., 2004 'Feeding in the peripatetic press tent: on being an Irish foreign correspondent', *Studies: an Irish Quarterly Review* 93 (369), 79–90.

Smyth, W.J., 2012a '"Variations in vulnerability": understanding where and why the people died', in J. Crowley, W.J. Smyth and M. Murphy (eds), *Atlas of the Great Irish Famine*, 180–99. Cork. Cork University Press.

Smyth, W.J., 2012b 'The famine in the County Tipperary parish of Shanrahan', in J. Crowley, W.J. Smyth and M. Murphy (eds), *Atlas of the Great Irish Famine*, 385–98. Cork. Cork University Press.

Soderberg, J., 1993 'A lost cultural exchange: reconsidering the Bologna Shrine's origin and use', *Proceedings of the Harvard Celtic Colloquium* 13, 156–65.

Soler, J., 2011 *Diles que son cadáveres*. Barcelona. Mondadori.

Souto, X., 2014 *Contos do mar de Irlanda*. Vigo. Xerais.

Spadzińska-Żak, E. (ed.), 2007 *Na końcu świata napisane. Autoportret współczesnej polskiej emigracji*. Chorzów. Videograf II.

Stalley, R., 1990 'European art and the Irish high crosses', *Proceedings of the Royal Irish Academy: Archaeology, Culture, History, Literature* 90C, 135–58.

Standún, P., 1999 *Das Vieh*. Transl. by G. Haefs. Bielefeld. Pendragon.

Standún, P., 2002 *Strigoiul Anvy*. Transl. by G.L. Sabau, Bucharest. Editura Pandora.

Standún, P., 2005 *Straszydło*. Transl. B. Sławomirska. Wadowice. Sagittarius.

Standún, P., 2006 *Kochankowie*. Transl. B. Sławomirska. Wadowice. Sagittarius.

Standún, P., 2006 *Umrzeć z miłości*. Transl. B. Sławomirska. Kraków. Sagittarius.

Standún, P., 2006 *Miłość kobiety*. Transl. B. Sławomirska. Kraków. Sagittarius.

Standún, P., 2008 *Dashnorët*. Transl. by J. Qirjako. Tirana. Dituria.

Standún, P., 2010 *Lyubovnitsy*. Transl. by A. Cherelova-Zheleva. Sofia. Zhar Publishers.

Standún, P., 2011 *Anvi*. Transl. by A. Cherelova-Zheleva. Sofia. Zhar Publishers.

Stec, Ł., 2014 *Psychoanioł w Dublinie*. Warszawa. Akurat.

Stifter, D., 2016 'Review of the critical edition of *Nauigatio Sancti Brendani* by Giovanni Orlandi e Rossana E. Guglielmetti, *Speculum* 91 (4), 1148–50.

Stokes, M., 1887 *Early Christian art in Ireland*. London. South Kensington Museum.

Stokes, M., 1895 *Three months in the forests of France. A pilgrimage in search of vestiges of Irish saints in France*. London. George Bell and Sons.

Strich, F., 1971, *Goethe and world literature*. Transl. by C.A.M. Sym. Westport CT. Greenwood Press. (Originally published as *Goethe und die Weltliteratur* 1945, Tübingen. A. Francke Verlag. Originally published in English 1949, London. Routledge and Kegan Paul.)

Studnicki-Gizbert, D., 2007 *A nation upon the ocean sea: Portugal's Atlantic diaspora and the crisis of the Spanish empire, 1492–1640*. Oxford. Clarendon Press.

Sturges, J., 1977 *The eagle has landed*. UK. Associated Films.

Supheert, R., 1995 *Yeats in Holland: the reception of the work of W.B. Yeats in the Netherlands before World War Two*. Amsterdam. Rodopi.

Suskiewicz, Ł., 2009 *egri bikavér*. Szczecin. Forma.

Swann, J., 1993 'Banville's Faust: *Doctor Copernicus, Kepler, The Newton letter* and *Mefisto* as stories of the European mind', in D.E. Morse, C. Bertha and I. Pálffy (eds), *A small nation's contribution to the world. Essays on Anglo-Irish literature and language*, 148–60. Debrecen. Lajos Kossuth University Press.

Sweeney, E.E., 2005 'Revisioning vision in the Bloody Sunday films', in J. Hill and K. Rockett (eds), *Film history and national cinema*, 154–64. Dublin and Portland, OR. Four Courts Press.

Swords, L., 1992-3 'Calendar of Irish material in the files of Jean Fromont, notary at Paris, 1701–30 in the Archives Nationales Paris: part I, 1701–15', *Collectanea Hibernica* 34–5, 77–115.

Tagliaferri, A., 1967 *Beckett e l'iperdeterminazione letteraria*. Milano. Feltrinelli.

Táin czyli uprowadzenie stad z Cuailnge (*The cattle raid of Cooley / Táin Bó Cuailgne*) 1986. Transl. by E. Bryll and M. Goraj-Bryll. Warszawa. Ludowa Spółdzielnia Wydawnicza.

Tanguy, B., 1977 *Aux origines du nationalisme breton* (2 vols). Paris. Union Générale d'Éditions.

Teage, P. and Donaghey, J., 2009 'Why has Irish social partnership survived?', *British Journal of Industrial Relations* 47 (1), 55–78.

Testa, F., 1999 '*Tristram Shandy*' in Italia. Rome. Bulzoni Editore.

Thiele, J., 2004 'Die große Versöhnung—Ruth Leuweriks vermittelnde Frauenrollen', in P. Mänz and N. Warnecke (eds), *Die Ideale Frau: Ruth Leuwerik und das Kino der fünfziger Jahre*, 33–40. Berlin. Henschel.

Tindbæk, B., 2009 'Irske Stemmer i Litteraturen—Januar/Februar 2009'. Available online: https://litteratursiden.dk/temaer/irske-stemmer-i-litteraturen-januarfebruar-2009. Accessed 12 December 2017.

Titley, A., 1991 *Tagann Godot*. Dublin. An Clóchomhar.

Titley, A., 1999 *Arriva Godot: tragicommedia in due atti*. Transl. by R. Barrone. Faenza. Mobydick Edizioni.

Titley, A., 2006a '*Tyda 2006*'. Available online: http://magazines.russ.ru/inostran/2006/6/avt18.html. Accessed 17 December 2017.

Titley, A., 2006b *Voilà Godot: tragédie comique en deux actes*. Transl. by L. Ó Baoill. Paris. Forsai Publications.

Tóibín, C., 2012 'A man of no mind', *London Review of Books* 34 (17), 15–16.

Tommasini, A.M., 1937 *Irish saints in Italy*. London. Sands and Company.

Toonder, J.G., 1970 *Kasteel in Ierland*. Amsterdam. Commissie voor de Collectieve Propaganda van het Nederlandse Boek.

Toonder, M., 1983 'De Keltische schemering', in A. van Dis (ed.), *Ierland. Verhalen van een land* (Bibliotheek voor de literaire reiziger), 7–15. Amsterdam. Meulenhoff.

Toonder, M., 2010 *Autobiografie*. Amsterdam. De Bezige Bij.

Tosi, M., 1985 'Il governo abbaziale di Gerberto a Bobbio', *Archivum Bobiense* 2, 195–223.

Tosi, M., 1978 *Bobbio Guida storica artistica e ambientale della città e dintorni*. Bobbio. Archivi Storici Bobiensi.

Tourism Policy Review Group, 2003 *New horizons for Irish tourism: an agenda for action*. Dublin. Tourism Policy Review Group.

Tucholski, K., 1927 'Ulysses', *Die Weltbühne* 33 (November), 792.

Tuori, S., Irni, S., Keskinen, S. and Mulinari, D. (eds), 2009 *Complying with colonialism: gender, race and ethnicity in the Nordic region*. Aldershot. Ashgate.

Tuuri, H., 2013 *Irlantilainen aamiainen: kertomuksia vihreältä saarelta*. Helsinki. Otava.

Tysdahl, B., 2004 'The reception of James Joyce in Norway', in G. Lernout and W. Van Mierlo (eds), *The reception of James Joyce in Europe* vol. 1: *Germany, Northern and Eastern Central Europe*, 103–10. London and New York. Continuum.

Untermann, M., 2001 *Klosterinsel Reichenau im Bodensee* (Arbeitsheft/ Landesdenkmalamt Baden-Württemberg vol. 8). Stuttgart. Konrad Theiss Verlag.

Urry, J., 1990 *The tourist gaze: leisure and travel in contemporary societies*. London. Sage.

van der Meer, V., 1995 *Spookliefde: een Iers verhaal*. Amsterdam. De Bezige Bij.

Van der Pol, F., 2006 'De Kerstening van het Noorden', in H. Selderhuis (ed.), *Handboek Nederlandse Kerkgeschiedenis*, 42–59. Kampen. Kok.

Van der Vegt, J., 1976 *Naar Ierland varen*. The Hague. Nijgh en Van Ditmar.

Van der Vegt, J., 2000 *A. Roland Holst: Biografie*. Baarn. De Prom.

Van Faassen, S.A.J., 1995 'Vestdijk en zijn Duitse vertalingen, 1937–1949: De correspondentie tussen S. Vestdijk, G.K. Schauer en de Rudolf M. Rohrer Verlag', *Vestdijkkroniek* 87, 1–74.

Van Winssen, T., 1996 'Leon de Winter', in L. de Winter, *Zoeken naar Eileen W.* (Series Grote Lijsters Nr. 4), 185–90. Groningen. Wolters-Noordhoff.

Vanderlinden, B. and Filipovic, E. (eds), 2006 *The manifesta decade: debates on contemporary art exhibitions and biennials in post-wall Europe*. Cambridge MA. Massachusetts Institute of Technology Press.

Vainonen, J., 2011 *Swiftin Ovella*. Helsinki. Tammi.

Vainonen, J., 2015 'Elämästä syntyy järkyttävä kauneus—W.B. Yeatsistä ja hänen runoudestaan', in *Torni ja kierreportaat: valitut runot*. Transl. by J. Vainonen, 5–22. Helsinki. Basam Books.

Vallet, F., 1982 'Trésors d'Irlande', in *Catalogue de L'exposition*. Paris. Association Française d'Action Artistique.

Varadkar, L., 2017 'Taoiseach addresses Queen's University Belfast, 4 August 2017'. Available online: https://merrionstreet.ie/en/News-Room/News/Taoiseach_ addresses_Queens_University_Belfast.html. Accessed 17 March 2018.

Vargas Llosa, M., 2010 *El sueño del celta*. Madrid. Alfaguara.

Vassiliou, A., 2012 'Commissioner Vassiliou's speech in Copenhagen', Press release 9 May. Available online: http://europa.eu/rapid/press-release_ SPEECH-12-345_en.htm. Accessed 18 August 2018.

Vendryes, J., 1921 *Le langage : introduction linguistique à l'histoire*. Paris. Renaissance du Livre.

Venema, A., 1991 *Schrijvers, uitgevers en hun collaboratie*, IIIb, *S. Vestdijk*. Amsterdam. De Arbeiderspers.

Verrier, A., 1989 *Ossianiques*. Paris. Orphée La Différence.

Vestdijk, S., 1939 'Hoofdstukken over Ulysses', in S. Vestdijk, *Lier en Lancet*, 90–125. Rotterdam. Nijgh en Van Ditmar.

Vestdijk, S., 1940 *Rumeiland*. Rotterdam. Nijgh en Van Ditmar. (Published in German, 1941, *Die Fahrt nach Jamaica*, transl. by G.K. Schauer; Brünn, Wien and Leipzig. Rudolf M. Rohrer Verlag. Also published as *Rum Island*, 1963, transl. by B.K. Bowes; London. John Calder.)

Vestdijk, S., 1946 'Afscheid van Joyce', in S. Vestdijk, *De Poolsche Ruiter*, 46–52. Bussum. F.G. Kroonder.

Vestdijk, S., 1950 *Ierse nachten*. The Hague and Rotterdam (6th edn). Nijgh en Van Ditmar. (First published in Dutch as *Iersche nachten*, 1946, Rotterdam. Nijgh en Van Ditmar.) Originally published in German as *Irische Nächte*, 1944, transl. by Kurt Schauer; Brünn, Wien and Leipzig. Rudolf M. Rohrer Verlag.

Vestdijk, S., 1951 *De vijf roeiers*. Rotterdam. Nijgh en Van Ditmar.

Vila-Matas, E., 2010 *Dublinesca*. Barcelona. Seix Barral.

Vila-Matas, E., Lago, E., Soler, A., Soler, J., Otero Barral, M. and Garriga Vela, J.A., 2010 *La orden de Finnegans*. Barcelona. Ediciones Alfabia.

Vila-Matas, E., Garriga Vela, J.A., Giralt Torrente, M., Lago, E., Monge, E., Otero Barral, M., Soler, A. and Soler, J., 2013 *Lo desorden*. Madrid. Alfaguara.

Villar García, M.B. (ed.), 2000 *La emigración irlandesa en el siglo XVIII*. Málaga. Universidad de Málaga.

Villar García, M.B., 2004 'Ingleses y irlandeses en España', in Antonio Eiras Roel and Domingo L. González Lopez (eds), *La inmigracion en España*, 31–76. Santiago. Universidade de Santiago.

Villar García, M.B. and Pezzi Cristóbal, P. (eds), 2003 *Los extranjeros en la España moderna* (2 vols). Málaga. Gráficas Digarza.

Von Pflugk-Harttung, J., 1891 'The Old Irish on the continent', *Transactions of the Royal Historical Society* 5, 75–102.

Von Pückler-Muskau, H., 1833, *Tour in England, Ireland, and France in the years 1826, 1828, and 1829 … In a series of letters*. Philadelphia, PA. Carey, Lea and Blanchard.

Völker, K., 1967 *Irish theatre I: Yeats and Synge*. Hanover. Friedrich.

Voskuil, J.J., 2006 *Gaandeweg. Voettochten 1983–1992*. Amsterdam. Van Oorschot.

Walker, D., 1997 *Modern art in Ireland*. Dublin. Lilliput Press.

Walsh, T.J., 1973 *The Irish continental college movement: the colleges at Bordeaux, Toulouse and Lille*. Cork. Golden Eagle Books.

Walter, B., 2011 'Including the Irish: taken-for-granted characters in English films', *Irish Studies Review* 19 (1), 5–18.

Wenell, L., 2015 *Den engelska ing-formen i nyöversättning: En komparativ grammatisk studie av två svenska översättningar av James Joyces Ulysses*. Uppsala. Uppsala Universitet.

Whelan, K.B., 2004 'Reading the ruins: the presence of absence in the Irish landscape', in H.B. Clarke, J. Prunty and M. Hennessy (eds), *Surveying Ireland's past: multidisciplinary essays in honour of Anngret Simms*, 297–328, Dublin. Geography Publications.

Whelan, S., 2018 'If you are not British, the UK Supreme Court case is irrelevant', RTÉ *News*, 25 January. Available online: https://www.rte.ie/news/2017/0124/847466-brexit-blog/. Accessed 15 April 2018.

White, H., 2008 *Music and the Irish literary imagination*. New York and Oxford. Oxford University Press.

White, H. and Boydell, B. (eds), 2013 *The encyclopaedia of music in Ireland* (2 vols). Dublin. University College Dublin Press.

Widukind Von Corvey, 1981 *Res Gestae Saxonicae (Die Sachsengeschichte)* E. Rotter and B. Schneidmüller (eds). Stuttgart. Reclam.

Wieteska, M., 2009 *Zielona wyspa*. Warszawa. Anagram.

Wilkinson, D., 2015 *Call to the dance* (The Wendy Hillton Dance and Music Series, no. 18). New York. Pendragon Press.

Williams, W.H.A., 2010 *Creating Irish tourism: the first century, 1750–1850*. London. Anthem Press.

Wilmink, W. and Gerritsen, W.P. (eds), 1994 *De reis van Sint Brandaan. Een reisverhaal uit de twaalfde eeuw*. Amsterdam. Uitgeverij Prometheus/Bert Bakker.

Winters, M., 2015 'Hans-Christian Oeser: translation strategies of a literary translator', in S. Egger (ed.), *Cultural/literary translators: selected Irish-German biographies II*, 211–24. Trier. Wissenschaftlicher Verlag Trier.

Wirth, F.P., 1959 *Ein Tag, der nie zu Ende geht*. Germany. Divina-Film.

Wittman, R., 'Print culture and French architecture in the eighteenth and nineteenth centuries: a survey of recent scholarship', in *Perspective, actualité en historie de l'art*. Available online: http://journals.openedition.org/perspective/5806?lang=en. Accessed 19 December 2017.

Wodak, R. and Meyer, M. (eds), 2010 *Methods of critical discourse analysis* (2nd edn). London. Sage.

Wojnarowski, M., 2008 *Okrutny idiota albo prywatny żart*. Poznań. Wydawnictwo EP.

Worthington, D. (ed.), 2009 *British and Irish emigrants and exiles in Europe, 1603–1688*. Leiden. Brill.

Worthington, D. (ed.), 2012 *British and Irish experiences and impressions of Central Europe, c. 1560–1688*. Leiden. Brill.

Wybranowski, T., 2012 *Nocne czuwanie*. Łódź. RC Solutions.

Wylie, C. and Murphy, E.K., 2009 *Willie Doherty: requisite distance—Ghost story and landscape*. New Haven, CT and London. Dallas Museum of Art and Yale University Press.

Wylie, P.L., 2006 *Ireland and the Cold War: diplomacy and recognition 1949–63*. Dublin. Irish Academic Press.

Xairen, G., 2015 *Iúl; Llegó el Momento de Saber la Verdad*. Seattle. Amazon Digital.

Yeats. W.B., 1905 'Samhain: 1903', in M. Fitzgerald and R.J. Finneran (eds), *W.B. Yeats. The Irish dramatic movement*, 20–6. New York and London. Scribner.

Yeats, W.B., 1914 *Tragedie irlandesi*. Transl. and Introduction by C. Linati. Milan. Studio Editoriale Lombardo.

Yeats, W.B., 1924a *Blæsten mellem sivene: digte og skuespil*. Transl. by V. Rørdam. Copenhagen. Haase og søns forlag.

Yeats, W.B., 1924b *Drømmerier over Barneår og Ungdom.* Transl. by V. Rørdam. Copenhagen. Haase og søns forlag.

Yeats, W.B., 1961a 'The Celtic element in literature', in *Essays and introductions.* London and Basingstoke. Macmillan Press.

Yeats, W.B., 1961b 'J.M. Synge and the Ireland of his time', in W.B. Yeats, *Essays and introductions*, 311–41. London. Macmillan.

Yeats, W.B., 1961c *Autobiographies: the collected works of W.B. Yeats.* London. Macmillan.

Yeats, W.B., 1966 *William Butler Yeats: Runoja.* Transl. by A. Tynni. Helsinki. WSOY.

Yeats, W.B., 1999 'The bounty of Sweden', in *Autobiographies: the collected works of W.B. Yeats* vol. 3, 389–409. New York. Scribner.

Yeats, W.B., 2012a *Ett kristalliskt rop: dikter i urval.* Transl. by A. Åklint. Lund. Elleströms.

Yeats, W.B., 2012b *Tornet.* Transl. by T Sjöswärd. Stockholm. Bromberg.

Yeats, W.B., 2014 *Valda Dikter.* Transl. by G. Artéus. Nacka. Sköna konster förlag.

Yeats, W.B., 2015 *Torni ja kierreportaat: valitut runot.* Transl. by J. Vainonen. Helsinki. Basam Books.

Young, A., 1780 *A tour in Ireland 1776–1779.* London. T. Cadell and J. Dodsley.

Yuste, C., 2010 *La mirada del bosque.* Alcalá de Guadaíra. Paréntesis.

Yuste, C., 2015 *Regreso a Innisfree y otros relatos irlandeses.* Zaragoza. Xordica.

Zanotti, S., 2004a 'James Joyce among the Italian writers', in G. Lernout and W. van Mierlo (eds), *The reception of James Joyce in Europe*, 329–61. London. Continuum.

Zanotti, S., 2004b *Joyce in Italy. L'italiano in Joyce.* Rome. Aracne.

Żuchowski, D., 2014 *The new Dubliners.* Dublin. Literary Publishing.

Zuelow, E., 2009 *Making Ireland Irish: tourism and national identity since the Irish civil war.* Syracuse, N.Y. Syracuse University Press.

Zwiers, G.J., 2007 *Mijn Ierland.* Amsterdam and Antwerpen. Atlas.

Contributors

David Clark was born in Edinburgh and holds degrees in English and American literature from the University of Kent at Canterbury and in philosophy and letters from the University of Alicante. He has lived in Spain since 1980, and his doctoral thesis on the work of Neil M. Gunn was read at the University of A Coruña, where he is a senior lecturer in and former head of English. He has published widely on Scottish and Irish literature. He is director of Amergin, the University Research Institute for Irish Studies, and has held executive positions in both national and international associations. He is currently editor of the journal *Papers on Joyce*.

Fiorenzo Fantaccini is associate professor of English and Anglo-Irish literature at the University of Florence. He is the author of essays on translation as well as on American, English and especially Irish literature, and of the book *W.B. Yeats e la cultura Italiana* (Firenze University Press; Firenze, 2009). He co-edited, with C. De Petris and J. Ellis D'Alessandro, *The cracked looking glass: contributions to the study of Irish Literature* (Bulzoni; Roma, 1999). He is also the co-editor, with O. De Zordo, of *Le riscritture del Postmoderno. Percorsi angloamericani* (Palomar; 2002); *altri canoni/canoni altri pluralismo e studi letterari* (Firenze University Press; Firenze, 2011), and *Saggi di Anglistica e Americanistica. Percorsi di ricerca* (Firenze University Press; Firenze, 2012). He has translated works by E.A. Poe, Hawthorne, Jane Austen, Brian Friel and Cónal Creedon. He is the general editor of the open-access journal *Studi irlandesi. A Journal of Irish Studies* (www.fupress.net/index.php/bsfm-sijis).

Anna Fattori is associate professor of German literature at the Faculty of the Humanities of the University of Rome 'Tor Vergata'. She has studied German literature and English literature at the University of Perugia and Pavia. She is a former holder of a *Bundesstipendium* at the University of Zurich. She has published on a variety of themes in Swiss-German literature, focusing in particular on Robert Walser. Her areas of special interest include the German novel of the eighteenth century, the theory of the novel, Anglo-German studies and literary stylistics. She has recently co-edited (with Corinna Jäger-Trees and Simon Zumsteg) *Heinrich Federer, In und um Italien. Plaudereien, Reisebriefe und Erzählungen* (Chronos; Zürich, 2015). She has recently published the Italian translation of *Reisen eines Deutschen in England im Jahr 1782* by K.Ph. Moritz. She is Erasmus coordinator for the German-speaking countries and Erasmus delegate for the Faculty of the Humanities in her university.

Joachim Fischer is senior lecturer in German at the University of Limerick and joint director of the Centre for Irish-German Studies. He has published extensively on Irish-German relations, travel writing and utopian studies; his current main area of research is Irish perceptions of Germany. Among his major book-length publications are *The correspondence of Myles Dillon, 1922–1925: Irish-German relations and Celtic Studies* (with John Dillon. Four Courts Press; Dublin, 1999), *Das Deutschlandbild der Iren 1890–1939: Geschichte. Form. Funktion* (Universitätsverlag Winter; Heidelberg, 2000) and *As others saw us: Cork through European eyes* (with Grace Neville, for Cork European City of Culture. Collins Press; Cork, 2005). He co-edits two book series, *Irish–German Studies* (Wissenschaftlicher Verlag; Trier) and *Ralahine Utopian Studies* (Peter Lang; Bern).

Anne Gallagher is head of the School of Celtic Studies and director of the Centre for Irish Language Research, Teaching and Testing at Maynooth University. She is a member of the executive committee of the Association of Language Testers in Europe (ALTE), of the Indicator Expert Group on Multilingualism at the European Commission and of the Royal Irish Academy's Languages, Literature, Culture and Communication Committee. She is a former chairperson of the Irish Association for Applied Linguistics and Raidió na Gaeltachta, and is currently chairperson of Údarás na Gaeltachta. In 2008 she was made *Chevalier dans l'Ordre des Palmes académiques* by the French government in recognition of her services to plurilingualism.

Paul Gillespie is a senior research fellow adjunct in the School of Politics and International Relations, University College Dublin and a 'World View' columnist and leader writer on international affairs for *The Irish Times*, from which he retired as foreign policy editor in 2009. His main research areas, journalism and publications are in European integration and political identities, Irish-British relations, Europe-Asia relations, comparative regionalism, media and foreign policy and the EuroMed region. Recent publications include: Dáithi

O'Ceallaigh and Paul Gillespie (eds), *Britain and Europe: the endgame, an Irish perspective* (Institute of International and European Affairs; Dublin, 2015); also 'News media as actors in European foreign-policymaking' in Knud Erik Jørgensen, Åsne Kalland Aarstad, Edith Drieskens, Katie Laatikainen and Ben Tonra (eds), *The Sage handbook of European foreign policy* (Sage; London, 2015).

Gisela Holfter studied in Cologne, Cambridge and St Louis, and worked as an assistant teacher in Belfast and as a lektor at the University of Otago in Dunedin, New Zealand, before coming to Limerick in 1996. She is senior lecturer in German and co-founder and joint director of the Centre for Irish-German Studies. Her research interests include German-Irish relations, German literature (nineteenth century to contemporary writing), exile studies, migration and intercultural communication. She is a member of PEN German-speaking Writers Abroad and has published many articles and edited a dozen books, the latest being *German reunification and the legacy of GDR literature and culture* (with D. Byrnes and J. Conacher, Brill, 2018). Her monographs include *Erlebnis Irland* (Wissenschaftlicher Verlag; Trier, 1996), *Heinrich Böll and Ireland* (CBS: 2011, paperback 2012) and *An Irish sanctuary: German-speaking refugees in Ireland 1933–1945* (with H. Dickel, de Gruyter; Amsterdam, 2017; paperback 2018). She is currently engaged in a project on Fontane's *Wanderungen durch die Mark Brandenburg* and one on German migration to Ireland since 1922.

Anne Karhio is an Irish Research Council Laureate Project Fellow at the National University of Ireland, Galway, where she works in the Republic of Conscience: Human Rights and Modern Irish Poetry project. Her previous project, Virtual landscapes: new media technologies and the poetics of place in recent Irish poetry, was co-funded by the IRC and by Marie Skłodowska-Curie Actions. Karhio is a co-editor of *Crisis and contemporary poetry* (Palgrave MacMillan; London, 2011) and the author of *'Slight Return': Paul Muldoon's poetics of place* (Peter Lang; Bern, 2016), and has published numerous journal articles and critical essays on contemporary Irish poetry, place and landscape; Finnish culture and art in Irish writing; and digital literature and aesthetics. She is also the secretary of the Nordic Irish Studies Network.

Linda King is a design historian, educator and consultant. She sits on the Board of the National Museum of Ireland, is the design curator for the television series *National Treasures* (RTÉ, 2018) and is the co-programme chair of the BA (Hons) in Visual Communication Design at the Institute of Art, Design and Technology, Dublin. Her research interests include the visual culture of tourism, with a particular focus on Aer Lingus, and the history of Irish design, on which she has published. She is co-editor, with Elaine Sisson, of *Ireland, design and visual culture: negotiating modernity, 1922–92* (Cork University

Press; Cork, 2011) and, with Oonagh Young, of *Transdisciplinary practice: images, objects and discourse across creative contexts* (Dublin, 2017). She is the visiting scholar in Design and Irish Studies at the School of Irish Studies, Concordia University, Montreal and sits on the editorial board of the *Canadian Journal of Irish Studies*. She is an invited member of the UNESCO affiliate the International Association of Art Critics (AICA).

Joanna Kosmalska works as a research-and-teaching fellow at the Department of British Literature and Culture, University of Lodz. She is a translator, editor of *DeKadentzya* literary journal, author, and, since 2004, coordinator of the research project Polish (E)Migration Literature in Britain and Ireland (emigracja.uni.lodz.pl). She has recently published on Polish writing in Ireland and the UK and has co-edited (with Jerzy Jarniewicz) an issue of *Teksty Drugie* on 'Migrant literature'.

Marieke Krajenbrink is lecturer in German and Comparative Literature at the University of Limerick and has been a member of the Centre for Irish-German Studies since 1998. She studied German language and literature at the Vrije Universiteit Amsterdam and has published widely on German and Austrian literature. Focusing on intertextuality and questions of memory and identity, her research interests range from Botho Strauß, German Romanticism and the reception of Richard Wagner, to Austrian and international crime fiction. She is a founding member of the International Crime Genre Research Network and the Comparative Literature Association of Ireland (CLAI). Her book publications include *Intertextualität als Konstruktionsprinzip. Transformationen des Kriminalromans und des romantischen Romans bei Peter Handke und Botho Strauß* (Rodopi; Amsterdam and Atlanta, GA, 1996); with Gisela Holfter and Edward Moxon-Browne (eds), *Beziehungen und Identitäten: Österreich, Irland und die Schweiz* (Peter Lang; Bern, 2004) and, with Kate Quinn (eds), *Investigating identities. Questions of identity in international crime fiction* (Rodopi; Amsterdam and New York, 2009).

Brigid Laffan is director and professor at the Robert Schuman Centre for Advanced Studies, European University Institute (EUI), Florence. She was vice-president of UCD and principal of the College of Human Sciences from 2004 to 2011. She was the founding director of the Dublin European Institute UCD in 1999, and in March 2004 she was elected a member of the Royal Irish Academy. In 2012 she received the THESEUS Award for outstanding research on European Integration, and in September 2014 was awarded the Lifetime Achievement Award by the University Association for Contemporary European Studies. In 2010 she was honoured with the *Ordre national du Mérite* by the president of the French Republic.

Fergal Lenehan received a BA and an MA from University College Dublin, a PhD from the University of Leipzig, and the formal German post-doctoral qualification of Habilitation from the University of Jena, where he teaches Intercultural Studies. He has published numerous chapters and articles in publications such as *Irish Studies Review, Interculture Journal, History Ireland* and the *Dublin Review of Books*. He has published two books: *Intellectuals and Europe: imagining a Europe of regions in twentieth century Germany, Britain and Ireland* (Wissenschaftlicher Verlag; Trier, 2014) and *Stereotypes, ideology and foreign correspondents: German media representations of Ireland, 1946–2010* (Peter Lang; Oxford, 2016).

Caoimhín Mac Giolla Léith is associate professor in the School of Irish, Celtic Studies and Folklore at University College Dublin. Among his recent publications on literature in Irish are co-edited volumes on two major twentieth-century poets: (with Liam Mac Amhlaigh) *Fill arís: oidhreacht Sheáin Uí Ríordáin* (Cló Iar-Chonnacht; Gaillimh, 2012) and (with Meidhbhín Ní Úrdail) *Mo ghnósa leas an dáin: aistí in ómós do Mháirtín Ó Direáin* (An Sagart; Magh Nuad, 2014). A selection of his published essays on modern poetry in Irish, *Raon na Geite: aistí ar an Nuafhilíocht* is forthcoming from Coiscéim. His many publications as an art critic include monographic essays for exhibitions at the Irish Museum of Modern Art, Tate Britain, Musée d'Art Moderne de la Ville de Paris, Museum für Moderne Kunst, Frankfurt, Kölnischer Kuntsverein, Kunsthalle Zürich and Bergen Kunsthall. He has curated exhibitions in Dublin, London, Amsterdam and New York and was a juror for the 2005 Turner Prize.

Bettina Migge studied in Hamburg, Yaoundé (Cameroon) and Berlin and received a PhD in linguistics from the Ohio State University. She worked as *Hochschulassistentin* at the Johann-Wolfgang Goethe Universität, Frankfurt am Main, and is currently professor of linguistics and head of the School of Languages, Cultures and Linguistics at University College Dublin, and a member of the research group Structure et Dynamique des Langues (SeDyL UMR 8202) in Villejuif, France. Her research interests are in the broad area of language contact, language documentation and sociolinguistics. Empirically, her research has focused on the Americas, specifically the Creoles of Suriname and French Guiana, and on migration to and language in Ireland. Her publications include book-length studies *Exploring language in a multilingual context: variation, interaction and ideology in language documentation* (with I. Léglise, CUP; Cambridge, 2013) and edited volumes *Support, transmission, education and target varieties in the Celtic languages* (with N. Ó Murchadha; Routledge; London, 2017), and *New perspectives on Irish English* (with M. Ní Chiosáin; John Benjamins; Amsterdam, 2012). She is currently engaged in a multi-year participatory dictionary project in French Guiana.

Edward Moxon-Browne holds degrees from the University of St Andrews in Scotland and the University of Pennsylvania in Philadelphia. He was the Jean Monnet Chair of European Integration and director of the Jean Monnet Centre of Excellence at the University of Limerick from 1992 to 2010. Before that he was lecturer, senior lecturer and reader in political science at the Queen's University Belfast. His principal research interests have been ethnic conflict, peacebuilding, political violence, and European integration. Among his publications are: *Nation, class and creed in Northern Ireland* (Gower; 1983); *Political change in Spain* (Routledge; 1989); *Who are the Europeans now?* (Ashgate; Farnham, 2004) and *A future for peacekeeping?* (Macmillan; London, 1998). He has held visiting appointments at Wesleyan University, Harvard University and Hollins University in the USA; as well as at Corvinus University in Budapest; Agder University in Kristiansand; the Ministry of Foreign Affairs in Tehran; and the UN Peace University in San Jose, Costa Rica.

Lynda Mulvin is associate professor at the School of Art History and Cultural Policy, University College Dublin, with specialist interest in classical antiquity and Irish medieval art and architecture and the reception of antiquity in the nineteenth century. She is Irish partner for the EU project, Connecting Early Medieval Collections of Europe (CEMEC), 2015–19, and her article on James Cavanah Murphy and unpublished drawings from his *Arabian antiquities of Spain* was published in *Muqarnas* in 2018. She was elected Fellow of the Society of Antiquaries in 2018.

Éamon Ó Ciosáin is lecturer in French, and also teaches Breton, at Maynooth University. He has published translations of modern literature between Irish and both French and Breton. He has published widely on Franco-Irish relations in the early modern period in particular, focusing on migration and literature. Among his other publications are a co-authored Irish-Breton dictionary and articles and reviews on twentieth-century literature in Irish.

Thomas O'Connor is professor of history in Maynooth University and holds a DEA and PhD from the Sorbonne. His undergraduate courses include the Spanish Inquisition, the French Wars of Religion and early modern migration. His research interests are in early modern European migration and religion, especially Jansenism, inquisitions, censorship, ideological controls, social discipline and religious conversion. He is co-director of the Irish in Europe project and editor of the history sources journal, *Archivium Hibernicum*. He is a member of the Irish Manuscripts Commission and of the Fondation Irlandaise (Paris). He has published several monographs in early modern European history, the most recent *Irish voices from the Spanish Inquisition: migrants, converts and brokers in Early Modern Iberia* (Palgrave; London, 2016).

Mervyn O'Driscoll is head of the School of History, University College Cork. His interests lie in twentieth-century international history, especially Irish relations with Europe and Germany. He has authored *Ireland, Germany and the Nazis 1919–1939* (Four Courts Press; Dublin, 2004; 2nd edn 2017); co-authored a report for the European Parliament titled 'The European Parliament and the Euratom Treaty' (Brussels, 2002); and coedited, with Dermot Keogh, *Ireland in World War Two: neutrality and survival* (2004) and, with Dermot Keogh and Jérôme aan de Wiel, *Ireland through European eyes: Western Europe, the EEC and Ireland, 1945–73* (Cork University Press; Cork, 2013). His latest monograph *Ireland, West Germany and the new Europe 1949–73: best friend and ally?* was published by Manchester University Press in January 2018. In addition, he has written numerous articles and book chapters. He chairs the Royal Irish Academy's Standing Committee for International Affairs and is a member of the RIA advisory committee for the *Dictionary of Irish Biography.*

Finola O'Kane is a professor at the School of Architecture, Planning and Environmental Policy, University College Dublin. Her books include *Landscape design in eighteenth-century Ireland: mixing foreign trees with the natives* (Cork University Press; Cork, 2004); *William Ashford's Mount Merrion: the absent point of view* (Churchill House Press; Tralee, 2012) and *Ireland and the picturesque; design, landscape painting and tourism in Ireland 1700–1830* (Yale University Press; New York, 2013). She has also published widely on Georgian Dublin, Irish urban history and Irish-owned Jamaican plantations. In 2017 she was elected a member of the Royal Irish Academy.

Harry White is professor of historical musicology at University College Dublin, where he has held the Chair of Music since 1993. He served as inaugural president of the Society for Musicology in Ireland from 2003 until 2006, and was awarded the society's Harrison medal in 2014. He is a fellow of the Royal Irish Academy of Music (2007). He was elected to the Royal Irish Academy in 2006 and to the Academia Europaea in 2015. His principal research interests are the cultural history of music in Ireland, the relationship between political and religious servitude and the European musical imagination in the early eighteenth century, and the history of Anglo-American musicology since 1945.

Index

Illustrations are indicated by page numbers in bold

language 207
Yeats, translations of 216
Déon, Michel xiii, 76, 90–2
D'haen, Theo 150, 165 n11–12
Dicuil 320, 322
diplomacy ix–x, 22–3, 24, 33
DIT Conservatory of Music and Drama
357, 358, 366 n16
Döblin, Alfred 185, 186, 200 nn53–4
Doherty, Willie 289, 290–3, 297
Donatus, bishop of Fiesole 53
Dorbhéne, abbot of Iona 310
Dornan, Jamie 407
Dorrestein, Renate 157, 158–60, 161, 168
n42
Dottin, Georges 227, 235
Douai, France 9, 10
Douglas Hyde Gallery, Dublin 289–90
Downey, James 422, 424
Doyle, Roddy 195, 208, 217, 228
Draak, Maartje 151
Draghi, Mario 60
Dublin City University (DCU) 375–6
Dungal of Pavia 322
Dunsany, Edward Plunkett, 18th Baron
of 100, 184
Durozoi, Gérard 87
Dutch literature
Celtic Twilight, Holst and 149–51
De Reis van Sint Brandaen 148
Dublin, portrayal of 157
fiction, twentieth century 148–9
Gothic novels 158–62
historical novels 151–4
Ierland is anders 148
intercultural encounters 154–6
Ireland and 148, 149, 157, 158–64
Irish identity, changes in 163
Irish literature and 157
Irish stereotypes 155
Irish women's voices 159
modern Irish society 163
Nazi occupation 153, 154, 167n31
Northern Ireland, perspectives on
156–8
travel literature 163
Dyer, Richard 408

E

Easter Rising (1916) 25, 120, 233
Eastern Bloc states 32, 35
Eco, Umberto 187
Economist, The 55–6
economy (Irish)
Anglo-American model 437, 438
corporation tax 67–8
dependence on Britain 27, 36, 38, 41
'Economic War' 27, 48 n19
EEC membership, effects of 55–7
employment (1950s) 36
foreign direct investment 22, 39, 40,
56, 68
growth 411
industrial protectionism 22, 35–6
Programmes for Economic Expansion
39, 43
recession (1980s) 56
social partnership 56
see also financial crisis (2008)
Edgeworth, Maria 179
Einhard 322, 323
emigration 36, 38, 139
see also Irish diaspora; migrants/
migration
Enright, Anne 208, 217
Epic Ireland 410
Erasmus programme 377, 380–1, 382
Espedal, Tomas 208
Europe
commercial expansion 4
Ireland une île derrière une île 20–1,
47 n1
Ireland/the Irish, perception of 14,
37, 38
Ireland's negative trade balance
39–40
Irish diaspora in xii–xiii, 4–5
Irish diplomats in 38
Irish neutrality, perception of 31–2
Irish trade with 4
official Ireland and 21
European Biennial 294
European Bureau for Lesser-Used
Languages 243
European Central Bank (ECB) 53, 59–61,
62, 373

F

Fabbri, A., *et al.* 238
Fáilte Ireland 401, 405–6, 409, 411
Farewell, James 262–3
Farrell, Colin 407, 408, 409
Farrell, Helen (artist) 285
Fay, William P. 36
Federal Republic of Germany (FRG) 22, 35, 39
Fennell, Desmond 431–2
Fernández Duro, Cesáreo 105
Fernández Fernández, Isaac 237
Ferreiro, Emilio 117 n3
Fianna Fáil 27, 28, 58, 419, 420, 431
Field, Thomas 11
financial crisis (2008) x, 59–60
    bank bail-out 60, 62, 63, 436
    bondholders, treatment of 62
    ECB and 59–61
    Troika and xiii, 53, 61, 373
Fine Gael 58, 62, 431
Fingen, abbot of St Felix 323
Finland 207, 211
    Beckett and 212–13
    cultural revival xvi, 210
    Irish art exhibition 285
    Irish plays and 219
    Yeats and 216
First World War xi, 22, 25, 28–9
FitzGerald, Garret 34, 392, 423, 431
Flaherty, Robert 333
Flanagan, Charlie 63
Flanders 165 n8
Fleischmann, Aloys 362, 364
Fleming, Lionel 420, 422
Fleuriot, Léon 77, 82
Flower, Robin 245
Flynn, Roderick 341
folk tales
    Buile Shuibhne 242, 285
    German translations 180, 227
    Irish 'otherworld' 152, 162, 167 n33, 227
    Tristan and Iseult 157, 158, 168 n42
Ford, John 341
Foreign Policy (magazine) 426
Forster, Lady E. 264–5

Foscolo, Ugo 176, 178
Foster, John Wilson 210
Foster, Roy 344–5
France
    Britain and 25
    diplomatic relations x, 24, 25, 33
    ECSC 37
    EEC 41, 42, 43, 44
    Irish art, perceptions of 289, 290
    Irish colleges 12, 13
    Irish language publications 13
    Irish migrants xiii, 7–9, 11, 12, 13, 77
    Jansenist disputes 11
    'L'imaginaire Irlandais' festival 235, 236, 249, 288–9, 290
    NATO and 45
    perception of Ireland xiii–xiv, 75–6
Franco, Francisco 29, 98, 101
Franco regime 100, 102–3, 116
Frankfurt Book Fair 232, 235
Frankfurter Rundschau 249
Frasca, Gabriele 189
Frears, Stephen 343
Freitag, Barbara 230
French literature 75–93
    analysis of Ireland's modernity 91–2
    Breton literature 78–82, 92
    Catholicism, the Irish and 79, 80
    Celts and the Celtic world 77–9
    Franco-Breton 77–8
    images of Ireland/the Irish 76, 77, 80, 88, 90–3
    Ireland as a theme 92–3
    Joyce's influence 85–7, 93
    medieval literature 76–7
    Navigatio Brendani, influence of 76–7, 84, 92
    Northern Ireland, portrayal of 87–90, 93
    religious divide, Ireland and 79, 80
    rêve/rêveurs 80, 82, 83, 84, 93 n3
    surrealism 87
    symbolism 181
    voyage literature 76–85, 92
French, Robert **274, 275, 276, 277, 278**
Friel, Brian 207, 230

G

Gadda, Carlo Emilio 178–9, 184
Gaffney, Gertrude 420
Gageby, Douglas 423, 424
Gainsborough, Thomas 265–6, **266**, 267
Galicia xiv, 6, 98–9
    Nós movement 99, 100, 116 n2
Galician-language literature 98–101, 116
    censorship 100
    Galician writers 99
    Irish influence 99, 100, 101
    Joyce's influence 100, 101
    Lebor Gabála Érenn 99, 100
    political texts 99
Gall, St 305–6, 310, 317
Gallagher, Frank 418, 419, 422
Garvin, Tom 433
Gathering, The 409
Gelbart, Matthew 354, 365 n4–5
gender, Irish writers and 216–19
Geographical Society of Lille 79
George, Stephan 181
George-Kreis 181
German Democratic Republic (GDR) 35,
    229–30
German literature
    Böll and post-war literature 190–3
    detective novels, Irish setting 193
    Fortunatus (chapbook) 174
    Ireland, two-sidedness of 180–1
    Ireland's literary impact 181–3
    Irish literature, role of 175–6, 177,
        178
    Joyce's influence 184–6, 228
    new literature 175
    Purgatorium Sancti Patricii and 174
    travel literature 179
German Studies 196
German-English-Gaelic literary texts 195
Germany
    Celtic Studies in xv, 174
    diplomatic relations x, 26
    industrial/political significance 25
    Ireland, Second World War and xii,
        174
    Irish literature, diffusion of xiii, 195
    Irish music and 350–1, 352–3

Keltologie 193–4
    music/art music 354, 361
    musical romanticism 353, 355
    Ossianic verse and 354–5
    perception of Ireland 228, 229
    post-war division 34–5
    reunification 231
    Tübingen conference xi
    see also Nazi Germany; Weimar
        Germany; West Germany
Gerold, Marianne 232, 246
Gibbons, Luke 333
Gids, De (journal) 150
Gil Soto, José Luis 105–6, 108, 116
Gillen, Aidan 407, 408
Gillissen, Christophe 46
Gilmore, Eamon 62
Giordano, Ralph 191
Gironella, José María 102, 103, 116
global financial crisis (2008) 59–60, 399
Global Irish (report) 409
Godwin, George 267
Goethe, Johann Wolfgang von 175–6
Goldsmith, Oliver xv, 175–6, 177
González de Matauco, Jorge 104
Good Friday Agreement (1998) 55, 64,
    65, 400, 413 n35
Goraj-Bryll, Małgorzata 121, 124, 241, 246
Gothic novels 158–62
Gourval, Alain 80, 82
Grall, Xavier 84–5
*Grand Prix du roman de l'Académie
    française* 81, 89
Great Famine (1845–9) 269, 271, 272
Greene, Graham 123
Greengrass, Paul 344
Gregory, Augusta, Lady 101, 150, 183,
    217
Greve, Jacob 205, 212
Griffith, Arthur 103
Griffith's Valuation 272, **273**
Gruchawka, Ryszard Adam 126, 135,
    136, 140
Guardian, The 114
Guattari, Félix 296
Guerrero, Mercedes 107, 108
Gunne, Sorcha 218–19

Italian literature 176–7
  Beckett and 189–90
  Goldsmith's influence 177
  Heaney and 190
  Ireland's literary impact xiii, 183–4
  Joyce's influence 186–7, 189
  Purgatorium Sancti Patricii and 174
  Sterne's influence 178
  Swift's influence 178
  travel literature 180
  Yeats's influence 188–9
Italy 23, 29, 37
  affinities with Ireland 196
  book industry 195
  Catholicism xv, 176, 180
  diplomatic relations x, 33
  EEC, Ireland and 41, 42, 43
  fascism 29
  German Studies in 196
  Ireland's links with 180
  Irish scholars/monks 3, 4, 53, 174
  Irish Studies in 194–5
  perception of Ireland 26

J

James II, King 12
James Joyce Stiftung Zürich 196, 199 n45
Jarniewicz, Jerzy 121, 142 n9, 242
Jenkinson, Biddy 250
Jesuits (Society of Jesus) 11, 13, 175
Joannon, Pierre 93
Jochum, Klaus Peter 215, 216
John Scottus Eriugena 4, 323, 330 n66,
    331 n67
Jones, Kirk 343
Jones, Sam 114
Joyce, James xiv, xv, 53, 82, 85–7, 183, 210
  Bloomsday celebrations 124
  canonical status of 205
  German literature, influence on
    184–6, 228
  intercultural institutions 196
  Italian literature, influence on 186–7,
    189
  Nordic literature and 203–6, 208
  'Order of Finnegans' group 109–11
  Polish writers/poets, influence on

121, 124, 125
  Queneau and 85–7, 93
  Spanish literature, influence on 100,
    101, 109–12
  Vestdijk and 151, 166 n22, 167 n24
  Dubliners 208
  Finnegans Wake 110, 186, 187
  *Portrait of the artist as a young man,
    A* 87
  Ulysses 85–7, 100, 111
  Ulysses, Broch's analysis of 185–6
  Ulysses translations 121, 183–4, 185,
    186, 203, 204, 212, 215
Joyes y Blake, Inés 8
Juncosa, Enrique 294

K

Kafka, Franz 199 n43, 244
Keane, Roy 407
Keatinge, Patrick 433
Keefe, Joan Trodden 247
Kelly, Liam 290
Keltologie 193–4, 233
    see also Celtic Studies; Irish Studies
Kennedy, Dennis 423–4, 426
Kenny, Enda 63
Keown, Gerard 120
Keyes, Marian 208, 217–18
Kilian, St 306, 310
Kimmich, Max W. 334, 337–8
Kirby, Peadar 144 n30
Kirsch, Hans-Christian (Frederik
    Hetmann) 227
Klein, Axel 361–2, 363, 364, 366 n21
Klitgård, Ida 215
Kobranocka (band) 121–2
Koeppen, Wolfgang 185
Kohl, Johann Georg 179
Kolasiński, Przemek 123, 132, 135
Koskinenen, Maija 285
Kosok, Heinz 181
Koumoutsi, Persefoni 238
Krasiński, Zygmunt 120
Krauss, Rosalind 295–6
Krautgarten (journal) 233
Krull, Hans Oldayu 285

L

La Capria, Raffaele 187
Labour Party (Irish) 58, 62, 431
Lago, Eduardo 109, 110
Lamprecht, Gerhard 339
Landy, Marcia 340
languages
    Bulgarian 241, 244
    Celtic languages 226, 232, 234
    Celtic/Indo-Germanic connection 174
    Czech xvii, 225
    English 383
    Finnish 207
    French 225, 382
    German 225, 382
    Hiberno-English 137
    Nordic 207, 209
    Romanian xvi, 225
    Sami 207, 209
    Scottish-Gaelic 232, 237, 250
    studied in Ireland 382–3
    translations of minority languages 225
    see also Irish language
Lanters, José 152–3
Lanthimos, Yorgos 347
Lappert, Rolf 192
Lasa, León 104
Laschen, Gregor 232
Laugersen, Peter 217
Lawlor, Mary 342
Laxness, Halldór 214–15
Le Braz, Anatole 79–80
Le Dû, Jean 236
Le Mercier d'Erm, Camille 80
Le Pen, Marine 67
Leader (magazine) 433
League of Nations 24, 25, 29, 30
Lean, David 333, 341
Lebesque, Morvan 84
Lee, Joseph 432–3, 437
Leerssen, Joep 165 n13, 169 n56
Lehman Brothers 59
Leipzig Bookfair 248
Lemass, Seán 39, 40, 41, 42, 43, 44, 391
Leoni, Franco 183
Libera, Antoni 121
Libération 87

Libre Belgique 36
Limburgsch Dagblad 34
Linati, Carlo 183–4, 195–6
Lisbon, Portugal 6, 9
Literature Ireland 226, 241
Literaturwerkstatt Berlin 231
Lithuania 287
Loach, Ken 344, 345
Lombard, Peter 11
Longley, Edna 219
Lönnrot, Elias 210
Loock, Ulrich 292–3
Louis XIV, King of France 8
Louvain University 9, 11–12
Luxembourg 23, 37, 41, 43, 306
Lynch, Jack 44, 46

M

Mac Annaidh, Séamus 237, 242, 244
McBride, Eimear 185
MacBride, Seán 32–3
MacCannell, Dean 398
Mac Cóil, Liam 231, 241, 244
Mac Con Iomaire, Liam 247
McDowell, Graham 407
McGahern, John 91, 195, 208
McGilligan, Patrick 25
McGonagle, Declan 288
McGuckian, Medbh 217
McIvor, Neil 392, 395
McKenna, Charlene **406**, 407, 408
McKenna, Siobhan 335
McLoone, Martin 333, 343
MacPherson, James 78, 176, 226, 354
McQueen, Steve 345
Mac Síomóin, Tomás 230, 232, 237
McTigue, Andrea 231, 232
McVeagh, John 280n7
Macron, Emmanuel 67
Madden, Deirdre 217
Magill, Elizabeth 285, 286
Magris, Claudio 196
Mahon, Derek 195, 217
Maleno, Carlos 109, 116
manuscripts *see* Hiberno-Latin
    manuscripts

Manzoni, Alessandro 177, 178
Markievicz, Casimir Dunin, Count 120
Markievicz, Constance, Countess 120
Markus, Radvan 241, 246
Marlowe, Lara 424, 425, 426, 428
Martin, Seamus 422, 428
Matasovic, Ranko 239, 240
Maude, Caitlín 238
Maude, Ulrika 209, 212–13
Maurin, Aurélie 232
May, Imelda 407, 409
Maynooth University (NUIM) 377, 379, 384
Méavenn (Fant Rozec) 84
Meid, Wolfgang 229–30, 250 n3
Melchiori, Giorgio 186–7, 200 nn58–9
Mendelssohn, Felix 350, 353–4, 357, 362,
    365 n5
Mercille, Julian 437
Michelsen, Paul 178
Michorzewski, Andrzej 122
Mickiewicz, Adam 120
migrants/migration
    Europe and 3–15, 174–5, 301
    France and 8–9, 12, 13, 77
    Irish monks and scholars xvii, 4, 53,
        174, 301, 312, 324
    military migrants 7–9, 13–14
    missionaries ix, 3–4, 14, 148, 301,
        304, 306
    peregrini 306, 320, 323, 325, 326 n2
    Polish writers in Ireland 122–33
    pre-historic 3
    religious migrants 15
    Spain and 4, 5–6, 7–8, 12, 14
    students 9–12
    trading diaspora 5–6, 13
    Viking incursions and 322
Mikhailova, Tatyana 242, 246
Miller, Daniel 391
Miłosz, Czesław 121
Mohrt, Michel 81, 83–4
Moi, Toril 211, 213
Molina, César Antonio 100
monasteries/monastic sites
    church of St Martin 316
    in Europe 3–4, 174, 313, 316–17, 324
    Honau on the Rhine 329 n41

Irish monasteries, layout of 312–13,
    316–17
Lindisfarne 302, 305, 313
Luxeuil 304, 305, 313, 316
monastic settlement of St Patrick
    313, **314**
oval-form layout 312–13
Patrician churches, layout of 313
St Gallen, Switzerland 3, 193, 313, 317
Scottus-monasteries 324
Montale, Eugenio 187–8
Moore, Thomas 120, 181, 355–6, 360
    influence in Europe 353, 355, 356,
        357, 363, 365 n8
    Irish melodies 120, 355, 356, 357, 360
    Lalla Rookh 356
    'Last rose of summer, The' 360, 361,
        362
Morash, Christopher 436
Morgan, Lady (Sydney Owenson) 180
Motin, Pierre 77
Muldoon, Paul 195, 207, 208, 217
Mullan, Peter 343
Munch-Pedersen, Ole 209, 217, 234, 246,
    247
Murguía, Manuel 99, 101
Murphy, Annalise 407
Murphy, Cillian 344, 407
Murphy, Gavin 295
Murphy, Robert 336
Murphy, Una 235
music xvii–xviii, 350–64
    Beethoven, folksongs and 356–9
    German art music xvii, 354, 356–7,
        361
    German musical romanticism 353, 355
    Irish air, German variations on
        359–62
    Irish art music 364
    Irish music xvii, 350–2, 355–62
    Irish musical identity in Europe
        362–4
    Ossianic verse 354–5
Musso, Jeff 337
Mussolini, Benito 28, 29
Myles na gCopaleen 229, 236, 237, 243
    see also O'Brien, Flann

N

O

O'Briain, Dara 407, 409
Ó Briain, Seán 13
O'Brien, Edna 157, 217
O'Brien, Flann 195, 228, 237
    see also Myles na gCopaleen
O'Brien, Mark 433
Ó Cadhain, Máirtín
    comparison with Joyce 244, 248, 249
    Cré na cille, translations 209, 241,
        243, 244, 246, 247–9
    Czech translation 241
    Danish and Norwegian translations
        209, 247
    English translations 244, 247
    Eochair, An, translation 233
    German translation 247–50
O'Casey, Seán 121, 184, 228
O'Clery, Conor 425, 426, 428
Ó Conaire, Pádraig 228, 238, 240, 241,
    242, 244
Ó Conghaile, Mícheál 232, 239, 240, 247,
    248
O'Connor, Barbara 389
O'Connor, Bernard 120
O'Connor, Frank 195, 243
O'Connor, Hugh 8
Ó Criomhthain, Tomás 229, 234, 235, 246
Ó Doibhlin, Breandán 235
Ó Doinnshléibhe, Aindrias 13
O'Duffy, Eoin 420
Ó Fithcheallaigh, Muiris 4
O'Flaherty, Liam 228, 229, 237, 338
Ó Gormaile, Pádraig 235
Ó hEithir, Breandán 229–30
Ó hUallaigh, Peadar 233
Olszewska, Kinga 134
O'Mahony, Jane 434
Ó Maol Chonaire, Flaithrí 11
O'Neill, Brian 419
O'Neill, Patrick 180
O'Neill, Terence 43
O'Reilly, Alexandro 8
Ó Ríordáin, Seán 235
Ó Searcaigh, Cathal 230, 232, 235, 238
Ó Siochfhradha, Pádraig (An Seabhac)
    228

Ó Snodaigh, Pádraig 238, 241
Ó Suilleabháin, Muiris 229, 235, 241
O'Toole, Fintan 113–14, 115, 345
Ó Tuairisc, Eoghan 238, 241, 242, 244
October (journal) 295–6
Ødegård, Knut 217
Oeser, Hans-Christian 229, 230, 232, 246
Order of Finnegans 109–11
Organisation for European Economic
    Cooperation (OEEC) 36, 38, 39
Orzeł, Magdalena 125, 132, 133, 137, 140
Oswald, Gösta 205
Otero Barral, Malcolm 109, 110
Otero Pedrayo, Ramón 99, 100, 101
Otherworld, *Purgatorium Sancti Patricii*
    76, 79, 174

P

Paluch, Anna 242
Panofsky, Erwin 333
Paris Biennale des Jeunes 287
Pascoli, Giovanni 190
patriarchal oppression 159, 162, 343
Patrick, St 76, 79, 106, 132, 305
Pearse, Patrick 228, 235, 236, 237, 242
Pedersen, Holger 234
Peroutková, Ivana 241
Petersen, Hans 230
Petrie, George 272
Pevsner, Nikolaus 267
Philip II, King of Spain 105
Piccolo, Lucio 188–9
pilgrimages 310, 323
pilgrims (*peregrini*) 301, 306, 320, 323,
    325, 326 n2
Pilný, Ondřej 241
Pippin II of Aquitaine 306
Pirmin, St 306, 316
Pizzuto, Antonio 187
Pokorny, Julius 227, 228
Poland x, 30
    affinities with Ireland xiv, 120,
        139–40
    Irish literature/drama xiv, 120–1
    migration to Ireland 122–3
Polish migrant writers